INTRODUCTION TO THE
SOCIAL SCIENCES

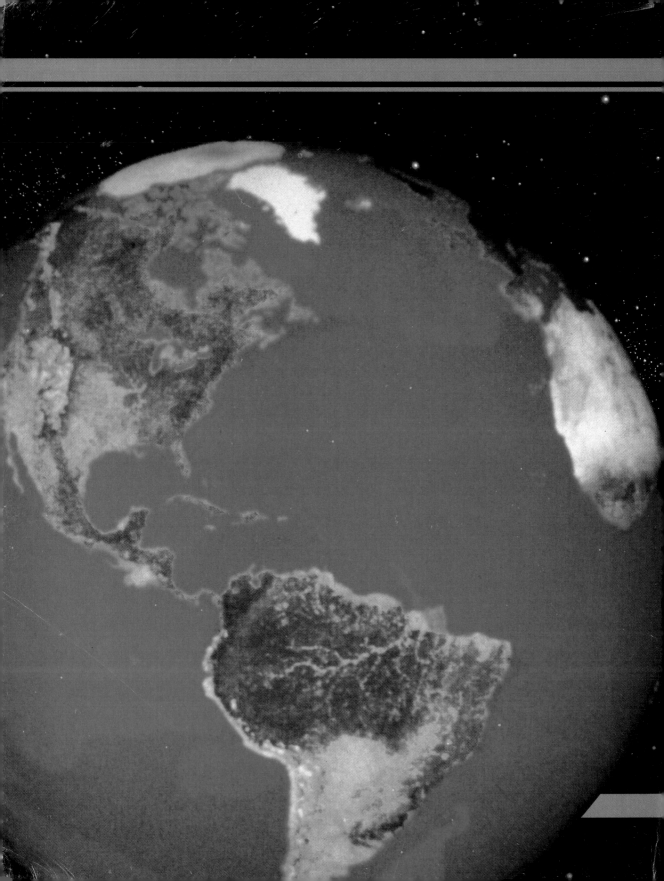

INTRODUCTION TO THE
SOCIAL SCIENCES

JOHN JAY BONSTINGL

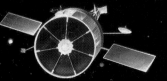

PRENTICE HALL

Needham, Massachusetts   Upper Saddle River, New Jersey

About the Author

John Jay Bonstingl is an international education consultant who has worked with school systems throughout the United States and with more than two dozen ministries of education around the world, helping them to create systems and processes in which all people can achieve their true potential. He is the author of several books and many articles in the fields of social sciences and education reform, and is a frequent keynote speaker at education conferences in this country and abroad.

As founder and director of The Center for Schools of Quality, Mr. Bonstingl conducts "Creating Schools of Quality" workshops worldwide, and teaches postgraduate seminars on topics ranging from "Effective Study Skill Development K-12" to "Education for the 21st Century: A Survival Kit."

This *Introduction to the Social Sciences* program is based upon the author's 17 years' experience as a social science classroom teacher at the middle school and high school levels. Mr. Bonstingl's academic degrees are in psychology, social science education, and history from Indiana University of Pennsylvania, and Carnegie Mellon University. He lives and works in Columbia, Maryland.

Dedicated to my family and to my former and present students.

Credits

Editorial Director: Tom Barber
Project Editor: Mary Ann Gundersen
Production/Manufacturing Coordinators:
  Robin Tiano, Holly Schuster
Design Director: Alison Anholt-White
Design Manager: Stuart Wallace
Production Design: Jack Pollard

Cover Design: Hannus Design Associates,
  L. Christopher Valente
Book Design: Carol H. Rose
Photo Researcher: Sue C. Howard, Russ Lappa
Text Maps: Function thru Form
Technical Illustration: Paul Foti/Boston
  Graphics, Inc.

PRENTICE HALL
A Division of Simon & Schuster
Needham, Massachusetts 02194
Upper Saddle River, NJ 07458

Printed in the United States of America

ISBN 0-13-412552-5

 2 3 4 5 6 7 8 9 03 02 01 00 99 98 97

Consultants

Peter Aiau
Boring, Oregon

Mary B. Allberry
North Platte, Nebraska

Christine A. Allen
Salem, Oregon

Samuel R. Bell
Elgin, Illinois

Peter N. Coutsos
Warren, Michigan

Fred Czarra
St. Mary's City, Maryland

Loyal L. Darr
Denver, Colorado

Billie Day
Washington, D.C.

Dominick DeCecco
Bethlehem, New York

Clarina DiPietro
Mt. Pleasant, Pennsylvania

Graydon Doolittle
Norman, Oklahoma

Patricia J. Dye
Plymouth, Massachusetts

Thomas Egan
St. Paul, Minnesota

James Elliott
Sanford, Florida

Phillip Ferguson
Waukesha, Wisconsin

Richard Flaim
Vineland, New Jersey

Dan B. Fleming
Blacksburg, Virginia

Sandra L. Fletcher
Lodi, California

Charles Fox
Kansas City, Kansas

Virginia Franklin
Greenbrae, California

Miriam Glessner
Columbus, Ohio

Barry Gomberg
Ogden, Utah

Franklin Greenough
Anchorage, Alaska

Robert Heinley
Media, Pennsylvania

Mary Kay Hemmes
Hartland, Wisconsin

Phyllis Henry
Chicago, Illinois

Rachel Hicks
Washington, D.C.

Phil Holland
De Kalb County, Georgia

Thomas Huff
Wayne, New Jersey

Ginny Jones
Denver, Colorado

William J. Kerewsky
Columbia, Maryland

Mary R. Krull
Peoria, Illinois

Marlene LaCounte
Billings, Montana

Sister Mary Louise Lisowski
Pittsburgh, Pennsylvania

Patricia Maguire
Burbank, California

Richard Moulden
Bellevue, Washington

Margaret Noe
Bartonville, Illinois

Ronald Hans Pahl
Rialto, California

Douglas A. Phillips
Anchorage, Alaska

Helen Richardson
Fulton County, Georgia

Judy Rogers
Littleton, Colorado

Brad Roghhar
Ogden, Utah

Maurice P. Shuman
Jacksonville, Florida

Dave Silberman
Montclair, New Jersey

Billie Jo Smith
Newport, Oregon

Sherrelyn R. Smith
Overland Park, Kansas

Jerald M. Starr
Pittsburgh, Pennsylvania

William Switala
Bethel Park, Pennsylvania

Susan E. Szachowicz
Brockton, Massachusetts

Dave Tidwell
Arabian American Oil
Company Schools
Dhahran, Saudi Arabia

Warren F. Tracy
Jacksonville, Florida

Larry Underwood
Brussels, Illinois

Robert Van Amburgh
Albany, New York

Richard J. Wagner
New York, New York

Roger K. Wangen
Minneapolis, Minnesota

William White
Jefferson County, Colorado

Gil Wilson
Temple Hills, Maryland

David W. Wolfe
Shawnee Mission, Kansas

Dale Zagrodnik
New Holstein, Wisconsin

CONTENTS

■ Readings
■ Experiments

UNIT 1 Critical Thinking Skills *xii*

UNIT **2** Effective Study Skills *48*

UNIT **3** Psychology *106*

U N I T 4 Sociology 150

U N I T 5 Anthropology 202

■ Readings ■ Experiments

UNIT 6 Geography 264

UNIT 7 History 342

UNIT 8 Political Science 404

UNIT 9 Economics 458

■ Readings   ■ Experiments

U N I T 10 The Future 534

UNIT 1

Critical Thinking Skills

PSYCHOLOGY

SOCIOLOGY

ECONOMICS

ANTHROPOLOGY

STUDY &
THINKING
SKILLS

POLITICAL
SCIENCE

GEOGRAPHY

HISTORY

Critical Thinking Skills

Luis and Sara are in the hallway after school, laughing and joking around. Kurt, a student they both know from history class, strides past them in a black, silver-studded leather coat. "That guy," Luis mutters under his breath. "I've never liked him." "Why not?" asks Sara, surprised. "Because he's got this big, ugly, loud motorcycle, and those guys always act like they're better than anyone else." Luis slams his locker shut. He and Sara begin walking. Sara moves slowly at first. "Luis. . ." she says quietly, "Have you ever actually talked to Kurt to find out what he's like?" "Don't have to," snorts Luis, "I've seen his motorcycle."

Logic is one way of arriving at conclusions. But if the logic used has a defect, the conclusion you reach may be false. In the Unit 1 readings you will be examining many critical thinking skills. In the Unit 1 experiments you will learn how to apply these techniques to help you avoid mistakes by drawing the right conclusions in your daily life.

Critical Thinking and You

We all can benefit from taking a fresh look at our usual way of thinking. Bad habits can be broken and good habits strengthened by paying attention to the ways we think. The questions below will help you see the importance of critical thinking skills.

1. Tossing ideas around with your friends can be fun. What are the drawbacks of this approach to problem solving? What are the benefits?

2. Can you think of an opinion you once held that you've changed over the past year to two? What new facts or impressions caused you to change your mind on this subject?

UNIT 1   CONTENTS

Learning To Think Critically

You have been thinking for as long as you can remember. Thinking is not new to you. Why, then, should you learn how to improve your thinking? And how do you *think critically,* anyway?

It is true that people think from the time they are born. But most people never examine the *way* they think. Their own ways of thinking seem normal and natural to them. And yet, some ways of thinking are more effective than others. Your thinking should lead you to the greatest possible success and satisfaction in life. Thinking critically is an important step in becoming a more successful student and in improving how you deal with other people.

Critical thinking is thinking clearly and with a purpose in mind. In this unit, you will have an opportunity to practice a variety of critical thinking methods, including a good way to solve problems. Our problem-solving process has three steps. First, you define exactly what the problem is. Then you collect and judge a variety of information related to your problem. Finally, you use the information to draw conclusions and solve the problem. It's one simple way you can improve your thinking every day.

We will also take a close look at how we gather information from our environment and use that information to create thoughts. We will explore the ways in which our actions come from our thoughts. And we will see that the way we perceive things helps to determine our thoughts and actions.

By the end of this unit you will be more aware of the ways in which you perceive,

It is important to think critically.

think, and act. You will notice more interesting things about your friends, your family, and the world around you. You may even become more confident, more successful, and happier with your life inside and outside of school. After studying this unit, you will also have better tools including the critical thinking skills to use in your study of the seven social sciences, which is what this book is all about.

READING REVIEW

1. What is this unit about?
2. Describe the three steps of the problem-solving process.

Critical Thinking

3. **Creating Good Questions** Before you read any further, think for a few minutes about your own thinking. Based on what you have just read, write down three questions you would like to answer by the end of this unit. Your questions should be about your own thinking processes.

Perception

Have you ever watched your baby brother or sister (or any baby for that matter)? Babies learn about the big new world they live in by experimenting. They play with their toes to see how they feel when wiggled, bent, and pulled. They lick the bars of the crib with their tongues and try to bite the bars with baby teeth. And with their big, unblinking eyes they stare at you and the world around them, trying to make some sense of it all.

These are examples of how babies know their environment by the process called perception. **Perception** is the process of taking in information from the environment through the senses. Although they cannot yet put their discoveries into words, all babies early in life perceive the people and things around them with their senses. Since babies are totally dependent on their five senses and have had little experience living in this world, they have something in common with you in the experiment performed in class today. What do you think that is?

As a "visitor from another planet" in "Experiment 1-A: Thinking About Thinking," you examined objects familiar to people on Earth. You had very little experience in your past, however, to help you identify those "strange objects." You couldn't tell your friends back on Planet Korton that you had held a "stone" or tasted a

In what ways does a child use perception *to learn about the world?*

"cookie" or felt an "ice cube." Those are all English words, used only on Planet Earth. To make things even more difficult, no one on your planet had ever seen a stone, a cookie, or an ice cube. And that was the first time you had ever seen them. So you had to try to describe these objects, first to yourself and then to your friends back home. What was the best way of doing that?

Critical Thinking Skills **5**

Now suppose that on your planet there are things called "snargs." Snargs, as everyone on Korton knows, are dry, cold, and hard, and taste bitter. "Grods" on your planet are also familiar items. Grods are hot when picked out of the sky, and as they get cooler they become wet and taste like water. This information you know from living on Korton all your life. Now how would you describe an ice cube to your friends back home?

You would probably say that an ice cube has some qualities of snargs and some qualities of grods. An ice cube is hard and cold like a snarg. Like grods, ice cubes are wet and taste like water. Your friends would then know what you are talking about, because you described the unfamiliar object in terms they could understand.

Babies learn about their world in much the same way. There are a lot of things they have never seen, touched, tasted, heard, or smelled. As soon as they are born, babies begin to store in their memory descriptions of things they encounter. Soon they begin to recognize both Mother and Father as two similar objects. Later they will know that Mother and Father are both "people." Still later, they will be able to associate Mother and Father with the *word* "people." They will be able to use this new word when referring to their parents.

As a child growing up, or as a visitor from another planet, you learn through your senses. Without your senses you could not perceive anything. Can you imagine what life would be like if you could not see, smell, hear, taste, or feel anything at all!

READING REVIEW
1. What is perception?
2. What part does perception play in everyday living?

Critical Thinking
3. **Recognizing Cause and Effect** Choose one of your five senses. Then describe 10 ways in which your life might be different if you were permanently without the use of that one sense.

READING 3

How Do We Think?

Perceptions come before thoughts. Remember the first time you bit into a big, juicy lemon? First, your eyes perceived the yellow skin of the lemon. Then your fingers touched the lemon. It felt waxy and a little bit soft. As you picked up the lemon and brought it toward your nose, you smelled its "lemony" odor. As you sunk your teeth into the lemon, your taste buds perceived its sour taste.

All of these perceptions came *before* you thought "Wow, is that sour!" Similarly your ears perceive a new song before you think "I like that song!"

Perceptions lead to thoughts. Thoughts lead to actions. However, single thoughts (for example, "I like that song!") do not lead directly to actions, unless they are joined by other related thoughts. Let's say you perceive (see and hear) a song performed on TV. You like the song very much and you would like to buy the compact disc (CD), but you don't have the money. Your thought is "I need money to buy the CD."

This one thought will not get you the CD. It must be joined by other related thoughts. Then all your thoughts together must lead to an action that will enable you to buy the CD. Take a close look at these thoughts:

1. My parents have a lawnmower.
2. My neighbors need their lawns mowed.
3. My neighbors may not have time to mow their lawns.
4. I could create a few hours of free time.
5. My neighbors might pay to have their lawns mowed.

If those five thoughts were combined with the thought "I need money to buy the CD," what action might result? Your answer might be this: "I will ask my parents if I can borrow their lawnmower so I can mow the neighbors' lawns in my spare time and earn the money to buy the CD I want." We call this connection of related thoughts leading to an action a **thought pattern.** Our example of a thought pattern may be diagrammed like this:

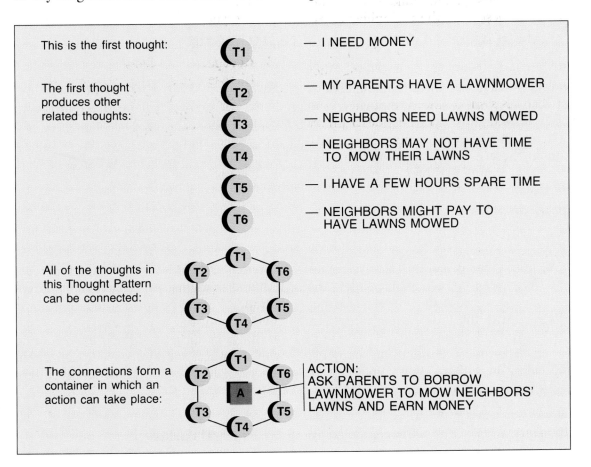

This is the first thought:

T1 — I NEED MONEY

The first thought produces other related thoughts:

T2 — MY PARENTS HAVE A LAWNMOWER

T3 — NEIGHBORS NEED LAWNS MOWED

T4 — NEIGHBORS MAY NOT HAVE TIME TO MOW THEIR LAWNS

T5 — I HAVE A FEW HOURS SPARE TIME

T6 — NEIGHBORS MIGHT PAY TO HAVE LAWNS MOWED

All of the thoughts in this Thought Pattern can be connected:

The connections form a container in which an action can take place:

ACTION:
ASK PARENTS TO BORROW LAWNMOWER TO MOW NEIGHBORS' LAWNS AND EARN MONEY

We usually think of an **action** as doing something physical. An action may also be a mental activity. Sometimes, actions may be defined as *not* doing something.

Stop now and think about a thought pattern you had today that led to an action. Identify the first thought in your thought pattern. Then, identify any other related thoughts you had. Finally, describe the action you took as a result of your combined thoughts.

READING REVIEW
1. What is the correct order of these steps: actions, perceptions, thoughts?
2. What is the connection of related thoughts leading to an action called?

Critical Thinking
3. **Identifying Central Issues** What is the central issue discussed in this reading?

EXPERIMENT **1-B   Combining Thoughts into Patterns   HANDOUT**

READING 4

Perceptions, Thoughts, and Actions

So far, we have examined the connections between perceptions and thoughts, and between thoughts and actions. Every thought grows from a perception, and thought patterns lead to action. We also know that the mind stores memories and draws them from storage when we need them. All of this can be diagrammed in what is called an **experience pattern.** An experience pattern has five steps. Let's begin this reading by studying just three basic steps:

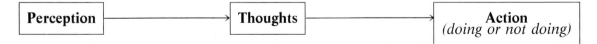

We know that perception always comes first. We cannot know anything unless the senses perceive something and feed that information to the brain. Our perceptions cause us to think thoughts about that information. Then we act upon our thoughts, responding by either doing something or not doing something.

Actually, there is a step between perception and thoughts. It is called **conceptualization.** After we perceive something in the environment, the brain tries to recall similar things in our past. If the brain comes up with an image, our mind conceptualizes (or imagines) it. Now, our experience pattern looks like this:

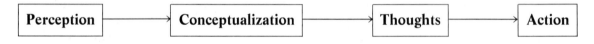

Of course, if we have never perceived something before, it is difficult or impossible to conceptualize it accurately.

The fifth and last step in the experience pattern is called **reaction**. After an action is performed (doing or not doing something), we almost always automatically evaluate the action. Was it good or bad? Should we have done something else? What should be done differently the next time? These questions are all part of evaluating the step of reaction.

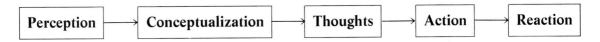

The brain recalls the reaction along with the conceptualization whenever the same situation comes up again. If your reaction was that your action was good, the brain tells you to repeat what you did before. If the reaction was bad, your brain will probably tell you to do something else. This is especially true if you stopped to figure out what went wrong (or right) and what action would have been better.

Here is an example of a complete experience pattern. You drive your car toward a railroad crossing. Your ears perceive a whistle and a rumbling sound. Your brain searches—quickly—for a similar experience pattern in your memory bank. You then conceptualize, or imagine, a train blowing its whistle and moving fast toward you. That image causes you to have thoughts about the danger of trying to cross the tracks until the train has passed. Your thoughts cause you to act: You decide to stop the car and wait. After the train goes by, you judge your action. You decide that it was wise to stop the car. Your reaction, therefore, is that your action was good and should be repeated next time. Now, when you perceive a similar whistling and rumbling sound, you will immediately conceptualize the train passing in front of your stopped car. You will act appropriately based upon your past experience pattern.

The example can be diagrammed like this:

Perception Ears perceive whistling and rumbling.	**Conceptualization** Brain identifies the sounds as those of a train. The mind pictures the train coming toward you fast.	**Thoughts** It's dangerous to cross tracks now. Better wait until it is safe.	**Action** Stop car and wait until the train passes.	**Reaction** Action was good. It paid to be safe. Do the same next time.

Now stop and think of an experience pattern you have had recently. First identify your perception, conceptualization, and thoughts. Then think about your actions. What was the action that resulted from your thoughts? What was your reaction?

How did your experience the first time affect your conceptualization of the situation the next time?

If you understand your own experience patterns, you are well on your way to improving your critical thinking skills. You will also be better able to understand why you think and act as you do. Your understanding of other people and why they behave as they do will improve. And you should be able to solve problems much more easily.

READING REVIEW

1. Write the five steps of a complete experience pattern in order.
2. What is conceptualization?

Critical Thinking

3. **Recognizing Cause and Effect** What effect does your reaction have on your perception and conceptualization the next time you encounter a similar situation?

EXPERIMENT 1-C   Creating Experience Patterns   HANDOUT

READING 5

Problem-Solving I: Identifying and Clarifying the Problem

Have you ever wondered why some people don't treat other people the way they want others to treat them? Have you ever wanted to know what you could do to make our planet a better, cleaner place? Have you ever wondered how you could get better grades than you do now?

Those are all good questions. Those questions are related to a few of the many problems social scientists are interested in solving. How do you think they go about this work?

Before you can solve a problem, you have to know exactly what the problem is. That is why the first step in our problem-solving process is called identifying and clarifying the problem. In this step, you describe the problem as clearly as you can.

Step 1: Identify and Clarify the Problem

Skill	Expressing Problems Clearly
Definition	The ability to focus on the exact nature of the problem and to put the problem into words
Everyday Example	The new athletic shoes you want cost $20 more than you can afford. You express your problem clearly: "How can I get $20 more, so I can buy the athletic shoes I want?"
Skill	**Identifying Central Issues**
Definition	The ability to identify the main point or idea contained in a piece of information
Everyday Example	Looking at a political cartoon, you are able to identify the cartoonist's point of view—the main idea of the cartoon.
Skill	**Creating Good Questions**
Definition	The ability to create thought-provoking questions that will lead to a deeper understanding of the problem
Everyday Example	Your grades aren't as high as they could be. You formulate questions to help you understand the issues behind your problem. "Why are my grades lower than they should be?" "How can I use my time more wisely to make better grades?"
Skill	**Making Comparisons**
Definition	The ability to perceive and describe similarities and differences
Everyday Example	You want to buy a good camera for the best price. So you examine the features of the cameras that are in your price range. As you compare the cameras, you notice their similarities and their differences.
Skill	**Determining Relevance**
Definition	The ability to decide which information is related to the problem and which information is unrelated to the problem
Everyday Example	You want to know the score of yesterday's game. After thinking about this problem, you decide that the comic pages of the newspaper would not help you solve your problem. You decide to look for the score in the sports pages instead.

Social scientists must learn how to pick out the main issues in their problems. They learn how to ask good questions. They compare and contrast pieces of information. And they figure out which pieces of information relate directly to the problem. They use the relevant pieces of information and put the others aside. Social scientists have found that by using these five critical thinking skills they can determine the exact nature of the problem.

Let's take a closer look at the skills you will learn in the first step of the problem-solving method. Study the chart on page 11 carefully before you go on.

READING REVIEW

1. Name the first step in the problem-solving method.
2. Describe the skills involved in this step.

Critical Thinking

3. **Identifying Central Issues** What is the central issue discussed in this reading?

READING 6

How To Express Problems Clearly

Have you ever listened to a friend tell about a personal problem? Maybe your friend started by telling you what happened at her home yesterday and for the past week. Your friend has not been getting along with her parents. Your friend says that there is too much pressure. "Parents expect too much!" your friend says. "I'm so frustrated and angry, I don't know what to do!"

After listening for a while, you wonder what the problem really is between your friend and her family. You want to help, but you aren't sure what the problem is actually all about. Finally, your friend tells you that all the trouble in her family started when she refused to go along with family rules about cleaning up and being on time. "Why didn't you tell me that sooner?" you ask. "It seems to me that the problem is not all your parents' fault. At least part of the blame is yours, don't you think?"

Sometimes it is difficult or even painful to be honest, especially when you are responsible for creating your own problem. And yet, you must be able to express your problem clearly if you want to discover good solutions to the problem. Our first critical thinking skill is called expressing a problem clearly.

Social scientists know that the first step in solving any problem is expressing the problem as clearly as possible. "Why is the world in such a mess?" is not a clearly expressed problem. This one is better: "Why is our planet so polluted, and what can we do about it?" The first question might lead us in many directions without ever getting to the problem of pollution. The second question is more clearly focused. It defines the problem better than the first question and it suggests that we should take action to solve the problem of pollution.

1. Why is it important to know how to express problems clearly?
2. Express as clearly as possible the problem you think is most important in your community.

Critical Thinking

3. **Expressing Problems Clearly** What happens when problems are not expressed as clearly as possible?

EXPERIMENT **1-D**

Expressing Problems Clearly

How clearly can you express a problem? Let's find out. In this experiment you will be examining 15 statements about Andy, a fictitious student in your school who has a problem. Some of the statements are important and others have little to do with Andy's problem. After reading all the statements, it will be up to you to decide what Andy's problem is.

1. Tonight is cold and rainy.
2. Andy's parents are not at home.
3. Andy has no brothers.
4. Andy is wearing his gray pants.
5. Andy is standing outside the front door to his home.
6. The doors and windows of Andy's home are locked.
7. Andy has one sister, who is four years younger.
8. The time is 9:35 P.M.
9. Andy's dog is named Spike.
10. There is an important test tomorrow, and Andy is not prepared for it.
11. Andy's sister and Spike are spending the night at a neighbor's house.
12. Andy's parents will be back around 10:00 P.M. tonight.
13. The key to Andy's house is in his blue jeans, which are in his room.
14. Andy is shivering.
15. Andy has tried to open all the windows and doors of his home, but with no luck.

Read all 15 statements one more time. On a separate sheet of paper, write one sentence that you think most clearly expresses Andy's problem. Try to express the problem in a focused way that suggests the possibility of action to solve the problem.

How To Identify Central Issues

Have you seen posters that say "Don't drink and drive!" and "Friends don't let friends drive drunk!"? The central issue in these posters is obvious. If you drink alcoholic beverages, you cannot drive safely. If your driving is unsafe, you risk harm—including death—to yourself and others.

In the process of solving our most important social problems, we must be able to identify the central issues in those problems. Driving while drunk is one example. Every year, thousands of people in the United States are killed as a result of drinking and driving. Many are teenagers. Groups such as SADD—Students Against Driving Drunk—work to focus our attention on the problem. They hope that their efforts will help people find solutions to the problem of drunken driving.

Social scientists know it is important to develop the ability to identify central issues in a problem. They know that sometimes it isn't easy to see the central issues right away. Sometimes the issues are hidden "between the lines." In order to persuade people to always be alcohol-free when they drive, social scientists need to understand the reasons why people drink and drive. Do they think that drinking and driving makes them more acceptable to others? Do they want to see how much they can get away with? Are they angry at someone and expressing their anger by being reckless?

These are all poor reasons to drink and drive—there are no good reasons—but social scientists understand that for some people, these are parts of the central issues of their drinking problems. Many social scientists believe that, until we work on the central problems of the individual driver, our society's problem cannot be solved.

Stephen Hawking, a noted physicist, identifies central issues clearly.

READING REVIEW

1. Why is it important to be able to identify the central issues in the process of problem solving?
2. Why is it sometimes necessary to "read between the lines" in identifying central issues?

Critical Thinking

3. **Identifying Central Issues** Identify two central issues facing you in your future.

Identifying Central Issues

*From Bill Amend, *Fox Trot*. (See Acknowledgements, pages 595–596.)

Can you identify the central issues in a cartoon or a poster? Here is an example of each. Examine the cartoon and the poster carefully. What is the main idea of each? Do you have to "read between the lines" in order to identify the artists' central issues? On a separate sheet of paper, write a paragraph explaining what the cartoon is trying to say. Then do the same for the poster.

Draw your own poster or cartoon that focuses on one central issue. Bring it to class and see whether your classmates can identify the central issue you are trying to communicate.

How To Make Comparisons

California faces a serious problem. There soon may not be enough water for the entire population to use for drinking, for showering and bathing, and for washing cars and irrigating crops. Social scientists and other professionals are working to solve this problem. For possible answers, they look to other states that are experiencing a similar problem. How have those other states attempted to solve the water shortage?

Social scientists also have to be aware of the differences that exist between California and other water-thirsty states. How is California different from those states? Would those differences make it difficult for California to solve its water problem by following other states' advice?

Social scientists know it is important to sharpen their ability to compare one set of information with another set. The better they can make comparisons, the more easily they can solve difficult problems.

Let's look at another situation. What do Israel, Great Britain, Pakistan, Nicaragua, and India have in common? Many answers may come to mind. They are all independent nations. They are all ruled by persons who are freely elected by the citizens of those countries. And each of these countries has been ruled by a woman at some time since the end of World War II.

Some social scientists wonder why the United States has not yet elected a woman president. To answer that question, we would need to look at the similarities and differences between our society and those of Israel, Great Britain, and the others mentioned above. By comparing and contrasting our values and beliefs with those of others, we can begin to understand ourselves better.

READING REVIEW

1. Why is it important to be able to compare similarities in the process of solving problems?
2. Why is it important to make contrasts and see differences in the process of solving problems?

Critical Thinking

3. **Making Comparisons** Compare the leadership of the American and British governments. How are they different? How are they the same?

Knowing how to make comparisons enables us to make good choices that please us and that help us understand ourselves better.

Making Comparisons

This experiment will help you sharpen your skill of making comparisons. Take a close look at the data in the table below. This table shows information about the average annual household income of white, black, and Hispanic households in the United States for two years: 1987 and 1991.

**Average Annual Household Income
in the United States**

Year	White	Black	Hispanic	All households
1987	$33,526	$20,743	$24,666	$32,144
1991	$39,523	$25,043	$28,872	$37,922

Source: *Statistical Abstract of the United States*

Here are five statements based on the information in the table. Some statements show similarities, while others show differences. On a separate sheet of paper, identify each statement with either "S" for similarity or "D" for difference:

1. Average household incomes for blacks, whites, and Hispanics went up between 1987 and 1991.

2. Whites averaged higher incomes than Hispanics in 1987.

3. The average income for all households in 1987 was higher than $15,000.

4. The average income for all households in the United States in 1991 was lower than $40,000.

5. The average black household income was lower than the average white household income in 1987.

How To Determine Relevance

In "Reading 3: How Do We Think?" you learned how several thoughts can be connected to form a thought pattern. And in "Experiment 1-B: Combining Thoughts into Patterns" you put that knowledge to work developing thought patterns of your own. Remember the thought pattern about earning money by mowing the neighbors' lawns? The thoughts in that thought pattern fit together like pieces of a puzzle, and together they formed the "container" in which the action took place. When thoughts can be connected like this, we say that the thoughts are **relevant** to each other. If thoughts have nothing to do with each other, we call them **irrelevant.** When thoughts are irrelevant, they cannot lead to an action. The process of finding out which thoughts are relevant is called determining relevance.

Sometimes, determining relevance is easy. Remember the problem expressed in Reading 3? It was "I need money." Several ideas grew from that problem, including these three:

• My parents have a lawnmower.
• Neighbors need lawns mowed.
• Neighbors would pay me to have their lawns mowed.

Are those ideas relevant in solving your money problem? Yes, each idea has something to do with the solution:

• I can earn money by getting my parents to loan me the lawnmower so I can mow the neighbors' lawns and charge them for my service.

People who are good at solving problems are usually also good at seeing relationships between pieces of information. They are also good at ignoring information that has nothing to do directly with the problem. Consider these thoughts:

• I prefer the color red and I don't like blue and orange.
• I am looking forward to my vacation this summer.

Are these thoughts relevant to the other thoughts above? No, they are irrelevant because they don't connect meaningfully with the other thoughts in the thought pattern and they don't seem to have much to do with making money by mowing lawns. This information is not essential to the solution of the problem.

Sometimes it is not as easy to determine relevance as you might think. Here is an example. What does a maple seed have to do with putting out fires? It may seem at first that those are irrelevant ideas. In fact, they are not irrelevant at all. The person who invented the automatic fire extinguisher couldn't think of a way to propel the liquid out of the container. He thought of everything that had already been invented. He searched his own experience patterns for clues. He asked experts for their opinions. Still no solutions.

Then one autumn day, he was relaxing under a maple tree and looked up to see a maple seed spinning toward the ground. It looked like the rotor of a helicopter. He jumped up, thinking "That's it! I've solved my problem! That's the missing piece of my invention!" He went home and made a metal part for his invention that looked like the "rotor." And it worked!

Sometimes, what seems like an irrelevant piece of information is just what you need to solve a problem. Next time you are ready to throw away a piece of information because you think it is irrelevant to your problem, think again. Often, if you are creative enough to see how that "irrelevant" piece connects with all the other pieces, you will find a workable solution to your problem.

READING REVIEW
1. What do we mean by relevant? By irrelevant?
2. What does relevance have to do with thought patterns?

Critical Thinking
3. **Determining Relevance** How does creativity help in solving problems?

Determining Relevance

Determining relevance is the critical thinking skill that makes it possible for you to decide which information is important to consider and which information is not essential in the process of solving a problem.

Here is a map showing the agricultural products of the countries of Central America. First, look closely at the map.

Which of the following answers can be found using this map of Central America? In other words, for which of these questions can you find relevant information on the map?

1. Honduras produces more bananas than Belize.

2. Both Belize and Honduras produce bananas.

3. Bananas are a more important crop in Belize than in Costa Rica.

4. The soil and climate of Panama is more favorable than that of Nicaragua for the production of bananas.

5. El Salvador does not produce bananas.

6. The population of Honduras is greater than that of Panama.

7. El Salvador is closer to Mexico than to Panama.

8. Costa Rica is wealthier than Belize.

9. Only one country in Central America produces lumber.

10. The capital of Costa Rica is San José.

Agriculture in Central America

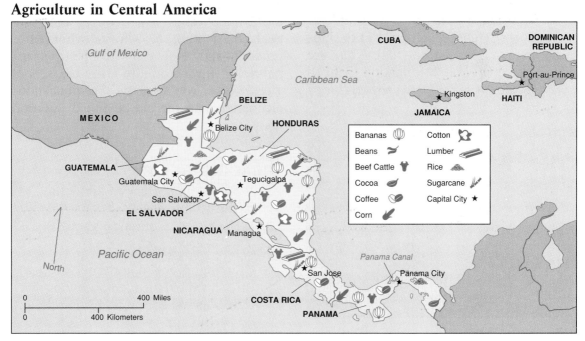

How To Create Good Questions

One of the most important critical thinking skills is the ability to create good questions. Questions lead us to find answers. Without questions, answers would not be possible.

Most problems in life have more than one right answer. Many problems have several good, workable solutions. In order to find those solutions, however, we need to ask the best possible questions.

The best questions are the ones that lead us to many possible answers and to many

What questions might you ask about the universe?

other possible questions. They are called "open-ended" questions. "Closed-ended" questions, on the other hand, lead only to answers of "yes" or "no."

Here is an example of a closed-ended question: "Could I work harder to make better grades?" This question can be answered either "yes" or "no." It doesn't lead you to other questions. It doesn't even suggest that a solution is possible.

A better question on the same topic would be this open-ended question: *"How could I work harder to make better grades?"* This question can be answered in a variety of ways. Open-ended questions like this one usually lead to other questions, which in turn lead to more answers, and so on. Some possible spin-off questions might include: "How can I use my time more effectively?" and "What long-term goals do I want to achieve with better grades?" and "How can I do a better job of balancing my social life with my school work?" Can you see how these questions are better than the closed-ended question above?

READING REVIEW

1. Why is it important to know how to create good questions?
2. What makes a question good?

Critical Thinking

3. **Creating Good Questions** Create three good open-ended questions that might lead to better grades in school.

Creating Good Questions

People who are good at critical thinking and problem solving are usually people who have practiced asking good, open-ended, focused questions. In this experiment, you will have a chance to practice creating good questions.

First, read the passage below. Then, on a separate sheet of paper, make two columns and label them *open-ended* and *closed-ended.* Under the column marked *open-ended,* create three good open-ended questions about the information in the passage. Under the *closed-ended* column, write three closed-ended questions that can be answered only with "yes" or "no." Notice how much better your open-ended questions are.

Stop Junk Mail*

We don't usually think of junk mail as an environmental hazard—just as a nuisance. But if you saved up all the unwanted paper your family will receive in the mail this year, you'd have the equivalent of up to one and a half trees. And so could each of your neighbors. And that adds up to about 100 million trees every year.

Did You Know

• Americans receive almost 4 million tons of junk mail every year.
• About 44% of the junk mail is never opened.

The League of Women Voters is a public-interest group that helps American voters create good questions about candidates running for political office.

• The average American spends up to 8 full months over a lifetime opening and reading junk mail.
• If only 100,000 people stopped their junk mail, we could save up to 150,000 trees a year. If a million people did, we could save up to 1.5 million trees.

*From The Earthworks Group, *50 Simple Things You Can Do To Save The Earth.* (See Acknowledgements, pages 595–596.)

Problem Solving II: Judging Information

So far in this unit, you have examined the first step in our problem-solving process: defining and clarifying problems. You have also learned how to use five important critical thinking skills in defining and clarifying problems.

Now, let's look at the second step in the problem-solving process: collecting and judging information related to the problem. In this step, social scientists identify facts, opinions, and inferences related to the problem. They check to make sure the information is consistent and they try to recognize the assumptions in that information.

Social scientists also identify false images, such as stereotypes, so they can be avoided. It is equally important for social scientists to recognize propaganda and bias. Social scientists find that by using these five critical thinking skills they can do a better job of judging information related

to a problem. Those skills make it easier to find good solutions.

Take a few minutes to carefully examine the chart on the next page before you go any further in this unit. The chart will help you understand the skills you will learn in the second step of our problem-solving method.

READING REVIEW ═══════

1. Name the second step in the problem-solving method.
2. Describe the skills involved in this step.

Critical Thinking

3. **Judging Information** How is the first step of the problem-solving method related to the second step?

How To Distinguish Facts, Opinions, and Inferences

Tomorrow morning the sun will come up, just as it has for millions and millions of days.

Is that statement a fact or an opinion? Or is it an inference? A **fact,** as you know, is a statement that can be proven. An **inference** is an "educated guess," or a conclusion

based on available evidence from past experience patterns. An **opinion** is not necessarily based on any evidence and it cannot be proven right or wrong. In this case, we made an inference about the sun (it will rise tomorrow) based upon evidence from the past (it has always risen).

CRITICAL THINKING SKILLS

Step 2: Judge Information

Skill	**Distinguishing Facts, Opinions, and Inferences**
Definition	The ability to separate statements that are proven from those that are not proven
Everyday Example	Your friend tells you to see a new movie, saying "It's the best movie you'll ever see!" You understand that your friend's statement is an opinion, not a fact.
Skill	**Checking Consistency**
Definition	The ability to compare two or more items to find out whether they agree or disagree with each other
Everyday Example	You know you should be making better grades and you want your grades to be much higher than they are. Yet, you spend most of your time watching TV. Your actions are not consistent with your desire for better grades.
Skill	**Recognizing Assumptions**
Definition	The ability to identify beliefs inside statements and experience patterns, even those beliefs not expressed directly
Everyday Example	Your new friend's family drives an expensive car and lives in a big house. You assume that your friend's family is rich. You later find out that they are deep in debt because they spend more than they can afford.
Skill	**Distinguishing False from Accurate Images**
Definition	The ability to identify stereotypes and clichés, especially about ethnic groups, religions, and minorities
Everyday Example	Everyone in a certain group is described negatively, allowing for no individual differences. "Well, what can you expect? *Those people* can't do anything right!"
Skill	**Recognizing Propaganda, Bias, and Ideologies**
Definition	The ability to perceive slanted messages that are designed to promote one set of beliefs over all others
Everyday Example	The TV commercial claims that Bloopie Bubble Bath is the best in the world. The commercial gives a slanted message to promote this belief so you buy their brand.

Being able to distinguish facts, opinions, and inferences helps us make good choices when trying to solve problems.

Being able to identify facts, opinions, and inferences can make you a better thinker and problem solver. On the other hand, if you mistake inferences and opinions for facts, your solutions may be misguided.

Here's an example. Mary has watched her friends sky-dive many times. Mary has an *opinion* that sky-diving is fun. Because her friends' parachutes have never failed, Mary *infers* that parachutes are always safe. She thinks her inference is a *fact*—parachutes never fail, so they don't have to be checked. Before her very first jump, Mary neglects to check her parachute, saying, "Parachutes never fail. Don't worry, I'll be perfectly safe." Mary is confusing her opinions and inferences with facts. What price might she pay for her confusion?

READING REVIEW
1. What is a fact?
2. Why might it be dangerous to confuse facts, opinions, and inferences?

Critical Thinking
3. **Distinguishing Fact from Opinion** Write two facts and two opinions about your school.

Distinguishing Facts, Opinions, and Inferences

Can you tell the difference between facts, inferences, and opinions? Let's find out.

Here are 15 statements. On a separate sheet of paper, identify each statement as either a *fact,* an *opinion,* or an *inference.* Explain the reason for your answer.

1. The brown dog has a beautiful coat of fur.
2. The Earth spins.
3. I will get older.
4. Everything you read in the newspapers is absolutely true.

5. Teenagers should not be allowed to stay out past 10 P.M.

6. Our country has the best government in the world.

7. Every human being has parents who are human.

8. The leader of the United States government is the President.

9. Our planet is polluted.

10. The Earth is beautiful when viewed from outer space.

11. My social science teacher will give me a grade.

12. New York is east of California.

13. My school is #1.

14. The world will come to an end in the year 2100.

15. The social sciences are interesting.

How To Check for Consistency

"This school year, I'm going to do much better! This is the year I am going to change my life and go for the gold!"

Have you ever made such a promise to yourself? Did your actions support your promise? Did you, for example, spend more time studying for tests? Did your words and actions agree? In other words, were your actions **consistent** with your promise? Inconsistency doesn't often lead to solutions to your problems. To be successful—in schoolwork, athletics, or business—you must be consistent.

The same idea holds true for solving problems. If the pieces of information you use to examine a problem are not consistent with each other, you will probably not be able to arrive at a workable, long-lasting solution. Look at this example:

"I firmly believe that women are equal to men. All men and women should be allowed to vote. Women and men should receive equal pay for equal work, too. It's shocking to think that women in this country earn less than two thirds what men make for doing the exact same work. Of course, there is only so much money to go around. I wish I could afford to pay the women who work for me the salaries they truly deserve. In the future, I'm sure that will happen."

Are the statements in the example consistent with each other? Are the speaker's actions consistent with what that person claims to believe? Chances are, as long as the speaker's words and actions disagree with each other, the problem of unequal pay will not be solved.

READING REVIEW

1. How can you tell if statements are consistent with each other?
2. Why is it important to be consistent in your words and actions?

Critical Thinking

3. **Checking Consistency** What relationship does consistency have with finding solutions to problems?

Checking Consistency

How good are you at spotting *inconsistencies?* Remember, any two things are consistent when they have a logical connection and they are in agreement with each other.

When a logical connection between two things is missing, there is an inconsistency. When two things are not in agreement, there is an inconsistency.

*From Bill Amend, *Fox Trot*. (See Acknowledgements, pages 595–596.)

1. Look at the cartoon above. What inconsistency is the artist trying to make you see?

2. Examine the statement below. What inconsistencies are in it?

"I believe that everyone should be sensitive to the needs of the handicapped. People who are in wheelchairs should be able to use public water fountains, restrooms, and doors as easily as everyone else. I really believe that. I also think taxes are too high, and it would cost a great deal of tax money to install new facilities in public places for the handicapped. I don't want to pay more taxes than I already do now."

Researchers at the Library of Congress check United States government documents for consistency.

How To Recognize Assumptions

We all take some things for granted. We make assumptions every day based upon past experience patterns.

You woke up again today, as you have every day during your lifetime. Based upon your history of waking up every day, you make an assumption. You naturally assume that you will wake up tomorrow, as you always have in the past. If you are good at recognizing assumptions, you will know that you probably will wake up tomorrow. You will also know that there is always a chance you won't wake up tomorrow.

Assumptions are hidden beliefs about something or someone. Assumptions are usually not put into words; they are *implied,* or indicated indirectly. If you see someone carrying an umbrella, you might make this assumption: The person with the umbrella thinks it might rain. That person doesn't need to say "I'm carrying this umbrella because I think it will rain." The act of carrying an umbrella implies a belief that the umbrella might be needed. We make that assumption, particularly if there are clouds in the sky.

Sometimes, however, our assumptions turn out to be wrong. What if the person with the umbrella is carrying it for self-defense? Or maybe the person sells umbrellas and is taking a new model to a store. Or maybe the person makes umbrellas and is testing this one out today. If any of these reasons were true, then we have made a false assumption by thinking that the umbrella is related to the weather.

Making assumptions can be dangerous, especially when we are trying to solve a

Drawing by Richter; © 1971 The New Yorker Magazine, Inc.

"My folks are in the gallery. If you can work it in, would you mind terribly calling me 'my esteemed colleague'?"

problem. When we make assumptions, we take the chance that our assumptions may turn out to be false. When that happens, our solutions can also turn out to be wrong or unworkable.

READING REVIEW

1. What is an assumption?
2. Why is it sometimes dangerous to believe our assumptions without making sure they are true?

Critical Thinking

3. **Recognizing Assumptions** What are two assumptions that you made today?

Recognizing Assumptions

In this experiment you will have an opportunity to improve your skills in recognizing assumptions.

PART ONE

Look at this series of statements, and then answer the questions that follow:

Four years ago, I ate an egg and it made me sick.

Three years ago, I drank some eggnog and it made me sick.

Two years ago, I ate an egg salad sandwich and it made me sick.

Last year, I ate a hard-boiled egg and it made me sick.

Last month, I ate an omelette and it made me sick.

Yesterday, I ate two soft-boiled eggs and they made me sick.

1. What assumptions could you make about this person and eggs?

2. What information would make your assumptions false?

PART TWO

In the next column is a poem by Goethe (Gêr tä), a German poet. In this poem, Goethe implies that there should be a special kind of relationship between humans and other living things, such as flowers. Read this poem carefully, then write a brief paragraph describing the assumptions you think Goethe makes about this special relationship.

Found

I walked in the woods
All by myself,
To seek nothing,
That was on my mind.

I saw in the shade
A little flower stand,
Bright like the stars
Like beautiful eyes.

I wanted to pluck it,
But it said sweetly:
Is it to wilt
That I must be broken?

I took it out
With all its roots,
Carried it to the garden
At the pretty house.

And planted it again
In a quiet place;
Now it ever spreads
And blossoms forth.

How To Distinguish False from Accurate Images

Have you ever been called a name just because you belong to a certain religion, race, or ethnic group? Have you ever heard people use negative words to describe others?

People who are good critical thinkers understand that every individual is unique. No two people look the same, think the same, or act the same. Everyone has a unique set of ideas about the world based on a lifetime of individual perceptions and conceptualizations. And yet, every person belongs to groups that make the individual similar to others who belong to those groups. If you are a good critical thinker, you know how to identify those areas of similarities, as well as those areas in which each person is different from all other individuals.

Good critical thinkers avoid **stereotypes** and **clichés.** A stereotype is an oversimplified view, usually negative, of a person or group of people. Stereotypes are based on a narrow perception of a person or group.

Those perceptions don't allow people to see the beauty and unique qualities of individual human beings. Instead, all people of a certain race, religion, ethnic background, or other group are lumped together as "inferior," "hostile," or "not like us." The sad thing about stereotypes is that they prevent us from getting to know other people just because they may be different from us in some ways. Most often, stereotypes arise out of fear. Once we learn how to overcome fear, it is often possible to form wonderful friendships and relationships based on respect.

Clichés also keep us from understanding and building our world. A cliché is a worn-out phrase or an old-fashioned, narrow expression. Some clichés make us groan because they are so out-of-date or because they have been overused. Other clichés are simply unfair to a person or a group. Here is an example: "A woman's place is in the home." Why is such a cliché unfair?

In 1984 Geraldine Ferraro became the first woman nominated for Vice President by a major political party. What stereotype did her candidacy help eliminate?

Critical Thinking Skills **29**

Stereotypes and clichés give false images of people. Clear thinking requires us to be fair and accurate in our images of everything and everyone. By thinking clearly, accurately, and fairly, we have a better chance of finding solutions to our most important problems. Thus, the challenges of everyday life will become easier to handle and the solutions we develop will be more pleasing. Besides, wouldn't you want everyone else to be fair and accurate in thinking and speaking about you?

READING REVIEW

1. Define: stereotype, cliché.
2. How does using false images about people and things keep us from solving problems?

Critical Thinking

3. **Distinguishing False from Accurate Images** Why would you want others to speak fairly and accurately about you?

EXPERIMENT **1-L**

Distinguishing False from Accurate Images

Now that you know what stereotypes and clichés are, take a look at these 15 statements. On a separate sheet of paper, explain why each statement produces false images that stand in the way of clear thinking.

1. A woman's place is in the home.
2. Once a crook, always a crook.
3. Kids can't be trusted to be alone.
4. The game isn't over until it's over.
5. All people who belong to that group are lazy.
6. Like totally awesome, dude!
7. The whole nine yards.
8. A diamond is a girl's best friend.
9. Out of the frying pan and into the fire.
10. Forever is a long time.
11. Sticks and stones will break my bones, but names will never hurt me.
12. Don't make waves.
13. If they're not for us, they must be against us.
14. Real men don't cry.
15. Poverty is the result of laziness.

What images does this rural Vermont town bring to mind?

How To Recognize Propaganda, Bias, and Ideologies

In the process of solving a problem, you usually have a great deal of information with which to work. Some of the information is reliable. Other information, however, may not be reliable because it is designed to appeal only to your emotions. Advertisements and commercials are often guilty of this. "If you want people to notice you, brush your teeth with Brand X toothpaste!" "Don't be left behind! Buy your very own wooget today!" Both of these slogans are designed to appeal to your emotions. Oftentimes, the information in such slogans is unreliable. Slogans such as these are called **propaganda.**

Sometimes, slanted emotional messages are designed to make you think something or someone is inferior. This is called **bias.** "Why are you hanging around with him? His kind of people aren't as smart as we are."

Emotional messages are sometimes used to make you accept a whole set of beliefs, which is called an **ideology.** Ideologies are not always biased, but some are. And it is important to be able to identify biased ideologies. An example of a biased or slanted ideology might be "Our group's way of thinking and living is the best. Everything else is not acceptable."

The Ku Klux Klan is a group that has used terror and violence to oppose the civil rights of blacks, Catholics, Jews, and other groups.

It is all right to want a wooget or Brand X toothpaste if you think it is the best and if you honestly have a good use for it. If you buy the toothpaste so that other people will notice you, however, then you are being controlled by the propaganda in the advertisement. If you plan to buy a wooget just because you don't want to be left behind, you might want to think again.

In solving any problem, it is important to recognize propaganda, bias, and ideologies. If you allow yourself to be controlled by emotional messages, the solutions you choose may not work for you. But they will probably work for those people who worked to convince you to believe their emotional messages.

People who recognize propaganda, bias, and ideologies are not easily controlled by others, so they feel better about themselves. They are also better at problem solving and critical thinking.

READING REVIEW
1. What is propaganda?
2. What is bias? What is an ideology?

Critical Thinking
3. **Recognizing Propaganda, Bias, and Ideologies** Create three good questions you might ask about an advertisement to judge whether it contains an emotional message.

EXPERIMENT **1-M**

Recognizing Propaganda, Bias, and Ideologies

Can you recognize propaganda, biased messages, and ideologies when you see them? Here are seven common propaganda techniques. They are used to make you believe biased messages and ideologies.

1. The Bandwagon "Everybody is wearing Loochie jeans. Do you own a pair?" The bandwagon technique tries to convince you to do something because "everyone else is doing it."

2. Appeal to Status This is the opposite of the bandwagon technique. "Only the best people belong to our club." "Why would you want to talk with her? She's not our kind of person." The message is "you (or we) are better than anyone else." This is sometimes called *snob appeal.* Ideologies

sometimes appeal to status: "Our group's set of beliefs contain the real truth; others are false."

3. Glittering Generalities "Kids just don't do good work anymore!" "Teachers are unfair!" Glittering generalities are broad, sweeping statements applied unfairly to everyone in a certain group. This technique is sometimes called *stereotyping.*

4. Plain Folks "Why, I'm not a celebrity. I'm just a country kid (or city kid) at heart, just like you." Plain folks statements are designed to make us think the speaker is just like us. If we identify with that person, we are more likely to believe him or her.

5. Statistics Statistics are numbers that describe something. "Four out of five doctors recommend Hexatron Tablets!" The numbers are supposed to impress you. Yet, how many doctors did they ask before they found four who recommended Hexatron?

6. Testimonial In this technique, a famous person tells why a product is terrific. Because that person is famous, we tend to believe him or her and follow that person's advice. But does the celebrity really believe in the product? Or is that person being paid to say those words? Sometimes this is called an *endorsement.*

7. Name-calling "Sam is ugly and dumb! No wonder his ideas are so bad." "People of her race (or religion or ethnic group) are ignorant (or greedy or inferior). Why would you want to be friends with someone like her?" In the first statement, instead of examining Sam's ideas, the speaker calls Sam names. Sam may have fine ideas, but the speaker refuses to consider them. The second statement makes a similar mistake. Rather than considering the individual, the speaker calls her names like "ignorant." This technique promotes biased ideas.

In this experiment, you will be putting your knowledge of these seven techniques to work. Find four advertisements that are examples of four of the techniques described above. Bring them to class and be prepared to explain how each of them is aimed at the emotions of the reader.

Problem Solving III: Drawing Conclusions and Solving Problems

So far, we have examined the first two steps in our problem-solving process. The first step is defining and clarifying the problem. The second step is judging information related to the problem.

The third (and final) step in our problem-solving process is called drawing conclusions and solving the problem. In this step, social scientists try to recognize cause-and-effect relationships. They identify alternatives so they can arrive at more than one possible solution to the problem. Social scientists try to predict consequences of various actions and they demonstrate reasoned judgment through their use of evidence. They also evaluate the evidence and synthesize, or draw together, the results. Finally, they draw conclusions and test those conclusions to see if they are the best solutions possible.

Before you go on, study the chart on the next page. It will help you to learn and apply the six skills in the last step of our problem-solving method.

READING REVIEW

1. Name the third step in our three-step problem-solving method.
2. Describe the skills involved in this step.

Critical Thinking

3. **Drawing Conclusions** How are the first two steps of the problem-solving process related to the third step?

Critical Thinking Skills **33**

Step 3: Draw Conclusions and Solve the Problem

Skill	**Recognizing Cause and Effect**
Definition	The ability to understand that some things cause other things to happen
Everyday Example	If detergents are dumped into a body of water, the water will be polluted. The detergents are the cause, and water pollution is the effect.
Skill	**Predicting Consequences**
Definition	The ability to forecast the most likely outcomes of a situation or an action
Everyday Example	The most likely consequence of committing crimes is going to prison.
Skill	**Identifying Alternatives**
Definition	The ability to see more than one solution for a problem
Everyday Example	You need money to buy a birthday gift for your friend and you think of five different ways to earn the money.
Skill	**Demonstrating Reasoned Judgment**
Definition	The ability to see relationships between similar pairs of items
Everyday Example	Cow is to milk as hen is to eggs
Skill	**Expressing Problems Clearly**
Definition	The ability to reduce a complex set of information to its simplest form and to judge its merits
Everyday Example	After listening to a friend telling you about a personal problem for 15 minutes, you are able to put the problem into one sentence.
Skill	**Drawing and Testing Conclusions**
Definition	The ability to arrive at solutions to a problem and make sure the solutions work well
Everyday Example	You notice that when a grocery store advertises a sale on several items, the prices of other items go up. You test your conclusion and you find out that it is correct.

How To Recognize Cause and Effect

Knowing how to identify cause-and-effect relationships can help you solve problems faster and better. If you can identify the direct causes of the problem, you stand a better chance of finding good solutions.

Here's a problem: Chris is spending today in bed with an upset stomach. Late last night, Chris ate an entire pepperoni pizza with double cheese, followed by a mint ice cream hot fudge sundae. Chris topped it all off with a dozen raw oysters dipped in ketchup and horseradish sauce followed by a large glass of buttermilk.

From the evidence you have, what are the most likely *causes* of Chris's illness? Chances are, one cause was the food Chris ate. There were too many varieties and too much quantity. It was also late at night so the food didn't have time to digest before Chris went to sleep. The *effect* of Chris's action is that Chris is sick today.

Cause-and-effect relationships can sometimes be difficult to identify correctly. "Ms. Jones is an unfair teacher. It's her fault I'm getting a bad grade. Other students come to school without their homework and they're not failing her class." This student sees Ms. Jones as the cause of the problem. Is it possible that this student is neglecting to recognize other possible causes of failing the class? Is it possible that Ms. Jones is actually *not* one of the causes of this student's failing grade?

It is likely that this student's bad grade in Ms. Jones's class has many causes. We call this **multiple causation.** What might be some of the multiple causes of this student's problem?

What effects did the actions of Rosa Parks have on civil rights?

When we examine a problem, it is important to be honest. It is easy to blame or identify people and situations that are not related to the problem. The best way to solve a problem is to find the causes of the problem, then to work on ways of changing those causes so they don't have the same negative effects in the future.

READING REVIEW

1. What is a cause-effect relationship?
2. What is multiple causation?

Critical Thinking

3. **Recognizing Cause and Effect** What are two good questions you might ask the student in Ms. Jones's class to help you recognize the causes of his or her problems?

Critical Thinking Skills **35**

Recognizing Cause and Effect

Based upon what you now know about cause-and-effect relationships, examine these six statements carefully. Each statement represents a problem in our country or in our world.

On a separate sheet of paper, tell whether you think the problem has one cause or multiple causes. Then for each problem, create two good open-ended questions you think might be useful in discovering the problem's most important causes. Remember, identifying the causes of a problem is often the most important step in solving it.

1. One third of the people living in poverty in our country are children.

2. High school drop-out rates in the United States are highest in the inner cities.

3. Many people believe that some products made in the United States are not as good as those made in Japan.

4. Some people believe that people are not as thoughtful of others as they once were.

5. Americans throw away an average of 1,930 pounds of garbage per person every year, which is the highest of any country in the world. (Great Britain, France, and Germany each throw away less than 800 pounds per person.)

6. Some people hate other people because of their skin color or because their religion or ethnic group is different.

How To Predict Consequences

In the process of drawing conclusions, you will need to know how to predict consequences of various actions and situations. A method called **induction** can help you accurately predict consequences. Induction is a pattern of thinking in which several examples of past experiences lead to a conclusion about the present. You have already seen an example of induction in "Experiment 1-K: Recognizing Assumptions." Let's take another look at the example from that experiment.

Four years ago, I ate an egg and it made me sick.

Three years ago, I drank some eggnog and it made me sick.

Two years ago, I ate an egg salad sandwich and it made me sick.

Last year, I ate a hard-boiled egg and it made me sick.

Last month, I ate an omelette and it made me sick.

Yesterday, I ate two soft-boiled eggs and they made me sick.

If I never ate eggs without getting sick, what would be your conclusion based upon the information above? We can use induction to collect past experience patterns, as we have here. By listing all the causes and effects of our actions in the past, we can more easily predict the consequences of our actions today.

One important warning: Past causes and effects must be consistent. If things do not happen the same way every time, predicting the exact consequences can be very difficult. In the example above, I tell you that I've had a long history of eating eggs, then getting sick. You might reason that, whenever I eat eggs, the consequence is sickness. Would you be correct? Would it make a difference in your conclusion if I told you that in the last four years, I ate 134 scrambled eggs, 62 egg salad sandwiches, and 103 hard boiled eggs—and in those instances, I did not get sick? In order to do the best job of predicting consequences, you must have as much accurate information about the situation as possible.

READING REVIEW

1. What is induction?
2. What is the relationship between consistency and predicting consequences?

Critical Thinking

3. **Predicting Consequences** What do you think are the likely consequences of studying the night before a big test?

EXPERIMENT 1-O

Predicting Consequences

In this experiment you will have an opportunity to sharpen your ability to predict consequences. As you saw in "Reading 19: How To Predict Consequences," we can predict consequences by using a method called induction. You remember that induction is the process of predicting consequences about the present or future, based upon past experiences.

PART ONE
Think of past experience patterns in your own life. On a separate sheet of paper, use your own experience patterns to write three examples of induction. Make sure your induction shows the consequences of your repeated actions. If you need a hint, review the "eggs" example described in Reading 19.

PART TWO
Refer back to the six problems described in "Experiment 1-N: Recognizing Cause and Effect." In that experiment, you created questions designed to find out the causes of those problems. In this experiment, use those same problems. This time write two questions for each problem, focusing on

the possible consequences if the problem is not solved in the very near future.

For example, Problem 1 deals with children living in poverty in our country. Here are some questions you might want to ask about the possible future consequences of this situation. How does poverty affect the health of children, now and in the future? What consequences does poverty have on the education of children? What will be the consequences of having lived in poverty when the children grow up?

How To Identify Alternatives

There are basically two kinds of thinking: *linear* and *lateral*. Both are used to figure out solutions to problems. Both are important in critial thinking. When you are trying to find the one right answer to a problem, linear thinking is best. (The word *linear* means "like a line, from one point straight to another point.") Induction and analogies are examples of linear thinking. When you want to identify as many workable alternatives as possible, you use lateral thinking.

With lateral thinking, you don't arrive at conclusions and solutions by using lessons you learned in the past. Instead, lateral thinking is a way of arriving at alternative solutions by finding new connections between ideas. When you think laterally, your ideas go wherever your mind takes you. Your creativity often works best when you think laterally. On the other hand, your common sense often works best when you think linearly.

Here is a problem. See if you can solve it. One hint: You can solve it most easily by thinking laterally. Look for an alternative that is different from what you might expect. Below are nine dots. Draw this nine-dot pattern on a sheet of paper. Then, connect all the dots with four straight lines.

You must make the lines without raising your pencil or pen from the paper. Does it look easy? Try it!

Turn to page 47 for the solution. In order to solve the puzzle, you had to find an alternative solution that allowed you to go outside the normal expected boundaries. Old thought patterns probably did not help you (unless you have done this problem before). You had to use creativity and lateral thinking to arrive at your alternative solution. Did you figure it out?

READING REVIEW

1. What is lateral thinking?
2. What is an advantage to identifying alternative solutions to a problem?

Critical Thinking

3. **Identifying Alternatives** What alternatives did you try before you solved the nine-dot puzzle?

Identifying Alternatives

As we have seen, lateral thinking is a way of identifying a wide variety of alternative solutions to a problem. One of the best techniques of lateral thinking is called **brainstorming.** This experiment will help you develop your ability to use the brainstorming technique to solve problems. It will also help you improve your lateral thinking and your creativity.

After your class has been divided into groups, choose a moderator for your group. The moderator will lead the brainstorming session. Also, choose a recorder. That person will write down the ideas that come up in the session. That person should write fast and have handwriting that is easy to read.

The moderator will be given a topic by your teacher. Your moderator will announce the topic to your group. After you have carefully read the directions below, your group will have five minutes to brainstorm as many solutions as you can to solve the problem. When the five minutes are up, the recorder and the moderator for each group will report their group's ideas to the class. Here are the directions for this brainstorming session.

1. All ideas are welcome, no matter how silly or fantastic they may seem. Some alternatives that seem to be funny or odd at first may turn out to be the best solutions! For this reason, it is important not to judge

What are the advantages to brainstorming, *or thinking in a group?*

anybody's ideas, whether you think they are terrific or awful. Watch your expressions! They sometimes communicate your judgment more loudly than your words do.
2. Express your ideas fast and without a lot of explanation. Explanations will come later. Now you are just trying to get as many ideas as you can.

3. If you have an idea that takes up where the last idea leaves off, say the word "Piggyback!" and the moderator will call on you next. That way, you can add to the ideas of another team member without losing the group's train of thought. If you are not piggybacking, raise your hand and your moderator will call on you.

How To Demonstrate Reasoned Judgment

When you use critical thinking skills you are using reasoned judgment because you allow your reasoning abilities to help guide your decisions. Every day you see relationships between different things. Understanding how things are related to each other helps you solve problems. You know, for example, that there is a direct relationship between your behavior in class and the grades you get.

Analogic thinking is a way of thinking about relationships. Analogic thinking uses a form called an **analogy.** Analogies are pairs of directly related items. Here is an example of an analogy:

RED:STOP::GREEN:GO

There are two pairs of directly related items in this analogy. Here is how to read the analogy: "RED is related to STOP in the same way that GREEN is related to GO." Can you figure out the relationship between the first pair? RED is the symbol for "STOP." Is that relationship similar to the relationship between the second set of words? Yes, because GREEN is the symbol for "GO." The relationships between the first and second set of items is the same, so this is a **true analogy.**

How about this analogy?

TRUE:FALSE::CORRECT:RIGHT

Is this a true analogy? No, this is a **false analogy** because the relationship between the first pair of words, TRUE and FALSE, is that of opposites. The relationship between the second pair of words, CORRECT and RIGHT, is that of synonyms, or words that have the same meaning.

Sometimes analogies are expressed in words. But they can also be expressed in numbers, drawings, and symbols. What is the best answer to each of these analogies? Study the three analogies carefully before you decide on your answer. Write your answer on a separate sheet of paper.

A. 1:100::2:_____

B.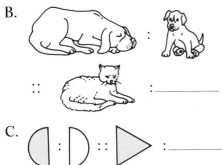

C. ◗ : ◖ :: ▷ :_____

READING REVIEW ══════
1. What is reasoned judgment?
2. What is an analogy? What is its form?

Critical Thinking

3. **Demonstrating Reasoned Judgment** What do you think might be one probable consequence of always using false analogies?

EXPERIMENT **1-Q**

Demonstrating Reasoned Judgment

In "Reading 21: How To Demonstrate Reasoned Judgment," you learned about analogies. In this experiment, you will have a chance to improve your abilities at analogic reasoning. Thus, you will be completing analogies, which is most often called *drawing analogies.*

Remember, an analogy is made up of two pairs of items. In a true analogy, the relationship between the first pair is exactly the same as the relationship between the second pair.

In the next column are 12 partially completed analogies. What would be the best word, number, symbol, or drawing to make each a true analogy? Study each analogy carefully before you decide. On a separate sheet of paper, write the entire analogy, including the last item for each, so that it is a true analogy. Be sure to check your answers carefully.

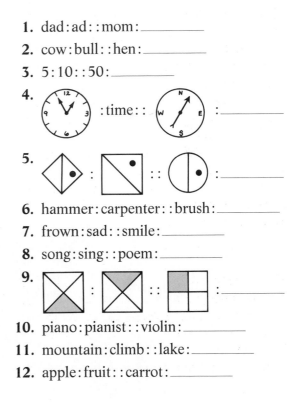

1. dad:ad::mom:_____
2. cow:bull::hen:_____
3. 5:10::50:_____
4. ⏰ :time:: 🧭 :_____
5. ◈ : ◹ :: ⊘ :_____
6. hammer:carpenter::brush:_____
7. frown:sad::smile:_____
8. song:sing::poem:_____
9. ⊠ : ⊠ :: ⊞ :_____
10. piano:pianist::violin:_____
11. mountain:climb::lake:_____
12. apple:fruit::carrot:_____

Critical Thinking Skills **41**

How To Draw and Test Conclusions

Lateral thinking is great for gathering a number of alternative ideas. Once you have many possible solutions, however, you need to find out which ones are best. Eventually, you have to draw conclusions about your problem. This is where linear thinking is most helpful. Once you have selected a possible solution, you must try it out to see if it really works. If it doesn't work, you can try one of the other alternatives you have created.

One method of drawing conclusions is a linear method called **deduction.** Deduction is a pattern of thinking in which two related statements, called *premises,* lead to a conclusion. This form of deduction is called a **syllogism.** If you understand deductions and syllogisms, you will be better able to solve problems by drawing and testing good conclusions.

A syllogism may show either good reasoning or faulty reasoning. Good reasoning is thinking that makes sense and that leads to workable conclusions. Faulty reasoning,

on the other hand, leads to poor conclusions and solutions that don't work well.

A syllogism is good if it has all three of the following characteristics:
1. The two premises are facts or inferences that have always been true and probably always will be true. (Example: Every human being is born and eventually dies.)
2. There is a logical connection between the two premises and the conclusion. The two premises should lead you directly to the conclusion.
3. The conclusion must be true.

If any of these conditions is missing, the syllogism is faulty and the conclusion may also be a mistake. Good critical thinking is always based on sound reasoning. Faulty reasoning leads us to mistakes in our thoughts and actions.

Here is an example of a syllogism:

Premise 1: All large men are football players.
Premise 2: John is a large man.

Are all football players large?

Conclusion: Therefore, John is a football player.

Is this a good syllogism? No, because the first premise is not true. All big men are not football players. That means that the conclusion is automatically questionable. In this case, we cannot tell whether John is a football player or not.

Make sure you understand the material in this reading before you go on to Experiment 1-R.

READING REVIEW
1. What is deduction?
2. What is a syllogism? How does it work?

Critical Thinking
3. **Drawing and Testing Conclusions** Create a syllogism using one of the seven propaganda techniques described in Reading 16. Is the syllogism faulty? Why or why not?

EXPERIMENT **1-R.**

Drawing and Testing Conclusions

Now that you have learned about deduction, try these syllogisms. Identify which are good and which are faulty. Then, explain how you could test each conclusion to see if it really works.

Syllogism A

Premise 1: When people dump garbage into waterways, the waterways become polluted.

Premise 2: Polluted water can make humans and other living things sick.

Conclusion: Therefore, if people didn't dump garbage into the waterways, the water would be less likely to be polluted and make humans and other living things sick.

Syllogism B

Premise 1: All people whose last names begin with the letter S have brown eyes.

Premise 2: Jane's last name begins with the letter S.

Conclusion: Therefore, Jane has brown eyes.

Syllogism C

Premise 1: All firefighters are hot-tempered.

Premise 2: Sam is a firefighter.

Conclusion: Therefore, Sam's dog has bad breath.

Syllogism D

Premise 1: A = B

Premise 2: B = C

Conclusion: Therefore, A = C.

Syllogism E

Premise 1: I could earn better grades if I worked harder.

Premise 2: I want to make better grades.

Conclusion: I should work harder in my school work to earn the better grades I want to make.

Critical Thinking Skills **43**

1 PERSPECTIVES

Social Scientists Look at Critical Thinking Skills

How do social scientists use critical thinking skills as they go about their day-to-day work? The following exercise focuses on the types of critical thinking skills social scientists might use if they were on a committee to study a proposal for a new waste disposal plant for Ourtown, U.S.A. Study the diagram below and then answer the questions on the next page labeled "Comparing the Social Sciences."

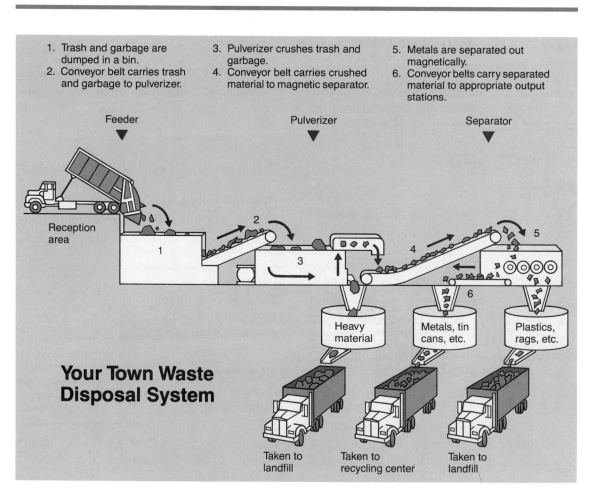

1. Trash and garbage are dumped in a bin.
2. Conveyor belt carries trash and garbage to pulverizer.
3. Pulverizer crushes trash and garbage.
4. Conveyor belt carries crushed material to magnetic separator.
5. Metals are separated out magnetically.
6. Conveyor belts carry separated material to appropriate output stations.

Feeder ▼   Pulverizer ▼   Separator ▼

Reception area

Heavy material

Metals, tin cans, etc.

Plastics, rags, etc.

Your Town Waste Disposal System

Taken to landfill   Taken to recycling center   Taken to landfill

Comparing the Social Sciences

Psychologists study the ways people react to things. If you were a psychologist testing ads for a waste-disposal program, what *critical thinking skills* would you need?

Sociologists study how groups behave. If you were a sociologist who wanted to convince a neighborhood committee that everyone would benefit from a waste-disposal program, what *critical thinking skill* would you need?

Anthropologists study cultures. What *critical thinking skills* would you need to find out if other cultures have more up-to-date waste-disposal programs than we have?

Geographers study the ways people use resources. If you were a geographer who wanted to show people that what they do with their trash today might affect the health of their children in 10 years, what *critical thinking skill* would you need?

Historians study the past. What *critical thinking skill* would you need if you were a historian who wanted to use the lessons of the past to help solve today's waste-disposal problems? Explain your answer.

Political scientists study politics. If you, as a political scientist, wanted to show that certain politicians were really against strict waste controls, no matter what they said, what *critical thinking skill* would you need?

Economists study the way people spend money. If you, as an economist, wanted to convince people to pay for an expensive waste-disposal program, what *critical thinking skill* would you need?

Volunteers at a recycling plant

GLOSSARY OF TERMS

action   doing or not doing something; for example, a physical or mental activity (page 8)

analogy   pairs of directly related items or ideas (page 40)

bias   a slanted view of something or someone (page 31)

brainstorming   a lateral thinking technique in which problems are solved by connecting ideas in new ways (page 39)

cliché   a worn-out phrase or an old-fashioned, narrow expression (page 29)

conceptualization   the picturing of a concept pattern in the mind; the step between perception and thoughts (page 8)

consistent   agreement between words and actions (page 25)

critical thinking   thinking clearly and with a purpose in mind (page 4)

deduction   a pattern of thinking in which two statements support a conclusion; also called a syllogism (page 42)

experience pattern   a pattern of learning that consists of five steps: perception, conceptualization, thoughts, action, reaction (page 8)

fact something that has been scientifically proven; that which is true (page 22)

false analogy an analogy in which the pairs of items are not related in a similar way (page 40)

ideology a set of beliefs (page 31)

induction a pattern of thinking in which several examples of past experiences lead to a conclusion about the present; the process of inference (page 36)

inference a conclusion based on evidence; a conclusion about the present or future drawn from past experiences (page 22)

irrelevant unrelated to the problem that needs to be solved; used to describe thoughts or ideas that do not fit together in a connected manner (page 18)

multiple causation the likelihood that an effect has many causes (page 35)

opinion a personal view, idea, or conclusion not necessarily based on fact; it cannot be proven right or wrong (page 22)

perception the process of gathering information from the environment into the senses (page 5)

propaganda information that is designed to convince people to do something or to believe something, based on emotion rather than reasoning (page 31)

reaction as used in this unit, the step of evaluation in the experience pattern (page 9)

relevant related to the problem that needs to be solved; used to describe thoughts or ideas that fit together in a connected manner (page 17)

stereotype an oversimplified view, usually negative, of a person or group of people (page 29)

syllogism two statements that lead to a conclusion; used in a deduction (page 42)

thought pattern connected thoughts that lead to an action (page 7)

true analogy an analogy in which the pairs of items are related in a similar way (page 40)

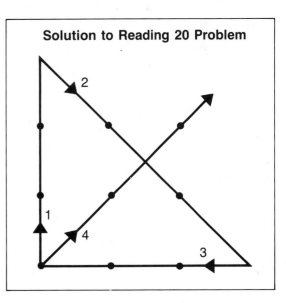

Solution to Reading 20 Problem

UNIT 2

Effective Study Skills

The wheel diagram labels: PSYCHOLOGY, ECONOMICS, SOCIOLOGY, POLITICAL SCIENCE, ANTHROPOLOGY, GEOGRAPHY, HISTORY, STUDY & THINKING SKILLS

Effective Study Skills

Panic time! That big history test that you thought was going to be next week has been moved up to *tomorrow*. You've got a ton of reading to do. If you had the full week, there would be no problem. You could have saved yourself by studying really hard over the weekend, maybe even asking your best friend to fill you in on what happened in class those two days that you missed. You could handle it. But now—no way. It's too much for a person to "cram" in just one night. And the teacher said this test will determine 50 percent of your grade for the semester. You're doomed!

Although the crisis pictured here may seem extreme, time is always limited when we seek to meet a challenge. Organizing our approach and concentrating our attention offers the best chance of success. The Unit 2 readings offer some tips on effective study skills. In the experiments, you will see how these study skills can make a difference in your life.

Study Skills and You

In a sense, effective study skills are a time-tested method of getting things done efficiently. The questions below will help you understand some possible uses for these skills in your own life.

1. When you have many tasks to accomplish in a short period, how do you organize your time? Where did you learn your method of studying? How might you improve your study habits?
2. How do you generally go about trying to learn more on a subject that strikes your interest? Describe how you would search for information in a library. What limitations apply to each of the sources you consult?

UNIT 2 CONTENTS

Learning How To Study

You are probably asking yourself, "Why should I take time and effort to learn how to study? I've been doing that all through school!"

You are right. You *have* been learning and studying since you began school. Actually, your learning experiences about yourself and the world began as soon as you were born. But the chances are good that you have never developed a *system* of learning. Few students have a well organized way of going about their classroom work and assignments. Those who do have a system of learning are the students who enjoy school work the most.

It is unfortunate that learning how to study is seldom taught in schools. This unit is all about learning how to study so that learning is easier and more enjoyable for you.

If you give these suggestions a fair trial, you should be able to cut your studying time in about half, without lower grades. In fact, your grades should go up. Your work

should improve, and you should find yourself enjoying your classes and assignments more. How are you going to do this? Very simple. You will be taking a close look at five secrets of good studying. They have been used by many students and they really work. You will be using them in practice sessions in this unit.

Often it seems difficult to understand what a teacher is driving at. You will examine this problem and find suggestions for dealing with it. Half the battle is learning exactly what it is that the teacher considers important.

A lot of work throughout your life (in school and out of school) requires the ability to memorize. And yet, most people—of all ages—have a hard time remembering things. So we will spend some time in this unit trying several ways to improve your memory.

Almost all of your school work and work later in life involves reading. There are many ways to read. *How* you read something should depend on *what* you are reading. You will take a look at secrets of effective reading. What you learn here will serve you throughout your life.

Through reading you get information. Facts, ideas, and concepts have a way of hiding unless you know *where* and *how* to look up the information. That skill is even more important in learning than memorizing. The library is one of the most central places for storing and looking up information. Sometimes this learning center is called a *media center* or *learning resources center.* You will see how a library is organized and how you can use it most effectively.

One last word. By the time they are teenagers most people think they have a fairly good idea of their abilities. But no matter what you think you can do—or can't do—you can improve your work greatly. Just try the suggestions in this unit. You must give them your honest effort or they won't work. Try them for a while and *think positively* while you do your school work. You will be surprised how well you do. After all, what have you got to lose?

READING REVIEW

1. Why should you learn how to study?
2. What study skills will you learn?

Critical Thinking

3. **Determining Relevance** (see page 17) How will you personally benefit from this unit?

READING 2

What Is the Teacher Driving At?

One of the biggest problems students have in school is understanding what the teacher is driving at. What does the teacher want you to learn? What does the teacher expect from you on an exam or assignment? What does the teacher want you to do in class?

Teachers are people. We know that no two people are the same. Also no two teachers are the same. You know from your experiences in school that every teacher teaches differently and expects different things from students. There are, however, some things which are common to almost all teachers. If you understand them, you will be able to do better work and to enjoy your classes more.

All teachers want their students to understand what they are saying. If you don't follow what your teacher is saying, speak up. Ask the teacher to explain again. (You are probably not the only student who doesn't understand!) If you can't figure out what the teacher is trying to get across to the class, ask!

In addition to trying to understand what the teacher is driving at, you should pay close attention in class. (If you are one who pays attention, you already know that you will have to spend less time after class studying the material.) And you know, it's amazing what a good class can do for a teacher. A good, interested class can actually make most teachers teach better. A dull, uninterested class can make any teacher discouraged and a "bad" teacher. If you don't believe that a good class can make a better teacher, try an experiment. Get your fellow students together to plan ways of improving your work in class. You may be surprised by the results.

Although you may never have been taught this, there are certain **objectives,** or goals, which your teacher tries to achieve in teaching you and the other students. For example, your teacher may have in mind the objective that every student should learn how to read maps. If every student can read maps by the end of the lesson, the objective is achieved.

When the teacher's objectives are achieved, it shows up in your school work. You understand the material, and you make better grades. Reaching objectives is a cooperative effort. It takes active involvement by both the teacher and the students.

Here the author, John Jay Bonstingl, discusses a point with a few students.

Your classes are based upon communication. When the communication between you and your teacher is not clear, or when it breaks down, nothing is accomplished. So it is important to understand what your teacher is trying to communicate to you. Let's begin by examining three types of objectives commonly used by teachers.

1. Cognitive, or "knowing," objectives. These objectives deal with your *knowledge* of facts such as dates and places. Most of these cognitive objectives can be reached by memorization of information. Also included in this category is your understanding of how facts fit together.

2. Affective, or "feeling," objectives. These objectives do not deal with facts as much as they deal with how you feel about something or someone. For example, some teachers may want to achieve certain objectives with the students concerning racial or sexual prejudice. When people *feel* about something, they are more anxious to do something about it.

3. Skill objectives. These objectives deal with your ability to *do* something, a skill. Map-reading objectives mentioned earlier are skill objectives. In shop class, a skill objective may be making a lamp base or a table. A skill is the ability to perform a certain act well many times. In this unit you will be sharpening your study skills. We will be concentrating on reading, memorizing, and researching (learning how to look up information).

If you know the teacher's objectives, you have a great advantage. You know what to look for. You know what is expected of you and the class. Try to understand the teacher's objectives as early as you can. Once you know what your teacher is driving at, you can begin to improve your ways of studying.

EXPERIMENT 2-B How Do You Study?   HANDOUT

EXPERIMENT   2-C

Making a Time Log

One of the most effective ways of finding out exactly how you spend your time is by making a **time log.** A time log is an accurate record of your activities, hour by hour. By keeping a time log, you will be able to see where you are wasting time and where you are spending time wisely. At first, this may seem a waste of time and energy. But it isn't. You may be amazed how much time you spend on tasks which should take only a fraction of the time.

In this experiment you will have a chance to make a time log. The spaces on the handout are divided into hours 1 to 24. If you want to divide each hour into half-hour or fifteen-minute segments, go ahead. Just be sure to write in each space an accurate description of how you spent that period of time. Your descriptions do not have to be long or complicated.

At the end of the twenty-four-hour log period, answer the following questions as honestly as possible. Remember, no one can really tell you what amount of time is good to spend on any activity. *You* are the judge in deciding whether you are spending your time wisely.

1. How much time (outside class) was used in doing work related to school? Was that time well spent, or did you take more time to do the work than you should have? Did you spend too little time doing school work? (In answering this question, consider the grades you would *like* to make.)

2. How much time was used in having fun? Did you really enjoy what you were doing? How could you improve this use of your time?

3. Do you think your time log for this period is typical of your life? What is different? What is the same? Do you think any changes in your normal activities would help you? If you can think of any, which ones would they be?

Work done, leisure time begins.

Secrets of Successful Studying

"But I really studied for that test! I can't understand why I got a low grade."

"Yes, I did read the assignment, but I can't remember very much about it."

"I never was the best student in school, so what can you expect?"

How many times have you or your friends made these remarks? The sad thing is that students often make studying much harder for themselves than necessary. They don't realize that they can do good work in much less time—and actually enjoy it. How? By using a few secrets of successful studying. It takes some effort at first, but as you get used to these ways of studying, they become easier. Soon they become habits which allow you to put less time into your studies, get better grades, and enjoy school more. Here are five secrets of successful studying to improve your school work.

1. Get excited about it. Even if you aren't interested in the subject you are studying, pretend that you *are* interested. Make yourself believe it. If you are studying science, for example, pretend that you are a scientist. Put yourself into your work. In a while, you won't be pretending any more. You will actually convince yourself. You will really start to enjoy the subject. When that happens you will find yourself getting better grades. You may even find that other subjects become more enjoyable.

2. Organize yourself and your work. Before you begin to do your work, make a **do list.** Write down all the things you *must* do at the top of the list. Put all the things you don't have to do immediately at the bottom. Also put at the bottom all those activities you would like to do for fun. Your list can be of things that need to be done in a part of a day, an entire day, a week, or any other period of time. Write the time period at the top of your list. Next to each thing you have listed, write the amount of time you think you will need to do it. Be realistic, allowing a little extra time for each item.

Then, begin your work. Start at the top of your list. Do everything on the list in the order you have listed it. Keep to your list until your time is up, or until you have done all the items. It won't take much effort to do this, and it will save time in the long run.

Making a "do list" to organize your time is one way of improving your work. But organization involves more than that. It also means putting papers, books, pens,

DO LIST
Monday 3:00 PM -- 10:00 PM

MUST DO:
1. Band practice -- 1 hour
2. Go to library to renew book -- ½ hour
3. Eat supper -- 1 hour
4. Watch evening news for history assignment -- ½ hour

LATER: Call John
Walk the dog
Finish Monopoly game started last night
Write letter to Mary

and other school equipment in a certain place every time. A little extra thought can save a lot of time hunting for things.

Save time, also, by organizing everything you need for an assignment before you begin. You will be surprised how much studying time you can cut by doing this.

Of course, organization is an important part of everything you do—not just school work. Try this kind of organization for all of your activities. It will make it easier for you to organize your studying and class work. Organization will become a matter of habit.

3. Find a good working environment. Try to find some place to do your work that is away from noises and distractions. It is good to have one special place for this purpose which you use all the time. Try a few places for studying before you settle on one way. Your working space should be well lighted. There should be some fresh air coming into the room. Stale air has less oxygen, and oxygen is needed for your brain to work at its best. It is better to have the room a little cool, rather than warm. Warm environments make you sleepy or bored more easily. Experiment with soft music in the background. If it becomes too distracting, and you find yourself listening to the music rather than studying, turn off the music. Remember, the object is to do your *best* studying in the *least* time. If you don't pay attention to that all-important fact, you are only fooling yourself.

4. Focus on what you are studying. Don't let your mind wander. Concentrate on what you are doing. Put your entire self into your work until it is done. If your mind wanders you will not understand what you are studying. You will also lose time, and you probably will not enjoy doing the work.

What makes this room a good environment for studying? How does your work area compare with it?

5. Don't be afraid to do good work.
Strange as it may sound, there are many people in this world who are actually afraid to do good work. They are found not only in school, but in every age group and job. One reason for this is that some people believe that if they prove themselves better than other people, those "others" will not approve. They fear that they will not be popular. The fact is, they could not be more wrong. You can do a lot more for yourself and for other people by doing your best. Just imagine what life would be like if everyone did a poor job. Not a pleasant thought. Doing your best will pay off in whatever you may try.

These five secrets of successful studying are not the only ways to improve your work, but they will start you on your way. We will be using these five steps through-out this unit. Be sure to keep them in mind as you go through this course and the rest of your school years. These steps of studying have worked for many, many people. With a little effort on your part they can work for you. Once you are able to use the steps, your studying should be much easier for you.

READING REVIEW ═══════
1. How can you be more successful in your studying?
2. What are the five secrets of successful studying suggested in this reading?

Critical Thinking
3. **Identifying Alternatives** (see page 38) How could you improve your studying environment at home?

READING 4

How To Improve Your Memory for Numbers*

Most of your work in school (and a lot of work out of school) involves memorizing. And yet, you probably have never learned how to remember facts and figures in an organized way. In this part of the unit you will experiment with some ways of improving your memory.

But first, let's see what memory is. We do not know exactly what causes you to remember something. There is no single part of the brain which controls memory. The entire brain is responsible for storing and recalling memories.

You have two kinds of memory: **short-term memory** and **long-term memory.** The first type is used to remember things for a very short time, from a few seconds to several minutes. The second type is used to remember things for days, weeks, and even years. When you remember a telephone number just long enough to dial it, you are using your short-term memory. You use your long-term memory to recall birthdays of friends and names and faces of people you meet. Of course, these are only a few uses of your long-term and short-term memory systems.

The night before a test some students memorize as much as they can, take the

*This reading is adapted from Harry Lorayne, *The Memory Book.* (See Acknowledgements, pages 595–596.)

Some study conditions are hazardous to your learning.

your short-term memory? Most people can recall between five and ten single numbers in order immediately after looking at or hearing a group of numbers in a row. This is not too difficult.

Below, on this page, there are nine lines of numbers. Each line after the first line has one extra number. Start with the first line. Read the line and then focus your eyes on the numbers as a group. Concentrate hard. Take a "picture" of the number in your mind, just as you might snap a photo of it with a camera. Keep concentrating on it until you think you have it in your short-term memory. Then look up and try to recite the number-group. Repeat this process with the next line until you find that you can't hold an entire number-group in your memory.

```
1 4 9 2
1 4 9 2 5
1 4 9 2 5 0
1 4 9 2 5 0 7
1 4 9 2 5 0 7 3
1 4 9 2 5 0 7 3 8
1 4 9 2 5 0 7 3 8 4
1 4 9 2 5 0 7 3 8 4 2
1 4 9 2 5 0 7 3 8 4 2 7
```

How many numbers in a row were you able to remember?

Now let's try remembering the numbers in a different way. Split the number group into smaller groups, or chunks, of two or three numbers each. This is called **chunking.** (You might do this on a separate sheet of paper.) Instead of trying to remember this number:

```
149250738427
```

test, and then forget what they learned. They forget because they used their short-term memory. If you want to remember a fact for a long time you must keep the fact "in the back of your mind." If you keep reminding yourself of it, the fact will become part of your long-term memory. By exercising your memory you can train yourself to remember more things. You can also remember them longer and more clearly with practice.

Let's begin our memory training by working with numbers. How many numbers in a row can you remember by using you will have a series of smaller number groups to remember:

149	250	738	427

By grouping the numbers this way you are able to focus on them more easily. Therefore, it is also easier to remember them. When you have anything large to memorize, split it into small parts. You will still have to concentrate hard, but your mind will find it easier to "digest" what you want to memorize. The telephone company recognizes this, which is one reason why your telephone numbers are split into groups of three, three, and four. It is much easier to recall this telephone number:

(332) 243–7825

than this number:

4052437825

which is not broken down into several small groups.

It is a good idea to practice remembering numbers a few minutes each day. After you feel comfortable with, let's say, six numbers, try to remember seven. Go slowly. Trying to increase your span too quickly might be discouraging.

Use these techniques regularly. Practice a few minutes each day, and you will be amazed how your ability to memorize numbers will improve!

READING REVIEW

1. What is the benefit of having a good memory in your school work and in your relationships with others?
2. What are the two kinds of memory?

Critical Thinking

3. **Recognizing Cause and Effect** (see page 35) Why is it easier for you to remember information if you "chunk" or group it in small bits?

READING 5

How To Improve Your Memory for Names and Faces*

In this reading we will see how you can remember names more easily. We will also see how to connect names with numbers and dates, and names with faces.

You have probably noticed that your memory works best if you really put your mind to it—if you really *want* to remember

*This reading is adapted from Harry Lorayne, *The Memory Book*. (See Acknowledgements, pages 595–596)

something. Long-term memory works for you only when you are determined to remember something important to you. Short-term memory works for a limited time because your mind holds information for only as long as you need it. When the need is gone, so is the memory.

The trick to remembering something for a long time is to make a very clear and lasting picture of it in your mind, whether it is

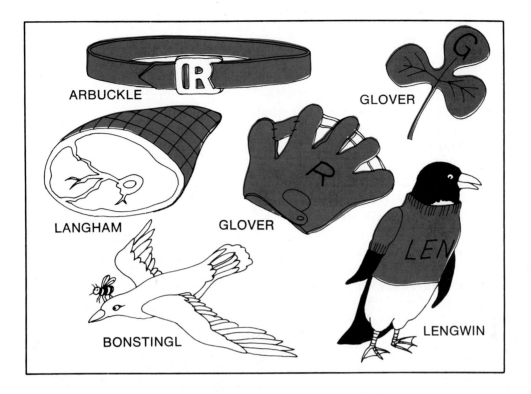

ARBUCKLE

GLOVER

LANGHAM

GLOVER

BONSTINGL

LENGWIN

a number, a face, or a name. Concentrate on it. Make your mental picture a funny or ridiculous one. Such a memory tends to last much longer. Remembering names and numbers requires concentration and organization. In remembering names we will use a system called **association.** Here is how association works.

Suppose you want to remember the name *Arbuckle.* Simply picture in your mind a belt buckle that looks like an "R." If you want to remember the name *Langham,* picture a long ham hanging from a meat hook. *Glover* can be recalled in two ways, depending on how the name is pronounced. If it rhymes with clover, picture a four-leaf clover with a big letter "G" inside it. If it is pronounced like "glove," then picture a big baseball glove with a huge "R" in the pocket of the glove.

The name of the author of this book is *Bonstingl.* One way to remember it is to take it apart this way. Picture a bee on top of a seagull. The bee is stinging the gull. Bee-on-sting-gull! If you want to remember a person whose last name is *Lengwin,* you could picture a penguin with the name of Len. Len the Penguin—Lengwin! Just use your imagination, and you can remember any name this way. Once you have the real name firmly in your memory, you will have no need to remember the original mental picture. You will forget the picture and recall the name very easily.

Suppose you want to remember a person's name and face. You need to concentrate on both the name and the face. Focus all of your attention on those two things. Do this with a firm intention to remember them for a long time. It may be helpful to write the person's name on a piece of paper and then to say it out loud. That way, three things about the person become printed on your memory: the pronunciation of the name, the spelling of the name, and the face which belongs to both.

Use the system of association to link faces with names. You just met a person whose name is Ms. Walters. As you shake hands, repeat her name out loud so that it becomes fixed in your memory. (Saying her name out loud is also considered polite: "Pleased to meet you, *Ms. Walters*.") As you say this, picture something in your mind that will help you recall the name and Ms. Walters' face. You might associate the name *Walters* with "wall tears" (picturing a wall crying). As you look at Ms. Walters, picture her at a wall crying. Or, try to see her face as a crying wall. It sounds crazy, but it works. As with the systems for remembering numbers, this system of association must be practiced in order for it to work for you.

Of course, there is another way of memorizing. It is the method you have probably been using all your life. It is **rote.** That means that you look at something, concentrate, and try to remember it. For some people, remembering by rote is easiest of all. Where it fails is in memorizing many facts at one time. The more you have to remember by rote, the more difficult it is to hold the facts in your mind.

Try association for a while without going back to rote. See how well it can work for you, both in and out of school.

READING REVIEW

1. What is association, and how does this technique help improve your memory?

Critical Thinking

2. **Identifying Central Issues** (see page 14) Give examples of how you could use association in three of your courses this year.

EXPERIMENT **2-D**

Improving Your Memory for Names and Faces*

By now, you should have developed a pretty good system for memorizing numbers. You may be using either rote memory or grouping. Use the system that works best for you.

In "Reading 5: How To Improve Your Memory for Names and Faces," you saw how easy it can be to remember names. The

*This experiment is adapted from Harry Lorayne, *The Memory Book.* (See Acknowledgements, pages 595–596.)

trick is to associate the name with a clear (and maybe funny) picture in your mind. Now let's suppose you are at a party and are introduced to six people you have never met. These are their names:

Ann Crosby	Jane Jeffrys
Cathy Koraido	Russ Baker
Jay Steinberg	Luis Valdez

How can you possibly remember all their names? Simple! Just associate each of the

Ann Crosby

Jane Jeffrys

Cathy Koraido

Russ Baker

Jay Steinberg

Luis Valdez

names with a picture of something that sounds like the name of the person. For example, for Ann Crosby, picture a cross and the letter "B" beside a big letter "N."

The picture is "N Cross B"—Ann Crosby.

Now you try the other names. On Handout 2-D describe your mental picture of each of the names listed.

Review in your mind each of these names and the mental pictures that go with them. Go over them several times. Then try to remember all the names. Can you do it?

If you have trouble remembering them all, try this trick. For each name, pick out a place in the room. Associate this place with the mental picture. For example, Ann Crosby could be associated with the teacher's desk. Picture a big "N" and a cross and a "B" (or a bee) on the teacher's desk. Do the same for each name and mental picture. Review them several times in your mind. Now can you remember all the names more easily? You can use this method of remembering for just about anything.

Now you have memorized each person's name. Would you be able to remember each person's name *and face?* Of course you would. Study their names and pictures on page 47. Look at each name and face and then look at the pictures below.

In order to associate each name with its face, picture each person doing something, in addition to your mental picture of the person's name. For example, picture Ann Crosby with a big N and a cross on her forehead. Or picture her carrying a cross with an N on it. Any vivid and clear picture will do, as long as it helps you remember the name. And when you have the picture of the person doing something in your mind, repeat the name to yourself. Say it out loud if you can. That will help you print the pronunciation of the name on your memory.

Once you have done that, review each mental image and face. Do you think you can identify each person by name now? If you think you can, go on with this experiment. If you are not quite sure yet, go back and review the names and faces once more.

The same photos appear again on page 64. This time they are scrambled. See how many mental pictures and names you can associate with the faces.

Well, how did you do? If you couldn't identify all the people by name, go back and review the names and faces once again. Go through the process of forming a mental image and associating the image with the photo. Then try naming the people once more.

Now you have systems for remembering faces, names, and numbers. How can you use these systems in your school work? If you are like most people, you have some trouble remembering a lot of facts, especially names and numbers. Suppose you had to remember a list of battles or wars and the years they began. How would you use your memory systems to do that? What other ways could you use these systems for remembering facts?

Later in life, you will find these memory systems very useful. People in the business world meet many people every day. Some of the people are familiar to them while many may not be. Regardless, it is very impressive to most people if you can remember their names immediately. It shows them that you consider them important. Your teacher has a similar job at the start of each new school year, memorizing dozens of new names and faces. It is helpful to have a good system for remembering them.

We have explored only a few of the ways you can use memory systems both now and later. Remember, the systems are yours only as long as you use them regularly. Keep using them and they will last you a lifetime.

How To Read Better

One problem shared by many students is poor reading habits. That's unfortunate because reading can be fun. It can also be your best source of information about yourself and the world around you. By now, you probably realize that reading is necessary for success in school. You will undoubtedly find that it is necessary for success later in life, too.

What if you had a chance to talk with someone who lived hundreds of years ago where you live today? What would you ask that person? What do you think he or she would talk about? Of course, you can't ask these questions face-to-face. But you can share that person's ideas if they were written down. Reading the ideas can be just as interesting as talking to the person who once spoke these ideas. Reading about the ideas and experiences of living persons can be exciting also. It is always good to get a letter from a close friend who is traveling or living a great distance from you. Reading the letter is almost as good as being there.

In the course of your lifetime, you will read billions of words. You will share the thoughts of many people who have written their ideas for you and others to read and think about. How much you understand of what you read will depend on *how* you read. Most people, including adults, don't realize that there are different types of reading material. Each type should be read in a different way. There are three basic types of reading material:

1. Pleasure reading Most novels (fiction), short stories, poetry, and articles from newspapers and magazines are written to entertain (and inform) the reader. This type of reading material can be read at any speed, depending on which style and speed gives the reader the most pleasure. It is generally read for entertainment. It is not used for memorization or tests, except perhaps in English classes.

2. Text reading This type of reading is used for studying and remembering. There is a greater need for concentration than there is with pleasure reading. One reads textbooks (such as this one) and almost all reading material used in school work for the purpose of learning specific information. Of course, that doesn't mean that text reading can't be fun. It can be if you think of it that way.

3. Reference reading Reference reading is different from both pleasure reading and text reading. The purpose of reference reading is to find facts. This type of reading involves using books of facts, numbers, and names. The books include: dictionaries, encyclopedias, almanacs, atlases, bibliographies, card catalogs, and indexes such as the *Readers' Guide to Periodical Literature*. We will examine each of these reference materials later in this unit.

Newspaper reading can be done for pleasure and to get information.

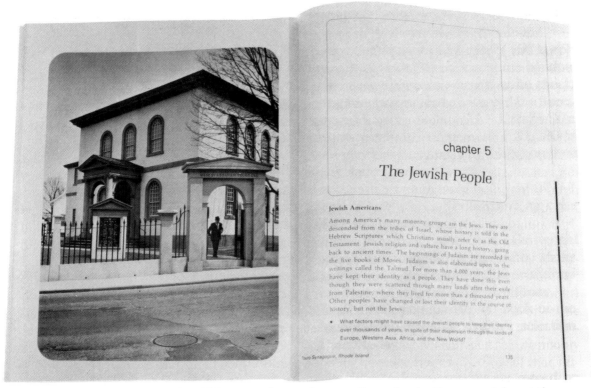

There are guideposts *you should know and use when reading a book. Can you pick out the following guideposts, or parts, in the two pages of text above: photo, caption, chapter title, subtitle, page number, and basic text? Before you begin to read any book, you should study whatever guideposts there are.*

Each type of reading requires a different attitude, or frame of mind. Text reading requires the most concentration for long periods of time. Reference reading can be done without such long periods of concentration, if notes are taken of the facts being researched. Both text and reference reading should be done in a serious frame of mind. These two kinds of reading are done with a goal in mind: to find and use facts and ideas.

Pleasure reading, on the other hand, is done primarily for fun. The goal of the reader is to enjoy reading, not necessarily to learn new facts or ideas. Textbooks and reference books are most often read for information. If you understand the three types of reading material, you will be able to get the most benefit from each.

READING REVIEW ═══

1. What are the three main types of reading?
2. From your own experience, give examples of the three types of reading material.

Critical Thinking

3. **Determining Relevance** (see page 17) Why is it important *how* you read something?

The SQ3R Method

One of the best and most widely known methods of text reading is called the **SQ3R Method.*** This method combines reading and studying in five steps:

S—Survey Don't just jump right into your reading. Warm up first, in a way that will help you to understand it better. The warm-up exercise in reading consists of reading all the titles and subtitles of the chapter. Look at the pictures and other illustrations and read the captions. If the chapter has an introduction and a summary, this is the best time to read them. Also, pay close attention to questions at the end of the chapter.

By surveying the chapter before you begin to read it, you have an idea of what the author will be saying. You will be able to follow the author's thoughts much more easily. In a way, it's like planning a long trip on a road map before taking off for the destination. The author includes titles, subtitles, pictures, and illustrations to help you follow the direction of her or his thoughts. If you use the Survey step you will understand the reading much better.

*The discussion of the SQ3R Method is adapted from Francis P. Robinson, ''Steps in the SQ3R Method'' in *Effective Study.* (See Acknowledgements, pages 595–596.)

Q—Question After the first step, S—Survey, you should have enough information about the chapter to begin asking yourself questions such as these: What is the chapter all about? What do I already know about the material in this chapter? What should I know when I am finished reading this chapter? What feeling and skill objectives does the author probably have in mind?

Take enough time and concentration to do the first two steps of the SQ3R Method well. They can save you a lot of needless, extra effort when rereading the chapter later. They will also help you remember and understand more.

R-1—Read Now you are ready to do what most people do right away—read the chapter from beginning to end. As you read, watch for the guideposts the author has given you. Notice how the introduction, titles and subtitles, and illustrations fit in with the rest of the book. Recall the questions you asked yourself in the second step (Q—Question). See if you can pick up any answers to those questions as you do the reading. If you have done a good job of surveying and questioning, you will find it easy at this stage to follow the author's thought patterns.

R-2—Recite Now close the book. Try to recall the important parts of the chapter. It is best if you can remember the author's thoughts step by step. Try to explain it to an invisible student or friend. Do this step out loud. If you understand it well enough to explain it to someone else, you know it well enough to pass any test. This step is well worth the extra time it takes. But it should be done as soon as possible after you finish reading, while it is fresh in your mind.

R-3—Review After you have recited, open the book again. See how much you covered in your recitation and how much you missed. Use this review to go over any material you were not able to explain to yourself in the recitation. Concentrate on making all the pieces fit together.

If your recitation was not very good the first time, close your book again and try reciting again. Then review a second time. Put the book aside now and do something else. Later, come back to it and try the last two steps again. Repeating this process will allow you to make the chapter's contents a part of the long-term memory. You will understand the material much better as a result.

If you want to improve your work even more, add one step to the SQ3R process. Add a *Writing* step after the Recite step. After you summarize the main points of the reading, write them down on a sheet of paper. Then take a few minutes to concentrate on what you have written. Picture your written summary in your mind. Finally, go to the Review step and complete the SQ3R Method. If you add the Writing step to the regular SQ3R Method, you will be studying the material in several different ways. You will be speaking and hearing the material, writing and seeing it, and thinking it. Of course, the greater number of ways you study something, the better and longer you learn it.

Although the SQ3R Method may sound like a lot of extra work, you actually *save time* with it. Most people separate reading from studying. In the SQ3R Method, reading and studying are combined. This saves a lot of time reading the material a second and third time. If you do it right the first time, you will not have to spend as much total time on the material, and you will understand it better and for a longer time.

READING REVIEW

1. For which of the three main types of reading material would you use the SQ3R Method?
2. Name the five steps of the SQ3R Method, and describe each step.

Critical Thinking

3. **Demonstrating Reasoned Judgment** (see page 40) Why is it good to add the *Write* step?

Improving Your Reading Skills

In "Reading 6: How To Read Better" we saw that there are three basic types of reading and that there is a special way to read each one.

Listed below are some types of reading material. Do you know how each one should be read? On a separate sheet of paper write the word "Pleasure" or "Text" or "Reference" to indicate which type of reading material each one is.

1. The introduction to a social science textbook
2. A poem
3. An article in an encyclopedia
4. A novel
5. A book on gardening
6. The sports pages of your newspaper
7. An entry in the dictionary
8. The telephone directory
9. A short story
10. A review of a movie
11. The *Readers' Guide to Periodical Literature*
12. An atlas
13. The owner's manual for a new car
14. Your science textbook

Using the SQ3R Method*

In Reading 7 you learned the five steps of the SQ3R Method. We added an additional step, *Write,* which will help you do the best

*This experiment is adapted from Francis P. Robinson, "Steps in the SQ3R Method" in *Effective Study.* (See Acknowledgements, pages 595–596.)

possible work in reading and studying. Now we will try to apply the SQ3R method to an actual reading.

Here is a selection from a geography textbook, *Our World and Its Peoples.* Read it, using the SQ3R Method. See how much better you understand what you are reading. Don't be discouraged if you think it is slower this way than reading it straight through. With a little practice the SQ3R Method can be done even more quickly than other ways of reading and studying.

When you have completed the reading, take the short test, which your teacher will give you on a handout, to see how much you understand. You may be surprised by the results.

Our Earth and its Natural Resources**

For many years, authors of science fiction wrote many stories imagining that some day rockets would reach the moon. After World War II, the United States began experimenting with space vehicles, chiefly at Cape Kennedy, Florida. The goal was reached when two American astronauts landed on the moon in 1969.

Let us join one of our real astronauts on an imaginary trip to the moon. At an average speed of 4800 kilometers (3,000 miles) an hour, it will take our space vehicle about three days to reach the moon. After landing, we will need to put on pressurized suits with oxygen tanks to explore the moon's surface. We immediately see that there is no sign of either human or vegetable life anywhere. This is true because the moon does not have the natural resources which make life possible for humans on earth. After returning from our imaginary trip to the moon, we can take a look at our earth to find out what natural resources are important for life on earth.

**From Edward R. Kolevzon and John A. Heine, *Our World and its Peoples*. (See Acknowledgements, pages 595–596.)

The Seven Kinds of Natural Resources

There are seven kinds of natural resources which make it possible for humans to live on earth. They are:

1. Sunlight   5. Forests
2. Air   6. Minerals
3. Water   7. Wildlife
4. Soil

Sunlight—Source of Light and Energy. Sunlight is the chief source of all the energy used by living things. Green plants use it to make the starches and sugars they need for growth. Plants are used by animals for food. In turn, humans use both plants and animals for food.

Sunlight also gives us our fuels. These include wood, coal, and petroleum. Water, evaporated by the sun, later falls as rain or snow. The water, flowing down the rivers, makes possible hydroelectric power.

It is the heat of the sun that warms the earth and makes it possible for us to live on our planet. Although most of the sun's rays never reach the earth, enough gets through to heat the surface of the earth. Some people believe that the day will come when we shall be able to make use of the energy of the sun even to heat homes, move automobiles, and run motors.

Our Ocean of Air. The earth is surrounded by an atmosphere which is sometimes called an "ocean of air." The oxygen in the air is so important to life that without it humans cannot live for more than a few minutes. Airplane pilots, climbing high into the atmosphere, must use oxygen tanks. Plants and animals also need oxygen in order to live.

Air is important in many other ways. It helps us to inflate the tires on our automobiles. Without air the wings of a bird or an airplane cannot be supported while in flight. The oxygen in the air is needed to keep the gas flame going in your stove or in your oil furnace. It may even surprise you to know that in a place that has no air there can be no sound. Although most people think that the only reason we need air is for the oxygen we breathe, it has hundreds of other uses.

The Importance of Water. Some doctors tell us that we should drink eight glasses of water a day. Water is also necessary for many other reasons other than health. In fact, it has been said that each person in the United States uses over 570 liters (150 gallons) of water each day. Water is helpful to man in other ways. It provides hydroelectric power for light, heat, and machinery. By wearing away rocks, water helps to form fertile soils for farming. Plants and animals also need water to live.

The fish that swim in the waters of our oceans and seas provide food each day for millions of people. From the waters of the Dead Sea scientists have been able to get such minerals as potash. Natural sponges also come from the waters of the world. No wonder some people have used the phrase, "mining the sea," to describe all the natural resources that man gets from the oceans.

Without water many factories would have to close. To make a metric ton of steel, about 272,000 liters (71,600 gallons) of water are needed. A metric ton of newsprint requires about 209,000 liters (55,100 gallons). Water is also needed to cool machines in factories. Automobiles and trucks on the highway, as well as other kinds of heavy machinery, such as tractors, use water to cool their engines.

The earliest highways were the waters of the rivers, lakes, and oceans. The waterways—then and now—provide easy methods to travel since they cost nothing to build and cost little, if anything, to maintain. Sending heavy goods for long distances over the water is usually the cheapest way to ship them. At times a country builds a canal, which is a man-made waterway, to join two other water highways. The Panama Canal, for example, connects the Atlantic and Pacific Oceans. It shortens the trip by boat from New York City on the east coast to San Francisco on the west coast by almost 12,800 kilometers (8000 miles).

Water has also become an important source of power. Water is so important that in a number of places in the world including Israel, Kuwait, and Florida's Key West, large machines have been built to convert sea water into fresh water to take care of the water shortage in these areas. De-salted (desalinated) water is rather expensive. However, people living in the areas where there are converters are willing to pay the higher price to get the important fresh water.

Soil Is Necessary. Why is soil so important to all of us? The next time you drive along a highway which cuts through the farmlands of the countryside look around and you'll be able to find clues to the answer. Wheat, corn, tomatoes, and trees need the soil—and the minerals found in that soil—to grow. In fact, all vegetation lives and grows in the soil.

Plants provide all of us with most of our food. Some are the vegetables and fruits which we eat at meals. Others are used to provide food for animals which, in turn, give us meat, milk, cheese, and butter. They also give us such materials to wear as leather, wool, and furs. Without soil there would be no forests and trees for our lumber.

Only 10 percent of the earth's land surface is farmed. Much of the rest cannot be used to raise crops. In other places people have misused the soil so that it can no longer be used for farming. Fortunately, science—through the use of fertilizers, machinery, and methods of irrigation—has made it possible for farmers to raise larger amounts of crops on a given piece of land. It has also made it possible to use certain areas for farming which once could not be used.

There are many different kinds of soil throughout the world. Those which are good for raising crops are said to be fertile. Those soils poor in quality, which do not produce good crops are said to be infertile.

One way in which you can tell if a soil is fertile is by its color. If it is black, the soil probably has a great deal of humus. Humus is made up of the decayed remains of plants and animals. This decayed matter helps make soil fertile. The "black earth" areas of the plains of the United States and Canada, the Pampas of Argentina, and the Ukraine are very fertile. On them large amounts of wheat and corn are grown.

Forests Are Helpful. The paper for the page you are now reading in this book was made from a tree. The paper for your daily newspaper also came from a tree. This is one way in which forest trees help people. Forests are also important because they provide wood for buildings, railroad ties, and furniture. Wood pulp is used in making paper; cellulose, made from wood, gives us rayon fiber. This fiber is used to make many different kinds of clothing. Wood is also used as a fuel to make fires for cooking food or heating a home.

Forests help to conserve the soil and prevent floods. When it rains, the roots of trees "drink in" the water. This prevents the rain from carrying away the soil and overflooding river banks. Trees also help to slow up the wind and thereby reduce the amount of soil blown away.

Almost one-third of the earth's land is covered by forests. Yet, so many trees have been used or destroyed by humans, insects, and fires, that we may soon face a shortage of forest resources. Presently, about 5 percent of our original forest in the United States still remains. However, much land has been replanted to grow new trees.

The Age of Minerals. It has been said that we live in the Age of Minerals. Improved transportation and communication would be impossible without minerals. Automobiles and airplanes use many minerals such as copper, chromite, tungsten, and petroleum. Every time we turn the switch for the electric light, toaster, or television set, the current travels through copper wires. Steel made from iron is used to make ships, locomotives, and trains. Telephone systems need no less than 14 minerals. Farmers need nitrates, phosphates, and potassium salts to fertilize their crops. The world would be very different without coal to provide power and heat, and iron to make machines and hold up buildings.

Minerals, unlike air, water, and forests cannot be replaced. Water running down a river valley will find its way to the sea, be evaporated, and fall again as rain. Young trees can be planted as older ones are cut down. But minerals, once used, are gone forever. Coal and oil, used as fuels, do not return to the earth from which they came. Some minerals, such as copper and petroleum, are used so widely that shortages have already developed.

Logs on their way to a sawmill. The United States uses wood faster than it can be grown. More trees need to be planted to meet the demand for wood.

Endangered species such as mountain gorillas are threatened both by hunters and by the destruction of the rain forest.

Many people believe that we are using up our mineral resources too quickly. However, scientists and engineers have tried to help us conserve our minerals by teaching us how to mine without being so wasteful. Also, they help us discover new places where minerals may be found. The increasing use of nuclear power will be helpful in providing another source of fuel and energy. Newer uses for such metals as aluminum, titanium, and magnesium should help offset the dwindling supply of some mineral resources. They can be substituted for those in short supply.

Wildlife Offers Many Gifts. This resource includes fish, birds, and other wild animals, many of which are important to people as food. The fisheries of the North Pacific provide the people of Japan with an important part of their diet. Salmon fishing and canning are key industries in Alaska. For hundreds of years, the fishing banks of the North Atlantic have given food to millions of people in Europe and North

America. Codliver oil and fertilizer are other valuable products of fisheries.

Hunters and people living in thinly populated places often depend upon wildlife for their food. In some parts of the world, such as the far North, people live chiefly by hunting. Fur trapping is important in several of the more northern parts of the world, such as Alaska, Canada, and Russia.

Some Wildlife Is Tamed. For a long time people have realized that animals can serve them in at least three important ways. The first is to give people such foods as meat, milk, cheese, cream and butter. Also, animals such as a horse, donkey, camel, elephant or water buffalo can help pull a plow, wagon, or sled. The hides of cattle and goats can be used to provide leather for shoes, belts, coats, or even furniture coverings. Wool from sheep or lambs makes warm clothes for people living in colder climates. These animals, once wild, and now tamed by humans for their own use, are known as "domesticated animals."

Getting the Main Ideas*

So far in this unit we have explored ways of improving your memory, reading, and studying. We have also seen what objectives are, and why they are important. All of this should help you become a better student and to enjoy your school work more. This reading is designed to help you get the points your teacher and your textbooks are making.

One way of picking out the main points is by **underlining** them in your book, lightly in pencil. If you don't *own* your textbooks, do not underline them. They belong to the school. In your own books, now and in later schooling, you may want to use the underlining method. We will see how this is done in class.

Another way of helping yourself understand the main ideas is by **outlining** material. Outlining can be done whether or not you own the book. It also has the advantage of being portable. You can make your outlines in notebooks, or on loose-leaf paper. Let's try a short exercise to see how outlining is done. Say, for example, that we have ten blocks that look like this:

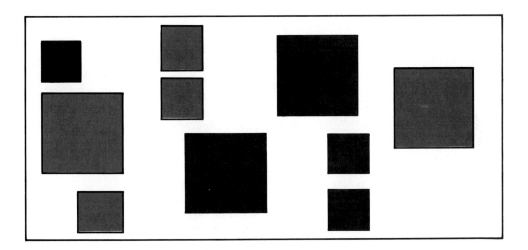

*This reading, together with the diagrams, is adapted from Robert A. Carman and W. Royce Adams, *Study Skills: A Guide for Student Survival.* (See Acknowledgements, pages 595–596.)

If you wanted to classify them into groups and subgroups, how would you do it? First, we could classify them all as *blocks*, even though there are different kinds of blocks. Next, we might classify the blocks into two groups: big blocks, and small blocks. Look carefully at the diagram below.

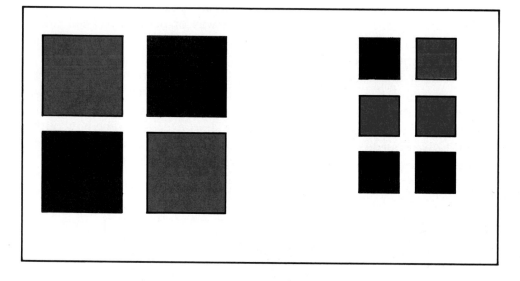

Now, we can classify them even further. The big blocks can be separated into big red blocks and big black blocks. The small blocks could be classified in two similar groups: small red blocks, and small black blocks.

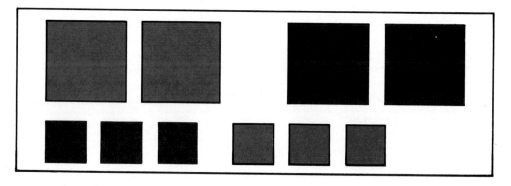

If we used these three classifications, we could make a **concept tree,** which is a method of organizing concepts and facts. The concept tree looks like this:

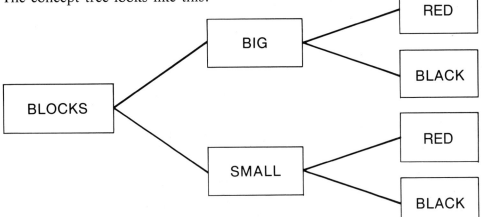

Now let's divide the concept tree into parts and make an outline from it.

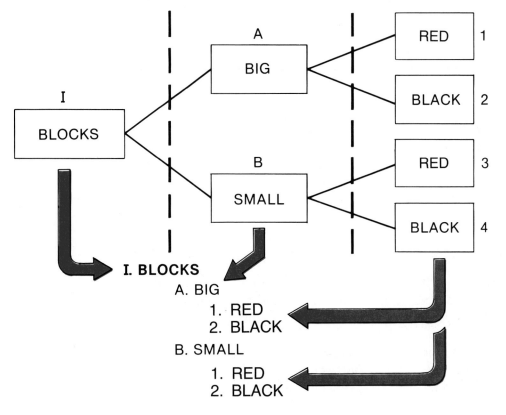

Of course, you don't often have to outline red and black blocks or make concept trees of them. But you *do* have to outline and make concept trees of ideas. Many students find it helpful to make an outline of the chapter of a textbook they are studying. You have probably used outlining in taking notes in classes.

So let's talk about using ideas, instead of blocks. Outlining is a way of organizing ideas. Your teacher may outline his or her class notes before the period begins. Outlining helps the teacher organize ideas and thoughts so that your notes can be clear and complete. Outlining can help *you* to organize the notes the teacher gives you and the information contained in your books. We will talk more about taking notes in class later in this unit.

Let's say you have the following words in your notes. How would you put them into an organized concept tree?

boxers	crows	birds
seagulls	rabbits	dogs
collies	beagles	hummingbirds
animals		

Would it look like the one below?

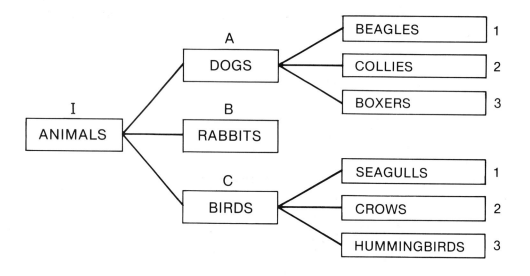

The word that describes all the others is *animals.* That is the main idea. The minor ideas are *birds, dogs,* and *rabbits.* You can then divide the birds into seagulls, crows, and hummingbirds. You can divide the dogs into beagles, collies, and boxers. The rabbits category can't be narrowed down any further because there is only one word that describes rabbits.

The concept tree in outline form would look like the representation on the top of the following page:

I. ANIMALS
    A. DOGS
        1. BEAGLES
        2. COLLIES
        3. BOXERS
    B. RABBITS
    C. BIRDS
        1. SEAGULLS
        2. CROWS
        3. HUMMINGBIRDS

Notice that in this type of outlining the main idea is written farthest to the left. A Roman numeral is placed in front of it. The minor ideas are written under the major ones and are placed more to the right.

That is one way of outlining. There is another way of arranging an outline, the bubble method. It was used by a recent presidential candidate. If he were outlining our concept tree, it might look like this:

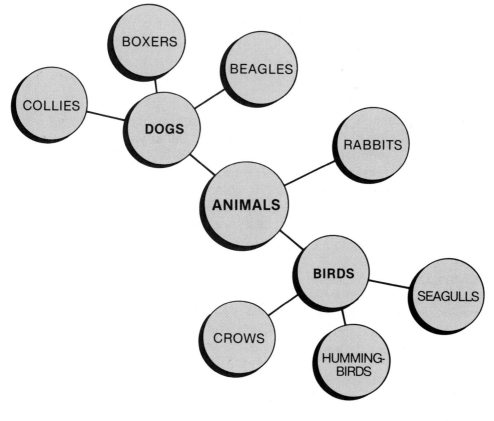

In this type of outlining, minor ideas shoot off from the major idea. You can tell which ones are the major ideas because they are at the center. This type of outlining is good for delivering a speech because the bubbles catch the eye of the reader who is making the speech. A speaker can read and follow it more quickly than the other type of outlining. It allows the speaker to spend more time looking out at the audience, instead of reading the paper containing the notes.

Both ways of outlining are good. You can use either the outline which is based on the concept tree or the "bubble" method. Which one is better depends on you. Try both of them and choose a style which is best for you. Whichever one you choose, your outline will help you organize the ma-terial you are studying. Outlining helps you organize your thoughts to make them more easily understood and remembered. Many students have discovered that when they have a good, clean outline to study, they can make better grades. They take a mental picture of the outline. This method saves a lot of time and effort.

READING REVIEW

1. What is a concept tree?
2. In a concept tree, where is the main concept placed?

Critical Thinking

3. **Recognizing Cause and Effect** (see page 35) How can outlining help you to organize your thoughts?

EXPERIMENT   **2-G**

Picking Out the Main Ideas

PART ONE

One of the most important things you should learn as a student is how to read a paragraph and then be able to put that paragraph into your own words. For example, what do you think the main ideas are in the paragraphs of this short reading taken from an American history textbook?

Extract 1*

The invention of the radio depended in large measure on the early work of Heinrich Hertz of Germany and Guglielmo Marconi of Italy. The money possibilities of radio were not at first obvious. It was in 1920 that the first musical broadcasts were made and baseball games were reported. In that same year the radio "commercial" was born.

The radio made it possible for the people to listen to descriptions of ball games and to hear music and plays. Melodramatic soap operas enlivened the day for many a housewife. . . . For the tired husband home from work, no day would have been complete without a half hour with the comedians Amos 'n' Andy. No Sunday would be complete without the mystery thriller "The Shadow."

People could now be reached by political leaders. Millions participated in the political events of the day as they had never before been able to do. They followed the

*Adapted from Gerald Leinwand, *The Pageant of American History*. (See Acknowledgements, pages 595–596.)

Smith-Hoover campaign of 1928. No politician made better use of radio than Franklin D. Roosevelt. With a radio voice that captivated his listeners, the President shared with the people his efforts to end the Great Depression. His "Fireside Chats" brought the Chief of State into every home. Through the radio the people in America—as well as in Germany—heard Hitler clamor for Czechoslovakia. And on the radio perhaps the most magnificent orator of them all, Prime Minister Winston Churchill, spoke to his countrymen and to Americans. He warned them that Hitler's threatened invasion was a serious challenge to democracy's survival.

Now try to pick out the main ideas in Extracts 2, 3, and 4. Try to think of a title for each of the extracts you read. This will also help you to organize your thinking. Extracts 2, 3, and 4 are immediately following.

Early radio entertainers

Extract 2*

A dramatic breakthrough came in sports when the Brooklyn Dodgers president, Branch Rickey, signed Jackie Robinson to

*From *The Black American in United States History* by Edgar A. Toppin. (See Acknowledgements, pages 595–596.)

a contract in the fall of 1945. At that time, not a single black athlete participated in organized professional baseball, football, or basketball. Moreover, none were admitted to play in any tournaments of the U.S. Professional Golfers Association or the U.S. Lawn Tennis Association. The hiring of Robinson by a major league baseball

Effective Study Skills **81**

After hitting a home run, Jackie Robinson is congratulated by a teammate.

club ended the disgraceful color bar that had excluded many great athletes.

Such great black baseball players as Rube Foster, Satchel Paige, Buck Leonard, and Josh Gibson had been barred from major league baseball. Major league professional contracts in football and basketball had been denied to black All-American college players. Football star "Brud" Holland and basketball star Don Barksdale, for example, were denied contracts. Such black stars as Fritz Pollard and Duke Slater had played in the early years of pro football. They played from 1919 to 1933, but were excluded thereafter. A black catcher, Moses Walker, starred for Toledo of the American Association from 1884 to 1888. At that time the association was considered a major league in baseball. But no blacks had played in organized baseball since then.

Rickey carefully selected Jackie Robinson to be the pioneer in ending the color bar in sports. Robinson was born in Georgia but his family moved to California in his childhood. Jackie starred in football, basketball, track, and baseball at U.C.L.A. (University of California, Los Angeles campus), before leaving school in 1941. His elder brother, Mack, was a track star who finished second to Jesse Owens in the 1936 Olympics. After military service, Jackie played for a black baseball team until Rickey signed him.

Robinson was placed on the top team of the Dodger farm system, the Montreal Royals. He endured in silence the taunts and insults of those players and fans opposed to his breaking the color bar in baseball. But his outstanding play soon won him the admiration of players and the support of fans. Playing the 1946 season in the minor leagues Robinson led his league in batting and in stolen bases. He then moved up to the major leagues. In ten seasons with the Dodgers, he led them to the league championship six times. Robinson was voted the National League Rookie-of-the-Year in 1947 and the Most Valuable Player in 1949. He had a lifetime batting average of .311 and was voted into baseball's Hall of Fame.

The ceremony of kowtow

Extract 3*

Tribute states had to accept the Chinese emperor as their ruler. They sent presents to the Chinese emperor as tribute. This showed they recognized the power and greatness of China. The ambassadors bringing this tribute also had to kowtow to the emperor.

The kowtow is a sign of loyalty and respect to the emperor. The Chinese had performed the ceremony of the kowtow for centuries. It went something like this:

People gathered and stood before the emperor. When the emperor was seated on his throne, an official called out: "Kneel down!" Everyone knelt. "Knock your heads to the ground!" The people touched their heads to the ground three times. "Stand up!" Everyone stood up. This ceremony was repeated three times.

*From *The Challenge of Change,* Learner-Verified Edition II, prepared by the Social Science Staff of the Educational Research Council of America. (See Acknowledgements, pages 595–596.)

Extract 4*

In the seventeenth century, most Europeans wore clothing made of wool. Cotton was expensive and hard to get. This was because most of the cotton cloth used in Britain was imported from India. Still, those who could afford it liked clothing made of Indian cotton. As the demand for cotton increased, a cotton cloth industry began to grow in Britain. After 1700, more raw cotton became available. The American colonies in the South began to grow large amounts of cotton, using slave labor. This, in turn, spurred the growth of the British cotton industry.

At first, cotton workers used the traditional methods and machines of the wool makers. Wool cloth has been made all over Britain for centuries. The thread was spun and woven into cloth in many homes

*From *The Interaction of Cultures.* Learner-Verified Edition II, prepared by the Social Science Staff of the Educational Research Council of America. (See Acknowledgements, pages 595–596.)

by the entire family. On market day, the farmer took the finished cloth to the nearest town to sell it. Wool cloth was an important part of most farmers' income.

Not all cloth making was done by individual families. Spinning was a very slow process. It took five or six spinners to produce enough yarn to keep one weaver busy. In the villages, weavers often bought a large amount of raw wool from neighboring farmers. Then they went from house to house in the village distributing the wool to spinners. In return, they paid the spinners a small wage. Traditional methods were used for making cotton cloth, too. Then a series of inventions made it possible for more cotton to be produced faster than ever before.

PART TWO

One way of picking out the main ideas in a reading is by underlining. This method should not be used unless the book or paper you are underlining is your own. An underline is simply a line drawn under the key words.

Here is an example of underlining, using Extract 1*, which you have already read.

The invention of the radio depended in large measure on the early work of Heinrich Hertz of Germany and Guglielmo Marconi of Italy. The money possibilities of radio were not at first obvious. It was in

*From Gerald Leinwand, *The Pageant of American History.* (See Acknowledgements, pages 595–596.)

1920 that the first musical broadcasts were made and baseball games were reported. In that same year the radio "commercial" was born.

The radio made it possible for the people to listen to descriptions of ball games and to hear music and plays. Melodramatic soap operas enlivened the day for many a housewife. . . . For the tired husband home from work, no day would have been complete without a half hour with the comedians Amos 'n' Andy. No Sunday would be complete without the mystery thriller "The Shadow."

People could now be reached by political leaders. Millions participated in the political events of the day as they had never before been able to do. They followed the Smith-Hoover campaign of 1928. No politician made better use of radio than Franklin D. Roosevelt. With a radio voice that captivated his listeners, the President shared with the people his efforts to end the Great Depression. His "Fireside Chats" brought the Chief of State into every home. Through the radio the people in America—as well as in Germany— heard Hitler clamor for Czechoslovakia. And on the radio perhaps the most magnificent orator of them all, Prime Minister Winston Churchill, spoke to his countrymen and to Americans. He warned them that Hitler's threatened invasion was a serious challenge to democracy's survival.

Now turn to the handout Part Two of "Experiment 2-G: Picking Out the Main Ideas" and put your underlining skills to work.

Concept Trees and Outlining

Underlining is one way to improve your studying skills. Outlining is another. As we saw in "Reading 8: Getting the Main Ideas," a good method of outlining is to make concept trees. Return to the same geography reading you used to practice the SQ3R Method. You will find it on page 71. This time, make a concept tree using the main points in that reading. Then, translate the concept tree into regular outline form. If you have difficulty, check "Reading 8: Getting the Main Ideas" again on page 75.

Taking Good Notes

"What did I read last night? I can't remember."

"What did the teacher say about that, again? I can't recall."

There is no need ever to have these discouraging thoughts. Doing good work in school can be easy and enjoyable if you really put yourself into it. There are very few students who do good school work without taking good notes. They take notes not only in class, but also when they do their reading assignments outside class. Why? Let's find out.

Journalism is one of many jobs which require good note-taking skills. A reporter must be able to take notes quickly and accurately.

Taking good notes is one of those secrets of successful studying we talked about earlier. It is a way of getting yourself organized. If you organize both the notes from your teacher's lectures and the material in your readings, you are well on your way to a solid understanding of the lesson.

Taking notes in outline form from the material in your textbooks is really simple. First, get a basic understanding of the material by using the SQ3R Method. (See Reading 7, page 68.) Use the Write step before the Review step. In the Write step, try to put the main ideas of the material into the outline form discussed in "Reading 8: Getting the Main Ideas." Then check your work in the Review step. You may find that some things you have written have to be changed. Some facts may be omitted completely. It is important that you do this *before* class, not after. *Expecting* what will be covered in class is a large part of effective studying. By preparing thoroughly for class it is easier to expect what the teacher is going to talk about and what the topics for class discussions will be.

Go into class with all assignments read and a basic outline of the reading. Put a few questions down on paper. Even if you don't ask the teacher those questions, keep them in the back of your mind while the teacher is giving notes or discussing key points.

To take good notes from class lectures, use the outlining method. If your teacher is organized in giving the class notes, you should have no trouble putting them into outline form. Be choosy about what you put in the notes. Write down only the important points. It's a good idea to put a star or arrow next to points which the teacher emphasizes. If the teacher says, "Now this is important," or, "If you don't remember anything else, I want you to remember

There were few books in the Middle Ages (A.D. 500–1500). Students had to rely heavily on the notes they took from the teacher's lectures.

this," you can bet you'll see it again— probably on a test. Next to any important point put an arrow, or star, or check mark, or anything else you can think of to remind you of its significance.

After class, go over your notes. If these are disorganized or poorly written, rewrite them. By reviewing your notes as soon as possible after class, you print them more firmly on your memory.

One of the most damaging things you can do in studying is to fall behind in your reading or notes. You can never really catch up. And what's worse, you will miss a lot by not knowing where the lessons are going. That can result in a feeling of being loaded down with work when you actually aren't. You soon begin to feel "what's the use" and then lose interest. Poor grades and a bad attitude follow close behind. Make the most of the time you spend on school work. It can only be more enjoyable.

READING REVIEW

1. How can your grades improve if you take good notes?

Critical Thinking

2. **Checking Consistency** (see page 25) Why is it helpful to review or rewrite your class notes as soon as possible?

EXPERIMENT 2-I

Taking Better Notes

The art of note-taking is one that every good student *must* learn. Through the centuries, teachers have found that the fastest and most personalized way of giving ideas and knowledge to their students is by lecturing and discussion. For the same amount of time, students have tried to find the best way of preserving the ideas and knowledge their teachers give them—at least until after the test. One of the best methods of doing this is by taking careful notes.

To take notes in class (or from your text book) all you really need is a piece of paper and a pen or pencil. Notebooks—the spiral type—and pens that don't smear are the two items that work best for some students. A spiral notebook has enough pages for at least a semester course, and it has the advantage of keeping all your notes together in one place. That way, you don't have to search for missing notes always.

Once you have the notebook and pen, you have to decide what to write. This is really the important part, because what you write will then determine how well you will be able to study from your notes. That, in turn, will affect how much you understand and ultimately your grade.

When taking notes from a lecture or tape recording (any *audio*, or hearing, source), the trick is to outline on paper only the most important ideas. How do you know what ideas are important? Here are a few hints to help you.

Sometimes, when giving notes in class, teachers make "asides." An aside is a joke or comment which is not important by itself, but something which helps the class to understand the point being made. Unfortunately, some students write down the aside and completely ignore the main point. Later, on a test or in a class discussion, they find out that they never understood that point. So, make sure your notes carry only the teacher's main points. Listen carefully when the teacher says something like, "And this is really important," or "If you don't understand anything else, know this. . . ." In cases like these, make sure you have in your notes the points the teacher is making.

Use abbreviations whenever you can. It is usually not necessary to write articles such as "a" or "an" or "the." The word "therefore" can be shown in your notes with the sign ∴ and "because" with the sign ∵ or *bc.* Names of people and places should be spelled out to make them clear in your mind. Generally, your notes should not be written in sentence form. It takes too long to copy the teacher's statements word for word. Besides, this just isn't needed. Write your notes in phrases. For example, instead of writing, "There were four major causes of the Civil War," write "4 maj causes Civil War."

A good idea is to rewrite your notes after class, especially if they are disorganized. Doing this has several benefits. Your notes will be better, more complete, and clearer. While rewriting them you can do one of the steps in the SQ3R Method: *Recite.* Recite the notes to yourself as you are recopying them. And finally, you will cut down on study time by redoing your notes while the ideas are still fresh in your mind.

These are some of the key "do's" in taking notes. Here is a very important "don't": *Don't* copy someone else's notes unless you absolutely have to. Notes are a little bit like shoes. The notes which "fit" other students may not fit you and your needs, even the notes of those in your class who make the best grades. Notes are very individual. Another person's notes may not mean much to you, especially if you are cramming for a test at the last minute. If you don't take good notes, don't expect miracles from someone else's notes. It is better to ask your teacher's help.

Now we will put all of this into practice. Listen carefully to the short lecture your teacher will give. It is an actual lecture. Take notes as if your teacher were giving the lecture for a test. Remember to use the hints we have discussed in this unit, especially the outline form for taking notes.

LECTURE: **The People Who Colonized America**

Yesterday we saw how the colonies in America became populated in the 16th and 17th centuries. We discussed the founding

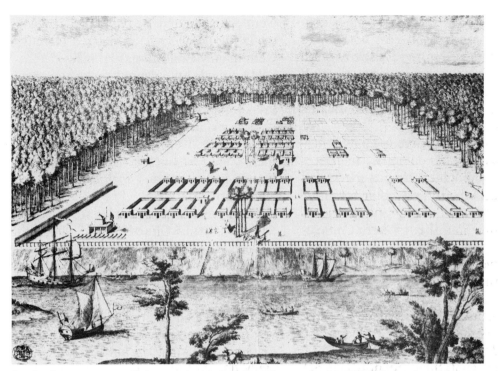

In the lecture you will learn about the American colonies. This is a view of the settlement of Savannah in the Southern Colony of Georgia in 1734.

of Virginia, Maryland, Plymouth, Rhode Island, the Carolinas, New York, New Jersey, Pennsylvania, and Georgia.

Today let's begin our discussion of the people who colonized America. What were they really like? Where did they come from? Why did they come to America?

Of course, it would be impossible to give all the details about these people. It is not possible to describe all the reasons people had for leaving their homelands and settling in a strange land. The reasons varied with individuals and groups. Some of the reasons included a desire for religious, economic, or political freedom. Another reason people left their homeland was because they were forced to.

There were, however, some common traits or characteristics among the European colonists—some common characteristics you should know. For the most part, Europeans who came to America were not satisfied with their lives in Europe. Some were wealthy, but most were poor. In those days, as today, it cost money to travel. Many people were able to pay for their passage by becoming a servant for seven to ten years to a wealthy master in the colonies. Such people were called indentured servants. Many others were taken from their homes in Africa without their consent and were forced into slavery.

One feature that the European colonists had in common was their geographic origin. Almost all of them came from Western Europe. The countries of Western Europe

Effective Study Skills **89**

were geographically closer and more convenient to the American east coast than were many other countries. Also, Western Europeans had the knowledge to reach America by ship. Most of the world did not have the desire or the means to sail its people to the Americas.

We have discussed some common characteristics of the early colonists: their economic and geographical origins. Now let's take a look at where these colonists chose to settle.

As we saw earlier, the Northern Colonies and the Southern Colonies were populated mainly by English people. The Middle Colonies were settled by Germans, or "Deutsch" people, who became widely known as the Pennsylvania Dutch. Through the years, the word "Deutsch," meaning "German," became "Dutch." Of course, the settlers were from Germany, not Holland. Farming was their main occupation.

There was a basic difference between the people who settled in the cities and those who sought the frontier. Frontier people were mainly from Scotland and Ireland, while the people who populated the cities were mainly English and French.

Here again, we cannot make too many generalizations. We would have found French people in the frontier. As a matter of fact, many of the most famous frontier fur trappers were of French origin. And there were many people from England and France in the countrysides tilling the soil and hunting.

What united these people into the country we call the United States? Once the European settlers left their homelands and began a new life in America, they slowly took on a new identity. They—slowly, mind you—became part of a new land. They developed common ideas, common values, and common goals. Within five generations, the families of these settlers would strike the armies and rulers of European countries from the American shores. By the 1770s they would be united in a cause, a cause in which they fought and won the independence that we enjoy today.

Looking Up the Facts

As you look over the number of paperbacks in a bookstore it's hard to imagine the time when only the very rich owned books. Several hundred years ago, books were lettered entirely by hand. Often, an entire book was memorized by people who traveled from town to town, retelling the stories in the book. After the invention of the printing press, it became much easier to own and keep books. More and more people learned how to read. Today most people in our society can read. Teaching children and adults to read is a national priority.

As a student you spend a lot of time with books and the facts in them. You read facts, exchange facts with others, put facts

This is a drawing of a stag and doe. It appeared in an Islamic book written in the thirteenth century. The book was a reference for the subject of natural history.

on tests, and look up the facts. It is difficult to understand anything if you don't have the facts. In this reading we will take a close look at methods of getting the facts. This is called **research.**

Many of the books and magazines you will use in doing research are in your library. We will talk about the library and its uses in the next reading. Now we will see the most effective way to use books and materials for research.

What is a book, anyhow? Well, it is a lot of pages with words and pictures on them. The pages are bound between two covers for protection. And there are ideas in the book. Is that all?

Most books are organized in a certain way. At the front of the book there are pages which give the **title** and **author.** In some books a **table of contents** comes after these pages. The table of contents tells you what is in the book. It gives this information according to the order of the chapters or units, from page 1 right through to the last page. Then comes the body of the book, which the table of contents has described. At the end of a book there is often an **index.** This is a listing of important things in the book. The list is in alphabetical order. The index also gives the pages on which those terms can be found. Sometimes the book also includes a glossary. (There is one for each unit in this book.) **Glossaries** are short dictionaries of terms used in the book.

In this reading we will be learning mainly about reference books. You recall that reference reading is one of the three ways of reading. (If you don't remember the three ways, review "Reading 6: How To Read Better.") Reference reading is done when you are researching facts. In doing research, you will be using dictionaries, encyclopedias, the *Readers' Guide to Periodical Literature,* the card catalog, almanacs, and many other reference materials.

Let's consider the **dictionary** first. The dictionary is probably the most familiar reference book to you. You have no doubt looked up the meanings of many words in dictionaries. Besides giving meanings for words, dictionaries have other uses, too. A good dictionary includes *synonyms* (words that have the same meaning) and *antonyms* (words that mean the opposite of each other). Examples of how a word can be used correctly are also given. And some dictionaries describe how the word came

Did you know that you must be over the age of 16 and have a license to fly a hot-air balloon? Where would you find that information —in a dictionary, almanac or encyclopedia?

into the English language. Here is an example of a dictionary entry:

el-e-vate (el′ə vāt′), *v.*, **-vated, -vating,** *adj.* —*v.t.* **1.** to move or raise to a higher place or position; lift up. **2.** to raise to a higher state or station; exalt. **3.** to raise the spirits; put in high spirits. —*adj.* **4.** *Poetic.* raised; elevated. [M E *elevat, t.* L: s. *ēlevātus,* pp.] —**Syn. 2.** elevate, enhance, exalt, heighten. . . . —**Ant. 2.** lower. . . .

We'll take this entry apart and see what facts we can get from it. The word *elevate* is followed by its pronunciation in parentheses (el′ə vāt′). The *v.* indicates that the word is a verb, or action word.

This is followed by two forms of the word: the past tense *elevated* and the adjective (adj.) *elevating.* Notice that only the last part of the word is printed after the hyphen (-) because only the last part changes. The first part (ele-) remains the same.

The symbol —*v.t.* further describes the type of verb. It is a **tr**ansitive **v**erb. Next, the dictionary entry gives four definitions of the word elevate. Then, a short history of the word is given in brackets [ ]. "ME" and "L" tell us that the word comes from **M**iddle **E**nglish and **L**atin words. Finally, synonyms (Syn.) and an antonym (Ant.) for the word *"elevate"* are given.

You see, there is a lot more to a good dictionary than just words and their meanings. Some symbols and organization of entries may be different depending on the dictionary. Check in the front of your dictionary for directions and explanations.

Now consider another familiar reference, the **encyclopedia.** You probably know that the encyclopedia is made up of many books arranged in alphabetical order. The entries in an encyclopedia are also in alphabetical order, and they tend to be longer than entries in a dictionary. The uses of an encyclopedia are somewhat different than the uses of dictionaries. While you use dictionaries to look up the correct spelling and meanings of a word, you use an encyclopedia to research facts about people, things, places, and events. Encyclopedias give more of a description and usually have more pictures and drawings than do dictionaries.

The **almanac** is still another familiar reference book. The people who make almanacs pride themselves on how many facts about almost everything they can put in those books. An almanac does not give as much description as an encyclopedia. It is used mainly for looking up specific facts very quickly.

Of course, these types of books are only three of the many reference books you can use to look up information. But the dictionary, encyclopedia, and almanac are three important, basic books with which you should become thoroughly familiar, and you can find copies of them in most school and public libraries.

READING REVIEW ═══════
1. What is research?
2. Name the parts of a dictionary entry.

Critical Thinking
3. **Making Comparisons** (see page 16) In what ways would entries about the same subject differ in an encyclopedia, almanac, and dictionary?

EXPERIMENT 2-J

Using the Dictionary, Encyclopedia, and Almanac

Three of the most useful reference books are the *dictionary,* the *encyclopedia,* and the *almanac.* Today we will practice using them. All three are good places in which to start looking for information. It is helpful to know what kind of information you can expect from each.

Using a standard classroom dictionary, find out as much information as you can about the following words:

dollar	stamp	constitution
flag	automobile	Atlantis
rise	drop	vegetable
judge	axis	warm
ground	learn	

Your teacher may substitute words for the ones printed above.

Referring to a good, recent edition of an encyclopedia, find out as much as you can about the following words. Then write a summary of each encyclopedia article *in your own words.* Use the methods of "getting the main ideas" which we discussed earlier in this unit. Notice the differences

The U.S. Post Office issues stamps to honor people, events, and ideas in American history. Dr. George Washington Carver, an American scientist, appears on this stamp. In what reference book would you find information about the history of stamps?

Effective Study Skills   **93**

between entries of the same word in the dictionary and in the encyclopedia.

automobile	Charles Chaplin
Helen of Troy	San Francisco
slate	stamp
astrology	Atlantis
Vancouver	football

Look up the answers to the following questions in an almanac, preferably one published this year:

1. What is the location of Burundi, and what is its language?

2. What baseball team won the World Series in 1903?

3. What natural resources are found in the state of Alaska?

4. How large was the population of the United States at the time of the most recent census?

5. What territory was purchased from Spain by the United States in 1819? How much did it cost?

6. What are the NATO countries?

7. What is the ZIP code for East Bridgewater, Massachusetts?

8. What is the "great red spot" on the surface of the planet Jupiter?

9. What American city has the largest population?

10. What part of every U.S. tax dollar is spent on military defense?

READING 11

Using the Library

Wouldn't it be wonderful to have all the facts you need built into your mind? Any time you wanted to have an answer to any question, all you would have to do is think about it. Automatically, the answer would pop into your mind! Who knows? Perhaps in the future, people will have that ability.

Unfortunately, people today don't have a built-in instant knowledge system. We have to work with the next best thing, a place where millions of facts are stored and organized so that anyone can get to them. That place, of course, is the library. In some schools, the library (combined with other facilities) may be called the *media center* or *learning resources center.*

The library can be the most effective tool you have for getting at the thoughts of others. It is, in fact, a kind of instant knowledge system, but that's only if you know how to use it. The more you use the library, the better you will understand its organization and the more "instant" the knowledge in the library will become for you.

An understanding of the system of the library is all-important. If you know the system, you know where to find the information you need. That is why order is so essential in a library. Can you imagine what would happen if all the books, magazines, and other sources of information were scattered throughout the library? You wouldn't be able to find a thing!

Let's examine the system of the library. Most libraries classify books into two major categories: fiction and nonfiction.

Identify the call numbers, the authors, and the titles of these books. Why does each book have a different call number?

These are placed on separate shelves. Fiction books are arranged alphabetically according to the last name of the authors. Nonfiction books are arranged according to topics and given a number.

In most libraries nonfiction books are given a number in the **Dewey Decimal System.** (This system is named after Melvil Dewey, its inventor. "Decimal" refers to the number 10 which is basic to the system.) The Dewey Decimal System classifies books into ten categories:

000—General Works
100—Philosophy and Psychology
200—Religion
300—Social Sciences
400—Language
500—Science
600—Applied Sciences and Useful Arts
700—Fine Arts and Recreation
800—Literature
900—History, Biography, Geography

The book's number, which is named its **call number,** is printed on the part of the book binding facing you as the book is shelved. In most libraries using this system, there is a second part of the call number. This number is placed under the Dewey number. It begins with a capital letter, which is the same as the first letter of the author's last name.

It would take time to search through all the books in one of the ten categories to find the books you wanted. That's why the library's **card catalog** comes in handy. The card catalog is a set of drawers containing cards or entries for every book. The cards or a computer database containing entries give the titles, authors, call numbers, and other information for every book in the library. You don't have to roam through stacks of books to find the ones you want. You simply use the catalog to get the numbers of the books. This process is also useful to make a list of books for a topic you are researching. Such a list is called a **bibliography.** The list may also include other reference materials, including films.

Cards in the card catalog are in alphabetical order. There are five types of cards.

The three main types are these:
1. the **title card,** which shows the title of the book first;
2. the **author card,** which shows the name of the author of the book first; and
3. one or more **subject cards,** which show the topics covered in the book.

Below and on page 97 are examples of each card. In the card catalog you will find that the cards are arranged in alphabetical order, depending on what kind of card it is. By using the three types of cards in the card catalog, you can research the information you need much faster and easier.

TITLE cards.

A – title of the book
B – name of the author
C – call number
D – cross references

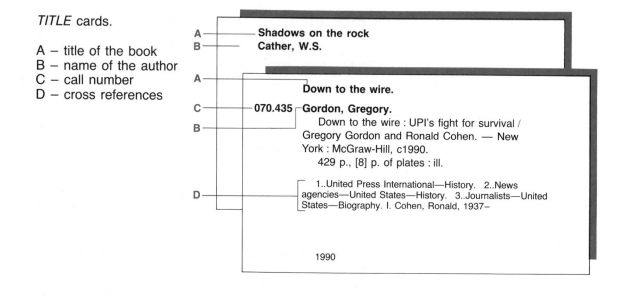

AUTHOR cards.

A – name of the author
B – title of the book
C – call number
D – publisher and date
of publication

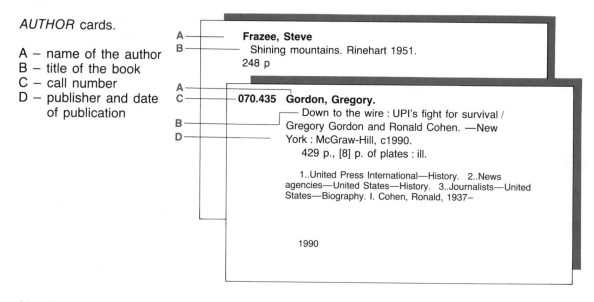

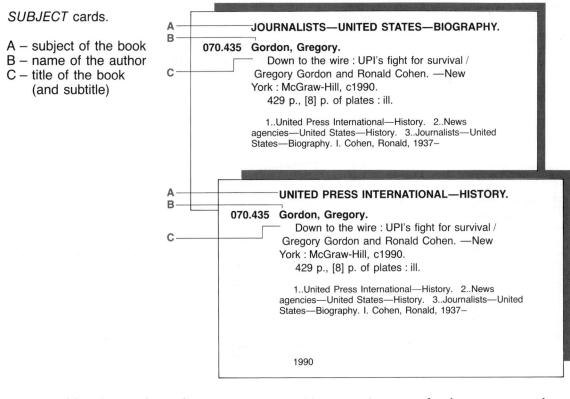

SUBJECT cards.

A – subject of the book
B – name of the author
C – title of the book
   (and subtitle)

A ———— **JOURNALISTS—UNITED STATES—BIOGRAPHY.**
B

070.435 **Gordon, Gregory.**

C ————   Down to the wire : UPI's fight for survival /
        Gregory Gordon and Ronald Cohen. —New
        York : McGraw-Hill, c1990.
          429 p., [8] p. of plates : ill.

         1..United Press International—History. 2..News
        agencies—United States—History. 3..Journalists—United
        States—Biography. I. Cohen, Ronald, 1937–

A ———— **UNITED PRESS INTERNATIONAL—HISTORY.**
B

070.435 **Gordon, Gregory.**

C ————   Down to the wire : UPI's fight for survival /
        Gregory Gordon and Ronald Cohen. —New
        York : McGraw-Hill, c1990.
          429 p., [8] p. of plates : ill.

         1..United Press International—History. 2..News
        agencies—United States—History. 3..Journalists—United
        States—Biography. I. Cohen, Ronald, 1937–

         1990

Some libraries and media centers no longer use card catalogs. Instead, they use *microfilm, microfiche,* or *on-line computerized catalogs.* Ask your librarian for more information about these systems.

Magazines can also be helpful in getting information, especially about very recent happenings. Many libraries have magazines (also called "periodicals") in *closed stacks.* "Closed" means that the stacks, or place where the periodicals are kept, are not open to the public. If you want a periodical, you must usually ask the librarian for it.

To research information from periodicals, use the *Readers' Guide to Periodical Literature.* This is the standard index for magazine articles. (An *index* is a listing of items in a collection and where they can be found. The card catalog is another kind of index.) The *Readers' Guide to Periodical*

Literature is a set of volumes arranged according to the month and year in which the magazine articles were published. An entry for an article may be listed under the name of the author of the article. Or it may be listed by the subject of the article. These entries appear in alphabetical order.

Here is an example of an entry in the *Readers' Guide* and how to interpret it. Let's say you want to find information in magazines about how environmental issues have influenced architecture. Look under "architecture" and you find this entry:

Architecture—Environmental aspects
Blueprints turn green. R. Gerloff. il *Utne Reader*
  p34–5+ N/D '93

The title of this article is given first. It is entitled "Blueprints turn green." The writ-

An architect designs and draws plans for buildings, bridges, and other structures. How do you think environmental issues have influenced the work of architects?

er's last name is Gerloff, and his or her first name begins with "R." The article is *ill*ustrated, which means that it has pictures or other types of illustration. The article was published in *Utne Reader* magazine. It starts on page 34. The plus sign (+) means that the article goes on for less than one full page after page 35. The article appeared in the November/December, 1993 issue of the magazine.

Suppose your assignment is to research Dick McCormick's views on the contributions Hispanics have made to the United States. This time instead of looking it up under "Hispanics" you would look under the author's name. Here is what you would find listed in the *Readers' Guide* under "McCormick":

McCormick, Dick
The importance of Hispanics to our nation [address, February 16, 1989] *Vital Speeches of the Day* 55:464–7 My 15 '89

From this entry you know that there is an article entitled "The importance of Hispanics to our nation" by Dick McCormick in volume 55 of a magazine called *Vital Speeches of the Day.* Inside the brackets, it tells you that the article is actually a speech given by Mr. McCormick on February 16, 1989. The article is found on pages 464 through 467 of the May 15, 1989, issue of the magazine.

article is found on page 108 of the December, 1983 issue of that magazine.

If you are confused about any abbreviations or symbols used in the *Readers' Guide,* study the first few pages of that volume for the explanations.

Just a few more tips on using your library. The reference works and indexes and catalogs we have talked about are very helpful. But there is one resource we haven't mentioned. Your librarian (or media specialist) is the most important resource of the library. The librarian's job is to help you get the most from the material in the library. The librarian is there to help. Don't be afraid to ask. Try to be as clear and to-the-point as possible about what you need. The librarian can be of much greater help if you can describe exactly the information you want.

Never go to do research in a library without taking a pen or pencil and several sheets of paper or note cards. When you are looking up a book in the card catalog or a periodical in the *Readers' Guide,* write down the information. Keep it some place where you won't lose it. A notebook is excellent for this. It is much easier to write down all the information about the book or magazine the first time around. If you leave information out, or find later that you can't understand the abbreviations you have made, you will have to look up the information a second time.

Most important—*Use* your library! The more you use it, the more enjoyable it will be for you.

READING REVIEW

1. What is the Dewey Decimal System? How well does it work?
2. What is the call number? Where is it found on a book?
3. How do you use the card catalog?

Critical Thinking

4. **Identifying Central Issues** (see page 14) How can your librarian help you find information?

EXPERIMENT **2-K**

Your Library—How Much Do You Know About It?

Your school or community library is a large system of information. If you know the system, you can find anything in the library very quickly. If you don't know the system, you might spend several hours trying to find something that should take only a few minutes to find. This experiment is designed to give you a good working knowledge of your library's system. Complete this experiment on a separate sheet of paper.

1. Where is your library located? Write it down.
2. What is the name of your librarian? If there is more than one librarian on the

staff, write down all their names.

3. Generally speaking, where are most of the books located? Where are the fiction books? Where are the nonfiction books?

4. Where are the magazines (periodicals) located?

5. For what length of time can you take books out?

6. Are you permitted to take periodicals out of the library? For how long?

7. Are there fines for not returning books and magazines on time? What are the fines per day?

8. What hours and days is the library open?

9. Can you listen to records and tapes in your library? Can you take them out?

10. Does your library have study areas? Where are they?

11. Is talking softly permitted in your library? Where and when?

12. What areas in your library are restricted (places where you are not permitted to go)?

13. What other places and rules of your library are important?

14. Suppose you could see your library from the ceiling. What would it look like? Draw a "floor plan" of the library, as you might see it from the ceiling. Label the shelves according to the categories we discussed in "Reading 11: Using the Library" ("fiction," "100s," "200s," "periodicals," "librarian's office," etc.).

EXPERIMENT **2-L**

Using the Card Catalog and the *Readers' Guide to Periodical Literature*

Your library has two major reference aids to help you find the information you need. They are the card catalog and the *Readers' Guide to Periodical Literature.* If you want to locate a book in the library, go to the card catalog. This is usually in a central place in the library. If you want to find a magazine or periodical, check the *Readers' Guide.*

(There are other indexes in your library besides the *Readers' Guide.* Ask your librarian for help in finding and using them.)

See how well you can use these two reference aids by doing this experiment. First, let's consider a few entries in the card catalog. Examine the information in the entries and answer the questions which follow.

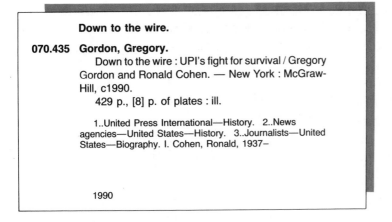

Down to the wire.

070.435 **Gordon, Gregory.**
  Down to the wire : UPI's fight for survival / Gregory Gordon and Ronald Cohen. — New York : McGraw-Hill, c1990.
  429 p., [8] p. of plates : ill.

  1..United Press International—History. 2..News agencies—United States—History. 3..Journalists—United States—Biography. I. Cohen, Ronald, 1937–

  1990

1. What is the title of this book?
2. Who is the author?
3. What kind of card is this?
4. What is the book about?
5. What is the call number of this book? Where do you find it?
6. Does the card give a short description of the book?

Here are some entries from the *Readers' Guide.* For each entry—A, B, C, and D—answer the questions that follow:

A **U.S. Customs Service**
  Soviet attempts to buy U.S. computers continue despite Customs crackdown. D. Hughes. *Aviation Week & Space Technology* 130:279+ Je 12, '89

B **Hersey, Brook**
  The truth about women and heart disease. il *Working Woman* 14:156+ Ap '89

C **Fitz-Haven Dairy**
  Successful family farm. J.R. Borcherding. il *Successful Farming* 87:44–6 Ap '89

D **High Definition Television**
  Get the picture! G. Kenny. il *Stereo Review* 54:69–73 Ap '89

1. What do you think this article is about?
2. Who wrote the article?
3. Is the article illustrated?
4. Which magazine contains this article?
5. What is the date of the magazine?
6. On what pages can this article be found?

EXPERIMENT 2-M Using the Dewey Decimal System HANDOUT

2 PERSPECTIVES

Social Scientists Look at Study Skills

How do social scientists use study skills in their day-to-day life? The following example focuses on study skills social scientists might use. Read the selection below by Kenneth T. Henson from *Secondary Teaching Methods* and then answer the questions on the next page under "Comparing the Social Sciences."

"During the first 250 years, instruction centered around recitation. In other words, students studied, memorized, and recited their lessons until they were committed to memory; students who failed received corporal punishment. In 1875 this method was openly challenged. Colonel Francis Parker, who, as an eight-year-old orphan was apprenticed to a farmer, had discovered that life on the farm was very educational. He had found school to be so hateful and unbearable that he attended it only about eight weeks every year. But instead of turning his back on education itself, Parker wanted to become part of the education process and to improve it. He believed that if education would be acquired so pleasantly in the fields, woodlands, and pastures, it could also be enjoyed in the schools. His dream was to become a great teacher; little did he know that his fulfillment of the dream would result in a revolution in American education.

In 1875 Colonel Parker was selected as superintendent of schools in Quincy, Massachusetts, a suburb of Boston. By establishing teacher's meetings, he gave to his forty teachers, not advice and knowledge, but questions and demonstrations. He did not tell them how to teach, he *showed* them. . . . To build a natural learning environment, Colonel Parker substituted games and puzzles for recitation and rote memorization. In the lower grades he instituted singing, playing, reading, counting objects, writing, and drawing. Above all, he wanted the experiences at his schools to be happy ones. . . .

This system, which became known as the Quincy System, gained national attention. In his own words Colonel Parker tells how enthusiastic the community had become over its schools. 'Throughout the centuries of Quincy's history, its people have ever manifested a deep interest in education, and I believe that I am right when I say that at no time in the past has this interest been greater than it is in the first year of the new century (of Independence).'"

Comparing the Social Sciences

Psychologists study how people learn. If you were a psychologist, how would you sum up the main idea of this passage? (*Identifying Central Issues*)

Sociologists study the way people behave in groups. If you were a sociologist, how would you describe the relationship between the teachers in Quincy and Colonel Parker? Explain. (*Drawing Conclusions*)

Anthropologists study subcultures—small cultures inside a society. If you were an anthropologist, what subgroup in Quincy would this reading help you study? (*Determining Relevance*)

Geographers study Earth's features. If you were a geographer, what could you learn from this passage about the natural setting near Quincy, Massachusetts? (*Demonstrating Reasoned Judgment*)

Historians study the past. If you were a historian, how would you compare the educational system proposed by Colonel Parker to today's schools? (*Making Comparisons*)

Political scientists study government and politics. If you were a political scientist and wanted to find out how Colonel Parker became school superintendent, what questions would you ask? (*Creating Good Questions*)

Economists study the way people earn a living. If you were an economist, what could you learn from this selection about the ways people made a living in Quincy in the late 1800s? (*Identifying Alternatives*)

A Winslow Homer painting of school children

GLOSSARY OF TERMS

almanac a reference work of specific facts concerning a wide variety of topics (page 92)

association a system of memorization in which two images are connected in one's mind (page 61)

author card a type of card in the card catalog that gives information about a book; it is filed alphabetically according to the author's last name (page 96)

bibliography a list of resources, such as books, magazine articles, and films (page 95)

call number the number printed on the bindings of books; used to help locate books in a library (page 95)

card catalog a library reference tool that lists all the library's books (page 95)

chunking a technique for memorizing by organizing (or "chunking") the information into small segments (page 59)

concept tree a method for organizing concepts and facts; useful in the process of outlining (page 77)

Dewey Decimal System the classification of nonfiction books into ten categories based on the decimal (page 95)

dictionary a reference book that gives the pronunciation, meaning, and uses of words (page 91)

do list a list of things to do, arranged in descending order of importance (page 56)

encyclopedia a reference work containing general information about a wide variety of topics (page 92)

glossary a list of the important words found in a book, along with their definitions; usually located near the end of the book (page 91)

index a list of the important names and ideas in a book or other work, with the pages on which the information is located; found in the back of the work (page 91)

long-term memory the retention of information by the brain beyond immediate use (page 58)

objective a teaching/learning goal; objectives are of three types: knowing, feeling, and skill (page 53)

outline the organization of facts and concepts in a logical way (page 75)

pleasure reading a type of reading done for enjoyment (page 66)

Readers' Guide to Periodical Literature a set of volumes listing magazine articles by author and subject (page 97)

reference reading a method of reading done in the process of researching facts (page 66)

research the process of looking up, recording, and using information (page 91)

rote memorization through concentration, without the use of memory aids such as association (page 62)

SUBJECT cards.

A — subject of the book
B — name of the author
C — title of the book
   (and subtitle)

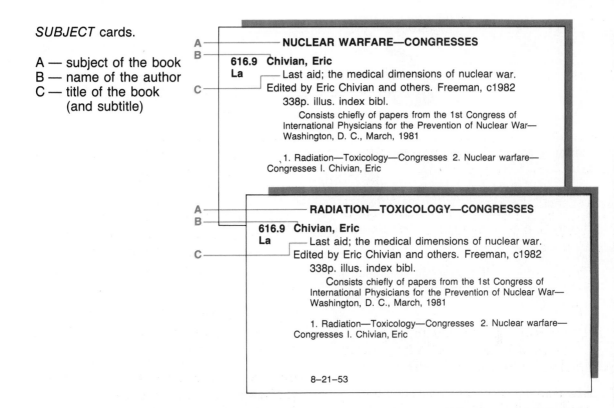

short-term memory the retention of information by the brain for immediate use (page 58)

SQ3R Method a method of studying with five steps: Survey, Question, Read, Recite, Review; a sixth step, Write, is often included (page 68)

subject card a type of card in the card catalog that gives information about a book; it is filed alphabetically according to the topic of the book (page 96)

table of contents a listing of main topics in a book or other work; found in the front of the work (page 91)

text reading a type of reading done with a textbook to gain new knowledge and understanding (page 66)

time log a record of personal activities, usually recorded hour by hour (page 54)

title the name of a book, article, or other work (page 91)

title card a type of card in the card catalog that gives information about a book; it is filed alphabetically according to the title of the book (page 96)

underlining a technique of studying by drawing a line under the most important words and ideas in a reading, used to draw the reader's attention to material when studying or reviewing (page 75)

UNIT 3 Psychology

PSYCHOLOGY

ECONOMICS

SOCIOLOGY

ANTHROPOLOGY

STUDY &
THINKING
SKILLS

POLITICAL
SCIENCE

GEOGRAPHY

HISTORY

This Is Psychology

Remember the time you and your friends went to visit the fun house at the carnival? The wiggly distortions from the trick mirrors inside made everyone laugh and scream. "Hey, look at this one over here!" someone probably yelled. "No, over here. This is wild!" someone else shouted. The experience made you doubt your own eyes. In one mirror your reflection came back straight, tall, and skinny as a ladder, while in the one right next to it you were a person who had been squashed down to the plump, rounded shape of a turnip. Later, after you got home, you may not have looked at yourself in the bathroom mirror quite the same way.

Our perceptions of ourselves, and other people, constantly change. In part, Psychology is the study of these subtle changes. Social scientists who work in this field are called **psychologists.** In the Unit 3 readings, you will learn how to think like a psychologist. In the experiments, you will see how Psychology is a part of your life.

Psychology and You

Psychology is a science concerned with individual behavior and feelings. The questions below will help you understand the place of Psychology in your life.

1. How do you feel when you lose at a game you're playing with your friends? Do you get mad? If you win, how do you act?
2. Sometimes it's nice to have time alone to think things through. Other times it's more enjoyable being with family and friends. When are you generally happier—when you're surrounded by others or when you're by yourself? Explain your answer.

UNIT 3   CONTENTS

How Much Do You Know About Psychology?

Before we begin this unit on Psychology, let's see how much you already know about the field of Psychology. On a separate sheet of paper answer the following questions, using the knowledge you already have about Psychology. All answers are either *true* or *false*.

1. The word "Psychology" comes from two Greek words meaning "the study of the mind."

2. Approaching a problem with a positive attitude is a very important step in reaching a solution.

3. *Personality* is another word for your physical appearance.

4. Heredity is much more important than environment in making you the person you are today.

5. Adults have fewer emotions than people your age.

6. It is good to feel emotions and to express them in ways that do not hurt yourself or others.

7. Good mental health is the ability to deal effectively with situations in life.

Psychology **109**

What Is Psychology?

For thousands of years people have wondered why they think and act the way they do. Only recently has a science of human behavior developed. The science is called **Psychology.** A person who studies the behavior of human beings is a **psychologist.** Like Anthropology and Sociology, Psychology is called a **behavioral science** because it is the systematic study of human behavior. The word "psychology" comes from two Greek words meaning "the study of the mind."

The ancient Greeks thought that every human being has two natures: a physical nature (the body) and a spiritual nature (the mind). It is the study of the spiritual side of humans that the ancient Greeks would call Psychology. Today we know that the two sides of human nature work together. Psychologists study how the mind works together with the body to produce thoughts that lead us to actions.

In this unit we will discover how the mind affects perceptions, conceptualizations, thoughts, actions, and reactions. If you studied Unit 1, you saw how thought patterns and experience patterns are made. In this unit we will see why we make certain thought patterns and experience patterns, and why we do not make others. We will see that no two people perceive exactly the same things, think exactly the same thoughts, or act exactly alike.

Psychologists use a variety of tools in researching these topics. One of these tools is **observation,** or watching human behavior and writing down what is seen. Psychologists try to see patterns of behavior, or actions that occur time after time. They also try to see exceptions to those patterns of behavior. And they attempt to analyze this information. **Analysis** helps psychologists figure out what those patterns and exceptions mean. It helps them understand why people do what they do.

Psychologists specialize in different fields. **Clinical psychologists** help individuals to understand themselves better. **Social psychologists** study how individuals behave in groups. **Developmental psychologists** study the psychological changes that normally occur as people get older. **Experimental psychologists** study the behavior of animals in laboratory settings.

All psychologists use the critical thinking skills described in Unit 1. It is important for psychologists to create good questions and to determine the relevance of information to the problems they are studying. Psychologists must use reasoned judgment, and they must be able to identify assumptions in their own work and the work of fellow psychologists. By using critical thinking skills, psychologists can be more certain that their discoveries are true and that other scientists will get the same results when they try the experiments.

In this unit, we will see what makes you unique. We will try new ways of solving personal problems. We'll look at how humans learn. We'll explore the world of creativity and learn how to increase your creative powers. We will discover what it takes to have good mental health. Finally, we will look at the psychological changes that normally take place as we get older.

In hang gliding the mind and body work together.

READING REVIEW

1. What is Psychology?
2. Which critical thinking skills and tools do you think are the most important to psychologists?

Critical Thinking

3. **Recognizing Assumptions** (see page 27)   When you began this unit, what assumptions did you have about Psychology and psychologists?

EXPERIMENT   3-B

Who Are You?

Take a blank sheet of paper. Fold the sheet of paper lengthwise in half. Label the left column "Facts," and the right column "Opinions." In the left column, list as many facts about yourself as you can. In the right column, list as many opinions (yours and other people's) about yourself as you can. Will you have more facts or opinions?

You will have ten minutes to complete each column.

Discovering Who You Are

Personality makes you different from everyone else.

Probably the most difficult task you will ever have is learning who you are. You may think that this should be easy. After all, you know your name, age, race, the color of your hair and eyes, and your other physical features. You know what you look like from mirrors and photographs. However your physical appearance is only a small part of the total "you."

What things and people are important to you? How do you act in many different situations? What experiences have you had? These make up the real you—inside your physical appearance. Some people call the "inner you" your **personality.** It is one thing that makes you different from all other people. No one has exactly the same personality as yours. How did you get to be the individual you are today?

Everyone has parents who bring them into the world. In the process of reproduction some characteristics of each parent were passed on to you. This process is called **heredity.** You may, for example, have your father's brown eyes and your mother's black hair. In some cases, your physical characteristics may go back to your grandparents or great-grandparents. Psychologists believe that some skills and abilities may also be inherited. Such abilities include writing, athletic, and artistic talents. Psychologists have discovered that your hereditary characteristics play an important part in making you "you."

Another important factor in the development of your personality is your **environment**—your surroundings, people, places, and things. You are born with certain hereditary tendencies. Throughout your life however your environment shapes your behavior. If you move from one part of the country to another, for example, some of your behavior changes to match that of the people in your new environment. Some of your perceptions change, and so do some of your thoughts and actions.

As you encounter different people and situations, your behavior changes. This process is called **adaptation.** Your behavior in school is different from your behavior at home, or when you are with your friends. Each of the three environments is different. Each requires different ways of thinking and acting. As you go from home to school, and from school to be with your friends, you change the way you act. You change your behavior because you know that the behavior your teachers expect is different from the behavior your friends and family expect. In other words, you adapt your behavior to fit the situation of which you are part.

Many great psychologists have studied the influences of heredity and environment on people's personalities. They have argued about which was more important: heredity

What effect does environment have on behavior?

or environment. Today, most psychologists agree that heredity and environment both play important parts in making every person who she or he is.

One of the first psychologists to study the human personality was Sigmund Freud, an Austrian who lived from 1856 to 1939. Dr. Freud believed that there are three parts to the personality. These parts are called the id, the ego, and the superego. The human being begins to develop the id at the time of birth. The **id** represents the person's most basic drives for food, water, survival, and pleasure. Throughout life, according to Dr. Freud, the id drives a person to satisfy these needs and desires. The id is the part of a person that seeks pleasure.

The **superego** is made up of the teachings of society concerning right and wrong. Parents, teachers, peers, and others teach the individual right from wrong as the person grows up. Those teachings form the superego. Some people call this the conscience. The superego works to control the pleasure-seeking id.

The **ego** is a sort of referee between the demands of the id and the superego. The ego helps a person be realistic, patient, and reasonable. In a well-balanced person, the ego is the strongest of the three. The stronger the ego is, the stronger the person's personality is.

A person with a superego that is stronger than the ego or the id is too much aware of what society says is right or wrong. This person tends to do exactly what society expects. A person with an id that is stronger than the superego or ego acts only to satisfy basic needs. He or she does not care what happens to others.

Can you think of examples in your own life of your id, superego, and ego?

READING REVIEW

1. According to Sigmund Freud, what are the three parts of the human personality? Define each.

Critical Thinking

2. **Testing Conclusions** (see page 42) Which is more important in the development of your personality: heredity or environment? Give reasons for your answer.

EXPERIMENT **3-C Heredity and Environment, Parts One and Two** **HANDOUT**

EXPERIMENT **3-D Emotions and You** **HANDOUT**

READING 3

Emotions and You

Can you imagine how dull it would be if you had no emotions? **Emotions** are feelings such as love, hate, happiness, sadness, and anger. (Can you think of others?) Emotions give your life excitement. Without them, we would be not much more than

machines. Your particular blend of emotions gives you a personality all your own. Some emotions can cause problems for you. For that reason you should try to understand them. The development of other emotions, however, can help make you a more interesting and fuller human being.

Knowing how the other person feels is a very important part of living. It is usually not possible to feel the other person's emotions as fully as that person does. However, it is important for you to try to understand and feel someone else's emotions. Have you ever tried to comfort a friend who was unhappy or disappointed? If you told your friend that you "know how he or she feels," you probably made your friend feel better. Emotional awareness can make any relationship stronger.

Emotions can also destroy friendships. Taking your frustration and anger out on a friend who has done you no harm can ruin a good relationship. Can you think of times when you should not have expressed an emotion? We all do this from time to time, and we regret it afterward.

Teenagers often seem to have more emotions than adults. This is not really true. Everyone feels emotions, but most people do not always show everything they feel. Many adults have found that certain ways of showing emotions may hurt people they care about. They may also be more careful about hiding emotions that may embarrass them. They have learned to hide some of their feelings. Even though they are hidden, emotions are felt by all people.

As you may have discovered in Experiment 3-D, not everybody feels the same emotions in the same situations. We have to consider this when we talk with others. What may make one person cry might cause another person to laugh or get angry. If we are truly considerate of other persons' feelings, we will always put ourselves in their shoes. This is called **empathy.**

Does this mean that we should treat others as we would like to be treated? Yes, but that is not enough. We have to know how the other person might react. People may react differently because of different experiences in their lives. For example, a joke about red-haired people might not bother you if you don't have red hair. Talking

about death may not make you sad, but it may sadden a person who has just lost someone in an accident.

You may have a completely different emotion in one situation than another. Differences in emotions are normal and natural. It is often helpful to remember that you do have many different emotions depending on the circumstances. That way, it is easier to avoid hurting yourself and others.

READING REVIEW

1. How can emotions be good? How can they be bad?

Critical Thinking

2. **Drawing Conclusions** (see page 42) What is empathy, and why is it important?

(see page 42)

EXPERIMENT 3-E

Can You Help Solve These Problems?

We all have problems from time to time. Sometimes it is easier to solve our own problems if we have helped someone else with the same problem. Do these six problems sound familiar? Can you help solve them?

1. John and Mary have been going together for two months. They like each other very much. People say that they make a "good looking couple." Lately, however, John has been touchy. His grades are down and he has been kicked off the school's football team. John has also been having problems

with his family. Yesterday, John told Mary that he wanted to break up with her. When Mary asked him why, he said he couldn't explain it. "It's just something," he said, "that I have to do." Mary was very upset and thought about John's decision all day.

What do you think Mary should do?

2. Carol's parents are very strict, and they want to know where she is at all times. They do not permit her to date and do not approve of dances. Carol met Bob last week, and they really like each other. Carol knows that Bob is not the kind of boy her parents would approve of. But she meets Bob every night after dinner anyway. Carol tells her parents that she is going to her friend Darlene's house to study. Darlene has agreed to lie, to tell Carol's parents if they phone her house that Carol is there. One day, Carol's grandmother died unexpectedly. Carol's parents tried to phone her at Darlene's home. Darlene's parents answered and said Carol had not been there all day. When Carol came home, her parents asked her where she had been. Carol said, "At Darlene's, studying." Then Carol's parents told her about her grandmother's death and waited for her to answer. Carol paused before she began.

What should Carol say? What would you do if you were Carol's parents?

3. Ellen and Jim have been married for almost a year. Both are very interested in politics. An important election is coming up, and there have been many disagreements over whom they should support. They can't seem to agree on which candidate to vote for. Jim is upset because Ellen is going to vote for his candidate's opponent. "Our two votes will do nothing but cancel each other out," he says.

What would you say to Jim if you were Ellen? Do you agree with Jim? Explain why or why not.

How does someone with a problem behave?

4. Karen has always been a good student with a pleasant personality. Her family has moved six times in the past ten years. They have lived in their present home for almost a year, and Karen has made many close friends. Karen has enjoyed this place more than anywhere she lived before. Yesterday, she found out that her family will have to move again next month to a city several hundred miles away. She is very depressed. She doesn't want to move again and leave her friends, but she doesn't seem to have a choice.

What advice would you give Karen as a friend?

5. Bob met Leon six weeks ago when Leon moved next door. They became good friends. Bob's old friends, Gary and Lynn, have become hurt and jealous that he is spending so much time with his new friend. They have been spreading lies about Leon to make him look bad. Leon does not know about these lies. Bob has heard the lies and believes them. Bob refuses to talk to Leon because he is angered by "what Leon said about him." When Leon asked Bob why he is acting strangely, Bob said, "You know why! There is no use talking about it. You know what you said." Leon is confused and doesn't know what to do.

What advice would you give Leon?

6. Ted has not been doing well in math this year. He has been absent thirteen days, and it is only October. Ted has a habit of missing more and more school as the year goes on. Although his absence from classes causes him to get bad grades, Ted complains that his teachers "have it in" for him. Ted says that they want to see him fail. He has told his friends, "If I fail the course, it's the teacher's fault. If he can't teach me anything, then he shouldn't be a teacher."

Do you agree with Ted? What would you say to Ted if you were his best friend? What would you tell Ted if you were his teacher?

How To Solve a Problem

If you are familiar with cars, you know that they don't run very well when their parts aren't adjusted. When all parts work smoothly, the car is in fine running condition. When it is adjusted, or tuned, the car can handle emergencies (a quick stop, for example). The car also uses less energy (gas and oil) and rides better.

Is it best to try to solve a problem alone?

Some problems can be solved just by talking them over with a friend.

In some ways, a human being is like a car. When a human being is well adjusted, he or she can handle emergencies better, use less energy, and operate better. What is a well-adjusted person?

Everyone has problems. It's what you do about your problem that counts. Well-adjusted people try to understand their problems and then try to do something about them. They know they can't hide from their problems because the problems will always be there. They understand that they can't take their anger and frustrations out on their friends. So they think about their problems and try to work them out. Sometimes, they talk with their closest friends

about their problems. Sometimes, they talk to parents, teachers, and to their guidance counselors. They may also seek help from their priest, rabbi, or minister.

Psychologists work with people who have serious problems. Many psychologists suggest six steps for solving any important problem. How do the following steps compare with the methods you most often use to solve your problems?

1. Define your problem and set a goal. Before you can do anything about your problem, you must make sure you know exactly what the problem is. Make sure you know all there is to know about the problem. If you are emotionally involved, don't rely on your feelings. Be sure you know the facts. Spell the problem out for yourself. Then decide what outcome you want. What goal could you reach which would solve your problem?

2. Approach the problem and your goal with a positive attitude. If you *think* you can solve the problem, you are halfway there. Do not avoid the problem. And don't tell yourself that it really doesn't matter, at least not until you think the problem through. After considering the problem thoroughly, maybe you *will* decide that it doesn't matter after all. For the time being, concentrate on solving the problem and reaching your goal.

3. Join forces with other people who have the same problem. Teamwork often gets things done which cannot be done by one person acting alone. Ask any player on a team. The individual player cannot win a game. He or she must depend on team members for help. In turn, that person must also help the teammates. The same thing applies to problem solving. If you have a problem, get together with others who have a positive attitude about the problem. Discuss ideas for solving the problem and reaching your common goal. Do not complain or feel sorry for yourself in this group. Try to keep a positive attitude at all times. That way, you can support your team members and help your group come to a good solution.

4. Talk with someone you know and trust about your problem. This person should be someone in whom you have confidence, someone you respect. Perhaps your parents can fill this need. Your guidance counselor or your teacher may be able to help. As we have already said, many people take their problems to their priest, minister, or rabbi. These persons help people with problems every day. Most clergy consider this part of their job and try to be as helpful as they can. Many people have a special, close friend they talk with about their problems. Sometimes you can solve your own problem just by talking with someone about it. It is always good to "get it off your chest" by talking about your problem as long as it is with someone you can trust.

5. When you are blocked from your goal or a solution to your problem, try to remove the thing or situation blocking you. After you have tried every way of solving your problem and reaching your goal, and you have not succeeded, try first to go around the obstacle. Try another way of doing it. If that fails, try to remove your obstacle. (As with any of these steps, you should be careful not to hurt someone else in the process.)

6. If everything up to this point does not work, think again about your goal. Is the problem really that important? Is it worth it to continue spending time and energy (and maybe money) on solving the problem and reaching your goal? If the answer is not a strong "yes" it might be a good idea to put the problem aside for a while. This should not be done until you have tried all of the other five steps. There is a time for putting all your effort into finding a solution. There is also a time for realizing that, in spite of everything you have done, there might not be a good solution to the problem. A well-adjusted person knows when to put effort into other activities when everything possible has been done.

Teamwork can get things done.

Have you ever tried to solve a problem using a method like this? Did you try all six steps listed here? How well did your solution work? If it failed, did you try another solution?

How could you solve a problem in the future using the six steps described in this section?

READING REVIEW

1. Name the steps in problem solving.

Critical Thinking

2. **Predicting Consequences** (see page 36) Why is problem solving considered important?

EXPERIMENT 3-F

Problem Solving

Read Reading 4 before working on this experiment. Think back on a problem you had recently. It should be a problem that took a lot of effort to solve. On a separate sheet of paper answer these questions:

1. What was the problem? State it exactly.
2. What kind of attitude did you have about solving the problem? Why?
3. Did you join forces with other people who had the same problem? Did it help?

4. Did you talk with someone about the problem? With whom? Did it help?
5. If you were blocked from your goal, did you try to remove the thing or situation blocking you? How? Did it help?
6. Did you solve the problem? How? Or did you put it aside for a while? Why?
7. Would it have helped to follow the six rules in Reading 4? Could the results have possibly been better?

READING 5

Taking Care of Your Needs

There is no one in the world exactly like you. Yet, there are many things about you that you have in common with everyone else. Your needs are an example. **Needs** are something one must have in order to survive and grow in a healthy way, both mentally and physically. We all have a basic need to eat, sleep, drink liquids, and guard against harm in order to keep alive. Everyone has a need to be loved and to have friends. Everyone has a need to feel good about herself or himself.

Many psychologists have studied human needs. Sigmund Freud was among the first. He believed that people are not always aware of their needs. Sometimes people's needs are hidden, even to themselves. Freud called these **unconscious needs.** For example, a person may have a strong desire or need to succeed. However that person may be so fearful of failing, that he or she will not try to succeed at all. That person may settle for constant failure because, for him or her it is more frightening to try hard and then fail than to not try and fail. Do you know someone like that? That person has a deep unconscious need for success. The need for success is so deep that he or she might not recognize it.

Other needs are not hidden, and they are called **conscious needs.** For example, you are aware of being hungry or thirsty, tired, or lonely. Your need for food, water, rest, and friends are all conscious needs, because you are aware of having those needs.

Every human has the need to protect himself or herself from emotional pain as well as physical harm. Dr. Freud taught that humans protect themselves from emotional pain by using **defense mechanisms.** Four of the most important defense mechanisms are projection, repression, denial, and rationalization.

Projection is the process of projecting one's own faults onto someone else. By doing this, the individual shifts blame or faults onto someone else's shoulders. "I'm not stubborn. *You* are the one who is stubborn. You always have to have your own way," is a common projection of people who want others to cater to their needs.

Repression is the process of putting painful memories out of one's conscious mind. By keeping such memories in the unconscious part of the mind, the individual does not have to face them directly. For example, if someone you love has hurt you deeply, you may unconsciously "forget" it without even realizing that you have done so. You "forget" in order to cover up the pain.

Denial is refusing to believe that something has happened, even when it is perfectly obvious. Some patients who are told that they have an incurable disease may practice denial. "It isn't true. It can't be true," they say. In an effort to hide their pain, they deny what is real.

Rationalization is a common defense mechanism. A person will make an excuse

An appreciation of dance is something people all over the world have in common.

for doing something but not realize that the excuse is not the real reason for the action. For example, a student might say that an assignment wasn't done because there wasn't enough time. The real reason, however, was that the student didn't understand the assignment.

Projection and repression and other defense mechanisms are done unconsciously. Defense mechanisms are not the best ways of dealing with problems, and they do not encourage people to be mentally healthy. Good mental health is the result of seeing your needs and problems for what they are, then working alone and with others to achieve your goals without hurting others.

Another psychologist who studied human needs is Abraham Maslow. According to Dr. Maslow we take care of our needs in steps. The first step consists of our physiological, or body, needs. These include the need to get enough of the right kinds of food, liquids, and air. Getting enough sleep and relaxation are other needs of our bodies. These needs must be taken care of before we consider the needs of step two.

Step two includes all our safety needs, those necessary to keep ourselves from harm. We all have the need to live in a situation free from attack. Imagine how difficult it would be to live if you were always

Self-actualization *includes liking yourself and working well with others.*

afraid of being hurt or killed. You could not work or have fun. You would always be looking out for an attack. Safety is a very important need, second only to the body needs of step one.

Step three includes our need to feel wanted and loved. When the needs of keeping alive and safe are met, we can consider the needs of step three. Belonging to a group and having friends are needs of step three. Loving people and being loved are important parts of living.

Step four includes the need to feel good about yourself. This is called self-esteem. Having a good reputation and the freedom to do what you think is right are part of good self-esteem.

Step five is the final step. It is called **self-actualization.** This simply means that you are constantly becoming the best person you can possibly be. You are developing confidence in yourself. You use your talents

wisely. You try to improve your attitudes about yourself and others all the time. Most of all, you really like yourself and other people. This is the best way to live, according to Dr. Maslow. Self-actualization is a step which we never completely reach. It is a continual process of self-improvement, a lifelong effort.

Dr. Maslow believed that you have to take care of your needs one step at a time. You cannot take care of step three needs if there are needs at step one or two that haven't been taken care of. Do you think he is right? Let's look at the following story. (After you have read the story, try to think of some other times when you must take care of certain needs before others.)

You have been on a desert island for two weeks. All your food and water are gone. If help doesn't come soon, you will die of hunger and thirst. Suddenly, a ship arrives with food and water. Two people are coming ashore. They are bringing the food and liquids you need to keep alive.

What would you do first? Would you take the food and water? Or would you first take time to become good friends with the people? First things first! You need to keep alive. Friendship would not keep you alive at that point. Your step one needs for food and water must be taken care of before you make friends (a step three need). You have to take care of your needs one step at a time.

READING REVIEW

1. What is the difference between unconscious and conscious needs?
2. List the five steps in Abraham Maslow's "ladder" of human needs.

Critical Thinking

3. **Determining Relevance** (see page 17) What is a defense mechanism? Are defense mechanisms useful for solving problems?

EXPERIMENT 3-H

Can You Believe Your Eyes?

We all perceive people and things. But sometimes it isn't easy to perceive what is really there. Sometimes your eyes and brain play tricks on you and throw your perception off.

1. Look at the center of this group of blocks. Stare at it for a while. What do you see between the blocks?

Between the corners of the blocks you see black dots. Are the dots really there?

2. What do you see here?

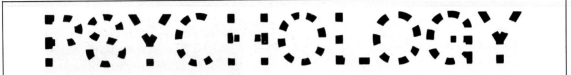

You recognize this word by making imaginary connections between the lines.
You are seeing things that aren't really there.

3. What do you see?

Did you see the young woman first? Or did you first see the old woman?

4. Follow the three poles on the left to the places where they are connected on the right.

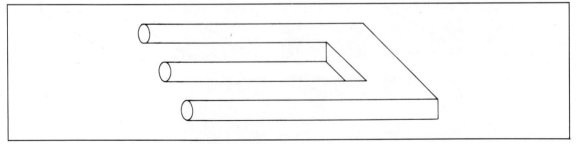

Why do you think your eyes were fooled?

5. Which inner dot seems larger?

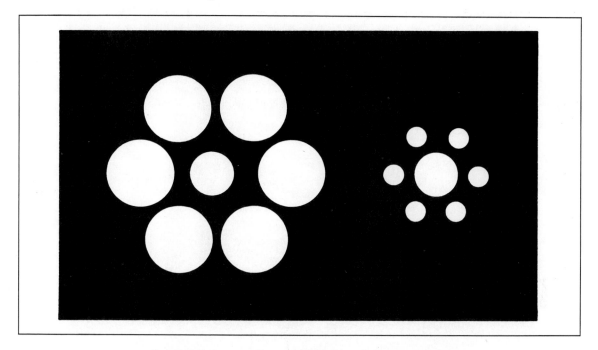

Measure both inner dots. Which one is larger?

6. Are these stairs going up or down? If you see them going down, try to see them going up. Pretend you are *in* the stairs. Do you see it now?

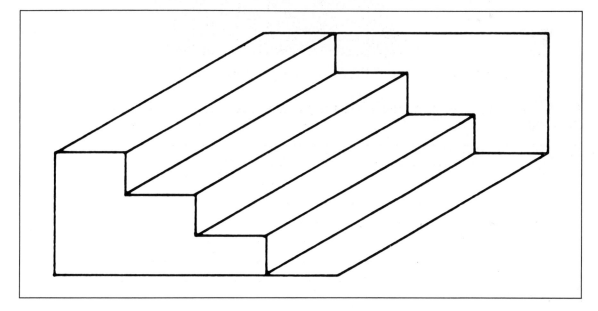

7. Why is this an impossible drawing?

Perception and Learning

Perception is the process of taking in information from the environment through the senses. That information is then used in thinking and acting. Perceiving correctly is often not as easy as you might think it is. A lot of things get in the way of our true perception of reality. One of these things is called a mental set. A **mental set** is an expectation of the way things should be or will be. Go back to page 128, and take another look at the waterfall. The artist tricked you into seeing water travel in an upward direction. (Some people see the water running along a flat surface.) From experience, you expect water to travel in a downward direction. In this case your mental set was wrong.

Mental sets can affect the way you think about yourself. If you carry strong expectations into your classes at the beginning of the school year, they will probably come true. For example, if you believe that you cannot be good at math, you carry a negative mental set into your math classes. That mental set will block you from really learning math and enjoying the subject. For a long time our society believed that boys were stronger in math ability than girls. People grew up believing this mental set. Many girls dropped out of math classes during their school careers, or simply didn't do well, because of a negative mental set our society had about girls and math. Boys, on the other hand, were expected to excel in math, and they did. Today, both boys and girls do well in math because our social mental sets have changed. Next time you are faced with a class you have not en-joyed, or one in which your self-confidence is low, try changing your mental set to a more positive one. "Psych" yourself up, and you will be amazed at how well you do.

Mental sets can also affect your relationships with other people. Here is an imaginary example. Dave has always been nasty toward you. Today, you see him coming toward you, yelling your name. "Oh no," you think, "here he comes! I wonder what nasty things Dave is going to say to me today? Can't he ever be friendly?!" You turn around and walk away from him. Later, you discover that Dave wanted to apologize for his behavior and was going to ask you to be friends. Your mental set was that Dave was mean and unfriendly,

OH, NO!

Dave = mean, yelling, unfriendly

and you thought and acted as if this would always be true.

Our perceptions of truth and reality can be wrong. It is necessary for us to continually examine what we believe and think to make sure it is true and real. We do this through a process called learning. **Learning** is defined as a change in behavior caused by experience. The change can often be permanent.

Here is how learning happens. We take in information through our five senses. This first step is referred to as *perception*. Information from the senses travels along the nervous system to the brain, where it is processed and the thinking process takes place. This second step is called *thought*. In a split second, in most cases, the brain decides what the body should do. Then the brain sends information back through the nervous system to the rest of the body, ordering it to act in a certain way. This third step is called *action*. An action may be either doing something, or not doing something. (If you are standing on the railroad tracks and you see a train in the distance approaching you, you may choose to stay where you are. Or you may decide to move, to reduce your chances of being hit. In either case, you have performed an action.) Once you have acted, you watch the results of your action. If the results are good, your brain stores information to repeat the action next time. If the results are not good, the brain stores information to do something different next time. This fourth step is called *reaction*. The four steps in learning are referred to as an **experience pattern.**

Learning may be beneficial or harmful. Some learning may be harmful if it prevents us from developing into healthy human beings. Learning how to cheat and steal is harmful learning. Learning how to get along with others and help them is beneficial learning.

Can you think of an experience pattern you have had recently that was a beneficial learning process for you? How did it help you to grow mentally?

Learning*

PART ONE: **The Star**

How do we learn? This experiment might help us come up with a few answers to that question. First, pick a partner. For Part One you will use Handout Pages A and C. You and your partner should also have a stop-watch or a watch or clock with a second hand. Exact timing is very important in this experiment.

To begin, place a piece of cardboard or any other barrier between your eyes and Page A. (See the picture on this page.) Place a mirror so that you can see the paper in it. Put your pencil on the dot inside the lines of the star. Watching through the mirror, try to draw a line inside the lines of the star all along the pathway back to the dot. Keep looking at the mirror. Don't peek at your pencil, hand, or paper. Try this experiment six times, while your partner times

*This experiment, Parts One, Two, and Three, is adapted from *Record of Activities and Experiments* for use with *Psychology,* Fifth Edition, by T. L. Engle and Louis Snellgrove. (See Acknowledgements, pages 595–596.)

you on each trial. Your partner will record your results for the six trials on Page C. Then switch with your partner while he or she tries the experiment. You record the time for each trial.

Finally, make a *learning curve* by plotting your results on the graph on Handout Page C. Your partner should do the same for her or his own results. What do the completed graphs tell you?

PART TWO: **Running a Maze**

You and your partner should have one cardboard with a hole in the middle. You should have one Handout Page B, which is a maze, for the two of you. You should each have Handout Page C to record your results.

The object of this experiment is to go from "Start" to "Finish" in the shortest possible time. Your partner should put the cardboard over the word "Start" so you can see the letter S. Have your partner time you as you move the cardboard along the line of the maze. When you run into a "dead end" you have to find your way back onto the right track. Continue until you reach the word "Finish."

Your partner should record your time for each of your six trials. Graph your own learning curve. Then time your partner as he or she tries the maze. Record your partner's time for all six trials. Your partner should then graph his or her learning curve. What do the graphs tell you?

PART THREE: **Doing a Jigsaw Puzzle**
You have probably done a jigsaw puzzle before. Did you know that doing puzzles involves a way of learning? Make a jigsaw puzzle from the magazine page or picture you brought to class. First, mount the picture on a piece of cardboard with glue or other adhesive. It is important that the *entire* picture be firmly attached to the card-

board. Cut the picture into twenty pieces. Make the pieces have curving edges like a real jigsaw.

Exchange puzzles with your partner, scrambling the pieces. Now try to put your partner's puzzle together while he or she times you. Do six trials. Your partner should record your times on your Handout Page C. When you have completed the six trials, graph your own learning curve on Page C. Then switch and allow your partner to try your puzzle while you time him or her and record the six trials on your partner's Page C. Your partner should graph his or her own learning curve. What do the graphs tell you?

When you have completed all three parts of this experiment, talk with your partner about what you both have learned about the process of learning. What helped in that learning process?

What Is Learning?

In Part One of "Experiment 3-I: The Star," you tried to do something which is normally an easy task, that is, drawing a line on a path. What made it difficult this time?

Your perceptions were changed! In the star exercise, you found out that your mental set did not work. Why? You had to learn a whole new way of perceiving—a completely different mental set. Only as you changed your mental set were you able to perceive accurately. You were then able to trace the line. After you did that, and practiced it for a while, it became easier for you to do the experiment. You *learned* to adjust your perceptions, thoughts, and actions to

fit a new set of conditions. Learning is defined as a change in behavior caused by experience.

One of the first persons to study the way we learn was Ivan Pavlov. In the late 1800s, he experimented with dogs. He wanted to make the dogs change their behavior. Pavlov knew that when the dogs were fed, they salivated (their mouths "watered"). Pavlov wanted to train the dogs to salivate anytime he gave them a signal. So every time he brought food to the dogs he rang a bell. The dogs developed the mental set:

Bell = Food

Pavlov noticed that, after a while, the dogs would salivate every time he rang the bell. It no longer mattered whether or not he brought food at the same time! Psychologists call this kind of training **classical conditioning.** The term *classical* means standard or traditional. *Conditioning* is a process of training. Let's see exactly how classical conditioning works.

Something in the environment which causes you to act is called a **stimulus.** (The plural of stimulus is *stimuli.*) The stimulus causes you to act, and that action is called a **response.** This can be diagrammed:

$$S \longrightarrow R$$

What was the stimulus in Pavlov's experiment? What was the response? There were actually two kinds of stimuli in the experiment. The bell was a *neutral stimulus.* It is called neutral because it did not mean anything to the dogs at first. The other stimulus, the food, had always meant something to the dogs. Food satisfied their hunger, and they normally salivated when it was brought to them. It did not take any training or conditioning to make the dogs salivate for food. We therefore call the stimulus of food an *unconditioned stimulus.* Pavlov conditioned the dogs to salivate at the sound of the bell. He did this by making the dogs associate the neutral stimulus (bell) with the unconditioned stimulus (food). The bell was then the conditioned stimulus. The response to *either* stimulus after a while was salivation. We can diagram it this way:

1. NS $\longrightarrow$ R
 (bell) (no salivation)

2. UCS $\longrightarrow$ UCR
 (food) (salivation)

3. NS + UCS $\longrightarrow$ R
 (bell + food) (salivation)

4. CS $\longrightarrow$ CR
 (bell) (salivation)

In the diagram:
  NS = neutral stimulus
  CS = conditioned stimulus
 UCS = unconditioned stimulus
   R = response
  CR = conditioned response
 UCR = unconditioned response.

A *conditioned response* is a response which the subject was trained to perform. An *unconditioned response* is one which

Examine this picture closely. Then explain how your mental set *affects what you* perceive.

the subject performs naturally, without having to be trained to do it.

Notice how Pavlov taught the dogs to associate the sound of the bell with food. Over time, the dogs learned to salivate at the sound of the bell, even though no food was presented to them.

If you have ever tried to train a dog to sit or to roll over, or to beg, you probably used another method of conditioning. Every time the dog came close to doing what you wanted it to do, you gave the dog a reward. Soon, the dog began to understand what you wanted, and you gave the reward for "getting closer" to your idea. Finally, you had the dog doing exactly what you wanted. To help the dog remember the trick, you gave the dog a reward every time the trick was repeated successfully. The dog was encouraged to repeat its response, or the trick, because it received a reward. This conditioning is called **operant conditioning.** Operant conditioning includes the process of **shaping** in which the behavior of the subject is gradually shaped into what the trainer wants.

A pioneer in the field of operant conditioning was Dr. B. F. Skinner of Harvard University. Dr. Skinner experimented with pigeons in a laboratory setting. His aim was to have the pigeons learn new patterns of behavior through operant conditioning. He put the pigeons in a specially made box, which is now called a "Skinner box." One is shown at the top of this page.

In a Skinner box the trainer wants the pigeon to peck at the round target. As the subject (the pigeon) walks past the target, the trainer releases a few pellets of bird food into the tray below the target. As the bird gets closer to the target, the trainer stops giving rewards for simply passing the target. Now, the bird will get pellets only by

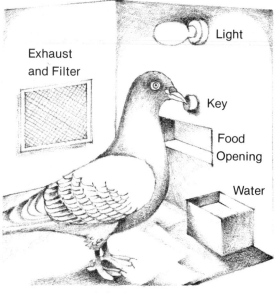

A SKINNER BOX

pecking close to the target. Eventually, the pigeon will peck the target every time and get pellets of food.

The reward in operant conditioning is sometimes called **positive reinforcement.** In some conditioning experiments, punishments are used to discourage unwanted behavior. Punishments are also known as **negative reinforcement.** Dr. Skinner and other psychologists have discovered that positive reinforcements are almost always more successful than negative reinforcements. Animals and people tend to learn better when they are rewarded than when they are punished. Why do you think this is so? Can you think of an example in which you learned better with a reward than with a punishment?

Some forms of operant conditioning are used today by practicing psychologists. The conditioning techniques are used to break people of destructive behavior patterns. The goal is to replace the "bad" habits with "good" ones, so that those people can lead happier lives.

Can you think of ways in which your behavior patterns are gradually changed by reinforcement by your friends? By your teachers? By your parents?

Classical conditioning and operant conditioning, or shaping, are two major kinds of learning. Another type is **trial-and-error learning.** In this type of learning, the subject tries different ways of doing an experiment. During each trial, the subject learns a little more from his or her errors. Finally, the subject discovers the "right" way to do it. From then on, the subject can more easily perform the correct actions. Running a maze and putting together a jigsaw puzzle are examples of trial-and-error learning. What other examples of trial-and-error learning can you think of?

EXPERIMENT 3-J

Making An Inkblot

The **inkblot test** is one of many ways some psychologists use to study personalities. The psychologist interprets what the individual perceives in the inkblot. Let's make and use a simple inkblot.

One way of doing this is to fold a piece of unlined paper in half. Open it up part way and pour a *small* amount of India ink in the middle of the fold. Close the fold again so that the two halves close with the ink inside. Open the paper and let it dry. Study the inkblot you have made. What does it look like to you? What do other people think it looks like? Are other people's perceptions of your inkblot different from yours?

Another way of making a kind of "inkblot" without using ink is to fold in half a piece of paper or construction paper. Cut designs into three sides of the folded paper, but not into the side with the fold. Open it up and flatten it. What does it look like? Compare your perceptions with those of others.

An inkblot. What do you see?

What Is Creativity?

No one knows exactly why some people have certain talents while others do not. Even identical twins, who have the same hereditary background, may not share the same talents.

Creativity is a talent. It is the ability to see, think, or do things in many new and different ways. Psychologists do not know exactly what factors determine a person's creativity. They do know, however, that some people are creative in one field while others are creative in other fields. Your mother may be creative in different ways than your brother or sister (if you have one). Perhaps you are creative in art, music, sports, or thinking.

You can develop creativity. How? Here are a few suggestions. Always try to be aware of what is happening to you and what is going on around you. Interesting things are happening all the time. Unless you are aware and tuned in to your environment, things will pass you by. Practice being aware. Open up all your senses. Notice how much more aware you become.

While you are practicing awareness, be sure to keep your mind open to new ideas and new things. Try doing something, such as bathing or eating, several different ways. Be willing to change to a better way. Or just try a *different* way to make routine things more interesting.

Completely absorbed in creating

Most important of all, don't allow others to discourage you from thinking and acting creatively. You can gain much by developing a creative mind.

Here are a few fun exercises to help develop creativity. Try them on your own.

■ Find someone else who also wants to become more aware, and share with that person an experience you have had in the past. It can be a funny experience or a sad one. Try to make your partner *feel* the way you did when you had the experience. Then your partner should share an experience with you. Your partner should close his or her eyes. As you give a brief description of the weather, the surroundings, or your feelings, your partner should try to paint in his or her mind what is being said. Then switch roles, with your partner giving you descriptions of something.

Using a camera is a different way to become aware of the world around you.

■ Everybody daydreams. Put your daydreaming to work for you. Concentrate on an activity which you do frequently. Picture yourself doing this activity as you normally do it. Try to "see" yourself doing this activity as you might watch it on television or at a movie. Once you are able to do that, picture yourself doing the same activity in new ways which you have never tried. Then try to picture yourself doing the same things in impossible or nearly impossible ways.

For example, "see" yourself going to school in the morning as you normally do. Then "see" yourself going to school in a slightly different way, walking if you normally ride, or riding if you normally walk. Next, try to imagine yourself going to school in really unusual ways. For instance, "see" yourself going outside your home, getting into your rocket, giving the count-

down, and blasting off toward your school at a very fast speed, landing safely outside the school, and going inside as you usually do. Or "see" yourself as a meteor high above the earth falling at an increasing speed right into your classroom. Or "see" yourself coming up from the center of the earth, crashing through layer after layer of rock, oil, sand, and water, finally crashing through the floor of your classroom, and then taking your seat. What expressions do you see on your friends' faces? What does it feel like to do that? Awareness of *feeling* is just as important as picturing yourself doing these things. Make up some other situations and practice "seeing" yourself doing the activities different ways.

■ To build awareness of everyday things which we all take for granted, try this: Go up to something you know very well. Examine it very carefully, as if you don't know what it is. Pay close attention to every detail. Can you describe everything about it to someone else? Try it! You can also do this exercise by examining and describing your partner's face or hands. Just make sure that your partner knows what you are doing. This exercise is especially good if your partner is your parent or a close friend. You may be amazed at how little you know about what they really look like, although you see them often.

Try these experiments many times in different situations. Have fun doing them, but take them seriously and really concentrate on what you are doing. You may soon find yourself becoming much more creative.

READING REVIEW
1. Can creativity be developed?

Critical Thinking
2. **Drawing Conclusions** (see page 42) What is important in developing your own creativity?

EXPERIMENT 3-L The Number-Word Talent Test **HANDOUT**

READING 9

You Can Do It If You Think You Can!

Recently you took part in an unusual experiment. You probably learned that your mental attitude has a lot to do with *what* you do and *how* you do it. If you were one of the people who was told you had no "talent," did you decide it was useless to try to develop the talent? Did you allow the teacher to make you believe that you had no talent? Did you give up before you really even began?

Many people don't succeed because they allow others to tell them what their abilities are. They accept someone else's opinion as fact. They accept failure before they even try for success. Sometimes, they think, it is easier to lose than to try to win.

Some people are not sure of themselves. They are afraid of people saying, "You have no talent!" so they take the easy way out. They quit before they begin. That way, nobody can hurt them or criticize their work. They would rather be sure of losing than take a chance at winning.

Who *really* wants to lose? Do you? Of course not. Everyone is born to win. Some people win in different ways than others. Everybody can win by building a **positive mental attitude.** Here are three steps you can use:

1. Everybody can win—no one should lose. If you always try to make the other

A positive attitude can bring success.

person lose so you can win, you have already lost. You can make yourself win while helping others to win. They will probably do the same in return. A winner is someone who gives credit where credit is due. If someone has a talent, compliment him or her. It makes a person feel good. It should also make you feel good. She or he will probably like you more, too.

2. If you think you can do something, you can do it! You can do many things! If it is physically possible and if you have a positive attitude about it, you can eventually do almost anything. It sounds crazy, but it's true. If you don't believe it, give it a try.

Sit down and *think* about what you would like to be successful at. Then *plan* how you will do it. Be sure to give yourself enough time. Then, *start thinking positively* about realistic goals. Think "I will do it!" and you really *will* do it. If you keep that one secret—a positive attitude—it will be just a matter of time until you succeed. Whether it is getting better grades, or being closer to people, or getting a job, you can do it if you *think* you can! The most successful people in the world today became successful because they knew this secret. They thought positively.

3. Recognize your own talents—And recognize your weak spots. Why do you need anyone telling you that you have no "Number-Word Talent"—or for that matter, any other kind of talent? Some of the greatest geniuses were not considered talented during their lifetime. Don't be discouraged. Just consider what your own strengths are and work from that point. Know what your weaknesses are, too. Don't try to hide them from yourself. Work on your weaknesses. Who knows? In time, these weaknesses may become your strengths!

Those are three secrets to being a happier person. How many ways can you think of to use them in your own life?

READING REVIEW ≡≡≡≡

1. What does "positive mental attitude" mean?

Critical Thinking

2. **Identifying Central Issues** (see page 14) What are the three steps in developing a positive mental attitude?

What Is Good Mental Health?

Psychologists help people work toward good mental health. When your body needs help from time to time, you go to a doctor. Likewise, when your mind needs help, you might decide to go to a psychologist. Let's suppose we asked some psychologists the question: What is good mental health? They might give us these answers:

Good mental health is the ability to recognize things for what they are. A mentally healthy person lives in the real world and enjoys it. He or she does not hide in a make-believe world.

Good mental health is being a winner and at the same time helping others to win. If

Living in the real world

everyone is a winner, how can *you* ever lose?

Good mental health is knowing that emotions are healthy and good. Putting your emotions to work for you is very important for good mental health.

Good mental health is having a positive attitude about your talents and your weaknesses. If you *think* you can do something, do it. You can if you *think* you can.

Good mental health is solving your problems as they come along. Try not to let them pile up. Take care of problems as soon as you can. People with good mental health know that they often cannot solve problems by themselves. They get help. They also know that some problems cannot be easily solved. They do as much as they can to solve the problem. If it cannot be solved, they either put it away for a while or think about whether the goals are really worth the effort.

Good mental health is knowing who you are. It is knowing how your heredity and your environment have affected you.

Good mental health is becoming a self-actualizing person (the last step in Dr. Maslow's "staircase") by becoming the very best person you can be. You have a lot going for you, no matter who you are. Think good things and there is no telling what you can accomplish.

READING REVIEW

1. Why is it important to work through your problems as they come along instead of letting them all build up?
2. Define "good mental health" in a single sentence.

Critical Thinking

3. **Determining Relevance** (see page 17) What does Dr. Maslow's last step in his ladder of needs have to do with good mental health?

Human Development

Each of us was born, and each of us will die sometime in the future. In between, we get older and we develop psychologically and physically. Many changes occur in the human body as time passes. Those changes make a person look, feel, and act older. **Developmental psychologists** study these changes, and through their work, we know that aging is a natural process.

While the outside of your body ages, the organs inside your body are changing, too.

Heredity has a lot to do with how fast you age. But we know that people who exercise regularly and eat properly tend to age more slowly and live longer. We also know that happiness is good for the body. Happy, friendly persons tend to be healthier and stay young longer than those who are always unhappy with life.

As your body ages, you will notice certain psychological changes taking place. Psychologist Erik Erikson believed that each person goes through eight stages of psychological growth in a lifetime. He has named those psychological stages the "Eight Ages of Man."*

In the first stage, early infancy, the individual reaches outside of himself or herself and learns to trust (or mistrust) others.

Stage two, during the second and third years of life, is a time of growing independence. The child takes pride in doing things without the aid of parents. Beginning with toilet training, the child discovers control over its own movements and behavior.

During the third stage, from age 4 to 5, the child is no longer simply saying "No!" to the requests of others. Instead, the child is now busy planning and doing things on his or her own. The child has greater control over body movements and is able to play physical games with other children.

By the fourth stage, from 6 to 11 years of age, the person has developed enough to enter the world outside the home. Making friends and finding out about the world becomes more important. The individual is able to understand and obey rules, making it possible to play more complicated games. Fairness becomes an important value. The person enjoys keeping busy by doing things, especially with other people of the same age. School gives the young person opportunities to do this. Adults other than parents begin to be more influential.

Stage five is generally from 12 to 18. We often call this stage *adolescence* or *puberty*. During puberty, the beginning of this stage, great changes take place in the body. The reproductive organs are now able to produce another human being. Interest in persons of the opposite sex increases. At this

stage it is normal to be confused about your identity. "Who am I, and how do I fit into this world?" becomes a very important question. Acceptance by peers takes on greater importance, too. The adolescent searches for a set of values to keep and live by throughout life. Preparation for a career usually begins at this stage.

Stage six is young adulthood. The individual now has a fairly good idea of who he or she is. Most young adults also have a direction in life. Many people in our society choose to have a love relationship during this stage. Traditionally, this has meant getting married and raising a family.

Stage seven is often called middle age. Many people at this stage are the creators and producers in our society. They are the decision makers in industries, government, and many other areas. A goal of this stage of life is to help the younger generation to grow and live in this world. This includes being good parents and good teachers.

The eighth stage is the final stage. It is the time when a person comes to the end of life's work. During this stage the individual looks back on a lifetime of experiences, taking pleasure in personal accomplishments.

One secret of a happy and healthy life is to make the most of every opportunity. No matter what stage you are in, enjoy it!

*Adapted from Erik H. Erikson, *Childhood and Society.* (See Acknowledgements, pages 595–596.)

READING REVIEW

1. How many "ages" does Erik Erikson include in his stages of human psychological development?

Critical Thinking

2. **Identifying Central Issues** (see page 14) Which of Dr. Erikson's stages is called adolescence? What are the characteristics of this stage?

The Aging Process: What Happens?

You can probably recognize the people in these photographs. They are (1) Leonard Bernstein, one of our country's greatest conductors, (2) Thurgood Marshall, our nation's first black Supreme Court justice, and (3) Queen Elizabeth II of Great Britain.

These three people are shown at three different stages of their lives. Look how their appearances have changed over the years. And yet, in some ways, they still look the same as when they were younger.

Can you identify some of the changes in their physical appearance as they grew older? What other changes do you think they went through in the course of their lives? As these people aged, how do you think their thoughts changed about themselves, their friends, and their world?

Careers in Psychology*

Do you like to watch people to try to figure out why they behave as they do? Do you enjoy listening to other people's problems and helping them decide what to do? If so, perhaps you should consider a career in the field of Psychology.

Psychologists today are involved in a great variety of activities. Most psychologists specialize in one of the many branches of Psychology.

Experimental psychologists study the behavior of humans and animals when they are rewarded and punished in many different situations. They examine how and why learning takes place.

Developmental psychologists study the ways people change and behave as they go through life.

Personality psychologists study human nature and differences among people.

Social psychologists study the behavior of people in groups—why some people become leaders and others remain followers.

Environmental psychologists study the effects of surroundings on a person's attitudes and behavior.

Population psychologists look at how different sizes and types of population affect people's behavior.

Physiological psychologists will study the influence of the body upon behavior.

Comparative psychologists compare the behaviors of human beings with those of animals.

Clinical psychologists specialize in helping people with their problems. Often, their work is done in their own offices. Their clients are scheduled for appointments of about one hour. During that time, the psychologist gradually guides the client to a better understanding of the reasons for his or her perceptions, thoughts, and actions. The work of a psychologist with one client may take several months or even years. The goal is to help the client to become a happier, more self-actualizing person.

School psychologists help students with both their personal and school-related problems.

Industrial psychologists work for companies and organizations. They try to learn the best way to treat workers.

Consumer psychologists study the psychological reasons why people buy the things they buy.

Psychologists go to college for four years and earn a Bachelor's degree in the field of Psychology or one of the other behavioral sciences. In addition, they study another two or three years in graduate school for a Master's degree. Almost all psychologists go beyond that level and earn a Ph.D. (Doctor of Philosophy) degree in a specialized branch of Psychology.

Some psychologists study even longer and earn a Medical Doctor, or M.D., degree. This usually takes another four to seven years. The combination of Ph.D. and M.D. degrees makes the person a psychiatrist. Psychiatrists are able to help people in the same ways as a clinical psychologist.

*Adapted from *Occupational Outlook Handbook*. (See Acknowledgements, pages 595–596.)

Psychiatrists are also able to treat clients with drugs.

There are over 130,000 psychologists of all types in the United States today. Some work for the government, at colleges and universities, and for private companies and organizations. Most psychologists have private practices and work with clients who need help with personal problems.

If you are interested in a career in psychology, you should be mature and emotionally stable. You should enjoy working with others, and you need to be able to deal with them effectively. If you are thinking about becoming a clinical psychologist, you must have great sensitivity and patience. The great reward of the clinical psychologist is in helping people.

Would you like more information on careers in Psychology? Write to the American Psychological Association, Educational Affairs Office, 1200 17th Street, N.W., Washington, DC 20036. They will send you printed information about career opportunities in any of the branches of Psychology.

READING REVIEW

1. What do psychologists do? What is the difference between a psychologist and a psychiatrist?

Critical Thinking

2. **Identifying Alternatives** (see page 38) Name a few careers you might be able to pursue with a background in Psychology.

Videotapes help comparative psychologists study animal behavior.

3 PERSPECTIVES

Social Scientists Look at Women in Sports

How do the ways psychologists think about a subject compare to the ways other social scientists think? You will explore these similarities and differences as you examine the selection about Jackie Joyner-Kersee. Read the passage below from an article by Janet Woolum in the book *Outstanding Women Athletes* and then answer the questions under "Comparing the Social Sciences."

❝Jackie Joyner-Kersee holds the world record in track and field's most grueling discipline, the heptathlon. "I like the heptathlon," Jackie once said, "because it shows you what you're made of." The heptathlon consists of seven events—the 200-meter dash, 100-meter hurdles, high jump, shot put, long jump, javelin throw, and 800-meter run—held over a two-day period. Heptathletes are awarded points based on individual performances in each event. In the 1988 Olympics, Joyner-Kersee outdistanced her closest competitor by nearly 500 points to win the gold medal, setting a new world record with 7,219 points and earning the title "World's Greatest Female Athlete."

Born to Alfred and Mary Joyner of East St. Louis, Illinois, on March 3, 1962, Jacqueline Joyner was named for then First Lady Jacqueline Kennedy. Jackie's grandmother predicted that "someday this girl will be the first lady of something." The first lady of track and field, Jackie began running and jumping at the Mayor Brown Youth Center near her home in an economically depressed area of East St. Louis. At age nine she entered her first track competition, finishing last. With the support of her parents and brother Al (husband of 100-meter world record holder Florence Griffith Joyner) Jackie continued to compete, specializing in the long jump. By the time she was 12, she could leap distances over 17 feet. . . .

If Babe Didrikson was the "female athlete of the first half century," then Jackie Joyner-Kersee may well be the "female athlete of the second half century." She clearly understands her place in history and the influence she has on the next generation of female track stars. Raised in the ghetto of East St. Louis, Joyner-Kersee is a role model for young women striving to escape the hardships brought on by poverty and lack of opportunity. "I remember where I came from," she says, "and I keep that in mind. . . . If a young female sees the environment I grew up in and sees my dreams and goals come true, they will realize their dreams and goals might also come true.❞

Comparing the Social Sciences

Psychologists study motivations. What could you as a psychologist learn from this passage about the motivations of sport champions? (*Demonstrating Reasoned Judgment*)

Sociologists study the role groups play in society. What could you as a sociologist learn from this article about the way women in sports are viewed in the United States? (*Recognizing Bias*)

Anthropologists study cultures. If you were an anthropologist, would you find anything in this passage that indicates that our culture is "youth oriented" and values a competitive spirit? (*Testing Conclusions*)

Geographers study Earth's features. As a geographer, what do you think were the causes of economic depression in East St. Louis where Joyner-Kersee was born? (*Recognizing Cause and Effect*)

Historians study about the past. If you were a historian, how would you determine whether Joyner-Kersee deserves the title "female athlete of the second half century?" (*Identifying Central Issues*)

Political scientists study government. Is there anything in this passage that would help you, as a political scientist, understand the role of the United States government with regard to sports? Explain. (*Recognizing Ideologies*)

Economists study the ways people spend their money. Could you, as an economist, explain why manufacturers might want Joyner-Kersee to endorse their products? (*Predicting Consequences*)

Jackie Joyner-Kersee

GLOSSARY OF TERMS

adaptation   a change in behavior to meet the needs of a changing environment (page 113)

analysis   the breaking up of an event or fact into smaller pieces in order to study it more closely (page 110)

behavioral science   the study of human behavior; Psychology, Anthropology, and Sociology are referred to as the behavioral sciences (page 110)

classical conditioning   the pairing of a neutral stimulus with an unconditioned stimulus in such a way that they become identified in a subject's mind and produce the same response (page 133)

conditioned response   a response that the subject is trained to perform (page 133)

conscious needs   those needs of which a person is fully aware (page 122)

creativity   the ability to see, think, or do things in many new and different ways (page 136)

defense mechanism   an unconscious way of protecting oneself from emotional pain and physical harm, according to Sigmund Freud; defense mechanisms include projection, repression, denial, and rationalization (page 122)

denial   a defense mechanism in which a person refuses to believe something even if it is obvious (page 122)

developmental psychologist   a social scientist who studies the many changes we go through as we grow (page 110)

ego   the strongest part of the human personality, according to Freud; helps a person be realistic, and balances the id and the superego (page 114)

emotions   feelings such as hate, love, and anger (page 114)

empathy   feeling as another person does; putting yourself in someone else's place (page 115)

environment   a person's surroundings, including people, places, and things; the nonhereditary part of a person's personality (see *heredity, personality*) (page 113)

experience pattern   a pattern of learning that consists of five steps: perception, conceptualization, thoughts, action, and reaction (page 130)

experimental psychologist   a social scientist who studies the behavior of animals in laboratory settings (page 110)

heredity   the passing of characteristics from parents to children through the process of reproduction (see *environment*) (page 112)

id   one of three parts of the human personality, according to Sigmund Freud; the id represents the individual's most basic drives for food, water, survival, and pleasure (page 114)

inkblot test   a psychological test in which patients describe what they see in general shapes made on paper with ink (page 135)

learning   a change in behavior caused by experience (page 130)

mental set   an expectation of how something should or will be. It determines what you perceive and what you do not perceive. (page 129)

needs   what humans require for basic survival and for living (page 122)

negative reinforcement a punishment given by the experimenter to the subject in operant conditioning after the subject performs an action that the experimenter does not desire (page 134)

observation the act of carefully watching and writing down facts and events (page 110)

operant conditioning the process of training a subject to perform a certain action by rewarding the subject when it performs the correct response (page 134)

perception the process of taking in information from the environment through the senses (page 129)

personality the "inner you"; the combination of experience patterns, hereditary factors, and environmental factors that make every human being a unique individual (see *environment, hereditary*) (page 112)

positive mental attitude thinking and believing that you really can do something you want to do (page 138)

positive reinforcement a reward given by the experimenter to the subject in operant conditioning after the subject performs an action desired by the experimenter (page 134)

projection a defense mechanism in which one's faults are shifted to someone else (page 122)

psychologist a social scientist who studies the ways the human mind works (page 110)

Psychology the study of how the mind and body work together (page 110)

rationalization a defense mechanism in which a person makes an excuse that is not the real reason for the action (page 122)

repression a defense mechanism in which a person puts painful memories out of his or her conscious mind (page 122)

response in conditioning, an action caused by a stimulus (see *stimulus, classical conditioning*) (page 133)

self-actualization the last step in Dr. Maslow's ladder of human needs; the process of trying to be the best person you can possibly be (page 124)

shaping a psychological technique used in training animals (see *operant conditioning*) (page 134)

social psychologist a social scientist who studies how individuals behave in a group (page 110)

stimulus in conditioning, something that causes a response (see *response, conditioning*) (page 133)

superego part of the human personality, according to Freud; the collective teachings of the society concerning right and wrong (page 114)

trial-and-error learning a method of learning by trying different ways of solving a problem until one works (page 135)

unconscious needs those needs of which we are not fully aware (page 122)

unconditioned response a response that the subject performs naturally, without being trained to do it (page 133)

UNIT 4 Sociology

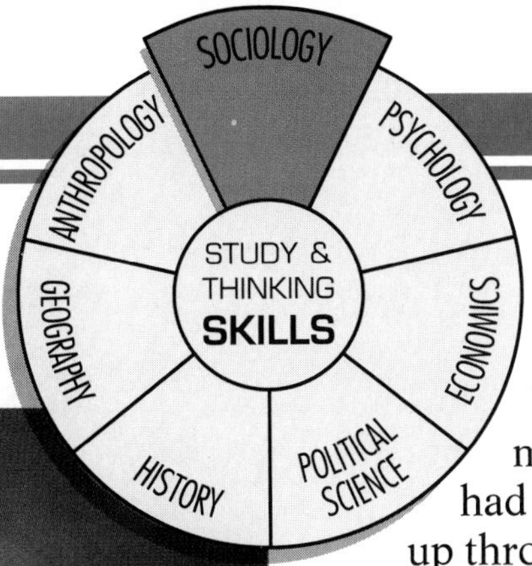

The circular diagram shows "STUDY & THINKING SKILLS" at the center, surrounded by: SOCIOLOGY, PSYCHOLOGY, ECONOMICS, POLITICAL SCIENCE, HISTORY, GEOGRAPHY, ANTHROPOLOGY.

This Is Sociology

When the dust settled in the bay area, a freeway lay mangled and torn. Huge sections of concrete and steel had collapsed onto the street below. Raging fires sprang up throughout San Francisco and Oakland. Many people had been killed. Some who had survived the earthquake could be heard moaning through the rubble. Within minutes, residents from neighborhoods near the freeway were clambering over the chunks of twisted steel, struggling to locate and free the survivors. Men and women formed human chains to hose down fires, remove concrete fragments from the shattered road, and clear a path for police and medical personnel. They worked until they were ready to drop, and when they finally turned away, others came to take their place.

Sociology is the study of how people behave in groups, whether in times of emergency or times of calm. Social scientists who work in this field are known as **sociologists.** In the Unit 4 readings, you will learn how to think like a sociologist. In the experiments, you will try new ways of looking at your family, friends, and community.

Sociology and You

The feeling of belonging, of being part of the group, is important to all of us. The questions below will help you understand more about the groups in your life.

1. What role do you play in your family? How has what you do with your family changed since you were a baby?

2. What groups do you belong to at school? Are you a leader in any group? What advice would you give someone who wanted to become a leader in one of these groups?

UNIT 4 CONTENTS

What Is Sociology?

Every day of your life you live, work, and have fun with other people. To do this, you must understand people and be able to get along with them. You should also understand how you fit into the groups of people in your environment. In other words, you need to know what your relationship is to other people and to different groups in our society. That is why Sociology is important to you.

Why is imitation of adult behavior such an important part of socialization?

Sociology is the systematic study of people's behavior in groups. Like Psychology and Anthropology, Sociology is a behavioral science because it is a systematic study of human behavior. A person who studies Sociology is called a **sociologist.**

The questions sociologists ask today are not new. The ancient Greeks were asking the same questions about human behavior thousands of years ago. The word "sociology" comes from a Latin word, *socio,* meaning "people together" and a Greek word, *logos,* meaning "the study of." And yet, the science of Sociology itself is relatively new. In the early 1800s, a French mathematician and thinker named August Comte gathered together the questions that the ancient Greeks and others had been asking for centuries and put them into one

new science. Comte laid the groundwork for other people to make contributions to the science of Sociology.

In this unit we will learn how sociologists work. We will use some of the tools that sociologists use. These tools include **observation** and **analysis** of human behavior, as well as **surveys** of public opinion, personal **interviews,** and **role playing.** By using those methods, we can better understand how the sociologist works.

We will also practice using the problem-solving method and critical thinking skills that sociologists use in their work. Every sociologist needs to know how to identify assumptions, create good questions, recognize stereotypes, and distinguish facts from opinions and inferences.

Using these methods and skills, we'll discover why people act differently when they are alone than when they are with other people. We will see what effects groups such as your family, school, and government have on the way you think and act. We will learn why groups put limits on your behavior. We'll also investigate the reasons for those limits.

Most important, we will find out about you, how you act when you are in different kinds of groups, and why you act the way you do.

READING REVIEW
1. What is Sociology?
2. What methods and critical thinking skills do sociologists use?

Critical Thinking

3. **Making Comparisons** (see page 16) Based upon what you already know, how is Sociology similar to another social science? How is it different?

Why Do People Live in Groups?

Many nonhumans live in groups. If you have ever watched an ant colony or a beehive, you probably discovered that each ant or bee spends its life doing the same things over and over. Some build the "home" while others go out to bring back food and water. Still others seem to be in charge of the workers. You may have noticed that when one ant is injured, other ants search for it and carry it back home. Of course, ants sometimes fight with one another, too. All of these activities are acted out in the ants' communities. In their groups, the ants have individual jobs to perform. By working in groups, the ants accomplish more than they could by working alone.

People also work in groups. No two human groups are *exactly* alike. No individual in our society can supply all of the things she or he needs and wants. So people work in groups to supply themselves with the things they want. Some human groups oppose other human groups because they may want different things. War is an extreme example of this. Think about your own needs and wants. Which of them are supplied by your town or community? Which can you take care of yourself?

In human societies there are many types of groups. In a **primary group** people usually have a very close relationship over a long period of time. They are emotionally involved with one another. They are loyal to each other and fulfill for each other the needs for love and "belongingness." Primary groups give the individual confidence

Judging from what you see here, is this a primary or a secondary group?

and strength to deal with "the outside world." Primary groups include families and close friends.

Secondary groups are usually larger and less loving than primary groups. Secondary groups are often no more than groups of people who need to do a job. A company or business is a secondary group. The people in this group are usually not as close to each other as members of a family are. And yet, there is a purpose for the secondary group: to get something done. Your city government is a kind of secondary group. Your school is also (except for your very close friends). What makes these groups "secondary groups"? What other secondary groups do you belong to?

A **community** is a group of people (or many groups of people) who often live close to each other and who work together for common goals. Your town or city is a community. What goals do the groups in your town have in common? What primary and secondary groups can be found in your community?

The largest kind of group is called the society. A **society** is made up of many primary and secondary groups and two or more communities. A nation, such as the United States, is an example of a society.

EXPERIMENT **4-A**

What Groups Do You Belong To?

In class you discussed why people live in groups. You also discussed some of the groups to which you belong. Let's take a closer look at these groups in this experiment. After you read carefully "Reading 2: Why Do People Live in Groups?", complete this experiment. Give it a lot of thought and answer the questions the best way you can. This experiment will be the basis of your work in this unit.

In column 1 on Handout 4-A, fill in the names of five groups to which you belong. These should be ones that are important to you, such as "Family" or "Basketball Team." Then in column 2, briefly explain the reason for the group's existence: What does the group do that makes it important to you? In the third column, give three main rules you must follow as a member of that group. In column 4, write whether your membership in the group is voluntary or involuntary. Lastly, in column 5, list three of the members of the group (do not name yourself).

When you have finished, take a close look at your answers. Do you notice any similarities among the groups? What are the major differences? What groups are missing from your list? Why did you omit them?

Can You Identify These Roles?

Anyone who has seen a movie or a play knows what a role is. Actors play out roles, depending on what the script calls for. The role might be "father" or "doctor" or "mountain climber." The script may call for the actor to play one, two, or many roles all at the same time.

In real life everyone plays many parts. Every person has many roles, depending upon the time, group, and other circumstances. Here are three photographs of people. As you study them ask yourself the following questions:

• What roles are being played by each of the people in the photos?

• How can you tell what their roles are? Are there any clues you can spot which help you identify those roles?

• What is the relationship of each person to others in the photo?

• What emotions do you think these persons are experiencing?

Rules, Roles, and Socialization

As we have seen, people live in groups. Living in groups is much different from living alone. When you live in a group, such as your family, you have to consider not only your own needs and wishes, but also the needs and wishes of other members of the family. Your family probably has certain rules which you are expected to obey. Some of the rules may never be spoken, but you somehow know what you are allowed to do and what you are not supposed to do. How did you learn the rules?

Every baby who enters the world also enters a society. The society she or he is born into has many communities, with many secondary groups and primary groups. Each of the groups to which a baby belongs—the primary group (family), secondary groups, the community, and society—has a set of rules by which people are expected to live. Individual members of each group teach the growing child the rules of the group. If the rules are broken in a group, someone who has authority punishes or corrects the child. The child is usually rewarded for obeying the rules. By rewarding and punishing the child, a group (or society) makes sure that the child grows up knowing what to do and what not to do.

Within a society, eating behavior is a norm. Is this norm in the category of folkways, mores, or laws?

This process of learning the rules is called **socialization** (sō′ shə līz ā′ shən). Sometimes the rules are obvious, such as the rule against killing other people. Most societies hold this rule, except in time of war or other unusual circumstances. Most often, however, the rules are less obvious than this and need to be taught. The rule against driving a car through a red light is an example. There is nothing natural about stopping when you see a certain kind of light. The light's meaning has to be explained.

Socialization also includes learning which rules, or standards, are to be taken more seriously than others. Sociologists call these social rules or standards **norms**. Norms tell us how to behave in the society. There are three types of norms:

1. Folkways are norms of politeness, or customs, such as eating properly or addressing a person by the right title—Mr., Ms., or Dr. If you break a folkway, you are not considered an evil person. After several offenses you might, however, find yourself with fewer friends, or be punished by your family or by some other group.

2. Mores (mŏr′ āz) are norms that are taken much more seriously than folkways. If you break such a norm, you may be punished severely or sent out of the society. Breaking mores against stealing and killing human beings is considered very serious by most societies. Such actions carry a moral judgment against the person who does the act. Those who break mores are considered "bad" or immoral by others in the society.

3. Laws are norms made and enforced by the government of a society. Laws are for-

What kind of norm has the owner of this car broken?

mal rules which are supposed to protect the people in a society from each other and from outsiders. Laws may or may not be mores. For example, you park your car at a parking meter and let the meter run overtime. When you come back to your car, you find a ticket on the windshield. You have broken a law, but not mores. No one would call you a "bad" person for breaking that law. But if you murdered someone, society *would* condemn you for your action. In that case, you would have broken both mores and laws.

The socialization process teaches us the society's folkways, mores, and laws. Socialization also does something else. It teaches us roles. A **role** is a name given to the kind of behavior that a person is supposed to have in a particular group or society. An actor in a play or movie acts out a role. You know what to expect of a person playing the role of detective or doctor or lawyer. If the actor does not act like the character she or he is supposed to be, you may be disappointed. People in any social group expect its members to act out certain roles, too. As long as these roles are acted out as the members expect them to be, everything is fine. When someone acts outside of his or her role, it may cause confusion or trouble.

Everyone plays many roles in life. The roles you play depend on your groups. You probably don't act the same way around your family as you do when you are with close friends. Chances are that you behave in school differently than you behave with your family and friends. That is because you have different roles, and rules, in each group.

How does society make us obey its norms and act out certain roles? Society gives rewards for obedience and punishments for disobedience. Sometimes rewards are called **positive sanctions** and punishments are called **negative sanctions.**

We will take a close look at socialization, roles, norms, and sanctions throughout this unit.

READING REVIEW

1. What is the process of learning the rules of society called?
2. What roles do you play in school, at home, and with your friends?

Critical Thinking

3. **Recognizing Cause and Effect** (see page 35) How do people in our society teach us how to behave?

EXPERIMENT **4-C**

What Are Your Roles?

Everyone plays many roles every day. Most of your roles probably agree with one another. You are a son or daughter, and you may also be a brother or sister. Those roles usually support one another. From time to time, however, you may find that two roles require you to be two entirely different kinds of people. The conflict you may have in such situations is called **role conflict.**

Role conflict may happen when you are expected to act in a certain way by one person or group, and at the same time you are expected to act in a much different way by another person or group. Role conflict is especially difficult to deal with when both persons or groups are important to you. Your friends may at times want you to act in a way that your parents or teachers would not approve. At times of such role conflict, you must decide how you will act. If you cannot please both sides, which side will you choose? Most people learn that it is easier if their roles do not conflict, and they try to build relationships that support one another.

Everyone plays many roles every day. Most of the roles you have probably agree with one another. From time to time, however, you may find that two roles require you to be two entirely different kinds of people. When this occurs, you experience what is called **role conflict.**

How many different roles do you play? Do any of them overlap or conflict with the others? You will diagram you and your roles. One of the most effective ways of doing this is to think of your life as a group of circles. Each circle contains a role which you play in your life. All the circles together make your *role diagram.* This represents you and your life. Here are two examples of a role diagram.

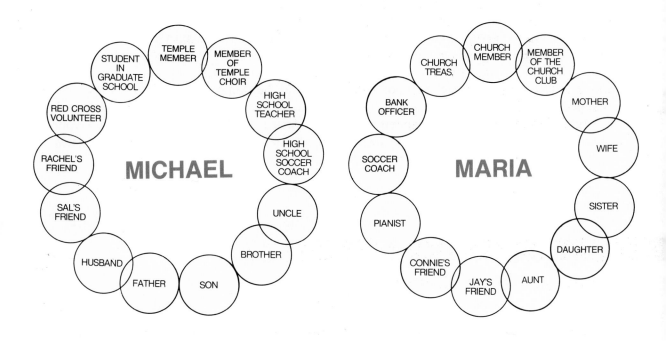

On a separate piece of paper complete these questions and activities:

1. Notice that some of Michaels' and Maria's roles overlap. Why? How are overlapping ones similar? Do any roles conflict?

2. Now try to do a diagram of *your* roles in life. Draw in as many roles as you can think of. Even part-time roles should be included. Draw in only those roles which you have at this point in your life. Where do they overlap and why?

How have traditional parenting roles changed?

3. Draw a second diagram of the roles you played five years ago. Again, include as many roles as you can think of and show which ones overlap. How have your roles changed? Have your values changed, too? Is your lifestyle (the way you spend your time) different from five years ago? In what ways? Are these differences shown early in both of your role diagrams?

4. Ask one adult to do a complete diagram of his or her roles. The adult you choose should be someone you know very well, such as a parent or relative or close friend. Compare this person's diagram with your own diagrams. How are they alike? How are they different?

Institutions

People live in groups in order to satisfy their needs. These needs may be satisfied in many ways. Over the centuries, most societies have found five ways of obtaining their most important needs. These ways are called **institutions.** Each of the five major institutions serves a particular need of the society.

The **Institution of the Family** meets the need for socializing children. The family (or marriage) also provides for the physical and "belongingness" needs of its members.

The **Institution of Education** helps the family teach children the society's values. Education (or schools) helps prepare children to enter the adult world.

The **Institution of Government** makes and enforces laws based upon the mores of the society. Government is supposed to keep the society running smoothly. It protects the members of the society from harm and punishes those who break the law.

The **Institution of Religion** (sometimes called the Church) meets the individual's need to worship God in a group.

The **Economic Institution** (or business) makes it possible for us to specialize in our work. Everyone can do a different job and produce different things and then "trade."

Family, Education, Government, Religion, and Economics—these five institutions have been important throughout the centuries.

Human institutions have existed for thousands of years. Take a close look at the picture above. What institution does this scene of ancient Greece represent?

READING REVIEW

1. What is a social institution? Name the five major social institutions.

Critical Thinking

2. **Making Comparisons** (see page 16) How does each of these five social institutions affect your own life and behavior?

EXPERIMENT **4-D**

Sanctions*

Every society sets rules, or norms, for its people to follow. Very serious norms are mores, and less important norms are folkways. Norms which are made by the government are laws.

Every society has ways of rewarding those who obey the norms and punishing those who disobey the norms. Rewards and punishments are part of the socialization process. Sometimes persons in authority give rewards and punishments, but most

often they are given by the people in society. These people include your family, neighbors, and friends.

Your society tries to control your behavior by giving you **sanctions.** A sanction is an action which supports a social norm. There are two types of sanctions: *positive* and *negative.*

A positive sanction is any reward given to you for obeying the social norm. A positive sanction may be given before you obey a norm, to persuade you to follow that norm. It may be given to you after you obey the norm, to reinforce your behavior. Soci-

*The "Sanctions" experiment is adapted from James A. Quinn, *Living in Social Groups.* (See Acknowledgements, pages 595–596.)

A positive sanction can be as simple as a smile and a hug of approval.

ety wants you to continue to obey that norm. By giving positive sanctions when you obey the folkways, mores, and laws, society makes sure you act in the "right" way. For example, if you study hard you not only get good grades, you also get approval from teachers and family. Such approval will probably have the effect of making you continue to study hard.

On the other hand, society gives you a negative sanction when you do something of which it does not approve. Negative sanctions may be disapproval, physical punishments, or the taking away of something you value. For example, if you are rude, society may show its disapproval by criticizing you. If you break a law, society may take away your freedom by putting you in jail. If your disobedience of a social norm is really serious, you run the risk of being ignored or "kicked out" of society. In some societies, for example, a person can be forced to leave the country for daring to criticize the government.

The Institution of the Family

The first group you encounter is your family. For this reason, the Family is called the primary social institution. Your father and mother (or their substitutes) care for your needs from the moment you are born. You are fed, clothed, and housed by them. You are socialized first by your family, then by other groups. Your parents and siblings (brothers and sisters) teach you very early in life what you should and should not do.

The folkways and mores of the society are passed on from one generation to the next by the family. You were taught the "right" way of acting by your parents. Your parents received their instruction from your grandparents, and so on, back many hundreds of generations. Thus, the mores and folkways of our society did not appear overnight. They were developed over many generations by millions of people.

In addition to teaching you the norms of this society, your family was the first to teach you about roles. Of course, when you were a baby, your parents did not give you lectures on how a father or mother or child should behave. They showed you these things by example. If you have observed a child closely (perhaps your sibling), you know how children like to imitate older people. That is how they learn roles. By playing roles they also learn about society's norms.

There are many types of families. Sociologists define a family as a group of people who are related by heredity or adoption. We often call the people in a family group "blood relatives." Sometimes, the family is just the mother, father, and their child or children. This small type of family is very common today. Sociologists call such a group a **nuclear** (noo′ klē ar) **family.** The word "nuclear" comes from "nucleus" which means "the center." If a nuclear family is considered the center, then an **extended family** is one in which the nuclear family lives with grandparents, aunts and uncles, and nieces and nephews. This family is larger than the nuclear family.

The Family, a primary group

Family Group, (1948–1949) Henry Moore

A type of family that is becoming more and more common is the one-parent family. Rising divorce rates in the United States and in other societies have caused families to "split." Oftentimes, one parent or both parents remarry. Children sometimes have two separate families as a result.

Marriage is the legal joining of two or more people, making a family. It may surprise you to think of more than two people united in one marriage. Although this form of marriage is illegal in our society, some societies throughout the world still approve of such marriages. The type of marriage in which a man has more than one wife, or a woman has more than one husband, is called *polygamy* (pə lig′ ə mē).

We can also categorize marriages on the basis of who rules the family. When the woman dominates the family, including her husband, we say that the marriage is *matriarchal* (mā′ trē ar′ k'l). On the other hand, a *patriarchal* (pā′ trē ar′ k'l) marriage is one in which the man dominates the family. Many marriages today in our society are moving away from both extremes. Instead, they are tending toward a more democratic arrangement in which both husband and wife share equally in the decision making.

READING REVIEW

1. Why is the Family known as the primary social institution?
2. What functions does the Family perform in the socialization process?

Critical Thinking

3. **Recognizing Ideologies** (see page 31) How does a matriarchal family differ from a patriarchal family?

EXPERIMENT **4-E Survey on Marriage and the Family** **HANDOUT**

READING 6

The Institution of Education

In societies of long ago, extended families taught their young everything they needed to know in order to get along in the world. Generally, the men instructed the boys in the arts of fishing, hunting, weapon making, and means of survival. The women taught the girls about taking care of the home and performing their role in the family. A few societies are structured this way even today.

As societies became more complicated, the family was no longer able to teach the youngsters everything. The idea of education and formal schooling developed. The school then continued the child's education which began in the home. People from the society became teachers to instruct the young people of the society.

Today, schools in the United States teach a variety of subjects in a great many ways your grandparents never imagined. Teachers and students are assisted in the learning process by films, computers, tape recordings, calculators, and many other devices.

In the first years of public education in this country many teachers were expected to teach all subjects from math to English to physical education. Today, teachers in our schools are trained to teach only a limited number of subjects. One reason for this is the enormous amount of knowledge in each field which has been developed in just the past few years. One teacher cannot be an expert on all subjects.

The institution of education in any society has three basic functions. First, education passes on the values, norms and roles of the society from one generation to the next. Education takes up where the family leaves off in the socialization of the young.

Secondly, education teaches the young how to adapt themselves to their environment and survive in it. In ancient times this meant teaching young people how to provide food, clothing, and shelter for themselves and their families. The young were educated in hunting animals, picking plants, and catching fish which would provide clothing, shelter, and food for survival. Today, the methods of education are different but the purpose is the same—survival in society. Education trains young people in specific fields, so they can get and keep a job. Money earned by working at a job pays for the food, clothing, and shelter which our ancestors had to get directly from their environment.

Students in Botswana, Africa, take part in a lab experiment. The institution of Education passes on the knowledge of society. It also helps to socialize the young people.

Thirdly, education teaches young people about the ideas and things of the past. Most societies are usually in a state of change. Societies which change too rapidly may lose much of the wisdom and experience of past generations. These societies may be greatly weakened or even doomed. Those societies which take the best of the past and mix it with wise decisions for the future have a good chance to grow and be healthy. Education, therefore, helps the society to grow, develop, and survive.

Education of the young is one of the most important and expensive activities of our American society. Americans pay over $350,000,000,000 (three hundred fifty billion dollars) in taxes every year to maintain schools, to pay teachers and administrators, to buy books and other supplies, and generally to keep the education process growing and healthy.

Today, education is no longer only for the young. Millions of adults are going back to school to learn in evening and summer classes. They take courses leading to a college diploma. They also take courses for self-improvement, such as guitar lessons, courses in painting or writing, psychology, or instruction in speaking a foreign language. For many adults, education makes their lives more interesting.

Think carefully and honestly about your own educational experience. How do you make the most of the opportunities school offers you? How would you evaluate what school offers you?

READING REVIEW

1. What are the three basic functions of education in any society?

Critical Thinking

2. **Distinguishing False from Accurate Images** (see page 29) Is it true that education in the United States today focuses entirely on the young? Explain your answer.

EXPERIMENT **4-F**

Schools Have Problems Too. Can You Solve Them?

In our modern industrial society, it is important for every member of society to get as much education as possible. This can be either academic or vocational education. Schools developed out of the need for well educated people to run the society. More tax money is spent on public schools in this country than almost any other single institution. This amounts to billions of dollars each year! In order to offer you and your classmates a good education, teachers must be hired and paid, books and supplies must be purchased, and school buildings must be maintained. Most schools also have full-time food preparation and janitorial staffs.

Running a school well is no easy matter. Difficult problems with students, teachers, parents, and administrators come up daily.

It takes many people working together to make a school run well. Those people are students, parents, teachers, school administrators, and school committees.

Also, every community group wants to have a voice in running the schools.

Let's see how difficult it really is to settle problems in a school. Your teacher will split the class into groups of six students each and pass out Role Cards to the group. Every member of your group will play a different role, depending upon what is written on his or her Role Card. The experiment calls for the following roles: Principal, Stu-dent Government President, President of the School Board, President of the newly formed "Concerned Parents" Group, Presi-dent of the Parent-Teacher Association, and a Representative of the Teachers. Remember to play your role. You *are* the person your Role Card says you are. It is very important that you *do not express your own feelings,* unless they agree with the role you are to play.

This meeting has been called by the President of the School Board to iron out some pressing problems of the school. Here are three problems your group is supposed to try to solve. As a group, try to come up with solutions to these situations:

1. There have been thefts in the locker rooms. One student's car keys and coat were stolen. Another student's watch and wallet were lifted. The thefts were committed during school hours. No one seems to know who stole these and other items from the lockers.

2. The elementary school building is old and should be replaced with a new, up-to-date one. Such a building would cost the taxpayers over twelve million dollars. Each taxpayer would have to pay fifty dollars more each year to pay for the building. It is apparent that many taxpayers, especially those without children, do not want to pay higher taxes.

3. It has been traditional at the school that the Pledge of Allegiance is said by everyone at the beginning of classes. Several students have refused to participate and the Principal has suspended them, against the protests of their parents.

The Institution of Government

So far, we have seen that the institutions of the Family and Education help to preserve the society and to educate its members. Without safety from harm for its members, no society can exist for long. The people in any society must feel that they are safe from each other and from outsiders. Otherwise, they will spend a lot of time and energy preparing to defend themselves and their possessions against the possibility of attack.

One of the main reasons why governments exist is to provide this protection for the members of their societies. In order to provide security for people, governments must do three things.

First, and most importantly, governments must protect *themselves* from harm.

Every government rules a territory, with clear boundaries. Everyone living and working inside those borders is under the control of the government which rules the territory. Unless a government is safe, and unless it has some control over the members of the society, the government cannot protect the people it represents.

Secondly, the institution of government, like those of family and education, passes the norms of society from one generation to another. The government does not do this by teaching. It does this by making and enforcing laws that protect the norms. Governments make laws to protect members of the society from one another and from outsiders. In the event that two or more members or groups of the society

A norm of American society is "equal justice under law." This norm is protected by the institution of Government.

have an argument, the government may play the role of "umpire" in settling the dispute. In the United States and many other countries, this is done through a system of courts and trials. Laws not only provide protection for the society, but also punishment for those who break the law. Most societies have a prison system to keep criminals away from the rest of society. Unfortunately, many societies have been slow in their efforts to help persons who have broken the law, so that they can go back into society and live normal, happy lives.

Thirdly, governments act as the representatives of their people in all dealings with foreign governments. You cannot make agreements with any other government without the permission of the United States government, for example. This protects you, the government, and our society.

An important aspect of government control is territoriality. **Territoriality** is the tendency to protect a certain territory as your own. The "territory" may be a piece of land, or sky, or time, or even another person. Governments try to protect the territories of lands they rule.

READING REVIEW

1. What is territoriality?

Critical Thinking

2. **Identifying Central Issues** (see page 14) What are the three things governments must do to provide for the security of the people?

Conducting a Survey of Public Opinion

The person taking a poll must know how to ask the right questions. Gaining the confidence of the person being interviewed also helps.

One way in which sociologists study a society and its members is by taking **surveys of public opinion.** These are sometimes called **opinion polls.** The person conducting a survey is known as the **interviewer.** Surveys are designed to find out what people think about certain issues at a specific time and place. You may have heard of the Gallup Poll and the Harris Poll. Both are professional organizations which take surveys of public opinion and publish their results in print or through the media.

Let's see what it is really like to make up and conduct your own survey of public opinion. Your assignment in this experiment is to do a small survey of your own

Survey Results (Sample)

Topic of survey: _____ Public opinion about the government _____
Population: _____ Adult residents of Ourtown _____
Sample: _____ 10 Adults living on Main Street _____
Interviewer: _____ John Jones _____

Questions:

1. Do you think our local government is doing a good job?

Yes	~~IIII~~ I	=	6
No	II	=	2
Und.	II	=	2

2. Do you agree with the President's tax program?

Yes	~~IIII~~ II	=	7
No	II	=	2
Und.	I	=	1

3. Should the federal government reduce spending?

Yes	~~IIII~~ II	=	7
No	III	=	3
Und.		=	0

4. Should ex-convicts be allowed to vote and hold public office?

Yes	III	=	3
No	~~IIII~~	=	5
Und.	II	=	2

5. Should 18-year-old people be allowed to drink alcoholic beverages in this state?

Yes	~~IIII~~	=	5
No	~~IIII~~	=	5
Und.		=	0

Conclusions: *The majority of my sample favored the President's tax program and our local government. The majority does not think ex-convicts should be allowed to vote and hold office. The sample was split equally on 18-year-old drinking. Most want federal spending reduced.*

and report your findings in class. Use the form supplied on Handout 4-G for recording your survey results.

Here is an example of a survey taken in "Ourtown" by a fictitious student named "John Jones." It is printed here to give you a better idea of how to conduct this survey.

You will be expected to bring your results to class, where you will have a chance to discuss your results.

Territoriality

Territoriality, the tendency for a government to protect itself and its people against harm, also applies to individuals. You tend to protect the people and things that are important to you. How far does this territoriality extend? It depends on the individual. Some persons are very protective of what they consider "theirs." Others are not so protective.

People protect not only their possessions and friends, but also the space around them, which is called **personal space.** Most people do not realize this. Going too far into the space territory of another person is called **spatial invasion.** In this experiment we will see how spatial invasion works.

A good place to find out about spatial invasion is at the dinner table. Everyone has a certain imaginary boundary line around her or his place at the table. Usually this personal space extends about a foot from the edge of the center plate on all sides. Most people do not realize that they have this territory "staked-out." It is perfectly all right for the holder of that place to put anything in his or her space. If anyone else tries to do that, watch that person become uneasy or annoyed.

At dinner, do not tell anyone about your assignment at first. Act normally, but every time you ask for the salt or ketchup or anything else on the table, replace it inside the space territory of another person at the table. When you do this, try to act as if you are doing nothing unusual. See how long it takes for the person whose space you have

In the animal kingdom the protection of territory includes the protection of the young. What appear to be fuzzy rocks to the left of the penguin are actually chicks, or young penguins.

invaded either to move the item out of his or her space or to say something about your actions. Notice the reactions you get each time you invade the person's space. After you get a definite response, explain the assignment to your family and show them this exercise.

If the dinner table experiment does not apply to your situation at home, try this one. People also have a feeling of personal space around them while talking face-to-face with someone. In our society it is not polite to be closer than about three or four feet from the person with whom you are talking. Try invading this personal space with several people and see what happens. Does it make any difference if the persons are strangers or members of your family or close friends? Why?

Try sitting "too close" to someone on the bus or standing "too close" to someone in an elevator. Observe carefully the behavior of the people whose space you invade. How do they react? Do they differ in their reactions?

Now try one of these territoriality experiments. Write a detailed account of what your actions and observations were. You will have an opportunity to share your experiences with the class.

The Institution of Religion

Since the beginning of time people have felt the need to understand the world around them. They have always wanted to know the purpose in living, working, and dying: What is the meaning of life? Many people believe in a spiritual force or God, or "the gods," or magic, or the devil. Societies often do not agree on questions about religion or the meaning of life. Yet, almost all societies have encouraged their members to practice a religion.

Most often, the religions which a society encourages are those which agree with the norms taught by the society's other institutions. Religions pass on the society's values from generation to generation, just as the family, government, and school do.

The Church is the formal religious institution. Often the Church (the organization with its members) is centered around a church (the structure where members of the Church worship). Notice that one word is capitalized, the other is not. The words "Church" and "church" describe two different things.

People in the Church have two roles basically. Most members have the role of lay people, while a special few are clergy (priests, ministers, rabbis). The clergy are in charge of the Church and are supposed to help the lay people practice their religion and become better human beings. In many Churches today the clergy must also raise money for Church programs and the maintenance of the church. Some Churches are encouraging their lay people to become more active. In some cases, lay people are taking over responsibilities and rights

This family is observing the traditions of the Buddhist religion.

that used to be the clergy's. In some cases, women are becoming members of the clergy for the first time. And a few women have even risen to positions of authority in traditional church organizations. You may know of instances where this has happened. Although the institution of Religion is changing, it continues to play an important part in many societies.

READING REVIEW ═══════

1. What are the two basic roles people have in an organized religion?

Critical Thinking

2. **Predicting Consequences** (See page 36) Will the role of religion grow in importance in the 1990s? Why?

EXPERIMENT **4-1** The Role of Religion **HANDOUT**

READING 9

The Economic Institution

As we have seen, social institutions throughout most of human existence have helped to satisfy people's needs and wants. One of the most basic needs of all people is the need to make a living—to survive in their environment. In the earliest days of

the human race, "making a living" meant hunting and fishing for food and making animal skins into shelter and clothing. If you lacked the skill to do these things, you could not survive. Most of the day was spent simply trying to stay alive. There was

In the American economy, people work to earn leisure time.

probably very little time to have fun. Work was an absolute necessity.

Have the times changed very much? For most people today, work is still an absolute necessity. As a matter of fact, our society tends to look down on those who do not work. One difference between our ancient ancestors and us is the *type* of work we do. We (at least most of us) do not hunt or fish to stay alive. Most people work at a job, either for themselves or for somebody else. Instead of taking home a catch of fish or a freshly killed animal at the end of the working day, most people today take home money earned at a job. They then spend their money on food, clothing, and shelter. A lot of money is also spent on luxuries—things we don't really need for survival, but that make life more enjoyable. Americans, for example, work billions of hours at their jobs every year to pay for movies, TV sets, cars, vacations, perfumes and cosmetics, food for their pets, and many other things.

The exchange of money for goods is a basic part of the economic institution. In this case, money is being exchanged for a radio.

We have come a long way from the daily struggle for survival of our ancestors. Something was responsible for this improvement in our way of life. It was the establishment of a rather recent social institution: the **economic institution.** This is also sometimes called "the economy."

A major part of the economic institution in our society (and in many others) is *industry.* Sometimes industry is called "business" or "the business world." Industry brings many people together in one place to work for a common goal. The common goal is usually to make money for the business. Ideally, the workers, or labor, in the business share in the good fortune of the business. The more they produce and the more the business makes, the more the workers should earn. Of course, that is the ideal. It sometimes does not work that way. Included in the category of industry are businesses such as farming, manufacturing, trading, banking, and many others.

Every institution we have studied has norms which its members are encouraged to follow. Each institution has rewards for those who follow the rules, and punishments for those who disobey. Industry, an economic institution, is no exception. If the workers in industry follow the rules of the place where they work, they are usually rewarded. If the norms are disobeyed time after time, however, workers are usually punished. What norms of industry can you think of? What rewards and punishments are there in the business world?

READING REVIEW

1. Define: industry, labor. How do they work together to make the economy of the country function?

Critical Thinking

2. **Testing Conclusions** (see page 42) Find out what kind of work your parents and grandparents did. Compare these jobs with what you want to do. Is it true that the type of work we do is changing in our society? Explain your answer.

READING 10

Values

"That sure is a fine looking car Jim has! Wish I had one just like it!"

"Mary hasn't been smiling lately. That isn't like her. I wish we could do something to cheer her up."

"Mark and Sally are going together now, and I think that's great. They were made for each other."

How many times have you heard (or made) remarks like these? They all have one thing in common: Each statement tells how the person speaking feels about something or someone. They show the speaker's values. Can you identify the values in each of the three statements?

A **value** is an idea or belief about the "goodness" or "badness" of a person, thing, situation, or action. We have all made thousands of value judgments. We hold our values as a result of the socialization process. From the time of birth, values

Sing shorter songs.

This gas company wants to sell you gas. In the ad the company wants to let you know it supports the American value of conservation. How does the gas company use that value to advertise its product?

are taught to us by other people and by institutions in our society. These people include the family, the Church, government, peer groups, and many others.

One value this society teaches most of us is that it is good to work for a living. We are raised to believe that laziness is bad and should not be rewarded. We are taught the value of working hard to get material things such as cars, stereo equipment, color televisions, and fashionable clothing. Even the titles we hold in our jobs are an important part of this "work value."

How can you tell what our society's values are? Just look at the norms. Norms usually develop from society's basic beliefs, its values. When society feels that something is good or bad, it tends to make norms to govern people's behavior. For example, our society feels that human life is valuable. It believes that the life of an individual should be continued as long as possible. That value is expressed in several norms, including mores against murder and suicide.

Norms enforce social values. Years ago, for example, people in our society developed an attitude against making noises while eating food. In other societies it is normal and expected behavior to show your enjoyment of food while you are eating. Burping, loud chewing and chomping, and making "mmmmm" sounds are actually encouraged in some societies, but not in ours. This value in our society has led to the establishment of a norm (in this case a folkway) which regulates the amount of noise we make with our mouths while eating.

Sociologists try to find out people's values by asking questions in surveys of public opinion. Another way to study values is to observe people's behavior in certain situations. By watching people, sociologists can form hypotheses about the values upon which people act. A person who buys many fine oil paintings probably values that kind of art, for one reason or another. A child who is polite and courteous probably comes from a home where those traits are valued and therefore taught.

Another way sociologists determine the values of a society is by examining the ways in which people spend time and money. In our society people spend time working for a living. Society encourages this. People earn money for the time they work and spend it on the things society produces. This is also approved by society. If you work eight hours per day, you are actually trading about one-third of your life for the things you need and want.

Sociologists attempt to understand the values of people by studying the ways they spend money. Industries often use findings of sociologists to determine how and what to produce and sell. For instance, the advertising industry uses sociological data to make ads which will convince people to buy certain products. In doing this, advertising people actually *create* social values. If you look closely at most ads, you will notice two things: the product being sold and the value supporting that product. In beverage ads a variety of people are often shown playing sports, having fun, and acting young. The social values of enjoyment and staying young are emphasized. Many people are influenced by such ads. The value is often sold along with the advertised product. Are you aware of how you are influenced by advertising?

Be on the watch for values in the ads you see on TV and in magazines and newspapers and on the radio. What are *you* buying: the product, the social value, or both?

READING REVIEW

1. What is a value?

Critical Thinking

2. Creating Good Questions (see page 20) What kinds of questions do you think sociologists ask to determine the values of a society? Give at least three examples.

EXPERIMENT **4-J**

Values in Advertising

As we saw in "Reading 10: Values," advertisements can tell us quite a bit about the values of a society. In creating a market for a product, advertisers often also create a value. Sometimes the value already exists in the minds of the people, and advertisers simply take advantage of it.

Look at these ads from old newspapers and magazines. What values and products are they selling? On a separate sheet of paper, list the product being sold and all the values you can "read into" the ad. Give reasons for your answers and be prepared to discuss them in class. Although the ads are old, many of the values in them are still held in this society.

Some day you'll buy her a
Frigidaire
why not for Christmas

FRIGIDAIRE
More than a MILLION *in use*

Rent this Electric
Floor Polisher
for $2 *a day and Beautify*
All *your floors and linoleum*
Quickly ~
Without Stooping, Kneeling or Soiling Your Hands

JOHNSON'S WAX
ELECTRIC FLOOR POLISHER

JOHNSON'S LIQUID WAX

ATWATER KENT RADIO

Sorting out the facts,
here's what you find

COACH BUILDERS
WE HAVE BEEN — OVER SIXTY YEARS
RAUCH & LANG
WORM DRIVE

Coach
Built Electric

THE Rauch & Lang is the only Coach Built Electric — the sole design conforming to high art standards — having harmonious contour — perfected scientific construction.

Ownership means unqualified assurance of service — of prestige — a result of sixty years leadership in coach building. No after regrets.

The Rauch & Lang is Worm Driven — (Top-Mounted — Straight-Type) the first Electric to offer successfully this advanced method of propulsion — Silence — No Adjustments — Longevity.

All the mileage you can use in a day — as fast as the law allows. *New models now being shipped.*

Dealers in all principal cities will gladly demonstrate. Catalog upon request.

The
**RAUCH & LANG
CARRIAGE CO.**
West 25th Street
CLEVELAND

BRANCHES

Values and Friendship

Let's take a close look at the values which affect our relationships with others. Relationships change with time, partly because we continuously change our values. How do our values affect our friendships? Does it also work the other way around? In other words, do our friends and friendships affect the values we hold?

On Handout 4-K is a list of characteristics and actions of different people. You might recognize some people you know. In the first column, indicate whether you strongly approve **(SA),** approve **(A),** don't care **(DC),** disapprove **(D),** or strongly disapprove **(SD)** of the person described. Circle the letters of the answers with which you agree. In the second column, tell whether or not you would keep the person as a friend. In the third column tell whether you would become new friends with such a person.

As you give your answers, think about your reasons. You will be given the chance to explain why you answered as you did.

Social Stratification and Status

The values of a society are demonstrated in many ways. They are shown in the society's norms and institutions. They are shown in the thoughts, perceptions, and actions of the members of the society. Social values are also reflected in the ways the society ranks its members. This ranking is called **social stratification.** The position an individual holds on the ladder of social stratification is called **status.**

Animal societies rank their members on the basis of size and strength. The biggest and strongest animals survive and rule over those smaller and weaker than themselves. This system of stratification is necessary for the survival of the animal species.

Stratification also exists in the world of human beings, although most often an individual's status is not determined by strength or size. Our society ranks individuals according to the values of society. In our ranking system a lot of emphasis is placed on education, wealth, power, salary, where you live, and what your (or your parents') occupation is. Your stratification level determines your roles, values, and your relationships with others. While your status makes it easier to get along in a society, it also limits your opportunities.

Everyone is born into a social status. In our society you are born into the status of your father and mother. Later you may change your status. Changing status is called **mobility.** There are three kinds of mobility. *Upward mobility* is a move up in status. *Downward mobility* is a move down in status. *Horizontal mobility* is mobility "across" on the same status level. In horizontal mobility, status is neither raised nor lowered. People who move horizontally usually go from one job to another job with similar status and salary.

As a reward for climbing the ladder of social stratification the individual acquires **status symbols.** These are things which tell everyone what the person's status is. Status symbols vary depending on the group to which one belongs. Since our society values material things that cost money, great emphasis is placed on cars, clothes, houses, televisions, and other material status symbols. A few years ago, owning a two-car garage (with two cars to put in it) meant that you and your family were "on the way up" (upwardly mobile). Titles such as "Doctor," or "Senator," can also be status symbols.

As an individual moves from one status to another, we say that he or she changes "class." Every **social class** has a status

Explain the status symbol in each of these photographs.

A neighborhood in a poor rural area of our country.

level. Generally speaking, there are three classes in our society. They are the *upper class,* the *middle class,* and the *lower class.* Each class can be identified by its own set of values and the actions and possessions of its members. In a relatively "open" society like the United States, it is much easier for an individual to move from one class to another. In closed societies such as India, mobility is almost impossible. The Indian class system has its origins in the Hindu religion, which most Indians practice. Although the government of India has tried to get rid of that class system (called the *caste* system), it has been difficult to change the attitude of people toward the custom. An Indian born into a certain caste tends to stay in that position for a lifetime. Indian children inherit their father's caste and pass it on to their children.

Let's examine three social classes in American society today: the upper, middle, and lower classes. Some sociologists divide society into still smaller classes, such as upper middle class, lower middle class, and so on. We will consider American society only in terms of three broad classes.

People in the upper class are wealthy. Many got their wealth from parents or grandparents. Upper class people usually have prestige. When we say that someone has prestige, we mean that people tend to "look up to" that person. Fame, honor, and respect usually go along with prestige. The reason upper class people have prestige is that they have what this society values: power, being born into the "right" family, and wealth and material things. Many of the people in this class do not have to work for a living. They tend to give a lot of money to churches, charities, and organizations which support the values of the business world. They live in relatively large houses or apartments which are well furnished. Their homes are almost always in an expensive part of town. They often send their children to private schools. These people often have a lot of power in the government, even though people from the lower and middle classes do not frequently see this involvement.

Middle class people make up the majority of American society. They are business and professional people, such as doctors, lawyers, teachers, architects, merchants, and managers in the business world. They put great emphasis on the value of education for themselves and their children. They make enough money to support a family, to own a car (sometimes two) and a home in the suburbs or an apartment in the city, and to give their children a good education. Their children often go to public schools and then to colleges and universities. Many middle class men and women join service clubs such as Rotary, Lions, and Kiwanis, as well as church groups and civic organizations such as the League of Women Voters and the Junior League. Middle class people live by a rather strict value system. They put great value on working hard to get ahead.

The lower class is the second largest group in the United States. Its members hold semiskilled or unskilled jobs. Many have never finished high school. They have limited opportunities to complete or advance their education. This affects what jobs they have and whether they can move into a better job. In turn, their jobs affect their status in society. Members of the lower class usually live in poor areas. Schools in these areas are often not as good as those in middle and upper class areas. People in the lower class do not live as long as those in other classes, and they suffer from poorer health. The lack of opportunities for people in the lower class can cause frustration, depression, and even despair.

Of course, these descriptions of classes are very general. They describe groups, not individuals. For many people, social mobility and status symbols are not as important as living a happy, satisfying life. For these people, material things are not as important as kindness and love.

READING REVIEW

1. What are the three major social classes in the United States?
2. What is social mobility?

Critical Thinking

3. **Determining Relevance** (see page 17) What is the connection between social stratification and status?

Status

Every society ranks its members. This is done on the basis of the individuals' wealth, education, power, where they live, and what they do for a living. The ranking is called **social stratification.** The position held by an individual in the stratification system is her or his **status.**

What determines status in our society? Let's look at some occupations:

How would you rank these occupations according to status? On a separate sheet of paper, write these ten jobs in order of highest to lowest status. Then try to find out: 1) how much each of these occupations pays, and 2) if there is a connection between job salary and status.

You will have an opportunity to discuss your findings in class.

lawyer
United States Senator
medical doctor
garbage collector
automobile mechanic
clergy (priest, rabbi, minister)
high school teacher
architect
ballet dancer
grocer

What status does this doctor have in our society?

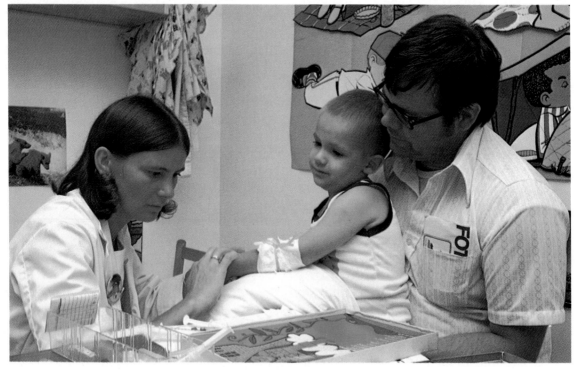

Communication

The Saturn car manufacturing company is known for its innovative style of communication within work teams and with customers.

In your relationship with other people, you communicate constantly in many, many ways. As a matter of fact, you communicate with others even when you are not talking to them or writing letters. How many times have you thought that someone was angry or "didn't care" because you hadn't heard from that person? Communicating with others is the main way you have of knowing what your relationships are with people. When you tell someone how you feel about him or her, you tell that person what kind of a relationship you have with each other. Or, you may be telling that person what kind of relationship you would *like* to have. **Communication** is basically a process of making, keeping, and changing relationships with others.

Communication isn't always easy. How many times have you thought: "I just don't understand him (or her). Why did she say that? Why did he do that?" Even when people try to communicate, they sometimes don't understand each other. Let's see why.

People communicate on two levels: the verbal level and the nonverbal level. The **verbal level** is that which is communicated by written and spoken symbols. What words and written symbols are used? In what order are the words used? What does the dictionary say the words mean?

One type of verbal communication occurs with the use of inflection, or "tone of voice." *How* you say something, the emphasis you give certain words, can be more important than *what* you say. For example, there are many ways of using inflection in the sentence, "Isn't she friendly." One could communicate sarcasm by saying, "Isn't *she* friendly!" in a mocking, sing-song way. If you honestly like her, you might say, "Isn't she *friendly*!" in a very enthusiastic tone of voice. If you have never met her, you might ask, "*Isn't* she friendly?" in a tone of voice that tells people you're not sure what she'll be like.

Sociology **187**

Much communication also takes place on the **nonverbal level.** This refers to communication done without words or written symbols. Ideas pass from people in ways other than by the use of language. Body language is an important kind of nonverbal communication. The way you pose yourself or move your body tells others much about what you think and feel. Sometimes body language tells people something quite different from what you actually say. For example, if you are frowning and in a slouched position, few people would believe that you are excited and happy, no matter what words you used. Body language gives clues about how you really feel.

So you see, there are many ways for us to communicate: with body language (nonverbal), and with words, symbols, and voice inflection (verbal).

Obviously, in order for communication to take place, there must be at least two people interacting with each other. Both people must want to communicate. Remember, communication in any situation takes place on both the verbal and nonverbal levels. Watch carefully the next time you see two people talking. Observe the words they use, the inflections they use, and the way they both act. Do the same whenever you communicate with others. You will be surprised at how much better you understand them.

READING REVIEW

1. On what two levels does communication take place?
2. What is body language?

Critical Thinking

3. **Distinguishing False from Accurate Images** (see page 29) What do you think it would mean if a person's body language contradicted what the person was saying?

EXPERIMENT **4-M**

Creating a New Language

People communicate in many different ways. Both nonverbal and verbal communication are important in understanding other people.

Behavioral scientists believe that one characteristic of human beings which sets them apart from animals is the ability to communicate by languages. A **language,** such as English, is simply a system of symbols used to communicate ideas and thoughts to others. These symbols may be letters or numbers or sounds. Whether the symbols are written or spoken they are arranged in a certain order to convey meaning. You think, read, and talk every day by using the symbols of a language.

If you tried to communicate with someone from another country, you might encounter a language problem. You would have to understand each other's language in order to communicate fully. Communication in another language can be a very difficult thing to do. In this experiment you will be creating a message in a language

The hearing-impaired (deaf) use a unique form of language called American Sign Language. Many different hand positions are used to communicate the symbols of the language.

you make up. As you try to communicate your message to a person in your class, you will discover the difficulties of "languaging."

Do this experiment in groups of three or four. Decide upon a simple, one-sentence message. Put the message into a language of your own creation. Do not use English words or words from a foreign language you may know. You may substitute your own sounds and symbols for English words, numbers, and letters. Take about fifteen minutes to create your message. Everybody in your group should help, because everyone will individually teach the group's message to someone outside the group. Keep your voices low so no one can hear what you are saying.

When every group has created a message in a new language, each group member should choose a person from another group and try to communicate the message to that person. Then switch roles, as the other person tries to teach her or his message.

While you may not use a familiar language (not even "pig Latin"), you may use body language, point to things, and make drawings. The important thing is that at the end of this experiment you will understand your partner's message (and something of a new "language") and your partner will understand yours.

When you have completed the experiment, be prepared to discuss the following questions:

1. What were your group's major difficulties in creating a new language for your message?

2. Was it easier for you to learn your first real language (probably English) than this new language? Why? What part did socialization play in learning your first language?

3. How did you go about teaching your partner the message? How did your partner teach you?

4. What good are symbols in communicating? Is it possible to communicate without the use of symbols? How?

5. How did body language help you communicate your ideas? How much did you rely on body language?

Nonverbal Communication

How many times have you heard the old saying, "Actions speak louder than words"? Many behavioral scientists believe this is absolutely true. People tend to communicate more with their bodies than with words and other symbols. Some sociologists claim that over 90 per cent of all human communication is nonverbal (without words) and not spoken or written.

Nonverbal communication is done in many ways. You communicate by your clothing, the way you use space and time, the way you move and position your body, and your facial expressions. Let's take a closer look at each of these.

You communicate to others by the kind of clothes you wear. What does the clothing you are wearing right now tell you about yourself? What do you think it tells others about you? Look around at your peers. What are they wearing? Is their clothing similar to yours? Why? Look at the clothes your teacher wears. How does it differ from yours? Does clothing tell you anything about different roles and social stratification?

People who work in the business world wear a certain kind of clothing, depending on the type of work they do. People who work with tools and machinery are called "blue-collar workers." They wear rugged work clothes, which can be washed after a hard day's work. "White-collar workers," on the other hand, usually work less with their hands and more with papers and pens. Often, blue-collar workers are employees of white-color workers.

The executive is a type of white-collar worker. If the executive is a man, he must wear a shirt, a tie, and some kind of dress

Clothing for work must be appropriate for the job.

jacket or suit. Women executives are expected to wear similarly dressed-up clothing, though their styles may vary more than men's. The executive is generally considered above both blue-collar and other white-collar workers. Notice that the higher a person goes in stratification, the more uncomfortable his or her clothes often become. Of course, blue-collar workers would find it difficult to do their jobs in ties and suits. They wouldn't have much freedom of movement, and their clothes would be ruined after one day. Working with papers and people doesn't require much freedom of movement, and the job usually isn't dirty. So the executive can more easily wear "good" clothes to work.

The clothes you wear are usually designed to make work, study, and play easier. They also communicate to others the

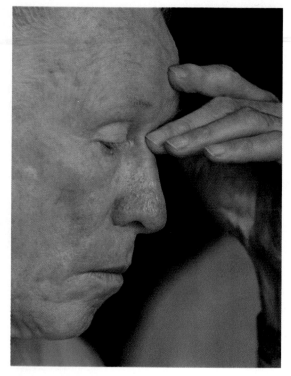

roles you play and sometimes the level of social stratification you occupy.

The use of space is another way of communicating. You have already discovered how territoriality and space invasion work. Often, without knowing it, people defend the invisible territory around them. They have staked it out for themselves. You tell others what they mean to you by your use of their space. Invading someone's territory may mean that you are friends, and therefore can feel free to invade each other's personal space without causing trouble. It could also mean that you do not consider the person to be your equal, so you can invade his or her space at any time. In addition, you can see how people communicate by the way they use space when talking to each other. In our society it is normal for people to stand closer to friends than to strangers. Lovers and very close friends tend to stand even closer to each other. Of course, two people who are about to have a fight also stand very close.

The principle of territoriality applies to the home "space." For example, some people feel it is impolite to visit without phoning ahead. Other people believe that one's home should be open to friends at any hour of the day or night. In Japan, overcrowding in the cities means very little personal space is available. It is not surprising that in many heavily populated societies, people prefer to entertain friends in restaurants or other public places and not in the home. The home is kept a very private place in Japan and other societies.

People also communicate by the use of time. For example, calling someone for a date at the last minute (especially to a for-

These three faces show that words are not always needed to communicate emotions.

mal dance, prom, or other personal event) tells that person a lot about you and the opinions you hold about him or her.

Time is valued a great deal in our society. Lateness is not approved. Whenever you are late some kind of excuse or apology is necessary. The later you are the better your excuse has to be. If you arrive late and offer no apology or excuse, you communicate something. Whoever is waiting for you will probably be insulted or hurt. When you invade someone's time by making that person wait for you, it is usually considered offensive in our society.

The use of clothing, space, and time are important ways of communicating nonverbally. But the most important means of nonverbal communication is body movement. It can often communicate much more than words.

Watch the expression on people's faces when you are talking with them. What do their facial expressions tell you? Are their words communicating the same idea or emotion as their expressions?

Look at these three pictures. Can you tell what emotions are being communicated? What do you suppose the person in each picture might be thinking or saying?

In class you will have a chance to find out how good you are at communicating nonverbally in the following game which is called "Body Language."

READING REVIEW

1. How do you personally communicate nonverbally?

Critical Thinking

2. **Demonstrating Reasoned Judgment** (see page 40) How do you communicate by your use of time and space?

Body Language*

Body language is an important part of non-verbal communication. If "actions speak louder than words," then we need to understand the actions of others in order to communicate with them effectively.

In this experiment, we will demonstrate the usefulness of communicating and understanding body language. You will play this game in teams of four. Your team will compete against another team of four players. If possible, put your seats in two rows facing each other. Leave a large space between the two rows so that you can easily act out the directions of the body language cards.

All teams are given a deck of 12 cards. On each card there are directions for the players to communicate their emotions and feelings. Players may not speak. They may use only facial expressions and body movements to communicate the emotion on the card. One person on each team should record the time it takes each player on the opposing team to convey the emotion on the card. Determine which team goes first. Then, a player from that team goes to the holder of the cards on the opposing team and chooses a card. The player reads the directions silently and gives the card to the members of the opposing team to read. The

player must communicate the emotion to his or her team in thirty seconds or less. Think carefully about what would be the most effective way to communicate the emotion. Use your imagination. Remember, you may use only body language. The player's teammates call out the emotion that they think the player is trying to show. If one of the player's teammates says the right word, matching the word on the card, the player's team gets one point. The opposing team does not get any points if the player fails to communicate the emotion. It is illegal for a player to use words or to "mouth" the answer. Should a player do either, the opposition team gets one point. No point is awarded to the player's team. The teacher will umpire in settling differences of opinion.

After the first player has had a turn, a player from the opposing team takes a turn, and so on. Each player should have three turns by the time the game ends. The team with the most points at the end of the game will be the winner.

If you and your teacher want to play a different version of this game, use a stopwatch or a clock with a second hand to time each player. Record the total seconds it takes for each team's players to communicate the emotions on the cards. The team with the lowest score wins. (The time limit on each turn should be no more than one minute.)

*The body language game was adapted from Layne A. Longfellow, "Body Talk" in *Psychology Today* (New York: Ziff-Davis Publishing Co. (See Acknowledgements, pages 595–596.)

What nonverbal message does the body language of these girls communicate?

Trust Me!

In Experiment 4-N we saw how we communicate by using our bodies. We called this type of nonverbal communication **body language.** A kind of body language which is hard to describe is the feeling of trust from one person to another. Can you trust someone you do not know very well? We will find out in this experiment. The class will play one of the games described below.

1. Divide into groups of two students each. Take turns with your partner closing your eyes tightly and following your partner's clues. Neither of you should speak. Only your touch is allowed. Notice how difficult it is to keep your eyes shut. Each partner should lead the other for about two minutes, then switch. Each partner should lead twice and follow twice. Is it easier the second time? Why or why not?

2. The class should sit on the floor in two rows (or arrange the chairs in two rows) facing each other, with about three feet between the rows. Blindfold one person at a time and have him or her go between the rows. As the person comes close to each person in the row, the row-persons should give directions out loud. The object for the blindfolded person is to avoid bumping against the rows. (After the blindfold is put on, change the direction and shape of the row.) How difficult is it to be the blindfolded person? Why? What does this experiment tell us about trust and human communication?

Mutual trust is a natural thing between close friends.

Careers in Sociology*

Did you enjoy the work of this unit? If you like observing people's behavior in groups, conducting surveys and interviews, and writing your results, you might enjoy a career in Sociology.

There are about 13,000 sociologists in the United States today. Most of them are teachers at the college and university level. Many sociologists do research into aspects of human behavior and publish their results in books and periodicals.

Sociologists study the groups that people form and try to learn about societies through an examination of their groups. Sociologists are concerned with how families help their children adapt to society and how primary and secondary groups function. They are curious about the reasons people have for joining groups, and they look at why people leave their groups.

Some sociologists, called criminologists, study the ways in which criminals behave in society and in prisons. Others look at the influence that society has on the health of individuals and groups, as part of the field of medical sociology. Still other sociologists study popular opinion.

If you want to be a sociologist, you should enjoy working with people, even those you don't particularly like. This requires patience and an even temperament. You should like to read, because your work will involve keeping up to date with recent findings by other sociologists. You must also be able to write well, so you can publish the results of your research about

The criminologist works to understand the social behavior of the criminal.

human behavior. Sociologists also should be open-minded in order to better understand the reasons behind the thoughts and feelings of other people.

For information on careers in Sociology, write to the American Sociological Association, Career and Research Division, 1722 N Street NW, Washington, DC 20036.

*Adapted from *Occupational Outlook Handbook.* (See Acknowledgements, pages 595–596.)

READING REVIEW

1. What work do most Sociologists do?

Critical Thinking

2. **Predicting Consequences** (see page 36) What characteristics do you think you should have if you want to become a sociologist?

4 PERSPECTIVES

Social Scientists Look at AIDS

How do the ways sociologists look at a topic compare to the ways other social scientists look at the same topic? You will explore the similarities and differences as you read the selection below about a unique memorial—a gigantic quilt with panels commemorating individual victims of AIDS (Acquired Immune Deficiency Syndrome). Read the passage below from *The Quilt: Stories from the NAMES Project* about the quilt's founder Cleve Jones and then answer the questions on the next page under "Comparing the Social Sciences."

❝Cleve's eyes still glisten, with both sadness and pride, as he reads such a letter. 'The Quilt shows that the most important thing is to love and be loved,' he says. 'Each letter breaks my heart.' This potential for expressions of love and compassion were central to Cleve's idea of a quilt as the form for this AIDS memorial. 'By providing a glimpse of the lives behind the statistics,' he states, 'It will create an extraordinary, dramatic illustration of the magnitude of the epidemic—to the president, to Congress, and to the country. Also, it's a way for survivors to work through their grief in a positive, creative way. Quilts represent coziness, humanity, and warmth.' For centuries, women have exchanged quilts for friendship, bridal or bereavement purposes. 'We want to create something that is beautiful,' Cleve says. 'The Quilt touches something in people that is pure and good—that is how the country should respond to the AIDS epidemic.'

Traditionally, quilts are collaborative works that include a vast array of colors and patterns, and the AIDS quilt specifically speaks to the diversity of lives affected by the disease. Although the remembrances sewn into each quilt panel can only hint at the person's life, and although the entire quilt records only about 10 percent of the nation's AIDS deaths, the disease's undiscriminating nature is easily seen in the range of people memorialized. They include a Colorado stockbroker, a mother of four teenagers in Atlanta, an Olympic athlete, a prize-winning Chicago journalist, a biker from Nevada, and a Stanford University professor. Some quilt panels name celebrities like Rock Hudson and Liberace. Others name people who were living on welfare, struggling to keep off the streets. There are policemen, schoolteachers, farmers, doctors, playwrights, ministers, chefs, lawyers, artists, and politicians.**❞**

Comparing the Social Sciences

Psychologists study human emotions. As a psychologist, what could you learn about the ways people close to AIDS victims are dealing with their grief? (*Identifying Central Issues*)

Sociologists study how people behave in groups. What could you as a sociologist learn from this passage about the value of groups? (*Recognizing Cause and Effect*)

Anthropologists study subcultures—small cultures within a society. What does this passage tell you as an anthropologist about the barriers between subcultures in the United States? (*Drawing Conclusions*)

Geographers study locations. What could you as a geographer learn about the spread of the AIDS epidemic from this article? (*Determining Relevance*)

Historians study about the past. Why might you, as a historian, regard the AIDS quilt as a valuable historical document? Can you think of other unusual sources of information? (*Determining Relevance*)

Political scientists study about government. If you, as a political scientist, wanted to pinpoint what policies the government had in place to deal with the AIDS epidemic, what questions would you ask? (*Creating Good Questions*)

Economists study the resources of governments as well as of individuals. Is there anything in this passage to indicate to you, as an economist, that the AIDS epidemic will have an effect on our nation's economy? Explain your answer. (*Demonstrating Reasoned Judgment*)

Displaying the AIDS quilt, Washington, D.C.

GLOSSARY OF TERMS

analysis the breaking down of an event or fact into smaller pieces in order to study it more closely (page 154)

behavioral science the study of human behavior; Psychology, Anthropology, and Sociology are referred to as the behavioral sciences (page 154)

body language a type of nonverbal communication in which body movements transmit messages, sometimes unconsciously, from one person to another (page 196)

Church, the a term generally used to describe organized religion or religious groups (page 175)

communication a process of making, keeping, and changing relationships with others (page 187)

community a group of people who work together for common goals and who may live close to each other (page 156)

Economic institution one of the five major ways in which a society survives; sometimes called *industry,* or *business,* in our society (page 178)

Education, institution of a major way a society survives, by training the young to take their place in the society as adults (page 162)

extended family a family structure composed of husband and wife, their children, and near relatives (page 165)

Family, institution of a group usually composed of at least a man, a woman, and their child or children (page 162)

folkway a custom in the society that is followed by persons in the society who are considered polite; a less serious norm than mores (page 159)

Government, institution of a formal organization within a society that regulates the activities of its members through a system of laws; one of the five ways in which society survives (page 162)

group two or more persons together; may be either a primary group or a secondary group (page 155)

interview a meeting at which information is gathered (page 154)

interviewer a person who conducts an interview, popular opinion poll, or survey (page 172)

language a system of symbols having meaning, used in communication (page 188)

law a norm established and enforced by government for the smooth running of society (page 159)

mobility a change in status within a society; mobility may be upward into a higher class, downward into a lower class, or horizontal across the same status level (page 183)

mores norms carrying a serious moral judgment against offenders (page 159)

negative sanction a punishment for violating a social norm (page 160)

nonverbal communication the passing of ideas from one person to another by ways other than language, including the use of space, time, clothing, and body movement (page 188)

norms rules of society that regulate the behavior of its members; they develop from a society's basic beliefs and values (page 159)

nuclear family family structure usually composed only of husband, wife, and children (page 165)

observation the act of watching and writing down facts and events (page 154)

opinion poll a systematic method of determining people's thoughts about certain issues at a specific time and place through interviewing; often called a survey of public opinion (page 172)

peer group individuals of about the same age, social class, and interests (page 179)

personal space the space, or territory, around an individual (page 174)

positive sanction a reward for obeying a social norm, or an inducement to obey a norm (page 160)

primary group a small group whose members have very close relationships over a long period of time, such as the family (page 155)

Religion, institution of the organization of beliefs concerning God or spiritual matters and their relationships with human beings and the material world; one of the five ways in which a society survives (page 163)

role a specific set of behavior patterns by a particular person or group of people in a society, conforming to the expectations of the society (page 160)

role conflict when roles require totally different kinds of behavior from an individual (page 161)

role play to act out the behavior patterns of a particular person (page 154)

sample a part of the survey population that supposedly represents the opinions of the larger population (page 173)

sanction a reward (positive sanction) or a punishment (negative sanction) that is used by a society to encourage its members to obey social norms (page 163)

secondary group a group that is usually larger and less loving than a primary group; it is often formed to do a job (page 156)

social class a group identifiable by the values, actions, and possessions of its members (page 183)

social institution a rather unchanging way that society has for survival; the Family, Government, Education, Economy, and Religion are five major social institutions in every society (page 162)

socialization process through which an individual learns the rules of society (page 159)

society a large group made up of many primary and secondary groups and two or more communities (page 156)

sociologist a social scientist who studies people's behavior in groups (page 154)

Sociology a behavioral science that studies people's actions in groups (page 153)

spatial invasion the entry of a person into the space territory of another person without consent (page 174)

status the position an individual holds on the ladder of social stratification in a society (page 182)

status symbols visible rewards that show an individual's status in the society (page 183)

survey population the entire group of people represented in a survey or opinion poll (page 173)

survey of public opinion a method in which questions are asked of a population sample to find out the opinions of the entire population; often called *opinion poll* or *interview* (page 154)

territoriality the tendency to protect certain people, land, space, and objects as one's own against invasion by others (page 171)

value an idea or belief about the "goodness" or "badness" of a person, thing, situation, or action (page 162)

Anthropology

ANTHROPOLOGY

SOCIOLOGY

GEOGRAPHY

STUDY &
THINKING
SKILLS

PSYCHOLOGY

HISTORY

POLITICAL
SCIENCE

ECONOMICS

This Is Anthropology

Walking home from school along a creek, you spy something small, dark, and pointed in the shallow, swirling water near the bank. You dip your hand in and fish it out: an arrowhead, made of flint. The stone dates back hundreds of years to Indian times. Once Indians used to hunt for their food around here—along this same creek, in fact. Now all that remains of their great culture is this bit of sharpened flint. The arrowhead is a clue to the mystery of that other time and place, one worth pocketing for a closer look later, when you get home.

Change lies at the heart of anthropology. Differences in language, behavior, and belief are all part of the picture of human variety through time. Social scientists who try to understand the cultures of the world, both past and present, are known as **anthropologists.** In the Unit 5 reading, you will learn how anthropologists think. In the experiments, you will have a chance to think like an anthropologist yourself.

Anthropology and You

Anthropology is the study of cultures. The questions below will help you understand how your culture touches all parts of your daily life.

1. What familiar items that you and your family use might puzzle anthropologists 1,000 years from now?

2. How has life changed between your parents' generation and your own?

3. Do you have any family members or friends from a different culture? How does their culture differ from yours? Do they eat different kinds of food? Speak different languages? Practice different religions?

UNIT 5 CONTENTS

What Is Anthropology?

One of the most enjoyable, necessary, and often difficult puzzles in life is understanding yourself and other people. This includes people from other countries who live differently than you do. The sciences that study how people perceive, think, and act are known as **behavioral sciences.** By studying one of these, Psychology, you can better understand yourself and others as unique and individual human beings. By

Beauty and richness in the Inuit, or Eskimo, culture.

studying another, Sociology, you can improve your understanding of how and why you and other people act certain ways in groups. In this unit, we will take a close look at a third behavioral science, called **Anthropology.**

The word "anthropology" comes from two Greek words: *anthropos,* meaning "humankind" and *logos* meaning "the study of." A person who studies Anthropology is called an **anthropologist.** Anthropologists study **cultures**—the ways people live in groups, their languages, their values, and their technologies. Anthropologists study the ways in which human groups change over the years.

The work of anthropologists is similar to that of sociologists. Sociologists, however, usually study the relationships among people in groups today in this country. Anthropologists study the ways human beings perceive, think, and behave in many different parts of the world and at many different times throughout history. Beginning with the earliest humans, who lived perhaps a million years ago, every part of the world where people have lived is of interest to anthropologists.

There are two branches of Anthropology. **Physical Anthropology** is the study of heredity and the biological evolution of human beings. **Cultural Anthropology** is the study of how people in different societies live and the effects their environments have on their life styles. This unit will focus mainly on Cultural Anthropology.

You may notice that some of the things we discuss and do in studying Anthropology are based on concepts and processes of the other behavioral sciences. In fact, we will be using some of the same tools that psychologists and sociologists use, including **observation** and **analysis** of human behavior.

We will be using many of the critical thinking skills described in Unit 1. Anthropologists need to understand how cultures develop stereotypes and clichés. They must identify the assumptions upon which people base their culture. They must also be able to create good questions to learn about and understand the ways of life that different cultures follow.

Anthropologists find out about cultures in several ways. One way is by living with the people in the cultures they are studying. In this way, anthropologists come into contact with the people's way of life every day, including their food, music, and work habits. Anthropologists try to live the same kind of existence as the people, so that they can better understand why those people do what they do. Anthropologists call this "living in the field" or a **field experience.** Anthropologists have discovered that it is easier to understand other people when you "put yourself in their shoes."

Another way anthropologists have of studying cultures is by reading the accounts of other anthropologists' findings. These accounts often give anthropologists a place to begin their own original research.

Unfortunately, not all cultures are still in existence today. Some cultures that were alive and prospering thousands of years ago have left things behind, often buried in the ground. Anthropologists use these ancient human-made things, called **artifacts,** to put together a description of how people in the culture once lived. They also study skeletons of human beings and animals to figure out how everyday life was carried on. In order to find artifacts, **excavation**—digging things out of the ground—is often necessary. Then up-to-date tools and technology, such as computers, are used to "date" objects, telling how old they are. Anthropologists who use this method of research are called **archeologists.** Their special field of study is called **Archeology.**

Why should we study Anthropology? There are many good reasons. Perhaps the best is this: We all live in a very small part of a very big world. There are many, many ways of living. Our way is just one of thousands. The earth changes, the environment changes, and humanity itself changes. By studying these different cultures in Anthropology, we discover that our ways of doing things are not the *only* ways. If we don't know the reasons behind the perceptions, thoughts, and actions of other cultures, we may think of them as weird or funny or not as good as our own. We may even find some of them offensive. By investigating other cultures and by putting ourselves "into" them, we can begin to appreciate their beauty and richness.

READING REVIEW

1. What is Anthropology?
2. How do anthropologists use critical thinking skills in their work?
3. Name three types of anthropologists and describe their work.

Critical Thinking

4. **Making Comparisons** (see page 16) How is Anthropology similar to, and different from, the other two behavioral sciences? How is it different?

Perception and Value Judgments

Look at each picture on page 209. How does each one make you *feel?* On Handout 5-A, Page One, put a check mark in the appropriate column after each number. Do not stop to think about your reactions. Simply record your first impressions. Spend only ten seconds on each picture.

When you have recorded your first feelings about each picture, turn to Handout 5-A, Page Two. Follow the directions. A class discussion will give you a chance to talk about your reactions.

What Is American?

Ask any five adults (including your parents, if you wish) this question: "Name five objects in our society which you consider to be 100 percent American." Their answers should be names of objects commonly found in our culture. Record their answers on a separate sheet of paper. Bring the results to class for discussion.

As American as Apple Pie?*

What is "American" about our American culture? Look at the list of objects to the right. Each of them is commonly found in our culture today. Which do you think originated in America, and which are from foreign cultures? On a sheet of paper make two columns, headed "American" and "Foreign." In the American column, list all those items you think had their start in our culture. In the Foreign column, list those things which you believe are from another culture.

*This experiment is adapted from the article "One Hundred Per Cent American" by Ralph Linton in *The American Mercury.* (See Acknowledgements, pages 595–596.)

1. Apple pie
2. Pajamas
3. Clock
4. Soap
5. Necktie
6. Forks and spoons
7. Oranges
8. Cereal
9. Umbrella
10. Railroad train
11. Steam radiator
12. Bathtub
13. Towels
14. Automobile

1

2

3

4

5

6

7

8

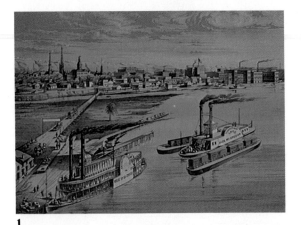

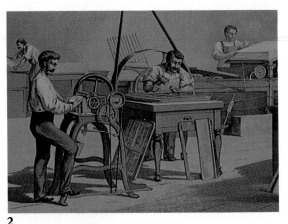

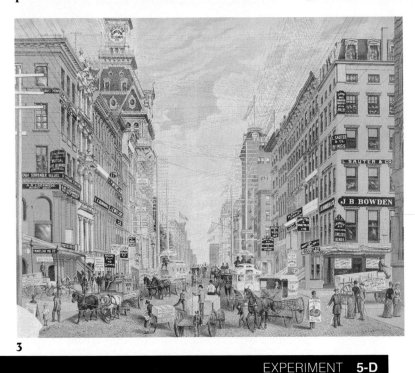

1. *Steamboat on Mississippi, early 1800s*
2. *Printing press, 1700s*
3. *New York City, 1900s*

How Has the American Culture Changed?

No culture remains exactly the same. Every culture is dynamic, or changing throughout the years. Values, fashions, institutions, norms—all of these may change in any culture. Our American culture is no exception.

Can you tell some of the changes that have taken place in our culture, using the photographs on these two pages as evidence? Look especially for changes in values and the way people live in our society.

Telephone, late 1800s

Factory conditions, 1900s

Willys-Overland automobile, 1920

Bicycling, Riverside Drive, N.Y., 1895

Child labor, 1900s

What Is Culture?

By this time you probably have a fairly good idea of what we mean by "culture." Yet, we have not actually defined the term. Describing what is meant by culture is a difficult task, since the word is used in so many ways. You have probably heard people say, "She (or he) is a very cultured person." They mean that she or he enjoys going to the opera, ballet performances, and symphony concerts. That person may also enjoy works of art, such as painting or sculpture. This is not how anthropologists use the term *culture.*

In Anthropology, **culture** refers to the entire way a society lives and is organized. This includes all the ideas, customs, values, norms, social institutions, attitudes, music and art, language, technology, and traditions of a society. Sometimes the term culture refers to several societies which have similar ways of life. For example, the "Western Culture" is shared by the people of North America and the countries of Western Europe.

The culture is learned by every person born into a society as part of the enculturation process. **Enculturation** refers to learning roles in the society and becoming part of the culture. (Sociologists call this process *socialization.*) As a person grows up, she or he is taught the culture by everyone in the society—parents, relatives, teachers, friends, and even strangers. Every person starts out in life with a unique heredity passed on by his or her parents. In time, heredity and culture combine to make the individual fully enculturated. The individual becomes a working part of the culture.

Every culture is made up of many parts, called **culture traits.** These traits are like the small pieces of a jigsaw puzzle. When the pieces are all in place together, they make sense. The small pieces support each other and make the jigsaw hold together. But if some pieces are missing, or are replaced by other pieces that don't belong there, the jigsaw picture would be ruined.

These pieces, or culture traits, include: marriage customs, the appropriate thing to say or eat at certain times, the proper use of clothing, the behavior at work or play of a person in a specific role or status, and many other features of the culture.

Sometimes, people in one culture view the people in another culture as backward or sinful or "not as good as us." This is called **ethnocentrism** (eth′ nō sen′ triz əm), or "culture centeredness." Ethnocentric people think that their culture is better than any others. They often think this way because they do not understand how the culture traits of other societies fit together to make a good, working culture.

Here is an example of ethnocentrism and its effects on a culture:

The first visitors from the United States to the islands in the Pacific found a society which had not changed for hundreds of years. The people were seemingly content, and they didn't have any sickness. Through the centuries the culture of the islanders had survived. Then the Americans came. The Americans were shocked to see the people of the islands wearing very little clothing. (In our country at that

The Japanese and Western cultures were very different from each other.
Was this painting done by a Japanese or Western artist? How can you tell?
Remember that people interpret other cultures by what they observe and
learn in their own.

time people wore many more clothes than they do now. They were more self-conscious about the human body.) Therefore one of the first things these American visitors did was to make clothing for the men and women of the islands.

The Americans also carried the germs of their environment. The islanders had not been exposed to American bacteria before, and they were not immune to American diseases.

The islanders, unlike the Americans, paid no attention to the rain. They worked and carried out other daily activities in the rain. Ordinarily they could do this, of course, since they wore little clothing which could get wet, and because they had been a traditionally very healthy people. But when the islanders began to wear clothing given them by the Americans they continued to go out in the rain, wearing their clothing even after they had become drenched with water. The combination of this practice and the introduction of new germs into their environment was fatal. A great number of the islanders caught pneumonia and died.

The Americans had changed only a few traits of the islanders' culture—a few pieces of the jigsaw puzzle. But they changed the entire culture forever.

There is some wise thinking behind the old saying, "When in Rome, do as the Romans do." What may be good in one culture, may be bad in others. Anthropologists know that in order to understand people in other cultures you have to change your mental sets to match those of the people you are studying. A swastika sign in the mental set of our culture may give us un-pleasant thoughts of Hitler, Nazis, and war. A swastika in the Hindu culture of India means something entirely different. In that culture, the swastika is a sign for Ganesh, a major God of the Hindus. For the Hindus, the swastika is a sign which gives *them* a *good* feeling. Culture traits (like the swas-tika) get their meanings from within the cultures. Can you see why it is dangerous to analyze culture traits without analyzing the cultures of which they are a part?

What is appropriate in one culture is not necessarily appropriate in other cultures. If someone said to you, "My eyes are your sacrifice!" after you gave a gift, you might think that these words were not appropri-ate. In Arab cultures, however, that is a perfectly good way of saying, "Thank you!"

An American may consider it impolite or even unpleasant to talk with someone who is standing only a foot away. Yet, this is the appropriate "talking distance" for most people from Latin America.

Misunderstanding culture traits may re-sult in hurt feelings or trouble. Can you think of any examples of this?

The first meeting of two different cul-tures is an exciting but touchy situation.

Eventually, both the cultures may get to know and understand each other. After a while both cultures may begin to accept each other's culture traits. This process is called **acculturation.**

No culture ever remains the same. Every culture is constantly changing, or **dynamic.** Sometimes changes come from inside the culture. Sometimes the change is from out-side the culture, through acculturation.

Every culture has smaller cultures inside it. These are called **subcultures.** A subcul-ture has most of the traits of the main cul-ture. It also has traits that are different from the main culture. One example of a subculture is the culture of the American teenager—a subculture of which you are a part.

READING REVIEW

1. Define: culture, enculturation, accul-turation, culture traits.
2. Give three examples of subcultures in your own community.

Critical Thinking

3. **Identifying Central Issues** (see page 14)   What do we mean when we say that all cultures are dynamic?

EXPERIMENT   **5-E**

The Teenage Subculture

PART ONE

You belong to a subculture of the main American culture. The teenage subculture of which you are a part has its own style of living, its own dress and language customs, and many of its own norms. Certainly,

many of the values of your subculture are different from those of the main culture. Many of these culture traits, of course, are similar to the larger culture's traits.

Think hard about what makes your teen-

Getting together with friends is a trait of the American teenage subculture.

age subculture different from the American culture. Look through magazines and newspapers for ads which support your thoughts. Search especially for those ads which are aimed at your age group and its values. Think of the ads as artifacts that tell something about the teenage subculture. Bring as many ads to class as you can find. They will be put to good use in the discussion and experiments.

PART TWO

During this experiment, the class will be broken into committees which will analyze the teenage subculture. Each group will discuss culture traits of the subculture, paying particular attention to the topic assigned. Here are the topics:

1. The family
2. Religion
3. Music/Art
4. Education
5. The business world
6. Transportation
7. Language
8. Peer groups and friendship

In your group, analyze the relation of your topic to the life style of the teenage subculture. Explain what values, roles, norms, and behavior patterns regarding your topic exist in your subculture. In this activity pretend that you and your committee persons are anthropologists looking at the teenage subculture from the "outside." Use the ads you and your classmates researched as artifacts. Show how those artifacts describe life in your subculture.

When your committee has completed this task, you and your group will have an opportunity to share your findings with the other groups. It should be interesting for you to see how well you understand your own subculture.

Developing a Culture

We have taken a close look at the main American culture and the American teenage subculture. You have analyzed traits of both. You have discussed and described the values, norms, and behavior patterns of our society.

Now stop and think: Would you have the same values, norms, and behavior patterns if you had been born into another culture? Would you and your family and friends care for your needs in the same way?

Chances are that your life style would be very different in another culture. Have you ever thought that whether you eat cornflakes, snails, or raw fish for breakfast depends on what culture you were born into? How would your life be different if you had been born into the Eskimo culture? Or born into a family of cave people thousands of years ago? Into the culture of China? Would your life be different if you had been born a member of a different race? How?

Environment determines how a society develops its culture.

Environment has a great part in determining how a society meets its needs and develops its culture. In this experiment you and the others in your group will discover what influence an environment has on someone's survival and on the building of a culture.

All groups should read the Background Information. Each group should then read the description of the group to which it has been assigned.

Background Information

You and the members of your group have been traveling by sea. Your ship sinks and you all climb aboard a lifeboat. After several days at sea, you spot land. You paddle toward shore. After landing, you and your group spend the rest of the day exploring your temporary home. You have no idea when (or if) you will ever be rescued. You have to make the best of the situation. The only things you have with you are the clothes you are wearing and enough food and water for everyone in the group for only one day. After looking around for other human beings, you discover that you and your friends are alone. You have only yourselves and the environment. How will you survive? How are you going to set up your society? Remember, you must be prepared for a long, long wait in your new environment.

No matter which group you are in, determine first what your group's basic needs are. How are you going to keep alive during the first few days? Then decide how you are going to structure your society. Who is going to have authority? What people are to perform what tasks? What norms are you going to establish, so things will run smoothly? If you are never rescued, how are you going to provide for family life? For

In a hostile environment which needs must be considered first?

education of children? For religion? How will you determine who gets possession of what? What values will your society have? In other words, what will this new culture be like?

Group One

In exploring your new land you find that the shoreline is part sandy and part rocky. The rest of the land, which is an island, is rocky with many boulders of various sizes. The ground does not seem good for agriculture. There are goats and a few sheep on the island. On the less rocky part of the island are several apple and maple trees. One of the people in your group discovered a cave, big enough to walk into, but not very deep. There is a natural ground spring in the middle of the island, and the water from it seems to be good.

Group Two

In exploring your new land, you find that the shoreline is sandy. In fact, the rest of this very large island seems to be mostly sand. In the first day of exploration, in which you and your group traveled around one-third of the island, you discovered an oasis with fresh water springing from the ground. Desert rats and wild dogs are frequently seen. In the northeast part of the island there is more fertile ground with wildflowers and several kinds of trees. Someone in your group spotted a few wild hogs; there may be more.

Group Three

In exploring your new land you find that it is mostly hot, humid jungle. The shoreline may be sandy, but the dense jungle is not more than twenty feet from the water's edge. Palm trees and thick tropical plants take up most of the land. Papaya, guava, and banana plants are everywhere. The sounds of jungle birds and monkeys can be heard throughout the island. It seems to rain frequently for brief periods of time.

READING 3

How Does a Culture Work?

We know that a culture is the total way of life in a society. Now let's see how a culture works within a society.

Every culture is made up of two parts. One part is the **material culture,** the things a society makes and uses. The material culture includes clothing, shelter, kinds of transportation and communication, and other things commonly used in the society for both survival and enjoyment. The material culture also includes the tools, machines, and knowledge of how to make things. This knowledge is called **technology** (tek näl′ ə jē).

The other part is the **nonmaterial culture,** which includes the society's ideas and values. A society's rules of behavior, or **norms,** are part of the nonmaterial culture. The three types of norms are **folkways** (fōk′ wāz), **mores** (môr′ āz) and **laws.** A folkway, or custom, is an approved way of doing something politely or with good judgment in a particular society. Mores are very serious rules of conduct. In order to enforce these norms, societies make laws. Breaking a law in any society usually leads to punishment of one sort or another. Anthropologists call those behavior patterns that the culture greatly disapproves of, **taboos.** In almost every culture, murder and theft are considered taboos. Breaking a taboo can lead to punishment, being sent out of the society, or even a death sentence.

The values of a society, including beliefs and attitudes, become part of the culture through the establishment of folkways, mores, laws, and taboos.

Every child learns all this from the time she or he is born into a culture. The culture is learned in everyday living, while the child is growing up with people who are older. The first group which teaches the child the ways of the culture is the family. This is true in every society, including ours. The child is also taught the culture by others, including friends and relatives. (Depending

The battle of Lexington. How did gunpowder contribute to the start of the American Revolution?

on the culture, the child's relatives may be a part of the family unit, living with the child's mother and father.) In some societies, such as ours, the child continues his or her education in formal schools. Religion, which is found in every culture, also plays a big part in teaching the child about the culture. This whole process of enculturation teaches the child the culture and the roles one must play in the culture.

We have seen that all cultures change. No culture ever remains exactly the same for long periods of time. Look at examples of this in the pictures in Experiment 5-D, page 210. Change in a culture does happen, but how?

There are many ways in which cultures change. Three significant ways cultures change are by **invention, innovation,** and **cultural diffusion.** You know that an invention is a new idea about how something can be made or done. An innovation is an improvement in a culture's technology. Many inventions and innovations are important because they satisfy a need of the culture. Throughout the history of the human race, such inventions as the wheel, the calendar, gunpowder, and the printing press have satisfied needs of society. Can you explain how? Once the inventions were accepted, great changes took place in society. Can you imagine what our culture would be like if those four inventions had never been thought of and developed?

Another way cultural change takes place is by **cultural diffusion.** This occurs when

The Spread of Papermaking from China to Europe

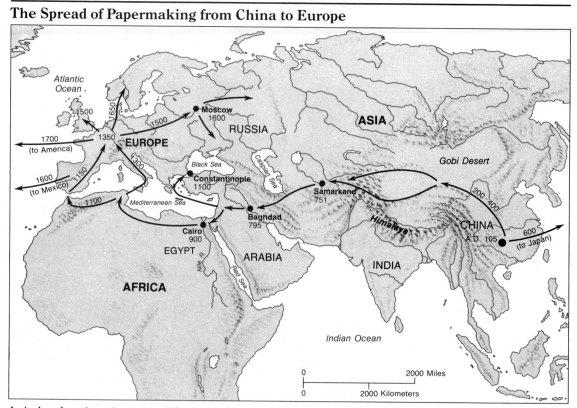

It is hard to imagine a world without paper. On the map, follow the spread of paper from its invention in China to other civilizations. How does this show cultural diffusion?

ideas from one culture are spread to other cultures. Paper, for example, was first used in China about a hundred years after the birth of Christ. By the year 1100 the idea and process of making paper had spread to Europe. Cultural diffusion may begin in a very simple way—by people talking to each other. In the case of paper, Arab traders are believed to have encountered paper while traveling in China. They brought samples of the paper to the people back home, where it became popular. Then that same experience was repeated with traders from other areas of the world, until paper finally reached Europe centuries later.

A well-known example of cultural diffusion is the spread of blue denim jeans. Most people today call them "blue jeans" or simply "jeans." People wear their jeans for recreation and play. Some people work in them or wear them to school. Jeans are available in a wide variety of textures, colors, styles, and prices. Jeans are known and worn in almost every country in the world today.

It may seem that jeans have been around forever, but they are actually a relatively recent American invention. Blue denim jeans go back as far as the mid-1800s, California lumberjacks and gold rush miners couldn't find pants that would stand hard use. When they bent their knees, the seams of their pants would split. Their pockets would tear when they tried to put tools and other things into them.

A merchant by the name of Levi Strauss moved to San Francisco in the 1850s. He established a store to sell clothing, canvas cloth, tents, and other merchandise to mining camps and frontier settlements. Jacob Davis was a tailor in the neighboring state of Nevada. In 1870, Davis and Strauss discovered a way to make life a little easier for lumberjacks, miners, and other frontier workers. They used Strauss's tough canvas cloth to make pants that would be strong and hold up well, even under the worst conditions. To make the pockets stronger, they pounded copper rivets into the corners of the front and back pockets. To prevent the seams from splitting, they double-stitched them. The following year, Strauss and Davis began making their pants from a French fabric called denim. (The word *denim* comes from the French words *de Nimes,* meaning "from Nimes," a town in France.)

The denim jeans were a tremendous hit! Between 1875 and 1900, blue denim jeans became the most popular of all clothing for workers in the West. When western movies in the 1930s showed John Wayne and other movie stars wearing jeans, the popularity of blue jeans skyrocketed from coast to coast. Suddenly, jeans were considered more than just work clothes.

During World War II, American soldiers took their jeans along with them to Europe. The Europeans saw them wearing jeans during their off-duty hours, and blue jeans have been popular in Europe ever since.

In the 1960s and early '70s, blue jeans became a symbol of students who protested against the Vietnam War. After the war, many Americans continued to wear jeans because they were comfortable and they last for years. In the 1980s, top designers created high-priced, high-fashion jeans.

Jeans have been acculturated into the life styles of people of all ages all over the world. By the early 1990s, more than a million jeans were sold every year worldwide. Jeans, American music, and movies—these are all enjoyed today by people in every part of our planet. All are examples of the spread of the American culture through the process of diffusion.

Jeans even show up on a skater in Gorky Park, Moscow.

Diffusion of ideas and things from culture to culture is much faster today than ever before. It took the invention of paper over a thousand years to be diffused from China to Europe. Today, information about new ideas can travel that same distance in a few seconds. The use of satellites, computers, and other modern technologies make it all possible.

In "Reading 2: What Is Culture?" there is a discussion of culture traits. Culture traits are small parts of a culture. Some culture traits fit together in meaningful groups, called **culture patterns.** For example, the idea in our society that work is good has led to the idea that it is good to work for a living. Working for a living is a culture trait. In some societies the burden of survival is not put entirely on the individual. Groups of people work together to furnish their needs and wants.

This attitude has helped the growth of the American business system. The business system also has other traits. They are efficiency (getting a job done well in the shortest possible time) and strict organization. The business world has a way of stratifying (or ranking) people according to

jobs and their importance to the organization or company. This tendency toward stratification is also a culture trait. All of these traits help make up one of the major culture patterns in American society, the American business system.

Culture traits and culture patterns are different from one culture to another. Take the pattern of friendship, for example. What *you* may think of friendship in your culture may not be typical of a friendship in many other cultures. What is a friend? Is a friend someone you can talk with honestly? Is she or he a person for whom you would give up your life? How do you know who is a friend and who is not? The friendship aspect of a culture is a fascinating one. We shall be examining friendship as a culture pattern in our society and in other societies.

READING REVIEW

1. Define: taboo, culture pattern.

Critical Thinking

2. Identifying Alternatives (see page 38) What are the three ways in which a culture changes? Describe each of the three ways.

EXPERIMENT **5-G**

Who Is a Friend?*

Friendship is a wonderful thing. Most of us go through life meeting a lot of people. But we have only a limited number of true friends. What is a friend? What makes a

*Adapted from an unpublished paper, "Friendship Module," by Susan Priester, Gloria Cohen, Charles Bullwinkle, Jim Kilmurray, George Renwick. (See Acknowledgements, pages 595–596.)

friend special in our culture? Are friends expected to act differently in cultures in other parts of the world?

We will be spending some time on the topic of friendship in our culture and other cultures. But first, let's see what friendship in our society means to you. Think very carefully about the exercises and questions

How does working together create a basis for friendship?

below. Answer them as honestly and completely as you can. It is important that you think those questions through in order to fully understand "Experiment 5-H: Friendship and Culture," which you will be doing in class.

A. First, pick out in your mind the name of one of your best friends. It can be a person of either sex. Keep that person in mind as you answer the questions that follow and on page 224.

1. When and how did you meet your friend?

2. What do you like to do together?

3. What do you give your friend, and how often? (Examples are gifts, clothing, books, and money.)

4. How long has your friendship lasted, and how long do you think it will continue?

5. How do you know when your friend is very happy? Depressed? Disturbed with you? Worried? Wants to be alone? Wants to have a serious talk with you?

6. How do you convey feelings to your friend? How do you know when she or he has "gotten the message"?

7. Do you turn to your friend for respect? For admiration? Support? Sympathy? Direction? Criticism? Acceptance? Do you turn to someone else for any of these?

8. What qualities in yourself do you think your friend most values? How do you demonstrate these values?

9. What types of emotions and feelings do you *not* like to share with your friend?

10. If your friend called you at two o'clock in the morning, got you out of bed, and asked for advice on a personal problem, how would you react? Has this type of thing ever happened to you? How did you respond?

11. What could you *not* ask your friend to do for you, and vice versa?

12. If you had only a limited time to spend with either your friend (assuming that your friend is outside the family) or a member of your family, with whom would you spend it? Why?

13. Do you think this friendship is typical of your peer group? Is it typical of your social class? Of your American culture, and the teenage subculture? In what ways is it similar or different?

B. Now, think of a friend who is older or younger than you by at least two years (if you do not have one, ask yourself why). What activities do you share with this person? What personal needs do you think this relationship fills for you? For your friend?

C. Next, think of a friend with whom you share a working relationship—either on a job, as a fellow student, or some other way. What topics would you not discuss with this person? If this person needed fifty dollars, and you had the money, would you lend it to him or her?

You will have a chance to discuss your thoughts to all of these questions.

EXPERIMENT 5-H

Friendship and Culture*

In preparation for this experiment you should have given a lot of thought to your own friends and friendships. "Experiment 5-G: Who Is a Friend?" was designed to help you do this. Now let's take a look at friendship in other cultures.

Case 1   This story takes place in Turkey.

Ahmet, a Turkish executive heard that

*Adapted from Susan Priester *et al,* "Friendship Module." (See Acknowledgements, pages 595–596.)

his friend Joe, an American on assignment in Turkey, had an opening in his office. Ahmet heard that Joe would be interviewing people for that job. Ahmet went to his friend and fellow Turk, Kemal, and told him about the job opening.

Ahmet was anxious to have his friend Kemal get the job in Joe's office. So Ahmet gave Kemal a letter to take to Joe, which would introduce the two men. Kemal made an appointment to meet Joe and brought along his letter of introduction. When the

Ankara, Turkey

two men met, they both said how happy they were to meet a friend of Ahmet. They both told each other what a fine friend Ahmet was. Then they went on to discuss Kemal's training for the job. Kemal was not as experienced as some of the other people who applied for the job. Joe told Kemal he would consider his application and let him know if he got the job.

Kemal left the interview pleased. After the interview, days went by. When he did not hear from Joe, Kemal grew more and more worried. What was the delay? Kemal finally found out that the job had been given to someone else.

When Joe called Ahmet to explain his decision, Ahmet grew very angry with Joe. Ahmet accused Joe of not being a true friend. Ahmet said, "How am I going to explain to Kemal? I told him you and I were friends. Friends help one another."

In Ahmet's culture it is expected that a job opening would be given to a relative or friend first. Less attention is paid in that culture to qualifications than they are in our culture.

Río de Janeiro, Brazil

What did Ahmet expect from his American friend? Do you think Ahmet had a right to expect this? Why or why not?

Do you think that friendship in the Turkish culture means something different than in the American culture?

When two cultures come into conflict, which set of customs and norms should be followed?

Case 2   This story takes place in Brazil.

Susan, an American doctor, came to Brazil to work with a Brazilian doctor, Sergio. Susan came to Brazil through an American government program. Sergio works in a public health program for the government of Brazil.

Brazil's laws do not permit certain drugs to be imported from other countries. This is done in order to build up Brazilian companies which manufacture drugs. Susan was allowed to bring drugs into the country, however, by promising that she would use them only for demonstration purposes. She promised that she would not give the drugs to sick people in Brazil, but use them only for experimentation in the laboratory.

While Susan was staying in Brazil, Sergio's daughter became seriously ill. Both Susan and Sergio knew that Susan had the medicine needed to cure his daughter. Because he could not get them, Sergio asked Susan to give him the drugs. Susan refused, saying that she had signed a pledge that she would not give away the drugs, even to sick people. As a result, Sergio grew very angry and broke off the friendship. The public health program which they were working on together suffered because of the coolness between Susan and Sergio.

Sergio did not feel guilty about asking Susan for the drugs, even though it would mean breaking the law. In his culture and in many others, taking care of one's family is often regarded as more important than obeying government regulations.

Susan, however, comes from a culture which does not view law in the same way. Susan knew that if she got caught, she would probably be sent home in dishonor. In such a case, the public health program would also have suffered.

What did each of the two persons expect from their friendship? Were their expectations created by the cultures in which they lived? How?

Why were Susan's and Sergio's friendship expectations not met?

Was there anything either of them could have done to save the friendship?

How do you think your parents would have responded to Susan's dilemma? How would you have responded?

How far should you be willing to "bend" the rules to help a friend?

Case 3   This story takes place in Thailand.

This is about an American couple, Jane and Bob, and two brothers, Nit and Pun, who are natives of Thailand. Nit is a friend of Jane and Bob. The American couple first met Nit a few years ago when they were all studying at the University of Massachusetts. Expecting to travel to the Orient on a honeymoon trip, Jane and Bob asked Nit for his address. Nit told them to visit him if they could. They decided to take Nit up on his offer. The skit below is about what happened when Jane and Bob arrived.

Scene One: *Nit's home. Bob and Jane have already entered Nit's home and stand waiting for him to receive them. Bob is dressed casually, in a colorful shirt, plaid pants, and sandals. Jane is wearing a blouse and pair of slacks. Nit walks into the room.*

NIT: Ah! I'm so glad to see you! *(Nit eagerly extends his right hand, and shakes hands with Bob and Jane, American style. They are all smiling happily.)*

BOB: We're so glad to see you again, Nit. We thought we'd never get here. *(At this moment, Pun, Nit's younger brother, enters the room. Pun has never been to the United States and speaks only a little English. Nit introduces Jane and Bob to Pun in English, then introduces Pun to Bob and Jane in Thai. Pun shakes hands with Bob and Jane. He bows slightly each time.)*

PUN: Hello, Bob. Hello, Jane.
(To show friendliness to Pun, Bob extends his left hand to pat Pun on the shoulder. Pun suddenly steps back, however, leaving Bob and Jane surprised and uneasy. Jane moves closer to Bob. They put their arms around each other, still watching Pun. Pun appears to be nervous, perhaps unsure of his actions toward the Americans. Nit senses the nervousness of Bob and Jane, and Pun.)

NIT: *(hastily)* Would you please be my guests for dinner this evening?
(Before Bob and Jane can answer, Pun, who appears annoyed, stares with disgust at the two Americans.

Royal Palace in Bangkok, Thailand

They have their arms around one another. Pun looks at his brother.)

PUN: Please excuse me, I have some work to do.
(He bows courteously to Bob and Jane, and then leaves the room. Bob and Jane try to appear at ease, but are somewhat unsure of what to do next.)

JANE: We would be glad to come to dinner tonight, Nit. What time should we arrive?

NIT: Seven o'clock would be fine.

BOB: Good. See you then.
(They shake hands, say good-bye, and Jane and Bob leave.)

Scene Two: *Bob and Jane in their hotel room.*

JANE: Bob, do you know what happened with Pun, back at Nit's place? I felt rather uneasy.

BOB: No, I'm not sure. It's not easy for Americans to understand the Thai. They do a lot of things differently from us. I feel a little bad that Nit's brother doesn't like me, though. I hope that's not a sign of *Nit's* feelings.

JANE: I hope so, too, Bob. Sometimes you just can never tell what people will be like. Maybe we'll have a good time tonight.

Scene Three: *Nit and Pun in their home.*

PUN: Do all Americans dress like that? Do all their men touch women like that while others are watching? And do all their women dress like that?

NIT: Yes, they do a lot of things differently from us. You know, you may have insulted Bob by not letting him pat you on the shoulder. An American does that to show he likes you. He meant no harm by using his left hand.

PUN: *(skeptically)* Well . . . I believe you, but I find it strange.

Why do you think Pun reacted as he did to the Americans?

Did the Americans do anything "wrong"? What?

Was anyone at fault? Is fault an important question here? Why or why not?

Could the misunderstanding have been avoided? How?

How would you try to correct this situation? Would you talk it over? Why? How?

Case 4 This story takes place in Tunisia.

Allen is a Peace Corps volunteer in Tunisia. For the past two years he has taught in the high school in the town where he lives. He and some other Peace Corps workers, Marsha and Bill, live in the home of Mr. Kadiri. They have lived there ever since their arrival in town about two years ago. Mr. Kadiri has treated all three of them as part of his family. Now the Americans have completed their two-year contracts with the Peace Corps. They are making preparations for leaving the town and returning to the United States. In the process of organizing their belongings for the trip, Allen, Marsha, and Bill have decided to sell a lot of their things before departing.

> **Scene One:** *A large bedroom, in the home of Mr. Kadiri. All chairs have open suitcases on them. Various things are strewn about the room. All three Americans are standing over their bags. Mr. Kadiri, standing behind them, is watching them go over their things. Mr. Kadiri seems to be unhappy at their departure. He is sighing, shaking his head, and fidgeting around nervously with a broom.*

ALLEN: Should I keep this overcoat, Bill?

BILL: No, sell it.

MARSHA: You ought to get about three dollars for it.
(Mr. Kadiri looks down, unhappily.)

BILL: Should I keep this hat?

MARSHA: Yes, keep it. It'll look great in the States.

BILL: Okay, maybe I will keep it. Yes, I think I will.

ALLEN: *(Picks up camera)* I wish I didn't have to carry this camera around with me anymore, but I guess it's worth it if I get a few decent pictures now and then.
(Mr. Kadiri looks up at camera, then looks sadly down again.)

BILL: *(Picks up a somewhat worn beach towel)* This is one thing I have used a lot. . . .

MR. KADIRI: *(Seeing the beach towel, he finally speaks.)* Bill, that is a beautiful towel. Why don't you let me have it?

BILL: Oh . . . well . . . ah . . . I'm sorry, but I hope to get more use out of it in the future.

Based upon what you already know, how would you describe the friendship of the three Americans and Mr. Kadiri?

Why do you think Mr. Kadiri asked Bill for his worn towel?

How would you have answered Mr. Kadiri under the same conditions?

> **Scene Two:** *On their last day in Tunisia, Allen came home from school and was intent upon packing the few*

A street in Tunisia

remaining items he had left in his room. He had not been in the room more than a minute, when Bill, who had also returned from school, asked him if he had seen his beach towel. Allen said that he hadn't seen it. He went over to his closet and opened the door. His overcoat, and camera were missing! Allen had planned on leaving that day and was furious that his plans would now have to be changed.

It seemed that the room was not broken into. The three Americans thought that Mr. Kadiri had left the door open, and that thieves may have entered the room while they were teaching. But then they remembered that Mr. Kadiri had asked especially for the towel, which was missing. All three of them went off in search of their landlord, Mr. Kadiri.

What thoughts do you think were going through the minds of the Peace Corps workers at this moment?

How would you interpret the situation at this point? How do you think this story will end?

Do you think that the landlord might be responsible for the missing items? Why or why not?

Scene Three: *The three Americans find Mr. Kadiri in his yard and begin to question him.*

ALLEN: *(in a moderately loud tone of voice)* I'm glad we found you, Mr. Kadiri. I'm missing my overcoat and camera, and I'm sure they were in my closet this morning before I went to school!

(Mr. Kadiri does not give an answer.)

ALLEN: *(To Mr. Kadiri)* Do you know where they might be?

MR. KADIRI: No.

ALLEN: *(His voice getting louder)* How could they disappear from my closet like that?!

BILL: We remembered that you wanted my beach towel the other day. . . .

ALLEN: And we hope there's no connection between your request and the missing items.
(Mr. Kadiri does not answer. He just looks down, standing over a rake.)

ALLEN: Mr. Kadiri, have you seen any strangers around here?

MARSHA: *(To Allen, in a low-keyed voice, but loud enough to be heard)* Ask him if he has a reason for taking the things.
(Mr. Kadiri looks away and appears restless. He moves a step or two in another direction.)

ALLEN: Did you take our things for any reason?
(Mr. Kadiri does not answer.)

ALLEN: Please tell us.

MR. KADIRI: No . . . I didn't take them.

ALLEN: *(Angered)* Yes, I think you did! Tell us where they are.
(Mr. Kadiri mumbles something, but walks toward the house as if he will lead them to their possessions. The Americans follow behind. He leads them into a basement, opens a cupboard, and reveals all the missing items.)

How do you account for this apparent "theft"?
Does this "theft" seem likely, considering the relationship between Mr. Kadiri and the three Americans?
What would you do if you were Allen, Marsha, or Bill?

Later, Allen found out something which helped to explain the "theft." Unknown to the Americans, it is a custom in Tunisia for a person who is going away for an extended period of time (or forever) to leave close friends a nice gift by which they can remember him or her.

Now what do you think of the "theft"?
Do you think Mr. Kadiri was correct to assume that the Americans should understand this cultural custom, and also his expectations and fulfill them? Why or why not?
Do you believe Mr. Kadiri was at fault? Why or why not?
How would you go about trying to correct this misunderstanding?

Language and Culture

Of all human culture traits, perhaps none is more important than language. A **language** is a set of signs and symbols used in communicating thoughts. It may be written, or spoken, or both. The symbols must be understood by the people who use them. Some anthropologists study language and its relationship with a culture. These anthropologists are called linguists. Their field is **linguistics.**

Just think how important language is. Without it, we couldn't collect and store information about ourselves or others. Without language it would be very difficult to tell other people what is on our minds. It would be very difficult to understand others. If we didn't have language, how would we learn? We would either have to experience everything ourselves, or be present when someone else has a learning experience. Reading a book or magazine would be impossible. Writing a letter to your best friend would be equally impossible. You would have to be right in front of your friend, using grunts, groans, and gestures to communicate your thoughts. Can you imagine TV or movies without language? We would have to go back to the days of silent movies. Imagine how simple the plots would have to be for us to understand them. In order to leave a record of our experiences, we would have to draw pictures and hope others could understand what we meant.

In fact, that is probably how written language began. Some of the oldest artifacts of human beings thousands of years ago are cave drawings of animals, weapons, and tools. These drawings show us something about human life before languages were invented. Some of the earliest letters of alphabets were actually drawings of animals and other objects. An example of this writing-drawing is Egyptian hieroglyphics which we will look at more closely later in this unit.

The words and language of a society tell us a great deal about the culture. Language is a product of the culture in which it is used. We can think of language as a mirror of the values and life styles of a society. How does the language of the teenage American subculture mirror the values and life style of your age group?

We have already seen that all cultures change. As cultures change, languages and words change. The more complicated a society becomes, the more complicated its language becomes. The more ideas and new things a society develops, the more words it needs to describe those ideas and things.

Practically all things have names attached to them. This includes people. If something or someone is without a name, people in the culture soon give it one. Just try thinking of one thing in our culture that does not have at least one name. Can you come up with any?

We can tell how important something is to a culture by the number of words the culture has for it. Did you know that the

The ancient Egyptians were one of the first people to develop a written set of symbols for their language. The symbols are called hieroglyphics. The Egyptians carved hieroglyphics on the walls of pyramids and monuments.

Inuit had many words to describe snow? Snow was very important to them. They had one word to describe falling snow, another one to describe "snow-water," still another to describe "igloo snow," and many more. Do you suppose that people living on a desert or in a jungle would have many words for snow? Of course not. Snow isn't important in deserts and jungles. In fact, snow does not exist in those climates. Would it surprise you to find out that people who live in the desert and jungle do not have a word for snow? In the Inuit culture, however, there were many words for snow, because snow was essential for survival. Snow provided many of the Inuit's daily needs. It gave shelter when it was made into igloos. Melted snow made

drinking and bathing water. Snow could also provide a natural refrigerator to keep food fresh.

Think of other cultures and the words they use. Would a lumberjack or paper manufacturer have just one word for "tree"? Would a fisher have only one word to describe "fish"? Why not?

Besides showing the values of the culture, words also help cultural diffusion. Ideas and things spread from one culture to another mainly through the use of words. Where a new word goes, the idea or object usually goes with it. Take the word "pajama," for example. Pajamas originated in India centuries ago. As the idea of wearing pajamas spread to other cultures outside India, the word "pajama" went along.

Browsing in a music shop. Spanish is the primary language of many Americans. English is often the second language. What two subcultures are represented here?

Today, that piece of clothing and the Indian word describing it are known in several cultures, including our own. There is one difference, however. Pajamas in India were worn as regular street clothes, but in America they are worn to bed.

Language is one ability all people have in common. Yet, language is also one of the things that keeps people apart. There are thousands of languages in the world today. Many languages have several **dialects,** or different ways of pronouncing the words. Some dialects are so different that people speaking one dialect can't understand other dialects, even though they are speaking the same language.

People communicate mainly with those who speak their own language and dialect.

This helps to produce unity among people. It helps people who speak the same language to develop a common culture. But language differences have also created barriers between people and have led to some undesirable traits in people. One is the attitude that "we are better than you, because you are different from us." Throughout history people have thought that other people and their cultures were inferior if they were different or strange. This attitude has led to misunderstandings, killing, and war. It has destroyed cultures instead of making them better.

We see that language is, indeed, very important. It is the foundation of culture. It is one thing that makes people different from animals. It is what makes us *us*.

Major Languages of the World

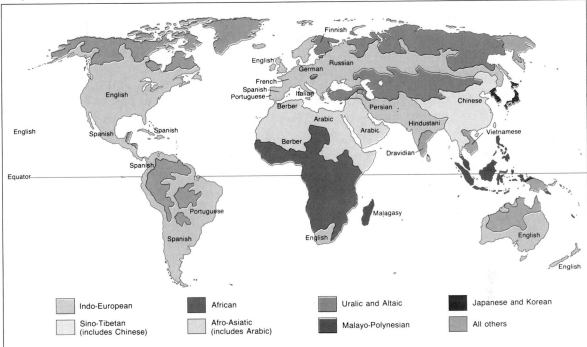

Approximately 50 percent of the people in the world speak an Indo-European language. Indo-European *refers to a family of languages that includes English. Using the map and the key, name some other Indo-European languages.*

Many languages use the same symbols as we do in the English language. Some words appear to be the same. They are usually pronounced differently though and have different meanings from the English language. Here are examples of German and English words that look alike but have different meanings:

Word *(English and German)*	Meaning in the German Language
ROCK	a coat or skirt
BRIEF	a letter
BAD	bath
KIND	child
RAT	advice
ELF	eleven
BRAVE	honest

ANGEL	fishing tackle
RANG	rank or station
PEST	sickness or plague
GANG	motion
LIST	crafty

READING REVIEW

1. What is linguistics?
2. Why is it important to study the language of a culture?

Critical Thinking

3. **Drawing Conclusions** (see page 42) What can be learned about the traditional Inuit culture by studying the Inuit, or Eskimo, language?

Language and Culture

Many anthropologists consider the study of languages very important. The symbols and sounds of a language tell an anthropologist a great deal about the culture. The branch of Anthropology which specializes in the study of language and culture is called Linguistics. .

Let's see how linguists, the people who study language, can get information about a culture by studying the language of that culture.

Example A

The ancient Egyptians wrote with symbols called **hieroglyphics.** These symbols were actually pictures and drawings, not letters as we know them. The following article describes the hieroglyphic "alphabet" and invites you to learn how to write in hieroglyphics. Try it!

Egyptians long ago wrote with pictures*

The next time someone tries to show off by writing something in Micmac or modern Urdu, why not go him one better by drawing your own name in ancient Egyptian hieroglyphics!

It's not as hard as it sounds: after all, any scribe in pharaonic times—and that lasted almost 3,000 years—learned the hieroglyphic alphabet from early childhood.

The knowledge of how to read hieroglyphics ended with the ancient Egyptian empire. Thirteen centuries had passed before anyone could figure out their meaning.

The breakthrough came in 1799, when some of Napoleon's soldiers unearthed in the Egyptian town of Rosetta an intriguing slab of black basalt. It has a long inscription on it in ancient hieroglyphics, and underneath an equally long inscription in Greek letters. It didn't take long for an interested French archaeologist, Jean-Paul Champollion, to realize that one inscription was a translation of the other. The "Rosetta Stone" overnight solved secrets previously hidden for over a millennium.

The hieroglyphic alphabet is composed of 23 signs representing different phonetic sounds. Most of these are consonant sounds since the ancient Egyptians, like the Jews and Arabs, tended to omit most of the vowel markings. Once you learn these phonetic signs, it is possible to write many names and word combinations. (See page 237.)

On page 238 are examples of modern first names as they might be written in hieroglyphics. You will notice after each name that there is a sign of a seated figure. This sign is called a "determinative," and is simply added to indicate whether the name is of a woman or a man.

Hieroglyphics may be written from left to right, as here, or equally from right to left. When written horizontally, the characters

*From Deborah Mason, "Egyptians Long Ago Wrote With Pictures" in *The Christian Science Monitor.* Reprinted by permission from *The Christian Science Monitor.* (See Acknowledgements, pages 595–596.)

SOME LETTERS IN THE HIEROGLYPHIC ALPHABET

Sign	Object pictured	Approximate sound equivalent	Sign	Object pictured	Approximate sound equivalent
	vulture	a as in *ah*		lion seated	l
	foot	b		owl	m
	hand	d		water	n
	horned viper	f		stool	p
	snake	soft g as in gem		mouth	r
	stand for jar	hard g as in goat		folded cloth	s
	shelter	h		pool	sh
	twisted rope	emphatic h		loaf	t
	reed leaf	i		tethering rope	th
	hill slope	k or qu as in *queen*		double reed leaf	y
	basket with handle	k		quail chick, bird	w

EXAMPLES OF AMERICAN NAMES

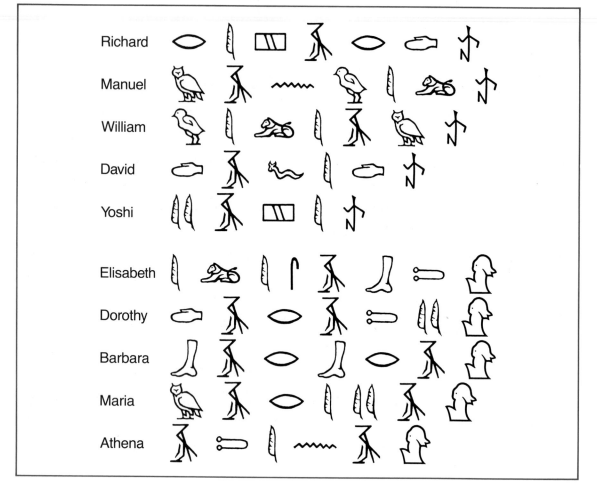

Richard

Manuel

William

David

Yoshi

Elisabeth

Dorothy

Barbara

Maria

Athena

always face the direction of the start of the word.

Some words, however, can be written from top to bottom and others in a circular fashion forming a small box. There are many variations in the positioning of the letters but they always represent the same sound.

Lest you think you can now read every inscription on an Egyptian tomb, don't be too optimistic! Between your present knowledge and that plateau lies a vast empire of grammatic rules and combinations that affect letter order and significance.

But even if you never reach the point where you could write a novel in hieroglyphics, at least you can now try something new and startling when you next sign your name.

Example B

The word for Japan in the language of that country is "Nippon" (pronounced nep′ pôn′). It means "land of the rising sun." The symbol for "sun" was originally ☼, which gradually became ⊙, and finally became 日. The symbol for "land of" was originally taken from the symbol for "tree" 米. This symbol was given one additional marking near the bottom 米 and became the early symbol for "root" or "origin." That symbol became 米 and finally 本. The symbols 日本 (pronounced nep′ pôn′) mean "land of the (rising) sun"—Japan.

The capital of Japan is Tokyo. The word Tokyo means "east capital." The symbol for "sun" 日 is combined with the symbol for "origin" 本 to make the symbol for "east" 東. This is pronounced Tō. The symbol for "capital" began as 宮 and became 京. It is pronounced Kyo. Together, the symbols 東京 make Tokyo, the East Capital.

The symbol in Japanese for "a man" is 男. This symbol is a combination of two symbols: 田 meaning "a field or rice paddy," and 力 meaning "the power to grip or work." What might this tell you about the traditional Japanese view of man's role? What do you suppose the traditional woman's role was in Japanese society?

Example C

The language of the Chinese also tells us about their culture. A figure standing on two legs represents a "man" 人. A figure with curves (similar to the one for man) represents a "woman" 女. A large-headed figure unable to stand 子 represents a child. The symbol of "one woman beneath a roof" 安 means peace and contentment. The symbol of two women under one roof 姦 is the sign for war or disturbance. The word for "good" in Chinese is made with the symbol of a woman beside a child. 好

Technology and Culture

People have always searched for easier and better ways of providing for their needs, such as food, clothing, shelter, and safety. In the early days of human life, survival was no easy matter. People spent almost all their time just trying to keep alive. Animals were sources of food and clothing, but they were dangerous. Keeping warm and dry in cold, wet weather was also difficult. Just finding and killing animals and eating their flesh was a full-time job. Early humans did not have an easy life!

Throughout the years, however, humans discovered and invented things to help them survive. About 300,000 years ago, they discovered that fire which destroyed could also be beneficial. They learned how to cook animal flesh. This process made the food taste better. Cooking also broke down the tissues of the meat, so that it could be eaten faster and digested better. Fire provided people with more hours of light in the day. Fires became central meeting places for people. They gathered around them to eat, to keep warm and dry, and to make tools and weapons for hunting. For many cultures, fire provided a spiritual experience—a good feeling that could be shared by people without the use of language.

Fire may have been discovered after a storm when someone saw the effects of a lightning bolt. Carrying the fire home on a stick, that person started a fire. There was only one problem: the fire had to be kept going. That meant that some people had to stand by the fire to make sure it did not go out. The need to keep the fire alive may have helped to bring people together. It may have helped to build a common culture among them. For another 100,000 years people had to guard the fire constantly, until they learned how to create fire themselves.

Another way the first people increased their chances of survival was by making tools and weapons from things in their environment. Spears and hand axes made of stone and bones were among the earliest tools and weapons. They were used for killing and skinning animals, and killing other people in war. It probably took people in early times many days to make just one spearhead or hand ax. They may look like simple, crude tools to you, compared to tools made today. Just try to make tools yourself with nothing more than the materials early people used. With this restriction, you would probably discover that it

Wind as a source of energy

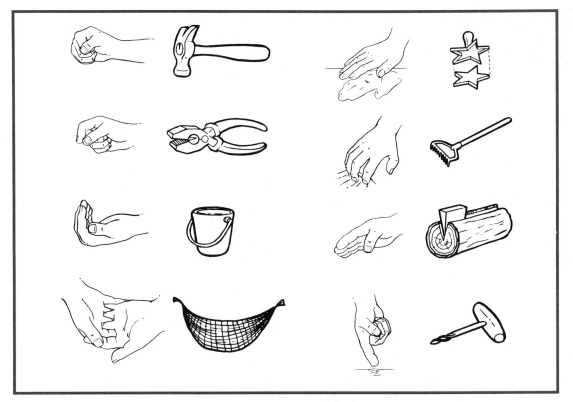

These drawings show how some simple tools invented by humans imitate what the human hand can do. For example, the tools can carry, strike, and hold, much the way the hand does. The tools make certain tasks easier.

takes months of practice to learn how to make a good spearhead or hand ax.

At various times, many cultures developed the bow to help them project the spear. Spears were changed somewhat to make arrows. With the bow and arrow, the hunter could be much more accurate at hitting targets farther away.

In addition to hunting animals for food, early people picked food from the ground and from trees and bushes. Only about 10,000 years ago (a very short time in human existence on Earth) did people begin to produce food by planting seeds and harvesting the crops. This process is referred to as *agriculture.*

Eventually, people learned how to use natural sources of energy to do work for them. Wind and water were the first energy sources to be tapped. A sail, attached to a flat platform or boat, allowed people to travel more easily on water. They found that wind would also move a windmill, which could provide energy.

People learned how to tame, or domesticate animals. The use of animals to do work made survival easier. Oxen and horses (and sometimes other humans captured in battle) were made to haul things. Dogs, once tamed, kept people warm at night, helped them hunt, and protected them from attack.

Without a doubt, one of the most important inventions of early people was the

Anthropology **241**

Technology refers to inventions other than the computer. Any invention which increases human control over the environment is an example of technology, even the windmill.

wheel. With the wheel, heavy loads could be carried long distances on vehicles. No longer did heavy loads have to be dragged or carried on a person's shoulders or head. Chariots (two-wheeled vehicles pulled by horses) were commonly used in wars. Wheeled vehicles, pulled by domesticated animals, became a way of getting from here to there in the shortest time and in the easiest way.

The invention and development of new ideas and ways of doing things by humans is called technology. A trait of every culture is the development of some sort of technology. The trait includes the sharing of that technology. The sharing of technology may have begun with the sharing of a fire. Today, people depend on each other for much more. Our way of life has become easier in some ways and harder in others. Most people in our society no longer have to worry about killing enough animals for daily survival. But we do have to work for

the money needed to buy things for survival. That alone takes more than a third of your lifetime!

We depend on our technology, our tools and ideas of how to provide for the things we need and want, to survive in the modern world. Our needs and wants are not exactly the same as those of early people. Yet, where would we be without fire and heat, tools and weapons, and the wheel?

What about technology and culture today? How does technology affect our culture? What changes are a result of technology? We will explore these questions in the remainder of this unit.

READING REVIEW

1. What is technology?

Critical Thinking

2. Recognizing Cause and Effect (see page 35) How did technology change the way humans survived?

Technology and Cultural Change

The invention of new ideas, tools, and methods of doing things makes up a culture's technology. An interesting way of observing cultural change is by analyzing changes in technology.

Interview several adults who remember what it was like to live in our culture thirty years ago. Find out what tools, machines, and appliances we have today that did not exist thirty years ago. From the information these people give you, make a list of at least twenty items.

When you have written your list, begin to think of the ways this culture has changed due to changes in technology. You will be putting these thoughts to use in class.

Men and Women

Below are thirteen jobs and characteristics of humans. Some are commonly associated with women. Others are thought of as belonging to men. On a separate sheet of paper, copy the list. Next to each, write an "M" if you believe it is primarily associated with men, or an "F" if you think it is associated with women. Even if you feel that the job or characteristic is equally common for men *and* women, choose the sex you think it applies to more often.

1. Brings home the money
2. Intelligent
3. Cries
4. Aggressive
5. Farmer
6. "The Boss" in business
7. Medical doctor
8. Emotional
9. Possessive
10. Strong
11. Controls money
12. Soldier
13. Cares for the children in the family

Would you have put "M" before Supreme Court justice? Sandra Day O'Connor was the first female in this position.

Anthropology   **243**

Stereotyping

Classifying people and things is something we all do every day. You cannot afford the time and energy to take a fresh look at every new thing or person you encounter. Instead you think back to a previous experience involving a similar person or thing. You then put the new person or thing into a category with those similar to the ones you encountered before.

This process saves time and energy, and it is generally useful. However, it can also be dangerous. Suppose you perceive that a new person or thing is like one you already know. What if your perception is wrong? From that moment on, you may have set yourself up to misunderstand that new person or thing.

Another point to consider is that no two people or things are exactly alike. You are unique. Every other person is also unique, with her or his own individual characteristics. Many people have a stereotype of an individual or a group of people. A **stereotype** is an oversimplified view, usually negative, of a person or group of people. Because the members of a group are perceived to have similar characteristics all are seen as the same and treated the same no matter how different the individuals may actually be. When a person is stereotyped he or she is not regarded as an individual but judged by a false picture. You can see how stereotyping can lead to discrimination and prejudice. Then that person or group is treated unfairly.

Until recently, our culture put men into roles in which they were expected to be more intelligent, stronger, more aggressive, better able to control money, and more naturally suited to a business career than women. The professions of doctor, lawyer, soldier, farmer, and many others were considered "men's work." Women, on the other hand, were considered weaker, more emotional, and unsuited for jobs in business and government. Since they were designed by nature to have children, all women were supposed to have the home and family as the center of their lives.

Or at least this is the way men and women were *expected* to be. Those were the accepted roles and stereotypes in our society. They are still held by some people who prefer the traditional roles. Ideas about sex roles and sex stereotypes are changing in our culture and throughout the world. Most areas of the world are, however, changing those stereotypes at a far less rapid rate than we are in the United States.

With the breakdown of sex stereotypes comes a greater freedom for every person to be the kind of individual she or he wants to be. Men are beginning to enjoy more freedom of emotion than before. Women are becoming more influential in the worlds of business and government. The cultural differences between the sexes are beginning to disappear. Men and women are beginning to share child-raising and housekeeping activities. There is a changing social climate. People are freer to choose different roles, whether they are traditional or non-traditional.

Stereotypes, of course, do not refer only to the sexes. They have also been applied to

In Israel women over 18 are eligible for the draft. Above is a researcher at the Weizmann Institute of Science, Rehovot, Israel. Are these typical roles for women?

people of other races, religions, and nationalities—to name only a few categories. How many times have you heard people condemn others just by referring to the group name? "Well, what do you expect? He/She is a _____!"

Stereotyping has led to misunderstandings, hard feelings, prejudices, hatred, and even wars. The unfortunate thing is that that kind of stereotyping is unnecessary. Think of each person as an individual, with his or her own good and bad points, tal-ents, and weaknesses. Isn't this how you want to be regarded?

READING REVIEW

1. What is treating people on the basis of a few similar characteristics called?

Critical Thinking

2. **Recognizing Bias** (see page 31) How are stereotypes of men and women changing in American culture?

How To Analyze a Culture

By now it should be fairly obvious that an anthropologist spends a great deal of time analyzing cultures—investigating how different cultures work.

We know that a culture is the way people live in society. In order to learn about the culture, we must find out what people think, feel, and do. One part of culture the anthropologist analyzes is its institutions. What is its technology like? What religion or religions are followed by the people? How is the family set up? How do the members of a society make their living? What is the government like? What roles are women, men, and children expected to play? How does the society provide for the education of its young people?

Another part of a culture which the anthropologist studies is the enculturation process. (Sociologists call this process socialization.) In studying enculturation the anthropologist asks many questions. How are individuals in the culture brought into the society? What norms do they learn? What sanctions (rewards and punishments) are imposed upon the individuals? What values does the society hold?

The anthropologist takes a close look at the social stratification system. Who is on top? Who is on the bottom? What determines the position or status you hold in the society? What roles are played by what people?

Communication is another important part of any culture. How do people send their thoughts and feelings from one person to another? How do the people communicate nonverbally (without words)? If the society is no longer living, have the people left any clues behind about their culture? The clues may be found in the form of writings, drawings, tools, or other kinds of artifacts.

Every culture has its art forms. In some cultures the form of art is painting. In others it may be dancing, music, sculpture, films and photography, or a combination of these. In most cultures, art forms serve several purposes. Art is a way to communicate feelings, ideas, and facts. It may also be a way for the artist to please himself or herself, even if the art doesn't please anyone else. The art work of cave people may have been done to record the important things in life at that time. It may also have been a way of teaching young people how to hunt (a kind of "how-to" manual), as part of their education. Or it may have been simply an early art form drawn to please the artist and the viewers.

The anthropologist tries to put all the parts of a culture together. Separately, they are meaningless. If you look at each culture trait as something which is complete in itself, you will probably make wrong guesses about the culture. Only when all culture traits are put together and viewed as a whole does the culture suddenly come to life. They then describe a living, breathing society, with people leading lives that make sense for them and are pleasing to them. Viewing all the traits of a culture together

is called **holistic** thinking. It is important to consider the *whole* culture. Holistic thinking is one of the most important methods used in anthropology.

READING REVIEW

1. Name six or more topics an anthropologist might study in the process of analyzing a culture.

Critical Thinking

2. **Determining Relevance** (see page 17) What is viewing all the traits of a culture together called? Why is this an important aspect of anthropological research?

How has the invention of the car influenced the life style of Americans? Their language (such as expressway)? Their landscape (such as the shopping mall)?

EXPERIMENT **5-L**

Analyzing Two Cultures

After studying "Reading 7: How To Analyze a Culture," you probably have a good idea of how an anthropologist puts it all together and comes up with a lifelike description of a culture. In this experiment you will have the chance to do just that—to examine photographs of artifacts and other pieces of evidence in order to try to understand the culture.

Examine the evidence presented on pages 248–253 for two cultures. On a sheet of paper write a description of each culture, based upon your interpretation of the artifacts. Later, you will be comparing your interpretations and reasoning with those of other students in your class.

Culture I: India Today

Note: You are making hypotheses about this culture using the photographs as evidence. A hypothesis is an unproved theory based on a limited amount of evidence. Additional evidence might cause you to change some of your hypotheses.

1

2 MATRIMONIAL

WANTED suitable match between 30–35 for post-graduate teachress (Brahmin) employed in Delhi. Caste no bar. Box XXXXX CA. Hindustan Times, New Delhi-1.
SUITABLE match for pretty accomplished homely* Punjabi Khatri Khukhran girl. M.A. B.Ed. 26. Father businessman. Box XXXXX Hindustan Times. New Delhi-1.
WELL placed Agrawal non-Singhzi engineer, doctor or Class 1 Govt. for handsome accomplished M.Sc. girl. 25 years. Respectable U.P. family. Early decent marriage. Box XXXXXX. Hindustan Times. New Delhi-a.
SUITABLE Kayastha match for beautiful Srivastava girl. 25 years. M.A. (Sociology). No dowry. Please reply Box XXXXXX. Hindustan Times. New Delhi-1.

1. *Western Railway headquarters, Bombay*
2. *Matrimonial column, New Delhi newspaper*
3. *Indian dress*
4. *Young Sikh*
5. *City Palace guard, Jaipur*

3

4

5

India

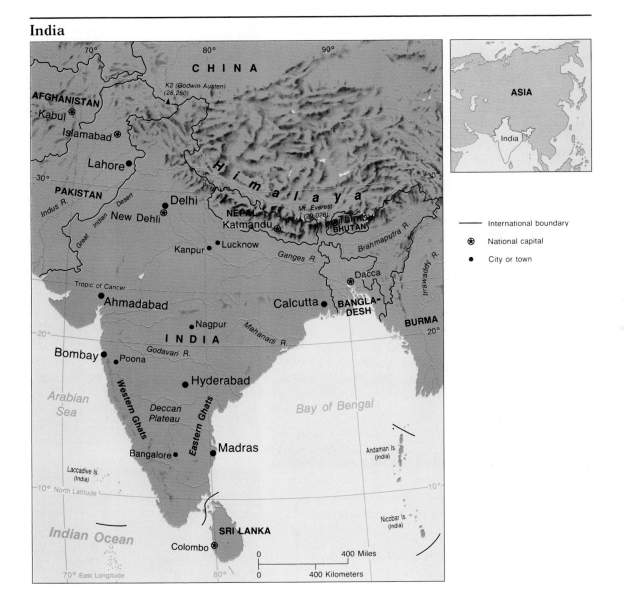

1

2

3

4

5

I am not interested in delay. I am interested only in things done.

Jawaharlal Nehru, Prime Minister of India (1947–1974)

1. Sorting tea
2. Jaipur market scene
3. Separating bajara (wheat-like grain)
4. Plowing implement
5. Parasnath Jain Garden Temple, Calcutta

Ancient Egypt

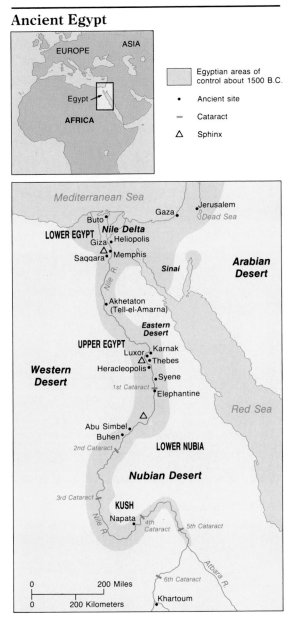

Egyptian areas of control about 1500 B.C.

• Ancient site

— Cataract

△ Sphinx

Mediterranean Sea

Buto
Gaza
Jerusalem
Dead Sea
LOWER EGYPT Nile Delta
Giza Heliopolis
Saqqara Memphis
Sinai
Arabian Desert

Akhetaton (Tell-el-Amarna)

Eastern Desert

UPPER EGYPT
Luxor Karnak
Heracleopolis Thebes
Syene
1st Cataract
Elephantine

Western Desert

Red Sea

Abu Simbel
Buhen
2nd Cataract
LOWER NUBIA

Nubian Desert

3rd Cataract
KUSH
Napata
4th Cataract
5th Cataract

Nile R.

Atbara R.

6th Cataract
Khartoum

0   200 Miles
0   200 Kilometers

Culture II: Ancient Egypt

Note: You are making hypotheses about this culture using the photographs as evidence. A hypothesis is an unproved theory based on a limited amount of evidence. Additional evidence might cause you to change some of your hypotheses.

1

1. *Tomb of Queen Hotshepsut, the first woman ruler known to history*

2. *Tomb of pharaoh Amenhotep IV*

2

Model of a boat from El Bersheh

Abu Simbel

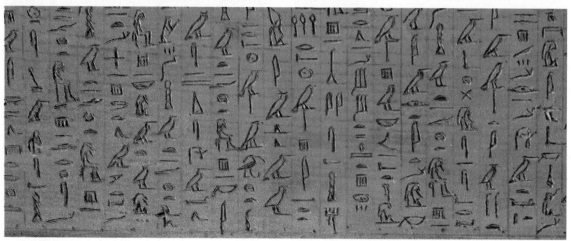

Hieroglyphics

Coffin of Tutankhamun, 1922

Egyptian tomb

Painting on tomb of Sennutem

Pyramids at Giza

Shadoof irrigation device on Nile River

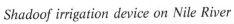

Digging Up the Past

So far in this unit on anthropology we have studied the ways anthropologists think about cultures and people. We have seen that anthropologists use the pieces of evidence about a culture—culture traits—to put together the puzzle of how people live in a culture. You may be wondering *how* the anthropologist gets this evidence and *where* this information is gotten.

One way of getting evidence is to live in a culture for a while. Anthropologists call this "living (or working) in the field." The anthropologist eats, works, sleeps, and plays with the people she or he is visiting and studying. By becoming an accepted member of the society, an anthropologist can find out firsthand what it is like in that culture. Since an anthropologist has not grown up in the culture, he or she can never completely understand it.

What if it isn't possible to "live in the field"? What if the culture is no longer in existence? Anthropologists then have to rely on the writings of other anthropologists. Or they can try to find clues themselves. One way of finding clues about past

These archeologists are working at a dig in Maine.

cultures is through **Archeology.** Archeology is the branch of anthropology in which the remains, or artifacts, of past cultures are studied. Archeologists dig up the past, uncovering cultures which have been covered through the years with dirt, water, and sand. The place where they choose to dig is referred to as a **site.**

As cultures die, they are often replaced by other newer cultures which are built right over the older ones. In the past, when a city was destroyed by fire or flood or some other disaster, the people who survived would leave. Years later (sometimes even centuries later) people would return. They would level the remains of the earlier culture and build new homes and buildings. Today archeologists find layers upon layers of ancient cultures. The culture found at each layer, or **stratum,** is older than the one just uncovered. The deeper the digging goes, the older the cultures are that are revealed. The artifacts found at each stratum tell the archeologist a lot about life in a culture at a particular time. Sometimes as many as twenty different strata have been uncovered, showing life at twenty different times in history!

The archeologist has to be very careful when digging up the precious remains of bygone cultures. One powerful thrust of the shovel could shatter and completely destroy a key artifact, ruining years of investigation by other archeologists and anthropologists. What is even worse, such an accident could ruin the chances of others who are just starting their work on that culture. Although they might mean no harm, many amateur anthropologists and archeologists have destroyed artifacts by being careless about their work. The destruction of artifacts has become such a problem that the government of the United States has passed laws against unauthorized people disturbing archeological sites.

Once at the site the archeologist excavates, or digs, to uncover the remains of one culture. Before the archeologist begins what is called the **"dig,"** he or she must first make a map of the site. Then the archeologist divides the site into squares. This is called making a **grid system.** Making a map and a grid system is necessary for the archeologist to keep track of exactly where all artifacts are found. The *location* of artifacts and other evidence may mean as much as the way they were made. Bones of people who lived long ago are important and useful to study. They tell us about the physical features of people in those past times. If the bones of many people are found in one place, we know more: the people in those times may have lived together in a society. If the bones of a large animal are found in the same place with human bones and arrowheads, we might guess that the people were killed by the animal. Another guess would be that the animal was slain by the survivors of the hunting party. Or, maybe the people killed each other over the right to keep the animal for food and clothing. At any rate, it is important to know exactly where each artifact (and bone) is found.

After making a map and grid system, the archeologist is ready to start excavating, or digging. Excavation is almost always done by a team of archeologists. The work is long and hard and usually lasts several years at each site. As they dig down, the archeologists mark each level with a metal disc, which has a number on it. When new maps are made, those numbers are used for identifying areas. Each stratum is dug out very carefully, so nothing is broken. When an artifact is found, it is removed and the dirt slowly taken off. It is then numbered and put away until later.

As artifacts and bones are collected, the archeologist tries to figure out how old they are. Science has ways of determining the age of the artifact.

By using various techniques, anthropologists can put together the pieces of the cultural puzzle. They hope to answer many questions about the culture. How long ago did these people live? What did they do? How did they keep alive? There are a million questions anthropologists and archeologists ask about life hundreds or thousands of years ago. Discoveries in the future may provide the answers.

READING REVIEW ▰▰▰▰▰
1. Define: stratum, dig, grid system, site.

Critical Thinking
2. **Expressing Problems Clearly** (see page 12) Why is it important to dig artifacts out of the ground slowly and carefully?

EXPERIMENT 5-M

An Archeological Dig

You should become familiar with "Reading 8: Digging Up the Past" before proceeding. You should now have a fairly good idea of how a dig is worked. In this experiment you will have an opportunity to put that knowledge to use. You will become an archeologist searching for artifacts which might tell you something about a culture.

You will be working as a member of an archeological team. Very few archeologists work alone, and for good reason. In any excavation there is a huge amount of work. All of the work must be done very, very carefully. It helps a lot when you have other people to share the joys of your discoveries—and the disappointments too. Good teamwork and team spirit is necessary for the success of any excavation. Your dig will be no exception. Here is a description of the site and how to work the dig.

The year is 2095. The place is Planet X-12 of the Helio Galaxy. You and your team have just received a container from the Central Space Agency. The container, you are told, is a sampling of a site on a planet which was recently destroyed. The site was not disturbed when it was lifted into this container. You and your fellow archeologists have in front of you a mini-site. Hopefully, this untouched site will give you some clues about the culture which once existed on the dead planet.

The first thing you must do is make a map of the site. Begin by measuring the dimensions of the site. Use Page A of Handout 5-M of this experiment to make the map. (Make sure you include width, depth, and length on your map. You may want to make more than one map to show these dimensions.)

Next, divide the site into squares to make the grid system you studied about in Reading 8. Mark the sides of the container, so as to set the boundaries of the squares. You

Artifacts from the Lost City, Colombia

may want to attach pieces of string or cord from the marks on one side of the container to the marks directly across on the other side. This will make the grid easier to see. You will probably want to remove the string while you are actually working on the grid, to make it easier to dig.

After you have marked the site, mark your map in the same way. Now give each square of the site a number. Also mark those numbers on your map. (In actual excavations of a site, the depth would also be marked into squares. For this dig only the surface of the site should be divided into squares.)

Before you begin your digging, look over Page B of Handout 5-M. On Page B is the "Archeological Survey Report." This is divided into two parts. In Part One you are to list the artifacts and their locations. This list is your **data,** or basic information. With this data you can go on to Part Two. In Part

Two you are to write a summary of your conclusions about the culture.

The most important rule of archeology is this: Be very careful! Dig slowly and carefully. You should not dig the artifacts out of the ground as fast as you can. A wise archeologist knows that one fast move can ruin the entire dig. So lift the dirt out of the container centimeter by centimeter, one square at a time. If you have a screen available, sift the dirt to make sure you haven't missed anything. When you find an artifact, dust it off gently (with a brush or old toothbrush if you have one). Then place the artifact on an index card. Label the card with the same letter used to identify the artifact in the "Archeological Survey Report."

When you have finished your dig, you should have all the artifacts on cards and labeled. Page B, Part One, of the "Archeological Survey Report" should be completed.

Turn again to your map of the site. On your map show where your team found every artifact. Use the letter you gave each artifact. Put the letter on the map. This information should be on your Survey Report. Now that you have the data, you and your team must try to put the pieces together. It is your job as a team to make sense of the puzzle. You must now make logical guesses about the culture in which these artifacts were used. What possible uses do you think the artifacts might have had in that culture? How might the artifacts have fit into the life styles of the people? (Remember, you are a total stranger to the culture in which these artifacts were used.)

After all the information gathering is done, you and your team should write a paper describing your findings. The paper should be as long as you think is necessary to make your conclusions clear. In your paper (which everyone on the team should help to write) make logical guesses about the uses of the artifacts. From these artifacts, what do you think the culture was like? What values do you think the people had? What were their life styles like? Can you make any guesses about their institutions? About their technology? About any other parts or traits of their culture? Put all your ideas down in writing. Let your imagination go. But make sure all your ideas are logical. Be sure to give reasons for the statements you make. Briefly summarize your conclusions on Handout 5-M, Page B, Part Two after you have written your paper.

You will have a chance to share your findings with those of the other archeological teams.

Careers in Anthropology

Do you like to observe people, especially in environments different from your own? If you do, a career in Anthropology might be for you.

Most anthropologists specialize in Cultural Anthropology. They live with groups of people in many societies, often far from home. They study the ways those people live, think, work, and play. In order to do this, anthropologists need to learn the language of the people. They also need to adopt many of the customs and lifestyles of the people. Sometimes this is difficult to do, since it requires giving up their old comfortable ways of thinking and acting.

Recently, cultural anthropologists have expanded their fields of study. They not only observe human behavior in societies outside the United States. They now observe also the behavior of people in this country. The topics of their studies range from drug addicts to business leaders and from politicians to homemakers.

The focus of other anthropologists is on linguistics. These anthropologists examine the sounds and structure of a society's language. Then they relate these to the behavior and thought patterns of the people in that society. Linguists show us that the way people use language may influence the way they think about things.

Physical anthropologists study human beings as organisms. They usually have a background in biology or anatomy (the study of the human body's structure). They study theories that explain how the human body got to be the way it is today.

Archeologists study cultures of the past by examining the artifacts they left behind. Some of their time is spent "in the field" digging up ancient skeletons and human-made objects. This excavation must be done slowly, a little at a time, so that nothing is damaged. Such work requires great patience, and a love of outdoor work in all kinds of weather. After the "dig," the archeologists take their work inside. In the laboratory, the items found are catalogued, examined, and dated. Then the archeologist tries to figure out how the items were used in their ancient cultures.

Most anthropologists today are oriented toward research. They seek to discover new information, and they publish their discoveries in articles and books. Many anthropologists combine this work with teaching.

About 15,000 Americans now work as anthropologists. Eighty percent are college teachers, who also do research and projects for government and business. A few anthropologists work in museums.

For more information about careers in Anthropology, write to the American Anthropological Association, 1703 New Hampshire Avenue N.W., Washington, DC 20009. If your interest is in Archeology, you can get information from the Archeological Institute of America, 675 Commonwealth Avenue, Boston, MA 02215.

The anthropologist above is studying art objects at the Louvre in Paris. What other job skills would this person need to have?

READING REVIEW

1. What do most anthropologists do today? What is the difference between a cultural anthropologist and an archeologist?
2. What traits should young people have if they want to be anthropologists?

Critical Thinking

3. **Distinguishing Facts, Opinions, and Inferences** (see page 22) Which area of Anthropology do you find most interesting? Why?

Social Scientists Look at Cahokia

How do the ways anthropologists think about a subject compare to the ways other social scientists think? You will explore these similarities and differences, as you examine a selection about Cahokia, the great trade and ceremonial center of the Mississippians. Its people flourished in the Mississippi River valleys from about A.D. 1000 to 1500. Located in Illinois just across the Mississippi River from St. Louis, Cahokia had a thriving population of between 30,000 and 40,000 people. Read the description of Cahokia below from Robert Claiborne's *The First Americans,* and then answer the questions under "Comparing the Social Sciences."

❝Yet Cahokia's most striking feature was not its protecting palisade or its market and spacious plazas, but the many mounds, large and small, that rose above the city. Some of the smaller ones held storehouses for corn and other crops, while larger mounds served as platforms for the houses of the city's more important citizens. For these upper-class Cahokians, a house that was elevated on a mound was a much coveted status symbol.

The biggest, most impressive mounds served less mundane purposes. One of them, a truncated pyramid not far from the city's southwestern entrance, was the location of sacrifices and other religious rituals; a conical mound looming beside it sheltered the graves of the city's illustrious dead.

Dwarfing all was the great steepsided mound that was Cahokia's religious and political center. More than 1,000 feet long—almost four modern city blocks—and nearly 800 feet wide, it rose in several enormous steps. On its topmost level, 100 feet above the city, was a post-and-wattle temple with a sharply peaked roof of thatch. From this vantage point the highest priest of Cahokia could keep an eye on another structure beyond the city wall but also under his jurisdiction—an immense circle of posts, more than 100 yards across, which the priesthood used as a combined calendar and solar observatory. Here, seated on a single post set near the circle's center, a priest kept track of the shifting seasons. By noting the position of the sun relative to the surrounding posts as it rose over the bluffs half a mile east of the city, he determined the propitious time for Cahokian farmers to plant their crops.❞

Comparing the Social Sciences

Psychologists study the reasons behind the ways people think about things. Why do you, as a psychologist, think it was the priest that kept track of the season? (*Identifying Assumptions*)

Sociologists study social classes—higher or lower groups in a society. What could you, as a sociologist, learn from this reading about the classes of the Mississippians? (*Drawing Conclusions*)

Anthropologists study cultures which include religion. What can you, as an anthropologist, learn from this reading about the Mississippians' religion? (*Demonstrating Reasoned Judgment*)

Geographers study the way people use the Earth and its resources. What question might a geographer have about the Missis-

sippians after reading this selection? (*Creating Good Questions*)

Historians study the past. Some researchers have argued that similarities of designs show that the Mississippian culture was influenced by the ancient Egyptians. As a historian, would you accept this theory? (*Testing Conclusions*)

Political scientists study the use of political power in society. Can you, as a political scientist, make a hypothesis about what gave the priests political power over the people? (*Drawing Conclusions*)

Economists study the way people make a living. What could you, as an economist, learn about the Mississippian economy from this reading? (*Demonstrating Reasoned Judgment*)

An artist's reconstruction of Cahokia

GLOSSARY OF TERMS

acculturation the process of making the traits of other cultures a part of your own culture (page 214)

analysis the breaking down of an event or fact into smaller pieces in order to follow it more closely (page 206)

Anthropology the study of humans in the environment; one of the three behavioral sciences (page 205)

anthropologist a social scientist who studies cultures (page 206)

archeologist a scientist who uses the research methods of Archeology (page 206)

Archeology a branch of Anthropology that attempts to find out what life was like in the past by examining things left behind by the people of a culture (page 206)

artifact anything made and used by people in past cultures that archeologists study to find out what life was like in the culture; a remain of a culture (page 206)

behavioral science the study of human behavior; Psychology, Anthropology, and Sociology are referred to as the behavioral sciences (page 205)

Cultural Anthropology a branch of Anthropology; the study of how people in other societies live, and the effects that environments have on their life styles (page 206)

cultural diffusion the spreading of ideas and ways of doing things from one culture to another culture (page 219)

culture the entire way a society lives, including customs, values, social institutions, attitudes, music and art, language, and tradition of society (page 206)

culture pattern a set of cultural characteristics, or traits, that are constantly repeated in a society (page 222)

culture trait a small part of a culture; a characteristic found in the culture (page 212)

data information; in Anthropology, the information researched about a culture (page 257)

dialect a different way of pronouncing the words in a language, usually shared by a people in certain geographical areas of a culture (page 234)

"dig" a nickname for an archeological excavation (page 255)

dynamic constantly changing; a characteristic of any culture (page 214)

enculturation the process of learning the roles one plays in a culture and becoming part of the culture; in Sociology this is referred to as *socialization* (page 212)

ethnocentrism the attitude that your own culture is better than any other culture; a kind of prejudice (page 212)

excavation the orderly and careful removal of artifacts from the ground by archeologists (page 206)

field experience living with the culture being studied (page 206)

folkways customs of politeness in a society; less serious than *mores* (page 218)

grid system the organization of an excavation site into square-shaped areas, used by archeologists to make it easy to record the location of each artifact (page 255)

holistic a method of thinking about a culture as a whole, rather than just a collection of separate parts (page 247)

innovation an improvement made on something that already exists (page 219)

invention the creation of something new from inside a culture; a means of cultural change (page 219)

language a set of signs and symbols used in communicating thoughts from one person to other persons (page 232)

law a norm established and enforced by government for the smooth running of society (page 218)

linguistics a branch of Anthropology that studies languages and their relationship to the cultures in which they are used (page 232)

material culture that part of a culture that includes the things a society makes and uses (page 218)

mores serious norms carrying a serious moral judgment against offenders (page 218)

nonmaterial culture that part of a culture that includes ideas and values (page 218)

norms the rules of a society that regulate the behavior of its members (page 218)

observation the act of carefully watching and writing down behaviors and events (page 206)

Physical Anthropology a branch of Anthropology; the study of human biological nature, heredity, and evolution (page 205)

site a place where an archeologist digs, or excavates, to uncover the remains of a culture (page 255)

stereotype an oversimplified view, usually negative, of a person or group of people (page 244)

stratum a layer of earth in an archeological dig that reveals a past culture (page 255)

subcultures smaller cultures within a larger culture, with traits similar to and different from the main culture (page 214)

taboo a behavior pattern that is strongly disapproved of by society (page 218)

technology the invention and development of tools and skills by humans (page 218)

UNIT 6 Geography

STUDY &
THINKING
SKILLS

GEOGRAPHY
ANTHROPOLOGY
HISTORY
SOCIOLOGY
POLITICAL SCIENCE
PSYCHOLOGY
ECONOMICS

This Is Geography

The mayor's golden shovel dug into the mound of soft, dark earth as the onlooking crowd clapped and cheered. Arbor Day in Taylorville had never been taken very seriously before this year, but times had changed. Pollution was making the Earth feel sick. Some kids at Taylor High got the idea to plant a grove of oak and maple trees on school grounds. They figured the trees' leaves would take carbon dioxide out of the air and in this way help fight global warming. By talking to their friends and neighbors, the students had hoped to collect enough money for 10 trees. Instead, 25 wrapped-and-bundled saplings stood ready to be planted beneath the clear blue sky.

Social scientists who study the interaction between people and their environment are known as **geographers.** These social scientists also map the features of the Earth's surface. In the Unit 6 readings, you will learn how to think like a geographer. In the experiments, you will see how Geography touches your life.

Geography and You

Geography affects you every day. It determines the weather around you, the food you eat, even the prices on the things you want to buy. The questions below will help you understand your connections with Geography.

1. What actions, if any, can a student like yourself take to help conserve the Earth's limited resources?

2. Imagine a perfect combination of physical features in a landscape where you would want to live. What features would you want this landscape to contain, and why?

3. Describe the area where you live. What are its most important physical features? What kinds of work do people in your area do?

UNIT 6 CONTENTS

What Is Geography?

The word *geography* comes from two Greek words: *geo,* meaning "Earth," and *graphos,* meaning "charting or mapping." People who study Geography are called **geographers.** To a geographer, Geography is much more than just the charting or mapping of the Earth. **Geography** is the study of where things are on Earth, why they are there, and their relationships to people, things, or other places.

There are two main branches of Geography, physical and human. **Physical Geography** is the study of the natural features of Earth, including the land, water, and atmosphere. **Human Geography** is the study of the impact humans have on our planet. This branch of Geography focuses on the ways in which people create cultures in their natural environments. It looks at how people use the resources of the planet and how people change the environment to suit their needs.

To help people understand the importance of learning about their world, one group of geographers has developed a framework of five themes—location, place, human-environment interaction, movement, and regions. These five themes can be used to examine both Physical and Human Geography. As we begin our study of Geography, we will use these themes to organize our knowledge and get a clear picture of the world around us. Read the chart on page 268 to learn more about these important themes.

In this unit, you will have an opportunity to develop some of the key skills that geog-

The study of physical geography includes vegetation such as this rain forest.

raphers use every day in making their important discoveries about people and our world. We will be asking some of the same

Five Themes in Geography*

Theme	Description
Location	Location is our position on Earth's surface. Geographers describe location in two ways, absolute and relative. Absolute location tells exactly where something is located. Relative location tells where something is located in relation to a place you already know. If you were giving friends the absolute location of your home (109 Third Street), you probably would also give them the relative location (five blocks north of the high school).
Place	No two places on Earth are exactly alike, just as no two human beings are exactly the same. The physical characteristics of a place, such as landforms, vegetation, and climate, combine in many different ways to give a place unique physical conditions. Human characteristics, such as language, religion, and beliefs, define a place's human character. Geographers use the physical and human characteristics of a place to identify and describe it.
Human-Environment Interaction	Everywhere on Earth, people have interacted with the environment to meet their needs. To do this, they have changed and adapted to their surroundings in many different ways. In the Middle East, irrigation has made it possible to turn vast areas of desert into land for growing crops. When industrialized countries, like the United States and Japan, ran out of room in their crowded cities, they built taller and taller buildings. Today, geographers study the interaction between people and their environment to learn how people use Earth's resources and how that use affects geographical systems.
Movement	People interact with each other as they move from place to place. By studying human movement, geographers can learn how we are all connected to each other. For example, Americans have been moving to the "sunbelt" of the south and away from the "snowbelt" of the northeast for the past 20 years. By studying this migration, geographers can better understand what effects this movement has had on people and the environment. People also interact with each other through the exchange of goods and ideas. Geographers might study, for instance, how blue jeans or the idea of democracy has spread from one place to other areas of the world.
Regions	A region is the basic unit of geographic study. Regions are areas that have certain characteristics in common. In a region people may speak the same language or they may share the same government or everyone may live on or near a certain mountain range. Geographers divide the world into regions because it is easier and more convenient to think about Earth and its people in smaller units.

*Adapted from *Guidelines for Geographic Education,* prepared by the National Council for Geographic Education and the American Association of Geographers. (See Acknowledgements, pages 595–596.)

Water buffalo seek relief from the afternoon sun in central Africa. How does the geography of this region affect the wildlife?

questions that geographers ask, such as Where is it? Why is it located there? and How is it related to other people, things, or places?

You will be working with maps and globes—two of the geographer's most important tools—to find the answers to questions like those. You will also be studying and analyzing information from tables, graphs, and charts to find out how people live in their environments in our own country and in countries all around the world.

Throughout this unit, you will have a chance to put yourself in the place of both the physical geographer and the human geographer. You will then be able to come to grips with some of the most important challenges that geographers face in studying the world.

READING REVIEW

1. From what two Greek words do we get our English word Geography? What do those two words mean?
2. What are the two main branches of Geography? What do geographers in each branch study?
3. Name the five themes of the framework developed by geographers to study our world.

Critical Thinking

4. **Identifying Central Issues** (see page 14) What do geographers believe makes one culture different from another—the ideas and preferences of the people or the features of the land they live on?

How Much Do You Know About Geography?

Let's see how much you already know about Geography. On a separate sheet of paper, answer the following questions as accurately as you can. This experiment will not count toward your grade.

1. On the map below, each continent is labeled with a letter. Identify each continent by its letter.
2. On which continent is the United States located?
3. What are some advantages and disadvantages of maps?

4. What are some advantages and disadvantages of globes?
5. In what direction do longitude lines run? What do they measure?
6. How do latitude lines run? What do they measure?
7. What are five characteristics of every good map and globe?
8. What is a system?
9. Everybody is connected to everybody else on our planet. Why is this statement true?
10. The United States depends upon cer-

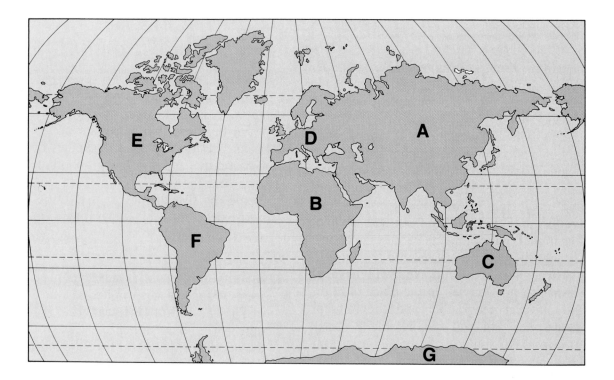

An isolated lighthouse, used to warn ships of shallow waters, stands in front of majestic mountains that surround a sheltered bay. On what features would a physical geographer focus? How does the focus of a human geographer differ from that of a physical geographer?

tain natural resources for its national well-being. Can you name five such natural resources and the foreign countries from which they come?

11. What effects does a constantly increasing population have on the Earth, its people, and its resources?

12. Why is the United States and practically every other country dependent upon many other nations to help supply its needs?

13. What is the difference between a developed country and a developing country? Can you name three of each?

14. How many children live in poverty in our country?

15. What is a time zone? Why do we have time zones?

16. Describe one important problem faced by our planet and its people.

17. What skills does it take to become a geographer?

Location: Where on Earth Are We?

"Where are you?"

If a friend asked you this question over the phone, how would you answer? You could say that you are in school or at home. That information wouldn't help very much, however, if your friend didn't know where your home or school is located. You would have to be more specific if you wanted that person to be able to find you.

You might say that the location of the school, for example, is the corner of Third Street and Gregg Street, which is five blocks south of your home. Or you might give the location of your home as 109 Third Street.

When geographers want to indicate the **location,** or position, of something on the Earth's surface, they usually use a globe or map. A **globe** is a small model of our round-shaped planet Earth. A **map** is a flat representation of Earth. Maps are more convenient to carry around and they are easier to duplicate than globes. A map's flatness, however, creates a special problem—there is no good way to transfer the globe's information accurately onto a flat surface. The Earth's round surface becomes distorted on a map. Carefully examine a globe. Then compare it with the maps on page 273.

Geographers describe the location of places on Earth in two ways. One of these, **absolute location,** describes the exact locations. The absolute location of your home is 109 Third Street. There is no other home except yours at that address.

Every place on our planet has an "address"—an exact description of its location

on Earth. Geographers put lines on their maps and globes to help them pinpoint exact locations of places. The lines run east to west and north to south, forming a grid. The east-west lines are called **latitude lines,** while the north-south lines are known as **longitude lines.**

All longitude lines eventually meet at the North and South Poles of our planet. Every latitude and longitude line is numbered. If you want to describe where Chicago is located, you can tell that city's "address" by identifying the numbers of the latitude and longitude lines that run through Chicago.

Your Town

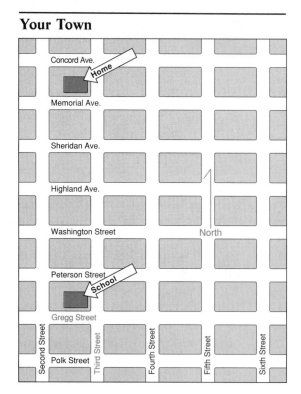

Types of Map Projections

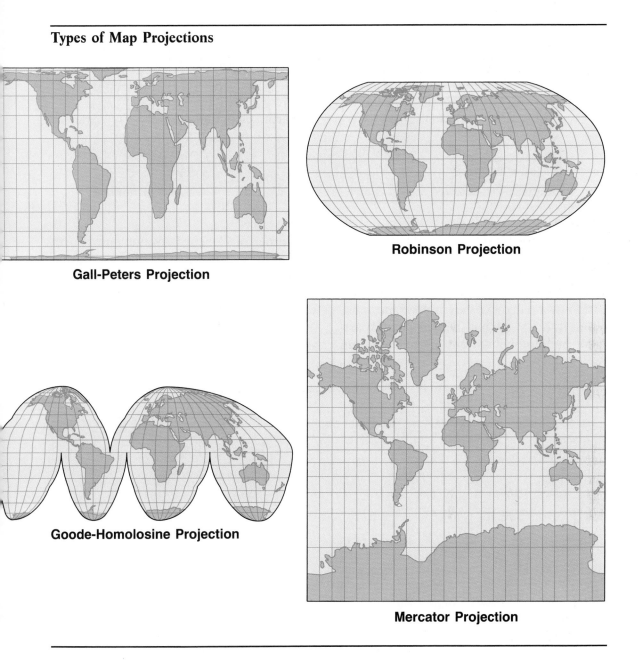

Gall-Peters Projection

Robinson Projection

Goode-Homolosine Projection

Mercator Projection

Those two numbers are Chicago's absolute location on our planet.

Geographers also want to know the relative location of places. **Relative location** is the location of a place in relation to other places. In relation to your home, the location of your school is five blocks to the south. The country of Vietnam is located more than 10,000 miles southwest of where we live. We could also identify Viet-

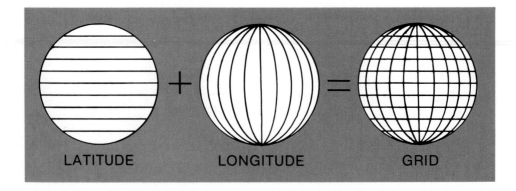

LATITUDE + LONGITUDE = GRID

nam's relative location as south of China, northwest of New Zealand and Australia, and east of India.

If we know the relative and absolute location of a place, we can understand more about it. Let's say that there is a new apartment building being built in your town on the corner of Concord Avenue and Fourth Street. There will be a lot of noise during the first year of construction. How close will the construction be to your home and your school?

The map of "your town" on page 272 shows you exactly where the corner of Con-

Vietnam: Relative Location

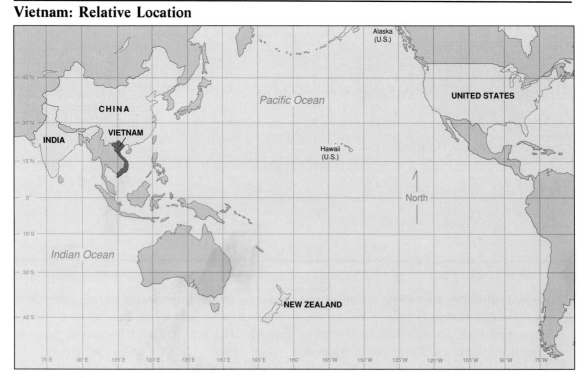

cord and Fourth is located—its absolute location. You look closely at the map and find that the new building will be built six blocks northeast of your school and one block northeast of your home—its relative location. By determining the new building's relative location, can you predict whether you might hear more construction noise from your home or from your school? Why can you tell this from the map?

In "Experiment 6-B: *Location:* Map Making," you will have a chance to use your understanding of relative and absolute location as you create a map of an area that is familiar to you.

1. What does a geographer mean by the term *location*?
2. How are maps and globes similar? How are they different?
3. Describe one advantage of maps over globes and one advantage of globes over maps.

Critical Thinking

4. **Determining Relevance** (see page 17) How are absolute and relative location important to the geographer's work?

Location: Map Making

When geographers want to show the location of something, they make maps. How are maps made?

First, the geographer surveys or measures the area to be mapped and then draws a picture of the area. To be sure the map is accurate, the geographer then makes a **grid,** or a pattern of lines running horizontally (across) and vertically (up and down). By numbering the lines, or using a combination of numbers and letters, the geographer can show the absolute location of a city, a lake, or any other human or physical feature.

The geographer also shows **direction** on the grid, usually by drawing an arrow pointing north, with a capital N near the arrow's point. (See Figure 1 on page 276.) It may take another form and show eight major directions. (See Figure 2 on page 276.) Direction helps the geographer to show relative location. For example, California is west relative to New York or Florida.

Most maps show **scale,** or how large the map's territory really is. Without knowing a map's scale, it is impossible to determine distance on a map. After all, it makes a big difference if the spaces in a grid represent 1 square mile or 1,000 square miles. If you are trying to reach a location shown on a map, but don't know the distance, it would be very hard to figure out how long it would take.

Scale can be shown in various ways. It may appear as a bar scale. (See Figure 3 on page 276.) Or, it can be shown as an inch- (or centimeter)-to-mile scale:

> **1 inch to 34 miles**
> **1 cm to 20 km**

Of course, every good map has a title telling what the map represents. It also has a **key,** or **legend,** telling what the map's symbols mean.

Now that you know about maps, how about making one yourself? Draw a map of one of the following: (1) your room at home, (2) the route from your home to school, (3) your neighborhood, showing roads, stores, buildings, and homes, or (4) your house or apartment.

Don't forget to include in your map the five main features of every good map: title, key, direction, scale, and a location grid showing lines that run vertically and horizontally. Mark the vertical lines with letters (A, B, C, etc.) and the horizontal lines with numbers (1, 2, 3, etc.). This will help anyone using the map to find a location.

Make sure your map is as accurate as possible. (What good is an inaccurate map?) Bring your map to class.

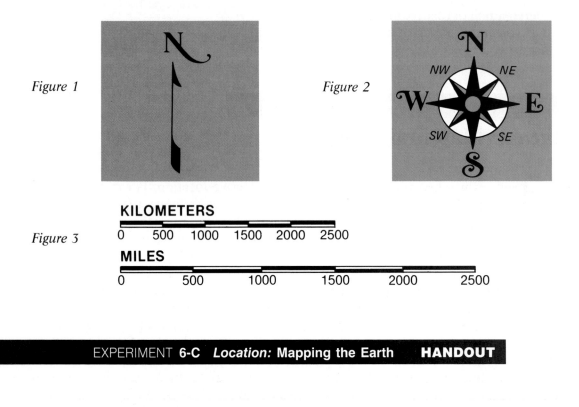

Figure 1

Figure 2

Figure 3

KILOMETERS

0   500   1000 1500 2000 2500

MILES

0   500   1000   1500   2000   2500

READING 3

Location: Types of Maps

There are many types of maps. Each type serves a different purpose. A *political map* shows the location of countries, states, and provinces, with the boundary lines separating those governments. On page 277 is a political map of Europe.

Europe: Political Map

Suppose you want to know the location of an area's physical features—lakes, rivers, mountains, plateaus, valleys, and seas. For this information, you would consult a *physical map*. On page 278 is a physical map showing the same area as the political map of Europe. Compare the information given on each. On a physical map you get an idea of the location of natural features of an area, such as mountain ranges and rivers. On a political map you see an area as it has been divided by governments. Boundary lines and names of countries may change from time to time on a political map. Such changes show the changes in government. Physical maps, on the other hand, do not change very much over the years. Why do you think this is so?

What kind of map would you use to find out the occupations and resources in an area? Political and physical maps would do you no good. To get that information, you would need an *economic map*. On the economic map of Poland on page 279 you can see the locations of natural resources, industrial areas, farmlands, and fishing areas.

The kind of map most car drivers use is still another type. It is a *road map,* or *transportation map*. Road maps show types of roads and the location of hospitals, airports, cities, and points of interest. Gas stations and motor clubs sell road maps.

Europe: Physical Map

Still other types of maps show temperature and rainfall, climate, vegetation (forests, grasslands, etc.) population density (the number of people per mile or kilometer), religion, language distribution, land use, economic data, and other information. In this unit you will see more examples of different kinds of maps.

All maps and globes are designed by geographers to help us learn more about the locations of people, places, and things in our world. As you can see, maps should be carefully selected to obtain the specific types of information for which you are looking.

READING REVIEW

1. What information does a political map give?
2. Describe the information shown in physical maps.
3. What does an economic map show?
4. What is the purpose of a road map?

Critical Thinking

5. **Identifying Alternatives** (see page 38) Think of two sources besides an economic map that you could use to get information about the occupations and resources in an area.

Poland: Land Use and Economy

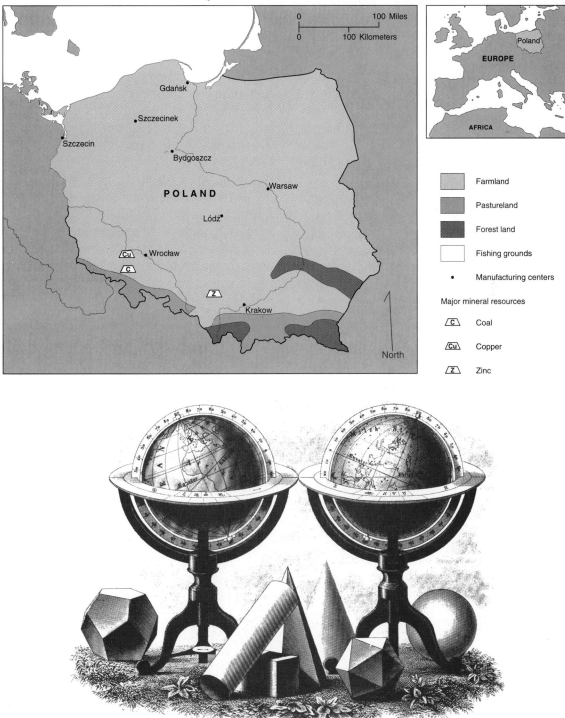

	Farmland
	Pastureland
	Forest land
	Fishing grounds
•	Manufacturing centers

Major mineral resources

/C\	Coal
/Cu\	Copper
/Z\	Zinc

EUROPE

Poland

AFRICA

Gdańsk

Szczecinek

Szczecin

Bydgoszcz

POLAND

Warsaw

Łódź

Cu Wrocław

C

Z

Kraków

North

0   100 Miles
0   100 Kilometers

Location: Interpreting Maps

In this experiment you will have a chance to interpret several kinds of maps. You will also be putting your knowledge to work about the five elements of a good map: title, key or legend, latitude and longitude, direction, and scale. Answer all questions on a separate sheet of paper.

PART ONE: **Road Maps**

Suppose you are planning to take an automobile trip throughout California. Before you start your tour of the state, you will need to consult an up-to-date road map. Using the road map of California on page 281, find the answers to these questions:

1. Look at the map's key (legend). What kinds of roads are shown? On the map, find one example of each kind of road.

2. You plan to drive from Los Angeles to San Francisco. In what direction will you be traveling? Which element of this map helped you determine your direction?

3. You decide that part of your tour will take you directly from Santa Cruz to Santa Barbara. Approximately how many miles are between those two cities? How many kilometers is that? Which element of this map helped you determine the distance?

4. If you decided to travel along the Pacific coast from Monterey to Morro Bay, what route would you take? If you preferred to take an inland route, what U.S. highway might you use?

5. You want to visit Lake Tahoe, located on California's eastern border. With what state does California share most of its eastern boundary?

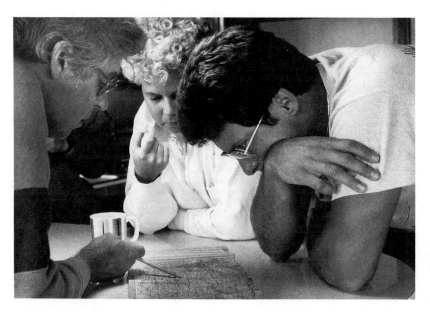

Planning an automobile trip requires the use of a road map. What information does a road map provide?

California Road Map

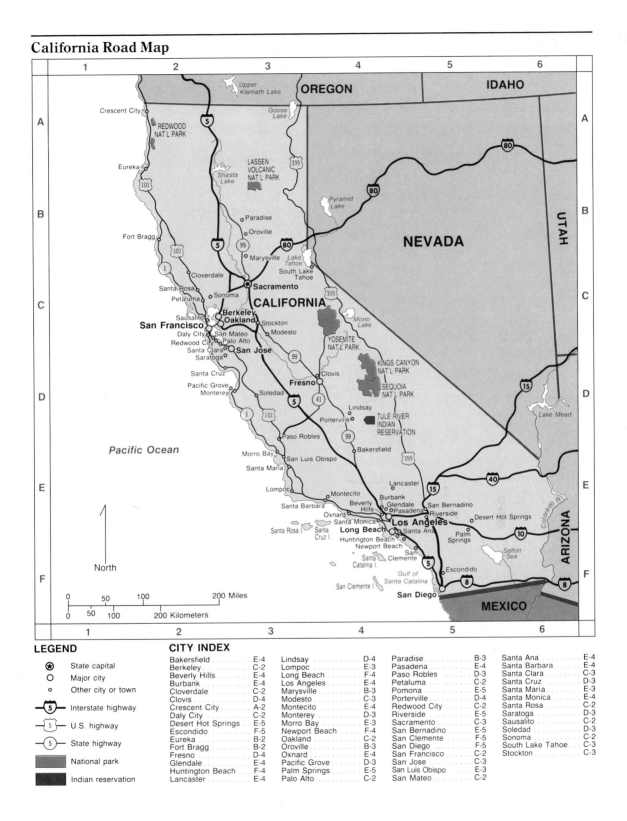

LEGEND

- ⊛ State capital
- ○ Major city
- ○ Other city or town
- 🛡5 Interstate highway
- 〔5〕 U.S. highway
- ⬡5 State highway
- ▬ National park
- ▬ Indian reservation

CITY INDEX

City	Grid
Bakersfield	E-4
Berkeley	C-2
Beverly Hills	E-4
Burbank	E-4
Cloverdale	C-2
Clovis	D-4
Crescent City	A-2
Daly City	C-2
Desert Hot Springs	E-5
Escondido	F-5
Eureka	B-2
Fort Bragg	B-2
Fresno	D-4
Glendale	E-4
Huntington Beach	F-4
Lancaster	E-4
Lindsay	D-4
Lompoc	E-3
Long Beach	F-4
Los Angeles	E-4
Marysville	B-3
Modesto	C-3
Montecito	E-4
Monterey	D-3
Morro Bay	E-3
Newport Beach	F-4
Oakland	C-2
Oroville	B-3
Oxnard	E-4
Pacific Grove	D-3
Palm Springs	E-5
Palo Alto	C-2
Paradise	B-3
Pasadena	E-4
Paso Robles	D-3
Petaluma	C-2
Pomona	E-5
Porterville	D-4
Redwood City	C-2
Riverside	E-5
Sacramento	C-3
San Bernardino	E-5
San Clemente	F-5
San Diego	F-5
San Francisco	C-2
San Jose	C-3
San Luis Obispo	E-3
San Mateo	C-2
Santa Ana	E-4
Santa Barbara	E-4
Santa Clara	C-3
Santa Cruz	D-3
Santa Maria	E-3
Santa Monica	E-4
Santa Rosa	C-2
Saratoga	D-3
Sausalito	C-2
Soledad	D-3
Sonoma	C-2
South Lake Tahoe	C-3
Stockton	C-3

Africa: Physical Map

EUROPE

ASIA

North Atlantic Ocean

Black Sea

Caspian Sea

40° North Latitude

ASIA MINOR

Iberian Peninsula

Strait of Gibraltar

NORTHERN HIGHLANDS

Madeira Is.

Atlas Mts.

Mediterranean Sea

COASTAL LOWLANDS

Nile Delta

Jebel Toubkal 13,665 ft. (4,165 m.)

Sinai

Canary Is.

S a h a r a

Qattara Depression

Nile R.

Tropic of Cancer

Libyan Desert

Lake Nasser

Arabian Peninsula

20°

Ahaggar Mts.

Tassili N'Ajjer

SAHARAN PLATEAU

Tibesti Mts.

Nubian Desert

Red Sea

Cape Verde

LOW AFRICA

NILE BASIN

Senegal R.

Niger R.

S a h e l

Atbara R.

Gulf of Aden

Socotra I.

Jallon Mts.

WESTERN   PLATEAU

Jos Plateau

Lake Chad

Chari R.

S u d a n

White Nile

Ras Dashan 15,157 ft. (4,620 m.)

Cape Guardafui

Lake Volta

Benue R.

Ethiopian Highlands

Cape Palmas

Niger Delta

Gulf of Guinea

Adamawa Massif

Ubangi R.

0° Equator

Principe I.

São Tomé I.

CONGO BASIN

Great Rift Valley

Lake Victoria

HIGHLANDS

Mt. Kenya 17,058 ft. (5,199 m.)

0°

Mt. Kilimanjaro 19,340 ft. (5,895 m.)

Kasai R.

Serengeti Plain

Pemba I.

Indian Ocean

South Atlantic Ocean

Lake Tanganyika

EASTERN

Zanzibar I.

Comoro Islands

Bihe Plateau

HIGH AFRICA

Zambezi R.

Mozambique Channel

MADAGASCAR I.

20°

SOUTHERN

Victoria Falls

20°

Tropic of Capricorn

Namib Desert

PLATEAU

Limpopo R.

Reunion I.

Kalahari Desert

Orange R.

Vaal R.

Drakensberg

North

Cape of Good Hope

Cape Agulhas

40° South Latitude

40°

| 0 | 500 | 1,000 Miles |

| 0 | 500 | 1,000 Kilometers |

40°

20° West Longitude

0° Prime Meridian

20° East Longitude

6. You are thinking about going to San Clemente Island (southwest of Long Beach) for a few days. In what body of water is San Clemente Island located?

7. You are trying to decide on other California places you want to visit. Using the map grid, locate the following places: Sonoma, San Bernadino, Fort Bragg, Lassen Volcanic National Park, Palm Springs, and Yosemite National Park. Indicate the number and letter you used to locate each place.

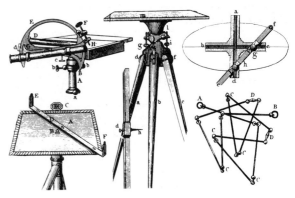

PART TWO: **Physical Maps**

Suppose your local travel agency is holding a geography contest. The contestant who can correctly answer the most questions about the continent of Africa will be declared the winner. The grand prize is a free two-week trip throughout Africa. You decide to enter the contest, and you begin studying maps of Africa. See how many of these questions about Africa you can answer by consulting the physical map of Africa on page 282:

1. What is the name of the mountain range located in northwest Africa?

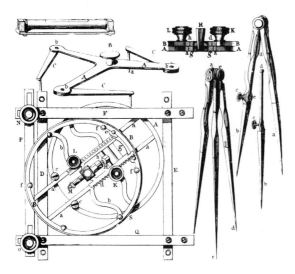

2. In what parts of Africa do you find deserts known as the Sahara and the Kalahari?

3. What degree of latitude runs through Madagascar? What degree of longitude on this map is closest to the Cape of Good Hope?

4. What body of water separates Africa from the Arabian Peninsula?

5. The Niger River (in northwest Africa) empties into the Niger Delta, which in turn empties into another body of water. What is the name of that body of water?

6. To go from the Mediterranean Sea to Lake Nasser, you could travel on which river?

7. What is the title of this map?

PART THREE: **Political Maps**

To prepare for the contest, you also study political maps of Africa. Find the answers to these questions, using the political map of Africa on page 284:

1. What countries border Liberia?

2. Through which country does the Congo River flow?

3. In what two countries are the Atlas Mountains located?

4. What are the capital cities of Ethiopia, Zaire, Madagascar, and Burkina Faso?

Africa: Political Map

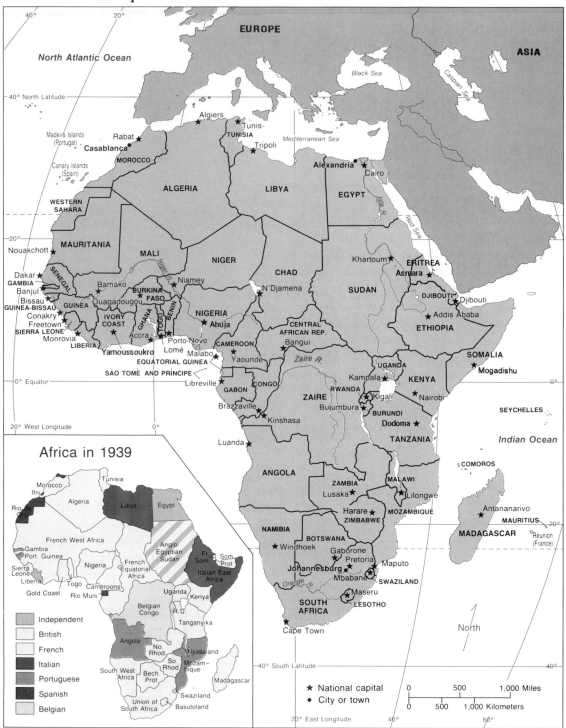

EUROPE

ASIA

North Atlantic Ocean

Black Sea

Caspian Sea

40° North Latitude

Algiers ★

Madeira Islands
(Portugal)

Rabat ★
Casablanca •

Tunis ★
TUNISIA

Tripoli ★

Mediterranean Sea

MOROCCO

Canary Islands
(Spain)

WESTERN
SAHARA

ALGERIA

LIBYA

Alexandria • ★
Cairo

EGYPT

Nile R.

Red Sea

20°

MAURITANIA

Nouakchott ★

MALI

NIGER

CHAD

Khartoum •

ERITREA
Asmara ★

DJIBOUTI
Djibouti •

Dakar •
GAMBIA
Banjul •
Bissau •
GUINEA-BISSAU
Conakry •
Freetown •
SIERRA LEONE
Monrovia •
LIBERIA

SENEGAL

Bamako •

Niamey ★

N'Djamena •

SUDAN

Addis Ababa ★

ETHIOPIA

BURKINA
FASO
Ouagadougou ★

GUINEA

IVORY
COAST

GHANA
TOGO
BENIN

NIGERIA

Abuja ★

CENTRAL
AFRICAN REP.

Accra •

Yamoussoukro ★

Porto-Novo ★
Lomé ★ Malabo •

Bangui ★

SOMALIA

CAMEROON

EQUATORIAL GUINEA

Yaounde ★

Zaire R.

UGANDA

Mogadishu ★

SÃO TOMÉ AND PRÍNCIPE

Libreville ★

Kampala ★

KENYA

0° Equator

GABON

CONGO

ZAIRE

RWANDA

Kigali ★

Nairobi ★

0°

20° West Longitude

0°

Brazzaville ★

Bujumbura ★
BURUNDI

SEYCHELLES

Kinshasa ★

Dodoma ★

Indian Ocean

TANZANIA

Luanda ★

COMOROS

Africa in 1939

ANGOLA

ZAMBIA

MALAWI

Lusaka ★

Lilongwe ★

Antananarivo •

MAURITIUS

Morocco
Ifni

Tunisia

Algeria

Libya

Egypt

Harare ★
ZIMBABWE

MOZAMBIQUE

MADAGASCAR

Reunion
(France)

Rio de
Oro

French West Africa

Anglo-
Egyptian
Sudan

Fr.
Som

Som.
Prot.

NAMIBIA

BOTSWANA

20°

Gambia
Port. Guinea

Nigeria

French
Equatorial
Africa

Italian East
Africa

Windhoek ★

Gaborone ★
Pretoria ★

Maputo •

Sierra
Leone

Liberia

Togo

Cameroons

Uganda

Kenya

Johannesburg •

Mbabane ★
Maseru ★

SWAZILAND

Gold Coast

Rio Muni

Belgian
Congo

R. U.

Orange

LESOTHO

Tanganyika

SOUTH
AFRICA

Angola

No.
Rhod.

Nyasaland

Mozam-
bique

Cape Town •

North

40° South Latitude

40°

South West
Africa

So.
Rhod.

Bech.
Prot.

Madagascar

Independent

British

French

Union of
South Africa

Swaziland

Basutoland

★ National capital

0   500   1,000 Miles

Italian

Portuguese

Spanish

Belgian

• City or town

0   500   1,000 Kilometers

20° East Longitude

40°

60°

5. Approximately how many miles are between Cairo and Khartoum? How many kilometers is that?

6. What are the main differences between the physical map of Africa and the political map of that continent?

7. Now study the map inset. You can see that major political changes have taken place in Africa between 1939 and today. Even if you don't know the history of Africa, you can understand something about it by examining these two maps. Describe as well as you can the political changes you think the two maps show.

8. What were these countries called in 1939: Zaire, Kenya, Ivory Coast, Chad, Somalia?

PART FOUR: **Economic Maps**

A foreign exchange student from Italy is studying at your school this year. You would like to get to know this student, so

Italy: Land Use and Economy

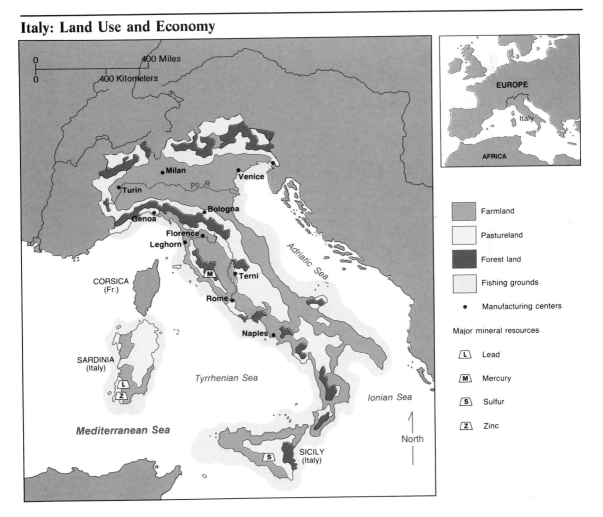

you begin to read about Italy. You want to be able to talk about Italy's land and economy with your new friend. Using the economic map of Italy on page 285, find the answers to the following questions:

1. Is more farmland located in the north or the south of Italy?
2. What two major mineral resources are located in the south of Sardinia, an island that is part of Italy?
3. Your Italian friend tells you that neighbors back home work in sulfur mines.

Based on the information in this map, where does your friend live?
4. Some of your friend's relatives work in the fishing industry. Where in Italy do you think those relatives might live?
5. Your friend's family is in the business of exporting products to neighboring countries. Which countries are located closest to Italy?
6. You know that Rome is Italy's capital and a major manufacturing center. Which three Italian manufacturing centers are nearest to Rome?

Place: The Earth and Its People

All **places** on Earth are different. A place is what geographers find at a location. All places have different absolute and relative locations. They also have different characteristics. When geographers want to identify and describe a place, they look at its physical characteristics and its human characteristics.

Earth's *physical characteristics* include its landforms, water, climate, and vegetation. Physical characteristics combine in many ways to produce a variety of natural environments from the lush tropical rain forests of South America to the cold, barren sweeps of the Arctic. If you look down at Earth from space, the marbled shades of blues, browns, and greens that you view only hint at the richness of the world below.

The colored patterns you see on Earth's surface are land and water. Land covers less than 30 percent of Earth's surface. The rest of the planet, over 70 percent, is covered with water.

The bodies of water on our planet are almost all connected with one another. The **oceans** are the largest water masses on Earth. Of the four oceans—the Pacific, the Atlantic, the Indian, and the Arctic—the Pacific Ocean is the largest. *Seas* are smaller than oceans. Examples of seas include the Mediterranean Sea, the Caribbean Sea, the North Sea, and the Black Sea. Other bodies of water include gulfs, lakes, rivers, streams, and ponds.

Earth's land mass is separated into seven major parts, known as **continents.** They are called North America, South America, Europe, Africa, Asia, Australia, and Antarctica. The land of our planet takes many different shapes called **landforms.** For example, level stretches of land with low elevations are called *plains*. Level land that is at least 300 feet (91 meters) above sea level is called a *plateau*. *Hills* are sloping landforms at an elevation of less than 2,000 feet (606 meters) above sea level. *Mountains* are landforms at an elevation of more than 2,000 feet (606 meters) above sea level.

Wrapped around Earth is a layer of air called the **atmosphere.** Carbon dioxide and oxygen, both necessary for life, are found in the atmosphere. A layer of ozone, which is invisible, protects all Earth's living things from the harmful effects of the sun's rays. The atmosphere is also where our weather develops.

There are many different **climates** in the world. A climate is the main kind of weather in an area. Differences in latitude, or how far an area is from the equator, is one reason for variations in climate. Many differences, however, are caused by Earth's atmosphere. The temperature, or amount of heat in the air, changes depending on where on Earth you are. The nearer you are to the equator, where the sun shines most directly, the warmer the temperature will be. Wind, or the movement of air from one area to another, causes changes in temperature. For example, winds that blow from the North and South Poles bring cold air. The amount of **precipitation,** or water in the air that falls as rain, hail, or snow, also makes a difference in an area's climate.

There are many natural vegetation regions on Earth. A **natural vegetation region** is an area that has common types of plant life. The kind of vegetation depends mainly on climate. You may be familiar with some natural vegetation areas such as deserts, forests, and grasslands.

Here are some natural vegetation areas you may not know. *Savannah* is grassland

This photograph of the Earth taken from the Apollo 17 *spacecraft clearly shows clouds.*

that is sometimes dotted with small trees. It is most often found in areas where there is both a rainy season and a dry season. *Steppe* is also grassland, but it is usually treeless. This vegetation area is found in climates where there is moderate rainfall throughout the year and mild summers and winters. *Tundra* refers to treeless plains of semi-frozen land that never completely thaws in summer. *Tropical rain forests* contain tall, densely growing evergreen trees and are usually found close to the equator. These forests grow in hot and humid areas that have heavy rainfall. Take a look at the map on page 288 to see where Earth's natural vegetation regions are located.

As you've read, every place on Earth has different physical characteristics. Almost every place also has human characteristics. The *human characteristics* of a place include the language, values, religion, ideas,

Natural Vegetation Regions of the World

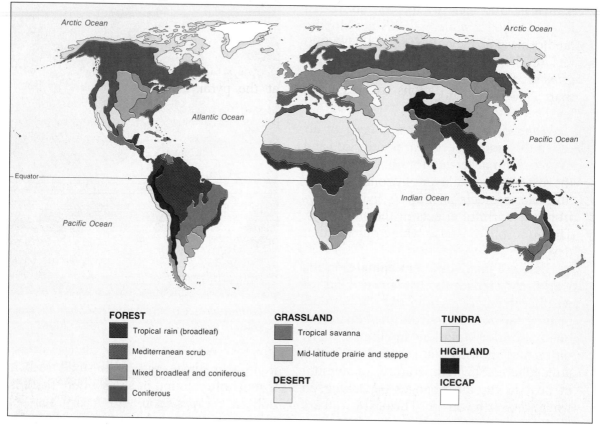

FOREST
- Tropical rain (broadleaf)
- Mediterranean scrub
- Mixed broadleaf and coniferous
- Coniferous

GRASSLAND
- Tropical savanna
- Mid-latitude prairie and steppe

DESERT

TUNDRA

HIGHLAND

ICECAP

art, customs, social institutions, and technology of the people who live there. Human characteristics combine to give a place its unique human identity. Just think of the rich diversity of cultures in our world. Compare, for example, the different ways of life in Japan and the United States. Both countries are highly industrialized and play an important role in the world, yet their language, values, ideas, art, customs, and social institutions are very different. Or think about the different places within the United States and the people living in these places. How have their backgrounds (English, Chinese, Mexican, German, Kenyan,

etc.) contributed to the unique character of the places in which they live?

The human characteristics of a place can be influenced by its history. For example, during colonial rule, wealth and power in Latin America were concentrated in the hands of the relatively few large landholders. Most of the rest of the people, unable to own their own land, were forced to work for the landholders. Even after Latin American countries won their independence from Spain and Portugal, people in countries like El Salvador and Nicaragua worked for low wages on the lands of rich landowners and foreign corporations.

These countries were characterized by social, political, and economic inequality as a result. Today, many Latin American countries are plagued by social unrest and war as people struggle for change.

Population statistics also help to describe a place. Large populations use resources differently than small populations do. The size of a population can be influenced by many things, including the availability of resources, birth and death rates, and immigration and emigration. Values influence population growth, too. For example, countries that have traditionally placed great importance on large families, such as India, often have large populations. A large population will need more water, food, and land than a small population needs. Sometimes there are not enough resources available to feed, clothe, and shelter everyone in a large population, and many people live in poverty.

Human characteristics include the things people have done to a place. Buildings, signs, and agriculture all tell us about the people who live in a place. When we look at the pyramids of Egypt, we can learn about the religion, social organization, values, technology, art, and customs of a powerful civilization that existed nearly 5,000 years ago. We can learn about many of the same things about the United States by looking at the skyscrapers of New York City or Chicago.

No two places on our Earth are alike. Every place has unique physical and human characteristics. Appreciating what makes places different from one another is important so we can understand the Earth and its people and prosper as a planet.

The human characteristics of Japan include the culture and social customs of the people.

The Egyptian pyramids tell geographers much about Egypt's ancient civilization.

READING REVIEW

1. Describe what is meant by the physical characteristics of a place.
2. What is the relationship between a location and a place?
3. What do geographers mean when they talk about the human characteristics of a place?
4. Why is studying the physical characteristics and human characteristics of a place important?

Critical Thinking

5. **Recognizing Cause and Effect** (see page 35) Why would the human characteristics of a place be likely to change over time?

EXPERIMENT 6-E   *Place:* Finding the Best Place To Live   **HANDOUT**

EXPERIMENT   **6-F**

Human-Environment Interaction: What Is a System?

Geographers are concerned with **systems.** A system is a working thing made of two or more parts. If a system is to operate properly, the parts must work together in a certain way. All parts must do their jobs. If just one part breaks down, slows down, or stops working, the entire system is unfavorably affected.

Let's examine several systems. The first system will be presented by your teacher. It is a system with which you are familiar. See if you can figure out what it is about that object that makes it a system. Use the definition of *system* given above.

There are two kinds of systems: open and closed.* An **open system** cannot operate on its own. It may need a starter, or it may need help to keep it going. A flashlight is an open system. It must be started by an outside source. Its bulb and batteries must be replaced when they wear out. Because a

*The discussion of open and closed systems was adapted with permission from *Teaching About Spaceship Earth, Intercom #71.* (See Acknowledgements, pages 595–596).

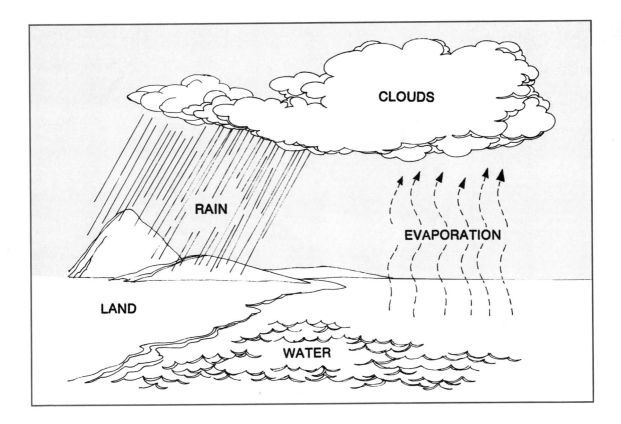

CLOUDS

RAIN

EVAPORATION

LAND

WATER

flashlight cannot operate on its own, it is an open system.

Closed systems, on the other hand, operate on their own. They start themselves and keep going by themselves. They need no outside source to operate. In many cases outside "help" can damage or even destroy a closed system. The Earth's water cycle is a closed system. Can you describe this system, using the illustration above?

Rube Goldberg, a writer and artist, created funny and unbelievable systems. On page 292 is an example of his work. Is this system open or closed? Can you figure out how it works? What would happen if just one part of the system were taken out? Pretend that any one part of the system

stopped working or was missing. What would happen to the system?

As you are beginning to see, systems depend upon their parts. In both closed and open systems, the parts of the systems are interdependent. That is, the parts are all dependent upon one another to make the system work.

Our Earth is a system. Earth's parts are its animals, plants, soil, minerals, water, air, and birds. All the parts work together without outside help or interference.

People are also a part of the Earth's system. When people began to live on the Earth, they started to interact with Earth. Sometimes these interactions disturbed the system. For example, fuels such as coal and

When you pick up morning paper(A), string (B) opens door of bird-cage (C) and bird (D) follows bird-seed (E) up platform (F), and falls over edge into pitcher of water (G) – water splashes on flower (H), which grows, pushing up rod (I), causing string (J) to fire pistol (K) – shot scares monkey (L) who jumps up, hitting head against bumper (M), forcing razor (N) down into egg (O) loosened shell falls into saucer (P).

Rube Goldberg © King Features Syndicate, Inc. 1928.

petroleum, which took nature millions of years to produce, were taken from the ground and used immediately. In many cases the animal life and plant life were chased away or destroyed in the process of mining and drilling. Layers of rich topsoil were dug up and destroyed. (There are other ways humans have interfered with the Earth's system. Can you think of any?)

The Earth's smooth-running system was interfered with because people were not wise or careful. Today, however, we know

that humans can exist with nature without disturbing the Earth's system. When parts are taken from the system they must be put back. Or, substitute parts must be found and put into the system. For example, we now know that after coal and minerals are taken from the ground, we should replace the soil and replant vegetation.

There is one thing we should never forget. We are all part of the Earth system. *Everything* we do to the Earth system—good *and* bad—will affect us in some way.

Human-Environment Interaction: Everything Is Connected To Everything Else*

As you have read, a system is made up of parts that must work together. If only one

part breaks down or is changed, the whole system is affected.

Our planet is a system of many parts. This Earth system is called the **ecosystem.** The study of our ecosystem is known as

*This reading, together with the diagram on page 295, is adapted from Barry Commoner, *The Closing Circle.* (See Acknowledgements, pages 595–596).

ecology. The first part of both words— *eco*—comes from a Greek word meaning "house." There are similarities between our planet and a house. Both need to be taken care of. And both can be ruined, or even destroyed, easily by the people who live there.

Geographers and many other people have become concerned, particularly in recent years, about the **interaction** of people with our ecosystem. They are worried about the impact we are having on the delicate balance of our planet's systems as we use Earth's resources.

The smoke from factory chimneys in the United States is releasing sulfur and nitrogen oxides into our air causing **acid rain.** Acid rain is killing fish, trees, and other forms of life. Smog caused by automobile exhaust is eating away at the beautiful Taj Mahal in India, killing millions of acres of pine trees in Europe, and polluting rivers in many countries.

The use of chemicals such as chlorofluorocarbons (CFCs) in refrigeration units and in aerosols is contributing to the destruction of the ozone layer in our atmosphere. Ozone in the atmosphere blocks out many of the sun's damaging rays. Without that layer of ozone, we would not be able to stay in the sun more than a few minutes at a time. In addition, the temperature of our planet would grow warmer. A planet that suddenly became warmer would result in great changes in climates around the world. The polar icecaps would melt, and large areas of the Earth would be flooded. This is what people mean when they talk about the **greenhouse effect.**

These are not just problems for geographers. They are everybody's problem. Barry Commoner is a scientist who is very concerned about the way we take care of the "house" we call Earth. In his book, *The Closing Circle,* Dr. Commoner gives four laws of ecology. These laws can help us understand our ecosystem and our responsibilities to it.

The first law of ecology is this: "Everything is connected to everything else."

This 1936 photograph of Pittsburgh, Pennsylvania, shows the effects of the pollution that once came from its factories.

This photograph, taken in the 1980s, shows the effects of clean-air legislation on Pittsburgh's environment.

Think of the Earth and every living person and thing on it as a system. It may be difficult to believe that if just one part is missing, the whole system can be upset. But it's true. Just think how you would have to change your whole way of life if just one part of the ecosystem—our ozone layer— were gone! No wonder some state and local governments are beginning to seriously consider how to limit the number of cars on our roads. Some states, such as California, have put restrictions on backyard barbecuing, which also contributes to air pollution and the destruction of the ozone layer. What harm could one more car or one more charcoal grill possibly do? If millions of people think that way, the problem

may only get worse, not better. We must work together to solve the problems of our planet.

Dr. Commoner's second law is this: "Everything must go somewhere." Consider the disposal of garbage. When the garbage we throw into the trash can is burned, some of it becomes carbon and gases. The carbon and gases then go into the atmosphere, contributing to the acid rain problem. Some garbage is buried. But we are fast running out of landfills in which to put our garbage. What will we do with it when there is no longer a place to bury it? The problem is severe, because only a small percentage of our trash is **biodegradable.** Something is considered biodegradable if its chemical parts decay over a few years and then return to the ground in usable form. Much of our garbage, unfortunately, doesn't decay at all. It is this kind of matter that is most dangerous to the ecosystem. Plastics, styrofoam, and certain other substances are not biodegradable, so they add to our mounting collection of garbage.

Sometimes, harmful substances actually become more harmful as they go through the ecosystem. Take the powerful poison DDT, for example. DDT was once sprayed on crops to kill bugs and insects that harmed the crops. DDT, however, was discovered to be more harmful to certain forms of life than it was helpful to the crops. Animals living near the area sprayed with DDT were affected. Small fish were also harmed, and in turn so were the larger fish and the birds that fed on them.

The drawing below shows what happens when DDT is used. Remember, all of this is

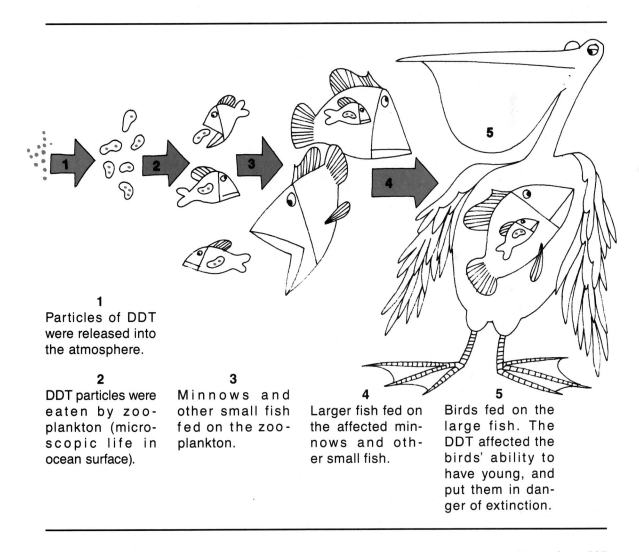

1
Particles of DDT were released into the atmosphere.

2
DDT particles were eaten by zoo-plankton (micro-scopic life in ocean surface).

3
Minnows and other small fish fed on the zoo-plankton.

4
Larger fish fed on the affected min-nows and oth-er small fish.

5
Birds fed on the large fish. The DDT affected the birds' ability to have young, and put them in dan-ger of extinction.

caused by just a small amount of DDT used to prevent crop damage. Everything must go somewhere. Look where the DDT goes after it enters the air, and look at the damage it does. When people interact with the environment, they must be careful to protect all the parts of the ecosystem.

The third law of ecology, which should be fairly obvious by now, is this: "Nature knows best."

Nature is a system that has taken millions of years to develop. With every change humans make in the ecosystem, with every part of the system that is destroyed, nature has to make changes in the rest of the system to keep it all balanced. Humans are capable of destroying in less than a lifetime what it took nature all those centuries to make.

The fourth and last law of ecology sums up the first three laws: "There is no such thing as a free lunch." Everything we do to our ecosystem has a cost. If nature cannot adjust to the demands humans place on the environment, we will pay the price.

The good news is that, over the years, humans have been able to think of ways to make otherwise hostile environments into places where people can live. Humans have adapted themselves to the heat of the deserts, the dangers of the high seas, and the flood plains of the world. We are more aware today than ever before of our responsibility to our planet. We know that water is not an unlimited **resource,** and we must use it wisely. We know the damage that auto pollution can do to the ecosystem, and we must act accordingly. We understand that the "gifts of the Earth" will run out if we do not use them carefully.

READING REVIEW

1. What is the Earth system called?
2. What is ecology?
3. What does the term *biodegradable* mean? Why is that word important?
4. Describe the four laws of ecology.

Critical Thinking

5. **Creating Good Questions** (see page 20) What are three good questions you could ask your local elected officials about their role in protecting the ecosystem?

EXPERIMENT **6-G**

Human-Environment Interaction: Everybody Is Connected to the Systems of Our Planet

PART ONE

How do humans, such as you, your family, and your friends, make an impact on our environment? How are you and your actions connected to our air, water, and land systems? Do those actions improve our planet, or do they help to destroy it?

People have always interacted with the environment. However, some kinds of interaction, like using non-biodegradable materials, have caused the Earth to become polluted. Recycling is one way to help control pollution.

In the next five minutes, focus on this question: What have my family and I done during the last 24 hours to make an impact on the environment? Write down as many things as you can think of. Next to each, print a plus sign (+) if it was good for the planet, or a minus sign (−) if you think it damaged any of the three Earth systems.

At the end of the five minutes, add up the plusses and minuses. What overall impact are you having on our planet?

PART TWO

More than 25 years ago, a songwriter named Tom Lehrer wrote the lyrics on page 298. He calls his song "Pollution." Do you think these words still apply to us? The song focuses on pollution in the city. Is that still a problem today? Does pollution today exist only in the cities, or is it a problem in the suburbs and in the country and rural areas as well?

In your group, think about Tom Lehrer's words. Then, as a group, create three good questions that focus on your own ideas about the impact humans have on the natural environment. Write those questions on the same paper you used for Part One. Be prepared to share your questions with the class.

Pollution*

If you visit American city,
You will find it very pretty.
Just two things of which you must beware:
Don't drink the water and don't
breathe the air.

Pollution, Pollution,
They got smog and sewage and mud,
Turn on your tap and get hot and
cold running crud.

See the halibuts and the sturgeons
Being wiped out by detergents.
Fish gotta swim and birds gotta fly,
But they don't last long if they try.

Pollution, Pollution,
You can use the latest toothpaste,
And then rinse your mouth
with industrial waste.

Just go out for a breath of air,
And you'll be ready for Medicare.
The city streets are really quite a thrill,
If the hoods don't get you,
the monoxide will.

Pollution, Pollution,
Wear a gas mask and a veil.
Then you can breathe as long as
you don't inhale.

Lots of things there that you can drink,
But stay away from the kitchen sink.
Throw out your breakfast garbage,
and I've got a hunch
That the folks downstream
will drink it for lunch.

So go to the city, see the crazy
people there.
Like lambs to the slaughter
They're drinking the water
And breathing (cough!) the air.

*From the song "Pollution" from the recording *That Was the Year That Was* by Tom Lehrer. (See Acknowledgements, pages 595–596.)

Human-Environment Interaction: Gifts of the Earth

As we have seen in Reading 5, natural resources are our "gifts of the Earth." Natural resources include a wide variety of things that grow and develop on our planet that humans use to survive and to build societies.

Some of the resources on Earth are **renewable**—they can be replaced. Food, livestock, and trees are some examples of renewable resources. Other resources are **nonrenewable.** They cannot easily be replaced, if they are able to be replaced at all. Petroleum and minerals take millions of years to form in the Earth, so they are considered nonrenewable resources.

Where are the "gifts of the Earth" to be found? Which parts of planet Earth are rich in natural resources? Which areas of our planet have a scarcity of resources?

Let's find out more about the distribution of resources in our world. Study the four maps on pages 300 and 301 carefully. Then, try to answer the following questions on a separate sheet of paper:

1. What areas of the world have the greatest population density? The sparsest population density? (Density refers to how many people there are per square mile or square kilometer.)

2. What areas of the world have the most cereals? Fisheries? Livestock?

3. What areas of the world have the most minerals and energy resources? Which areas have none of those resources?

4. Using your answers to Questions 2 and 3, can you guess which areas of the world have the richest and poorest populations? Why? What areas do you think do the most trading with other areas of the world? Why?

5. Why do you think it is important to use resources wisely? Why is it especially important to use our planet's nonrenewable resources wisely?

Replacing valuable timber resources is vital if future needs are to be satisfied.

World Resources: Food

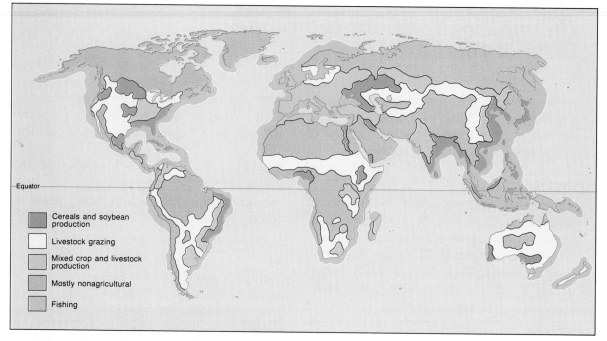

Cereals and soybean production

Livestock grazing

Mixed crop and livestock production

Mostly nonagricultural

Fishing

Equator

World Resources: Minerals

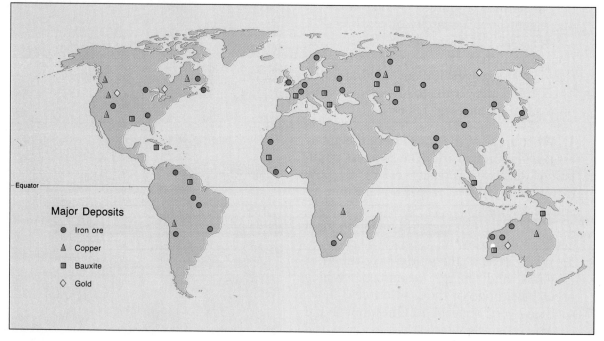

Equator

Major Deposits

● Iron ore

▲ Copper

■ Bauxite

◇ Gold

World Resources: Energy

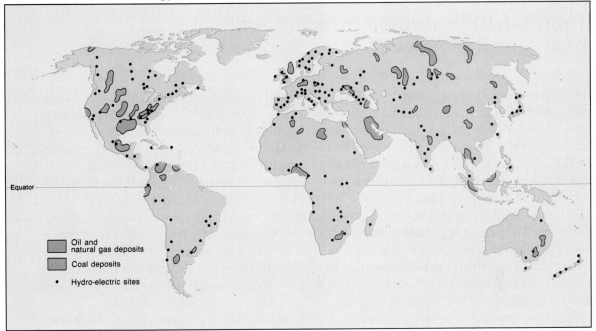

Equator

Oil and natural gas deposits

Coal deposits

• Hydro-electric sites

World Population Density

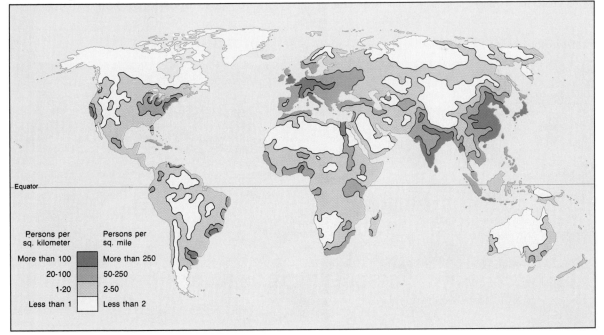

Equator

Persons per sq. kilometer	Persons per sq. mile
More than 100	More than 250
20-100	50-250
1-20	2-50
Less than 1	Less than 2

Human-Environment Interaction: Strategic Resources*

Every day, people in our country use thousands of products made from natural resources. Some of those products make life more enjoyable. Your daily newspaper and the book you are reading now would not be possible without trees. The fireworks you enjoy on the Fourth of July would not be possible without a natural resource called antimony. Your compact disc and tape collections would not be possible without the petroleum from which they are made.

Other resources are necessary for our country's security. Four minerals you may not know—titanium, beryl, chromite, and

*Sources: Life Lines, a publication of the U.S. Navy, and other sources. Thanks also to the National Strategy Information Center for assistance in preparing this experiment.

bauxite—are necessary components of jet planes. Our national defense requires those resources and many others.

All of these are examples of **strategic resources** that our country needs for our industries and for national security. The United States is blessed with great natural resources. Yet, there are many raw materials we must import. What are these resources, and where on Earth are they found? What can the raw materials be used for? Which ones do we absolutely need, and which could we do without? These are some of the important questions that the geographer, as well as our national leaders, must answer.

In this experiment you will find some answers to these questions. You will also

International trade plays a key role in transporting of resources.

The Alaskan Pipeline transports billions of gallons of crude oil across the Alaskan wilderness.

examine examples of strategic materials imported from other countries. You will discover their uses and find out which countries produce them.

Your teacher will distribute handouts to you, including: (1) a world map, and (2) data sheets for recording information about strategic resources. You will be working in small groups to share information and ideas.

The countries that supply the United States with strategic resources have been numbered on the world map. These source countries are also listed on pages 304–307. Only three of the source countries are listed for each resource. These three are not the only countries from which we import strategic resources. For each strategic resource choose *one* source country. Draw a line

from that country to the United States. Label the line with the name of the resource being imported. Try to choose a different country for each resource. (For the other countries that supply the same resource to us, trace an imaginary line from each of them to the United States.) The strategic resources listed on pages 304–307 are just a few of those our country imports.

After you have completed the map handouts, turn to the data sheet handouts and fill in the required information. Then, in your small group, decide which of all the strategic resources you consider most important. Which three resources could we absolutely not do without? Be prepared to report your decision to the class, along with the reasons for your choices.

Strategic Resources

Antimony

Uses:	Sources:
Ammunition	Republic of
Metal Sheets and Pipes	South Africa
Fireworks	Mexico
Matches	China
Ceramics and Glass	
Rubber Products	
Adhesives	
Industrial Chemicals	
Medicines	

Beryl

Uses:	Sources:
Spark Plugs	Brazil
Nuclear Reactors	France
Telephones	Argentina
Household Appliances	
Jet Engine Parts	
Keys for Woodwind	
Instruments	
Space Navigation	
Instruments	
Business Machines	

Asbestos

Uses:	Sources:
Cement Products	Canada
Floor Tile	Republic of
Textiles	South Africa
Plastics	Finland
Protective Suits for	
Firefighters	
Electrical Insulations	

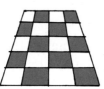

Chromite

Uses:	Sources:
Stainless Steel	Philippines
Jet Engines	Turkey
Ammunition	India
Petroleum Refining	Brazil
Equipment	
Furnace Repairs	
Household Appliances	
Heating Coils of Electric	
Toasters, Heaters, Ranges	
Printing Inks	
Tanning (Leather)	

Bauxite

Uses:	Sources:
Pots and Pans	Jamaica
Window Frames	Australia
Aircraft Fuselage	Dominican
Auto Pistons	Republic
Paper Making	
Water Treatment	
Children's Toys	
Spark Plugs	
Dye	

Cobalt

Uses:	Sources:
Jet Engines	Zaire
Tool Steels	Zambia
Lacquers, Varnishes,	Finland
Paints, Enamels, Glazes,	
Inks	
Dental Restorations	
Artificial Limbs	

Columbium

Uses:	Sources:
Refinery Equipment	Brazil
Jet Engines	Canada
Rockets and Missiles	Nigeria
Gas Pipeline Steel	
Corrosion Resistant Materials	

Copper

Uses:	Sources:
Electrical Conductors	Peru
Industrial Tubes and Pipes	Canada
Bearings	Chile
Wire	
Coins (dimes, quarters, half dollars)	
Roofing, Gutters, Downspouts	
Alloys for Ship Hulls	
Railroad-car Boxes	

Fibers—Abaca, Sisal, Henequen

Uses:	Sources:
Slippers	Mexico
Paper Manufacture	Philippines
Furniture Padding	Brazil
Tea Bags	

Iron Ore

Uses:	Sources:
Ships	Canada
Railroad Engines and Rails	Venezuela
Automobiles	Liberia
Kitchen Stoves	
Safety Pins	
Nails	
Knives and Scissors	
Typewriters	
Factory Machinery	
Office Furniture	

Lead

Uses:	Sources:
Ammunition	Canada
Brass and Bronze	Mexico
Paints and Pigments	United Kingdom
Decorative Arts	
Gasoline Additives	
Batteries	

Manganese Ore

Uses:	Sources:
Stainless Steel	Brazil
Fertilizers	Gabon
Disinfectants and Deodorants	Australia
Ceramics	

Nickel

Uses:	Sources:
Stainless Steel	Canada
Jet Engines	Norway
Magnets	Dominican Republic
Gas Turbines	
Oil Refineries	
Rocket Motor Cases	

Petroleum

Uses:	Sources:
Motor Gasoline	Canada
Aviation Gasoline	Venezuela
Lubricating Oils	Saudi Arabia
Asphalt	
Road Oil	
Liquefied Gas	
Plastics	
Synthetic Rubber	

Potash

Uses:
Agricultural Fertilizers
Glass
Batteries
Drugs
Rocket Fuel

Sources:
Canada
Israel

Rubber

Uses:
Tires and Tire Products
Medical and Surgical
  Goods
Waterproofing Textiles
Footgear
Mattresses
Sporting Goods
Flooring

Sources:
Malaysia
Indonesia
India

Silver

Uses:
Photographic Film
  Emulsions
Mirrors
Jewelry
Dental Work

Sources:
Canada
United
  Kingdom
Belgium/
  Luxembourg

Sugar

Uses:
Candy and Gum
Beer and Liquor
Soft Drinks
Canned, Bottled, and
  Frozen Foods
Jams, Jellies, and Preserves
Bakery Products
Cereals
Ice Cream and Dairy
  Products
Syrups and Molasses
Food Seasoning
Industrial Products

Sources:
Philippines
Dominican
  Republic
Brazil

Tin

Uses:
Tinplate (Tin Cans, Sheet
  Metal, etc.)
Solder
Bronze and Brass
Pipe and Tubing
Molten Float Bath for
  making large plates of
  very smooth glass for
  automobiles and other
  industries
Anti-Rodent Sprays

Sources:
Malaysia
China
Indonesia

Titanium Concentrates

Uses:
Supersonic Aircraft
  Frames
Jet Engines
Space Vehicles
High-Speed Precision
  Tools
Ceramics
Paper

Sources:
Australia
Canada
Republic of
  South Africa

Tungsten

Uses:
Incandescent Lamps
Radio and Television
  Tube Filaments
Jet Engines
Gas Turbines
Waterproofing
Fire-Retarding Fabrics
Surgical Instruments
Stainless Steel
Chemicals and Ceramics
Tire Studs

Sources:
Canada
Peru
China

Uranium

Uses:	Sources:
Weapons and Explosives Applications	Republic of South Africa
Ship and Submarine Reactors for Main Power Propulsion	Canada
Nuclear Power Reactors (Electric Power Utilities)	France
Test, Research, and Teaching Reactors at Universities and Research Centers	
Industrial Measuring Applications	

Zinc

Uses:	Sources:
Production of Bronze and Brass	Canada
Paints, Varnishes, Lacquers	Mexico
Tubes and Pipes	Spain
Medicines	

Zircon

Uses:	Sources:
Nuclear Reactors	Australia
Spark Plugs	Canada
Synthetic Rubber Production	Republic of South Africa

READING 6

Human-Environment Interaction:
The Distribution of Resources

Some nations of the world are blessed with many resources, while others have very few. The resources of our Earth are not distributed equally.

Natural resources existed on our planet long before humans appeared. In some places the land was rich with resources. In other places the land was poor. When the first people began to live on Earth, they used very few resources. Rocks and tree limbs were used as weapons. Caves and dried grass were used for shelter. The waters gave fish, and animals on the land provided meat. Animal skins were used for clothing to keep the body warm and protected from exposure. Human needs for resources were very limited in those times. Keeping alive, warm, and fed were as much as any person could hope for.

Then, gradually, people's needs changed. Keeping warm and staying alive were not enough. It became important to improve the quality of life as much as possible. Forms of transportation changed. So did housing, communication, weapons, and just about everything humans used in daily life.

With improvements in living, people required different kinds of resources and more of them. Over a period of time, those resources were used in greater and greater quantities. Early humans had no use for some resources we consider essential to our way of life today.

In our modern world, coal, natural gas, and petroleum for fuels are important in providing energy for heating, cooling, transportation, and industry. Iron ore,

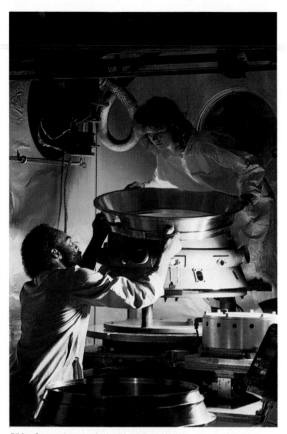

Workers in a developed country assemble highly technical equipment. Developed countries are high-tech leaders.

bauxite, aluminum, nickel, tin, diamonds, copper, tungsten, rubber, and zinc were practically useless to people several thousand years ago. Today, those natural resources bring wealth, power, and comfort. The people who don't have such resources, or aren't able to use them, live much the way ancient people did. For the have-nots, life is usually a daily struggle to survive.

Social scientists study human ways of life in many cultures and countries. For purposes of comparison they sometimes divide the countries of the Earth into two different groups or categories.

The first group of countries includes the industrialized, wealthy nations of Europe, the former Soviet Union, the United States, Canada, Japan, Australia, New Zealand, and South Africa. They are the richest nations of the world, and they consume most of the resources of our planet. They are often called **developed nations.** Most of these countries believe in capitalism. In other words, private individuals and companies use capital (money, buildings, and equipment) to own and operate businesses. There is relatively little control of businesses by the government. Developed countries are leaders in high technology. They are often the first to develop new ways of making information and communication systems such as computers and communication satellites. They were the first to install robots in factories and homes to do work humans had done before.

The second group, or category, of countries consists of countries with developing economies. These countries are often referred to as **developing nations** or **less-developed nations.** The less-developed countries of the world include the countries of Africa (except for South Africa), Latin America, the Caribbean, Asia (except for Japan), and Oceania (except for Australia and New Zealand). The people of these countries generally have much less education than do people in developed countries. The literacy rate is low. That is, relatively few are able to read and write. Those people are usually the minority who are very rich in a land where almost everyone is poor. There are schools and colleges in less-developed nations, but only the wealthy can afford to attend. Many of the rich send their children to developed nations to be educated. Some less-developed countries, such as Ethiopia in Africa and Bangladesh in Asia, are so poor they cannot provide enough food for all their people. These countries must import food using the money they earn from exports or by borrowing money from banks and other institutions. When countries must use their money to import food, it means that they cannot use that money to build roads, schools, hospitals, or airports. Some poor countries have borrowed so much money in the past that they spend a great deal of their income on interest on their loans and paying off their debt. This leaves even less money for food and economic development.

Less-developed countries often make parts for the products made by developed countries. The people of less-developed countries usually work for companies at much lower wages than people in developed countries get for the same kind of work. Entire computers, television sets, and other finished products such as clothing, batteries, and toys are assembled in less-developed countries. Then these products are shipped to the developed countries, where they are packaged and sold around the world.

Farmers in less-developed countries usually do not have modern machinery. This farmer in Latin America still relies on methods that developed countries would consider quite primitive.

Some less-developed countries have valuable natural resources that have helped raise their standard of living. The Arab nations, Venezuela, and Nigeria fall into this group. They produce petroleum that is needed by developed countries. With enormous profits from oil exports, these nations are working to improve their levels of industry, education, and wealth.

Most less-developed countries are not fortunate enough to have such a precious resource as petroleum. Their development will likely be much slower. Many less-developed countries receive aid from the United States and other industrialized nations. This aid takes the form of food, education, medicine, technology, and equipment for farming and industry. Sometimes it also takes the form of military weapons.

READING REVIEW

1. Why do people today use more natural resources than people did 1,000 years ago?
2. Which nations are considered "developed"? Who owns businesses in these countries?
3. What do less-developed countries have in common? What changes are taking place in these countries?
4. How do developed countries use workers in less-developed countries?

Critical Thinking

5. **Making Comparisons** (see page 16) How do developed countries compare with less-developed countries?

Human-Environment Interaction: What Does It Feel Like to Be Poor?*

Poverty is a relative term. If you have a few million dollars in the bank, you might consider someone with only $50,000 poor by comparison. But compared with most people of the world, both you and the person with $50,000 would be considered very wealthy. So would someone earning $10,000 a year, which is below the poverty

*Information in this experiment is based upon data from: Heifer Project International, as reported in *USA Today;* Robert L. Heilbroner, *The Great Ascent: The Struggle for Economic Development;* and other sources. (See Acknowledgements, pages 595–596.)

level in our country for a household of four people. For many poor people on our planet, $1,000 would be a fortune!

Poverty exists worldwide. It is a global problem. Millions of people in this world live at a subsistence level. **Subsistence** means making just enough to get by, just barely enough to keep alive from one day to the next. This is the kind of poverty that most Americans have never seen or experienced. But this is the kind of poverty that over half of our planet's people have to endure throughout their entire lifetimes!

Homelessness has become a serious problem in most major American cities, including our nation's capital.

In our own country, more than 12 million children live in poverty. Their families cannot afford to buy the goods and services they need. Most of those children don't get enough to eat and go to bed hungry every night. Many have only one set of clothes, and some do not even have a home.

In other parts of the world, the life-and-death struggle with poverty also goes on day after day. What would it be like to live in the worst kind of poverty—the kind of poverty millions of people encounter every day of their lives? Suppose you had been born into a poor family in one of the poorest countries of the world. How would your life be different than it is today? How would your future be changed?

Could you live on $100 a year? More than half of all the people in our world live on less than that! Think about what that would mean to you and your family. To live on $100 a year, here is what life will be like for you and your family:

Your car and all your furniture will have to go, except for one chair and one table. You will not have any TVs, radios, phones, or lamps.

All your clothing will go, except your oldest dress or suit. One pair of shoes may be kept for the head of the family.

All the appliances and food from the kitchen will go. You can keep a small bag of flour, some sugar and salt, a few potatoes and onions, and some dried beans.

The electricity, gas, and water will be shut off. You will have to carry all your water from a well, which is polluted. You will spend most of your day transporting water and fuel to your home, so you will not have time for school. But never mind, there's no school for miles.

Throughout the twentieth century, most Americans have enjoyed the luxury of kitchen appliances that were unknown in many developing countries.

You must move out of your house and into a toolshed, which has more space than many homes in less-developed countries. Your neighborhood will be a shantytown, and that is what you will call "home."

You won't be reading any newspapers, magazines, or books. You can't afford them. Besides, you are not able to read or write.

You have money for an emergency, but it is only $5. You have no insurance and no bank accounts. Your parents will have no social security or income when they retire. They will rely on your support in their old age.

You cannot afford any type of medical or dental care, except that provided by a small clinic run by missionaries that is five miles away. The clinic must be reached by foot.

You may farm three acres of land as a tenant farmer. Chances are there will be a drought, but if you are successful you may earn a few hundred dollars in cash crops. After you pay one third of your earnings to your landlord and 10 percent of your earnings to the moneylender, you and your family may keep the rest to pay all your expenses for an entire year.

Government services must go. No postal service, no garbage collection.

You will not get enough to eat. Hunger will be a constant companion. You will wake up hungry and go to bed hungry.

Because your body doesn't get the nourishment it needs, you will look and feel much older than you should. On average, your life will be 25 to 30 years shorter.

You may be able to find work, doing simple tasks. If you live close enough to a factory, you may get a job assembling products for companies. Your pay is great compared with the poverty of your neighborhood. But you are making less than 10 percent of the salary you could make at the same job if you lived in a developed country. If you cannot find work, you may have to scavenge, or sift among the garbage dumps for your food and clothing.

You will sleep in the same room with your parents and your brothers and sisters. Your family is very fortunate if there is one mattress in your home.

Your family's new poverty will take away almost everything you take for granted in your life style. But your poverty will also give you some things you don't have today:

You will smell the odors of poverty all around you. There are no toilets, no plumbing. There is no way to dispose of garbage.

A nearby stream is filled with rotting garbage and human waste. It carries bacteria that have already killed many people you have known in your neighborhood.

This woman in India prepares a meager meal on a simple outdoor stove.

Flies, rats, and other pests surround you. They carry diseases to you and your family and neighbors.

You have almost no hope of ever getting out of this situation. If you get married and have children, they will share the same fate.

To get a better idea of what it would be like to live in poverty, make a list of the 20 features of your everyday life that you value the most. Then take another look at your list. Cross out every item you would have to give up if you lived in one of the many areas of the world where people subsist on only $100 a year. How many items are left on your list? What would it mean to you if you had to give up every one of those things forever?

READING REVIEW

1. Why is poverty a global problem?
2. What is meant by a subsistence level of living?
3. Name 10 things you now own that you probably would not have if you had been born into a poor family in one of the least developed nations of the world.

Critical Thinking

5. **Identifying Central Issues** (see page 14) Many governments and international organizations, such as the United Nations, work to end poverty in countries like Ethiopia and Bangladesh. Why do you think ending poverty is so difficult?

EXPERIMENT 6-K

Human-Environment Interaction: Global Development

There are great differences among nations and the natural resources they possess. The resources of a country are directly related to the quality of life there. In most cases, the richer the country is in resources, the better the people live. In areas of the world with little or no natural resources, people starve or barely make a living.

Using what you already know, as well as the graphs and charts included in this experiment,* answer these questions about global development on a separate sheet of paper. This experiment is designed to sharpen your ideas about the developed nations (rich and industrial), and the developing nations (agricultural and poor).

1. On page 316 is a map of the world showing the average gross national product (GNP) per person for countries of the world. Compare the information on the map with your answers to Question 4 in "Experiment 6-H: *Interaction:* Gifts of the Earth" on page 299.

*Sources: The material in the chart and graphs on pages 316 through 325 was compiled by the author from various sources, including publications of the United Nations, Unicef, the World Bank, the Food and Agriculture Organization, the Population Reference Bureau, and agencies of the United States Government.

laborers work in jobs that are related to agriculture? In what countries does 10 percent or less of the labor force work in agriculture?

8. Which regions shown on Graph 6 on page 321 have the highest percentage of their population under age 15? Over age 65?

9. According to Graph 8 on page 323, in which regions—less developed or more developed—do the majority of people live in rural (farm) areas? Which regions have the largest total population?

10. Approximately how many people live in rural areas in Asia? In urban areas (cities) in Asia?

11. Why do you think a greater percentage of people in less-developed countries live in rural areas, compared with the developed countries? For help, refer back to the information you found in Questions 6 through 10.

12. Examine Graph 9 on page 323. Based on this graph which countries have the faster growth in population: the developed or less-developed countries?

To answer questions 13 through 19, refer to the "Statistics of Development" table on pages 324–325.

13. A high literacy rate is very important to a developing country. To build up the country, a large number of workers, planners, and managers must be literate. Education is the key to literacy. Of all the countries in the table, which ones have a literacy rate above 80 percent?

14. Which countries have a literacy rate below 20 percent?

15. In your list of countries for Questions 13 and 14, which are developed and which are developing?

16. Choose one *developed* country and one *developing* country. Make a chart in which you compare those two nations on the basis of the following information: (a) number of persons per telephone, radio, and television; (b) daily calorie intake per person; (c) number of persons per physician; (d) life expectancy at birth; (e) infant mortality rate; (f) adult literacy rate; (g) persons per motor vehicle; (h) percent of population living in cities; and (i) public expenditure on education per capita.

17. Choose three developing nations and three developed nations (other than the ones you chose for Question 16). Make a chart comparing the adult literacy rate for each country with the public expenditure on education per capita. Is there a connection between the ability to write and read as an adult and public spending on education?

18. Write the GNP per capita for these five nations: India, the United States, Peru, China, and Israel. Beside each, write what percent of the country's population has access to safe water. What does the wealth or poverty of a country have to do with access to safe drinking water? What are some of the possible costs of providing safe drinking water to people? What other factors may be related? (Hints: Look at the data on urbanization and population and consider size, and climate.)

19. Write a description of the developing countries and the developed countries in terms of what you have learned about the following: literacy, equality of educational opportunity for males and females, GNP per capita, urban and rural populations, farming and non-farming populations, calorie intake, life expectancy and infant mortality, population growth rates, and the availability of physicians, communication, and transportation.

The following terms are those you need to know in order to read Graphs 1–9 (pages 319–323) and the table "Statistics of Development" (pages 324–325).

INA: Information Not Available

urban population: percentage of total population living in cities

work force in agriculture: percentage of total population who farm for a living

adult literacy rate: percentage of adult population who are able to read and write

gross national product (GNP): the total value of all new things produced in the country in a year

gross national product (GNP) per capita: GNP of the country divided by the total population. "per capita" means "per person." GNP per capita is *not* the income every person receives. In Saudi Arabia, for example, less than 5 percent of the total population controls almost all the country's wealth. The $11,261 GNP per capita is, therefore, misleading.

average daily calorie and protein intake per person: According to the Food and Agriculture Organization, the minimum daily requirement of protein is 100 grams. The usual minimum daily requirement of calories is 3,000 for men and 2,200 for women. It is impossible to remain healthy if daily intakes always fall below these levels.

infant mortality rate: the number of children who die before their first birthday, per 1,000 births

life expectancy at birth: the average lifespan of a person in that country. This is *not* the maximum age most people in the country reach. It is an average age, calculated by adding the ages of all persons at the time of death, then dividing the total by the number of persons who died. If, for example, the total number of persons who died was 10, and if half of them died on their second birthday while half died on their 70th birthday, the life expectancy in the country would be calculated in this way:

$$5 \times 2 = 10$$
$$5 \times 70 = 350$$
$$350 + 10 = 360$$
$$360 \div 10 = 36 = \text{Life Expectancy}$$

Infants who die before their first birthday are not counted in statistics for life expectancy. This means that life expectancy is a completely different statistic from infant mortality.

Specialized land use such as terrace farming increases productivity, thus helping to raise the region's standard of living.

GRAPH 1: AVERAGE GROSS NATIONAL PRODUCT (GNP) PER CAPITA

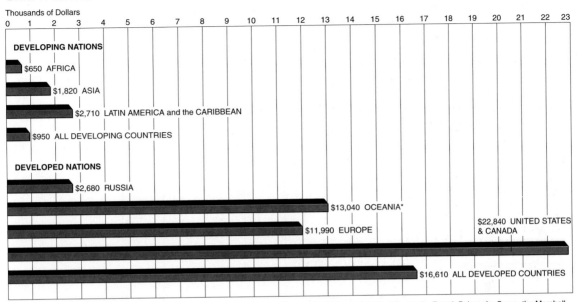

Thousands of Dollars

DEVELOPING NATIONS

$650 AFRICA

$1,820 ASIA

$2,710 LATIN AMERICA and the CARIBBEAN

$950 ALL DEVELOPING COUNTRIES

DEVELOPED NATIONS

$2,680 RUSSIA

$13,040 OCEANIA*

$11,990 EUROPE

$22,840 UNITED STATES & CANADA

$16,610 ALL DEVELOPED COUNTRIES

* Oceania includes Australia, New Zealand, Fiji, Papua-New Guinea, Western Samoa, the Solomon Islands, Micronesia, French Polynesia, Guam, the Marshall Islands, New Caledonia, and Vanuatu
Source: Population Reference Bureau, Inc.

GRAPH 2: AVERAGE LIFE EXPECTANCY AT BIRTH

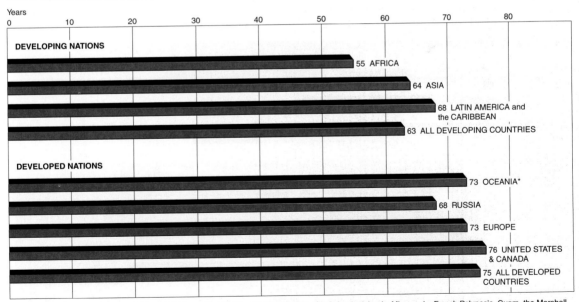

Years

DEVELOPING NATIONS

55 AFRICA

64 ASIA

68 LATIN AMERICA and the CARIBBEAN

63 ALL DEVELOPING COUNTRIES

DEVELOPED NATIONS

73 OCEANIA*

68 RUSSIA

73 EUROPE

76 UNITED STATES & CANADA

75 ALL DEVELOPED COUNTRIES

* Oceania includes Australia, New Zealand, Fiji, Papua-New Guinea, Western Samoa, the Solomon Islands, Micronesia, French Polynesia, Guam, the Marshall Islands, New Caledonia, and Vanuatu
Source: Population Reference Bureau, Inc.

GRAPH 3: AVERAGE INFANT MORTALITY RATES

Infant Deaths (before age 1) per 1,000 live births

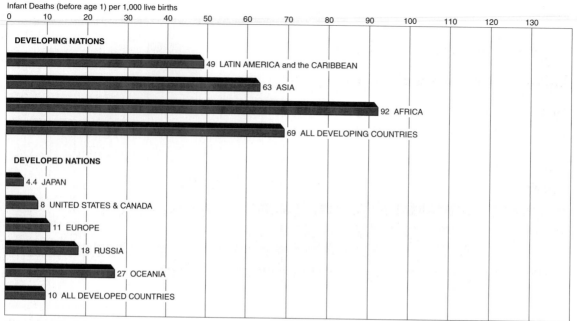

DEVELOPING NATIONS

49 LATIN AMERICA and the CARIBBEAN
63 ASIA
92 AFRICA
69 ALL DEVELOPING COUNTRIES

DEVELOPED NATIONS

4.4 JAPAN
8 UNITED STATES & CANADA
11 EUROPE
18 RUSSIA
27 OCEANIA
10 ALL DEVELOPED COUNTRIES

Source: Population Reference Bureau, Inc.

GRAPH 4: AVERAGE PERCENT OF PRIMARY SCHOOL STUDENTS ENROLLED IN SCHOOLS

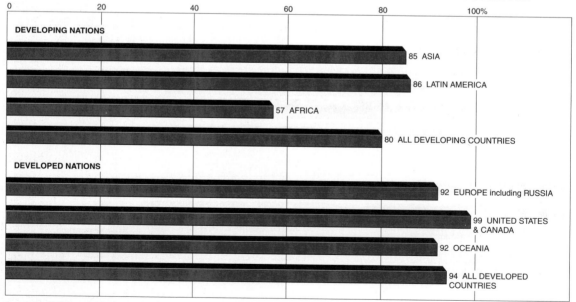

DEVELOPING NATIONS

85 ASIA
86 LATIN AMERICA
57 AFRICA
80 ALL DEVELOPING COUNTRIES

DEVELOPED NATIONS

92 EUROPE including RUSSIA
99 UNITED STATES & CANADA
92 OCEANIA
94 ALL DEVELOPED COUNTRIES

Source: World Military and Social Expenditures

GRAPH 5: AVERAGE PERCENT OF SECONDARY SCHOOL STUDENTS ENROLLED IN SCHOOLS

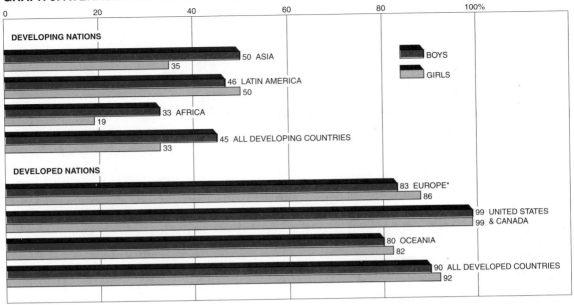

Source: Population Reference Bureau, Inc.
* Not including Russia or the former Soviet Republics.

GRAPH 6: AVERAGE PERCENT OF POPULATIONS UNDER AGE 15 AND OVER AGE 65

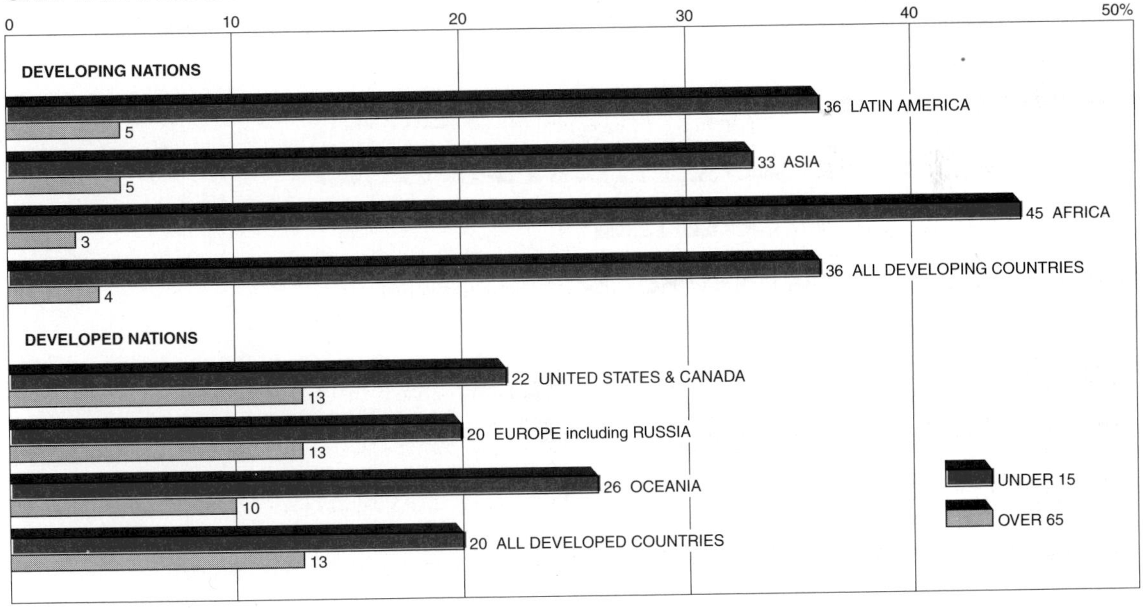

Source: Population Reference Bureau, Inc.

GRAPH 7: AVERAGE PERCENT OF POPULATIONS WORKING IN AGRICULTURE

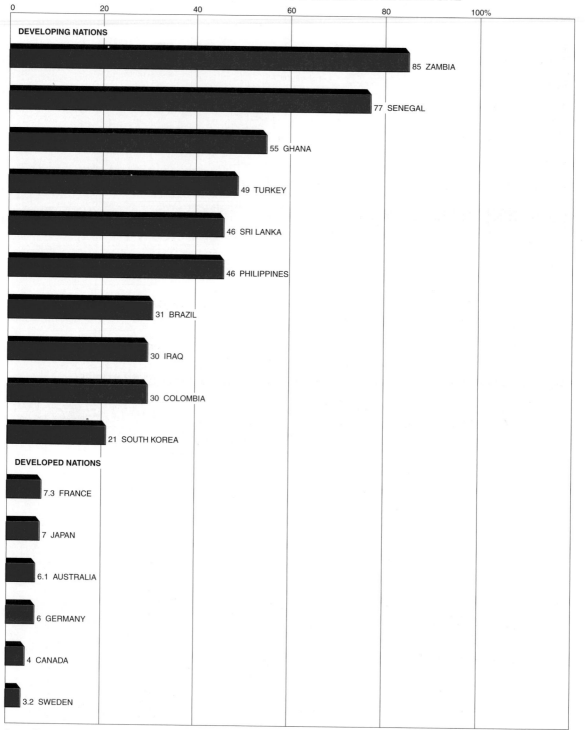

Source: The World Factbook, Central Intelligence Agency

GRAPH 8: URBAN AND RURAL POPULATION OF SELECTED COUNTRIES AND REGIONS

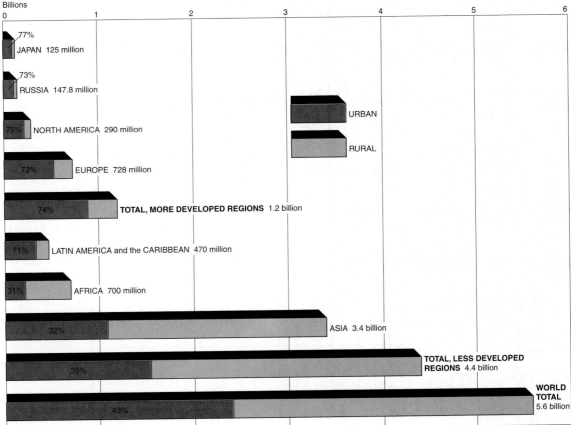

Billions

| | 0 | 1 | 2 | 3 | 4 | 5 | 6 |

77% JAPAN 125 million

73% RUSSIA 147.8 million

URBAN

RURAL

75% NORTH AMERICA 290 million

73% EUROPE 728 million

74% **TOTAL, MORE DEVELOPED REGIONS** 1.2 billion

71% LATIN AMERICA and the CARIBBEAN 470 million

31% AFRICA 700 million

32% ASIA 3.4 billion

35% **TOTAL, LESS DEVELOPED REGIONS** 4.4 billion

43% **WORLD TOTAL** 5.6 billion

Source: Population Reference Bureau, Inc.

GRAPH 9: POPULATION GROWTH

Billions of People

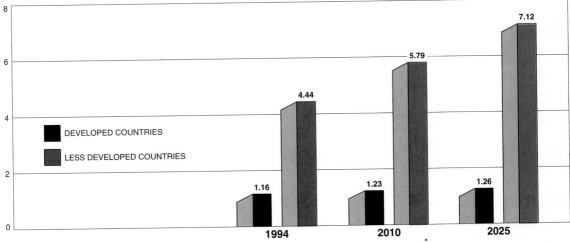

■ DEVELOPED COUNTRIES

■ LESS DEVELOPED COUNTRIES

	1994	2010	2025
Developed	1.16	1.23	1.26
Less Developed	4.44	5.79	7.12

Source: Population Reference Bureau, Inc.

Statistics of Development INA-Information Not Available	POPULATION IN MILLIONS	URBAN POPULATION (%)	WORK FORCE IN AGRICULTURE (%)	ADULT LITERACY RATE (%) MALE/FEMALE		PERSONS PER TELEPHONE	PERSONS PER RADIO	PERSONS PER TELEVISION	PER CAPITA COMMERCIAL ENERGY CONSUMPTION (IN BARRELS OF OIL EQUIVALENT)	PUBLIC EXPENDITURES ON EDUCATION PER CAPITA ($US)
AFGHANISTAN	17.8	18	68	M:44	F:14	443	11	156	.7	INA
ALGERIA	27.9	50	24	M:70	F:46	24	4.6	16	6.9	228
AUSTRALIA	17.8	85	6.1	M:98	F:98	1.8	2.4	2.7	32.8	611
AUSTRIA	8	59	8.1	M:98	F:98	1.8	1.6	2.9	INA	935
BRAZIL	155.3	76	31	M:83	F:80	11	2.5	4.2	3.6	64
CANADA	29.1	77	4	M:99	F:99	1.3	1.2	1.7	47.5	1,201
CHAD	6.5	32	85	M:42	F:18	555	4.5	1,050	.2	4
CHINA, PEOPLES REPUBLIC OF	1,192	28	60	M:84	F:62	103	9.4	9.0	3.6	8
COLOMBIA	35.6	68	30	M:88	F:86	13	7.3	6.0	3.9	35
CUBA	11.1	73	20	M:95	F:93	19	3	5.0	6.9	82
EGYPT	58.9	45	34	M:63	F:34	34	3.8	15	3.3	40
ETHIOPIA	55.2	15	80	M:11	F:5	324	5.6	503	.2	5
FRANCE	58	74	7.3	M:99	F:99	1.2	1.2	2.0	7.8	942
HONDURAS	5.3	44	62	M:76	F:71	63	2.6	26	INA	34
INDIA	911.6	26	67	M:62	F:34	189	16	43	1.3	11
IRAN	61.2	57	33	M:65	F:43	25	4.9	25	6.2	114
ISRAEL	5.4	90	5.5	M:97	F:93	2	2.2	4.2	13.4	765
JAPAN	125	77	7	M:99	F:99	1.8	1.3	1.8	18	1,107
MEXICO	91.8	71	26	M:90	F:85	9	5	6.6	8.2	71
NETHERLANDS	15.4	89	6	M:99	F:99	1.5	1.2	3.2	34.8	902
PERU	22.9	71	37	M:92	F:79	30	5.1	11	2.8	33
POLAND	38.6	62	27	M:99	F:98	7.8	3.7	3.9	23	72
SAUDI ARABIA	18	79	16	M:73	F:48	8.5	3.5	3.8	30.2	408
SOMALIA	9.8	24	30	M:36	F:14	971	19	2,270	INA	1
SWEDEN	8.8	83	3.2	M:99	F:99	1.1	1.2	2.3	24	1,486
SWITZERLAND	7	68	6	M:99	F:99	1.1	2.5	2.9	18.1	1,392
TAIWAN (REPUBLIC OF CHINA)	21.1	75	15.6	M:96	F:86	2.8	1.5	3.0	INA	172
UNITED KINGDOM	58.4	92	1.2	M:99	F:99	1.9	1	2.9	24.5	601
UNITED STATES	260.8	75	4	M:99	F:99	1.3	.5	1.2	45.8	1,095
RUSSIA	147.8	73	13	M:99	F:98	INA	INA	INA	INA	166
VIETNAM	73.1	21	65	M:92	F:83	537	9.4	30	1.8	INA
ZAIRE	42.5	40	75	M:84	F:61	1,026	10	1,707	.3	2
ZIMBABWE	11.2	27	74	M:74	F:60	31	21	68	3.4	67

Statistics of Development

INA-Information Not Available

	GROSS NATIONAL PRODUCT (GNP) PER CAPITA IN U.S. DOLLARS	PERSONS PER MOTOR VEHICLE	PERCENT OF POPULATION WITH ACCESS TO SAFE WATER	DAILY CALORIE INTAKE PER PERSON AS A PERCENT OF REQUIREMENTS	PUBLIC EXPENDITURES ON HEALTH CARE PER CAPITA	INFANT MORTALITY RATE	LIFE EXPECTANCY AT BIRTH: MALE/FEMALE	NUMBER OF PERSONS PER PHYSICIAN
AFGHANISTAN	INA	236	21	83	INA	168	M:42 F:43	6,931
ALGERIA	1,830	20	71	119	36	58	M:66 F:68	2,433
AUSTRALIA	17,070	1.7	99	121	696	6.6	M:74 F:80	512
AUSTRIA	22,110	2.4	100	133	890	6.7	M:73 F:79	470
BRAZIL	2,770	8.7	87	115	46	66	M:64 F:71	1,114
CANADA	20,320	1.6	97	131	1,123	6.8	M:74 F:81	446
CHAD	220	396	57	73	1	122	M:46 F:49	39,172
CHINA, PEOPLES REPUBLIC OF	380	224	74	112	4	31	M:69 F:72	1,072
COLOMBIA	1,290	24	88	112	10	33	M:68 F:73	1,102
CUBA	INA	27	98	136	43	10.2	M:75 F:79	306
EGYPT	630	38	73	133	7	62	M:60 F:63	834
ETHIOPIA	110	751	19	72	1	110	M:50 F:53	63,975
FRANCE	22,300	2	100	138	1,140	6.7	M:73 F:81	371
HONDURAS	580	40	65	99	24	50	M:64 F:69	1,760
INDIA	310	225	86	101	3	79	M:57 F:57	2,614
IRAN	2,190	26	89	132	42	66	M:64 F:65	3,297
ISRAEL	13,230	5	98	124	179	8.1	M:74 F:78	490
JAPAN	28,220	2.1	98	126	638	4.4	M:76 F:82	638
MEXICO	3,470	8.9	71	131	6	35	M:67 F:73	1,126
NETHERLANDS	20,590	2.5	100	117	919	6.3	M:74 F:80	399
PERU	950	35	61	93	7	81	M:63 F:67	1,078
POLAND	1,960	6.4	89	134	58	13.8	M:66 F:75	482
SAUDI ARABIA	7,940	3.2	94	119	229	24	M:69 F:72	619
SOMALIA	INA	243	37	82	<1	122	M:45 F:49	16,967
SWEDEN	26,780	2.2	100	110	1,554	4.8	M:75 F:80	322
SWITZERLAND	36,230	2.1	100	132	1,432	6.2	M:74 F:81	345
TAIWAN (REPUBLIC OF CHINA)	INA	7.8	93	INA	119	5.7	M:72 F:77	911
UNITED KINGDOM	17,760	2.6	100	125	663	6.6	M:73 F:79	715
UNITED STATES	23,120	1.3	100	139	1,012	8.3	M:72 F:79	416
RUSSIA	2,680	INA	100	132	89	18	M:62 F:74	225
VIETNAM	INA	INA	42	103	INA	36	M:63 F:67	2,974
ZAIRE	INA	185	33	90	2	93	M:50 F:53	14,810
ZIMBABWE	570	36	66	96	21	59	M:54 F:57	7,844

Movement: Earth's Travels in Time

We are a society that pays a lot of attention to time. In many ways, we are actually ruled by time. Look at the importance we place on birthdays, celebrated once each year on the same date. Getting to class on time is very important. People who work must get to work on time. Not being ready on time for a friend can result in hurt feelings or even an argument. Because time is so important to us, clocks and watches are everywhere—on walls, wrists, town halls, and so on. We can even get the time over the phone by dialing a special number.

You might not associate time with the subject of Geography, but you can't study Geography without understanding time. **Time** is really a measure of the Earth's movements, on its own axis and around the sun. The Earth rotates, or spins, on an imaginary pole that runs through its center from north to south. The pole is called the **axis.** The rate of the Earth's rotation is 15 degrees (15°) an hour. Every circle has 360 degrees (360°). There are 360° around the Earth's middle, or **equator.** It takes the Earth 24 hours to complete one **rotation** of 360°. A rotation of Earth is the time between one sunrise and the next sunrise (or between noon of one day and noon of the next, and so forth).

Until the late 1800s there were many different time systems around the world. Most cities and towns kept their own time, and these times had no relation to other places. This made traveling very confusing. In the United States alone, every railroad line had its own time system for a total of 53 different time systems!

As travel became faster and more important during the 1800s, it became difficult, if

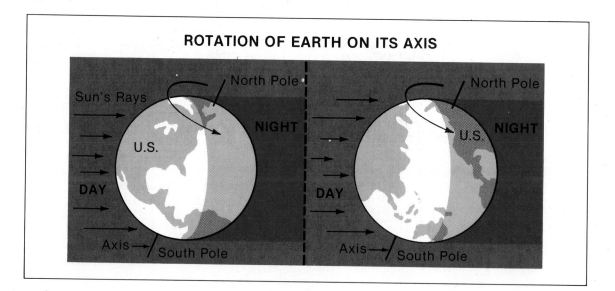

ROTATION OF EARTH ON ITS AXIS

Sun's Rays • North Pole • NIGHT • U.S. • DAY • Axis → South Pole

North Pole • NIGHT • U.S. • DAY • Axis → South Pole

Time Zones of the World

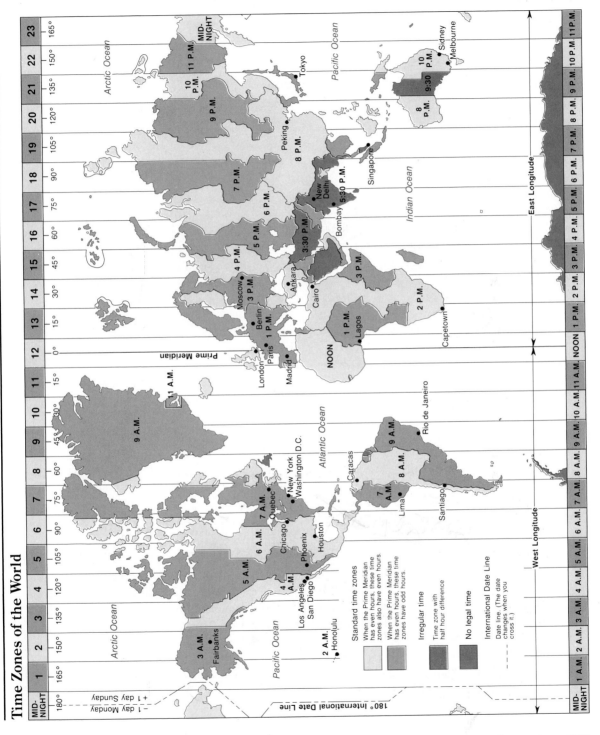

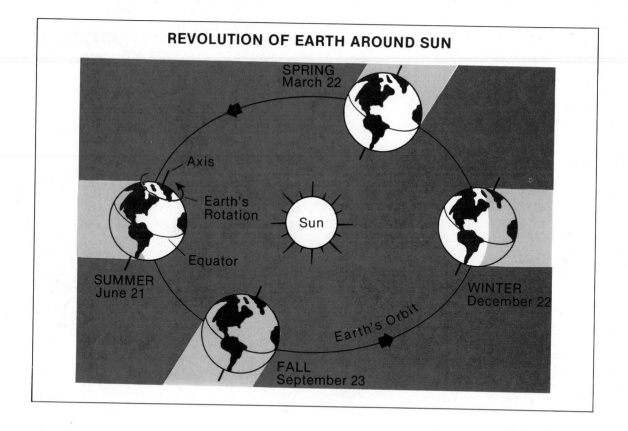

REVOLUTION OF EARTH AROUND SUN

SPRING
March 22

Axis

Earth's
Rotation

Sun

Equator

SUMMER
June 21

WINTER
December 22

Earth's Orbit

FALL
September 23

not impossible, for travelers to know the correct times in the cities they were passing through. Nor could they know the correct time of the place to which they were going. Something had to be done. So in 1884 a conference was called in Washington, D.C. It was attended by delegates from countries around the world.

The delegates agreed on a time system called *Standard Time.* According to the system, an imaginary line was drawn through Greenwich (gren′ ich), England. That line, running from the North Pole to the South Pole, was called the **Prime Meridian.** Meridian is another word for longitude line. From the Prime Meridian, all other lines of

longitude were drawn. Seven and a half degrees to the west of the Prime Meridian another time zone (one hour earlier) would begin. Seven and a half degrees to the east of the Prime Meridian is another time zone. There, time would be one hour later than at the Prime Meridian zone. Notice that every time zone (including the Prime Meridian zone) consists of 15° (7½° + 7½° = 15°).

On page 327 there is a map of the 24 times zones. Notice how the time zones are arranged in 15° intervals. Time zones make it possible for travelers to know the correct time, anywhere in the world. The system of time is tied in with the rotation of the Earth on its axis.

The Earth has another movement related to time, which we call the *year*. While spinning on its axis, the Earth moves in a sphere-shaped path around the Sun. This is called a **revolution.** It takes one year for the Earth to make the trip. On this year-long trip, the tilt of the Earth remains the same, but as it moves around the Sun, the seasons of the Earth change. As you can see from the diagram on page 328, the rays of the Sun directly hit the Northern Hemisphere during the last part of June. (The Northern Hemisphere is the area of the Earth north of the equator.) Because of this, the Northern Hemisphere has warmer weather in June than December, when the Sun's rays are directed at the Southern Hemisphere.

This movement of the Earth accounts for changes of seasons during the year. The Northern and Southern Hemispheres have opposite seasons. When it is spring in the United Sates, for example, it is autumn in Argentina. When it is summer in Korea, it is winter in Australia.

So you see, Geography is really the basis for time systems. The hours of the day, the seasons, and the years are figured by the rotation of the Earth on its axis and by its yearly trip around the Sun.

READING REVIEW

1. Define: Prime Meridian, time zone, axis.
2. Describe the relationship between the Earth's rotation and time.
3. Describe the revolution of planet Earth and its relationship to time.
4. What improvement in the system of keeping time was brought about by the 1884 Washington conference?

Critical Thinking

5. **Drawing and Testing Conclusions** (see page 42) How important is time to you? Count the number of watches, clocks, and other timepieces that you and your family own. (Don't forget to count the clocks in cars and on microwave ovens, VCRs, and other appliances.) Divide that number by the number of people in your household. The result is the number of timepieces per member of your family. What does this tell you about the importance you and your family place on time? Does our society put a lot of emphasis on time? How can you tell?

EXPERIMENT **6-L**

Movement: Measuring Time and Space

Using an atlas or globe, answer the following questions as accurately as you can. This experiment is designed to see how much you have learned about systems of measuring time and space.

1. What is the location in longitude and latitude of the following places?
   a. Cairo, Egypt
   b. Sidney, Australia
   c. Arequipa, Peru

d. Toronto, Canada
e. Madrid, Spain

2. What places would you find at the following locations?
   a. 52° S 59° W
   b. 60° N 86° W
   c. 30° N 90° W
   d. 1° S 33° E

3. According to Standard Time zones, when it is 12:00 noon in London, what time is it in the following cities?
   a. Sidney, Australia
   b. Beijing, China
   c. Moscow, U.S.S.R.
   d. Tokyo, Japan
   e. Cairo, Egypt
   f. Rio de Janeiro, Brazil
   g. Honolulu, Hawaii
   h. New York, New York
   i. San Diego, California

4. When it is summer in Chicago, what season is it in the following cities?
   a. Wellington, New Zealand
   b. Stockholm, Sweden
   c. Ottawa, Canada
   d. Cape Town, South Africa

5. You are planning a plane's flight pattern from John F. Kennedy International Airport in New York City to the four cities listed below. Your job, using a globe, is to plan the most direct route to each city. What is the approximate distance you would have to travel to each city? With an average speed of 600 miles (approximately 965 kilometers) per hour, how long would it take to get to each city?
   a. Hong Kong
   b. Leningrad, U.S.S.R.
   c. Buenos Aires, Argentina
   d. Paris, France

READING 8

Movement: Everybody Is Connected To Everybody Else

As we saw in "Reading 7: *Movement: Earth's Travels in Time,*" our planet is in constant movement. Earth's movements connect our days and nights, as well as our seasons and our years. The land, air, and water systems of our planet move and change, too, as do the animal and plant life systems. It would be accurate to say that our Earth today is not the same planet it was 1,000 years ago, 100 years ago, or even yesterday.

Along with our Earth, the people of our planet are also moving and changing. No longer are we a world of isolated places. Improvements in transportation and communication have connected our world as never before. People can move easily and quickly from place to place. Today, people all around our planet have many more opportunities to meet one another and gather information about places far from them than their parents or grandparents had. You don't even have to leave your home. You can turn on your television and see what is happening all over the world. You can pick up your home telephone and within a few seconds your voice is transmitted and can be heard thousands of miles away.

Transportation and communication networks have made it possible for people around the world to do business with one another at an astounding pace. Clothing designers here in the United States can call their suppliers in Asia and order a thousand new items. The designer may use the telefax to send exact information and sketches. Ten thousand miles away, those sketches are received in seconds. Computerized equipment makes it possible for the Asian factory to send the designer a finished product by air delivery.

This constant, speedy movement of people, ideas, and products around the planet is creating an exciting world market. It is also creating some challenges for us. As a world we are more **interdependent** than ever before. This means people and nations rely upon each other. Individual actions and thoughts that once affected only our community or our country are now felt worldwide. When we travel and trade with other nations we interact with environments everywhere.

Who, then, should be held responsible for the pollution of air and water systems halfway around the world? Should people everywhere be paid the same wages for similar work? How should the people of rich countries interact with people from poor countries? Those are just some of the questions and challenges that face the world community.

Everybody is connected to everybody else. How can we use our connections with other humans and with our planet's systems to make a better world for all of us?

READING REVIEW

1. How are you connected to people in places you have never seen?
2. Why does the survival of our planet depend upon the cooperative efforts of all people?

Critical Thinking

3. **Predicting Consequences** (see page 36) How do you think your choice of products at the stores where you shop would be affected if the United States stopped trading with other countries?

Computer networks have made it possible for people around the world to communicate with one another at an astounding pace.

READING 9

Regions: Understanding Our World

So far, we have looked at location, place, human-environment interaction, and movement. Those are four of the five themes that geographers use to study our planet. The fifth theme is regions. A **region** is made up of areas that have common characteristics. It is possible to divide our planet into regions in many different ways. Below is a map of Europe, showing *language* regions. These are regions in which common languages are spoken. Can you identify the language groupings?

On the top of page 333 is another map of Europe. This time, the continent is divided into *economic* regions. On this map we see the countries of Europe that have economic ties with each other and, as a result, form an economic region known as the European Union.

Agricultural regions are shown on the map of Europe on the bottom of page 333. Can you identify each of the regions, according to types of agriculture?

The *political* regions of Europe are

Europe: Language Regions

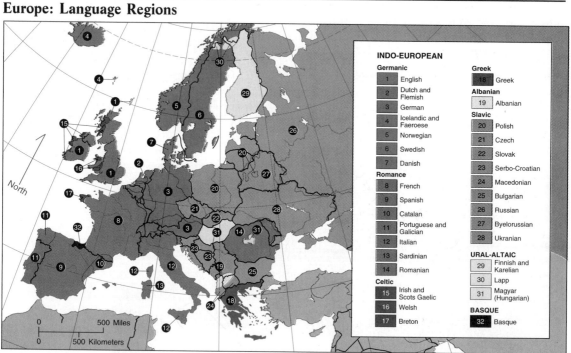

Europe: Economic Regions

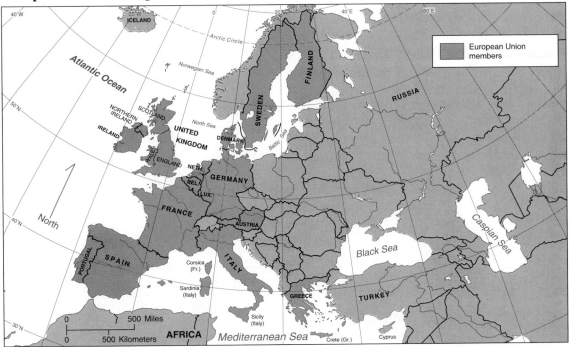

Europe: Agricultural Regions

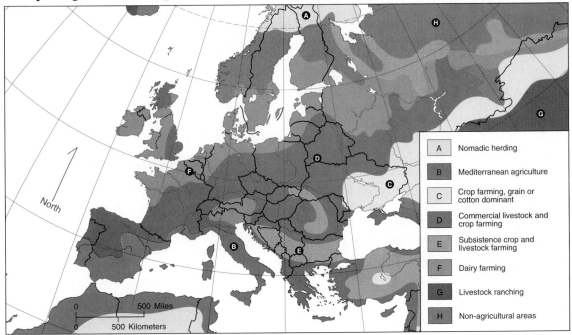

Europe: Political Regions

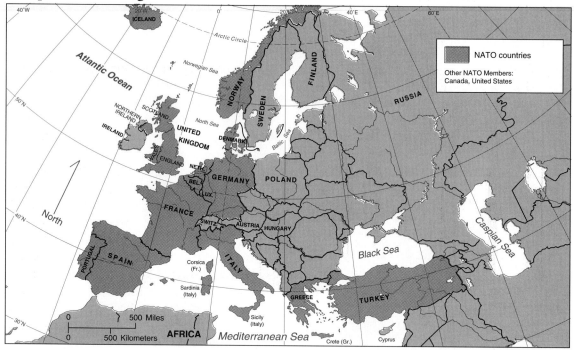

shown in the map on page 334. Can you identify the political alliance that connects some of the countries of Europe?

Those are only four of the many ways in which geographers divide Europe into regions. The same may be done for our entire world. Geographers like to study regions because they provide a larger picture than studying local areas. Studying single regions is also more manageable than trying to study the entire planet.

Regions help geographers understand the differences that exist between one part of our world and all other areas of the globe. Each region is unique, unlike any other on the planet. But studying one region often helps geographers understand other regions better. If people learned how to grow crops in the Sahara, for example, geographers might be able to apply that knowledge to other deserts around the world. By studying the effects of destroying the tropical rain forest in Brazil, geographers can better understand the impact of such destruction in other countries.

In "Experiment 6-N: *Regions:* Focusing on Today," you will have a chance to put your understanding of regions to work, as you examine important current events of today.

READING REVIEW

1. What is a region?
2. Name three kinds of regions.

Critical Thinking

3. **Making Comparisons** (see page 16) Compare the region of the United States in which you live with another region. What similarities do you find? What differences exist?

Regions: Focusing on Today

If you read the daily newspaper or watch the evening news, you know that important events are happening in our country and around the world all the time. In fact, our world is changing faster than ever before. If you want to know about your world, you must keep up with the news in every region of the planet. Fortunately, with today's technology we are able to do this. News stories reach us in only a few seconds from anywhere on our planet. Instant news reports are available around the clock on TV and radio. Satellites make it possible for newspapers to include up-to-the-minute information in their stories.

Do you keep yourself informed about current events? The most successful people in our country and in our world make it a habit to keep up with the news. They know that information is often the source of power. Knowing what is going on in the world can give you an important advantage in life.

In this experiment, you will be given a map of the United States and a series of regional maps of the world. Using the newspaper or magazine you brought to class, identify 10 recent events outside the United States and 5 events inside our country. On your maps, place numbers marking the locations of those 15 events. Then, write a short description of each event on the reverse side of the map. Be prepared to discuss those current events in class.

Reading the newspaper everyday will help you keep informed about the day's events in your area and throughout the world.

Regions: Focusing on Tomorrow

In this unit, you have learned about our planet from a geographer's point of view. You know how important it is to be part of the solutions for the challenges we face today and in the future. There is a lot of truth in the old saying "If you're not part of the solution, you are part of the problem."

In this experiment, you and your group should first choose any one region of the world. Identify one challenge faced by the people of that region. The challenge might be a human problem—poverty, homelessness, hunger, or illiteracy, for example. Or the challenge might be environmental—air pollution, water shortages, garbage, destruction of the rain forests, or contamination of the waterways.

As a group, write an original news story about the challenge you have chosen to focus on. Describe the problem and the region. Explain why the challenge is an important one to the people of that region. Then make at least two good suggestions for solving the problem.

Choose one person from your group to present your news story to the class. Every member of the group should be prepared to answer questions after the presentation.

READING 10

Careers in Geography*

Do you think you might be interested in a career in Geography? Geographers are employed in a wide range of occupations. Most geographers are teachers in secondary schools and colleges. Some geographers write articles and books on their areas of interest. Others are researchers and analysts who gather information for businesses, organizations, and the government.

Some geographers are cartographers, or map makers. The National Geographic Society employs a staff of cartographers who draw beautiful, precise maps for the society's books and its magazine. The United States Government employs cartographers and other geographers to make maps for the armed services, the FBI, the CIA, and other federal agencies. Local and state governments also hire geographers to study problems of ecology and the uses of land, water, and air.

Business and industries need people trained in Geography to make studies of transportation and marketing systems. Industries use the information geographers produce to determine the best locations to build factories, and office buildings.

*Adapted from *Occupational Outlook Handbook.* (See Acknowledgements, pages 595–596.)

A geographer gathers information about the ecology of a wetland area.

Some geographers study climates and weather patterns. They use their information to help farmers produce greater harvests. They help preserve wildlife by making studies of the migrations of wildlife throughout the year. Medical geographers study the effect of the environment on the health of people and animals. They recommend ways of improving the environment so that people live longer, healthier lives.

Urban geographers study cities. They analyze the ways houses and other dwellings are placed. Their recommendations often result in housing patterns that are better for urban living and working.

Some geographers are employed by organizations that protect the environment from pollution and other dangers. They study ways of protecting the plants, animals, and sea life of Earth. They are also concerned with providing for human needs and the needs of government and industry.

Training in Geography provides a good background for many careers, in addition to the ones we have just described. Most high schools and over 300 colleges offer courses in Geography. Government agencies and industries sometimes hire students as interns during the summer. Interns learn about the real world of Geography, and at the same time they learn about government and business. Internships often provide important contacts with people with whom you can later talk about careers and full-time employment.

If you want to be a geographer, you should enjoy reading, studying, and doing research. That is because geographers need to know the most current information about their fields. Curiosity and creativity are also important personal characteristics. Patience and hard work are also essential. Many geographers need these qualities for the long hours they spend making their work the best it can possibly be.

For more information about careers in Geography, write to the National Council for Geographic Education, Indiana University of Pennsylvania, Indiana, PA 15705. Another good source of information is the National Geographic Society, 1710 Sixteenth Street N.W., Washington, DC 20009.

READING REVIEW

1. What occupation do most geographers practice?
2. What are some other occupations for geographers today?

Critical Thinking

3. **Making Comparisons** (see page 16) What similarities do you see between careers in Geography and careers in any of the other social sciences? What differences do you see?

PERSPECTIVES

Social Scientists Look at the Destruction of the Rain Forests

How do the ways geographers think about a subject compare to the ways other social scientists think? You will explore the similarities and differences as you examine a selection about the Brazilian rain forest. Read the passage below from an article in *National Geographic* and then answer the questions that follow under "Comparing the Social Sciences."

"The rush had slowed somewhat now, but large numbers of men and women from the ranks of the dirt poor continued to arrive, chasing dreams of a better life—riches, even—through the vast dank chambers of Amazonia, which stands today as probably the last great seductive frontier on earth.

Mostly they make their way to the state of Rondônia, in western Brazil, along the border with Bolivia. Given large tracts of land there by the federal government, they first fell and burn the trees (not the mahogany and cherry, though; those are sold), and then they hack and clear until the . . . acres lie blackened and scarred like a battlefield in war.

In Rondônia's capital city of Pôrto Velho, steamy and swollen now with a population of 450,000, there are people who tell of a time not far back when the jungle tightly girded what was then a lightly populated outpost on the frontier. The place lay fast by the Madeira River, a . . . tributary of the Amazon with the promise of gold in its sands. . . .

But then a road was scraped through the length of the state, eventually linking Pôrto Velho with Cuiaba, the capital of Mato Grosso state. An ambitious highway through the Amazon, it is called BR-364. At first the 900-mile road was dirt, so when the tropical rains came each year, starting in September, it all went to thick red mud.

Still the mass movement of people to Rondônia began in those years of the early 1970s; by 1984, when the paving of BR-364 was completed, the migration was turned to full throttle. There has been nothing like it since the rush to the American West by settlers. The damage to the environment has been severe. As much as 20 percent of the rain forest may have been destroyed. Socially Rondônia has mirrored the excesses of other frontier openings: the undercurrent of lawlessness . . . and a haphazard lifestyle gripped by uncertainty.

. . . [T]here are Indian players in this frontier drama. They are being pushed into corners, sometimes murdered."

Comparing the Social Sciences

Psychologists study human emotions. As a psychologist, what could you learn about the feelings of the pioneers headed into the Amazonian jungle? (*Demonstrating Reasoned Judgment*)

Sociologists study group behavior. As a sociologist, what different changes might you expect the continuing population growth to bring to the Pôrto Velho residents? (*Predicting Consequences*)

Anthropologists study cultures. As an anthropologist, what questions would you ask pioneers to find out the new ways of living they developed in Amazonia? (*Creating Good Questions*)

Geographers study natural resources. If you were a geographer, which details from this article would you pay most attention to?

Explain your answer. (*Demonstrating Reasoned Judgment*)

Historians study the past. As a historian, what similarities or differences do you see between the westward movement in Brazil today and the rush to settle the American West in the nineteenth century? (*Making Comparisons*)

Political scientists study the role of government. As a political scientist, how would you describe the role of Brazil's government in the development of the rain-forest region? (*Identifying Central Issues*)

Economists study the way people use resources. As an economist, what do you think the state of Amazonia's resources will be in 10 years if this trend continues? In 50 years? (*Predicting Consequences*)

Billowing, smoke from the burning rain forest

GLOSSARY OF TERMS

absolute location   exactly where something is located on Earth (page 272)

acid rain   rain that contains sulfur and nitrogen oxides gathered from factory smoke and automobile exhaust (page 293)

atmosphere   the layer of air covering Earth (page 287)

axis   an imaginary pole on which Earth spins (page 326)

biodegradable   the chemical quality of a substance that allows it to decay and be broken down into its individual parts (page 294)

climate   the main kind of weather in an area (page 287)

closed system   a system that operates on its own; it does not need outside help to start or to keep going (page 291)

continent   one of seven major land masses on Earth (page 286)

developed nations   the wealthy, industrialized nations of the world (page 308)

developing nations   the poorer nations in the world seeking to use their resources to develop industry; sometimes referred to as *less developed* (page 308)

direction   as used in this unit, the arrow pointing North on maps and globes (page 275)

ecosystem   the Earth system of life, made up of all living things and beings on this planet (page 292)

ecology   the study of the ecosystem (page 293)

equator   Earth's halfway point from the North Pole to the South Pole; zero degrees latitude line (page 326)

geographer   a person who studies the Earth and its people (page 267)

Geography   the study of Earth and its people; divided into Physical Geography and Human Geography (page 267)

globe   a miniature model of the planet Earth, usually showing landforms, waterways, and political boundaries (page 272)

GNP   Gross National Product; total value of everything produced in a country in a year (page 318)

grid   a pattern of lines running horizontally and vertically that cross each other at right angles (page 275)

greenhouse effect   warming trends over parts of the Earth caused by heat from the Sun trapped beneath a layer of pollution in the Earth's atmosphere (page 293)

Human Geography   the study of people and how they interact with the environment (page 267)

interaction   people's relationship with the environment, particularly how they use the environment and the impact they have on it (page 293)

interdependence   in a system, the reliance of one part upon other parts; the reliance of people upon people and nation upon nation in the systems of Earth (page 331)

key   that which explains the symbols on maps and globes; also called a legend (page 276)

landform the shape land takes; types of landforms include plains, plateaus, hills, and mountains (page 286)

latitude lines the imaginary lines on maps and globes running east and west; used to locate places (page 272)

legend see *key* (page 276)

less-developed nation see *developing nations* (page 308)

location the position of something or someone on Earth's surface (page 272)

longitude lines the imaginary lines on maps and globes running north and south; used to locate places (page 272)

map a flat projection of some aspect of Earth's surface, such as landforms and waterways, political regions, economic regions, and so on (page 272)

natural vegetation region a region of Earth characterized by a particular kind of plant life (page 287)

nonrenewable resource a resource that cannot easily be replaced, such as petroleum (page 299)

ocean one of Earth's four largest bodies of water (page 286)

open system a system that cannot operate on its own; needs something to start it or keep it going (page 290)

Physical Geography the study of Earth's natural features (page 267)

place what you find at a location; every place has unique physical and human characteristics (page 286)

precipitation water in the air that falls as rain, hail, or snow (page 287)

Prime Meridian the zero meridian (0°) that passes through Greenwich, England, and from which east and west longitudes are measured (page 328)

region a group of areas that share certain common characteristics (page 332)

relative location the location of a place compared to a known, familiar place (page 273)

renewable source a resource that can be replaced (page 299)

resource a part of nature people use (page 296)

revolution one complete trip around the Sun, lasting a year (page 329)

rotation the spinning of Earth on an imaginary axis that runs through its center and from north to south (page 326)

scale the size of an area on a map or globe compared with the actual size of that area on Earth (page 275)

strategic resource a resource that is important for our country's industries or national security (page 302)

subsistence a level of existence in which there are only the barest means to stay alive (page 310)

system a working thing composed of two or more parts that work together and are interdependent; there are two types: open and closed (page 290)

time a system used to divide the Earth's rotation on its axis and its revolution around the sun into seconds, minutes, hours, days, months, years, and so on (page 326)

UNIT 7 History

HISTORY

GEOGRAPHY

ANTHROPOLOGY

POLITICAL SCIENCE

STUDY & THINKING **SKILLS**

SOCIOLOGY

PSYCHOLOGY

ECONOMICS

This Is History

Imagine that you woke up one morning and had lost your memory. Think of all the ways this would change your life. You probably would not know even a simple thing like how to get to school. Once at school, how would you decide which room to go to first? How could you pick which person to ask, of all those rushing past you in the hall, if you could not recognize your teachers, classmates, or friends? Almost every decision we make during the day depends in one way or another on memory. Memory guides us, helping us avoid unnecessary mistakes.

History is like memory. It helps us learn from our past experiences. Social Scientists who study the past are called **historians.** In the Unit 7 readings, you will learn how historians think. In the experiments, you will have a chance to think like a historian yourself.

History and You

History is not just something that happened to other people far away and long ago. History is happening here and now—to you, your friends, and family. The questions below will help you understand your connection to History.

1. What are five things from your home that communicate something about your family's past? Where did the objects come from? What's the significance to your family?

2. Name several household objects that you take for granted today that people did not have 30 years ago. How have they changed the way you live?

3. If the only thing from your life that your great-grandchildren had to examine was your collection of records or CDs, what would they think of how you and your generation lived?

UNIT 7   CONTENTS

Getting a Line on Your Past

History, as we all know, deals with the past. Let's begin by taking a look at your recent past, the last 24 hours. On a sheet of paper, draw a straight line and then determine which is the beginning and end of the day. Mark your line, showing when important events happened. Label those events. What you have created is called a **time line.**

After you have drawn your time line, study it closely. Are there any events on the time line that might have caused other events to happen? What are they? In what ways are the events of the past 24 hours related to each other?

When you think you can answer those questions, write a description about your time line. Make it a history (a true story) about your life during the last 24 hours. Be sure to show how the most important events are related to each other.

Once you have done this you are well on your way to understanding what history is all about. That's because you examined events and saw how they were related. You then wrote as accurately as possible a history of those events. This is what professional historians do when they reconstruct the past.

Does your time line look something like the one below?

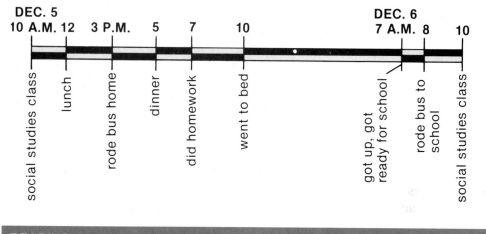

DEC. 5
10 A.M. 12   3 P.M.   5   7   10

DEC. 6
7 A.M.   8   10

social studies class · lunch · rode bus home · dinner · did homework · went to bed · got up, got ready for school · rode bus to school · social studies class

What Is History?

Of all the social sciences, History is probably the one you have studied most. It may also be the one you understand least.

What is History, anyhow? Is it mainly a collecton of names, dates, and facts? Is it about wars and battles? Is it a record of human accomplishments? Is it a record of the effects of local, national, and global events upon people's lives?

History is all of this and more. History is what you wore to school today, and why you wore it. History is the day you were born and all the generations of births in your family leading up to that day. History is the reason you live where you do. History includes the reasons why we face important challenges in our future.

Historians, those who study and write about History, include all of those topics under the category of "History." In this unit, we will take a close look at the tools historians use to write accounts of past events and their causes. In fact, you will be using many of the historian's tools yourself. You will discover that the work of a historian is much like the work of a detective. Historians, like detectives, try to figure out what really happened, and why. They want to know who made it happen, as well as the perceptions, thoughts, and actions behind it all. They want to know what the consequences were, and what cause-effect relationships developed.

Like detectives, historians use many methods to arrive at their conclusions. They use their powers of observation to watch people and events very carefully. They study important events, and read as much as they can about those events. They try to discover as many interpretations of the events as possible, so that every possible angle is covered.

The historian's critical thinking skills really come in handy when studying such events. Historians must be able to identify slanted messages and propaganda, because such evidence is often biased and not trustworthy. They must be able to recognize their own assumptions, as well as those of other historians, and they should be able to identify the assumptions that are false.

The end result of the historian's work is the accurate, truthful record of our past. It's important that future generations will know *what* happened and *why* it happened. By studying the successes of the past, we can take pride in our accomplishments. And by studying the failures of the past, we can possibly learn what to do now and in our future.

So you see, **History** is a lot more than just a story of the past with facts, names, and dates. It is the ever-changing story of the human race. History is a useful and interesting tool for examining ourselves.

Finding out about yourself and the people who came before you can be fascinating.

Until now, History may have seemed dull and boring to you. This unit is unlike any History course you have ever taken. You will have an opportunity to see how a historian works. You will see how historians use the tools of their trade to put together their stories of the past. And, most important of all, you will be writing a historical account yourself. By "doing" History, you will have a better understanding of how all those facts, names, and dates got into your History books.

READING REVIEW

1. What is History?
2. What are the methods historians use in their work?

Critical Thinking

3. **Predicting Consequences** (see page 36) Based upon what you already know, describe two possible consequences of your own work in this unit.

EXPERIMENT **7-B**

A Family History on Maps

Many Americans today are on the move. Studies show that people in this country move about five times during their lifetimes, on the average. Some move more often, while some don't move at all. In your family history, your ancestors moved to this land from other places. Everyone living in this country has ancestors who came from another land. Even the native American Indians at one time, perhaps 20,000 years ago, came here from Asia.

Where did your ancestors come from? When did they arrive in America? Where did they live? Where did they move? It is understandable that you might not know where *all* your ancestors came from, lived, and moved to. Chances are, however, that you know at least some of the answers to these questions. Those you are not sure about may be answered by your parents or grandparents, or by family records.

First make a list of the ancestors you plan to trace, beginning with your grandparents. If your grandparents did not come from another country, try tracing your great-grandparents. Beside each ancestor's name, put the country of origin. On the outline map of the world on Handout 7-B, locate and label the places from which your ancestors came. Then locate and label where they settled in America. Draw lines connecting the places they left to the places in which they settled. You might want to use different colored lines to represent the different branches of the family.

On the outline map of the United States on Handout 7-B, trace the route your immediate family took over the years in moving from place to place. Label the cities in which your immediate family has lived. If you can find out the dates they lived in each city, include the date beside the city. Your family may have moved from or lived in another country. If so, put the name of the country, or countries, on the right of the map on the space provided. Draw your lines from the map to the name of the country and back to the map.

This activity will give you a better idea of your own history and your family's history.

Some of your ancestors may have been part of the expansion west. This painting by Thomas Otter, called On the Road, *shows people traveling west by both covered wagon and by train.*

Your Family Tree—Getting To Know Your Past

You have traced your family's movement from place to place and have drawn the routes on maps. Now let's do some more research.

What do you know about your ancestors? What sort of people were they? Do you realize how important your ancestors are to you? If one of your ancestors had decided not to come to America, you might have been born in another country. Your life might have been completely different. Who you are, where you live, and what you do—all of these are partly the result of your ancestors' actions.

One way to find out more about those important people in your past is to make a family tree. This is sometimes called a lineage chart. A family tree is similar to any other kind of tree. It has both "roots" and a "top." The roots are your ancestors, and the top is you.

On page 350 is a model family tree. Notice that it has been turned on its side. Real family trees are usually more complicated than this if you include the brothers and sisters of all the people from whom you are directly descended. It is further complicated if divorces, remarriages, and step-relatives are included. Notice that the name of the person is given above the line. The date and place of birth are written underneath the line. You will be setting up your own family tree on Handout 7-C.

Information about your family will probably be more and more difficult to find as you go further back in time. However, try to get information for your tree as far back as possible.

Photographs of ancestors may reveal family resemblances. What resemblances do you see here?

How are you going to get the information you need to do your family tree? One obvious source is your parents. Ask them to recall the data you need. Perhaps they have some pictures of your ancestors you can add to your family tree. (Here's a tip: Make a photostatic copy of the photographs and keep the originals at home. It's safer that way.) Other relatives—aunts, uncles, cousins, and grandparents—might also be able to help you.

While you're talking to those people about the family history, take the opportunity to ask them some questions. What was life like when your grandmother was your age? What kind of music was popular then? What did people your age do for fun? Why did some of your ancestors, or even parents, move to the United States? (Think of some other questions.)

You will have a while to work on this project, so do the best job possible. Make an adventure of it, a once-in-a-lifetime chance to find out everything you've wanted to know about you and where you came from.

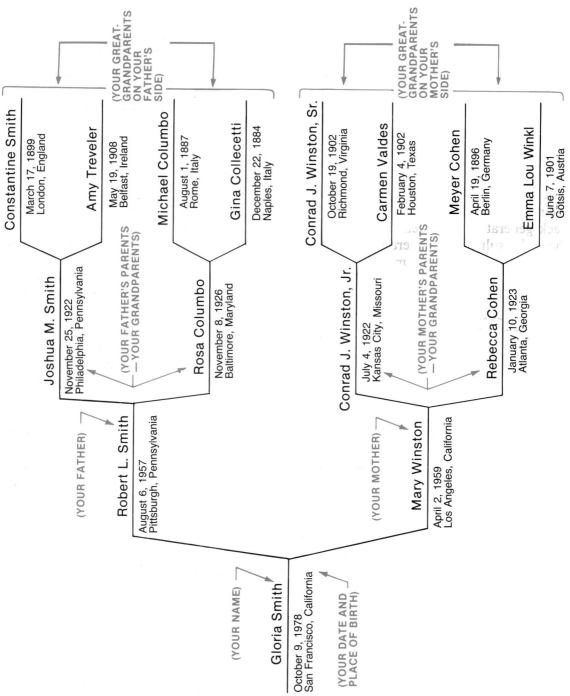

(YOUR GREAT-GRANDPARENTS ON YOUR FATHER'S SIDE)

Constantine Smith
March 17, 1899
London, England

Amy Treveler
May 19, 1908
Belfast, Ireland

Michael Columbo
August 1, 1887
Rome, Italy

Gina Collecetti
December 22, 1884
Naples, Italy

(YOUR GREAT-GRANDPARENTS ON YOUR MOTHER'S SIDE)

Conrad J. Winston, Sr.
October 19, 1902
Richmond, Virginia

Carmen Valdes
February 4, 1902
Houston, Texas

Meyer Cohen
April 19, 1896
Berlin, Germany

Emma Lou Winkl
June 7, 1901
Götsis, Austria

(YOUR FATHER'S PARENTS—YOUR GRANDPARENTS)

Joshua M. Smith
November 25, 1922
Philadelphia, Pennsylvania

Rosa Columbo
November 8, 1926
Baltimore, Maryland

(YOUR MOTHER'S PARENTS—YOUR GRANDPARENTS)

Conrad J. Winston, Jr.
July 4, 1922
Kansas City, Missouri

Rebecca Cohen
January 10, 1923
Atlanta, Georgia

(YOUR FATHER)

Robert L. Smith
August 6, 1957
Pittsburgh, Pennsylvania

(YOUR MOTHER)

Mary Winston
April 2, 1959
Los Angeles, California

(YOUR NAME)

Gloria Smith
October 9, 1978
San Francisco, California

(YOUR DATE AND PLACE OF BIRTH)

You Have a History

As an individual you have quite a history. In class you began an investigation into your history and the history of your family. You may have discovered that your personal history really goes back centuries before you were born. You are here because certain events led your mother and father to meet; your mother and father in turn are here because events led to the meeting of their mothers and fathers. And so it goes, back generation after generation. You are the end result of one generation giving life to another generation, multiplied many times over.

Looking into your past can give you a much better idea of who you are. Dr. Mary Matossian, a professor at the University of Maryland, believes that you can learn a lot by studying your ancestors. She says that a family is an "emotional system." Each member develops a pattern of behavior toward every other member of the family. Dr. Matossian thinks that these behavior patterns repeat themselves from one generation to the next. Research was done on hundreds of families before she could arrive at that conclusion.

Those findings make sense. After all, can't you see some similarities between your behavior and ideas and those of another member of your family? (Even if you can't see the similarities, chances are that your close friends can see them. Ask them!) You learn much more than you think from the ways your parents act and talk.

That doesn't mean you will be a carbon-copy of your parents. (Not unless you want to be.) It simply means that you have a tendency to be more like your parents than anybody else. While your family and its history have a strong influence on you, you are nevertheless unique. You can do much to determine the course of your own life. As long as you are alive, you have the opportunity to change. There has never been anyone exactly like you, and there never will be. You have an identity like no other person in the past, present, or future.

Can you describe the person who is *you*? It's a difficult thing to really know yourself. Oftentimes, it is much easier to know other people than it is to know yourself. But you need to understand yourself in order to understand your history.

Let's suppose you have an opportunity to tell future generations about yourself. You may briefly describe yourself in writing. You cannot, however, use just a description of yourself. You should use only those objects which give clues about yourself. What will you choose? What things best describe the real *you?* What pieces of evidence would you leave behind? Think about it!

READING REVIEW

1. Why is it important to study your family history, according to Dr. Mary Matossian?

Critical Thinking

2. **Recognizing Cause and Effect** (see page 35). Why aren't you destined to be a carbon-copy of your parents?

How Will They Know Who You Were 200 Years from Now?

If you had the chance to let future generations know about you, what clues would you leave them? What pieces of evidence would you want to leave your great-great-great-great-great-great-grandchildren to give them a clear idea of your personality, your ideas, and your actions?

In this experiment you will be given a chance to do just that. You will be permitted to select only five pieces of evidence to represent yourself. Only one of them can be a description of yourself in fifteen words or less. The other four must be objects which would tell something important about you.

One of the objects may be a photo or drawing of yourself.

Think seriously! What would you choose to describe the real you? Bring in five pieces of evidence for the next class period. Label each item with your name in a place where it can't be easily seen. Bring the items to class in a paper bag and keep them there until your teacher collects the bag. If an object is too impractical to bring to class, prepare a small sketch of it. Or, bring something that represents the object.

Your class will be deciding how well your clues describe yourself.

Gathering Evidence

Evidence is the key to solving a mystery. It is also the key to history. A good historian knows that the right kind of evidence is essential. Without it the historian cannot know what happened in the past and cannot interpret past events. For the historian, **evidence** consists of records of the past. These are used to study how people and events affected each other. As you can see, history can't be written without evidence.

In preparation for this experiment, you selected five clues, or pieces of evidence about yourself. Each piece was chosen because you thought it would describe something important about you. Your classmates did the same for themselves.

This is a follow-up to the work you did in "Experiment 7-D: How Will They Know Who You Were 200 Years from Now?" Consider the types of evidence each "mystery" student used to describe himself or herself. Try to answer the following questions as completely as you can on a separate sheet of paper.

1. What was each piece of evidence?
2. Which evidence was most effective in describing the person who brought it in? Why?
3. Which evidence was not obvious or helpful in describing the person? Why?

4. How much evidence, in some cases, was needed before you could decide who the person was?
5. What if the teacher had shown a piece of evidence taken from another person? What problems would have occurred as a result of being shown an incorrect piece of information?

You should begin to see that the historian's evidence and the five pieces of evidence you brought to class today have a lot in common. The best kinds of evidence for historians are those which show as closely as possible the true nature of the person or event being studied. Unless all the evidence by which you judged a person was genuine, your conclusion about the person's identity would have been wrong. Unless historians have accurate, genuine and sufficient evidence with which to work, they will make wrong conclusions. Their interpretations of events and people will be distorted.

Evidence

When you read a history book you are reading the product of the historian's work. Where did all those facts, names, places, and dates come from? How does the historian know which facts are important and which ones are not important enough to include in the work? How does the historian know how one event affects another event? How does the historian know how to interpret the events of the past?

It isn't easy. Some historians begin by asking an important question about a historical topic. For example:

"George Washington is called the Father of our country. Does he deserve this honor more than anyone else?"

Newspaper Rock in the Petrified Forest National Park in Arizona has ancient Indian carvings. To a historian this would be a valuable piece of evidence in the study of Indian life.

"North Vietnamese PT boats attacked the U.S. destroyer *Maddox* in August 1964. Why did President Lyndon Johnson call for a congressional resolution to defend American interests in Asia?"

"Why did the Roman Empire rise to power, then collapse?"

Personal topics would also be worth investigating. You could ask:

"What were the reasons my ancestors moved to America?"

"How did my town (city) develop in the early 1900s?"

"What was the importance of transportation in my state during the 1800s?"

(If any of these topics interest you, why not ask your teacher to give you credit for researching them?)

Once a topic or question has been determined, the historian begins to search for evidence. This stage of research is something like the work you did in "Experiment 7-D: How Will They Know Who You Were 200 Years from Now?", only in reverse. In that experiment you saw evidence about the identities of students. You were trying to discover who the evidence was about. In doing historical research, most often you already know the subject about which you are going to write. You then look for evidence that will help you to know as much as possible about the person or event.

What kinds of clues are helpful to the historian? There are many. Letters, books and magazines, tape recordings, journals, photographs, maps, conversations with people living at the time—all of these can be helpful in piecing together the story which the historian will finally write.

Historians classify evidence into two types: **primary evidence** and **secondary evidence.** These are often referred to as *primary sources* and *secondary sources.* Primary evidence is a record that comes to us *directly* from the past. It is evidence recorded by people who witnessed the event or knew the person. There are different kinds of primary evidence: for example, letters, diaries, and even a film of an event shown on the evening news. The thing to remember about primary evidence is that it is a firsthand account. If you were researching the history of the American Revolution, you would consider a letter written by a colonial leader to Benjamin Franklin as primary evidence. If you were researching the history of baseball, old films of baseball heroes such as Babe Ruth or Roberto Clemente would be used as primary evidence. Can you think of other kinds of primary evidence?

Another kind of record used by historians is secondary evidence. Just as the term implies it is evidence about a person or event that is *secondhand.* It may be just as accurate as primary evidence, but it was not recorded by a person who was there or by someone who was an eyewitness. Also, secondary evidence is recorded *after* the event, at a later time. Most history books are secondary evidence. An account of a Civil War battle written in 1990 is another example of a secondary source.

Both primary and secondary sources of evidence are important to the historian. Is one better than the other?

Primary sources often give the "flavor" of the times. There is something fascinating about holding in your hands a genuine letter by Ben Franklin in which he describes life in colonial Philadelphia. Just as thrilling is hearing a recording of the words of the first astronauts as they viewed the Earth from far out in space. Primary sources are exciting. Also, because they were made at the time an event happened, the details in them are usually accurate. Sometimes primary sources contain false information. Sometimes primary sources do not agree with one another. This can make the historian's job difficult. Nevertheless, historians will usually seek and use primary materials first because they are firsthand evidence.

Secondary material can be useful, too. Suppose you have two accounts of the Revolution in America. One is a primary source: a pamphlet urging the colonists to rebel against England. The other is a secondary source: an account found in a book published two hundred years after the pamphlet was printed. The author describes the effects it had on the colonists.

Which is of value to the historian? The answer is: Both! The original pamphlet was printed and handed out by people who were angry and anxious to break away from England. Because the people were emotional, some of the facts in the pamphlet may not be accurate. The pamphlet is still valuable, however, because it shows the mood and excitement of the times. It also gives the historian a good idea of some of the arguments used by the revolutionaries to spark their fellow colonials into rebelling against England.

On the other hand, the secondary source about the Revolution was written far from the heat of the times. The author of the secondary source was not personally wrapped up in the cause of revolution and had a calmer attitude toward it. She or he was in a better position to look at all sides of the issues and to write an account of the situation that is fair to all sides. In many ways, the author writing today has more information available about the Revolution than the writer of the pamphlet had in the 1700s.

Good historians recognize the benefits of both primary and secondary sources. They use both to write the best possible historical accounts.

READING REVIEW

1. Where does the historian get information to write historical accounts?
2. Give one advantage and one disadvantage of primary and secondary sources.

Critical Thinking

3. **Making Comparisons** (see page 16) What is the difference between primary and secondary sources? Give an original example of each.

In 1898 there was a terrific explosion on the USS Maine, *anchored in Havana Harbor, Cuba. The battleship (shown here) was destroyed and hundreds of lives were lost. Many Americans blamed the Spanish, who controlled Cuba at the time. The Spanish-American War that followed was brief and was won by the United States. In what kind of source would you probably find this photograph?*

Evaluating Evidence

The historian looks for all possible evidence and sources, but only those sources which are directly related to the topic are used. A good historian has one main goal: to write an account that is accurate and fair to all sides.

When a historical account is fair and accurate, we say it is **objective.** An objective historical account is based on facts. It is not influenced by the historian's opinions and feelings. Of course, some historians deliberately choose evidence that supports what they want the reader to believe. When the writing of a historian, or any author, is influenced by personal opinion and feeling, it is called **subjective** writing. No responsible historian ever knowingly writes history in a subjective way.

Good historians are very careful about the evidence they use. It is important that the sources are **reliable.** You can trust the truth of a source if it has the quality of reliability. You pick friends whom you can trust, and who will not lie to you or "stretch" the truth. In the same way, historians choose sources that have a reputation for reliability.

It is also necessary that all sources be **authentic.** Authenticity is the quality of being the "real thing," not a fake. Do you trust people who are "fakes"? Of course not. Good historians study their sources to make sure they are genuine. Sources that are shown to be not authentic can ruin many long hours or years of research and writing.

An authentic diary is a reliable source of evidence. Above: Anne Frank, author of The Diary of Anne Frank.

If you were a historian, would you trust sources that might not be reliable or authentic? As a reader of history, would you trust the word of a historian who uses many unreliable and unauthentic sources? Why not? Historians are usually very careful that their accounts are as objective, reliable, and authentic as possible. To make sure of this, they use a process called **corroboration.** A historian corroborates an account by finding several pieces of evidence that tell the same story, or at least support each other. By corroborating the account, the historian is more sure of reporting history accurately.

If you are writing history, it is important to be as fair and accurate as possible. If you are reading history, you should try to be

An unauthentic source of evidence: The Secret Diaries of Hitler, *published in 1983.*

critical. Is the writing objective or subjective? Are the historian's sources reliable and authentic? Has the historian corroborated his or her sources? These tasks sound easy, don't they? They aren't. In this unit you will begin to discover why.

Historian Yigael Yadin studying the Dead Sea Scrolls of Palestine.

READING REVIEW

1. Define: objective, subjective, reliable, authentic, corroboration.

Critical Thinking

2. **Testing Conclusions** (see page 42) As a reader of history, how can you tell if the historical account is one you can believe?

EXPERIMENT **7-F**

Watch What You Do With Your Evidence!

Evidence, like any tool, is only as good as the historian using it. The greatest, most exciting evidence in the world won't make your historical account a good one, unless you handle it properly. Today we are going to examine things every good historian should know.

Let's begin with this photograph. Consider it as evidence of an event. Study what is happening in the photo, and then on a sheet of paper write a description of what you see.

Now compare your description with those of the members of your class. Are they similar? How? How are the descriptions different? What might explain those similarities and differences?

Now, examine the next piece of evidence, a series of four photos. See page 360. The photo on page 359 was taken from this series of shots. Examine your new evidence closely. After viewing all the evidence in this series, write a new description on a sheet of paper. How did your description differ with those of your classmates? Why did your opinion change about what you saw in the first photo?

At the beginning of the experiment you examined a photo. On the basis of what you saw, you interpreted the "action" in the photo. Your interpretation, however, was not a fact. It was an **inference,** a guess or a theory about what was taking place in the picture. In this case it was a wrong inference because you did not have all the evidence available. When you saw the rest of the evidence, the series of photos, you were able to make a correct inference. In order to prove an inference true or false, all available evidence must be examined. If all the evidence agrees with the inference, then the inference is a **fact.** A fact is something which can be proven. The series of photos proves that the building was being demolished.

This exercise points out a difficulty in the study of history. One piece of evidence should never be examined outside its natural setting, or **context.** This is taking evidence **out of context.** Leaving out some of the evidence affects the interpretation, as you saw above. When evidence is left out intentionally, the result is dishonest, subjective, and bad history. After seeing the first photo placed in its natural context, in the series of photos, you probably felt that you had been tricked. This feeling should help you understand why good historians never use evidence out of context.

Now look at the picture on Handout 7-F, "Downtown." Many different things are going on. What do you see? How would you describe what is going on? If you were a historian, what would you write about the events of this day and place in the picture?

No doubt the things you say about this picture will depend on your **frame of reference.** Everyone has a frame of reference. That is, we all tend to view people and events according to our own individual feelings, values, customs, and experiences. Since we all have different experiences, it cannot be expected that everyone will view the world and events in the same way.

Suppose you are a television news reporter. Your assignment is to report on the events happening today in the downtown area pictured on Handout 7-F. How would you report the events you see? What would you show the viewing audience? What would you say about the events? You will have an opportunity to decide those questions and design your own one-minute television report.

First, get together with one other person with whom you would like to work. One of you will be the reporter, and the other will be the camera operator. You will work closely as a team to produce a well-written, well-photographed television report.

Next, your teacher will distribute an index card to each team. Place the card horizontally (lengthwise) and draw a 5 cm × 8.5 cm (2 in. × 3 in.) rectangle (again lengthwise) in the center of the card. Very carefully cut out the center rectangle. This will leave an open space which you will use as the camera eye to "film" the downtown area on the handout.

With your partner, survey and discuss what is happening in the downtown area. What is worth reporting to your viewers? Examine the picture closely. Are any events causing other events to occur? What events seem unrelated?

Put your index card "screen" over those areas you want to show your viewers. Move the screen around to show the most important scenes. The reporter should write a one-minute script to go with the visual presentation. Make sure that the "camera" is showing what your script is describing.

Be very careful as you are writing your report and choosing your camera shots to go along with your words. Pay attention to the words you are using, as well as the interpretation you are giving to the events you are reporting. Try to be as objective and fair as possible with the information in your report. Be prepared to present your report as soon as possible.

Perception: An Important Key To History

If history were only a list of events in the order in which they occurred, the job of historians would be much simpler. Such a list which is called a **chronology,** does not explain how and why the events occurred.

Historians use chronologies. But history is much more than a simple chronology. Historians are concerned about not only *what* happened, but *why* events happened. They try to explain the past by studying the relationship of **cause and effect.** Every event is caused by something or someone. Getting a good grade in this class is an example of an event. What were the causes? Probably, the causes included doing homework, studying, and paying attention in class. These causes led to the effect, or end result, of getting good grades. Historians attempt to show the relationship of cause and effect. In studying the Vietnam War, for example, historians already know that the end result (the effect) was America's

longest war. To try to determine the causes of that war they study a variety of historical documents. Firsthand accounts, documents, interviews, periodical articles, and many other types of evidence may be used. In the end, the historian not only wants to know *what* happened, but *why.*

Oftentimes, historians will use the same evidence, yet disagree on their interpretations of that evidence. This is normal and natural. All of us rely upon our senses for information about our world. Our senses constantly take in information, interpret it, and use it. The process of absorbing and interpreting information from the senses is called **perception.** Two persons may see the same event with their eyes, yet perceive it entirely differently. Differences in perception lead to differences in descriptions of the same event. How does this illustration and poem tell about some of the differences in perception?

The Blind Men and the Elephant*

It was six men of Indostan
To learning much inclined,
Who went to see the Elephant
(Though all of them were blind),
That each by observation
Might satisfy his mind.

The *First* approached the Elephant
And, happening to fall
Against his broad and sturdy side,
At once began to bawl:
"God bless me! but the Elephant
Is very like a wall!"

The *Second,* feeling of the tusk,
Cried, "Ho! what have we here
So very round and smooth and sharp?
To me 'tis mighty clear
This wonder of an Elephant
Is very like a spear!"

The *Third* approached the animal
And, happening to take
The squirming trunk within his hands,
Thus boldly up and spoke:
"I see," quoth he, "The Elephant
Is very like a snake!"

The *Fourth* reached out an eager hand
And felt about the knee.
"What most this wondrous beast is like
Is mighty plain," quoth he;
" 'Tis clear enough the Elephant
Is very like a tree!"

The *Fifth,* who chanced to touch the ear,
Said: "Even the blindest man
Can tell what this resembles most;
Deny the fact who can,
This marvel of an Elephant
Is very like a fan!"

The *Sixth* no sooner had begun
About the beast to grope
Than, seizing on the swinging tail
That fell within his scope,
"I see," quoth he, "the Elephant
Is very like a rope!"

And so these men of Indostan
Disputed loud and long,
Each in his own opinion
Exceeding stiff and strong.
Though each was partly in the right,
All were also in the wrong!

John Godfrey Saxe

*From John Godfrey Saxe, "The Blind Men and the Elephant" in *The Poetical Works of John Godfrey Saxe* (Boston: Houghton Mifflin.) (See Acknowledgements, pages 595–596.)

Perception is an important key to history. Your perception depends partly on your frame of reference. If you were reporting on the events of the American Revolution, your perceptions would depend on whether you sided with the American colonists or with the Loyalists, those loyal to Britain. Your frame of reference would be much different as a revolutionary than it would be as a person who wanted British rule to continue. Can you tell why?

Take a close look at these two engravings of the Boston Massacre. Both are visual interpretations of the same event. Which one looks more like a "massacre"? Which one would have stirred up the anger of the colonists against the British? Which gives us the impression that the colonists had prepared for this battle? Why do you think these two pictures are so different from each other?

The picture on the left shows a merciless British attack on unarmed American colonists. The soldiers are firing from a line, at very close range. The picture on the right shows a different interpretation. Here the Americans are obviously as ready to fight as the British soldiers. Dead men from both sides are lying in the street. Does it surprise you to find out that the picture on the left was made by a revolutionary named Paul Revere? His frame of reference is obvious. What was the frame of reference for the other artist?*

Your frame of reference influences the way you write or interpret historical accounts. Sometimes historians want to tell about the past so that their readers feel good about what happened. Sometimes historians may omit important facts, changing the meaning of an event. Here are two accounts of the last days of World War II. Both are taken from Soviet textbooks. This first account was published in 1974.

*The concept sequence presented here is adapted from Jack Block, *Understanding Historical Research: A Search for Truth.* (See Acknowledgements, pages 595–596.)

On 26 July 1945, the U.S.A., England, and China demanded unconditional surrender from Japan. The Japanese government rejected this demand.

The Soviet government agreed with the statement of those three countries, and on 8 August 1945, carrying out its alliance, declared war on Japan. This resulted from the necessity to quickly end the war, to restore general peace, to liberate the people from further sacrifices and suffering, to restore the rights of the Soviet Union to the Russian land which had been taken away, to provide for the government interests of the USSR and the safety of our far eastern boundaries. . . .

On 9 August, Soviet troops began attacking hostile troops on three sides. . . .*

Nowhere in the account is there any mention of the atomic bombs dropped on Nagasaki and Hiroshima. The impression you get is that the Japanese surrendered only because the USSR entered the war! By omitting one fact—the American atomic bombing of the two Japanese cities—the entire historical account is changed!

In the mid-1980s, the Soviet government began a policy called *glasnost,* which means "openness and honesty." Textbooks began to be more honest, although they still showed a Soviet frame of reference. Here is an account of the end of the war, taken from a 1985 Soviet textbook. What differences and similarities do you see, compared with the 1974 account?

On August 6, 1945, three days before the USSR's entry into the war with Japan, the American Air Force dropped an atomic bomb on the Japanese city of Hiroshima, and on August 9, the day the USSR began its war with militarist Japan, dropped a second bomb on the city of Nagasaki. More than 200,000 people perished as a result of the atomic bombing. In later years, more than 170,000 people died from radiation. . . .

The fate of the Japanese aggressors was decided not by atomic bomb blasts, but by the actions of the Soviet Armed Forces. . . .

On September 2, 1945, on board the American battleship "Missouri" in the Gulf of Tonkin, Japan signed an unconditional surrender.†

This account corrects the earlier one by mentioning the atomic bombing. However, it makes the bombing seem unimportant in ending the war. If you compared the Soviet accounts with the account in your American History textbook, what differences do you think you would find?

Perception, frame of reference, and objectivity are important in any historical account. Subjectivity, unfairness, and the omission of key facts are always dishonest. Sometimes, honest historians write accounts that are incomplete or inaccurate. This may be the result of carelessness. The historian also may not be aware of being subjective. Or the historian's evidence may be incorrect or misleading. These are problems a historian (and reader) faces.

Sometimes faults are easy to pick out in an historical account. Very often they are difficult to spot because skillful historians can control words to present their view in a believable way.

*From *The History of the USSR During the Epoch of Socialism.* (See Acknowledgements, pages 595–596.)

†From *Contemporary History (1939–1984).* (See Acknowledgements, pages 595–596.)

READING REVIEW

1. What does perception have to do with the writing and reading of History?
2. What is a chronology? Explain the statement: History is more than a chronology.

Critical Thinking

3. **Determining Relevance** (see page 17) What is frame of reference? What is the importance of frame of reference in writing and reading History?

EXPERIMENT **7-G**

What's in a Word?

As for many other professionals, the main tool of the historian is language. By the use of language—spoken and written symbols—the historian gathers information, records observations, and connects many kinds of clues. Language makes it possible to understand cause-effect relationships. Without language it would be impossible to communicate. History would not exist because no one could communicate the events and causes of the past.

We know that words are the major ingredient of language. In addition we know that historians use words to write historical accounts. In this experiment we will take a look at how historians choose words and how those words are used. We will see that it is possible to record the same event in many different ways and from many different frames of reference, just by the way words are used.

There are two ways of interpreting a word. One way is to take the dictionary definition of a word. The dictionary meaning is called the word's **denotation.** Let's

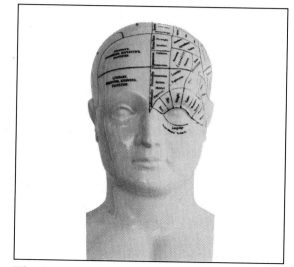

The human mind can understand and remember the meaning of many thousands of words in a language. It is also capable of recognizing the emotional meaning that often goes with a word.

consider the word "unemployed." Look at the following:

out of work   between jobs   loafing

All of the above terms can mean unemployed. And yet, there are differences among them which limit how they are used. For example, you would not suggest to an unemployed friend looking for a job that he or she was "loafing." Your friend might be insulted if you said that. But chances are your friend would not be offended if you referred to his or her unemployed state as being "out of work." To a friend who is enjoying being unemployed, you could say, "You are loafing," and probably not offend that person.

Many words also carry emotional meanings which need to be interpreted. The emotional meaning of a word is called its **connotation.** Those words which carry a pleasant emotional meaning are said to have a positive connotation. Words which carry an insulting or unpleasant emotional meaning have a negative connotation.

Look at this list of words. Can you think of a positive and a negative connotation word for each?

denotative word(s):	connotative words	
	negative	*positive*
automobile	(?)	(?)
thin	(?)	(?)
many people together	(?)	(?)
child	(?)	(?)
person who doesn't change his/her mind	(?)	(?)

Choose a denotative word from the list above and use it in a sentence. Then write the same sentence twice, using first the negative connotation and then the positive connotation of the word. Can you see how the meaning of an idea can be changed just by the words you use? Here are two statements:

1. Great Britain lost the war.
2. The American colonists, while struggling for freedom against the mightiest army and navy in the world, handed Great Britain a stunning and humiliating military defeat in winning their hard-fought War for Independence.

Both of these statements say basically the same thing. But the second one is full of connotations. None of the connotations make Great Britain look favorable. The second statement could have been said by an American revolutionary after the war was over. It appears to be from an American revolutionary's frame of reference. On the other hand, a British soldier of the time might have simply stated that "Great Britain lost the war." It is simple and to-the-point. Who really likes to talk about losing?

In "Reading 5: Perception: An Important Key to History" are two pictures of the Boston Massacre. Consider the name of

What is a favorable connotation for the word city? *A negative connotation?*

that armed meeting between British soldiers and American colonists: Massacre. The word has definite negative connotations about the British, doesn't it? Who do you think originated the phrase "Boston Massacre"?

It is very important to watch for the negative and positive connotations in written history. They can give you clues about the author's frame of reference. The connotations may also indicate that the historian is writing subjectively.

It is equally important to look for the emphasis placed on certain words and phrases. This is true especially when history is passed on orally, by word of mouth. Compare these questions, giving added emphasis to the italicized words:

1. *Where* did you get that *car*?
2. Where *did* you get that car?
3. Where did *you* get that car?
4. Where did you get *that* car?

Here again, all four questions consist of the same words in the same order, but all four questions carry a different meaning. What meanings can you understand from each of the four questions? What feeling do you think each of the questions brings with it?

How many different connotations can you give these statements, just by putting emphasis on different words each time?

1. George Washington is considered to be one of the greatest military leaders of his time.
2. While in jail, Adolf Hitler wrote *Mein Kampf,* his blueprint for taking over the world by force and trickery.
3. The typical 18th-century American colonial person was a farmer.

Historians may change their accounts by the use of positive and negative connotations. They may also change the entire meaning of accounts by omitting certain key facts. As you saw earlier, when facts are omitted the results are a distortion of the truth and an unfair reporting of the events.

It is common practice when quoting material to use three periods (. . .), called *ellipsis points,* to show where words or phrases have been left out. But important facts should never be omitted.

Movie ads provide a humorous example of how the omission of key facts or words can change the meaning of an account. Here is an ad for a movie:

"A triumph. . . ! You must see it. . . !"

But this is what the movie critic really wrote:

"A triumph for idiocy! You must see it to understand how bad this movie really is!"

The ad writer, by omitting words, completely distorted the original review. Look at this ad:

"A once-in-a-lifetime performance by the star. . . . A fine film . . . made by a master. . . !"

That came from this review:

"A once-in-a-lifetime performance by the star is what you pay good money for. But what do you get? To say that it is a fine film would be false. To tell you that it was made by a master would be false! The film is boring and not recommended."

This type of omission in the writing of history is easy to find, especially in those countries which control communications and education. You have already seen an example of historical omission of facts in Reading 5, page 362. Go back to it now. What effect did the omission of atomic bombings of Japanese cities by the United States have on the Soviet account of the end of World War II? Was the Soviet version accurate? Was it honest, objective, and fair?

Facts and Inferences

PART ONE

A historian deals with facts. Facts must be collected, sorted, arranged in order, and then interpreted. The final result of this process is **history.**

The process of writing history is far more difficult than it seems. The historian has to determine what is factual and what is not. This is the process of determining authenticity. Unless a document or an eyewitness account of an event can be proven authentic—true and genuine—it is of no value to the historian.

Another problem for historians is separating facts from inferences. On page 359 in "Experiment 7-F: Watch What You Do With Your Evidence!", you made an inference about the first picture, which showed a building and "smoke." Your inference was probably proven wrong by the series of pictures that followed. Your inference was a theory, not a fact. What that picture really showed was obvious when you saw

What would cause you to make the inference *that this police officer is on duty? Is your inference a theory or a fact?*

the rest of the pictures. In order to discover the facts of history a historian must have all available facts about the event. Otherwise, wrong conclusions are reached, and the historian's account is incorrect.

Let's see how good you are at spotting inferences. Here is an article from the San Rafael *Independent Journal* about a man's sudden death.

SAN FRANCISCO (AP)—Police said a suspected burglar suddenly bumped against a drawn gun while being searched in a Nob Hill bar, discharging a bullet into his heart.

He fell dead.

Police identified the man as Richard L. Klebenow, 30, named in an all-points bulletin put out by San Diego for a burglar there Friday.

Mrs. Olive Trahan, 48, manager of a six-story apartment at 801 Jones Street, called police on hearing noises in the cellar. She said a prowler used the same cellar Thursday to gain entry to an alley, break into the rear door of the bar at 808 Jones Street, and steal $700.

Patrolmen William Arietta and Gene Haudbine went to the cellar at 3:30 a.m. today, then pursued a man they saw run down the alley into the bar. Arietta said the six-foot suspect, while being searched, whirled and struck the officer's revolver with his shoulder, discharging it.

From the *Independent Journal.* Reprinted by permission of The Associated Press, New York, N.Y.

The morning after that article appeared, the San Francisco *Chronicle* published this account of the same event.

A burglary suspect was killed early yesterday in a Sutter Street tavern when he shot at a policeman who was searching him.

Police said Richard L. Klebenow, 30, a recent arrival from San Diego, died with a bullet through his heart.

He was being searched by Patrolman William Arietta, 29, who with Patrolman Gene Haudbine, 26, responded to a report of a prowler in the 808 Club, 808 Sutter Street, 3:30 a.m.

Klebenow was found in the bar and ordered to lean with hands on the wall. He whirled on the officer, fired and missed, police said.

From the San Francisco *Chronicle.* (See Acknowledgements, pages 595–596.)

Homicide Inspector William Armstrong gave the police department's version of the incident to *The Sunday Ramparts.*

The apartment house, the basement of which was used as entry, is at 801 Jones Street; the bar at 808 *Sutter.*

The suspect, while being searched by Patrolman Arietta whose gun was drawn and cocked, suddenly turned and the weapon went off.

It was discovered *after* the suspect was dead that he was wanted by San Diego police.

A search of the corpse revealed not a gun but an eight-inch screwdriver.

Befuddled newspaper readers notwithstanding, the conflicting aspects of the press reports were, obviously, of little moment to Richard L. Klebenow, 30.

From *The Sunday Ramparts.* (See Acknowledgements, pages 595–596.)

Note: These three newspaper articles were drawn on material from Nancy Shingler Messner and Gerald Messner, *Patterns of Thinking.* (See Acknowledgements, pages 595–596.)

Obviously, readers of the *Independent Journal* were given a different set of inferences and facts to work with than readers of the *Chronicle.* Can you separate the facts from the inferences? What would you be led to believe about the incident if you read only the *Independent-Journal* account? Or if you read only the *Chronicle* article? How did both articles differ from the "facts" of the case given by Mr. Armstrong of the police department?

Make a chronology of this incident, based upon the three accounts. It will be helpful in determining the facts and separating them from the inferences and wrong information. In doing your chronology, simply make a list of the things that happened in the order they occurred.

Then make two other lists: one of the inferences and wrong information in each account; and the other of the true facts of the case. How did you determine what facts were true or false?

Now let's consider an event in American history about which a fantastic number of inferences was made. The event was the destruction of the battleship *Maine* before the outbreak of the Spanish-American War, in 1898. Cuba at that time was ruled by Spain. In 1895 a group of Cubans, working from headquarters in New York, proclaimed themselves revolutionaries. Their aim was to free Cuba from Spanish control. They proclaimed Cuba independent and free. Spain, however, continued to rule the island. Conflicts between Spanish soldiers and revolutionaries in Cuba increased. Because of his cruelty and ruthlessness in suppressing the revolutionaries, the Spanish governor-general Weyler was given the nickname "Butcher Weyler."

The following is an account of the Spanish-American War. It is taken from an American history textbook.

Why Did the United States Go To War over Cuba?*

The Spanish-American War (April 1898-August 1898) is often referred to as a turning point in American history. Up to that time, by and large, the United States desired to play only a limited role in world affairs. After that war, the United States could not help but play a major role in world affairs.

By 1895 Americans had substantial business interests in Cuba, largely in sugar and tobacco. These interests seemed threatened by the continuous revolts in Cuba. Many Americans were, however, moved by humanitarian, not economic interests. They were moved when they read of atrocities (brutal or cruel acts) visited on Cubans by "Butcher Weyler." He drove Cubans into camps where they were beaten and mutilated and allowed to die by starvation or disease. The gory details of such horror stories made fascinating, although grim, reading. The American press took advantage of them to sell papers. These newspapers gave the people what they wanted to read. In so doing, they prepared a climate in which American intervention in Cuban affairs would be hard to resist. The newspapers encouraged the growth of "jingoism" or "super-patriotism." All the old desires for Cuba mounted for all Americans. *Cuba libre,* "free Cuba," became the cry. And the American's attitude was that if this took war, "by jingo," so much the better.

President Cleveland had successfully resisted pressure to intervene. But pressures were building up which eventually forced President McKinley to declare war. Fever for action in Cuba mounted when Cuban rebels released a telegram sent by Dupuy De Lôme, Spain's ambassador to the United States. In the telegram, De Lôme called McKinley a "weak bidder for the admiration of the crowd." The American public was further incensed when the battleship USS *Maine* was blown up in Havana Harbor. "Remember the Maine," became a war cry heard far and wide. But it could never be clearly shown that it was the Spanish who had blown it up.

McKinley demanded that the fighting in Cuba stop. He insisted that the practice of herding Cubans into concentration camps also end. Spain began to change its policy by granting some self-government to Cuba. But the Cuban rebels demanded full independence. By 1898 the simple truth was that most Americans wanted war. Congress had appropriated the money to fight it. Assistant Secretary of the Navy Theodore Roosevelt had sent Admiral George Dewey to the Pacific. In the event of war—a war that [Secretary] Roosevelt desperately wanted—Dewey could attack the Spanish in the Philippines. When McKinley hesitated before asking Congress for a declaration of war, Roosevelt scornfully criticized him as having the "backbone of a chocolate eclair."

*From Gerald Leinwand, *The Pageant of American History.* (See Acknowledgments, pages 595–596.)

Had McKinley been stronger, war might have been avoided. He did have powerful support for peace. Yet he asked Congress to declare war, and Congress gave in to his request. Spain was shocked. In a fit of self-righteousness, Congress passed, in addition to the war declaration, the Teller Resolution. The Resolution said America was fighting for Cuban independence and would never seek to govern that island. To many thoughtful Americans, however, this act of self-denial defied reason. It was

Are the inferences from both the headlines and the cartoons sufficient to reach conclusions about the facts of this incident? How do you think this information affected the readers in 1898? What other sources would a historian use to write an unbiased account of the destruction of the Maine?

asking too much to believe that the United States would give up a land that, in nearly every decade of its existence, it had sought to purchase or conquer.

American business interests in sugar and tobacco in Cuba were large. But most businessmen wanted peace. It was the "average" American—spurred on by the stories and the lurid pictures in the "yellow" press—who wanted war. The use of sensationalism to win and influence public opinion is called "yellow journalism." Hearst of the *New York Journal* and Pulitzer of the *World* competed for readers. What better way to win readers than to dramatize the brutality, the revolution, and the atrocities in Cuba?

Who really blew up the *Maine?* The answer to that question is still a mystery. No matter who was responsible, the destruction of that American ship was the spark which started the four-month war between the United States and Spain.

Take a close look at the newspaper headlines on page 374. What inferences can be drawn from them? What is the frame of reference in which they were made? Do the cartoons support the same inferences?

PART TWO

Your teacher may give you an assignment, which is to get two newspapers or magazines and then compare accounts in them of a single incident. Do the accounts use words with strong positive or negative connotations? Do they lead you to draw inferences? How do the articles differ? Bring your results to class.

READING 6

Oral History

Some of the most exciting history is what we call **oral history.** It is "talking history"—accounts of past events handed down through the years by people telling other people what happened and why. If you have ever listened to a good storyteller, you know how fascinating talking history can be.

One way of capturing the excitement of oral history is to have a cassette tape recorder ready to use when an opportunity arises. It is a good idea to use recorders with built-in microphones. That way, you can just set the recorder down and it does all the work. Also, you won't be making people nervous by pointing a mike in front of their faces.

It is usually better to record oral history in an atmosphere that is natural to the person being interviewed. Family reunions, town picnics, or even Sunday dinner at your grandmother's would be ideal for oral history recordings. Planned recording sessions are less natural, although they can also be valuable in getting oral accounts of the past. A photograph of your father from

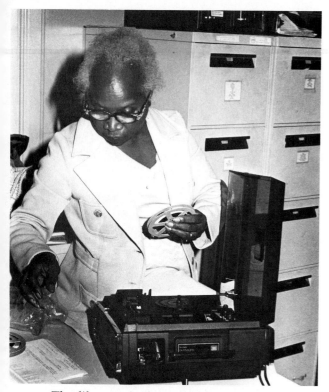

The library of this woman is filled with interviews of her neighbors.

the family album, or a record from your mother's teenage years might stir up memories and make it easier for them to talk about the past.

The oral historian has a great deal to work with: People! Every person you know has many fascinating stories about what life was like in the past. Since people are natural primary sources, their accounts often have great authenticity and value.

Apart from the tape recorder and perhaps a pen and notebook, the most important assets an oral historian can have are enthusiasm, imagination, and an attentive ear. It is also important to let the person you are interviewing do most of the talking. That way, your "source" can have a steady

train of thought. Only once in a while, when your subject is at a complete loss for words, should you ask a short, open-ended question. What do we mean by open-ended? An open-ended question is one which allows the subject as many different ways of answering as possible. Here is an open-ended question:

"You must have grown up when trains were still running through town. What was it like back then?"

In this open-ended question, you not only ask about trains, but about the town, the local happenings during those days, and the subject's life as a younger person. It is a good question because it leads the subject to give a lot of information.

Now, here is a closed-ended question:

"Were there train tracks running through town when you were my age?"

There are only two possible answers to this question: *Yes* and *No*. Asking this type of question wouldn't encourage the person to talk about trains and tracks and how the town developed because the trains ran through town. Can you see why this type of question is not as good as the open-ended type of question?

Practice asking open-ended questions. That will help you polish your oral history interviewing techniques.

READING REVIEW

1. What is oral history?

Critical Thinking

2. **Identifying Central Issues** (see page 14) How does an oral historian work?

Recording Oral History

In this experiment you will have an opportunity to record oral history. If you have a tape recorder, or if you can get one from school, use it in this experiment. You'll want to get a long tape (90- or 120-minute cassettes are best) so that you don't run out of tape in the middle of the best part of your subject's story.

If a tape recorder is not available, use a notebook and pen. Write down the important parts of your subject's stories. Don't try to take down every word, or you will miss most of what is being said. Just jot down the essentials, especially those words which will later remind you of the entire story. As you conduct your oral history interviews, write your questions and the responses on Handout 7-I for this experiment. Use your own paper if you run out of room on the handout sheet. When you are finished, remember to thank your subjects for their time and courtesy.

Take a few minutes now to think about what you would like to investigate as an oral historian. If you need help, your teacher or your librarian might be able to suggest some good topics and sources. Good luck!

Why would a family reunion provide a good opportunity to record oral history?

Interpreting History: Vietnam—What Really Happened in the Gulf of Tonkin?

Introduction

Thus far in this unit you have studied the nature of History. You have learned what evidence and sources are, and you have seen examples of each. You have seen how the use of words, photographs, and cartoons can affect one's interpretation of events. You have learned about oral history and you have learned some basic principles of writing history.

Now let's put it all together. In this experiment you will be developing a historical account. You will be gathering and interpreting evidence—primary and secondary sources, a chronology, maps, and photographs.

The subject is an event that happened off the coast of North Vietnam in August 1964. The consequences of what happened then have an important impact upon our nation and our world even today. In this experiment you will discover for yourself what happened in the Gulf of Tonkin that led to America's fighting a war in southeast Asia during the 1960s and 1970s.

The basis for American involvement in Vietnam is rooted in the cold war—the tensions that developed between the United States and the Soviet Union after World War II. The United States and the Soviet Union had been allies during World War II. After the war, however, the Soviet Union began to force its communist system of government on the countries of Eastern Europe. In 1949 mainland China also fell to the communists. In response, the United

Vietnam

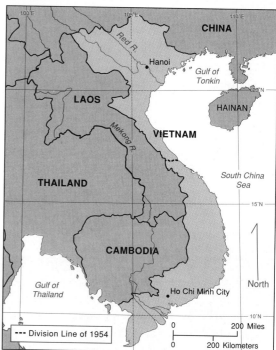

Vietnam, on the coast of Southeast Asia, became the site of America's longest war.

States developed a policy of "containment." This policy was designed to limit the expansion of communism.

Containment was an outgrowth of the "domino theory," which claimed that nations were like dominos. When one domino falls, all the others fall in a row. This was the reason that in the early 1950s United States troops made up the largest part of the United Nations' forces fighting against the communists in South Korea. For the most part the United States followed the policy of containment until the late 1980s.

After World War II, the Vietnamese wanted independence. But France, assisted financially by the United States, fought to reestablish control over Vietnam. In 1954, France admitted defeat and Vietnam was divided into a communist North and an anti-communist South. The North Vietnamese never accepted the 1954 division and invaded the South to reunify the country. The United States sent money and military advisers to South Vietnam to repel the attacks from the North. Then in the early 1960s, President John F. Kennedy increased aid to South Vietnam. By the end of 1963, about 16,000 American troops were serving in South Vietnam as advisers.

Throughout 1964, the fighting between the communist Viet Cong and the South Vietnamese increased. American "advisers" were losing their lives in Vietnam. Then in August 1964, the news came that North Vietnamese torpedo boats had attacked the United States destroyer *Maddox* in the Gulf of Tonkin, off the coast of North Vietnam. What happened there set the stage for a much wider war in which the United States would give up its role of military adviser. Instead, United States troops became the primary fighting force against the communists.

Historians are still trying to determine exactly what happened in the Gulf of Tonkin during that first week of August 1964. In this experiment, you will have a chance to examine a wide range of historical evidence, including newspaper accounts and the words of President Lyndon B. Johnson and his staff. As you go through the evidence, be alert to all the things we have discussed in this unit.

When you read each source, ask yourself these questions: Does the evidence seem to be objective or subjective? Does the speaker or writer benefit in any way if people believe his or her words? Do the words have a negative or positive connotation? Are any facts taken out of context? Can you spot any inferences and opinions? Can you tell which statements are facts? What are the frames of reference of the sources of this information? Are any key facts omitted? Think about these questions for a while. Make sure you know how to apply the necessary skills to answer the questions before you continue with this experiment. If anything is not clear to you, be sure to take the time to go back through this unit and review the material you are uncertain about.

In this experiment you will confront a great amount of evidence. Not all of the evidence is in agreement, so you will have to make decisions about which evidence to believe and which evidence you do not trust enough to use in your own historical account.

Some of the sources you will use may be difficult to read. But if you can learn to read, understand, and interpret the material presented in this experiment, you will have acquired valuable skills. Even if you do not choose a career as a professional historian, you will be using those skills for the rest of your life.

Your assignment is to use the evidence in this experiment, along with all the historian's skills you have learned so far, to develop your own original historical account of the events in the Gulf of Tonkin during the first week of August 1964. Your account should be approximately 1,000 words in length. Be prepared to share your work with the class.

Sources for the Gulf of Tonkin Case Study

Source A

This article appeared on the front page of the New York Times *on Monday, August 3, 1964. Similar front-page articles in newspapers across the country told readers of a conflict between a U.S. destroyer and North Vietnamese patrol (PT) boats off the coast of North Vietnam. As you read this article, ask yourself what your reaction might have been if you were a teenager reading this in 1964. After you read the article, try to summarize the facts. Ask yourself: "What happened in the Gulf of Tonkin on Sunday, August 2, 1964?"*

Red PT Boats Fire at U.S. Destroyer on Vietnam Duty
Maddox and Four Aircraft Shoot Back After Assault 30 Miles Off Coast

By Arnold H. Lubasch
Special Correspondent to the *New York Times*

WASHINGTON, AUG. 2—Three North Vietnamese PT boats fired torpedoes and 37-mm. shells at a United States destroyer in international waters about 30 miles off North Vietnam today.

The destroyer and four United States aircraft fired back, damaged them and drove them off.

The incident was announced here in an official statement by the Defense Department. It said that neither the destroyer nor the aircraft sustained casualties or damage.

The statement said that the destroyer, the 3,300-ton *Maddox,* was on a routine patrol when an unprovoked attack took place in the Gulf of Tonkin. . . .

Goverment officials said later that the attack was not regarded as a major crisis. They said the United States Seventh Fleet had been patrolling the area for some time, would continue its patrols and had sufficient strength on hand.

Admiral U.S. Grant Sharp Jr., Commander in Chief in the Pacific, was advised of the incident by radio as he flew back to his Pearl Harbor headquarters from a visit to South Vietnam.

The Defense Department statement said that the boats were damaged by gunfire from the *Maddox* and the four carrier-based jet aircraft. The statement said:

"While on routine patrol in international waters at 4:08 A.M., E.D.T. [Eastern Daylight Time], the United States destroyer *Maddox* underwent an unprovoked attack by three PT-type boats at latitude 19-40 north, longitude 106-34 east, in Tonkin Gulf. The attacking boats launched three torpedoes and used 37-mm. gunfire.

"The *Maddox* answered with 5-inch gunfire. Shortly thereafter, four F-8 aircraft from the U.S.S. *Ticonderoga* joined in the

In the early 1960s, President John F. Kennedy sent more advisers to Southeast Asia to help stop the spread of communism.

defense of *Maddox,* using Zuni rockets and 20-mm. strafing attacks.

"The PT boats were driven off with one seen to be badly damaged and not moving and the other two damaged and retreating slowly. No casualties or damage was sustained by the *Maddox* or the aircraft."

The attacking boats, which displayed no flags or other identifying marks, were picked up on the destroyer's radar, kept coming and opened fire, according to the Defense Department officials.

After the attackers were driven off, they said, the United States forces resumed their patrol. No effort was made to sink the PT boats, because the fleet was not at war, they said.

The *Maddox* was apparently carrying out a surveillance mission, according to officials here. They said there was no ready explanation why the PT boats would attack the powerful Seventh Fleet.

State Department officials noted that Seventh Fleet patrols in the area were nothing new and would continue, although shooting incidents could not be precluded. They indicated that the United States did not plan an immediate diplomatic protest as a result of the incident.

One reason the Seventh Fleet patrols the area of the incident is that it attempts to maintain surveillance on supplies that might be moving by sea from ports in Communist North Vietnam to Communist guerrillas in South Vietnam.

On August 2, 1964, the United States destroyer U.S.S. Maddox *was attacked by North Vietnamese PT boats. Inset: A naval officer points to a bullet hole reported to have resulted from the attack.*

Source B

The next day, Tuesday, August 4, this follow-up news story appeared on the front page of the Los Angeles Times. *What new information does it give you that you did not find in Source A? Does this information seem to agree or disagree with Source A?*

Johnson Orders Navy to Destroy Viet Attackers
American Fleet, Air Power Bolstered in Area of Raid on Ship

By Richard Reston
Times Staff Writer

WASHINGTON— . . . In the wake of Sunday's "unprovoked" torpedo boat attack on the U.S. destroyer *Maddox,* the President ordered a second destroyer into the Gulf of Tonkin and directed air combat patrols to protect these ships. The Navy announced that the destroyer *C. Turner Joy* had joined the destroyer *Maddox.* . . .

Shortly after Mr. Johnson acted, the State Department announced it is sending to North Vietnam a formal protest against the attack on the *Maddox.* . . .

The Defense Department released details of Sunday's attack in which one of three Communist PT-boats apparently was sunk when the *Maddox* and four Navy F-8 Crusader jets returned the fire.

Officials gave this account:

The three high-speed patrol boats began a close-formation run at the *Maddox.* All three boats were traveling at approximately 50 knots.

They were observed several miles away by radar on the *Maddox,* but since all the boats were in international waters, and no state of war exists between the United States and North Vietnam, the destroyer did not fire first. . . .

The three boats turned slightly toward the *Maddox* and fired one torpedo each. At this point the destroyer turned hard to port, avoiding two of the torpedoes by about 100 and 200 yds. respectively. The other torpedo was not seen to run.

The *Maddox* opened fire with its 5-inchers, hitting one boat directly.

Meanwhile, air support was on its way from the carrier *Ticonderoga,* which was cruising some 300 miles to the south. The jets, arriving in less than 30 minutes, damaged the two fleeing boats with rockets and 20-mm strafing attacks.

The chairman of the Senate Armed Services Committee, Sen. Richard B. Russell (D-Ga), told reporters, "there have been naval operations in the Gulf of Tonkin by South Vietnamese and this could have confused the North Vietnamese. . . ."

The State Department also rejected as "without foundation" two recent charges made by North Vietnam. The charges, made over the weekend, were that four U.S. fighter-bombers had launched an attack from Laos on a North Vietnamese village near the border and that American and South Vietnamese ships shelled two North Vietnamese islands last Thursday.

Asked about possible reasons for the North Vietnamese attack, [press officer at the State Department, Robert J.] McCloskey said any such speculation on this point would be "ill-advised." But, he added, the North Vietnamese attack is "part of continued aggressive actions against the South Vietnamese."

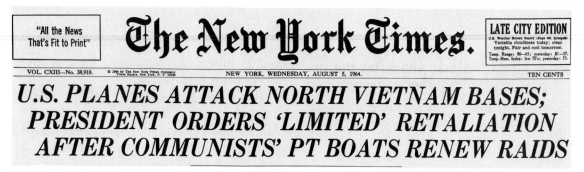

The New York Times.

LATE CITY EDITION
U.S. Weather Bureau Report (Page 60) forecast:
Variable cloudiness today; clear
tonight. Fair and cool tomorrow.
Temp. Range: 86—65; yesterday: 81—57.
Temp.-Hum. Index: low 70's; yesterday: 73.

VOL. CXIII—No. 38,910. © 1964 by The New York Times Company   NEW YORK, WEDNESDAY, AUGUST 5, 1964.   TEN CENTS
Times Square, New York, N.Y. 10036

U.S. PLANES ATTACK NORTH VIETNAM BASES; PRESIDENT ORDERS 'LIMITED' RETALIATION AFTER COMMUNISTS' PT BOATS RENEW RAIDS

The New York Times, as well as other newspapers across the country, carried headlines of President Johnson's response to North Vietnam.

Source C

The following article from the Wednesday, August 5, Washington Post *tells the story of a second incident in the Gulf of Tonkin, which the writer says happened two days after the first incident. As you read this article, ask yourself these questions: What does the writer say happened? Why did the North Vietnamese attack U.S. destroyers in the Gulf of Tonkin for the second time in two days? What was the response of the United States government to this new incident? What was the North Vietnamese version of this story?*

Johnson Orders Action, Stresses It Is Limited; U.N. to Hear Charges

By Murrey Marder

President Johnson last night ordered United States "air action" against "gunboats and certain supporting facilities in North Vietnam" after the second attack in three days upon American warships by Communist torpedo boats. . . .

But it was emphasized last night that the intent of the United States is not to esca-late the war but only to retaliate against the Communist attacks. . . .

The President has already asked Senate and House leaders for action "immediately" on a congressional resolution expressing United States unity in a determination "to take all necessary measures in support of freedom, and in defense of peace, in Southeast Asia."

The official news of the latest attack yesterday on U.S. vessels off the North Vietnam coast came at 6 p.m. in a Defense Department announcement calling it "a second deliberate attack."

Again it was repeated that there was no American casualties or damage. It was believed that at least two Communist PT boats were sunk and two others damaged, out of six or more attacking vessels.

Yesterday's attack was double the scale of the first shooting encounter on Sunday in the Gulf of Tonkin, off the North Vietnam coast. This time, in a three-hour night battle, attack aircraft from the American carriers *Ticonderoga* and *Constellation* joined in beating off the torpedo boats.

The new assault added major dimensions to what appeared to be a whole new pattern of boldness by the Communists in challenging overwhelming U.S. naval power in the Pacific.

On Sunday the United States took the position that the first attack on the destroyer *Maddox,* that reportedly occurred about 28 miles from the Vietnam coast in international waters, may have been an "isolated incident." The second attack was much farther out in international waters—65 miles, the Defense Department said. . . .

The Defense Department's official announcement of the second attack, issued at 6 p.m. yesterday by Assistant Secretary of Defense Arthur Sylvester said:

"A second deliberate attack was made during darkness by an undetermined number of North Vietnamese PT boats on the USS *Maddox* and USS *C. Turner Joy* while the two destroyers were cruising in company on routine patrol in the Tonkin Gulf in international waters about 65 miles from the nearest land.

"The attack came at 10:30 p.m. local time (10:30 a.m., Aug. 4, Washington time).

"The PT boats were taken under fire by the destroyers and thereafter by attack aircraft from the *Ticonderoga* and the *Constellation*.

"The attackers were driven off with no U.S. casualties, no hits, and no damage to either destroyer.

"It is believed that at least two of the PT boats were sunk and two others damaged.

Fight in Bad Weather

Defense officials said that during the three hours of battle there were some lulls and new attacks. The weather was described as "miserable," with rough seas, an 800-foot ceiling and scattered thunderstorms. . . .

The PT boats were said to have fired torpedoes repeatedly, scoring no hits. Because of the darkness, the bad weather, and the swirling attack, American officers do not know exactly how many PT boats were engaged, although some reports referred to six.

Most of the damage to the PT boats probably was done by destroyers, it was thought, as the American jet pilots could see little in the dark.

When officials were asked how they knew the attacking boats were North Vietnamese, they replied "We're satisfied" that they were. Officials expressed similar conviction in Sunday's attack, while declining to disclose their precise method of identification. . . .

After news of the second PT-boat attack in the Gulf of Tonkin reverberated around Washington, there was a rush of policy conferences at the State Department, Pentagon and White House.

According to the gunnery officer, this blurry photograph, taken from the U.S.S. Maddox, *shows a North Vietnamese PT boat fleeing the scene of the attack.*

United States fighter planes such as these were sent to bomb targets in North Vietnam.

view of the fact that the United States obviously can bring superior air and naval power to bear against North Vietnam. . . .

American officials who have been debating these questions since the first attack, now are under much greater pressure to come up with a conclusion since the second attack ruled out the "isolated incident" premise. Many were convinced from the outset, despite the official party line, that the first attack indicated the pattern that the second attack proved.

Hanoi Accuses U.S.

Radio Hanoi in its first comment on Sunday's attack on the USS *Maddox* said early today that the incident occurred in North Vietnamese territorial waters.

"Our boats came into action to protect our territorial waters and our people and to chase the enemy ship out of our waters," the radio said.

It accused the U.S. Seventh Fleet of aggressive action and said the United States was attempting to cover up its "aggression" with a story of a so-called unprovoked attack on North Vietnamese boats.

The broadcast contained a warning that North Vietnam would take the necessary steps in case of further American aggressive acts.

North Vietnam on Sunday charged that the United States and South Vietnam had sent warships "to shell the Hon Me and Hon Ngu islands in the territorial waters" of North Vietnam. Those islands are near the area where the *Maddox* was attacked on Sunday. Hon Me is used as a naval base, American sources said, and Communist PT boats have been seen in the area.

Then the President, facing the greatest international test of his Administration, called in the National Security Council for a decision at 6:15 p.m.

This challenge for President Johnson embraced a broad combination of international uncertainties over an anti-Communist conflict where more than 16,000 U.S. servicemen are already serving in South Vietnam, with several thousand more on the way. . . .

The great questions confronting United States policy makers are these: Were the North Vietnamese, perhaps encouraged by their Chinese Communist allies, deliberately trying to provoke the United States into a direct retaliatory attack on North Vietnam? If so, what is the motivation, in

The United States has denied that any of its warships shelled the islands of Hon Me and Hon Ngu. However, despite some reports published yesterday, the State Department denial did not [clear] South Vietnam. It only denied American participation.

Speculation on Attack

There are some indications, however, that the South Vietnamese may in fact have attacked the two islands. American officials have declined to discuss that, although U.S. warships on occasion reportedly have escorted South Vietnam vessels part-way to their targets. . . .

U.S. officials, however, were explicit on that point. They said they had no reason to believe Sunday's attack was the result of accident or confusion in any way. The second attack yesterday appeared to confirm that.

Source D

This Chicago Tribune *article appeared in the August 5 edition on the second page. It is reprinted here in its entirety. How does this account differ from the North Vietnamese story in Source C? What new information does this article give you? How does the viewpoint of the North Vietnamese differ? Why do you think the facts are different here? Which set of facts do you think are more reliable? Why?*

No. Vietnam Calls Attack Story a Lie

SAIGON, South Vietnam, Aug. 5 [Wednesday] [Reuters]—Communist North Vietnam today denied reports of Tuesday night's attack on the American destroyers *Maddox* and *Turner Joy*. Radio Hanoi was quoted here by the Vietnamese news agency as saying the news of the second attack on the United States warships was "completely invented and fabricated by the United States."

"It is part of United States imperialists' new scheme for provocations and is aimed at covering up their illegal acts of flagrantly violating the security of North Vietnam and further aggravating the situation in southeast Asia," the radio was quoted as saying.

Source E

On Friday, August 7, after brief discussions, both houses of Congress overwhelmingly passed the Southeast Asia Resolution *that President Johnson requested. Why do you think that the Southeast Asia Resolution is usually called the Gulf of Tonkin Resolution? What reasons are given for the passage of the Resolution? What powers were given to the President? To Congress?*

Southeast Asia Resolution (The Gulf of Tonkin Resolution)

Whereas naval units of the Communist regime in Vietnam, in violation of the principles of the Charter of the United Nations and of international law, have deliberately and repeatedly attacked United States naval vessels lawfully present in international waters, and have thereby created a serious threat to international peace;

Whereas these attacks are part of a deliberate and systematic campaign of aggression that the Communist regime in North Vietnam has been waging against its neighbors and the nations joined with them in the collective defense of their freedom;

Whereas the United States is assisting the peoples of southeast Asia to protect their freedom and has no territorial, military or political ambitions in that area, but desires only that these peoples should be left in peace to work out their own destinies in their own way: Now, therefore, be it

Resolved by the Senate and House of Representatives of the United States of America in Congress assembled, That the Congress approves and supports the determination of the President, as Commander-in-Chief, to take all necessary measures to repel any armed attack against the forces of the United States and to prevent further aggression.

SEC. 2. The United States regards as vital to its national interest and to world peace the maintenance of international peace and security in southeast Asia. Consonant with the Constitution of the United States and the Charter of the United Nations and in accordance with its obligations under the Southeast Asia Collective Defense Treaty, the United States is, therefore, prepared, as the President determines, to take all necessary steps, including the use of armed force to assist any member or protocol state of the Southeast Asia Collective Defense Treaty requesting assistance in defense of its freedom.

SEC. 3. This resolution shall expire when the President shall determine that the peace and security of the area is reasonably assured by international conditions created by action of the [U.N.] or otherwise, except that it may be terminated earlier by concurrent resolution of the Congress.

Source F

The following statement was given by President Johnson's press secretary at a news conference held early in the afternoon of August 7 at the White House. The statement expresses President Johnson's viewpoint on the passage of the Gulf of Tonkin Resolution by Congress. As you read, think about the following questions: What did the second Gulf of Tonkin incident have to do with the passage of this resolution by Congress? Why did President Johnson feel so strongly about this? Why did President Johnson thank Congress for passing the resolution? Why do you think the President was "sure the American people" joined him in thanking Congress?

Statement by the President on the Passage of the Joint Resolution on Southeast Asia
August 7, 1964

The 414-to-nothing House vote and the 88-to-2 Senate vote on the passage of the Joint Resolution on Southeast Asia is a demonstration to all the world of the unity of all Americans. They prove our determination to defend our own forces, to prevent aggression, and to work firmly and steadily for peace and security in the area.

I am sure the American people join with me in expressing the deepest appreciation to the leaders and Members of both parties, in both Houses of Congress, for their patriotic, resolute, and rapid action.

Source G

On Saturday, August 8, the President invited journalists to his Texas ranch for a barbecue and press conference. In this excerpt, reporters ask President Johnson for his opinions on the motives for the second North Vietnamese attack on U.S. destroyers in the Gulf of Tonkin. As you read this brief excerpt, ask yourself: What did President Johnson think North Vietnam's motives were for the second Gulf of Tonkin attack? Do you think it is important to know what Johnson was thinking at the time?

President Lyndon Johnson speaks to reporters at his Texas ranch.

The President's News Conference at the LBJ Ranch
August 8, 1964

Q: Sir, have you been able to better establish the motives in the two Vietnamese attacks?

THE PRESIDENT: You had better find out about their motives from them.

Q: Do you have any ideas or do you assume why?

THE PRESIDENT: The same answer would go to that same question. I am unable to speak with any accuracy on the imaginations or motives or ideas they might have had in mind on what they did. It would be pure speculation and I don't care to indulge in that.

Source H

Lyndon Johnson had won the 1964 presidential election by an overwhelming margin. Although Johnson was eligible for reelection in 1968, the fighting in Vietnam had gone so badly in the previous four years that he went on nationwide television to announce that he would not run again for president. Three years later, Johnson told this version of the Tonkin Gulf incident in his autobiography. How does this agree with or disagree with all the sources you have read? What do you think accounts for the differences?

In August 1964 an unexpected crisis developed, one that threatened for a time to change the nature of the war in Vietnam. During the early hours of Sunday morning, August 2, a high-priority message came in reporting that North Vietnamese torpedo boats had attacked the destroyer USS *Maddox* in the Gulf of Tonkin. The duty officer in the White House Situation Room gathered all the available data, prepared a summary and sent it to my bedroom. The report began:

Mr. President:

Early this morning the USS *Maddox* was attacked by three DRV [Democratic Republic of (North) Vietnam] PT boats while on patrol approximately 30 miles off the North Vietnamese coast in the Gulf of Tonkin.

The Captain of the *Maddox* returned the fire with 5-inch guns and requested air support from the carrier *Ticonderoga* on station nearby in connection with reconnaissance flights in that area.

Ticonderoga jets arrived shortly and made strafing attacks on the PT boats resulting in one enemy boat dead in the water, two others damaged and turned tail for home.

The *Maddox* reports no personnel or material damages.

The *Maddox* was on what we called the DeSoto patrol. One purpose was to spot evidence of Hanoi's continuing infiltration of men and war supplies into South Vietnam by sea. Another was to gather electronic intelligence. The actions and objectives of the patrol were similar to those of Soviet trawlers off our coasts and to the intelligence activities of many nations throughout the world. In an important way our DeSoto patrol was far more justified, for Hanoi was sending troops south to kill Americans.

I called a meeting of key advisers later that morning in the White House. . . . We studied the latest reports and discussed what we should do about this attack on the high seas. We concluded that an overeager North Vietnamese boat commander might have been at fault or that a shore station had miscalculated. So we decided against retaliation, but I ordered the Navy to continue the patrol, add another destroyer, and provide air cover. We were determined not to be provocative, nor were we going to run away. We would give Hanoi the benefit of the doubt—this time—and assume the unprovoked attack had been a mistake. . . .

Though we had decided to treat the first North Vietnamese strike against our destroyer as a possible error, we drafted a stiff note to the Hanoi regime. We said that our ships had always operated freely on the high seas, and added: "They will continue to do so." We advised the North Vietnamese to be "under no misapprehension as to the grave consequences which would inevitably result from any further unprovoked offensive military action against United States forces." When prompt delivery to Hanoi proved impossible, we broadcast the note on Voice of America radio and released it to the world press.

Two days later the North Vietnamese struck again at our destroyers, this time at night (midmorning Washington time) on August 4. A few minutes after nine o'clock I had a call from [Secretary of Defense] McNamara. He informed me that our intelligence people had intercepted a message that strongly indicated the North Vietnamese were preparing another attack on our ships in the Tonkin Gulf. Soon we received messages from the destroyer *Maddox* that its radar and that of the USS *C. Turner Joy* had spotted vessels they believed to be hostile. The enemy ships appeared to be preparing an ambush. The *Maddox* and the *C. Turner Joy* had changed course to avoid contact, but they then sent word that the enemy vessels were closing in at high speed. Within an hour the destroyers advised that they were being attacked by torpedoes and were firing on the enemy PT boats. As messages flowed in from Pacific Command Headquarters, McNamara passed along the key facts to me.

We had scheduled a noon meeting of the National Security Council. . . . We immediately took up the crisis in the Tonkin Gulf. McNamara gave us the latest available information. [Secretary of State] Rusk said that he and McNamara were developing a set of options for response but that the proposals were not yet ready for presentation. I closed the NSC meeting and asked Rusk, McNamara, [NSC members] Vance, McCone, and Bundy to join me for lunch. The unanimous view of these advisors was that we could not ignore this second provocation and that the attack required retaliation. I agreed. We decided on air strikes against North Vietnamese PT boats and their bases plus a strike on one oil depot. . . .

Action reports continued to arrive from our destroyers, and from the Pacific Command. A few were ambiguous. One from the destroyer *Maddox* questioned whether the many reports of enemy torpedo firings were all valid.

I instructed McNamara to investigate these reports and obtain clarification. He immediately got in touch with Admiral U.S.G. Sharp, Jr., the Commander in Chief, Pacific. . . . McNamara and his civilian and military specialists went over all the evidence in specific detail. We wanted to be absolutely certain that our ships had actually been attacked before we retaliated.

Admiral Sharp called McNamara to report that after checking all the reports and evidence, he had no doubt whatsoever that an attack had taken place. McNamara and his associates reached the same firm conclusion. Detailed studies made after the incident confirmed this judgment.

I summoned the National Security Council for another meeting at 6:15 P.M. to discuss in detail the incident and our plans for a sharp but limited response. About seven o'clock I met with the congressional leadership in the White House for the same purpose. I told them that I believed a congressional resolution of support for our entire position in Southeast Asia was necessary and would strengthen our hand. . . .

As we considered the possibility of having to expand our efforts in Vietnam, proposals for seeking a congressional resolution became part of the normal contingency planning effort. But I never

President Johnson confers with two key members of the National Security Council, Dean Rusk (left) and Robert McNamara (right).

adopted these proposals, for I continued to hope that we could keep our role in Vietnam limited.

With the attack on our ships in the Tonkin Gulf, the picture changed. We could not be sure how Hanoi would react to our reprisal strike. We thought it was possible they might overreact and launch an all-out invasion of South Vietnam. They might ask the Chinese Communists to join them in the battle. Any one of a dozen things could have happened, and I wanted to be ready for the worst. Part of being ready, to me, was having the advance support of Congress for anything that might prove to be necessary. It was better to have a firm congressional resolution, and not need it, than some day to need it and not have it. This was the thinking behind my decision to ask Congress for its backing. . . .

Nine Senators and seven Congressmen [members of the House of Representatives] joined me in the Cabinet room for that meeting. . . . We discussed the advantages and disadvantages of a congressional resolution. . . .

At the close of the meeting I felt encouraged by this show of solidarity and support. As Speaker [of the House of Representatives], McCormack said near the end of our discussions, we were presenting "a united front to the world."

Source I

The New York Times, Newsweek, Time, *and virtually all of the most widely read and the most influential American periodicals published accounts of the Tonkin Gulf incidents that were in agreement with the official White House version. Not all of the world press, however, printed the White House version of the story. On August 14, 1964, the following article appeared in the* New Statesman, *a British publication. How does this information differ from the information in the previous sources. Is it reliable? How do you know?*

The Guns of August

By Karl E. Meyer

. . . In the retrospect of a week, the incidents in Vietnam do not seem quite so simple as the initial headlines indicated. Last Friday, the conservative *Washington Star* published an account by its Pentagon correspondent, Richard Fryklund, which threw a new light on what happened in the Gulf of Tonkin. According to Fryklund, the South Vietnamese navy landed guerrilla forces on the island of Hon Me [which is part of North Vietnam], about 10 miles off the coast of North Vietnam on Saturday 1 August. These guerrilla raids . . . are coordinated with "American advisors" in Saigon, who failed to notify the American Seventh Fleet of these operations.

Thus on the fateful Saturday the destroyer *Maddox* was on a wholly unrelated reconnaissance mission when she happened to sail past Hon Me Island, which is about 30 miles from the PT-boat base subsequently attacked by US planes. Apparently, the North Vietnamese thought that the *Maddox* had been shelling the island or had been escorting the raiding vessels. Hence, the first attack on the *Maddox,* which Washington sought to [minimize] in the belief that the incident was caused by an error. On Monday, there was the second attack, this time on the destroyers *Maddox* and *C. Turner Joy.* But because of foul weather, it was impossible to tell how many boats had attacked, according to the official account.

Observers familiar with Vietnam and naval warfare are puzzled by this detail, since radar blips are not affected by bad weather. Is it possible that the destroyers could not count the attacking vessels because they could not be distinguished from South Vietnamese craft that were engaged in another raiding mission? There is so little trust in official accounts about Vietnam that the suspicion is surely understandable. . . .

Source J

On August 15, 1964, The National Guardian *published this story on its front page. The National Guardian was a weekly "alternative" newspaper. It published stories that the larger national daily newspapers either reported in a different way or did not report at all. How do the facts and opinions here differ from accounts in the other sources you have read? How are they similar? What important questions does this article pose to you?*

Tonkin Gulf: The Questions

By David Wesley

On Aug. 5 the United States, after nearly two decades of brinksmanship in its self-proclaimed Cold War with the Communist world, finally plunged over the brink with a direct assault on the territory of a Communist state. . . . [T]he "ravaging" three-hour air attack on five coastal areas of the Democratic Republic of Vietnam (DRV) had been launched, the Johnson administration announced, in retaliation for the two North Vietnam torpedo boat attacks, Aug. 2 and 4, on . . . U.S. destroyers patrolling the Gulf of Tonkin. . .

In the non-Communist world . . . the dominant feeling was that Johnson had "over-responded" because of his election race with a hardliner, Sen. Barry Goldwater. . . .

The American press lined up almost unanimously behind the act of brink-plunging. In essence, the editorial comment . . . added up to the contention: "We cannot allow the American flag to be shot at anywhere on earth if we are to retain our respect and prestige."

The DRV government, while fully acknowledging the Aug. 2 skirmish, denounced the charge of a second attack by its boats as "sheer fabrication" devised to extend the war to North Vietnam. Peking [the Chinese Communist government] called it "an out-and-out lie" and declared: "In fact, the so-called second Tonkin Gulf incident of Aug. 4 never occurred. That night the DRV did not have a single war vessel on the waters where the U.S. warships were."

In spite of these protestations . . . the word of the U.S. government was accepted implicitly throughout the . . . press of the western world. The crisis thus showed how easily a manufactured provocation could set off World War III.

The nature of the two incidents differed in every respect. This was indirectly recognized in Western comment, which found the quick hit-and-run raid on the *Maddox* Aug. 2 a standard naval defensive maneuver, but the second four-hour engagement far out at sea completely baffling since its purpose could only be to provoke a war-escalating response from the Americans, something that even Washington officials admitted both Hanoi and Peking had shown a desire to avoid.

[T]he known facts of the affair are highly suggestive that the South Vietnamese, seizing on the opportunity afforded by the Aug. 2 incident . . . staged a phony, but far more provocative raid on the destroyers two days later. . . .

No matter whose gunboats were churning around the *Maddox* and the *Joy* in the Gulf of Tonkin on the night of Aug. 4, the portentous fact about the encounter is that the U.S. did not know whose they were.

The president launched a devastating retaliatory blow not on a known enemy, but on an assumed one. . . . Yet in retrospect it is clear that the assumption was not an airtight one at best. . . .

One unanswered question remained in the aftermath of the crisis. What, in fact, was the *Maddox* doing in the Tonkin Gulf at that time? . . . [T]he Administration tried to create the impression that the *Maddox* "patrol" was "routine". . . .

The *Maddox* thus seems to have been on a specific mission in the gulf, part of it carried out close to, or within, the limits of DRV territorial waters. . . . The mission may not, after all, have been purely routine, nor may others in the future.

Now that you have examined all the evidence, go back and compare the sources. Use these questions as a guide:

1. Which sources are in agreement with each other?

2. Which sources disagree?

3. Which sources do you believe?

4. Are some sources more reliable than others?

5. Which sources seem more objective and which seem more subjective?

6. Can you spot words with negative connotations that the writers have used?

7. Can you identify those words that have positive connotations?

8. What do you think the writers wanted their readers to think when they used those words?

9. Which writers had reasons for wanting people to believe their stories? What were those reasons?

10. Are you willing to trust what those writers say?

After you have carefully examined all of the sources, you will be ready to develop your own account of what happened in the Gulf of Tonkin during the first week of August 1964. Your readers will want to know why the events of that week are important. Be sure to give them enough information about the context of that week's events by telling them what led up to those events and what happened as a result of the events of August 1964.

Like every good historian, you should focus your account on what happened, why it happened, who was involved, where it happened, and how it happened. Historians also explain why the event is important today. Be sure *you* include the importance of the Gulf of Tonkin incident today.

Your account should be titled "What Really Happened in the Gulf of Tonkin." It should be approximately 1,000 words. You should be prepared to share your work with your class.

Good luck!

Historical Bibliographies

One of the historian's most important tools is the **bibliography.** A bibliography is a list of sources that may be useful in conducting research. Good bibliographies give important information about books and articles, so people who are interested in the topic can find those sources easily.

A bibliography gives the following information for every book: the author or authors, the title of the book, the place of publication, the name of the publishing company, and the year of publication. For articles, a bibliography gives this information: the author or authors, the title of the article, the name of the periodical, the date of publication, and the pages on which the article can be found.

The style we are using in this book is one of several popular styles of bibliographic writing, called the MLA* style. Your teacher may be able to show you others.

Here is a brief bibliography on the topic of this unit's case study:

American troops evacuate Vietnamese villagers during the war. American involvement in South Vietnam did not prevent a communist takeover.

The Vietnam War: What Really Happened in the Gulf of Tonkin?

Books

Berman, William C. *William Fulbright and the Vietnam War.* Kent, Ohio: The Kent State University Press, 1988.

Gibbons, William Conrad. *The U.S. Government and The Vietnam War.* Princeton, New Jersey: Princeton University Press, 1986.

Karnow, Stanley. *Vietnam: A History.* New York: The Viking Press, 1983.

*Modern Language Association (M.L.A.) Style Sheet

Mabie, Margot C.J. *Vietnam There And Here.* New York: Henry Holt, 1985.

Moore, John Neal. *The Vietnam Debate: A Fresh Look at the Arguments.* University Press of America, Published by the Center for Law and National Security, 1990.

Summers, Harry G., Jr. *Vietnam War Almanac.* New York: Facts on File Publications, 1985.

Williams, William Appleton, *et al.,* editors. *America in Vietnam: A Documentary History.* New York: W.W. Norton, 1975.

American civilians, diplomats, and some South Vietnamese officials were rescued from the American embassy in Saigon after North Vietnamese troops overran South Vietnam in early 1975.

Periodicals

Lubasch, Arnold H. "Red PT boats fire at U.S. destroyer on Vietnam duty," *The New York Times* (3 August 1964) 1, 6.

"Making sense of a war that shaped your world," *Scholastic Update* (29 March 85) 3.

Meyer, Karl E. "The Guns of August," *New Statesman* (14 August 1964) 205–206.

"The phantom battle that led to war: Can it happen again?" *U.S. News and World Report* (23 July 1984) 56–67.

"The war that won't go away," *Newsweek* (15 April 1985) 34–67.

Let's look first at the books in this bibliography. Notice that the list of six books is arranged in alphabetical order, according to the last names of the authors. In each instance, the author's last name is followed by a comma, then his or her first name or initials. Then comes the title of the book, which is underlined or *italicized*, followed by a period. Finally, the place of publication, a colon, the publisher, a comma, the year of publication, and a period.

Now look at the list of periodical, or magazine, articles. This list is also arranged alphabetically, according to the last names of the authors. The author's last name is followed by his or her initials or first name, and a period. The name of the article comes next, and it is in quotation marks. (Book titles are underlined or *italicized*, but articles are in quotes.) Then comes the name of the periodical in italics followed by the volume of the periodical. Next will come the date of publication in parentheses, a comma, the page numbers on which the article can be found, and a period.

A good historian composes bibliographies of historical sources when he or she is doing research. The historian obtains the sources in the bibliographies, and reads and studies them. Information is taken from the sources. This information includes names, places, dates, and other facts about the topics being researched. The historian then uses the information to do several things: to make an outline, to make a chronology, and to begin figuring out what happened and why it happened. All of this is used by the historian in creating the final product: History. Many historians also include their bibliographies at the end of their histories. That way, their readers know about additional sources of information on topics that interest them.

READING REVIEW

1. What is a bibliography?

Critical Thinking

2. **Demonstrating Reasoned Judgment** (see page 40) In what ways does a historian use bibliographies?

EXPERIMENT **7-K**

Writing a Bibliography

In this experiment you will be putting your new skills to work by writing a bibliography. First, choose a history topic in which you have an interest. Your topic may be a famous person in history, or an important place, or an event. Here are some sample topics to choose from:

Christa McAuliffe
Sigmund Freud
Mahatma Gandhi
Sojourner Truth
Mikhail Gorbachev
Jeannette Rankin
I. M. Pei
The Vietnam War
Auschwitz
Antique automobiles
The U.S. Open tennis tournament
The United States Football League
Pablo Picasso
The Beatles

You and your teacher may be able to think of many others. Once you have chosen a topic, look for periodical articles and books on your topic. You do not have to check out the articles and books from your library or media center. If you are interested in doing research on your topic at a later time, you will need to find the materials and read them. For this experiment, however, you only need to research enough information to write a bibliography. (If you would like to do research on your topic after writing the bibliography, perhaps you could ask your teacher for extra credit in this unit.)

Ask your librarian for help in researching the information you need. A good starting point for books is your library's card catalog. For periodicals, your best bet is a set of reference books called the *Readers' Guide to Periodical Literature*. (See pages 84–86 for an explanation of how to use the *Readers' Guide*.)

Be sure to write your bibliography as a good historian would. Pay close attention to the style, making sure that even the commas and periods are in the right place.

Careers in History*

If you enjoyed the work of this unit, perhaps you would be interested in a career in History. As you have seen, historians try to discover what happened in the past, and why the events happened as they did. They use many varieties of primary and secondary sources. Most historians write their findings and publish them in books and periodicals. Some historians lecture on their findings, and make a living by their public speeches.

There are about 75,000 professional historians in the United States. Almost all historians combine careers in researching and writing history with teaching. Some are secondary school teachers, while others teach at colleges and universities.

Historians sometimes combine their knowledge and love of History with careers as librarians. Would you enjoy the challenge of finding sources and pieces of evidence for other people to use in doing research? If so, maybe this career is for you. Most of these historians are called archivists. They identify, classify, and catalog items in museums, libraries, and other institutions. They may help to preserve historical treasures and documents, such as the Declaration of Independence.

Other historians are biographers. They write the life stories of people who have made an impact on our world. Biographers enjoy looking through old books, diaries, and personal letters for clues that tell them about these persons.

Geneaologists are historians who trace family histories. They use birth and death records, marriage certificates, court records, records of real estate purchases, and personal interviews to gather information. Some geneaologists make a living by writing books containing the family histories of people who pay them for this service.

More and more historians are becoming involved in preserving old buildings and sites. Many of these historical structures have a great value for society. When they are destroyed, a part of American history goes with them. Historians do research into the history of such old buildings. They find out who lived and worked there, what those people did in their communities, and other information.

Federal, state, and local governments employ historians as archivists, researchers, and writers. Historians also work in government agencies where old buildings, landmarks, documents, and artifacts are preserved.

Most historians go to college and earn a Bachelor's degree in history. They then specialize in certain fields of history, as they work for a Master's degree and the Ph.D. (Doctor of Philosophy) in History.

To become a historian takes a great deal of patience and curiosity. You probably found that out as you did the experiment on the Gulf of Tonkin controversy. Historians must also stick with a project until it is done, which may take years. Historians must enjoy spending a lot of time by themselves, writing and researching. But they must also enjoy talking with others about their work,

*Adapted from *Occupational Outlook Handbook.* (See Acknowledgements, pages 595–596.)

Dr. Mary Frances Berry is a former president of the Organization of American Historians. Dr. Berry is a lawyer and a historian specializing in constitutional history. She was assistant secretary of education under President Carter.

interviewing people, and lecturing on their findings.

Needless to say, historians really enjoy reading, and they read volumes of material in their work. They also enjoy writing. Their written works must have good grammar and correct spelling. But more than that, they must be interesting to the readers. These are qualities most historians try to develop.

If you think you might be interested in a career in History, you can get more information from the American Historical Association, 400 A Street S.E., Washington, DC 20003. You may also write to the Organization of American Historians, Indiana University, Bloomington, IN 47401.

Are you interested in a career as a museum archivist? Write to the Office of Museum Programs, Smithsonian Institution, Washington, DC 20560. If you think you would like to work for the preservation of buildings, write to the National Trust for Historic Preservation, 1789 Massachusetts Avenue N.W., Washington, DC 20036.

READING REVIEW

1. Define: biographer, genealogist, archivist.

Critical Thinking

2. **Determining Relevance** (see page 18) What personal qualities are needed to become a historian?

Social Scientists Look at The Vietnam War

How do the ways historians think about a subject compare to the other social scientists? Below you will explore the similarities and differences, as you examine a selection about the Vietnam War. Read the passage from the novel *Going After Cacciato* by Tim O'Brien, a Vietnam veteran and then answer the questions under "Comparing the Social Sciences."

"The platoon of twenty-six soldiers moved slowly in the dark, single file, not talking. One by one, like sheep in a dream they passed through the hedgerow, crossed quietly over a meadow and came down to the rice paddy. There they stopped. The leader knelt down, motioning with his hand, and one by one the others squatted or knelt or sat. For a long time they did not move. Except for the sounds of their breathing, . . . the twenty-six men were silent: Some of them excited by the adventure, some of them afraid, some of them exhausted from the long night march, some of them looking forward to reaching the sea, where they would be safe. At the rear of the column, Private First Class Paul Berlin lay quietly with his forehead pressed against the black plastic stock of his rifle, his eyes closed. He was pretending he was not in the war, pretending he had not watched Billy Boy Watkins die of a heart attack that afternoon. He was pretending he was a boy again camping with his father in the midnight summer along the Des Moines River. In the dark, with his eyes pinched shut, he pretended. He pretended that when he opened his eyes, his father would be there by the campfire and they would talk softly about whatever came to mind and then roll into their sleeping bags, and that later they'd wake up and it would be morning and there would not be a war, and that Billy Boy Watkins had not died of a heart attack that afternoon. He pretended he was not a soldier.

In the morning, when they reached the sea, it would be better. The hot afternoon would be forgotten, would not have happened; he would bathe in the sea, and he would forget how frightened he had been on his first day at the war. The second day would be better. He would learn. . . ."

There was a sound beside him, . . . and then a breathed . . . "Hey! We're *moving* . . . Get up." . . . Private First Class Paul Berlin blinked. Ahead of him, silhouetted against the sky, he saw the string of soldiers beginning to wade into the . . . waters. . . . [H]e was afraid, for it was his first night at the war. . . . "

Comparing the Social Sciences

Psychologists study human emotions. As a psychologist, what could you learn about emotions from this passage? (*Drawing Conclusions*)

Sociologists study group behavior. As a sociologist, what group would you say Private First Class Paul Berlin belonged to? What role did he play in the group? (*Demonstrating Reasoned Judgment*)

Anthropologists study subcultures—small cultures inside a society. What could you, as an anthropologist, learn from this reading about how the U.S. military subculture in Vietnam differed from the mainstream American culture? (*Making Comparisons*)

Geographers study the planet Earth. What could you as a geographer learn from this passage about the land forms and vegetation of Vietnam? (*Drawing Conclusions*)

Historians evaluate evidence for reliability. If you were a historian, would you accept Tim O'Brien's account of a night patrol in Vietnam as a trustworthy source of facts? Why or why not? (*Drawing Conclusions*)

Political scientists study public opinion. By writing *Going After Cacciato* in 1967, O'Brien hoped to sway public opinion about the war. Can you, as a political scientist, tell whether O'Brien supported the position of the hawks or doves concerning the war? Explain your answer. (*Recognizing Bias*)

Economists study the way things are produced. One of the factors of production is land. If you were an economist, could you learn anything about Vietnamese products from this passage? Explain your answer. (*Recognizing Cause and Effect*)

A platoon in Vietnam

GLOSSARY OF TERMS

authentic true and genuine; a necessary condition for evidence in historical research (page 357)

bibliography a list of sources used in doing research, including historical research (page 397)

cause and effect a sequence of events, in which one event or person causes another event or events to happen (page 362)

chronology a listing of events in the order in which they happen—there is no explanation of causes and effects (page 362)

connotation the emotional meaning of a word; may be either positive (favorable) or negative (unfavorable) (page 367)

context the setting; in History, the setting into which facts are placed. (Taking facts out of context gives them different meanings.) (page 361)

corroboration the process of finding pieces of evidence that support each other in order to check the authenticity and reliability of a source (page 358)

denotation the dictionary definition of a word (page 366)

evidence in the study of History, the records of the past used by historians to analyze the effects of events and people upon each other; also called *sources* (page 352)

fact a proven statement (page 361)

frame of reference   a person's own set of perceptions and experiences through which he or she views the world and its events and people (page 361)

history   the study of people and events of the past, including what happened and why it happened (page 370)

inference   a theory based upon one's perception (page 361)

objective   without bias or prejudice; with the least amount of personal opinion influencing interpretations (page 357)

oral history   accounts of the past transmitted (carried) by word of mouth (page 375)

perception   the intake of information by the five senses, leading to thoughts and actions based upon the perceptions (page 362)

primary evidence   a direct record of the event or person being studied, most often done by a person who was there at the time; also called a *primary source* (page 355)

reliable   trustworthy and believable (page 357)

secondary evidence   a record of an event or person of the past done a long time after it happened by a person who was not there at the time; also called a *secondary source* (page 355)

subjective   with bias or prejudice; the result of personal opinions and goals influencing one's judgment (page 357)

time line   a straight line with beginning and end points that shows significant events of the past and present (and, sometimes, the future) (page 345)

8 Political Science

POLITICAL SCIENCE

HISTORY

ECONOMICS

STUDY &
THINKING
SKILLS

GEOGRAPHY

PSYCHOLOGY

SOCIOLOGY

ANTHROPOLOGY

This Is Political Science

"The deep grass in the outfield of the neighborhood park ripples in the wind. It's unbelievable that the town plans to turn this beautiful baseball diamond, where my friends and I have played so many great games, into a parking lot. I remember that day last August when Yoshi hit three homers in a row. This is a great place—and not just for kids, either. Old folks like to walk here because the springy turf is easy on their legs. New parents bring their babies on nice warm days. Dad was saying some people intend to protest the parking lot idea with a big march to City Hall next Saturday. Well, I'll be one of those people. I'll be there making the most noise of anyone."

Individuals taking action are a vital part of life in a democracy. Social scientists who study government and power are called **political scientists.** In the Unit 8 readings, you will learn how to think like a political scientist. In the experiments, you will discover how government touches your life.

Political Science and You

Political Science is the study of government, power, and politics. This may sound complicated, but the questions below will help you understand your connection to Political Science.

1. How do you feel when your friends outnumber you in a vote and you are forced to go along with something you really don't want? What can you do to influence the next group decision?

2. Describe your impressions of the candidates in the country's last presidential election. Where did you pick up these impressions? Why might election coverage in a newspaper, magazine, or TV show be slanted to favor one candidate over another?

UNIT 8 CONTENTS

What Is Political Science?

In just a few years, you will be old enough to vote. It will not be long until you and your classmates will have the power to participate in politics and government. Most people participate by voting and by telling their elected representatives how they feel about the problems the country faces.

Political Science is the study of politics, power, and government. Let's see what each of those three terms means and how they are related. **Government** is a system of rule over territory and people. **Power** is the means to rule the people and the government. **Politics** is the process of using power in government. Political Science developed out of people's need to know how power, politics, and government work.

People who examine this field are called **political scientists.** Political scientists use various tools and processes to do their work. They conduct **interviews** of those who hold office, they **analyze** information about the people and their leaders, and they take **surveys** of public opinion. Political scientists study the governmental systems of our own country, as well as those of other nations around the world.

Political scientists, like other social scientists, use many of the critical thinking skills described in Unit 1. They need to be able to identify central political and social issues. They make comparisons between the positions of various politicians and groups. They must be good at differentiating facts from opinions. Political scientists should know which pieces of information are objective and which are simple ideologies and biased statements.

In this unit you will use some of the political scientist's tools to discover ways in which power, politics, and government influence the lives of people in a nation. You will examine the various forms of government to see how they work. You will take a close look at the process of running for public office in our government. You will discover the difficulties of writing an international treaty. And you will explore some of the features of our nation's court system.

Some people consider government so important that they run for public office themselves. Why not think about a career in government for yourself? Government is always looking for young people who want to help run the country or their state, city, or town. In the future, you could be a mayor, a state legislator, or a member of the U.S. House of Representatives or Senate. Impossible? Well, maybe that is what the President of the United States once thought.

READING REVIEW

1. What is Political Science?
2. Define: power, politics, government.
3. What skills should a political scientist have?

Critical Thinking

4. **Making Comparisons** (see page 16) Give one example of a fact about politics and one example of an opinion about politics. How can you tell one from the other?

EXPERIMENT 8-A

Creating a Government

If you could create your own government, what kind of a government would you want? Would it be a government with a lot of control over you and others? Or would it have very little power? Who would run the government? Would you want to have some control over the government? How much control would you want other people to have?

In this experiment you will answer questions such as these by creating a government on paper. Your challenge is similar to the one which our country's founders faced in 1789. You must create a government which you think will be best for yourself, your family and friends, and your country.

In creating a working government, our nation's founders wrote a **constitution**—a general outline of the government and how it is supposed to work. Your job is to write a simple constitution with your fellow students in your committee. Do not look for answers in the United States Constitution. Remember, the government you are creating is *your* idea of how a government should work.

Many written constitutions follow a pattern similar to the American Constitution, which is divided into four parts: (1) the preamble, (2) the structure of government, (3) the roles of citizens in the government, and (4) ways of amending the Constitution.

In 1990, Namibia gained its independence as a result of an agreement signed in late 1988. Above, United States Secretary of State George Schultz joined other United Nations delegates at the signing of the agreement.

Does that sound complicated? It really is not as difficult as it appears. Let's look at it one step at a time.

1. The **preamble** comes first. It is an introduction to the rest of the Constitution. The preamble tells why the creators of the government planned it as they did. It describes the values of the government. (The American Constitution's Preamble lists these as values: justice, peace, liberty, and the well-being of the people.) In your preamble, describe in sentence form the values you think are most important in your model government.

2. A description of the structure of the government is next. This part of a constitution creates offices (such as chairperson, or president, or senator, or judge) and gives

those offices specific powers. In this part of your constitution, you must create offices

From the *Rotarian*, June 1972. By permission of the publisher.

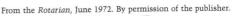

"Now, you try to get a fire started while I draft a constitution."

and decide what powers they should have. Who should rule? How should those people be chosen? How are laws made? How are the laws to be enforced?

3. Next describe the roles of the citizens. What rights will citizens such as yourself have? What responsibilities will they have?

4. Finally, explain how the constitution can be *amended,* or changed. Who will be able to amend the plan of government you have created?

Think about those four parts and your ideas of what a government should do. Talk about it with your committee. Then, on the handout for this experiment, write the constitution you and your committee create. Be prepared to defend your constitution in class.

What Kind of Government Is Best?

The uses of politics and power vary widely throughout the world today. They have varied throughout history. Not all governments give power to the people, as our government does. In some nations, the freedom we enjoy every day is not permitted to anyone except a few rulers. In some countries, the government controls the industries. In others, such as ours, private individuals control industries, although there are government rules they must follow. In some countries, monarchs (such as kings or queens) may rule. In other countries a prime minister, president, or dictator may rule. There are many forms of government. Is one best?

Here are a few of the forms of government most commonly found in existence in the world today.

Republic The term republic comes from the Latin words *res publica*. It means "the thing of the people." A republic actually belongs to the people. It is a form of government in which the people elect the representatives who rule the country. The representatives are responsible to the people for the laws that are made. The people can reelect the representatives if they are pleased with the government. In most republics, the right to vote is held only by the citizens of the country. Ancient Rome and the United States are two examples of republics. A republic is sometimes referred to as a *representative* democracy.

Democracy In a democracy, like a republic, the people hold the ruling power. The difference is that the people rule directly in a democracy. The word democracy comes from two Greek words which together mean "power of the people." Instead of electing representatives to rule the government, citizens in a democracy meet to make laws and run the country themselves. (The idea of democracy began in the city-states of ancient Greece, particularly the city-state of Athens.) Today, there are few pure democracies. Some villages in New England and Switzerland are small, working, pure democracies.

Oligarchy The form of government known as an oligarchy also comes from ancient Greece. The word means "rule by a few." In an oligarchy, a few powerful families or people run the government. The rest of the people have little or no power. This kind of government exists in most communist countries, including the People's Republic of China.

Dictatorship The term dictatorship refers to the unlimited use of power by an individual or group over an entire nation or group of nations. The word dictator comes from a Latin word meaning "to speak with authority." In a dictatorship the people have no power. All power is exercised by the dictator or dictators. An example of a dictatorship is Adolf Hitler's Germany before and during World War II.

Monarchy In a monarchy, usually one person rules. A monarchy is a government ruled by a person of royalty, such as a king or queen, prince or princess. Power is passed from one generation to another in the same family. Usually, the power to rule is passed from the monarch to his or her first-born son. The term *monarch* comes from the Greek and means "one person ruling." There were many monarchies during the last thousand years of Western history, but there are few today. An example of a constitutional monarchy is the Netherlands.

King Henry VIII ruled England from 1509 to 1547. Today, England is one of the few countries that still has a monarchy. The monarchy, however, has no real power in governing.

Anarchy Anarchy is not really a form of government. In fact, anarchy is the absence of government. The word anarchy comes from Greek words and means "rule by nobody." This lack of government forces everyone into the position of looking out for his or her own welfare. It is not hard to imagine what this leads to. Riots, killing, and stealing are common when there is anarchy. This lack of government usually does not last long before someone steps in and takes control. Anarchy is most often followed by some form of dictatorship or oligarchy. There was anarchy for a while during the French Revolution in the late eighteenth century. Then Napoleon Bonaparte rose to power as dictator of France.

These are some of the major forms of government that have appeared throughout the centuries. Most still exist. Which form of government do you think is best? Under which one would you like to live? Under which would you least like to live? In which government do you think you might like to be the ruler? In which would it be easiest to become a ruler?

READING REVIEW

1. Define: dictatorship, oligarchy, monarchy.

Critical Thinking

2. **Making Comparisons** (see page 16) What is the difference between a democracy and a republic?

EXPERIMENT **8-B**

Comparing Different Governments

In "Reading 2: What Kind of Government Is Best?," you studied several different forms of government. And in "Experiment 8-A: Creating a Government," you had a hand in creating a model government. Now put it all together. Use what you have learned about governments to complete the chart below on a separate sheet of paper. The first item has been done as an example of what you are supposed to do.

Type of Government	Where Does the Name Come from?	Rule by	Example
1. Republic	"Res Publica" —thing of the people	Citizens through representatives	Ancient Rome; U.S.
2. Democracy			
3. Oligarchy			
4. Dictatorship			
5. Monarchy			
6. Anarchy			

How and Why Nations Make Treaties

Nations are a lot like people. They have lives of their own, but interact with each other. They get along with some nations and not with others. They may work together to achieve common goals, or they may fight with each other. They also trade goods and services.

In order to get along with each other, nations may write treaties saying what their relationship should be. Also, a treaty may concern a disagreement, rather than an agreement. A treaty is one way to set down the terms of the relationship. The treaty is worked out and signed by representatives of each country. A **treaty** is an agreement between two groups or nations, or among several nations. The treaty may be a trade agreement, a peace treaty, a treaty limiting weapons, or an agreement on almost any topic. In general, a treaty is a sign that the nations involved expect to have a rather permanent relationship.

A treaty is something like a contract between two nations or people. It is a paper on which there are definite promises. Both parties agree to follow the treaty.

The important thing to remember is that when nations enter into a treaty relationship, they do so in the belief that it will be of some benefit to them. The benefit may

A historic treaty or agreement was signed by Palestinian Liberation Organization Chairman Yasir Arafat (right) and Israeli Prime Minister Yitzhak Rabin (left) in 1993. The agreement led the way to Palestinian self-rule in Gaza and the West Bank town of Jericho.

be short-term or long-term, but there must be some advantage in signing it. Otherwise, there would be little sense in signing it.

You probably know that treaties end wars. And you may even be familiar with some of them, such as those which ended World Wars I and II. But did you know that there are actually *thousands* of international treaties in operation today? According to one political scientist, there is an average of two treaties signed by the United States every day. So now you will have a chance to participate in an experiment on making a treaty and see what kind of international diplomat you can be.

READING REVIEW

1. Why do nations enter into treaties with each other?

Critical Thinking

2. **Demonstrating Reasoned Judgment** (see page 40) In what way is a nation like a person?

EXPERIMENT **8-C**

Making a Treaty

In this experiment you will learn about power and politics in international relations. You will take part in making a treaty. There are four fictitious (pretend) nations—Boksylvania, Zorrone, Condinia, and Frebia. You have been assigned by your teacher to the National Committee of one of these nations. The National Committee is concerned with the welfare of the nation. It must find ways to have good relations with other nations. One of the ways to do this is to make treaties. A treaty contains the terms of agreement on a topic, such as the establishment of national boundaries. Both parties agree to observe the terms of the treaty.

The nations in this experiment want to make treaties in three topic areas: Trade; Pollution; and Population and Migration. Each nation will send a representative to an International Subcommittee. There is an International Subcommittee for each topic area. (There may be two or more subcommittees for a topic depending on the size of the class.) You will be a representative of your nation on one of the subcommittees. You are expected to be a specialist in the topic area to which you have been assigned. You should be a well-informed representative.

As a representative and specialist you should study the description of the other nations as well as that of your own. The descriptions are on pages 400–404. It is important to know as much as you can about the nations with which you will be dealing. Also become familiar with the map of the four nations on page 419. Trade specialists should study Charts 1–4 on pages 421–424.

Before sending representatives to the International Subcommittees, each National Committee should discuss the priorities of its nation in each topic area. What priorities would the committee be willing to change? What priorities would the committee *never* give up? Decide among yourselves how you will achieve your priorities when you meet with the representatives from the other nations on the International Subcommittees. Remember, those people will also be hoping to achieve the priorities they have worked out in their National Committees. On Handout 8-C: "Treaty Negotiations: Master List of Priorities", record what your nation "wants" and what it is willing to "give" in return.

As a representative for your nation you will have a certain role to play, depending on your topic. You will have one of the following roles:

Trade Specialists will try to agree on how the nations should trade with one another. They will try to decide what trade will be allowed and what trade will be forbidden.

Pollution Specialists will try to agree on how to stop the pollution of water, land, and air. (They may decide that certain levels of pollution are acceptable.)

Migration and Population Specialists will try to decide how, why, and if migration and population should be limited.

William Penn founded the colony of Pennsylvania in 1681. He made a treaty of friendship with the Indians living there.

Specialists on the three topics are to meet in their respective International Subcommittees. Each International Subcommittee is to make a treaty in its area of specialization. The treaty should be as satisfactory as possible to all specialists. It should also give *your* nation a "good deal."

After you and the other specialists have hammered out a treaty, you will take the treaty back to your respective National Committees. Those committees will discuss all the agreements from all the International Subcommittees. Thus each National Committee will be discussing one or more treaties on three topics: Trade; Pollution; and Migration and Population. It will approve or reject (veto) each of the treaties. Your National Committee may choose its own method for accepting or rejecting the treaties. If there are two or more treaties for a given topic, your National Committee must make some decisions. Should it combine the treaties? Should it reject one and accept the other? In any case, the terms of one treaty must not contradict the terms of another.

When the treaty you worked on is approved, go back to your International Subcommittee. By now the other representatives in your subcommittee should have had the treaty ratified by their National Committees. If all National Committees ratified the treaty, the representatives may sign the final treaty. If, on the other hand, your National Committee rejected the treaty, report that fact to your International Subcommittee. It may be that only a few or none of the treaties were ratified by the National Committees. In real-life treaty negotiations it is often difficult to come to an agreement. Sometimes the parties are not able to reach any agreement and give up entirely. This experiment is intended to give you an idea of the processes involved in treaty making.

Boksylvania

Boksylvania is north of the country of Frebia and west of the country of Condinia across the Loka Channel. The Bok population is eight million. The people living in the midwest region of the Bok Mountains are poor and uneducated. The farmers of the northeast region are somewhat better off, but the highest standard of living is found in the major cities of Loka, Senzare, Bok, and North Presia. North Presia is the capital of Boksylvania.

The conflict between the Bok people and the Frebians at the border of Boksylvania and Frebia has increased in recent months. The issue is the pollution of the Fertilia River by Boksylvania. The river runs south from Boksylvania to Frebia. The Boks use the river for disposal of waste from the iron ore mines in the Bok Mountains and the gigantic steel mills in North Presia. The water pollution is carried by the Fertilia River into the once rich farmland of Frebia, the fishing areas of the Gulf of Peace, the Loka Channel, and the Gulf of Frebia. The iron ore and steel industries are essential to Boksylvania's economy. Frebia demands that Boksylvania use anti-pollution devices in these two industries. But those devices would cost $20,000,000 at today's prices. This would raise the cost of producing iron ore and steel to about twice the current market price. Boksylvania would lose customers to its competitors.

Boks forbid immigration into the country. Nor do they permit their own citizens to move to Condinia, the country across the Loka Channel. Condinia and Boksylvania are longtime rivals and enemies. This is in spite of the fact that Boksylvania needs

Condinia's coal to make steel. Despite the hostility, the two countries have traded successfully with each other for the past four years. Boksylvania and the country of Zoronne, on the other hand, are traditional allies. They coexist in peace.

Boks believe in hard work and the need for fighting in defense of their country. They are viewed by other nations as war lovers and destroyers of the environment, especially regarding Frebia. As a matter of fact, the tension between Boks and Frebians has grown more and more serious in the past few weeks. This is especially true in the City of Presia, which is split in half between the two countries. North Presia is in Bok country, while South Presia is part of Frebia.

Boks view foreigners with suspicion. They tend to believe that their way of doing things is the only right way. They believe in education and would like to build a college in North Presia. However, the Frebian conflict and lack of necessary money ($20,000,000) have delayed this project. Boks have a very low birth rate. They want their population to be even lower in the future. Boksylvania also needs a hospital, a high priority. But here again, the cost is too high: $50,000,000.

The government of Boksylvania is a republic, led by a president. He or she is appointed by an elected legislature to a nine-year term. This long term of office gives the president almost dictatorial powers.

Zoronne

Zoronne is an island kingdom to the south of Condinia. It has a population of ten million. Most of the country's wealth (90%) is owned by the Zors. The Zors conquered the island a hundred years ago. They have controlled the land since then, even though they are only ten percent of the population. The country is overpopulated. The poor, uneducated Zoks make up ninety percent of the population. The Zors feel that in order to cure the overpopulation problem at least three million Zoks should be deported (sent) to other lands. There has been a lot of pressure on the legislature and King Roz to do this. The Zoks, however, would fight against their deportation. The problem is made more difficult because the Zoks are uneducated and unskilled. They are not untrainable, however.

Zoronne is very unpopular with Condinia and Frebia because of the pollution of the waters by waste matter coming from the gold and silver mines. The mines are

This water pollution control device can filter millions of gallons of water each day.

Zoronne's only source of wealth. The pollution affects the fishing industry of Condinia and Frebia.

Zoronne society is split between the Zoks and the Zors. Fighting and hatred inside the country are strong and constant. The Zors are determined to keep control of the country, even if it means a civil war which might cut off all shipments to foreign nations. Zoronne is dependent upon the trade of gold and silver for other goods.

Zoronne has recently convinced the best experts on the problem of pollution to move to Zoronne. They will be professors in the famous University of Zoronne.

Zoroneville is the location of the capital of Zoronne.

Condinia

Condinia is a large country to the north of Zoronne and to the east of Boksylvania. It is the only nation of the four which has nuclear secrets and the uranium to develop nuclear power, including nuclear weapons. But Condinia needs people from other lands in large numbers (over five million more) to fully develop their coal, oil, and uranium reserves. Condinia's population of six million is too small to develop all the potentials of the country.

Condinia is ruled by a very powerful oligarchy, who have as their goal the military conquest of the world. Condinia contributes to the pollution of the Zorcon Strait. Actually, it would rather not contri-

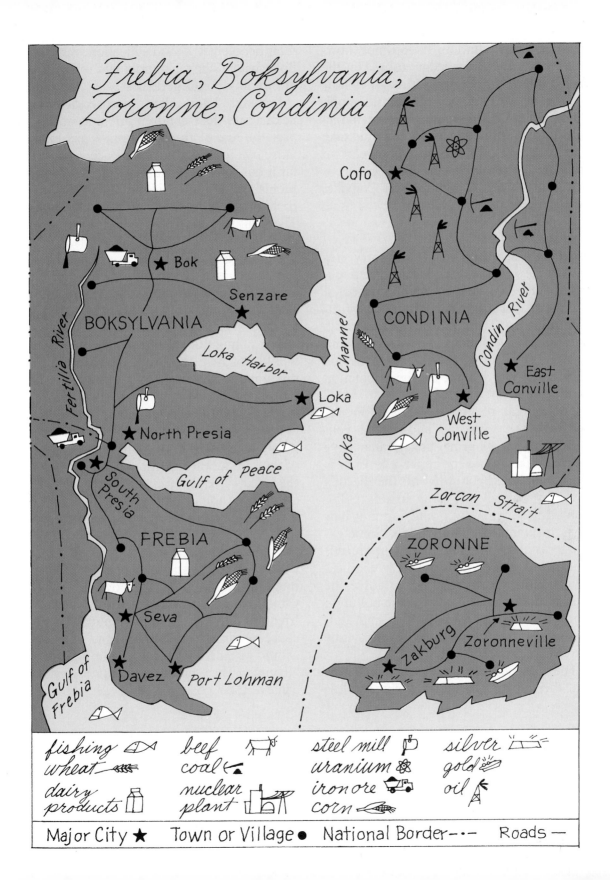

bute to water pollution. It does not, however, have the knowledge to make the antipollution machinery, although it now has the necessary money to control the pollution. Even if Condinians could manufacture antipollution machinery, it would take $100,000,000 over the next five years to carry on the research.

Condinia's capital city is West Conville, on the Great Condin River.

Frebia

Frebia is a beautiful lowlands country situated to the south of Boksylvania. The population of Frebia is only four million, most of whom are workers in the farming and fishing industries. These industries are vital to the country's economy. Although the population is small now, Frebians are carrying on a campaign to increase the population within the next five years.

The capital of Frebia is South Presia. Several demonstrations and armed conflicts with neighboring Boksylvania have recently taken place in Frebia. The issue is the continuous pollution of the Fertilia River by Boksylvania. Due to this pollution, damage to fishing and farming harvests in Frebia is running high. Some experts say that output (amount produced) will be cut in half. This means in the next two months prices will rise to twice the market price they are now. If the pollution continues, market prices of fish and agricultural products may triple by this time next year.

The folk of Frebia are poor and know that their poverty cannot be helped unless their people get a good education. But, like Boksylvania, the main problem Frebia faces in building a college is cost.

Frebians know that because of poor health care their children often do not live past the age of three. Condinia has many more medical doctors than it needs. But so far it has refused to let the doctors move to Frebia, or even to allow them to treat Frebian patients who come to Condinia. The health care problem in Frebia is further aggravated by the lack of hospitals.

Although Frebia needs more people, Frebia can just about produce enough food to feed the present population. Frebia must sell food to other countries yet have enough food left to feed the native Frebians. A larger population would add workers but would not help the problem of food production. A larger population would eat more. It would also reduce Frebia's profits in trading with other countries.

Frebians believe in their socialist government. The legislature rules almost as it wishes, under the direction of King Frebran the Great. The government controls almost all parts of the economy. The government owns all the land of Frebia, which Frebians rent on a yearly basis.

Frebians are anxious to learn about other peoples and possibly convert (change) them to their lifestyle. The governments of Condinia and Boksylvania have never been friendly with the Frebian government because of disagreements on how a nation should be ruled. Frebians do not believe in violence. They prefer peaceful means to achieve their goals.

CHART 1: **Zoronne**

Resource	Domestic Production	Domestic Consumption of Domestic Production	Additional Amount Needed	Available for Trade	Explanation of Need
Oil	0	0	60,000,000 liters	0	Needed for transport and mining fuels in Zoronne.
Steel	0	0	200,000,000 kilograms	0	Needed to make mining machinery in Zoronne.
Coal	0	0	180,000,000 kilograms	0	Needed for mining fuels in Zoronne.
Iron Ore	0	0	0	0	
Corn	0	0	170,000 bushels	0	
Wheat	0	0	170,000 bushels	0	
Beef	0	0	4,500,000 kilograms	0	
Dairy Products	0	0	130,000,000 kilograms	0	
Fish	0	0	450,000 kilograms	0	
Gold	90,000 kilograms	9,000 kilograms	0	81,000 kilograms	Limited amount is kept to back up currency, to pay government debts, and to make coins.
Silver	130,000 kilograms	13,000 kilograms	0	117,000 kilograms	

Note: 1 liter = approx. 0.26 gallons; 1 kilogram = approx. 2.2 pounds

CHART 2: **Boksylvania**

Resource	Domestic Production	Domestic Consumption of Domestic Production	Additional Amount Needed	Available for Trade	Explanation of Need
Oil	0	0	80,000,000,000 liters	0	Needed for industrial and transport fuel in Boksylvania.
Steel	700,000,000 kilograms	500,000,000 kilograms	0	200,000,000 kilograms	
Coal	0	0	700,000,000 kilograms	0	Needed for steel production (with iron ore).
Iron Ore	400,000,000 kilograms	270,000,000 kilograms	0	130,000,000 kilograms	
Corn	35,000 bushels	35,000 bushels	140,000 bushels	0	
Wheat	100,000 bushels	100,000 bushels	70,000 bushels	0	
Beef	900,000 kilograms	900,000 kilograms	3,600,000 kilograms	0	
Dairy Products	5,500,000 kilograms	3,600,000 kilograms	0	1,900,000 kilograms	
Fish	1,800,000 kilograms	1,800,000 kilograms	2,700,000 kilograms	0	Needed to back up currency, pay government debts, and make coins.
Gold	0	0	50,000 kilograms	0	
Silver	0	0	80,000 kilograms	0	0

Note: 1 liter = approx. 0.26 gallons; 1 kilogram = approx. 2.2 pounds

CHART 3: **Condinia**

Resource	Domestic Production	Domestic Consumption of Domestic Production	Additional Amount Needed	Available for Trade	Explanation of Need
Oil	150,000,000,000 liters	32,000,000,000 liters	0	118,000,000,000 liters	Would decrease if industry develops in Condinia.
Steel	90,000,000 kilograms	90,000,000 kilograms	360,000,000 kilograms	0	Needed for full industrial development in Condinia.
Coal	900,000,000 kilograms	180,000,000 kilograms	0	720,000,000 kg.	
Iron Ore	0	0	180,000,000 kilograms	0	Needed for steel production (with coal) in Condinia.
Corn	35,000 bushels	35,000 bushels	100,000 bushels	0	
Wheat	35,000 bushels	35,000 bushels	100,000 bushels	0	
Beef	900,000 kilograms	900,000 kilograms	2,700,000 kilograms	0	
Dairy Products	0	0	18,000,000 kilograms	0	Condinians love dairy products.
Fish	5,400,000 kilograms	3,600,000 kilograms	0	1,800,000 kilograms	
Gold	0	0	23,000 kilograms	0	Needed to back up currency, pay government debts, and make coins.
Silver	0	0	23,000 kilograms	0	

Note: 1 liter = approx. 0.26 gallons; 1 kilogram = approx. 2.2 pounds

CHART 4: **Frebia**

Resource	Domestic Production	Domestic Consumption of Domestic Production	Additional Amount Needed	Available for Trade	Explanation of Need
Oil	0	0	16,000,000,000 liters	0	Needed to run farm equipment in Frebia.
Steel	0	0	9,000,000 kilograms	0	Needed to manufacture farm equipment in Frebia.
Coal	0	0	0	0	Coal pollutes more than the oil Frebians use.
Iron Ore	0	0	0	0	No steel manufacturing in Frebia.
Corn	600,000 bushels	105,000 bushels	0	495,000 bushels	
Wheat	560,000 bushels	105,000 bushels	0	455,000 bushels	
Beef	16,000,000 kilograms	3,600,000 kilograms	0	12,400,000 kilograms	
Dairy Products	12,000,000 kilograms	3,600,000 kilograms	0	8,400,000 kilograms	
Fish	10,000,000 kilograms	3,600,000 kilograms	0	6,400,000 kilograms	
Gold	0	0	13,000 kilograms	0	Needed to back up currency, pay government debts, and make coins.
Silver	0	0	22,000 kilograms	0	

Note: 1 liter = approx. 0.26 gallons; 1 kilogram = approx. 2.2 pounds

A political candidate's success depends largely on the campaign efforts of his or her supporters.

Making Government Work for You

We have been talking a lot about priorities: priorities in your life, priorities in government. A **priority** is something so important that it comes before everything else. It is absolutely essential to know what your priorities are. And yet, not everyone agrees on what the most important priorities of our government should be. In fact, some of the priorities you and the class received from the people you interviewed probably do not

agree. Some people might have said that lower taxes are most important, while others might have said that we should spend *more* money on transportation, or helping the poor and aged, or on military weapons and defense.

To whom will the government listen? Whose priorities will the government adopt? The answer to these questions usually depends on who has the most power.

In our republic, where the people elect representatives to govern them, we have a great deal more power than do the citizens under a dictatorship and some other forms of government.

If you believe in a priority for our government, let your elected representatives hear your ideas. Government often listens to the people who talk the most and who make the most sense. If you remain quiet, how can your government work on your ideas? It is important in our free society to become involved. If you have a suggestion to make, make it. If you have a question about a certain issue, ask it. If you have a complaint, tell the people in government about it.

There are many things a citizen can do to make the government better and to urge officials to accept her or his priorities. One way is to vote only for the people you think are going to do the best job of representing you and your ideas. In just a few years you will be legally able to vote. Voting is a right which relatively few people around the world have. Until you are able to vote, you can offer your time and talents to the candidates in whom you have the most confidence.

There are many things you can do, no matter what age you are. People running for office always appreciate help. Just walk into the candidate's office or headquarters and ask if there is anything you can do. You will be greeted with open arms. There are many benefits for someone who works in a campaign. You can get an inside look at how the political process works in this country. You support the candidate you believe in and try to get that person elected to office. And, an extra bonus is that people in politics and government get to know you. You have an "in" if you want to express your ideas or priorities. And you have a possible source of support in case you decide to run for office yourself.

Of course, campaigns are carried on during a rather short period of time. When you cannot work for candidates, what can you do to help and to be heard? Many people write letters to the editors of newspapers in their towns and to the editors of magazines such as *Time* and *Newsweek*. These magazines reach millions of people across the United States and the world. Some people write to the *New York Times* and the *Washington Post*, two powerful and widely read newspapers. The more people you tell your ideas to, the more support you have. A reader in another city across town or across the country may read your ideas, agree with them, and start a campaign in his or her area. As your ideas become accepted and known by more and more people, the government becomes more interested. Eventually, your ideas may be accepted as priorities and made into laws.

Writing to your legislator (your representative in the state legislature or U.S. Congress) is perhaps the best way to make your ideas known. Your elected representatives want to hear from you. They want your support in order to be reelected.

Joining forces with other people who believe in your priorities is an excellent method of spreading your ideas. There are some formal organizations you can join either in Washington or in your state capital. These organizations work full-time for the passage of laws based on your beliefs. They specialize in influencing lawmakers to their ways of thinking. They are called **lobbies.** *Lobbyists* are the people who work in them. The name comes from the days when people used to wait in the "lobbies" of Congress to talk to the legislators. Now, lobbies have their own offices and full-time staffs. Another common term for lobbies is **special interest groups.**

Of course, the most direct way to have your ideas heard by other people is to run for office yourself. Already there have been people under twenty years old elected to office.

READING REVIEW

1. What is a priority?

Critical Thinking

2. **Identifying Alternatives** (see page 38) Explain two ways a citizen can help to improve the government.

EXPERIMENT **8-D**

Survey on Government Priorities

By now the concept of priorities should be familiar to you. You and your class have examined priorities in your own lives. You also participated in an experiment in which you determined your nation's priorities for the purpose of making a treaty.

Now take the concept of priorities and apply it to another situation. By conducting a short survey, try to determine the priorities the people in your community expect the local, state, and national governments to have. Ask any five adults in your community the question: "What do you think should be the most important priorities of our local, state, and national governments today?" Record their responses on the Experiment 8-D Handout. You should get from each person you interview at least one priority for each of the three levels of government.

Mayor Dennis Archer of Detroit has made it a priority to attract new businesses and industries to his city.

Senator Fred Thompson (left) of Tennessee is shown here taking the Senate oath of office from Vice President Al Gore (right). Former Tennessee Senator Howard Baker is holding the Bible during the ceremony.

Working for a Priority

In "Reading 4: Making Government Work For You" you saw that there are many ways of making yourself and your ideas heard. One of the most effective ways of doing this is to write your elected representatives.

In this experiment you will be writing such a letter. First, find out the names of your state and federal government representatives. They are the people who represent you in your state legislature and in the United States Congress.

Then take one priority from the survey you took on government priorities in "Experiment 8-D: Survey on Government Priorities." It should be a priority with which you strongly agree. Express your ideas concerning your priority in a letter to one of your elected representatives. Make your argument a convincing one, so that your representative will agree with you. Be sure to explain *how* you think your priority can be achieved. What actions and measures are necessary to make your priority work? Your letter should be approximately 150 to 200 words. Remember, a government representative is not impressed by the length of letters, but rather by the quality of the writer's argument.

Bring your letters to class, where you will have a chance to share your ideas. See if you can convince your fellow students that your priority is an important one.

The Political Spectrum

Have you ever heard someone referred to as a "conservative" or "liberal" or "moderate"? Do you know what those terms mean? They are words that describe the general political thinking of an individual or of a group. When the words are placed on a line, they form what is referred to as a **political spectrum.**

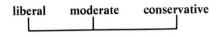

Generally speaking, a **liberal** is one who works for changes, while a **conservative** wants to keep things the way they are. A **moderate** sees the value in both positions, liberal and conservative. Moderates choose to follow a "middle of the road" course, sometimes taking a liberal position and sometimes a conservative position. The liberal position is often referred to as "the left" or "leftist," while the conservative position is referred to as "the right" or "rightist."

In this country all three—conservatives, liberals, and moderates—believe in the American government system. They work to accomplish goals within that system.

There are two more positions on the political spectrum. They are **reactionary** and **revolutionary.** The reactionary person takes the conservative position to extremes. A reactionary believes not only in keeping what exists, but also in going back to the way things were in the past. The position of the reactionary is to the right of conservative, and it is sometimes called "far right" or "radical right."

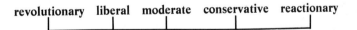

Revolutionaries, like the liberals, work for change. However, revolutionaries want to see changes happen as a result of overthrowing the government. They believe that the laws do not work for them, and they sometimes break the law to get what they want. The position of revolutionaries is to the left of liberal, so they are sometimes called the "far left" or the "radical left." Most reactionaries and revolutionaries think it is acceptable to use force and to break the law to achieve their goals.

Have you ever heard of Nazis? They were the members of Adolf Hitler's political party in Germany before and during World War II. The Nazis were **fascists,** or super-patriots, who believed that Germany had to recapture its lost glory and power. They were reactionaries who gained control of the government through elections.

After the elections, Hitler set himself up as dictator of Germany and tried to conquer the world. The term **fascist** refers to a person at the far right on the political spectrum. A person who is a fascist believes in dictatorship.

Take another look at the political spectrum. Which of the five positions do you think best describes you? Your parents? Your teachers? Which position do you believe is the best one for the country? Why?

1. What is the meaning of "the left?" "the right?"
2. What qualities do revolutionaries and reactionaries have in common?

Critical Thinking

3. **Recognizing Ideologies** (see page 31) From left to right, write the five positions on the political spectrum.

EXPERIMENT **8-F Working With the Political Spectrum** **HANDOUT**

READING 6

Governments in the United States

We often speak of "the government." But actually there are many governments in the United States. Each of our fifty states has its own state government. Every county (in Louisiana they are called *parishes*) has its own county government. Every city and town has its own government. Then, of course, there is the federal government which rules over the entire country.

When the founders of our country created the national government back in 1789, they wanted to make a government which would stand the test of time. They wanted to prevent any possibility that the United States would turn into a monarchy. Americans had had enough of British kings and queens who ruled the colonies for over a century and a half.

To ensure that no person would ever have full control of the government, those who created our government built in many safety features. The first of these features

was the **separation of powers.** This divided both the federal and state governments into three branches: (1) the **legislative branch,** to make the laws; (2) the **executive branch,** to enforce the laws; and (3) the **judicial branch,** to interpret the laws.

In our national government the legislative branch is made up of the two houses of **Congress.** These are the *Senate* and the *House of Representatives.* In most cases, both houses and the President must approve a bill in order to make it a law. The state governments also have legislatures made of two houses. (The only exception is Nebraska. This state has a one-house legislature.)

The number of members of the United States House of Representatives is 435. There are 100 members of the Senate. Altogether, there are 535 members of Congress. Every state elects two Senators, but the number of Representatives a state may elect is determined by the size of its population. The state with the largest number of Representatives is California with 52. Six states have very low populations, and have only one Representative each.

A Representative must be at least 25 years old, and a citizen of the United States for at least seven years. A Representative serves in office for a term of two years, then must run for reelection. Each member of the House of Representatives represents about 550,000 people.

A Senator must be at least 30 years old, and a citizen of the United States for at least nine years. Senators serve a term of six years, then may run for reelection. The two Senators from each state represent all the people in the state.

All members of the United States Congress must live in the state from which they are elected. Almost all Senators and Representatives live in or near Washington, D.C. for most of the year, in order to be close to their job.

The second branch of government is the executive branch. In the federal government, the executive branch is headed by the President and Vice President of the United States. The executive branch also includes a large number of federal departments and agencies. There are 14 departments, each of them headed by an officer known by the title "secretary." The departments deal with almost every aspect of American life. Here are the names of the departments and their main functions.

Department of State conducts America's relations with other nations.

Department of Defense provides for the military protection of the United States.

Department of Justice enforces all federal (national) laws. ˈ

Department of the Treasury supervises the printing of all money and provides protection for the President, the Vice President, their families, and important visitors.

Department of Energy encourages the development of energy resources.

Department of Education funds public school and college programs.

Department of Health and Human Services (HHS) directs programs that give help to the old, the disabled, and the poor.

Department of Transportation helps the states develop safe and efficient transportation systems by land, sea, and air.

Department of the Interior protects the nation's natural resources, such as timber, minerals, and water.

Department of Housing and Urban Development (HUD) helps cities to rebuild and provides assistance to poor people for low-cost housing.

Department of Labor protects the rights of workers.

Department of Commerce encourages the growth of trade inside the United States, as well as foreign trade.

Department of Agriculture helps farmers grow better crops and provides food programs for schools and the needy.

Department of Veterans Affairs protects the interests of the men and women who have served in the armed forces.

The secretaries of these departments and their employees all work for the President of the United States, who appoints them to their jobs. So it is with all the people who work for numerous agencies and bureaus within the executive branch. More people work for the executive branch than for the other two branches combined.

The executive branch of every state is headed by a Governor and a Lieutenant

Governor. State executive branches include many departments and agencies similar to those in the federal government.

The third and last branch of government is the judicial branch, a system of courts headed by judges or justices. It is the job of the judiciary to conduct trials. Through the trials, the judges interpret the laws passed by the executive and legislative branches. There is a federal system of courts, the highest of which is the United States Supreme Court. There is also a system of courts in every state, modeled after the federal system.

The government systems we have described are set up so that none of the three branches can completely rule the other two. This is a safety measure referred to as the **balance of power.** It is also called **checks and balances.**

Another safety measure is a **division of powers** between the federal government and the state governments. The state governments created the federal government and gave it certain powers, called **delegated powers.** The state governments kept some powers for themselves, called **reserved powers.** Some powers are shared by both

From the Supreme Court to a small claims court such as this one, our citizens use the judiciary to settle disputes.

the federal and state governments. They are called **concurrent powers.** The power to print money is a delegated power of the federal government. So is the right to make war and declare peace. The regulation of trade between the United States and other countries is also a delegated power held by the federal government. Reserved powers of the states include the right to determine legal ages for marriage, voting in state elections, and the purchase of alcoholic beverages. A concurrent power held by both state and federal governments is the right to tax citizens.

Governments of countries, towns, and cities, are often referred to as **local government.** Local governments are of many different types. Although we will not discuss local governments in this unit, they are very important. In many ways, your local government affects your life more directly than the federal and state governments. It is a good idea to find out as much as you can about your local government.

That, briefly, is how the governments in the United States are structured.

READING REVIEW

1. Define: separation of powers, division of powers, unicameral.
2. What qualifications must a member of the U.S. Senate have? A member of the House of Representatives?

Critical Thinking

3. **Making Comparisons** (see page 16) Name the three branches of government and describe the function of each.

EXPERIMENT 8-G How Much Do You Know About Governments **HANDOUT**
in the United States?

EXPERIMENT   **8-H**

The American Political Process

In this experiment you and your class will learn a great deal about power, politics, government, and the American election process. You will actually have a role in an election campaign. A **campaign** refers to the process by which a candidate tries to get elected to public office. No matter what role you play in the campaign, your work will be vital to the success of the experiment. (Unnecessary absences during this time will hurt the effectiveness of the experiment for the whole class.)

Once you have been assigned your role in the experiment, study first the Data Base which is most important to your role. If you are a candidate, study Data Base 1. If you are a campaign manager, study Data Base 2. And if you are a researcher, study Data Base 3. People in special interest groups should refer to Data Base 4, while those in the media are directed to Data Base 5. *Everyone* should become familiar with Data Base 1 and Data Base 6. (For this experiment, you should also refer to the Glossary for important vocabulary words.)

When you have read the Data Base that relates to your role, read all the other Data Bases. This will help you understand the perceptions and roles of the other players. You will need to know how they are going to act in this experiment. It is to your advantage to understand how all the roles are to be played.

From there on, just do what you think is appropriate. The more you put into the experiment, the more you will learn about power, politics, government, and the American election process. So, make the effort. Get involved!

Contents

Miss Peach—*courtesy Publishers-Hall Syndicate*

Data Base 1
The Candidate:
How To Run for Public Office

A **candidate** is someone who runs for a publically elected office. As the Candidate for public office in this experiment, you are the center of the campaign. The eyes of the voters are on you almost all the time. You will find, as the campaign rolls along, that the constant attention you receive has its good points and bad points. Naturally, you want the public's attention so that they can get to know you and what you stand for.

But you must give up a certain amount of privacy in order to win the election. Your Campaign Manager and Researcher will not be as visible to the public as you are. A **campaign manager** is responsible for the overall running of the candidate's campaign. The **researcher** supplies the candidate with facts about the key issues. That person also communicates the feelings of the people on the issues. It is the job of the

Campaign Manager and the Researcher to make you look as good as possible to the voters. To do this they must stay in the background of the campaign. You, of course, will be giving public appearances, following the advice of your Campaign Manager and Researcher.

Before you can even run for public office, you must take care of some "red tape" (official procedures). First, you must file for office. To do this you must obtain a petition from your local Board of Elections. A **petition** is an official form requesting permission from the government to run for office. It is filed with the government's Board of Elections. (In this exercise, the teacher will act as the Board of Elections official.) Be sure to follow the instructions on the peti-

tion carefully. You must get at least five signatures on it. Hand the petition back to the Board of Elections in completed form before the deadline, which is stated at the bottom of the petition. This procedure is called *filing your petition*. When you have filed your petition, you are officially in the race for public office. You must now kickoff, or begin, your campaign.

There is no substitute for an effective and attention-getting kickoff speech in a campaign. Remember that first impressions, in politics as in life, are very often the most lasting impressions. So make your kickoff a good one, giving an impression of yourself as an outstanding Candidate in the minds of the public. Here are some hints on how to do this.

A candidate for office delivers a kickoff speech. It is important to make a positive impression early in a campaign.

Political Science **435**

First, issue a public statement. Arrange (through your teacher) for a news conference, in which you state before the class that you have become a Candidate for public office. Specify the title of the office, for example: "the office of Governor" or "the office of Senator." You and your Campaign Team should have a brief press release printed and ready to hand out to those who want it, especially reporters from the media. **Media** is a word describing all public communication forms, such as newspapers, magazines, radio and television. In both the press release and in the public statement you make, you should let the public know the following: you are serious about winning the election; you are qualified to hold the office; why you think you are qualified; and the reasons why you decided to run for public office. You may also mention your concern about several important problems facing the people (called "key issues"). However, it is usually best not to be too specific at this early stage in your campaign.

During the campaign let your Campaign Team find out what people want. You will make your position on the key issues more clear as the campaign continues. Remember, your goal is to be elected. You are elected to fulfill the wishes and expectations of your **constituents** (the people— your classmates—you want to represent). You can do this best by getting to know what the voters want you to do if they elect you. So *listen* to the voters, *then act* on what you think their wishes are.

You will also need to listen to special interest groups in determining key issues of your campaign. A **special interest group** is an organization of people concerned about a particular issue. They join together to influence the making of laws and public pol-

Keeping a candidate's name and face before the public is essential. Teddy Roosevelt (U.S. President 1901–1909) ran this "PR" banner in the election of 1904.

icy about that issue.

Prepare your "platform" on the basis of the voters' wishes. A **platform** is a list of views and priorities you and your Campaign Team believe in and want to accomplish if elected to office. The statements in a platform are sometimes referred to as "campaign promises."

The kickoff speech is your first bit of publicity in the campaign. Publicity during the remainder of the campaign will have to come from other activities. In a campaign such as yours, in which the number of constituents is small, there is no substitute for *personal* contact. Talk with the voters, individually and in groups. Try to convince them that your ideas and their ideas are very much alike and that you would do a good job for them if elected. If your classroom situation allows, other publicity tools may be used. You and your team should check with your teacher to see which ones might be available.

In an election campaign, **public relations,** or **PR,** is very important. The term PR refers to activities which help you gain a good relationship with the public.

Posters are an absolute necessity in any election. They are the best way of keeping the name of the Candidate and the issues she or he represents in the public eye during the entire campaign. Leaflets and handbills are effective, too. All of these forms of PR should have one thing in common: they should be attractive and simple. People have very little time to read detailed posters and leaflets. So put just enough on your material to keep your name, qualifications, and the main issues before the public. Also, do not flood the public with such handouts. The public may think of your material as "junk" if they receive too much of it. You do not want this to happen.

Campaign buttons have long been popular in American politics. These buttons are from Teddy Roosevelt's campaigns.

Campaign buttons are another way of keeping your name constantly in the public eye. Simple buttons can be made of thick paper with slogans marked on them with felt tip pens. The buttons can be attached to clothing with pins.

Your most important PR is your personal contact with the people and Interest Groups. There are many "special interest" groups, most of whom will have entirely opposite ideas about what your platform should be. You cannot please all of them, but you must satisfy most of them in order to be elected. In politics, it does not pay in the end to be dishonest in your promises or unfair in your methods of campaigning. The people who elected you because they believe in you will not reelect you if you do not carry out your promises.

Personal contact with the voters can be done in many ways. Your team should schedule meetings (through your teacher) with special interest groups and voters. Be on the lookout for those voters who seem to be most influential in getting other people to vote their way. Get to know these people, so that they can help you win the favor of others in their circle of friends. If possible, get endorsements from as many groups and individuals as possible. An **endorsement** is a public statement made by a voter or group of voters that they support you fully in the campaign. The more people you can get to endorse you, the more likely it is that others will do so too.

Money is a necessary evil in any campaign. Everything in the campaign will have a price tag on it. Interest Groups will be given stage money by the teacher. You will need to get that money in order to "buy" the right to make posters, buttons, handbills, etc. You will also need the money to "buy" television and radio commercials, to pay your staff, and to take care of many "expenses." You must pay in advance. The Treasurer will help keep track of how the money is handled. This game of politics then becomes more difficult. You must persuade the Interest Groups to give you money. You have to rely upon voters' contributions in order to produce the PR you need to spread the word of your candidacy. (You may be interested to know that in real politics, money is so important in waging a successful campaign that it costs over five million dollars to become a U.S. Senator in some states. The money spent on a recent presidential election is estimated at over one hundred million dollars.)

Your Campaign Team is made up of your Manager and Researcher. They are there to help you. Use their talents as much as possible to make as many good contacts with voters and groups as you can. They should be doing most of the background work for you, especially in researching the best positions for you to take. They should be talking with the people and digging up facts in the school or community library. (Your school librarian will be of great help to you—if you ask for help.) You certainly will not have time to do all that work by yourself, so rely on their information and advice. In your spare time, especially after class, it would be wise to do some reading on how candidates in the real world of politics carry on successful campaigning.

Before the end of the campaign, your team should prepare for a debate against your opponent (on Day 3 of this exercise) and a closing speech which you will deliver on the day before the voters go to the polls to cast their ballots. Both should be strong outlines of your position on the key issues, combined with a request for votes. After your speech, your team will have a brief amount of time to talk to the voters to find out what your chances of winning are and to find out with what issues they agree or disagree. If you are winning at this point, you and your team should try to make the voters' decisions as firm as possible. If you are losing, you may be able to gain votes by changing your positions on some issues. Be careful to hold fast on those issues which are your strongest source of support and in which you believe most strongly. Your changes of position must now be publicized as widely as possible. However, be careful to avoid giving the impression that you are panicking and insincere, and that you are just trying to get a few quick, last-minute votes. You must change your mind on the issues only if it is in the best interest of the public.

The day before balloting is the last day of campaigning. At that point, there is little to

After the campaign is over a politician often realizes the work has just begun. Communication with the people does not stop when the election is won. Here, Representative John Conyers of Michigan is shown holding a news conference.

do but sit back with your team and wait for the results. If you win, that's fine. It is the goal of every politician to win the election. But if you lose, do not feel badly. You have accomplished some great things if you and your team have worked hard on the campaign. First, you made a name for yourself. The voters will remember you the next time you run for public office. Secondly, you gained a great deal of knowledge about yourself and others—and the world of politics—from your experience. And perhaps most importantly, you have contributed to the effective functioning of government by

running for office. If you had not opposed the other Candidate, he or she could easily have been elected without giving the public any choice. In that case, everyone would have been the loser.

There are a few last words of advice. Make it a point for you and your team to keep in constant touch with your teacher for information on meeting times with groups and voters, for hints on how to conduct your campaign, and for scheduling parts of the classroom and other school facilities. Next to your Campaign Team, your teacher will be of greatest help to you. (Do not expect your teacher to take sides, though. She or he will give you help only when you specifically ask for it.)

Finally, one of the most important pieces of advice for you and your team members is this: COMMUNICATE with one another. You cannot win if you and your team are pulling in many different directions. If the voting public has the impression that your team is disorganized, you are beaten even if your opponent is not a particularly good candidate. Stick together and work as a team, and you will be amazed at the results.

Good luck to you and your team. May the best Candidate win.

Data Base 2
The Campaign Manager in an Election Campaign

As the Campaign Manager, you have one major goal: You must guide your team to victory. To do this you must 1) help your Candidate make the best possible appearances and 2) publicize the Candidate's strong points. You are your Candidate's primary backup person, the one she or he will rely on to make all arrangements for publicity, meetings with various groups and individuals, finances, and speeches. You are, in fact, the Candidate's right-hand person. Without your full support and one-hundred-percent effort, your Candidate cannot win. In general, you are in charge of selling your Candidate to the voting public. Here are some hints on how to be a Campaign Manager:

1. First, your Candidate must file a petition to run for office. A petition is an official form obtained from the Bureau of Elections, a part of the U.S. government. (In this exercise, your teacher represents the Bureau of Elections.) Your Candidate must fill in the information on the petition, have a specified number of voters (five) sign it, and hand it back to the Bureau of Elections by the deadline stated on the form. You must make certain that your Candidate does this, or he or she cannot run for public office. The petition is government approval to enter the campaign.

2. Once the petition is filed, or handed back to the Bureau of Elections in completed form, your Candidate is then in the race. Now you must work closely with the Candidate on the kickoff speech. This is your Candidate's first official public appearance as a candidate for office, so everything must go right. The public's first impression of your Candidate is a lasting one. So prepare for it carefully. Arrange with your teacher for a kickoff speech (call it a "news conference") in which your Candidate will state publicly for the first time that she or he is a candidate for public office. Specify the title of the office, which has been determined in advance through class discussion.

You should also work closely with the Candidate to prepare a brief press release. This should be ready to hand out to those who want it, particularly reporters from the media. (Media describes all public communications forms, such as TV, radio, newspapers, and magazines.) In the kickoff speech and press release the Candidate should let the public know that he or she is serious about winning the election, that he or she is qualified to hold the office, and why he or she decided to run for office. The Candidate should also state a deep concern for several important problems facing the public at this time. These are called **key issues,** but it is usually best not to be too specific at

CONNOLLY
he's only just begun ... working for you.

PAID POLITICAL ADVERTISEMENT

The campaign manager is one of the busiest people in a campaign. He or she must spend a lot of time on the phone, writing letters, and performing other organizing activities.

this early date in the campaign. You and your team's Researcher should find out what the people want during the campaign. As you find out more and more exactly what the voters think, help your Candidate make positions on the key issues clearer. As the public's opinions become clearer to you, you will be able to help the Candidate plan the campaign platform. The platform states what your Candidate and team believe in and want to accomplish if elected.

3. In a small campaign such as yours, where the number of constituents is small, personal contact is most important. Constituents are people your Candidate will represent, if elected. Do your best, as Campaign Manager, to arrange meetings with the various Interest Groups for your candidate. Before she or he talks to them, try to

find out what they want the Candidate to support and oppose. You can tell the Candidate this information and prepare to make a favorable impression on the group. You should also take advantage of all PR (public relations, or publicity) devices you can to promote your candidate. Here are some that can be used in most classroom situations.

a *Campaign buttons.* Convince people who support your Candidate to wear a button with the Candidate's name on it. You will also be in charge of manufacturing the buttons. These can be made easily with thick paper and felt tip pens and attached to clothing with pins. Very few words should be printed on the buttons. Usually the Candidate's name is sufficient.

Political Science **441**

Preparation of campaign posters is a basic task people can do to help support a candidate.

b *Posters, handbills, and leaflets.* These are absolute necessities in any election. They are the best way, next to buttons, of keeping the Candidate's name and platform before the public at all times. Make all these forms of PR simple and always to-the-point. Remember, people usually do not take the time to read long and detailed posters, leaflets, and handbills. So put on them just your Candidate's name, qualifications, and the main issues. One warning: Do not flood the public with this written material. Flooding the voters with them may create a negative attitude toward the material and they may dismiss it as "junk." It may hurt rather than help your Candidate by irritating voters.

c *Finding out the issues.* This is mainly the job of your Researcher, but you should also be active in finding out what the key issues are in this campaign and reporting them to *your* Candidate and Researcher. Together you will work out a platform to please the greatest number of voters.

d *Financing the campaign. Everything* in the campaign will have a price tag on it. Interest Groups will have a special type of money, distributed by the teacher. You will have to get it in order to "buy" the right to make buttons, handbills, and leaflets, and to broadcast radio and TV messages, etc. The game then becomes more difficult, as well as more realistic, because you must then rely on contributions from groups in order to produce the PR materials you need. (You may be interested to know that in real politics, money is so important in waging a successful campaign that it costs over five million dollars to become a U.S. Senator in some states. And the money spent on a recent past presidential election is estimated at over $350 million.)

e *Endorsements.* An endorsement is a public statement by a person or group that supports your Candidate and is a declaration to vote for him or her. You should try to get as many endorsements as you can. The more you have, the more likely others are to endorse or vote for your Candidate. Individuals and groups can help in other ways, too. They can work to convince other voters to support your Candidate. They can also help prepare and distribute PR materials. They can help research the key issues. So do not be afraid to ask for their help. The people who are most involved in your Candidate's campaign will feel that they have a stake in your candidate's winning the election. Therefore, they will be more eager to get others to vote for your Candidate.

4. When the campaign politicking is winding to a close, take a poll of the voters to see what the chances are of your Candidate's victory. The best time to do this is probably on the day before the election. If it looks like your team will win, try to make your supporters' promises of votes as firm as possible. If it appears that your Candidate might lose the election, you may be able to gain some votes by having your Candidate change her or his position on some issues. But be careful to hold firm on those issues which are the strongest source of support. Those positions which are changed must be done for the public good, not just because you want to pick up a few last-minute votes.

5. In your politicking, be on the watch for those individuals who seem most interested in the campaign and your Candidate. If you can get them to join you, they are often influential in winning others to your side. Try to get such persons as involved as possible in your Candidate's campaign.

6. You and the Campaign Team may want to come up with slogans, campaign songs, and other gimmicks to help draw attention away from your opponent and focused on your Candidate. In all these arrangements, keep in close contact with your teacher. Next to the persons in your campaign team, your teacher is the greatest source of help to your team. He or she will give you information on meeting times with groups and individual voters, hints on how to conduct your campaign, and details concerning the scheduling of parts of the classroom and other school facilities. (Your teacher will give help only when asked, and should not be expected to take sides.)

7. Finally, one of the most important pieces of advice for you and the Campaign Team is this: COMMUNICATE with one another. You and your Candidate should know exactly what each other is doing. The same, of course, applies to your Researcher. You cannot win if you and your team are pulling in different directions. If the voters have the impression that your team is disorganized, you may be beaten even if your opponent is not a particularly good candidate. Stick together to win!

If your Candidate wins, congratulations. You did a fine team job. If he or she does not win, do not feel badly. You accomplished some great things, if you gave one-hundred-percent effort to the campaign.

Newspaper headlines reflect a campaign manager's dream come true.

First, you helped your Candidate make a name for himself or herself. The voters will remember the Candidate the next time he or she runs for office. You are also known for the quality of work *you* did in the campaign. Secondly, you and your Candidate probably got to know each other better than most people ever will. You and the rest of the team gained a great deal of knowledge about yourselves and others—and the world of politics—from your experience. And perhaps most importantly, you and your team have contributed to the effective functioning of government by your participation in this campaign. Without your opposition the other Candidate could have been elected without giving the voters

what they wanted. In that case, everyone would have been losers.

Good luck to you and your team. May the best Candidate win!

Data Base 3
The Researcher in an Election Campaign

As the Researcher for your Campaign Team, your job is to help get your Candidate elected. You should work closely with the Candidate and the Campaign Manager. Provide him with the information necessary for the Candidate to understand the key, or major, issues in the campaign. Your position is a very important one. The Candidate must know as much as possible about the key issues. He or she must be able to take a stand on them and talk intelligently to the voters about them. The Candidate will not be able to do this unless you detail a complete picture of each important issue. Your team needs information in order to win.

What are key issues? Key issues are problems about which the voters feel strongly. Of course, not all voters believe in the same solution to any one issue. For example, a key issue today is whether or not there should be gun control. The use of guns in crime and murder has increased tremendously. Citizens as well as law en-

Many Americans protest high taxes, or at least want a say in how taxes are spent. Tax reduction is an issue many politicians must consider including in their platform.

forcers are alarmed about this problem. Some people urge this solution: *all* ownership of guns by private individuals should be outlawed, and only police and the military should be allowed to own and operate firearms. They favor strict gun control. Others argue that all guns should *not* be outlawed. Guns are a source of enjoyment to hunters and others who use guns in a sport. These opponents to gun control are just as concerned about guns and crime, but they feel strongly that guns should not be outlawed. Other opponents of gun control claim that the ownership of firearms is a right of every citizen of the United States protected by the Constitution. Some people believe there is another solution to the gun control issue. They feel that gunowners should have their firearms licensed by the government. If gunowners were licensed, they could be identified in the event of a shooting or crime. So, although various groups are concerned about the abuse of guns, they disagree completely on the best solutions to the problem. Gun control is certainly a key issue. It is likely to be an unresolved issue for some time.

Gun control is only one key issue. Your Candidate will have to know a lot about this issue and many others. At the very beginning of the campaign you, the Campaign Manager, and the Candidate must get together to work out campaign strategy. Together you will decide what the key issues are. You will have to determine what the voters think your Candidate should do about each of the issues. You will work closely with the other Campaign Team members in writing a campaign platform. The platform is a list of things the candidate believes in and will do if elected. You and the Campaign Manager will have to talk to the voters individually and in groups to determine whch issues they want your Candidate to support.

Not all key issues will be obvious at the beginning of the campaign. Many of the issues will emerge as the campaign runs its course. You must be on the alert for any issues that arise. Supply your Candidate with the information necessary to keep him or her well prepared. This is one reason why you will be working daily throughout the campaign with the Candidate and Campaign Manager.

One source of information in the research process is the voter. You will listen to voter arguments for and against certain solutions to the key issues. Some of your time will be spent in the library looking up facts on the key issues to make your Candidate's speeches, posters, handbills, and other public relations (called "PR" or "publicity") devices strong and to the point. The public is much more likely to elect someone who knows what she or he is talking about than one who does not know the key issues and has not prepared a platform on them. It is also necessary to make your Candidate's positions on those key issues attractive to the voters. The public is not going to elect a person to office who holds solutions to key issues in which they do not believe.

It is fairly easy to research the issues if you know where to go to find information. A good place to start is your community or

Health care reform has been a key issue in many recent elections.

school library. To research current topics, go first to the *Readers' Guide to Periodical Literature*. This is an index of all major magazine articles. All articles are listed by topic, author, and date of publication. The card catalog may also be of help, especially in researching issues which were also important in the past, such as pollution. Ask your librarian for help.

Information on the key issues can be gathered from many other sources. Ask your family and older friends for their viewpoints on the key issues. Listen to radio and TV news commentators and newspaper columnists and personalities. They are usually informed about issues. Local news people may be willing to talk to you. Consider interviewing them.

An excellent source of arguments pro and con (especially in city areas) can come from associations, clubs, and other groups which have an interest in a particular key issue. For example, both the National Rifle Association and the Sierra Club have an interest in the gun issue, but disagree on possible solutions to the problem. You will probably not have time to write such groups for information. But you can visit nearby offices and headquarters, or phone them for information. A good place to check for organizations is the Yellow Pages of your area, or that of Washington, D.C., New York, Los Angeles, or any other major city. Listings found under the heading "Associations" in the Yellow Pages should provide you with several good sources for your research. Do not be afraid to approach these organizations. Most of them are anxious to talk with young people who are concerned about the same issues for which they work hard day after day.

The job of Researcher is not an easy one. As in the job of Campaign Manager, much hard work is needed to be successful. To help your Candidate win, you have to give a great deal of effort. You and your team will learn much about one another, about the world of politics, about the key issues in the community and the United States today, and about your class.

If your Campaign Team wins, congratulations! It is, of course, the goal of every Campaign Team to work together for the election of its candidate. If you lose, don't feel badly. Your team has done a great job, if you all gave one-hundred-percent effort to the campaign. You have strengthened the American political process by your participation. You have made a name for your Candidate if she or he decides to run in another election. You have made a name for yourself as an excellent Researcher and team player. And most importantly, you and your team provided the other Candidate with opposition. Without opposition the other Candidate could have won easily without giving the voters a choice. In that case, everyone would have been losers.

Good luck to you and your team.

Data Base 4
The Special Interest Group in an Election Campaign

A *special interest group* (most often called simply an "interest group") is an organization of people who believe in the same values and who unite to reach a common goal. Some examples of interest groups today include the following:

the American Medical Association, which tries to promote the best interests of the medical doctors of this country

Vermont citizens marching in support of a nuclear arms freeze form a strong interest group. Local government officials must pay close attention to the concerns of their constituents.

the National Rifle Association, which, among other things, fights against the laws controlling the ownership and use of firearms in our country

the Audubon Society, which attempts to influence legislators to pass bills protecting our environment

Other interest groups can be found in the Yellow Pages of the telephone directory under the heading "Associations." Since many interest groups have their headquarters in New York City and Washington, D.C., the Yellow Pages of those cities are especially helpful.

Each interest group has a membership, large or small, which is very interested in a specific key issue. When a key issue comes

up in an election campaign, there is often an interest group behind it. Interest groups try to influence candidates to accept their views. If a candidate supports the views of an interest group, that group tries to help the candidate's campaign in many ways. One way is by donating (giving) money to the candidate's campaign. It costs a lot of money to run a successful campaign, so the money donated by the voters (including interest groups and their constituencies) is always welcomed by candidates.

In this exercise, your Interest Group should first determine your priorities. Make a list of priorities you would like either Candidate, or both Candidates, to make part of the campaign. Try to convince both Candidates to make campaign promises which favor your priorities. You will be given money (not the real stuff, unfortunately) to use in the campaign. Pretend that the money has been raised by members of your Interest Group. In order to do the most good for your Interest Group and its priorities, the money should be spent. Hanging onto the money past the election serves your group no purpose. You and your group are going to have to determine early in the campaign just how you will use this money. When the Candidates make requests for money from your Interest Group, you will want them to make certain promises in exchange for your contributions. If the Candidates do not agree with your views, you may choose to wait awhile. As time goes on, the Candidates will need more and more money. They may be willing to change their positions on the issues later in the campaign. Therefore, it may be to your group's advantage to wait before giving generously.

In addition to giving money, your group can help a Candidate who supports your views by endorsements. An **endorsement** is a public statement of support for a particular candidate. An endorsement tells other voters that you and your group are solidly behind a candidate. It is a promise that she or he will get your vote. It is in turn a promise by you that you will help that candidate in the campaign. A successful campaign depends on this kind of relationship.

Your group can also work for a Candidate by becoming part of the Candidate's Campaign Team. There is always a lot to do in a campaign. Ask the Candidate or his or her Manager if there is anything you can do. As an added bonus, you will be involved in the inner workings of a campaign. That is where much of the political action is.

Data Base 5
The Media in an Election Campaign

One of the most exciting roles during an election campaign is that of a member of the Media. The term **Media** refers to all forms of public communications—newspapers, radio, television, magazines, etc. A member of the media may be a reporter, a news commentator or announcer, a publisher of a magazine, or a columnist.

In this exercise you are a member of the Media. It is your job to report to the people what the candidates are saying and doing. It is important that you bring to the public's attention as much as you can about all Candidates. The voters need a lot of information on which to base their votes. The more they know about each Candidate, the more wisely they will be able to choose.

How can you supply this very important service for the people? First, get together with your fellow Media persons. You should act as a team. Decide how you will report the election campaign. For example, you may decide to publish a daily magazine or newspaper in which you inform voters about the recent progress of the campaign. You should discuss this idea with your teacher. It is less important to have a good looking publication than it is to do a thorough job of reporting. (Perhaps a duplicating machine can be made available for your use.) Feel free to interview the Candidates and Interest Groups about where they stand on the key, or main, issues. You may, for example, want to ask the Interest Groups what progress they are making in convincing Candidates to accept their points of view. Candidates may be asked how they will go about carrying out their

Today's candidates know that their use of the media can affect the outcome of an election. Appearing on talk shows and taking part in debates are ways politicians make use of television.

campaign promises, or platform, if elected. Ask questions about any issues of possible interest to the voters which are also relevant to the campaign.

A tape recording of an interview with a Candidate, or his or her Campaign Manager, may be played in class as a "radio broadcast." You should get your teacher's permission to do this. If videotaping facilities are available, you could interview the Candidates on a TV show taped for playback in the class period.

Your Media group must also select one Media person to be a moderator. She or he will moderate the debate scheduled for the final part of the campaign.

The ways for the Media to cover the election campaign are endless. The Media has

an important role. The course of the campaign and the outcome of the election could be influenced by your choice of words. It could even be influenced by your facial expressions while reporting the campaign. Just remember one thing: Be as fair and impartial as you can.

Data Base 6
A Guide for New Voters

After you have participated in the campaign as a citizen and member of a special Interest Group, and you have listened to the Candidates' platforms (their promises and beliefs) on the key issues, it will be time to vote. How are you going to vote?

What is going to determine how you vote? Here are some things to consider in making your decision.

1. Is the Candidate sincere? Does your choice really mean what he or she says, or is it obvious that the Candidate cares only about your vote, but does not care about you and your beliefs?

2. Does the Candidate agree with you on the key issues you feel most strongly about?

No Candidate can or will agree with you fully on all issues, so be selective. Decide what issues are most important to you, then choose the Candidate whose views come closest to yours.

3. Does the Candidate express her or his views clearly, or does she or he tend to hedge on those issues about which you feel strongly? Make your Candidate take a firm stand, promising to support the issues you

Preparing to cast your first vote is both a right and a responsibility.

think are most important. Look for clues that the Candidate might be making promises to other people which contradict those made to you. Such a candidate would not be a good public official if elected to office and does not deserve your vote.

4. Does the Candidate work well with other people? Does she or he seem to be able to lead the Campaign Team (Researcher and Campaign Manager) and get it all together, or does she or he seem to be disorganized and poorly prepared? Does the Candidate seem to like working and talking with her or his constituents (the people she or he will represent if elected—including you)? Or, does the Candidate seem to view you only as a steppingstone to getting elected? A good candidate likes people and is well organized and prepared.

5. Some people vote for a Candidate because she or he is good looking, popular, seems always to be at the right places at the right time with the "in" people, and other

such reasons. But you only have one vote. You should consider seriously investing your vote in the Candidate who really wants to support what you believe in. That Candidate will probably do the best job for you in office.

In the last election, millions of Americans went to the polls to vote. And millions did not. Consider what would happen if you and others in your class did not vote for any candidate in this election exercise. Could you be sure that the Candidate you favored would win?

In the real world, what might be the outcome if you did not register and vote? Would you have any right to complain about the government if you did not bother to register and vote?

The type of government we have in the United States has been in existence for 200 years. It works. But it works best only when we put the best people into office. Maybe you would be a good candidate for office in the near future. Think about it.

EXPERIMENT 8-I Government Crossword Puzzle **HANDOUT**

READING 7

Careers in Political Science*

Did you enjoy this unit in Political Science? How did you feel about participating in the election campaign? Did you enjoy the process of using power to create an international understanding in the treaty experiment? Did you like being involved in the

creation of a new government, deciding what roles citizens should play and who would hold power in the society?

If you found the experiments enjoyable and challenging, and if you would like to learn more about government, politics, and power, a career in Political Science might be for you.

*Adapted from *Occupational Outlook Handbook.* (See Acknowledgements, pages 595–596.)

Some people study Political Science in order to learn more about running for a specific political office. Some people run for election themselves, while many others work in election campaigns for the candidates they support. Once elected, the successful candidates must do what they are elected for: they must hold office and work to fulfill their campaign promises. They must do what needs to be done in government to benefit their people and to make it possible for them to be reelected.

There are about 14,000 political scientists in the United States today. Many never enter the world of politics and government themselves. Instead, they study it from a distance. Four out of every five political scientists study power, politics, and government from positions in colleges and universities. They teach Political Science courses, and they do research on topics related to the main elements in this field. And sometimes they act as consultants.

Some political scientists work in interest groups as lobbyists who try to convince legislators to pass certain laws. In order to do this, lobbyists must know a lot about the individual legislators. They also need to do much research to support their arguments and to convince the legislators to support the position of the interest group.

Political scientists live and work in every part of the United States. Naturally, many are drawn to Washington, D.C., which is the national headquarters of many interest groups, unions, and other political organizations. Others are employed as representatives of the United States government and work overseas as Foreign Service Officers.

Would you like to get more information on careers in Political Science? For general information in this field, write to the American Political Science Association, 1527

Elizabeth Dole answers reporters' questions. Her successful political career has included two cabinet posts—Secretary of Transportation and Secretary of Labor.

New Hampshire Avenue NW, Washington, DC 20036. If you are interested in representing the United States as a Foreign Service Officer, write a letter to the Board of Examiners, Foreign Service, Box 9317, Rosslyn Station, Arlington, VA 22209.

READING REVIEW

1. What do most political scientists do for a living?
2. What personal characteristics should you have if you want to be a political scientist?

Critical Thinking

3. **Identifying Alternatives** (see page 38) Name four types of occupations open to political scientists.

PERSPECTIVES

Social Scientists Look at the Rise of Democracy in Eastern Europe

The years 1989–1990 saw profound changes in Eastern Europe and the Soviet Union. Poland's Communist government surrendered power to trade unionist Lech Walesa's Solidarity party. East Germans began taking down the infamous Berlin Wall and held a democratic election for the first time in 50 years. In the Soviet Union Mikhail Gorbachev's policies eventually led to the breakup of the Soviet Union. This process of democratization is illustrated in the cartoon below. Study the cartoon by Auth and then answer the questions under "Comparing the Social Sciences."

Comparing the Social Sciences

Psychologists study the way people see or perceive things. How would a psychologist explain the massive size of the sand castle representing the Soviet Union? (*Identifying Assumptions*)

Sociologists study groups. How would you, as a sociologist, interpret the links among the political groups shown as the sand castles? (*Demonstrating Reasoned Judgment*)

Anthropologists study world cultures. If you were an anthropologist looking at the cartoon, would you think that the cultures of the countries shown in the cartoon were similar or different? Explain your answer. (*Making Comparisons*)

Geographers study regions of the world. If you were a geographer, what would you point to in this cartoon to show that these countries make up a region? What political or cultural traits are shared in this region? (*Recognizing Ideologies*)

Historians study the past. What events would you as a historian say are represented in this cartoon? (*Demonstrating Reasoned Judgment*)

Political scientists study the status of governments. As a political scientist, what does the cartoon suggest to you about the status of the governments shown? (*Identifying Central Issues*)

Economists study the ways goods are produced and distributed. How would you, as an economist, explain the recent changes in the ways the countries in this cartoon produce and distribute goods? (*Identifying Central Issues*)

Tearing down the Berlin wall

GLOSSARY OF TERMS

analyze the breaking down of an event or fact into smaller pieces in order to study it more closely (page 407)

anarchy the absence of government (page 411)

balance of power the more or less equal distribution of powers between the judicial, executive, and legislative branches of government; also called *checks and balances* (page 432)

campaign the process by which a candidate tries to become elected to a public office (page 433)

campaign manager the person in a campaign team responsible for the candidate's public appearance and the overall running of the campaign (page 434)

candidate a person running for public elected office (page 434)

checks and balances (see *balance of power*) (page 432)

concurrent powers those constitutional powers that are shared by the federal and state governments (page 433)

Congress the legislative branch of the American government, made up of the Senate and the House of Representatives (page 430)

conservative a person who works to keep things as they are; a position on the political spectrum to the left of reactionary and to the right of moderate (page 429)

constituents those people represented in government by an elected official (page 436)

constitution a basic plan of government that outlines the distribution of power, responsibilities, and the liberties of the people (page 408)

delegated powers those powers, according to the Constitution, that the states gave to the federal government (page 432)

democracy a government in which the people rule directly (page 410)

dictatorship a government in which an individual or group exercise unlimited use of power (page 411)

division of powers the assignment, according to the Constitution, of certain powers to the states and other powers to the federal government, with some powers shared by both (page 432)

endorsement a public statement of support for a candidate (page 438)

executive branch that section of the government responsible for enforcing the laws; headed on the federal level by the President and Vice President, and on the state level by the Governor; additionally on the federal level are 14 departments, each headed by a Secretary (page 430)

fascist a super-patriot who supports reactionary government actions; for example, a follower of Hitler and the Nazis before and during World War II (page 430)

government a system of rule over people and territory (page 407)

judicial branch that section of the government responsible for interpreting and applying the law, especially in court cases (page 430)

interview a meeting at which information is gathered (page 407)

key issues topics considered important by candidates or their constituents in an election campaign (page 436)

legislative branch that section of government responsible for making laws; the U.S. Congress (page 430)

liberal a person who works for change within the system of government; a position on the political spectrum to the left of moderate and to the right of revolutionary (page 429)

lobby a group of people who work for the passage of laws based on certain beliefs and goals; a special interest group (page 426)

local government the governments of counties, towns, and cities (page 433)

media a word describing the combined newsgathering and news reporting outlets, including newspapers, radio, magazines, and television (page 436)

moderate a person who supports both liberal and conservative viewpoints; a position on the political spectrum to the left of conservative and to the right of liberal; middle of the road (page 429)

monarchy rule by one person, usually royalty, with the right to govern passed through blood lines (page 411)

oligarchy rule by a few (page 411)

petition a formal, written request by a person to run for an elected office, filed with the government's Bureau of Elections (page 435)

platform the combined campaign promises of a candidate on key issues in an election campaign (page 437)

Political Science the study of power, politics, and government (page 407)

political spectrum a line showing the five major political views in their order from reactionary to revolutionary (page 429)

politics another term for Political Science; the practicing of power and government (page 407)

power in politics, the strength and influence necessary to rule or govern (page 407)

preamble the introduction to a constitution, detailing the reasons for establishing the government in the way spelled out in the rest of the constitution (page 409)

priority an issue of greatest concern that should be done first (page 425)

public relations communication with the people, usually through the media; often called PR or publicity (page 437)

reactionary a person who works to make conditions as they were in the past, often by working outside the system of government; a political position to the right of conservative; also known as the far right (page 429)

republic government in which the citizens elect representatives who rule in their place (page 410)

researcher person in a campaign team responsible for supplying the candidate with facts on the key issues of the campaign and the feelings of the constituents on those issues (page 434)

reserved powers those powers, according to the Constitution, that were kept by the states for themselves (page 432)

revolutionary a person who works for change by stopping or overthrowing the government; a position on the political spectrum to the left of liberal, also known as the far left (page 429)

separation of powers the assignment, according to the Constitution, of certain specific powers to each of the three branches of government (page 430)

special interest group a group of people who work for the passage of laws based on certain beliefs and goals; a lobby (page 436)

treaty an agreement between nations, usually concerning trade, warfare, and other common interests (page 413)

UNIT 9

Economics

ECONOMICS

POLITICAL SCIENCE

PSYCHOLOGY

HISTORY

STUDY & THINKING SKILLS

SOCIOLOGY

GEOGRAPHY

ANTHROPOLOGY

This Is Economics

The audience inside the hall is restless and excited. People are still filing in behind you and nabbing the last few seats. Blue, green and red shafts of light cross on the immense, darkened stage, which is stacked high with speakers. This is going to be some concert. You've waited six months for your favorite band to make it to your town. Now they're here and you and your friends have got the best seats in the house, front and center. Not cheap, but hey—what is, these days? Your mother couldn't believe it when you told her the ticket price. She said in the old days, rock music was about 10 times cheaper than now. That was a long time ago, Ma. . .

From rock music to beeswax, Economics is the study of how things are produced and distributed. Social scientists who work in this field are called **economists.** In the Unit 9 readings, you will learn how to think like an economist. In the experiments, you will see how Economics plays a role in your life.

Economics and You

The coins in your pocket make you a participant in the economy. Whatever you choose to buy or not to buy has an immediate effect on the American economic system. This, in turn, affects other world economies. The questions below will help you understand this connection better.

1. Have you ever worked at a part-time job to earn extra money? What factors determined how much you were paid?

2. When you decide you want to buy something, how do you generally go about finding good value? For example, do you talk to friends, consult reference books and magazines, or compare prices at several stores?

UNIT 9 CONTENTS

What Is Economics?

Every day you have to make choices. Should you go to the ball game or stay at home and watch TV? Should you spend money on new clothes or buy a radio? Should you spend the next half-hour daydreaming or exercising? There are thousands of choices you must make every day. Some decisions are very important, and some are routine.

Economics is the social science that deals with making choices about how we use our resources, including money and time. Economics also deals with the use of natural resources such as coal and water.

The word "economics" originally came from the Greek language, and means "household management." The ancient Greeks knew that taking care of a home was not easy. A limited amount of money came into the household, and the person who managed the household had to know how to spend that money wisely. Otherwise, the household would go into debt.

Today, **economists**—people who study Economics—are concerned with the way people manage their households. But they also study groups other than households, including industries, labor unions, retail stores, and everyone who makes and spends money. All these parts of society have important effects upon the entire economic system. When one part of a society doesn't manage its economic business properly, other parts of the economic system are affected for better or for worse.

Economists use a wide variety of tools in their work. They observe human behavior as people earn and spend money and as they use resources. Economists analyze graphs, charts, and information to get a better understanding of the reasons for human behavior.

Like other social scientists, they use many of the critical thinking skills described in Unit 1. For example, economists learn how to recognize cause-effect relationships between the supply of goods and the price of the goods. They make comparisons between our type of economy and other economies around the world. They also try to predict the consequences of government spending. And they determine the relevance of information to the specific problems they are studying.

In this unit you will find out how economists work. You will see what makes money valuable and what determines the prices you pay for the things you buy. We will look at reasons why people buy some things and not others. Your class will try to make money playing the stock market. (But we won't be using real money. Sorry!) And you will have a chance to run your own mini-advertising campaign.

Through this unit, you will learn how economists think about the field of economics. You may even pick up some good ideas about running your own "household" in the future.

READING REVIEW

1. What is Economics?
2. Describe the work economists do and the methods they use.

Critical Thinking

3. **Demonstrating Reasoned Judgment** (see page 40)   What benefits do you expect to get from studying this Economics unit?

EXPERIMENT   **9-A**

Managing the Household

PART ONE

The word economics comes from two Greek words meaning "household management." The household is a basic economic group. What would happen if all the households in the United States suddenly did not buy anything? Can you imagine how many businesses would have to close? The way households are managed has a great influence on our economy. Because they buy certain things, households tell producers what to make. When certain other things are not bought, households tell producers what not to make. Therefore, what is produced and available for sale in our society depends to a large degree on what households buy.

How well do you think you could run a household? Do you know how much money it takes to buy needs and wants for a family? A **need** is something essential to live. A **want** is a luxury, not absolutely necessary to live. Do you know how much time and effort is involved in managing a household? Let's try to find out.

On a separate sheet of paper make a list of all the things you think a typical family in our society would have to buy in one year. Next to each item on your list, estimate the cost of that item. Remember, your list of items is for one whole year. Be as complete in your listing as possible.

PART TWO

In Part One of this Experiment you listed what you think are a typical family's needs for a year. Next to each item you wrote an estimate of its cost for the year.

Review your list with your mother or father (or whoever manages your household finances). Have that person suggest additions and corrections. Bring your revised list to class.

Greek vase illustrating a Shoemaker's Shop, 520–510 B.C. "Household management" is the original meaning of Economics.

Well, You Can't Have Everything!

How often have you heard that phrase? It's a fact of life that you can't have everything you want. That fact is the basic law of Economics. It is called the *law of scarcity.*

Everyone would like to have more. More money or more time or more friends or more . . . anything. You might like to have a color television or a new stereo set.

Maybe you would like a shiny new sports car. You might just want more time for yourself, without someone telling you what to do. Yet, there are certain things that you know you will have to do without. Why? The **law of scarcity** states: *All things are limited. In order to get something you always have to give up something else.*

Let's think of some examples of this rule. If you want a job, you have to give up some free time. If you want a stereo, you have to give up some money (or somebody else has to give up money). Someday you will be on your own and away from your parents' restrictions. You will need a job and money to support yourself, which means you lose free time.

When economists talk about scarce goods, they mean those material things which are limited in number. Not everyone who wants something can get it. Notice that a good has to be *wanted* in order to be scarce. Porcupine teeth are rare, but we couldn't call them scarce. Who really wants a complete collection of porcupine teeth? Since nobody really wants them, there is no *demand* for them. Therefore, porcupine teeth are not scarce.

The problem of scarcity means that you have to decide what you want most, and what you are willing to give up to get it. You must choose which goods you want and which ones you can do without.

There are always many choices to make. People have limited resources, but unlimited wants and needs. Our resources are scarce. Therefore, the more we produce of one thing, the less we can produce of something else. Let's say that this country has one billion dollars to spend. We might want to spend part of it on defense and part of it on the production of such items as cars, stereos, foods, and clothes. The more

money we spend on consumer goods (things people can buy), the less money is left for defense. (And vice versa.)

Your family makes similar choices. The money your parents earn has to take care of all the needs of your family. Food, clothes, rent, phone bills, insurance, gasoline, and a lot of other things come out of your parents' salaries. If money is left over after the family's needs have been cared for, your parents can then take care of some of your wants. A **need** is something essential for living. A **want,** on the other hand, is not necessary for you to live, but makes life more enjoyable. A choice then has to be made. How should the extra money be spent? Who should get their wants satisfied—the parents or the children? Or both? Should the money be spent on a vacation, or a new television, or a car? Should it be put into the bank as savings? Your family works with the basic fact of scarcity, just as this country does.

Because of scarcity, we need to make choices. Every society has three major questions it must answer in making economic choices. They are the following:

1. What should be produced?
For example, should more cars be made? Or should we make buses and other public transportation vehicles? Should we continue to spend money on exploration of outer space, or should we invest more money in producing food and clothing for people on Earth?

2. For whom should we produce?
In some societies, things are produced for the rulers and the wealthy. These people also decide what should be produced. In our economy, things are produced for the people who can buy them. Should everyone

receive goods equally? Or is it fair for some people to have more than other people? Who should be satisfied?

3. How should we produce?

Machines are rapidly taking over the work which has always been done by people. This makes it possible for goods to be manufactured more quickly and cheaply. But it also puts people out of work. If people are out of work, how can they buy the goods? How to produce the goods has become a major problem.

Which photograph on this page represents something people need? *Which one represents something people* want?

READING REVIEW

1. What is the law of scarcity?
2. What makes something scarce?

Critical Thinking

3. **Creating Good Questions** (see page 20) What are the three questions every society must answer when making economic choices?

OFFERED BY

FOR SALE

F

FORBES

REALTORS

Making Economic Decisions

We know that our resources are limited, while our wants and needs are unlimited. This means that we are constantly faced with choices. What should be produced? How should we produce it? For whom should it be produced? The problem of scarcity forces the consumer to decide what to buy with a limited amount of money. How much should you buy? Where should you buy it?

The ideas economists work with can be difficult to understand. To help us understand the concepts of scarcity and limited resources, they use graphs and tables, such as the ones on this page.

Let's look at the problem of scarcity for the consumer. Say that you have $50 to spend. You decide that you need new clothes. You also want some new compact discs (CDs). You plan to buy all you can of both CDs and clothes. Obviously, you can buy only a limited amount of both with $50. You are faced with a number of choices. Your situation can be graphed like the one at the top of the page.

The amount of money ($50) you spend on clothes is measured on the *vertical axis* of this graph (line running up and down). The amount of money ($50) you spend on CDs appears on the *horizontal axis* (line running straight across, from left to right). Notice that the more you spend on CDs, the less you have left to buy clothes. You might choose to spend your $50 by buying $10 of CDs and $40 of clothes. That possibility is shown by point A on the graph. Or, you might decide to spend all your money on CDs, shown by point B. Or you might

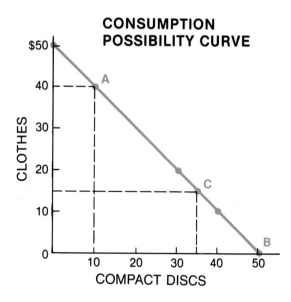

CONSUMPTION POSSIBILITY CURVE

choose to spend $15 on clothes and $35 on CDs, as shown by point C. With every gain, you have a loss. With every loss, you have a gain. Whatever you decide to buy, you have to give up something.

Now on Handout 9-B in the rest of Table 1: *Consumption Possibilities* (also shown below). Use the graph above as a reference. In filling in the missing figures, each combination of CDs and clothes should have equalled $50. Did they?

TABLE 1	
Consumption Possibilities	
Compact Discs	Clothes
$50	$ 0
$40	$____
$____	$20
$____	$15
$ 0	$____

The problem of choice in this example is a typical one for consumers. Consumers must deal with a limited amount (or scarcity) of money. Now let's look at the problem of scarcity from the viewpoint of producers. **Producers** are those who make, or manufacture, goods to sell. They also make what the consumers buy.

Imagine that you are the president of Ajax Metal Products Company. Your company makes wire coat hangers and nails. You have to decide how much of each to produce. You must know what choices are open to you before you can make that decision. You know that with the money and raw materials you have, you can produce 1,000 coat hangers or 20,000 nails per hour. It is up to you whether you produce *all* hangers or *all* nails. You might also decide to produce some of each. If you figure out how much of each item you could produce, you might make a Production Possibility Curve like the graph in the left column. You can choose from many possibilities. Five of your possibilities are marked A, B, C, D, and E. Study the graph and then write these possibilities in Table 2: *Production Possibilities* on Handout 9-B.

TABLE 2 **Production Possibilities**

Point	Nails	Coat Hangers
A	0	1,000
B	_____	_____
C	_____	_____
D	_____	_____
E	_____	_____

There are many factors which you must consider in order to decide what you will produce. For example, let's say that you can make twice the profits making nails as you can making hangers. If that is the case, which would you want to manufacture— nails or hangers? What if the cost of making hangers were half the cost of making nails? Would that influence your decision about what to produce? How would your decision be affected by what people wanted to buy? How would each of these questions affect your decision?

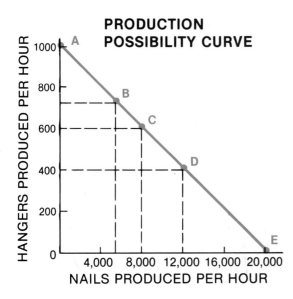

PRODUCTION POSSIBILITY CURVE

HANGERS PRODUCED PER HOUR (vertical axis): 0, 200, 400, 600, 800, 1000

NAILS PRODUCED PER HOUR (horizontal axis): 4,000 8,000 12,000 16,000 20,000

Be a Smart Consumer!

A **consumer** is a person who buys or rents goods and services, and consumes (uses) them. You have been a consumer since you were born. Your family bought goods and services for you when you were younger. Now you are purchasing many of your own goods and services. Stop and think of all the goods and services you buy in a month.

What kind of research could you do before purchasing a bicycle?

Include your purchases at music stores, grocery stores, and shopping malls. And don't forget to mention the food you buy at school and at fast food restaurants.

Every consumer is faced with the law of scarcity. You only have a limited amount of money and time. How can you get the most for your money? How can you save time and get the best products at the lowest prices?

The field of consumer economics deals with these questions. According to consumer economists, there are many things you can do to sharpen your skills as a consumer. Here are several tips:

First, do some research. See what the experts say about the quality and worth of the items you are interested in. Read *Consumer Reports* and other consumer magazines that compare similar items. Narrow your choices by eliminating those items that are really not what you are looking for. Consider the quality of the items as well as the general price range.

When you have decided on one or two brands of the item you want, be sure to shop around for the best buy. Some stores may charge twenty or thirty percent more than other stores for the same items. Save yourself time and effort by phoning several stores before you go there to buy. Make sure you give the salesperson an accurate description of the item you want to purchase, including its model number, color, and size. Also tell the salesperson how much money you want to spend. The more information you can give, the more help the salesperson can be.

Be sure to ask about the guarantee. For what length of time will the guarantee be in effect? What does the guarantee cover? Does it cover labor and parts? Does it guarantee replacement if the original item cannot be fixed? Can it be fixed in the store, or must it be sent back to the factory for repairs?

If you have any doubts about the reputation of the seller, don't buy anything. Ask other people who have made purchases there if they have been satisfied with the goods and services. It is often a good idea to contact your area's Better Business Bureau. Ask the Bureau about the reputation of the person or store where you want to do business. The Better Business Bureau is an organization of businesses. Its job is to keep consumers like you happy with the services and goods of its member stores.

When you buy the item, send the guarantee card in as soon as you can. In this way, you are protected from the very start, in case the item does not function as it should.

If the item doesn't work after you get it home, take it back to the store. Ask for a replacement, or ask for your money back.

Most stores will replace the item, unless it is obvious that you damaged it yourself. If this doesn't work, use your guarantee to have the item repaired.

If the item does not carry a guarantee, and if the store will not replace it or return your money, what can you do? A smart consumer in this situation goes immediately to the Better Business Bureau or the local Chamber of Commerce. Both organizations may help you get your money back. You can also complain about the store to your local television station. Many TV stations have consumer advocates. These people are paid to research consumer complaints, and they report their findings on the news programs. Sometimes the idea of being embarrassed on the news is enough to make stores return your money.

If you have an unworkable item and none of these ideas help you, go to your local government. Every city or county government has a consumer affairs department. Talk with them, and explain your problem. There may be some way you can get your money back by using the government system.

The most important thing a smart consumer knows is: *There is no substitute for a careful purchase.* There is a Latin phrase for this: "Caveat emptor." It means "let the buyer beware!"

Use these tips consistently. They will help you become a smarter consumer.

READING REVIEW
1. Define consumer.

Critical Thinking
2. **Demonstrating Reasoned Judgment** (see page 40) Why is it true that there is no substitute for a careful purchase?

READING 4

What Do We Have To Work With?

Everything in this world is limited in supply. Many things are scarce. And scarcities mean that we must constantly make decisions. What should be produced? How should it be produced? For whom should it be produced?

People must answer these basic questions of production or nothing would ever get done in our economy. But in order to answer them we must first know what we have to work with. It would be pointless to decide to produce steel if we didn't have any iron ore or coal. It also probably wouldn't make much sense to produce air conditioners for people in the Arctic region.

What do we have to work with? In any economy, there are four things which are necessary to produce anything. They are called **factors of production:**

1. Land
If you are building a factory, you need land to build it on. Also in this land category are all the natural resources needed to carry on production. People are becoming more and more aware that natural resources are scarce and must be used wisely if we are to avoid a world of shortages in the near future.

2. Labor

This factor of production includes all kinds of human effort used in production. The strength of human muscle power and human brain power are both considered labor. Both muscle power and brain power are needed for production.

3. Capital

You probably are familiar with the meaning of the word "capital" as the city where the state government is located. Sacramento, Albany, and Indianapolis are all state capitals.

In economics, capital has a different meaning. Capital refers to the money, equipment, machines, buildings, and other things needed to turn raw materials and labor into finished products. Companies make profits on what they produce. They pay their workers with some of these profits. They spend money on research to develop new products and to improve old ones. And they buy new machinery and build new factories. These invested profits are forms of capital.

Money is a form of capital, since it is used to buy and make those things needed for the production of goods and services. Such capital is often borrowed from banks and other financial institutions. Sometimes it is obtained through the sale of stock, which is a share in the ownership and profits of a company. You will learn about stocks later in this unit.

THE FOUR FACTORS OF PRODUCTION

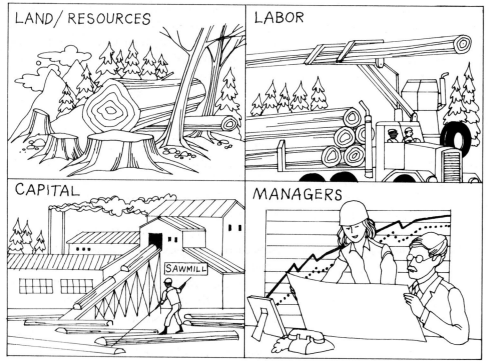

LAND/RESOURCES

LABOR

CAPITAL

SAWMILL

MANAGERS

4. Management

It takes somebody to bring land, labor, and capital together to begin production. That "somebody" is called an **entrepreneur,** or **management.** That person (or persons) is often called "the boss." It is up to this person or group of persons to organize the business. It is management's job to stay in business, to make a profit, to reinvest capital, and to make the business grow. Without management, the other three factors of production would not combine to do an efficient job. This is true for both large and small companies.

READING REVIEW ══════

1. Every society works with four major factors of production. What are they?

Critical Thinking

2. **Determining Relevance** (see page 17) For each item below, name the factor of production to which it belongs: (a) coal used to make steel; (b) the owner of a cinema; (c) a student who works at a repair shop; (d) a telephone in the boss's office; (e) money to build a restaurant.

READING 5

Three Main Types of Economies

Throughout human history, people have lived in groups. At first, these groups were simply family units. These units grew into communities of several families. These grew into villages, then cities, then nations. Throughout the centuries the people in each of these groups have faced the same economic problems we face today. They had to decide how to deal with the problem of scarcity.

We can imagine what economic life was like for early humans. For them, life was a constant struggle for survival. We are not certain how they decided who would kill the animals, who would skin them and make clothes, and who would get the animal meat to eat. But we can guess that it probably took a few thousand years to develop rules and traditions about these basic questions.

As societies grew, governments began to take shape. Large areas of land and the people living on that land were ruled by people who were strong enough to conquer them. **Traditional economies** developed. In these economies the basic questions of production were settled by tradition—rules which had developed over the years, and which most people accepted as good and correct.

Traditional economies existed in Europe during the Middle Ages (A.D. 500–1500). Monarchs followed the tradition of giving serfs the right to farm the monarch's land. In return for this right, the serfs would give a part of the year's harvest to the monarchs. In addition, the serfs promised loyalty to the monarchs in time of war. This practice lasted for many centuries. During its existence the traditional economy benefitted both the monarch and the serfs. Each was fed and given safety. In some parts of the world where there are few cities and industries, traditional economies still exist.

While members of the nobility look on, serfs harvest the year's crop of wheat. What kind of economy existed in the Middle Ages in Europe?

As cities began to appear, traditional economies died. In the cities, people started to specialize in the production of one kind of good. Specialization meant that trading had to take place. If you were a bootmaker, for instance, you spent all your time making boots. In order to get food, clothes, weapons, and other needs filled, you had to trade your boots for them. A simple system of exchange developed, called barter. **Barter** was the trading of one good for another. Sometimes, barter included exchanging services, such as repairing worn-out boots in exchange for help during the harvest.

Barter was the beginning of what we today call the *market economy*. The market economy answers the basic economic questions of production in a different way from the traditional economy. In a traditional economy, people make what they need in order to live. People are self-sustaining. They are able to live on what they produce themselves and are not dependent on others for economic survival.

In the market economy people are more dependent upon each other. In market economies today, individuals no longer make everything they need for survival. Instead, they work at specialized jobs to make money. They then use that money to buy goods and services produced by many other people in *their* specialized jobs. Sellers and buyers exchange money for goods and services based upon supply and demand. If you are a bootmaker in a market economy, you must find people to buy your boots, or you will not be able to make a living. People are not self-sufficient in a market economy, and so they must rely on others to produce what they need, and they rely on others to buy what they make.

So far, we have seen that basic economic questions are answered either by *tradition* or by the *market*. There is still another kind of economy, called the **command economy**. This kind of economy answers the basic economic questions differently than the market and traditional economies. In the market economy, decisions about what and how to produce and whom to produce for are made by the people. Whatever people don't want to buy won't be produced because the producer would lose money. In traditional economies, decisions about production are made on the basis of accepted rules of the past.

In a command economy, production decisions are made by the rulers. The rulers decide what will be produced with the limited resources of the society. They decide who will work in what industries and who will be paid what amounts. The rulers decide who should get the goods produced in the economy. They also decide how the goods and services are to be produced. As you can imagine, a lot of power is in the hands of the rulers in a command economy. The former Soviet Union was an example of a command economy.

READING REVIEW

1. What are the three main types of economies?
2. Define barter. In which of the three types of economies was barter most widely used? What took the place of bartering?

Critical Thinking

3. **Making Comparisons** (see page 16) Who decides what should be produced in each of the three types of economies?

EXPERIMENT **9-C**

Managing a National Economy

The method for managing an economy varies from country to country. Depending upon whether the economy is free enterprise, traditional, or command, the national economy is managed differently.

In a command economy, for example, a great amount of power is vested in a central group of rulers. The traditional economies of the world operate on the basis of old values and beliefs. Free market economies work on the basis of supply and demand. American values are not held by all people in other countries and other economic systems. You will need to deal with that fact of life in this experiment.

Transylvania, an imaginary country, has a traditional economy. Five people rule Transylvania. They are called the Council of Elders. The Council meets daily to decide how to use their limited resources.

Transylvania's economy is a simple one. The economy depends upon three products to meet the needs of the people: wooden knives, fish, and fishing nets.

The people of Transylvania live a simple life. They use wooden knives to hunt and kill animals. They also eat fish. Nets are used to catch the fish. Not all men fish with nets, however, as the Transylvanians have only ten nets. The rest of the men catch fish with their bare hands. Those who fish with their hands usually catch a fish a day. Those who use nets catch about ten fish a day. It takes one man thirty full days to make a good strong net.

Wood is needed to produce knives. Transylvanians find wood in a nearby forest. There is more wood than the Transylvanians need. It is not scarce, so there is no need to plan how it should be used.

Labor, however, is scarce. People would like to spend time making knives and nets but they never seem to have much time for this. Up until now, the Transylvanians have succeeded in producing 25 knives. Women and children are not allowed to work on the nets or the knives.

There are 150 people living in Transylvania. Sixty are men. Ninety are children and women. It takes 150 fish a day to feed the community. In addition to fish, Transylvanians eat plants that they grow outside

their huts. The children dig for clams and occasionally trap a turtle resting on the shore. But the main item in everyone's diet is fish.

A neighboring community is threatening to take over Transylvania. The foreigners claim that the Transylvanians are fishing in their waters. The Transylvanian Council of Elders has been called together. The Council decided that each Transylvanian man should be provided with a knife to defend the community. Since there are now only 25 knives in all of Transylvania, 35 more will have to be produced to meet this goal. If the men are able to make knives only in the evenings, one knife can be produced each week. Working full time, a man can produce a knife in a day. It has also been suggested that some men should remain in the village at all times to be prepared to defend it in case of attack.

If you were called upon to give advice to the Council of Elders, what would you suggest the Transylvanians do? Could you come up with a plan that would make full use of the resources available to the Transylvanians? Your suggestions should also answer the Council of Elders' objectives, which include providing for food and for the survival of the people of Transylvania. The Council does not want to change the people's customary ways of living, if that is possible.

Your group should come to one main decision. Most economic advisory groups have "secondary" plans, just in case the main plan doesn't work. It would be helpful to the Transylvanians if your group also gave them a secondary plan, in addition to your main plan.

At the end of the experiment, you will compare your economic plans with those of other groups in your class.

Supply and Demand in a Market Economy

Left, a buyer for a store checks an order of yogurt. Right, shoppers decide what yogurt to buy. Before 1960, few Americans knew what yogurt was. Then they began to "discover" it. Today, most grocery stores have many different brands of yogurt for sale. How does the popularity of yogurt show the influence of demand *on producers and what they are willing to* supply?

The market economy operates on the basis of what the people want to buy. If there is no demand for the goods and services which you produce, you will go out of business. You must produce what you can sell. If you are a good business person, you will supply the people with as much as they demand and also make a profit.

Of course, running a business isn't quite that simple. If it costs you more to produce something than the price people are willing to pay for it, you lose money. If you produce more of something than the people

want to buy, you lose money again. If you invest capital in a new building or a new piece of machinery and then business goes bad, you could lose even more money. Producing goods and services in a market economy can be risky. Producers must know what they are doing, or they have a good chance of losing money or going out of business.

How do producers know what to produce? How do they know what to charge for their goods and services? How do they figure out who will buy them? How do they determine how much to produce at any one time?

All of these questions can be answered by using the laws of supply and demand. The **law of supply** is this: *As prices go up, producers are willing to produce more. As prices go down, producers tend to produce less.* **Supply** is the amount of a good or service for sale at a particular price and at a certain time.

The **law of demand** is this: *As prices go up, people demand less. As prices go down, people demand more.* **Demand** is the ability and willingness of people to buy something. If you want something but don't have enough money to buy it, that is *not* demand. Demand is indicated by what people actually buy.

Economists use graphs to make the laws of demand and supply clear. On every graph, the price is given on the *vertical axis* (the line running up and down on the left side). The quantity, or number of goods, is given on the *horizontal axis* (the line running across). Both the supply curve and the demand curve can be drawn on the same graph. This is a *supply curve:*

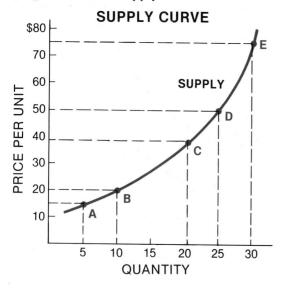

The supply curve always goes from lower left to upper right. The supply curve tells us how much of a certain good producers are willing to make at various prices. In this particular supply curve, we see that producers are willing to make 5 of whatever-it-is at $15 per unit (each item). Or, 10 of them at $20 per unit. Or 20 of them at $40 per unit. Or 25 at $50 per unit. Or even 30 at $75 each. From this supply curve, we can make this list, called a *supply schedule:*

	Supply Schedule	
Point	*Price per Unit*	*Quantity Supplied*
A	$15	5
B	$20	10
C	$40	20
D	$50	25
E	$75	30

Why does it make sense that producers are willing to make more goods at higher prices than at lower prices? (If you need to make this clear in your mind, multiply the price per unit by the quantity at each point. At which point does the producer make the most money?)

Of course, the producers are not the only ones who make decisions in a market economy. The consumers (buyers) also make decisions. Consumers make their decisions about what to buy on the basis of what costs the least and gives them the most satisfaction. Producers want to make more things at higher prices. But consumers want lower prices. They want to buy the best goods and services at the lowest possible prices. That is the law of demand. It can be graphed as shown at the top of the next page.

DEMAND CURVE

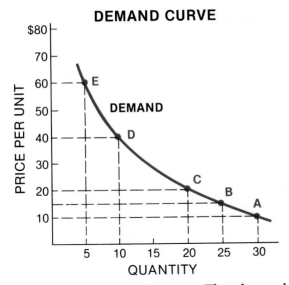

This is a *demand curve*. The demand curve always goes from upper left to lower right. It shows how much of a certain good consumers are willing to buy at various prices. Here we see consumers are willing to buy 30 of this item at $10 each. Or they would buy 25 of them at $15 each. Or 10 at $40 each. But consumers would only buy 5 items at $60 each.

The demand curve shows the law of demand: *As the price goes up, consumers are willing to buy less.* We can make this *demand schedule* from the information on the demand curve:

Demand Schedule

Point	Price per Unit	Quantity Demanded
A	$10	30
B	$15	25
C	$20	20
D	$40	10
E	$60	5

Demand for goods can increase or decrease. The supply of goods can increase or decrease. Changes in supply and demand can also be shown on a graph. When the supply curve shifts to the right, it shows an *increase* in the quantity produced. The original supply curve is always marked S, while the shifted curve is marked S^1. In this graph, there is an increase in the production of goods priced at $25 each.

INCREASE IN SUPPLY CURVE

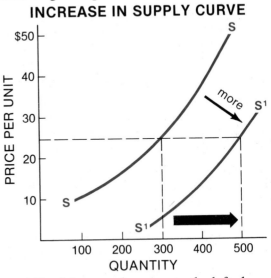

A shift of the supply curve to the left shows a *decrease* in the quantity produced. The graph below shows a decrease in the production of goods priced at $25. How many goods were not made?

DECREASE IN SUPPLY CURVE

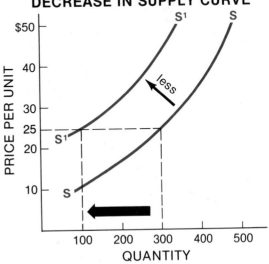

Now let's look at changes in the *demand* curve. When the demand curve shifts to the right, it shows an increase in the quantity of goods people demand. In the graph below, people are now willing to buy more of the item priced at $25. How many more items did they buy?

INCREASE IN DEMAND CURVE

DECREASE IN DEMAND CURVE

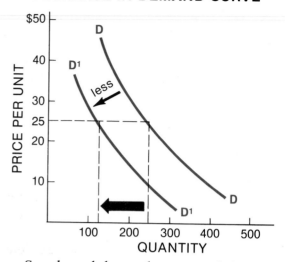

Supply and demand are two of the most important concepts in economics. Make sure you understand them before going on.

A decrease in demand is shown by a shift of the demand curve to the left. In the graph opposite, people were originally willing to buy 250 of the $25 item. By how much has demand decreased? In this case, there is half the demand there was before.

EXPERIMENT **9-D** **Working With Supply and Demand: Review**   **HANDOUT**

EXPERIMENT   **9-E**

Working With Supply and Demand: Graphs and Schedules

By now you should have a knowledge of supply and demand. You should know how supply and demand work together in a mar-

ket economy such as ours. (You have completed "Experiment 9-D: Working with Supply and Demand: Review.")

Now let's take a closer look at demand in a market economy. As we saw in "Reading 6: Supply and Demand in a Market Economy," demand refers to the ability and willingness of people to buy something. That "something" can be either material goods or services. A **service** is a specific action performed by one person for another person. The person who performs the service receives a payment. Fixing a TV set or a car is a service. We can enlarge the definition of demand. The term demand includes all people who are willing and able to buy a particular good or service *at all prices at a specific time.*

For example, here is a demand schedule for frozen yogurt in Ourtown on June 5 of last year:

Schedule A
Demand for Frozen Yogurt in Ourtown
June 5

At this price:	*People would buy:*
$2.90	500 pints
$2.70	550 pints
$2.50	600 pints
$2.30	700 pints
$2.10	850 pints
$1.90	1000 pints
$1.70	1200 pints

The demand for frozen yogurt in Ourtown includes all the frozen yogurt (the good) bought at all prices (from $1.70 to $2.90) at a specific time (June 5). The demand for frozen yogurt in Ourtown on June 5 includes the 600 people who are able and willing to buy frozen yogurt at $2.50 per pint. (Or it may have been less than 600 persons, with some persons buying more than one carton of frozen yogurt.) It includes the 500 who would have bought the frozen yogurt even at $2.90 per pint. Actually, the demand includes *everyone who is willing and able to buy frozen yogurt at any and all prices* along the scale.

Where there is an increase in demand, there are more people willing and able to buy *at all prices.* That is why the demand curve shifts upward and to the right. It shows that a greater quantity of each item is demanded at all prices. Why do you suppose that a decrease in demand is shown by a shift of the demand curve downward and to the left? Would it tell you that there are *fewer* people who are able and willing to buy at all prices? Why?

Notice on the demand schedule (Schedule A) that there were 100 more people who would buy frozen yogurt on June 5 at

$2.30 than there were people who would buy frozen yogurt at $2.50. But this change is not a change in demand. It is simply a difference in price. The 700 people who would buy frozen yogurt at $2.30 and the 600 who would buy it at $2.50 are all part of the same demand schedule and curve. There is no change in demand. The only difference is that 100 persons would *not* buy yogurt at $2.50 but *would* buy yogurt at $2.30.

Before we continue, it would be helpful if you made a graph of Schedule A (a demand curve) on Handout 9-E. Mark the demand curve "D."

Okay. Now set your graph aside and take a look at the following schedules of demand for June and July.

Schedule A
Demand for Frozen Yogurt in Ourtown
June 5

At this price:	People would buy:
$2.90	500 pints
$2.70	550 pints
$2.50	600 pints
$2.30	700 pints
$2.10	850 pints
$1.90	1000 pints
$1.70	1200 pints

Schedule B
Demand for Frozen Yogurt in Ourtown
July 5

At this price:	People would buy:
$2.90	600 pints
$2.70	700 pints
$2.50	750 pints
$2.30	800 pints
$2.10	900 pints
$1.90	1100 pints
$1.70	1500 pints

Does Schedule B show a change in demand for frozen yogurt in Ourtown from the demand described in Schedule A? Why?

Take your graph of Schedule A on Handout 9-E and add to it the demand curve of Schedule B. Mark the new curve D1. What do the positions of the first curve (D) and the second curve (D1) on the graph tell you? What might be some possible reasons for the change in demand?

That brings us to some very important questions raised in Economics—why do people want certain things at certain times, and in certain places, and at certain prices?

The next set of examples should help us answer those questions. Look carefully at the two demand schedules on page 481. Once again, the first one is Schedule A. The second one is Schedule C.

Schedule A

Demand for Frozen Yogurt in Ourtown
June 5

At this price:	People would buy:
$2.90	500 pints
$2.70	550 pints
$2.50	600 pints
$2.30	700 pints
$2.10	850 pints
$1.90	1000 pints
$1.70	1200 pints

Schedule C

Demand for Frozen Yogurt in Ourtown
November 5

At this price:	People would buy:
$2.90	100 pints
$2.70	150 pints
$2.50	250 pints
$2.30	300 pints
$2.10	350 pints
$1.90	450 pints
$1.70	500 pints

Does Schedule C represent a change in demand from Schedule A? If so, what kind of change is it? Graph Schedule C on Handout 9-E to help you see it more clearly. Label that curve D2. Can you suggest a reason for the change it shows?

Suppose that most of the adults working in Ourtown are employed at the Ajax clothing company. In mid-July, the company lays off half the employees. There is no change in the town's unemployment situation by the end of November. How do you think unemployment would affect demand for frozen yogurt in late November? Graph a demand curve on Handout 9-E to show that change in demand. Label the curve D3.

Now suppose that on July 10th, the Ourtown Daily Press published an article stating that three cases of typhoid fever had been reported. A rumor circulated through the community that typhoid was spread by contaminated milk products, such as yogurt. Graph a demand curve on Handout 9-E to show the change in demand you think would occur. Label the curve D4.

Now let's take a close look at the other side of demand—*supply.* We have seen that demand can be shown by a schedule which lists the quantities of a good or service that consumers are willing and able to buy at various prices at a particular point in time. In a similar way, supply can be shown by a schedule that lists the quantities which suppliers (producers) are willing to sell or produce at various prices at a particular point in time. A change in supply is a change in the number of units produced at all points along the supply curve.

In the first part of this experiment, we examined the *demand* for frozen yogurt in Ourtown. In this part, we will look at the *supply* of frozen yogurt in Ourtown and see just what causes the supply to increase and decrease.

The supply of frozen yogurt in Ourtown on June 5 might be shown:

Schedule D

Supply of Frozen Yogurt in Ourtown
June 5

At this price:	Producers supply:
$2.90	1100 pints
$2.70	850 pints
$2.50	600 pints
$2.30	500 pints
$2.10	350 pints
$1.90	100 pints
$1.70	50 pints

Why are producers willing to supply more frozen yogurt at higher prices? Graph Schedule D as a supply curve on Handout 9-E. Mark the curve S.

Suppose on August 20 lightning struck the largest dairy farm in the area. It caused a huge fire. All the buildings and a large part of the herd were destroyed. Yogurt makers in the area depended on this farm for a large amount of the raw materials that are used in making yogurt. Would this scarcity of raw materials cause an increase or a decrease in the supply of frozen yogurt in Ourtown? Why?

Schedule E

Supply of Frozen Yogurt in Ourtown
September 5

At this price:	Producers supply:
$2.90	_?_ pints
$2.70	_?_ pints
$2.50	_?_ pints
$2.30	_?_ pints
$2.10	_?_ pints
$1.90	_?_ pints
$1.70	_?_ pints

On Handout 9-E draw a new supply curve to show an appropriate change in supply. Mark the curve S1.

Early in April, the Frosty Milk Products Company purchased a brand new yogurt-making machine. The machine is able to produce about twice as many gallons of yogurt as the older machines at a lower cost per gallon. However, the machine is very

expensive. None of the other dairies in Ourtown can afford to buy it. The machine was installed and ready for use in the Frosty yogurt plant on July 10. Would this new machine cause an increase or a decrease in the supply of frozen yogurt in Ourtown? Why? On Handout 9-E, draw a supply curve to show an appropriate change in supply. Label it S2.

We have worked with both supply and demand. Now examine the exercises you did in this experiment. Can you identify some things which affect supply? What factors cause an increase in supply? What factors cause a decrease in supply? What are some things which cause demand to change? Identify some factors which cause an increase in demand. What causes a decrease?

Supply and demand do not work separately. They work together and are related to one another. In "Reading 7: What Is the Price?" you will find out what happens when supply and demand work together.

What Is the Price?

You have probably bought many things in your life with money that you earned or was given to you. Everything that you buy has value. And the value of a product or service is indicated by its **price.** But have you ever wondered just how prices are determined? Of course, we all know that the price of a good or a service must cover the cost of production. That is, the raw materials, salaries for workers, energy costs, new machines and buildings, the repair of old machines and buildings—all of these, and others, are included in the cost of production. In addition to paying for these costs, the producer must make a fair profit. (Why stay in business unless there is a profit?)

On the other hand, we know that consumers look for bargains. They are not really concerned about a company's profits. They want the best quality items at the lowest possible prices. Consumers look around for the goods and services which give them what they want at prices they can afford.

Both producers and consumers follow the laws of supply and demand, whether they realize it or not.

But that doesn't answer our question: How are prices determined? For the answer, we have to dig deeper into the laws of supply and demand. We also need to understand how the law of supply and the law of demand work together to create prices.

We already know that producers are willing to supply more goods as prices increase. They stand to make more profit. As prices go down, producers tend to supply less. Otherwise, they will lose money. That is the law of supply.

We also know that consumers will buy more at lower prices and less at higher prices. That is the law of demand.

When producers and consumers "agree" on how much money a good or service should cost, that sets the price. It's that easy!

Let's take a closer look. Suppose we have the following demand schedule for shoes in Ourtown:

Demand Schedule
Shoes in Ourtown

At this price:	Consumers would demand, or buy:
$50	20 pairs
$40	30 pairs
$30	50 pairs
$25	70 pairs
$20	100 pairs
$15	150 pairs
$10	250 pairs

We could graph this demand schedule like this:

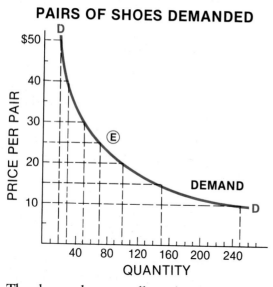

PAIRS OF SHOES DEMANDED

The demand curve tells us how many pairs of shoes the people of Ourtown would be willing to buy at various prices. Notice that both the demand schedule and curve show that people are willing to buy more at lower prices than at higher prices.

Let's look at the supply schedule for shoes in Ourtown at the top of the next column.

At this price:	Producers would supply
$50	200 pairs
$40	170 pairs
$30	110 pairs
$25	70 pairs
$20	50 pairs
$15	20 pairs
$10	0 pairs

We could graph the supply schedule like this:

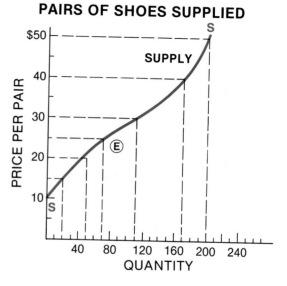

PAIRS OF SHOES SUPPLIED

The supply curve tells us how many pairs of shoes the people who make shoes in Ourtown would be willing to supply at various prices. This supply curve and schedule show that producers are willing to make more goods at higher prices than at lower prices. They want to make the most money on what they produce.

Examine both schedules and both curves very closely. In each case, there is a point where the supply curve and demand curve meet. It is where people will buy the shoes producers will supply. It is the same point where the supply schedule and the demand schedule agree on a price (point E). That point is the **equilibrium point.** *Equilibrium* means "balance." So the equilibrium point is the point where the consumer's wishes and the producer's wishes are balanced. It is the price at which supply equals demand, and there is neither scarcity nor surplus.

If we combine the supply curve and the demand curve, we can see how supply and demand work together to make the equilibrium point:

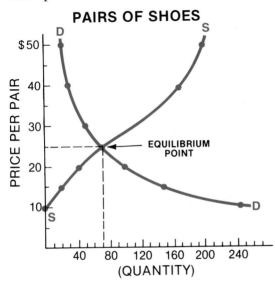

PAIRS OF SHOES

The equilibrium point is just as easy to see by combining the supply schedule and the demand schedule:

Price	Quantity demanded	Quantity supplied
$50	20 pairs	200 pairs
$40	30 pairs	170 pairs
$30	50 pairs	110 pairs
$25	70 pairs	70 pairs
equilibrium point		
$20	100 pairs	50 pairs
$15	150 pairs	20 pairs
$10	250 pairs	0 pairs

According to this combined schedule of supply and demand, the equilibrium point is where consumers and producers are willing to agree on a price of $25 for each pair of shoes. Both also agree on 70 shoes. The producers will make 70 pairs and sell them at $25 per pair. Consumers will buy 70 pairs at the $25 price, and there is no shortage or surplus of shoes for the producer. Of course, this "agreement" is never spoken or written. It just happens.

We know that not all shoes in Ourtown will be sold for $25 a pair. Some will be priced at $50 a pair because there are some people who are willing to spend that amount. If you look back at the demand schedule, you notice that only 20 pairs of shoes are demanded at $50. If producers were to make as many shoes as they were willing to supply at $50, how many shoes would not be sold? (Subtract the quantity demanded from the quantity supplied.) There would be 180 pairs of unsold shoes at $50 per pair. Economists refer to this as a *surplus* of 180 pairs of shoes.

A **surplus** occurs when there are more goods and services than there is demand for them. In other words, there are more products than consumers are willing to buy.

Look at the demand schedule again. Notice that consumers demand 150 pairs of shoes at $15 a pair. But the producers are not willing to supply 150 pairs at that price. They would probably lose money. But they are willing to sell 20 pairs at $15 each pair. (See the combined supply and demand schedule.) The shoes are probably not made as well as more expensive shoes, but they *are* shoes, and they are for sale at $15. In this case, there are more shoes demanded than supplied. Subtract 20 from 150, and you find that there is a *shortage* of 130 pairs of shoes at $15 a pair.

A **shortage** occurs when there are not enough goods and services available to meet demand. In other words, there are more consumers willing to buy than there are products being produced.

How does a change in demand or supply affect price? When consumers demand more of a certain good at all prices on the demand curve, there is an increase in demand. We know that this is shown by the demand curve shifting up and to the right. When we combine the supply curve with the original demand curve (D) and the new demand curve (D¹), we can see what happens to the price.

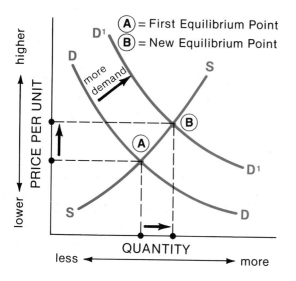

What happens to the price per unit consumers are willing to pay? What happens to the quantity producers are willing to produce at that price? Both price and quantity increase. This results in a new equilibrium point (B).

When there is a decrease in demand, just the opposite happens. Consumers demand less of the good at all prices along the demand curve. This is shown by the demand curve shifting down and to the left. We can see what happens to the price by looking at the combined supply and demand curves.

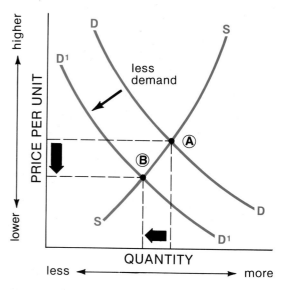

As you might have guessed, the decrease in demand results in a lower price and a decrease in the quantity consumers buy. A new equilibrium point (B) is reached.

Producers realize that lower prices attract buyers. So the producers may lower their prices to try to increase consumer demand for their goods. They may do this for a short time, even if it means losing money. Some return of the money they have spent in production is better than no money at all.

What happens to the price when there is an increase in supply? Let's see. An increase in supply is shown by a shift of the supply curve downward and to the right. When we combine the demand curve with both the old supply curve (S) and new supply curve (S¹), look what happens to the price.

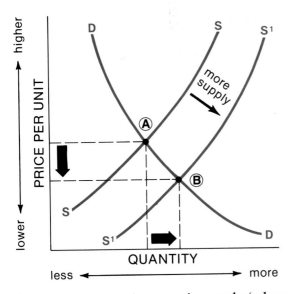

As you can see, an increase in supply (when demand remains the same) results in lower prices and a greater quantity sold.

A decrease in supply has just the opposite effect on price. The graph below shows a shift of the supply curve upward and to the left. Notice also the change in the equilibrium point.

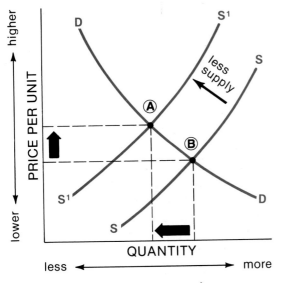

A decrease in supply causes prices to go up. The same number of people want to buy the goods, but there aren't as many goods available. That means that people have to compete against each other to buy the scarce goods. All of this results in higher prices for the goods that people want to buy. Producers may then increase production to meet the demand.

We can make a table to explain the effects of changes in supply and demand upon the prices of goods and services. The table is shown below.

You will be doing more with shifts in supply and demand, equilibrium points, and prices. So be sure you understand this reading before you continue.

when **Demand:**	and **Supply:**	then the **Price:**
Increases	Remains the Same	Increases
Decreases	Remains the Same	Decreases
Remains the Same	Increases	Decreases
Remains the Same	Decreases	Increases

READING REVIEW

1. Who determines prices in a market economy: consumers, producers, or both?

Critical Thinking

2. **Identifying Alternatives** (see page 38) What happens to the *price* when there is: (a) a decrease in demand as the supply remains the same? (b) an increase in demand as the supply remains the same? (c) an increase in the supply as demand remains the same? (d) a decrease in the supply as demand remains the same?

Working With Supply, Demand, and Prices

In "Reading 7: What Is the Price?" we saw how prices are determined. Supply and demand work together to make an equilibrium price. Other prices also exist, although there are shortages and surpluses at those prices.

Look at this combined supply and demand schedule. Can you tell what the approximate equilibrium point is? How?

Schedule A

Price	Quantity Demanded	Quantity Supplied
$80	10 shirts	200 shirts
$60	15 shirts	180 shirts
$40	25 shirts	150 shirts
$30	50 shirts	120 shirts
$20	100 shirts	90 shirts
$15	170 shirts	60 shirts
$ 5	300 shirts	0 shirts

Between what two prices would you expect to find the equilibrium price? About how many shirts would consumers buy and producers supply at the equilibrium price?

On Graph 1 on Handout 9-F, Page 1, draw a graph of Schedule A. Show both supply and demand curves on the graph. Label the equilibrium point.

Can you tell from Schedule A what surpluses and shortages there would be at each price? Fill in Table 1 on Handout 9-F, Page 1, with the correct figures.

Now let's examine four situations which show changes in supply and demand of shirts. We'll also see how those changes affect prices.

The Marvo Clothing Company is the largest manufacturer of shirts. This company introduced a new kind of shirt onto the market. The shirt is much easier to wash and is more comfortable than others on the market. The people who own the Marvo Company were so certain of instant success that they produced great quantities of these shirts. The quantity of new Marvo shirts added to the quantity of shirts pro-

FLOOD WIPES OUT STOCK AT MARVO SHIRT CO.

duced by other manufacturers gives us this new supply schedule:

Schedule B

Price	Quantity supplied
$80	300 shirts
$60	270 shirts
$40	200 shirts
$30	160 shirts
$20	130 shirts
$15	70 shirts
$ 5	0 shirts

The Marvo Company was convinced that consumer demand for their shirts would be high. But consumer demand for shirts did not change when the Marvo shirts hit the market. What do you suppose happened to the price of shirts? To the equilibrium point? To the surplus of shirts and the shortage of shirts at various prices?

Turn to Graph 2 on Handout 9-F, Page 1. Graph the "Quantity Demanded" figures of Schedule A. Substitute the "Quantity Supplied" figures of Schedule B for those of Schedule A. Figure out the new equilibrium point. Then fill in Table 2 with the new figures of surpluses and shortages at each price.

A flood in Ourtown wiped out the complete stock of Marvo shirts. It also destroyed most of the shirts manufactured by other companies. Immediately after the flood, the quantity of shirts which all the companies could offer for sale at various prices was greatly decreased. Schedule C shows this change in supply:

Schedule C

Price	Quantity supplied
$80	100 shirts
$60	80 shirts
$40	70 shirts
$30	50 shirts
$20	30 shirts
$15	10 shirts
$ 5	0 shirts

Despite the decrease in the number of shirts for sale at various prices, the demand remained the same. Consumers were not anxious to buy more shirts than previously, no matter how little they cost. How do you think the equilibrium point was affected?

Graph the "Quantity Demanded" figures of Schedule A on Graph 3 on Handout 9-F, Page 2. This time substitute the "Quantity Supplied" figures of Schedule C for those of Schedule A. What is the new equilibrium point? Figure out the shortages and surpluses of shirts caused by the flood and by the decrease in supply. Fill in Table 3 with the correct figures.

The three major shirt producing companies in Ourtown all gave their employees a raise in pay of $2,000 per year. This caused the demand for almost all goods and services, including shirts, to increase. (Remember, employees are also consumers.) With more money to spend, the consumers were willing to buy more. The demand for shirts now changed:

Schedule D	
Price	*Quantity demanded*
$80	15 shirts
$60	25 shirts
$40	50 shirts
$30	100 shirts
$20	170 shirts
$15	300 shirts
$ 5	450 shirts

How do you think this new increase in demand affected the price of shirts?

Graph Schedule A and add the demand curve of Schedule D on Graph 4 on Hand-out 9-F, Page 2. Where is the original equilibrium point? What is the new equilibrium point?

Fill in Table 4 with the new surpluses and shortages.

* * *

The Whammo Futuristic Clothing Company just began to manufacture a new kind of shirt made of a plastic chemical. It is very convenient and it doesn't feel uncomfortable. It is also must less expensive than regular shirts. The consumers of Ourtown were very enthusiastic about the new plastic shirts. As a result, everyone wanted to buy the new shirts. Sales of old-style cloth shirts went down. Schedule E shows this decrease in demand for cloth shirts at all prices:

Schedule E	
Price	*Quantity demanded*
$80	2 shirts
$60	5 shirts
$40	10 shirts
$30	15 shirts
$20	25 shirts
$15	35 shirts
$ 5	50 shirts

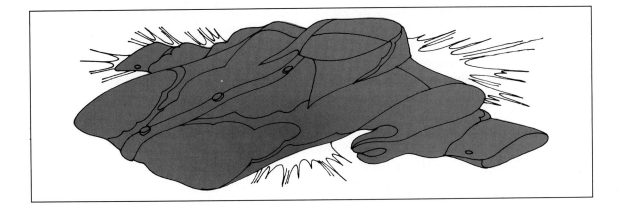

Graph this new demand schedule on Graph 5 on Handout 9-F, Page 2. Add the supply and demand curves of Schedule A. Where are the new and the old equilibrium points? Fill in Table 5 with figures representing the new surpluses and shortages.

Now that you have worked with supply and demand, shifts of supply and demand, changes in prices and equilibrium points, and shortages and surpluses, you should have a much better idea of how a market economy functions.

The Market Economy

The American economy is a **market economy.** It is also called a **capitalist economy.** This economy is named after the use of capital in businesses by groups and individuals. Still another name for the American economy is the **free enterprise system.** This simply means in an economy such as ours that it is relatively easy to start your own enterprise, or business. In other economic systems, such as communism in the People's Republic of China, it would not be as easy to own and operate your own business. Although government control of the economy in China is changing, there are still many restrictions on private ownership of businesses. Only limited forms of private ownership are allowed by the government, and these are carefully regulated. In a strict, more traditional communist system, the government claims that all the people own and operate all businesses together. Critics of the communist system say that this is not true. They claim that only a very small group of people have a voice in how the businesses and the government are run.

The American economy is not completely free from control, either. Our economy cannot be called a *pure* free enterprise economy. In fact, there are no pure free enterprise economies in the world today. A

Economics   **491**

pure free enterprise economy has no government rules which affect business. A pure free enterprise economy also forbids businesses to agree on prices. ("Fixing" prices prevents the consumers from shopping around for the best price.)

Our economy has both government rules and some price-fixing by companies. Therefore, it is more accurate to call the American economic system a **mixed economy.** This system is someplace between a controlled economy and a pure free enterprise economy.

Generally speaking, the rules of supply and demand work in our mixed economy. When people demand more of a good or service, the price usually goes up. In order to supply more goods and services to the people who want them, companies produce more. When demand goes down, so do prices, and businesses respond by cutting production. You can see then how demand affects production.

In our mixed market economy there are three main types of business enterprises. The simplest is the **single proprietorship.** In this case a business is owned and operated by one person or one family. Corner grocery stores and hardware stores, especially in small towns, are sometimes single proprietorships. However, these are fast disappearing. Large supermarkets and chains of hardware stores (many stores owned by one company) are taking the place of the single proprietorships. There is a disadvantage to single proprietorships in a market economy: The owners can't buy their goods in large quantities. They sell less than bigger stores. Therefore, they can't buy as many goods at one time from the wholesalers (people who buy from the factories and sell to the stores). The more an owner buys from the wholesalers, the cheaper the cost is. Large stores and chains are able to buy goods from wholesalers more cheaply. They can then offer the goods at lower prices to the consumers. Large stores also are able to give the consumers more variety.

Single proprietorships do have advantages, though. They are usually more friendly to the consumers. The owner of such a store may know you personally and call you by name. Because you and the store owner are on friendly terms, he or she may treat you more specially than a large store's employees do. Another advantage is that if you are the owner of a single proprietorship, you work for yourself. You decide how many hours a day you want to work. You decide whether you should hire an employee, or fire one. You are the boss. Your only concern is pleasing your customers and making a fair profit.

Another kind of business enterprise is the **partnership.** In a partnership there is more than one owner. The partners share in the profits and the losses of their business. A partnership is something like the single proprietorship in that it tends to be a personal, friendly sort of business. The partners also can determine what hours they will work and whom they want to employ or fire. The partners usually have more capital between them than the single proprietor does. So the partners are able to run a larger business. Often they can sell their goods and services more cheaply than the single proprietor.

But this type of business enterprise is not perfect either. Whenever two or more people work as partners and have different ideas about running the business, trouble can start. Sometimes, this situation ends up with the partners competing against each other. Or even making decisions of which the other partners aren't aware. One of the biggest drawbacks to a partnership is that all partners are responsible for the actions of one another. If you are in partnership with another person, and that person runs away with all the money, you are responsible for any debts your partner leaves behind. Needless to say, partnerships sometimes do not last for very long.

A good way to avoid the hassles of a partnership is to form a **corporation.** The owner or owners of a business can form a corporation by applying for a charter from the government. A charter is a written document in which the government recognizes the business as a corporation. A corporation is a business which has a legal personality. The owners have unlimited liability in single proprietorships and partnerships. They can be sued in court for all of their earthly possessions. However, if you have a corporation, you can't be sued for a business dealing. The *corporation* is sued.

Owners of the corporation have limited liability. They can lose only the amount of money they have invested into the business. The personal savings and property of the owners cannot be taken away by a lawsuit.

Forming a corporation also enables you to sell stock in your company. **Stock** is a share in the company's earnings, in return for an investment of money into the company. There are millions of stockholders (or shareholders) in the United States today. Each of them owns a part of a corporation. Depending on the kind of stock they own, stockholders have the right to vote for the people who run the corporation. The more shares of stock you own, the more votes you can cast.

Of course, a possible disadvantage to forming a stock corporation is the loss of direct control over your company. When you own a single proprietorship or partnership, you decide what the company will do. When you turn the company into a stock

This is a stock certificate issued by the Communications Satellite Corporation. It tells the person who bought the certificate that he or she owns a certain number of shares in the corporation.

corporation, the stockholders decide what the company will do.

Stockholders make money from their investments in a corporation in two ways. First, when the corporation makes money, the stockholders receive dividends. Dividends are a share of the company's profits and are usually paid once a year. Secondly, stockholders can profit from their investments by selling their shares at a higher price than they paid for them. Of course, they can't always do this. A company's stock can go down in price when people lose confidence in the company. This happens when the company is in trouble or isn't performing as well as it should. Under these circumstances people pay low prices for stocks. But when people think the company will make money they pay high prices for stocks.

The role of a corporation in a market economy will be our next subject. In an experiment you will have a chance to "buy" stock in a corporation and watch its ups and downs. We will also take a look at advertising in a market economy. You will be able to try your hand at finding tricks and gimmicks in advertisements. And we will see how creative you are in making your own ads.

READING REVIEW

1. What terms are used to describe the type of economy in American society?
2. What are the three main types of business enterprise in the United States? Who is the owner of each type?
3. Give one advantage and one disadvantage of each of the three types of business enterprise.

Critical Thinking

4. **Identifying Alternatives** (see page 38) In what two ways can stockholders make money?

EXPERIMENT **9-G**

The Free Enterprise Market Game*

As we saw in "Reading 8: The Market Economy," a pure free enterprise economy works without government rules directing what happens in the market. Businesses are allowed to operate as they wish. Trading, buying, and selling go on freely.

Here is a game to play to make the opera-

tions of a free enterprise system clearer. In any market, business deals are conducted between buyers and sellers. In this market game you will play the role of either a buyer or a seller in a wheat market. Buyers will decide whether or not to buy wheat. Sellers will decide whether or not to sell. Together, buyers and sellers will decide the price of wheat. And every time you make a decision to sell or buy, you will affect the price at which wheat can be sold and bought. (Prices here may or may not be true market prices.)

*Game concept adapted with permission from "Role Playing in Teaching Economics" by Myron Joseph in *The American Economic Review*, and from *Economics Readings for Students of Twelfth Grade American Democracy* by Mindella Schultze, prepared by the Developmental Economic Education Program of the Pittsburgh Public Schools. (See Acknowledgements, pages 595–596.)

With every decision you make you help determine how scarce resources should be used. Every time you buy wheat in a market economy, you actually cast a vote *for* the production of wheat. Every time you refuse to buy, you cast a vote *against* the production of wheat. As you play the game, see if you can figure out why this is so.

Here are the instructions for playing the game. Try to understand these directions before you play the game. If there is any-thing you don't understand, ask your teacher about it.

1. Each student will be given an armband to wear. If you are a SELLER, you will wear a *white* arm band. If you are a BUYER, you will wear a *blue* arm band.

2. Each BUYER will be given a "buyer's card" and each SELLER will be given a "seller's card." Buyer's cards look like this:

WHEAT BUYER'S CARD

Buy 30,000 bushels of wheat for *no more than*

$ _____

Try to get the best price you can *below* this price. *Do not* buy any wheat above this price. If you haven't bought any wheat after five minutes, get another buyer's card.

As you can see, the buyer's cards tell the buyers how much they can afford to pay for bushels of wheat on the market. Of course, it would be more profitable for the buyers to purchase wheat from the sellers at lower prices than the ones that are listed on their cards.

Seller's cards look like this:

WHEAT SELLER'S CARD

Sell 30,000 bushels of wheat for *no less than*

$ _____

Try to get the best price you can *above* this price. *Do not* sell any wheat below this price. If you haven't sold any wheat after five minutes, get another seller's card.

Wheat is a major export of the United States. Here equipment is shown which is used to move vast amounts of this commodity.

Seller's cards tell the sellers the lowest prices at which they can sell wheat to buyers. The higher the price they can get, of course, the more profits they will make.

Neither the sellers nor the buyers should tell anyone the information written on their cards. Buyers and sellers should have only one card at a time.

3. When the teacher says "START," sellers and buyers should meet and try to agree on a price for 30,000 bushels of wheat. Any buyer can talk to any seller, and any seller can talk to any buyer. If they haven't made a deal after five minutes, both the seller and the buyer should get new cards from the teacher.

4. As soon as a buyer and seller agree on a price for 30,000 bushels of wheat, each should go at once to the teacher's desk and report the agreement. Buyers and sellers should carry a piece of paper to record their profits (or savings) for each transaction. A *profit* is the difference between the amount on the card and the amount of the transaction.

5. Once an agreement has been reported, the teacher will write the price on the board. Watch the board for the posted prices.

6. After the buyer and the seller have reported an agreement, they should get another buyer's card and another seller's card and go back to the market and try to reach another agreement with the other buyers and sellers. They can make another deal with each other if they wish.

7. Both buyers and sellers should do as well as they can. Do not violate the instructions on your cards. If you are a seller, never sell wheat lower than the price on your card. If you are a buyer, never buy wheat higher than the price on your card.

8. Transactions should end in zero cents ($1.70, $1.80, $1.90).

9. Pay attention to your teacher for further instructions, including when to stop.

READING 9

The Stock Market

Corporations in a market economy need capital. Capital is the money used to pay the expenses of starting or expanding a business. Corporations get capital in several ways. One way, which is discussed in "Reading 8: The Market Economy," is by the sales of shares of stock in the company. There are two kinds of stock: **common stock** and **preferred stock.** Both types of stock give the stockholder a part ownership of the company. Both types of stock may pay **dividends** to the stockholder. Dividends are shares in the profits of the company.

There are some differences between common and preferred stock. Owners of common stock are entitled to vote for the directors of the corporation at the annual meeting of shareholders. Common stock owners vote according to the number of shares they hold. Common stock may pay dividends according to how well the company did in the last year. If profits are up, higher dividends on common stock are frequently given. When profits go down, so may the dividends.

Preferred stock is called "preferred" because the holders of that type of stock are given special treatment over holders of common stock. Holders of preferred stock are paid dividends before holders of common stock. However, preferred stock will usually pay dividends at a fixed rate. For example, preferred stock in one corporation may yield $5.00 per year for every share. Whether the corporation makes a large profit or not, holders of preferred stock can only expect to be paid $5.00 a share. Owners of preferred stock are usually not entitled to vote for company officials, even though they are considered part-owners of the corporation.

Corporations also raise capital by selling bonds. A **bond** is actually an IOU. A corporation borrows money from people like you, usually in $1,000 amounts or more. In return for a person's investment in the company, the company promises to pay the investment back in a fixed number of years. The company also promises to pay a certain amount of interest each year on the money borrowed. Interest is figured in percents. For example, a $1,000 bond at 10% interest would pay you your original $1,000 back in a stated number of years. Each year, however, you would receive $100 for the use of your money. When you collect at the end of your time agreement with the company, you get $1,000.

Bonds, unlike common and most preferred stocks, do not allow you to vote in the company. Nor does holding bonds make you a part-owner of the company.

Stocks and bonds are considered property. They can be bought, sold, or traded. They can be inherited at the death of the owner. Dividends and profits (dividends and the money made by selling stock at a higher price) are taxable. This is also true of bonds.

Stocks and bonds are sold by people called *stockbrokers*. They are licensed to

A buyer and a seller on the floor of a stock exchange. They have just agreed on a price for some shares of stock. To reach the price, they had to compromise. The seller (and customer) had to take a lower price for the shares than he originally wanted to. The buyer (and customer) had to pay a higher price than he originally wanted to.

READING NEWSPAPER STOCK TABLES

New York Stock Exchange Transactions — Thursday, February 16, 1984

52-week		Stocks	Div.	PE	Sales 100s	High	Low	Last	Chg.
High	Low								
48⅝	31	Alcoa	1.20	19	3496	39½	38½	38⅞	+⅜
36¼	26½	AvcoCp	1.20	6	435	28	27¼	27⅜	−⅜
59	46	Gen El	2	12	6623	54	48	53⅜	+⅛
80½	56	GMot	3.20e	6	7848	71½	70⅝	70¾	---
52¼	43⅛	GMot pf	5	--	4	49⅝	49¼	49⅝	+⅛
74½	55¾	McDnld	1	11	2947	66⅛	65	65⅛	+⅜
90½	74⅜	MMM	3.40	14	1814	77½	76⅝	76¾	+⅜
38⅜	22	RCA	.90	15	2291	31¾	31¼	31¾	+¼
45⅛	29	Sears	1.76	10	8244	37¼	36⅝	36¾	−¼

1 2 3 4 5 6 7 8 9

2 The price range indicates the highest and lowest prices per share paid for this stock on the Exchange during the last 52 weeks — in this case, $36.25 and $26.50.

3 Rate of annual dividend — for this stock, $2.00. This amount is an estimate based upon the last dividend payments.

4 Letters following the dividend number indicate additional information. Here, for example, the "e" designates the stated amount as declared or paid so far this year. Other symbols are explained in tables appearing in the stock market quotation pages of the newspaper.

5 The abbreviation "pf" following the name indicates a preferred stock.

6 The price-to-earnings ratio (PE) indicates the earnings divided by the price of the stock.

7 The number of shares reported traded for the day, expressed in hundreds. For this stock the number was 181,400.

8 The highest and lowest prices paid for a share of the stock during the day's trading. In this case, the highest price was $31.75, the lowest was $31.25.

9 The closing price or last sale of this stock before the newspaper went to press. In this stock it was $36.75. And this, Thursday's closing price, was $0.25 less than the closing price of the previous day, as indicated by the "−¼."

sell stocks and bonds. They are also members of a stock exchange. A stock exchange is like a market place. In fact, another name for stock exchange is stock market. A **stock exchange** is a central place where stocks and bonds are bought and sold by an agent of the stockbroker's office. When you ask a stockbroker for, let's say, 100 shares of stock in the Ford Motor Company, he or she sends the order for stock (by teletype or telephone) to the stock exchange. There an agent of the stockbroker's office will buy the shares of stock on the "floor" of the stock exchange. The floor is where the stock is traded, bought, or sold. The agent will try to buy the stock from someone who wants to sell. That person, like the buyer, is represented on the floor by an agent from a stockbroker. Both agents try to get the best possible price for the customer they represent. Eventually they come to an agreement on the price for the shares of stock. The customers are then told the price. The buyer decides whether to buy or not, and the seller decides whether to sell or not.

The two major exchanges are the New York Stock Exchange and the American Stock Exchange. Both are located in New York City. As we saw earlier, the price of stock tends to go up when the corporation is making a profit and seems to have a good future. Prices go down when it looks like the company is in trouble or has an uncertain future.

For his or her efforts, a stockbroker charges a fee based on a certain percentage of the total purchase of stock. The charge is usually estimated at 1 to 6 percent. When you want to sell your stock, you go back to your stockbroker. For another 1 to 6 percent charge the stockbroker will send the order to sell your stock back to the exchange. There someone will (hopefully) buy the stock.

The prices of stock traded in the exchanges are printed in many daily newspapers. They can normally be found in the Financial Section of a newspaper. Before you continue this reading, get a copy of

today's newspaper and find the stock market report in the Financial Section. You will also need this section for class.

Look closely at the stock market report. What company issued the stock? With what exchange is the stock listed? Different exchanges carry different corporation stocks. Now look at the columns of words and figures. They are abbreviated so that you can check the price of your stock quickly. Now study the model stock market table on page 499. Compare it with the one in your newspaper.

READING REVIEW

1. Define: common stock, preferred stock, bond, stockbroker, stock exchange.

Critical Thinking

2. **Demonstrating Reasoned Judgment** (see page 40)   How can you tell if the value of a stock has increased or decreased?

EXPERIMENT **9-H**

The Stock Market Experiment

In this experiment we will find out how the stock market really works. We will do this by "buying" stock, keeping track of its progress, and then "selling" it at the end of the experiment for a profit or a loss.

You will be given $1,000 to buy any stock you choose from either the New York Stock Exchange or the American Stock Exchange. (Unfortunately, the $1,000 is not real. Better luck next time!) With the

$1,000 you can purchase stock of only one company. Don't forget, also, that a stockbroker's fee must come out of that money. In this experiment we will set the fee at $50, which is a five percent fee. (Most fees are between one and six percent.) So actually, you have only $950 left to buy stock.

Record as much information as you can on the Daily Tally Sheet on Handout 9-H of this experiment. Each day write down the closing price of a share of your stock and record the stock's progress on the Progress Chart on Handout 9-H.

At the end of the experiment complete the Daily Tally Sheet and figure out how much money you profited or lost in your stock market dealings. To do this, just fol- low the formula on the Tally Sheet.

It is very important to keep an accurate daily record of your stock's prices. Without that record it will be impossible for you to chart the stock's progress, and it will be dif- ficult for you to figure out how well you did in the experiment.

This is a "trading post" on the floor of a stock exchange. Here, agents from various stockbrokers compete with each other to get the best price for stock.

Business Cycles

The American economy has gone through some good times and some bad times. One of the worst times was during the 1930s, during the Great Depression. One out of every four adults was unemployed during the Depression, and most people were severely affected by it. Many people could not afford housing, or new clothing, or automobiles. Luxuries were owned by very few persons.

One of the best economic times was during World War II. Industries were hiring as many people as they could find. Everything was being produced for the war effort, and American business made great profits. Those profits were passed on to the workers in the form of paychecks. Many workers labored for 60 and 70 hours per week, and were paid higher salaries for it. Everyone had money to spend and to save.

Every economy goes through good times and bad times. Economists see this as part of the business cycle. A **business cycle** is an up and down pattern of change in the

GNP FOR 1930 THROUGH 1990

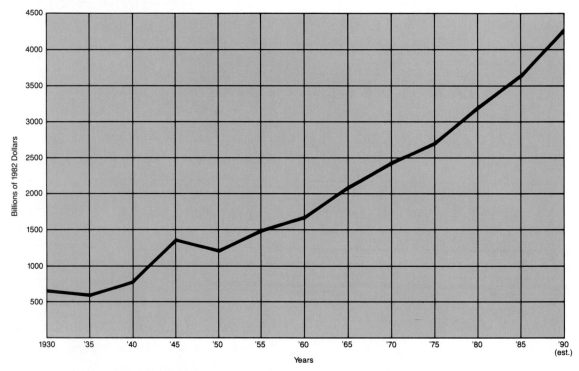

Sources: Budget of the United States Government, Fiscal Year 1990
U.S. Bureau of Economic Analysis, OMB

Unemployment line, New York City. When the GNP is high, how is unemployment affected?

economy. Every cycle includes a high point (or peak) and a low point (or trough), and the points in between. A high point is when the economy is prosperous. People buy goods and services. And usually there is high employment. After a high point in the business cycle the economy begins to slow down and enter a recession. A **recession,** very simply put, means that there is less business growth. The low point in the business cycle is a **depression.** In a depression there is little business growth. Unemployment is high and people do not have much money to spend or save. After a while the economy begins to enter another stage in the cycle. It gets better and moves toward prosperity.

An economy does not go smoothly from one stage of the business cycle to the next. It may remain in different stages for varying lengths of time. Predicting the ups and downs in an economy is difficult.

Another thing you should know in order to understand the business cycle is the GNP. The **GNP,** or **Gross National Product,** is used to measure a nation's economic health. It refers to the total money value of all the new goods and services produced in the country in a year. When the GNP is high, the nation's industries are producing a lot of goods and services. During such times, employment is high and people have money to spend.

When the GNP is low, however, the nation's production of goods and services is low. People are unemployed and do not have money to spend or save. A high GNP means an upward-moving business cycle and economic good times. A low GNP means a downward-moving business cycle and economic hard times. When the GNP goes down for six months in a row, the economy is said to be in a recession. When the GNP declines for a longer period of time and remains low, the economy is in a depression.

It is normal to have some changes in production and sales in any economy over a year, however. The owners of department stores will tell you that their busiest time of year is between Thanksgiving and New Year's Day. Nearly half of all yearly sales in some industries are made during the winter holiday season.

A nation's business cycle is affected by many things. Events in other parts of the world may play a large part in the cycle. During the early 1970s the flow of Arab oil to the United States was drastically reduced. As a result, American industries and consumers did not have enough energy to operate factories and cars. Business suffered, and the economy declined for a period of time.

The business cycle is also affected by the decisions companies make about employees. When production is up many people are employed, people spend money more freely. This, in turn, increases demand for goods and services, which means people buy more. The GNP increases, and unemployment goes down. When companies lay off or fire employees, they cannot afford goods or services, so the GNP goes down.

Sometimes government decisions and laws affect the business cycle. The United States government spends hundreds of billions of dollars every year. Most of this money is given to American companies to produce military goods and other government requirements. When government spending goes up, industries make more money. The business cycle rises. But cuts in government spending usually make the business cycle go down.

The economy is a system. Each part of the system influences the other parts. To have a healthy economy, most or all of the parts must help the others to succeed.

Advertising in a Market Economy

Nine out of ten doctors recommend . . .
You can't afford to miss our fantastic, gigantic sale . . .
Be the first in your neighborhood . . .

Every day you are bombarded by advertisements. On TV, on radio, in newspapers, magazines, and even books, on buses, trucks, and highway billboard signs. Ads are everywhere. And all those ads are trying to tell you something. An **advertisement** attempts to sell a product or service to you and the rest of the public. It uses persuasive messages to get you to buy. In a market economy like ours, advertisements bring together the people who produce goods and services with the people who might be interested in buying those goods and services. Ads form a link between consumers and producers. They make it easier for the market economy to work.

In the early days of advertising, a few hundred years ago, getting the producers and consumers together was a lot easier than it is today. In those times, if you produced guns you simply hung a sign (called a "shingle") outside your store. The words on the shingle told the world what you do for a living: "John Snyder, Locksmith." Those words told everyone what goods and services you sold. The message was simple because a locksmith sells only locks and keys and services related to locks and keys.

Today, very few businesses sell only one product. Take drugstores for example. At one time, drugstores used to sell only drugs. Then it became popular for drugstores to sell also refreshments like Coca-Cola, ice cream floats and sodas, and ice cream cones. In the 1940s and '50s, high school students "hung out" after classes in the neighborhood drug stores, which had actually become part-restaurants by that time. By the 1960s that kind of drugstore had disappeared. Now a drugstore can be expected to sell such things as books, paper, pens, and a whole range of other products. They also sell drugs. However, many drugstores no longer keep the word "drugs" in their names. Chances are that for every prescription you fill at a drugstore, you buy ten products which are not drugs. So drugstores must find a way to tell the consumers what they have for sale. Advertising is one answer.

Of course, drugstores are not the only businesses that have expanded their range of products for sale. Most enterprises have discovered that they must offer a greater variety of goods in order to compete with other, larger companies. Advertising answers the need for telling the public about a company's new goods and services.

It shouldn't surprise you to discover that advertising has become a big industry in itself. Companies pay advertising firms more than $100 an hour to create advertisements and commercials that will help sell their products. Companies also pay television networks large sums of money for the air time to show their commercials. For example, thirty seconds during the Super Bowl Game costs approximately $1,000,000. A minute of prime time (dur-

Reproduction of an 18th century fabric shop sign. Why are "shingles" no longer used?

ing the evening hours) costs about $300,000 for a commercial seen across the nation. That amount can be much less or much more, depending upon the size of the audience that the program attracts. The more people across the country who watch a program, the more it costs to advertise on that program. More viewers mean more possible customers. During the Saturday morning cartoons a one-minute commer-

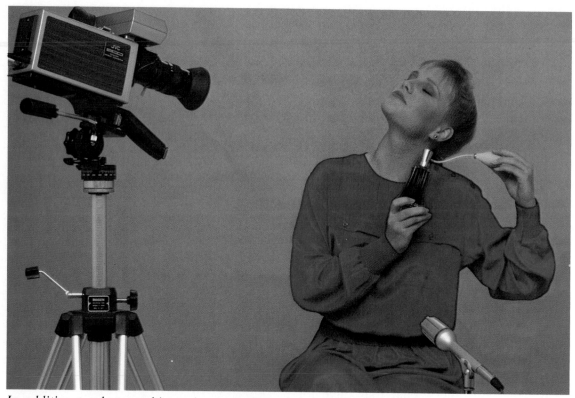

In addition to photographic equipment, what other costs contribute to producing an ad?

cial runs about $30,000. Air time on a local radio station in a major American city costs as much as $500 per minute.

If you wanted to buy a full-page color ad in *Newsweek, People,* or *Time* magazine, or any other national magazine, it would cost you around $140,000. A full-page ad in a major daily newspaper costs about $10,000. In our biggest cities—Los Angeles, Chicago, and New York—that figure jumps to $40,000 or more.

These costs do not include the costs of producing the ad or commercial itself. TV commercials, for example, usually require actors, a camera crew, lighting and sound crews, makeup artists, musicians, and a staff to write the commercial and direct its production. Sometimes a commercial requires expensive special effects or computer graphics, which can dramatically increase the cost of the commercial.

One award-winning TV commercial for a computer company cost over a million dollars to be produced. It was shown only once—during the Super Bowl. The company paid a lot of money for one minute, but it was worth it. The commercial introduced a new line of computers. As a result of that one minute of commercial air time, demand for the new computers was exceptionally high, right from the start.

When businesses have to pay that much money for advertising, they expect to get something back: profits. By carrying on an effective advertising campaign, an unknown manufacturer can become a household name within a year. Advertisers know that people tend to buy products with familiar names. So it makes sense to put the name of your product and your company in front of the consumers. The consumer must not only recognize the product name, but also think of it in a good way. That is the business of advertising agencies—to make consumers recognize a brand name, associate it with something pleasant, and buy the product.

Advertising makes the consumers aware of new products and reminds them of older products. Advertising in a market economy creates needs and wants, and that creates demand. Demand, in turn, creates a greater supply and variety of goods and services from which to choose. This helps companies to grow. Growing companies hire more people. The new employees spend money in the economy, which makes other businesses grow. In short, advertising can help make our economy expand, so this society's standard of living is improved.

READING REVIEW

1. State the main purpose of advertising.

Critical Thinking

2. **Recognizing Cause and Effect** (see page 35) How is the price of an ad or commercial determined?

Creating Your Own Advertising Campaign

Ads try to catch your attention, and then persuade you to do something. Is this ad effective? Why or why not?

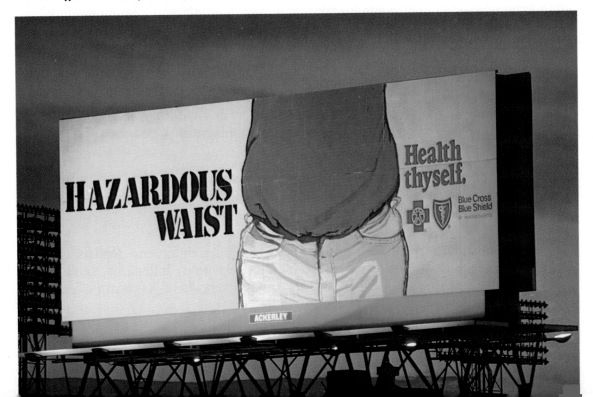

After thinking about "Reading 11: Advertising in a Market Economy," try this experiment at home in preparation for class. Choose something that you own. It can be anything from an old rag doll you haven't used in years to something you use every day. If you were going to sell that object, how would you do it?

You would first have to put yourself into the place of the consumers. If you were a consumer, why would *you* want to buy it? What possible uses could you put the object to? Write down as many answers to these questions as you can think of.

Now you already have the basis of your own advertising campaign. You've got an object to "sell," and you've thought of some reasons why your "market" should want to buy it. All you have to do at this point is to convince the consumers. That is not quite so easy as it sounds. In fact, the entire advertising business in our market economy spends a great deal of time and money trying to find the best ways of selling products to consumers.

Of course, you won't be expected to have a fully professional sales campaign for your object. (Let's call it your *product,* as the ad people do.) It should be fun to see how well you do in an advertising campaign.

In case you haven't already guessed, you will be trying to "sell" your product in class. To do that, you should prepare a one-minute presentation, which you will give in front of the class. Here are a few hints:

1. No matter what your product is really like, make it seem appealing and useful. What can you say about it that will make your classmates want to buy it? Some visuals (things they can look at while you are talking) might help. Certainly, one visual should be the product itself. Other visuals might be signs or charts. Use your imagination. The possibilities are endless.

2. Don't tell lies about your product. Be truthful, but emphasize the good points about your product. In the real world of business and advertising, people who are disappointed in a product usually don't buy it a second time. And they tell their friends to do the same. In the long run, lying in ads is certainly not the best policy.

3. Be prepared. You only have one minute. Use the time wisely by preparing what you have to say *before* you get up to say it. (You already know that advertising costs per minute on radio and television are very high.) Whether it is a good or poor ad will depend on the time and thought you put into it.

4. Don't be afraid to be creative. We all know how boring some commercials are. Make your commercial the way you would like all ads to be—make it interesting and enjoyable.

Bring your product and visuals to class, along with anything else you need to do your commercial. Good luck.

How Are You Influenced by Advertising?

Everyone is influenced by ads. According to advertising experts you are exposed to nearly 15,000 ads every day! Ads in newspapers, magazines, and leaflets. Ads on radio, television, billboards, buses, taxis. Almost everywhere you turn there are ads.

Chances are that you know some ads word for word. Often, the words of an advertisement will be put to music. Some of the ad songs are as hard to forget as the most popular songs on the "top ten" list. And no doubt, you recognize many slogans connected with advertised products, even for some of the older ads.

Let's see if this is true. Look at the following advertising slogans and nicknames. Most of them are several years old. Which ones can you still identify with the product they represent?

1. Just do it! (athletic shoes)
2. The choice of a new generation. (soft drink)
3. This is the new generation of _____. (automobile)
4. Sometimes you need a little _____ _____, sometimes you need a lot. (shampoo)
5. I love what you do for me! (automobile)
6. Make it last a little longer with _____ _____. (chewing gum)
7. The heartbeat of America is today's _____. (automobile)
8. The _____ blimp. (tire and rubber products)
9. Just for the taste of it. (diet soft drink)
10. We bring good things to life. (electric appliances)

What other slogans are popular today? Try naming as many slogans as you can, along with the products with which they are associated.

Slogans, nicknames, and images (bringing good things to life, for example) are used because they stick in the consumer's mind. They help to create a good feeling (hopefully) about the product. A slogan like "just do it!" helps you put away all

What is the process called when an advertiser links a name and an image with its product?

your excuses for not exercising. It's a powerful, quick, and imaginative message.

A good slogan put to music is equally hard to beat. Take the "heartbeat of America" jingle, for example. The commercial links an American-made car to the heartbeat of our country and its people. The advertiser's message is powerful, emotional, and even patriotic. The actors in the television commercials for this car are young and full of energy. Do you identify with them? The advertiser hopes you do, so you will buy its cars instead of its competitors' automobiles.

Linking a product with slogans, nicknames, and images is called **product identification** in the ad business. It is considered an essential part of selling products. What sort of product identification did you build into your own advertising campaign?

The Role of Labor and Unions

We have concentrated in this unit on the roles of consumers and producers in an economy. Now let us focus on the role of labor, the people who work for the producers. Without labor, production and consumption of goods and services would not be possible. Every type of economy needs labor.

However, the rights and duties of workers differ greatly from one economy to another. The former Soviet Union, as you have seen, had a command economy. The government kept tight control over the factors of production, including labor. In market economies such as the United States the government exercises far less direct control over labor.

Early in the nineteenth century workers began to organize in the United States. They formed free and democratic **labor unions.** These are organizations dedicated to improving the salaries, working conditions, and living standards of the workers. Workers realized that they could do very little by acting as individuals. They needed to speak and act with one voice to get what they wanted. They needed to be independent of political parties, the government, and the producers.

At first, the management of companies and industries did not allow labor unions to form. Eventually, however, workers were able to unite, and unions were recognized by the producers as the legal representatives of their members. Unions grew more and more powerful over the years. Today, unions in market economies are sometimes as powerful as the industries in which their members are employed. Unions today are able to get many benefits for their members.

Labor unions in our economy have four basic rights:

(1) They have the right to organize. The law forbids industries to get in the way of workers who want to start a labor union where they are employed. Employers are also forbidden to discourage employees from joining a union.

(2) Unions have the right to elect their own leaders. Industries, political parties, and the government are not permitted by law to decide who leads the union. The workers elect their own union leaders and their own representatives.

(3) Unions have the right to bargain collectively for the workers. This means that the workers' union representatives have the power to speak for the workers. Union leaders meet with representatives of management to work out agreements which concern salaries, working hours, working conditions, and other problems.

(4) Unions have the right to strike. Union leaders, with the consent of workers they represent, may call a strike. A strike is a temporary stopping of work and production. It is used to bring pressure on the employer to agree to union demands in collective bargaining.

State and federal laws in the United States usually guarantee labor unions these four rights. There are some exceptions. For example, some government employees have the right to organize, the right to elect union leaders, and the right to bargain col-

As machines and computers replace human workers, people become less eager to unionize.

lectively, but they do not have the legal right to strike. Some government employees (firefighters and police, for instance) must be on the job for the public good. If they went on strike, the safety of the people might be threatened.

In recent years, American unions have been growing less powerful. Machines and robots have replaced human workers in many factory jobs. And computers have replaced many office workers. These machines often work faster and more efficiently than human workers. In the long run, they are almost always less expensive than human labor. As machines have replaced humans in their jobs, people have become less anxious to unionize.

Critics of the American unions say that the unions are at least partially to blame for the loss of jobs. In the last twenty years, unions in the largest industries have demanded and received high wages for their members. Those high wages encouraged industries to accept new ways of production which are now replacing many union workers.

Unions still provide many benefits to their members, however. And the American government still protects the rights of people to organize in unions that are free from government control.

In command economies the rights and duties of workers are much different. In the former Soviet Union, for example, almost all workers belonged to labor organizations. Sometimes these organizations were called unions. However, Soviet unions had none of the four basic rights of American unions. The goal of Soviet labor organizations was not to protect the workers. Instead, labor organizations in the former USSR had one main goal: to assist the Communist Party. Union leaders were most often leaders in the Communist Party.

The Communist Party not only ran the government and industry in the Soviet Union. It also ran the labor organizations. Soviet workers were taught that the Communist Party was the best labor representative they could possibly have. They were commanded not to strike or ask for higher wages. To do so would hurt their country and Soviet industry. Soviet workers were told that any action against the industry or

Workers in the former Soviet Union had limited choices about what they could buy. The government decided what would be produced.

the Communist Party would be unpatriotic. In fact, workers who criticized the Communist Party or its labor organizations were sometimes fired, put in jail, or given an unpleasant job. The Soviet government, managed by the Communist Party, controlled almost all jobs in the USSR. So, it was very easy for the Party to control the workers.

Wages in the Soviet Union were fixed by the government. The government also determined where the individual worker was employed. And it often determined where the workers and their families would live.

Unions in the former USSR sometimes provided workers with vacations (if the workers produced more than they had to). These unions also ran the social programs for their workers. They also ran some hospitals. Unions in the USSR played a small role, if any, in getting higher wages for the workers. And, since they were run by Communist Party members, the unions did not protect the workers from the Soviet government which was "management" in all Soviet industries.

The wages of workers in the former Soviet Union remained low, while prices of goods and services were usually high. Consumer goods such as cars and clothing were not as easily available. Some necessities were very expensive. Food bills cost the average Soviet worker more than half of his or her salary. Although apartment rent and medical care was much lower in the USSR than in American cities, most apartments were very small and were shared by two families. Unlike American unions, Soviet unions were powerless to improve the workers' standards of living.

Labor is a necessary factor of production in every economy. But, as you have seen, the way workers live depends upon the economy in which he or she lives.

READING REVIEW

1. What is a labor union? What is the purpose of a labor union?
2. What four basic rights do labor unions have in this country?

Critical Thinking

3. **Recognizing Cause and Effect** (see page 35) Why have American labor unions been growing less powerful in recent years?

READING 13

Money

Question: What do stone wheels, cigarettes, beaver skins, whiskey, salt, and beads have in common?

Answer: They were all at one time or another used as money. In the economies in which they were used, each of those goods was accepted by most people as payment for other goods and services.

Barter is the oldest system of exchanging goods and services. It was used in Europe in the Middle Ages. No money was involved. If you had, let's say, five bushels of wheat and you wanted to trade them for a hunting dog, you had to find someone who owned a hunting dog and who wanted to trade the dog for wheat. That kind of trading took a lot of time and effort.

These merchants exchange sacks of wheat for cloth. In the Middle Ages in Europe people used the barter system to get the goods they wanted. Now turn to page 461. In terms of economic activity, what is the basic difference between the man buying gas and the people shown above?

With the growth of the market economy a new and better means of trading goods and services was found. Money became a go-between in trading. Instead of bartering a hunting dog for your five bushels of wheat, it became possible to sell the dog for money. Then the money could be used to buy anything, including wheat. Money became a *measure of the value of goods and services.* Instead of figuring that a hunting dog is worth five bushels of wheat, we can say that a hunting dog is worth a certain amount of money. A bushel of wheat is also worth a certain amount of money.

Money also became a *medium of exchange.* It became possible to exchange money for goods and services. With money, you can buy and sell at separate times and places. In bartering, the exchange of goods must take place at one time.

With money you can also buy something now and pay for it later through a system called credit. Usually, buying on credit means that you pay a higher price for the goods and services in the end. In this way money is a *standard for payment in the future.*

Money provides us with a *way of saving wealth.* Paper and metal money are called **currency.** They can be put away for a while. It is difficult to save such things as bushels of wheat or hunting dogs. Dogs grow old and lose value, and wheat rots after a short time. Money usually keeps its value and doesn't rot or grow old.

So, **money** provides four main services: It is a measure of the value of goods and services, a medium of exchange, a standard of payment in the future, and a way of saving wealth.

Until recently, paper and metal currency and stocks and checks were the major kinds of money. Credit cards, such as American Express, Visa, and MasterCard, let you buy almost anything around the world and pay for it later. They don't get rid of the need for currency, but they do make it easier for many people to buy goods and services when they need them.

In the future, paper and metal currency may disappear. They will probably be replaced by computer recordings of money transactions. When you get paid for a good or service, a message will be sent from the buyer's bank computer to your bank computer. The message will put money into one bank from another almost instantly. Paper and metal money will not even touch your hands!

But that is in the future. Today, we use the common forms of money in our day-to-day dealings. What makes money valuable? Just that people are willing to agree that money is valuable. The government of the United States promises that American money can be traded for goods and services. Foreign governments and people accept the American dollar in payment for

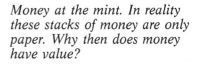
Money at the mint. In reality these stacks of money are only paper. Why then does money have value?

goods and services. They do so because they believe in the value of the American dollar. Besides, they know that the people who produce goods and services in the American economy will continue to do so. Production "backs up" the dollar and builds confidence in American money.

Another reason the dollar is accepted by other countries is because of international agreements. It is easier to do business if one country accepts the currency of another. Without such agreement, countries would have to go back to bartering. So would the people in those countries.

The value of money does not always stay the same. Sometimes the American dollar is worth more, sometimes less. In recent years, the value of the dollar has been decreasing. That means that it takes more dollars to buy the same goods and services. When this happens, the economy suffers from **inflation.** Why is inflation a problem for consumers? Inflation is particularly difficult for people who live on "fixed incomes." These people are mainly older people who are retired and who get only a certain amount of money every month from their retirement funds and from the government.

When the value of the dollar becomes stronger, it takes fewer dollars to buy goods and services. This is called **deflation.** Which do you think is better: inflation or deflation?

Money is a fascinating topic. It is a subject you will be talking about and thinking about for most of your life.

READING REVIEW

1. Describe three functions of money.

Critical Thinking

2. Expressing Problems Clearly (see page 12) Why is it incorrect to say that credit cards replace the need for money?

EXPERIMENT **9-K**

Working With Money

PART ONE
Every country uses money to trade with other countries. If you go to another country, you will probably have to change your American dollars into the currency of the foreign country. When you buy a foreign product, the American dollars you pay for it are given to the foreign manufacturer, often in the currency of his or her land.

Some people may think of American dollars as "real money" and other currency as somehow less valuable. This is seldom true.

The currencies of all nations are valuable, and each kind represents the national economy of a real government.

In this experiment we will see how much American dollars are worth in other currencies. And we will find out how foreign currencies can be turned into American dollars. Exchanging one form of currency for another is done every day in major banks. Try it yourself.

First, by using the figures on the board, determine how much of each foreign currency you could buy with one hundred U.S. dollars ($100):

- British pounds sterling
- Mexican pesos
- Australian dollars
- German deutschmarks
- Italian liras
- Russian rubles
- Indian rupees
- Japanese yen

Now, convert the following currencies into American dollars:

- 100 British pounds sterling
- 3,000 Mexican pesos
- 450 Australian dollars
- 6,000 German deutschmarks
- 900 Italian liras
- 100 Russian rubles
- 4,000 Indian rupees
- 100,000 Japanese yen

From the top to bottom left, the paper currency is from France, Great Britain, and the United States. From the top to bottom right is paper currency from Canada and Germany. Can you name the different currencies?

In figuring out how many yen or liras (or whatever you can get for an American dollar) there are some factors you should consider. The things which you can buy in the United States for a certain amount of money cannot be bought in another country for an equivalent (the same) amount of that currency. For example, an apartment which costs $1,300 a month in New York City may cost 938 pounds (about $1,500) a month in London.

Tariffs also affect the prices consumers pay for goods. A tariff is a tax on goods imported from other countries. India puts a high tariff on goods coming into the country. This means that a new car from the United States costs almost twice in India what it does in this country. Taxes make up about half of the cost of the car. The taxes go to the government of India. As we will see later, governments often put high tariffs on incoming products in order to discourage people from buying foreign goods. A tariff raises the price of foreign goods above the price of domestic goods (made in the country). This encourages industries inside the country to produce. People prefer to buy the cheaper domestic goods, and the domestic industries make profits. Those profits are then shared with the government in the form of taxes.

Government control of the economy in foreign countries may also influence the worth of money and goods. An example of government control of the economy is the sale of blue jeans in the former U.S.S.R. The Soviet government controlled all industries and did not manufacture blue jeans. And yet, blue jeans were very popular among the Soviet people. It was illegal to buy jeans from foreigners, and yet many Soviets did exactly that. The jeans which foreigners brought into the Soviet Union (illegally) were sold on the black market—an illegal, underground market—for over $200 a pair! The same jeans would have cost you one-sixth that amount of money here in the United States.

On the other hand, some goods did cost less in the U.S.S.R. than here. The Soviet government controlled all factors of production in the U.S.S.R. Because the government controlled the economy, the government could keep the cost of renting an apartment very low. A small apartment in a large city like Moscow once cost a family about $25 to $50 a month. Its equivalent in this country would have been $300 to $600 a month, depending on where it was located.

So, as you can see, it is difficult to translate U.S. dollars into foreign currency and tell *exactly* what that money will buy.

PART TWO

It is fairly easy to figure out rates of exchange for American and foreign currencies. But it is not so easy to agree on how money should be spent because we all think differently and have different values. How important is money? What should money be used for?

Suppose that a very wealthy person died and left $1,000 in a will for your class. The will simply states that the money should be spent by the class within one month and cannot be distributed among the members of the class. According to the will, the money will be spent by the class *as a unit*. This means that everyone in the class must agree on the money's use.

See if you as a class can come up with a solution.

Banks—How Do They Work?

The business of a bank is money. Banks are as old as the market economy. They began as places to put money and jewels and precious metals such as gold, to guard against robberies. Moneylenders at one time served as banks. They took people's money and kept it for them until they wanted to spend it. For that service, the moneylenders charged a fee. Today, in any modern bank you can still deposit jewels, official papers, and other important and valuable things by renting a safe deposit box. The safe deposit box is locked up in the bank's safe. There it is protected against theft and natural disasters like fire and flood.

Moneylenders, like modern banks, made money by giving out and taking in money. They made loans at sometimes high interest rates. This way their supply of money to lend was always growing. Of course, their profits grew at the same time. Today, the rate of interest a bank can legally charge is set by the federal government. Extremely high interest rates are not allowed.

Banks called **commercial banks** are the ones with which we are most familiar. Commercial banks are found in almost every town and city in the world. You or your parents more than likely have a savings account or a checking account in a commercial bank.

The modern commercial bank has many more services to offer than the old moneylenders. So do other types of banks, called *savings banks, trust companies,* and *savings and loan associations.* Commercial

Most communities in the United States have banks. They are all part of a nationwide banking system. Without that system our economy could not exist.

Economics **519**

When you shop in a department store, it probably does not occur to you that the store uses a bank much the way an individual does. For example, a store borrows and deposits money. It depends on a bank for many services.

banks generally give more services than the other three types of banks. They are sometimes referred to as "full-service banks."

There is one other type of bank, called the Federal Reserve Bank. There are twelve Federal Reserve Banks in this country. Each one services a different area of the United States. You do not have direct dealings with a Federal Reserve Bank. They are banks for other banks. **Federal Reserve Banks** are United States government banks. They make loans to commercial banks. And they accept money deposits from commercial banks. They also help commercial banks transfer money by check. Federal Reserve Banks act as the bankers for the federal government. They keep a watchful eye on the activities of commercial banks. They make sure the banks are healthy and that they are obeying the laws of banking.

Let's take a look at a commercial bank and find out how it works. You can have a **savings account** at a commercial bank. This is often called a time deposit because you earn money by keeping your money in the bank account for a certain period of time. You can draw your money out of a savings account at any time. The longer you have your money on deposit, though, the more interest you make. **Interest** is the profit depositors earn from banks for depositing money in a savings account.

Another service of a commercial bank is called a **checking account,** or demand deposit. This account lets you deposit and withdraw money any time you want to. You simply write a check. Your deposit is available to you upon your demand. Some banks charge a service fee for a checking account.

So, commercial banks take in money two ways: through savings accounts and checking accounts. What do they do with all that money?

Like the moneylenders of former times, banks use money deposits to earn more money. Banks give loans to responsible businesses and individuals. Banks charge higher interest rates for loans than the interest rates they give on savings accounts. This means there is more money coming in than going out. Therefore, banks make a profit. They are required to keep a great deal of money on hand so that depositors can withdraw their money at any time. Commercial banks also invest large amounts of money in stocks and other investments. These earn additional money for the bank.

What happens if a bank runs out of money? Although it seldom happens, there is little for the depositor to worry about. Savings and checking accounts are guaranteed by an agency of the federal government. They are backed by the money of the Federal Reserve Banks. Each account is insured by the government up to $100,000 per account.

What uses could you make of banks in your area?

READING REVIEW

1. What role did moneylenders play in past times?
2. Define: interest, checking account, savings account.

Critical Thinking

3. **Making Comparisons** (see page 16) What is the difference between a commercial bank and a savings and loan institution?

EXPERIMENT 9-L

Using the Services of a Bank

Banks can give you a variety of services. Most banks offer savings accounts (time deposits), checking accounts (demand deposits), and loans. You can also rent containers called safe deposit boxes, in which you can store valuable papers and goods. At all banks you can buy United States savings bonds and travelers checks. At some banks you can exchange foreign currency for American dollars, or dollars for foreign currency. Some banks also offer advice to their best customers on how to invest

money. Loans are given by banks to businesses and individuals for many reasons.

Of all the services offered by banks, the two most frequently used are the **checking account** and **savings account.** In this experiment you will see how both of these accounts operate.

First, let's consider the *checking account.* This type of account, also called a demand deposit, can be opened at most banks by depositing an amount of money with the bank teller. You then receive a checkbook from the bank. You use this when you want to draw money out of your checking account. When you write a check to someone, that person can cash it at his or her bank and at some stores. The check then goes to your bank, and the money is taken out of your account. It is important to keep a record of the money you deposit and withdraw. You cannot take more money out of your account than you have in it. When you take more out than you have in, you overdraw your account. Many banks charge you a service fee of up to twenty dollars or more for overdrawing your checking account.

Below is a typical check. The second blank space down in the upper right corner is for the date. When you write a check, put that day's date on the check. If you postdate the check (dating it with a future date) it is usually returned to you, along with a service charge. Dating the check more than a month behind can bring the same results. So be sure you are accurate in dating your checks.

Below the date line is another line beginning with the words "Pay to the Order of" or simply "Pay." On this line you should write the name of the person to whom you are making the check. Or, if you want to draw money out for yourself, usually at your bank, you can write the word "Cash" on this line.

At the end of the same line is a dollar sign ($), and then the line is continued. After the dollar sign, write in numerals the amount of the check you are making. Be sure to include a period between dollars and cents. For example, fifty-seven dollars would be written $57.00. On the line underneath spell out the same figure— "Fifty-seven and no/100". "No/100" means there are "no cents." Then draw a line to the word "Dollars." Now let's put this all together. If the amount were $57.12, the number would be written "Fifty-seven and 12/100 Dollars."

Finally, there is a line at the bottom right corner for you to sign your name. It is important that you sign your name the same way every time you write a check. The bank has a record of your signature. If a check is returned with a signature that doesn't look like yours, the bank may think it is a forgery. That could cause a lot of trouble and confusion.

☆☆ FOUR STAR CITY BANK
☆☆ Brightown, TX 01234

NOT NEGOTIABLE   No. _____

_____ 19 _____   29-9
                         213

Pay to the
Order of _____ $ _____

_____ Dollars

_____

⑆0213⑆0009⑈ 130⑆0099⑆9⑆43⑈

In these ways checks are alike. Also, some checks have a space at the top right for you to number the checks. Some checks are already numbered for you. Check numbers are important in keeping an accurate record of the money in your account.

On some checks there is a place for you to indicate the reason for writing the check (for example, "Rent for August" or "2-year subscription to 'Rolling Stone'").

Some check books have stubs. The stubs are used for recording the amount of each check, the date, to whom it was made and your *balance* (the amount you have left). Stubs are attached to one end of the check. After writing the check and recording the information on the stub, you tear the check off. You keep the stub in your records. Here is what one type of stub looks like.

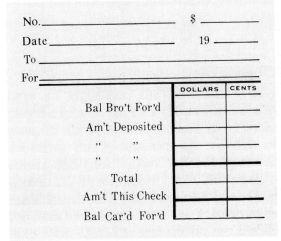

So far, we have been talking about how to make a check payable to someone else. But what about checks other people make out to you? How can you cash this check? It is really very simple. All you do is take the check to your bank. Endorse (sign) the back of the check and hand it to the teller. The teller will put the amount of money stated on the check into your account, or, if you wish, give you the cash amount.

Now let's write a few checks and keep a correct record of them. Using the handout given to you by your teacher, write checks out to the persons listed. Record the necessary information in your check stubs. You are starting with a balance of $1,200 in your checking account. Put this amount on the balance forward line.

Check #1. Pay Jo Guffey $895.45 for color TV set. Dated today.
Check #2. Pay Georgene Cartwright $25.00 for a beagle puppy. Dated today.
Check #3. Cash a check for $50, withdrawing money for yourself. Dated today.
Check #4. Pay $12.85 to the Book-of-the-Month Club for this month's selection. Dated today.

Be sure to keep an accurate record on your stubs. After all four checks are written, how much money do you have left in your account? On stub #5, record the fact that you have just added $503.10 to your balance. Now how much do you have in your account?

Now let's take a look at *savings accounts,* which are sometimes called time deposits. You can open a savings account in a manner similar to checking accounts. You simply deposit a certain amount of money with the bank teller. A bankbook or statement will be given to you, showing the amount of money you deposit. As time goes on, the money you deposit earns interest. The interest is added onto the original amount, and all that money earns more interest. As you can see, money in a savings account is not supposed to be withdrawn. In many banks you can withdraw money from a savings account at any time.

Other banks may require a 90-day notice. You may lose a lot of interest if you draw money from a savings account.

Here is a page from a typical bank statement. Can you explain what each of the figures means?

Most banks issue a monthly statement that shows the number of deposits and withdrawals you have made during the month. The amount of money that is left in your account once all the withdrawals are subtracted is called your balance.

Economic Interdependence

Nations, like individuals, have to manage their "households." They have to deal with the problems of scarcity, supply and demand, and the needs and wants of their people. As we have seen, all countries have a different way of dealing with these problems, depending upon the kind of economy they have. But each nation has much the same responsibility: To keep itself going and to satisfy (at least to some extent) the desires and physical needs of the citizens.

There are poor countries and rich countries. There are some which have abundant natural resources. And there are those which have to import most of the goods and services used in the economy. There is a way of measuring the value of the goods and services produced in a nation in any given year. It is called the Gross National Product (GNP). The GNP is the total money value of all new goods and services produced in a national economy during a *fiscal* (business) year. In many countries, including the U.S., the fiscal year is from July 1 until June 30. Let's say General Motors produces a new car. That new car adds to the GNP of the United States for that year. But when you buy a used car, your purchase does not contribute to the GNP. That's because the car is not a newly produced item.

A nation which produces and consumes (uses) all that it needs is said to be self-sustaining. Such countries are rare today. Industrialization has brought with it great specialization. This means that nations (as well as people) depend on each other through trade for the raw materials and the goods and services needed to keep their economies going. This is called **economic interdependence.** It is one of the most important concepts in our world today.

Look at the maps below and on page 526. They show economic interdependence. The United States trades with countries which supply us with the raw materials we need in order to produce finished products. Map A shows the countries which send us materials to make various chocolate products. If it were not for those raw materials, we could not make many chocolate products, such as the candy bar. In this country chocolate manufacturing is a multi-million dollar business. Many people are employed by businesses which manufacture chocolate products. Map B shows the goods the United States ships to those countries which supply us with the raw materials for chocolate products.

What would happen if trade between the United States and all those countries stopped? How would the manufacture of chocolate products be affected? (What would happen to *other* industries which

Selected Raw Materials Imported by the United States for the Manufacture of Chocolate Products   A

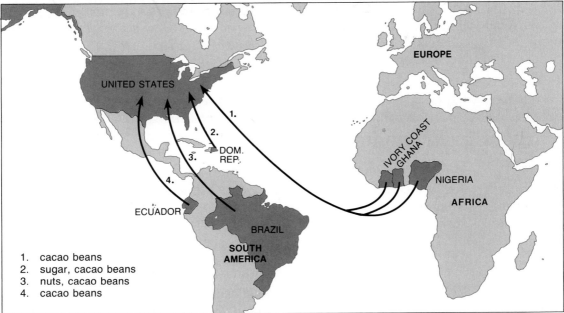

1. cacao beans
2. sugar, cacao beans
3. nuts, cacao beans
4. cacao beans

Selected Goods and Raw Materials Exported by the United States   B

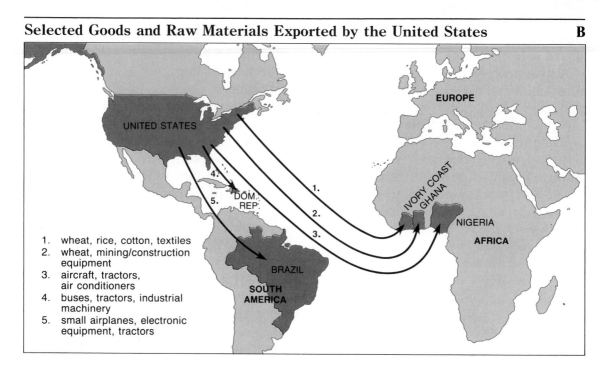

1. wheat, rice, cotton, textiles
2. wheat, mining/construction equipment
3. aircraft, tractors, air conditioners
4. buses, tractors, industrial machinery
5. small airplanes, electronic equipment, tractors

rely on imported raw materials?) What would happen to the economies of the countries with which we trade?

By now it should be clear that all the nations of the world rely heavily upon each other. We are all interdependent. And with more sophisticated technology, interdependence will increase.

READING REVIEW
1. Define: fiscal year, GNP.

Critical Thinking
2. **Recognizing Cause and Effect** (see page 35) How are nations economically interdependent?

READING 16

Careers in Economics*

Are you interested in a career in Economics? Economists study the way a society uses resources such as land, labor, capital, and management. They help to determine the best uses for these scarce resources.

*Adapted from *Occupational Outlook Handbook.* (See Acknowledgements, pages 595–596.)

Some economists focus on the needs of our society and the world to find new sources of energy. Others study how the money supply affects the way people live in a society. Most economists are concerned with economic decisions in specialized fields such as labor, agriculture, transportation, health services, and many others.

Economists are concerned with economic decisions in the areas of labor, agriculture, transportation, and health services.

Economics is the largest social science field. About 130,000 persons are employed as economists in the United States today. Three-fourths of these people work for private industries such as factories, banks, insurance firms, and investment companies. Most other economists teach at colleges and universities or work in government. Many economics teachers combine their teaching with consulting that they do for businesses.

The largest number of economists live and work in Washington, D.C., and in New York City. Many economists work in New York because it is the financial capital of the United States. Others work in Washington because many international organizations have headquarters there.

If you are interested in a career in Economics, you must have a thorough understanding of economic theories, such as supply and demand, equilibrium point, business cycles, and many others. It is helpful to have training in computer science, mathematics, and business. Economists work with details, and must be very careful with their statistics. You must be exact in your work if you want to be a successful economist. It also helps to be patient, and to stick with problems until they are solved.

Economists should be able to express themselves well orally and in writing. Creativity and curiosity about the way Economics really works are essential.

If you would like more information on careers in Economics, write to the American Economic Association, 1313 21st Avenue South, Nashville, TN 37212. For more information on careers in business economics, write to the National Association of Business Economists, 28349 Chagrin Boulevard, Suite 201, Cleveland, OH 44122.

READING REVIEW
1. Where do the largest number of economists live and work?
2. How many economists are there in the United States today?

Critical Thinking
3. **Identifying Alternatives** (see page 38) Name six fields in which economists are employed.

Social Scientists Look at Advertising and the Youth Market

How do the ways economists think about a subject compare to the ways other social scientists think? Below you will explore the similarities and differences as you examine the advertisement. Read the Bonjour International ad carefully and then answer the questions that follow under "Comparing the Social Sciences."

"WE CAN SAVE THE WORLD

No matter who you are and where you're from, there's one thing we all have in common: the earth is our home. A home is something to take care of and protect, not abuse and destroy. We know this and yet we continue to contribute toward the destruction of the planet. Why? Perhaps we say, 'I can't make a difference.' Well, we can. But only if every one of us decides to take action. That's why at the beginning of the summer, we are issuing millions of hangtags containing simple instructions on how we can save our world. Different tags will be found on each BONJOUR fashion item for every woman, man, and child in stores all over the world. Get hold of them, read them, have your family, friends, and neighbors read them, and do your share.

Let's save our world.

We have nowhere else to go.

Charles Dayan, President, BONJOUR INTERNATIONAL**"**

Comparing the Social Sciences

Psychologists study human motivations. Why do you, as a psychologist, think this advertiser decided to run an ad about ecology when the product being sold is jeans? (*Identifying Central Issues*)

Sociologists study how groups behave. What groups do you, as a sociologist, think this advertiser is targeting? (*Demonstrating Reasoned Judgment*)

Anthropologists study the values of a culture. As an anthropologist, what two values of American culture can you identify as being mixed in this advertisement? (*Recognizing Ideologies*)

Geographers study how humans change the Earth's features to meet their needs. Do you, as a geographer, agree with the advertiser's view about the importance of taking care of the Earth? Explain your answer. (*Testing Conclusions*)

Historians study the past. Do you, as a historian, think that the makers of jeans in the days of the California gold rush would have used this kind of advertisement? Explain your answer. (*Making Comparisons*)

Political scientists study government. Do you, as a political scientist, agree with the passage that saving the world should be up to the individual rather than up to the government? Explain your answer. (*Testing Conclusions*)

Economists study the way goods and services are distributed. Do you as an economist see a connection between this advertisement and how jeans are distributed? (*Determining Relevance*)

Shopping for jeans

GLOSSARY OF TERMS

advertisement a persuasive public notice that certain goods and services are for sale (page 504)

barter a system of trading one good or service for another good or service, without the use of money (page 472)

bond a kind of IOU in which a corporation or government pays back the full amount plus interest in return for the use of the investor's money for a specific period of time (page 498)

business cycle an up-and-down pattern of change in the economy; includes a high point, a low point, and points in between (page 502)

capital a factor of production; the money, equipment, buildings, and other things needed to turn raw materials and labor into finished products (page 470)

capitalist economy one in which capital is used in business; also referred to as the market economy (page 491)

checking account popular name for a demand deposit; a bank account that enables a person to deposit money and withdraw it at any time by issuing a check (page 520)

command economy an economic system in which decisions regarding the factors of production are made by government leaders (page 473)

commercial bank a business establishment that offers a full range of services to the consumer, including checking and savings accounts, loans, and the use of safety deposit boxes (page 519)

common stock a certificate that gives the holder part ownership in a corporation; also pays dividends on a regular basis (page 497)

consumer one who buys or rents goods or services and consumes or uses them (page 467)

corporation a form of business, authorized by a government charter, that is recognized as a legal person and that carries certain privileges not given to other forms of business (page 493)

currency the money issued by a government, in modern times usually of paper and metal (page 514)

deflation an economic condition in which the value of currency increases while the cost of goods and services decreases (page 516)

demand the ability and willingness of consumers to buy a good or service at a certain price and at a given time (page 476)

depression a stage in the business cycle in which there is little or no economic growth (page 503)

LAND/ RESOURCES

LABOR

dividend the money paid by a corporation to stockholders as a sharing in the profits of the company (page 497)

economic interdependence a situation in which nations depend on each other through trade for the raw materials, goods, and services necessary to keep their economies going (page 525)

Economics the social science that deals with ways in which scarce resources are used; the study of wealth (page 462)

economist a social scientist who studies how we use our resources (page 463)

economy a country's basic way of producing and trading goods (page 462)

entrepreneur a person who begins a business and manages the factors of production of that business (page 471)

equilibrium point the price at which supply equals demand, and there is neither scarcity nor surplus (page 485)

factors of production those four things necessary to produce anything: land, labor, capital, and management (page 469)

Federal Reserve Banks United States Government banks, which service commercial banks and act as bankers for the federal government (page 520)

CAPITAL

free enterprise system an economy in which it is relatively easy to start and manage a business without government interference or ownership (page 491)

Gross National Product the total value of goods and services produced in an economy within a given year (GNP) (page 503)

inflation an economic condition in which the value of currency decreases while the cost of goods and services increases (page 516)

MANAGERS

interest   a sum of money paid for the use of capital (page 520)

labor   a factor of production that includes both mental and physical human labor used in the process of production (page 510)

labor unions   organizations of workers whose goal is to improve working conditions of the worker (page 510)

land   a factor of production that includes all natural resources needed to carry on the process of production (page 453)

law of demand   as prices rise, people demand less (page 476)

law of scarcity   an economic law that states: all things are limited; in order to get something, you always have to give up something else (page 464)

law of supply   as prices rise, producers produce more (page 476)

management   a factor of production; the person or people responsible for the direction of the other factors of production; sometimes called *entrepreneur* (page 471)

market economy an economic system in which buyers and sellers exchange goods and services on the basis of supply and demand; also referred to as the capitalist economy (page 491)

mixed economy an economic system in which free enterprise is affected by governmental regulations (page 492)

money any material that serves as a recognized medium of exchange; a measure of the value of goods and services; a standard of payment; a means of saving; currency (page 514)

need something essential to live (page 462)

partnership a form of business in which two or more people are owners and share in the profits and losses of the business and are liable for each other's business dealings (page 492)

preferred stock a certificate giving the holder rights to corporate dividend payments, usually in fixed amounts and distributed before common stock dividends (page 497)

price the value of a good or service in money (page 467)

producer one who makes, or manufactures, goods to sell (page 467)

product identification linking a product with slogans, nicknames, and images (page 509)

recession a time of little business growth, when the GNP is down for at least six months in a row and unemployment rises (page 503)

savings account the popular name for a time deposit; a bank account in which a person deposits money for use by the bank in return for interest payments (page 520)

service an action done by one person for another, such as repairing a car, for a price (page 479)

shortage a condition in which there are too few goods or services to meet the demand (page 486)

single proprietorship a form of business owned, and often operated, by one person (page 492)

stock a certificate of investment and usually part ownership in a corporation, expressed in terms of number of shares (page 493)

stock exchange a central place where shares of stocks and bonds are exchanged; also called a stock market. The New York Stock Exchange and the American Stock Exchange are two leading stock markets. (page 499)

supply the quantity of a good or service available for sale at a particular price and at a given time (page 476)

surplus a condition in which there are more goods or services available than there is demand for them (page 485)

traditional economy an economic system in which the questions of production are settled by rules accepted as good and correct (page 455)

want a luxury; not absolutely necessary for living (page 462)

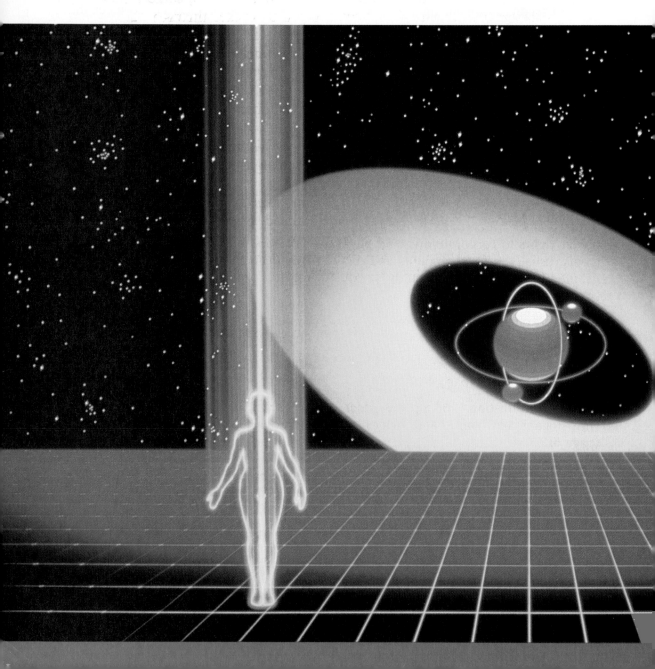

10

The
Future

The wheel diagram labels: PSYCHOLOGY, ECONOMICS, POLITICAL SCIENCE, HISTORY, GEOGRAPHY, ANTHROPOLOGY, SOCIOLOGY, with center **STUDY & THINKING SKILLS**

This Is the Future

When you get home from school today, spin around and look behind you. Do you see yourself coming home from school? It's doubtful. Even so, some scientists predict that as people begin to rocket through outer space at high speed, something called a "wormhole" may permit travelers to peer backwards in time. Wormholes in space are like wormholes in an apple—shortcuts. A rocket darting through such a tunnel might even be in time to see itself entering the wormhole. What would happen if a little girl were then to wave to this earlier image of herself? Would the early image wave back? And if so, would the little girl remember being waved at by another little girl as her rocket entered the wormhole?

Everyone spends some time wondering about the shocks and surprises that lie ahead. Social scientists who plan for the future are known as **futurists.** In the Unit 10 readings, you will learn some ways of thinking about the future. In the experiments, you will learn ways to plan for the future.

The Future and You

The future is where the present leads us, as surely as water spills downhill. The more we plan for the future, the better off we tend to be, both as individuals and as a society. The questions below will help you appreciate the importance of your own future.

1. Where would you like to be and what would you like to be doing in 5 years? In 10 years? In 25 years?
2. Can you see yourself in the role of parent at some time in the future? Where will you look for guidance to meet the challenge of raising your kids?

UNIT 10   CONTENTS

Why Study the Future?

The future. For centuries, people have feared it and worried about it. They have also awaited it with hope and excitement. Now we are about to enter the twenty-first century. What will it be like to live in the future?

Only time will tell us what will actually happen in our future. But some experts, called **futurists,** are watching current events very closely in an effort to predict what the future will be like.

Futurists use many techniques to study the future. They study past events and current trends. They spend a great deal of time and effort thinking of good questions to ask experts in many fields, such as science, the arts, business, and education, among many others. They use specialized techniques called decision trees, future wheels, and cross-impact matrices. In this unit you will have an opportunity to try all of these methods of studying the future.

To forecast future events, futurists must know about our past. In past eras, people had far less control over their lives than they do today.

Diseases such as the plague, which killed millions of European people throughout history, could not be predicted. And no effective cures were known. A common remedy for many diseases was bloodletting. This operation was performed by a barber,

People have always wondered what the future holds. Making plans for the future helps us to lead successful, happy lives.

who in those times was also a surgeon. To make the victim well, the barber would cut open the body to allow the "bad humors" to escape. That kind of surgery most often killed the patient.

Today we know much more about the many causes of disease, thanks to scientific advances and improvements in technology. The future is a little safer for all of us because of this knowledge.

Some futurists study the relationships between science, technology, and society. The study of these three is sometimes shortened to STS. We will take a close look at STS in this unit, and we will see how science and technology affect almost everything we do.

We will also see how ideas change the future. Ideas cannot be seen or touched or experienced by any of your senses. And yet, ideas have always had a tremendous impact on the futures of civilizations. The ideas of preventing disease by cleaning the body with soap and water, of sending pictures and sound through the air, and of launching rockets into space to explore our universe were all considered crazy at one time.

Tiny microchips hold the key to the future for humanity as we approach life in the twenty-first century.

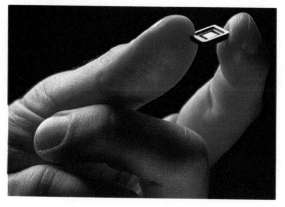

Yet, the people who believed these things were possible put up with the ridicule from other people, and they kept working on their ideas. Eventually, through many years of hard work and dedication to their dreams, those ideas became reality.

One of the most powerful ideas of all time is the idea of democracy, the belief that all people should govern themselves rather than being ruled by a monarch or dictator. This idea turned the world upside down in the past, and it continues to make dramatic changes in people's lives all around the world, from Eastern Europe to China.

The idea that people should rule themselves first appeared in ancient Greece. During most of European history, the idea of democracy was suppressed by kings and queens who ruled their countries with a firm hand. Then, in the eighteenth century, the rule of monarchs was challenged. The American colonies rebelled against the King of England. The colonies claimed that the king ruled them without the consent of the people.

Partly as a result of the American Revolution, democracy spread to other parts of the world. The countries of Eastern Europe, once dominated by the Soviet Union, are now experimenting with their own versions of democracy. If the founders of our country had been able to see into the future, would they have been surprised to see how great an impact their ideas had on the entire world?

In this unit we will take a look into our future. We will examine possible futures for ourselves and our world. We'll see futures that are probable, or most likely to happen. We will determine which ones we would like and which ones we would like to avoid.

You will have an opportunity to examine some of the most serious challenges facing you and your generation as you go into the future. These problems include poverty in the United States and throughout the world, hunger and homelessness, drug abuse, and the protection of our Earth's environment. We will take a close look at the energy crisis and ways of creating alternatives to our current energy choices. And we will look at the issue of security as we try to find ways of making our world safer.

Most important, we will see that much of what the future will be like is up to all of us. The decisions you make and the actions you take today help to determine what tomorrow will bring. We will spend the rest of our lives living in the future. The more we know about our choices today, the wiser our decisions will be. What kind of a future do you want for yourself, your friends, your family, and your world? What sort of a world would you be proud to leave behind for future generations to enjoy?

READING REVIEW

1. Why is it important for people to study the future?
2. What are people called who study the future, and what are some of the methods they use?
3. How did the idea of democracy change the world? Can you think of another great idea (not one from this reading) that had a great impact on changing the world for the better?
4. Why is it important to study the effects of science and technology on our society and on our world?

Critical Thinking

5. **Recognizing Assumptions** (see page 27) Identify two assumptions you have held about your own future. Explain why you have believed each idea and describe what actions you could take to improve your possibilities for the future.

EXPERIMENT **10-A**

Surveying Your Future

PART 1: **A Personal Opinion Survey on the Future**

In this unit we will consider the future—your own personal future, the future of this country, and the future of this planet. One of the best ways to prepare for the future is to think about it before it happens. That way, you can better plan the way you want your future to turn out. Thus, the future may be less of a surprise to you.

You can have more control over the future if you plan for it today. And, believe it or not, it is possible that what you do in your future may influence the future of the world. (If you find this hard to believe, think of the influence this handful of people have had on our world: Thomas Edison, Queen Elizabeth I, Henry Ford, Queen Isabella and King Ferdinand, Martin Luther King, Jr., and Susan B. Anthony.

This sphere, a symbol of spaceship Earth, stands at the entrance to EPCOT Center in Orlando, Florida.

In this experiment you will have an opportunity to predict what will happen by the year 2010. It is not that far away. (How old will you be in 2010?)

Look at the handout you have been given. There are 20 statements. Each statement predicts something. Tell whether you think the prediction will come true before the year 2010 by checking either the "will happen" or "won't happen" blanks in Column 1. Then tell whether you would approve or disapprove of that prediction happening by checking one of the blanks in Column 2.

After you have completed the activity, you will find out how the rest of the class has responded to this survey. Compare and discuss your predictions.

PART 2: Challenges in Your Future

One way to prepare for the challenges in your future is to study the directions in which you seem to be going. Then figure out where you may be if you continue in those directions. It is also helpful to study trends in our society and in the world. A **trend** is the way in which something is going or changing. For example, the trend in the 1970s and early 1980s was toward the manufacture of smaller American automobiles. Throughout the 1900s, the length of women's dresses has constantly varied. Is the trend today toward longer or shorter dresses? What are the current trends in the types of energy we use? The kinds of food we eat? Trends affect the daily lives of us all. What trends do you see in your own life?

In this activity, first make a list of six goals you want to reach during your lifetime. They can be as general or specific as you wish.

Next, make a list of five events that are almost certain to happen in your lifetime. These events should be ones that will have a great effect upon you. They are different from the six goals because they are events that you may not be able to fully control, or perhaps not control at all. One example is your own death.

Now make a time line. At the left end point of the time line make a mark and show the date of your birth. Divide the time line into 15-year sections, like this: Between your birth and your age now, record four very important events that have happened in your life. They should be events that have made you the person you are today. Those events may be pleasant or unpleasant. If you or your family consider these to be private or personal, do not describe them. Include the year in which each of those four events occurred.

On the time line, record your six goals for the future. Show on the time line how old you think you will be when you may achieve each of the six goals. Include the year in which you think each goal might be achieved.

Also record on the time line the five events that are almost certain to happen in your lifetime. Show the year and your age as you have done with your goals and your important past events. Predict your age at death. Base this prediction upon your family's health history.

Finally, study your completed time line. Write a paragraph telling how you feel about the time line you have drawn for yourself. Bring all your work to class.

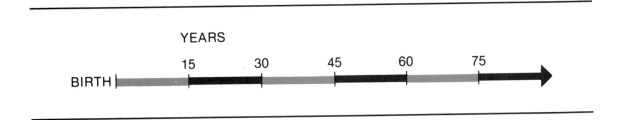

Methods of Studying Possible Futures

Predictions about patient recovery made only a few years ago are becoming obsolete. A computer measures spinal-column activity as a patient walks.

What if you could see into the future? Would it be shocking? Disappointing? Happy? Confusing? Would you really want to know what will happen to you and to the world in the next 20 or 30 years?

Some science fiction writers have been remarkably accurate in predicting the future. Edward Bellamy published a novel entitled *Looking Backward* in 1888. In this book he described a world in which electrically powered machines do the cooking and laundry. Jules Verne, writing in the late 1800s, described a flight to the moon in a spaceship similar to the one used by American astronauts in the 1960s.

In his novel *1984*, George Orwell described a world of the future in which personal privacy is unknown. The government controls the actions of people through electronic spying equipment. Some of the principles found in *1984*, such as hidden cameras and electronic listening devices, are at work today in various parts of the world.

In the depression years of the 1930s, the adventures of Buck Rogers in the comic strips helped people forget their miseries. Buck Rogers, a space adventurer of the future, became famous for his ray gun. Laser beams, similar to Buck Rogers' ray, are now used in photography, medical research, communications, and weapons.

How could these writers have known what life would be like 60 or even 100 years in the future? Of course, they had no ability to see into the future. They used their fine imaginations and sharp minds to make reasonable guesses about what the future might be like.

There are many people who not only want to know the future, but actually make it their business to know as much about the future as possible. These people work for businesses, governments, and organizations of many kinds. They are writers, thinkers, and planners. They are people concerned with this world.

How it is possible for these people to "see" into the future? We can make some pretty good guesses about the future, based on what we know about the present and the past. And if our guesses are accurate, we can have more control over the future.

One method of seeing into the future is called **projection,** or **trend analysis.** In this method, researchers gather as much information as they can find about a particular topic. They research the topic as it exists today and also as it existed in the past. Then the researchers compare their findings about the present and the past and draw conclusions based on that information. By using these conclusions, it is possible to project into the future.

For example, if you know that the city of Ourtown (an imaginary place) had a population of 5,000 in the year 1920, and that the population has increased by 100 every 10 years since then, you can tell how many

people were living in Ourtown in 1970. Can you figure it out? The answer is 5,500. Now project that **trend** (+100 every 10 years) into the future. If that trend continues, how many people will Ourtown have by the year 2000? (Answer: 5,800). As long as the trend continues, our projections will continue to be accurate. What could cause them to be inaccurate? Think of several factors that might affect the population growth trend.

Another way to analyze the future is to plan scenarios. A **scenario** is a description of life in the future based on what is known about current trends. Scenarios usually deal with only one or a few ideas about the future. World population in the year 2000 and its effect on human life styles is an example of a scenario topic.

A third way to analyze the future is to make a decision wheel. A **decision wheel** can be used to examine the direct and indirect effects of a decision about the present or the future. The first step is to place a decision in a circle at the center of the wheel. The next step is to identify several direct effects of this decision. The direct effects are then written in circles connected to the center. Indirect effects of the decision are written in an outer ring of circles.

A growing population is a likely trend of the future.

Finally, the effects are connected by lines, forming the "wheel." The completed decision wheel shows how one decision can have far-reaching results.

A fourth way of looking into the future is called the **Delphi method.** In this method, questionnaires are sent to experts in a field. They are asked for their opinions. When the experts send back their opinions the results are fed into a computer. The computer sorts, tabulates, and summarizes the information, and it is then sent back to the experts. The experts comment on what the other experts have said and their comments are fed into the computer again. The process continues in this way until there is enough information to make projections.

A fifth way to understand the future is to think about how one thing influences other things in the present. For example, what influence does pollution in rivers and oceans have on the fish we eat? On our children? On *their* children? On the future of the human race? On the future of all living things on this planet? This method is the **cross-impact matrix,** or **CIM.**

A sixth way to analyze the future is to make a **decision tree.** This method is based upon the effects of YES/NO answers to questions about decisions to be made both in the present and the future. The first step in the decision-tree method is to pose a question that can be answered YES or NO. Then future possibilities are matched with both YES and NO answers. In this way, alternatives are thought out before action is taken.

You will learn more about these methods in this unit. By using these six methods, we can analyze possibilities for the future.

This futuristic truck allows the driver to concentrate on the road, rather than watch the instrument panel.

READING REVIEW

1. Name two predictions of science fiction writers discussed in this reading that have come true.
2. What are some reasons for studying possible futures?
3. Name the six methods of analyzing the future presented in the reading.

Critical Thinking

4. **Determining Relevance** (see page 17) Think about the methods of analyzing the future described in the reading. Determine one way in which information gathered by these methods will benefit you.

Trend Analysis: Population Growth

As you learned in Experiment 10-A, a trend is a pattern that reappears over a period of time. In Reading 2 you learned that projection, or trend analysis, is a method of exploring and looking into the future. This method allows people to "project" into the future by helping them analyze and compare what has happened in the past and what is happening now.

To project into the future, we first have to gather evidence. We start by looking into the past for trends. A simple example of a trend is the pattern of celebrating your birthday. If you have celebrated your birthday yearly on August 10 since you were born, it would be safe to say that next August 10 you will celebrate still another birthday.

We can project trends in population growth the same way, by looking at the patterns in the past. Here is the population for Ourtown from 1920 to 1990:

1920	5,000
1930	5,100
1940	5,200
1950	5,300
1960	5,400
1970	5,500
1980	5,600
1990	5,700

On the basis of this pattern of population growth, you can predict that Ourtown will have a population of 5,800 by the year 2000. What will be the population of Ourtown by the year 2100? If the trend of 100 more people every 10 years is continued into the future, by the year 2100 Ourtown will have 6,800 people.

Demographers, social scientists who study population growth, most likely used trend analysis to make the predictions in these charts.

World's 10 Most Populated Countries	
1994	*2025 (Est.)*
China	China
India	India
United States	United States
Indonesia	Indonesia
Brazil	Pakistan
Russia	Nigeria
Pakistan	Bangladesh
Japan	Brazil
Bangladesh	Iran
Nigeria	Russia

Source: Population Reference Bureau, Inc.

Ten Cities Estimated to Be World's Largest in 2000	
Tokyo/Yokahama, Japan	29,971,000
Mexico City, Mexico	27,872,000
Sao Paulo, Brazil	25,354,000
Seoul, South Korea	21,976,000
Bombay, India	15,357,000
New York City	14,648,000
Osaka-Kobe-Kyoto, Japan	14,287,000
Tehran, Iran	14,251,000
Rio de Janeiro, Brazil	14,169,000
Calcutta, India	14,088,000

Source: *1995 World Almanac*

Concentric Growth Rings of the New York Urban System

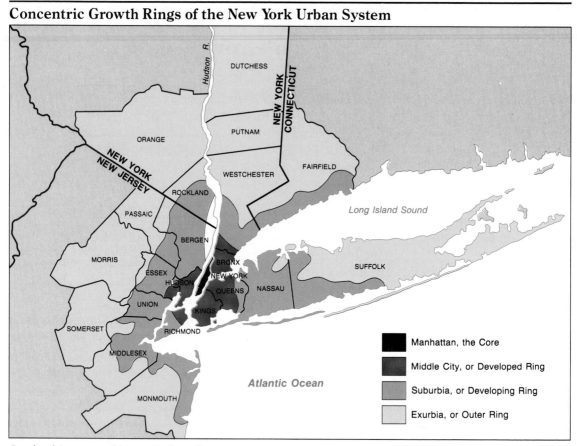

Manhattan, the Core

Middle City, or Developed Ring

Suburbia, or Developing Ring

Exurbia, or Outer Ring

Study this map of New York. What projection might be made about growth around Manhattan in the future?

Now put that population trend into graph form. On Handout 10-B, there are two grids. Use both grids to make a graph.

Graph 1 is titled "Population of Ourtown." On that graph show the total population of Ourtown every 10 years beginning in 1920. Do this by putting a dot at the point where the year and population intersect (meet). Do the same for every year and population figure. Then draw a line connecting all the dots. Show your projection beyond 1990 by continuing the line. Beyond 1990 use a broken line, rather than a solid one, to show that the projection is not

yet a fact. After 1990 does your graph show the same population trend as it does before 1990?

The population trend for Ourtown shows a steady increase. The increase is the same number every 10 years: 100 persons. The graph illustrating this increase shows a straight line.

If the population of Ourtown increases by 100 persons every 10 years, when will the population be 10,000? In other words, when will the population double?

This projection method has at least one major problem. It takes for granted that the same trends of the past will continue into the future. It supposes that no new factors will change the trend. What factors could possibly disturb our predictions about the population growth of Ourtown? Take time now to think of some factors that could make our projection wrong.

Now you know how the projection method works. It is often much more complicated than the simple problems in this experiment. The projection method may be used to get information of all types about the future. Using that method, researchers can forecast how long our natural resources may last. Many similar trends can be predicted for our cities, our nation, and the world by using the projection method of studying the future.

Science, Technology, and Society: Visions of the Future

If someone told you that in your lifetime it would be possible to travel around the world 168 times faster than it is today, what would be your reaction? How would you respond if someone predicted that the following events and developments would all happen within your lifetime?

1. The wealth of the world will grow to six times what it is today.
2. The planet will be populated by three times as many people as today.
3. New inventions in communications will bring you into immediate contact with beings you have never seen.
4. There will be four major wars that will kill millions of people.
5. An economic depression will last for a decade and put millions of people out of work.

Would you want to live in such a world? Chances are you would have mixed feelings. You would probably feel that some aspects of that world would be exciting. Some parts of that vision of the future, or **scenario,** would also be frightening.

If you had been asked to respond to the predictions above in the year 1900, you might have shaken your head and declared, "I don't believe those things could happen." But since 1900 they have actually happened. It is now possible to travel around our planet in less than 90 minutes. Astronauts have orbited the Earth in that amount of time. (In the year 1900 it took three weeks to go around the globe by ocean liner.)

All the wealth in the world is six times greater today than it was in 1900. There are three times as many people in the world today as in 1900, and today's people are living longer and healthier lives. (At the present rate of growth the population of the world will triple again in your lifetime.) The radio, telephone, TV, and space satellites have brought millions of people into contact with people, things, and cultures that they have never seen. World War I,

Modular housing, which is easy to assemble, may become increasingly commonplace in the future.

World War II, the Korean War, and the War in Vietnam have claimed the lives of millions of people. And the Great Depression caused worldwide suffering as millions of people lost their jobs. All of this has happened since 1900.

Looking back helps us to see how far we have come in such a short time. It helps us understand how fast our ways of life have changed. It is a way of understanding how the world might be in the near future—in your lifetime.

As far back as 1970, author Alvin Toffler helped promote the study of the future. His best seller *Future Shock* helped to make popular the study of the future.* In the first part of the book, Toffler shows how the rate of change has greatly speeded up during human life on Earth. He suggests that one way to understand this rate of change is to divide the last 50,000 years of human existence into lifetimes of about 62 years each. (Sixty-two years is an average lifetime

*The following discussion is adapted from Alvin Toffler, *Future Shock*. (See Acknowledgements, pages 595–596.)

in our society during the twentieth century.) According to this method of figuring, there were about 800 lifetimes in the last 50,000 years.

In the first 650 lifetimes, humans lived in caves. Only during the last 70 lifetimes have humans known how to communicate messages by writing. The printing press was invented only eight lifetimes ago. Only during the last four lifetimes have we known how to measure time with precision. The electric motor was invented two lifetimes ago. And almost everything we use in daily life today was developed in the present lifetime—the 800th!

What can you expect in your future? Some futurists predict modular homes for the people of the future. Modular homes will be put together, taken apart, moved, and then put together again in another place. Every person will have his or her own module.

Today we have throw-away bottles, paper clothes, and plastic knives and forks. Tomorrow we may be able to dispose of the damaged parts of our bodies and get new parts to replace them. Actually, this is already being done. People are living longer today because of kidney and heart transplants, and even an artificial heart. Plastic surgery makes it possible to appear younger than you are. And artificial limbs now are constructed to replace lost arms and legs.

Scientists are also learning more about human genes—the basic unit of heredity. By changing the internal structure of a person's genes, scientists might be able to find a cure for several serious diseases, including cancer. In the future, many life-threatening illnesses may be eliminated.

Robots and computers may have five (or more) senses and act in very "human" ways. If all this happens, will it change the ways we view ourselves as human beings? Who should have the power to make the decisions concerning artificial hearts and limbs, genetic changes, and the programming of robots and computers? What do you think?

What will school be like in the twenty-first century? In the book *July 20, 2019,* Arthur C. Clarke discusses his predictions about the classroom of the future. Clarke describes a "teleclass" in which a student at home can ask questions of a teacher who is hundreds of miles away in a video studio. But the teacher appears in the student's room as a life-sized, three-dimensional image!

Clarke predicts that most people will attend school throughout their life. There are a number of reasons for this. Fast-changing technology will require workers to learn new job skills or to train for different careers. New careers, such as underwater farming, will create the need for additional schooling.

Clarke also points out that technological advances will create more leisure time. People will return to school for recreational, or fun, learning! (If you want to observe this trend, look at the number of adult education courses offered by your local community college.)

How can you prepare for the technological changes you will face in the future? How can you choose a career when that career may not exist by the time you are ready to enter the work force? Part of the answer lies in the thinking skills you acquire today. Most educators agree that the key to future success is the ability to think critically, to balance opposite points of view, and to analyze alternatives in order to make sound judgments.

The world we live in is changing faster every day. Whether or not you know it, you are caught up in this rapid change. As change occurs at a faster and faster rate, we are increasingly in danger of not being able to keep up with it. We may be headed for what Alvin Toffler refers to as "future shock." Or we may take advantage of opportunities to gain a broad-based education that will enable us to prepare for a successful life in the future.

READING REVIEW

1. List three changes that have taken place since 1900 because of advances in technology.
2. How did Alvin Toffler help promote the study of the future?
3. What changes in education did Arthur C. Clarke predict for the future?

Critical Thinking

4. **Drawing Conclusions** (see page 42) What is the best way you can prepare for future changes in technology?

Scenario: What Will Everyday Life Be Like in 20 Years?

"In the year 2001..."

Have you ever thought about what people will be like in the future? What thoughts will they have? How and where will they live? Will work no longer exist? How will people of the future treat one another?

In this writing activity, use your imagination to think about what an average person will be like 20 years in the future. What might the world be like in 20 years?

First, describe your "average person." What is the person's sex? Age? Height? Weight? Is the person married, single, divorced, or some other status?

Then describe the person's family and educational background. Write what you think the person's goals might be. Explain how the person feels and thinks about life, the future, the country, and so on. Describe how the person lives. If you want to, take your person through a typical day from start to finish.

Let your imagination go! You may be asked to bring your written description to class. It should be interesting to compare your "average person of the future" with those of the rest of the class.

Today Is Where the Future Begins

"Today is the first day of the rest of your life." Have you ever heard that saying? Think about it. If you are in your teens, most of the rest of your life will be spent in the twenty-first century! What you do today will in large part determine the world you will live in for the rest of your life.

Of course, the responsibility for the future is not yours alone. But you are part of the generation that will become the world's leaders in the next century. Your decisions will affect the lives of your children, your grandchildren, and all future generations. During your lifetime, you are the caretakers of our planet for all those not yet born.

In Reading 3 you read that acquiring thinking skills is one way to prepare for future changes. Now we will consider some other strategies. The first step is to identify possible and probable futures.

One possible future is the world Alvin Toffler describes in his book *Future Shock*. In the world Toffler foresees, everything will be more temporary, from your car to your relationships with other people. Toffler predicts that we will have to get used to temporary cars and apartments. We will also have to get used to temporary friends. A symptom of future shock is the feeling that making friends is useless, because you will move to a new place before you have time to enjoy them. Or maybe your new friend will move and you will be left behind. It is an empty feeling.

Other possible futures include children being raised by a computer nanny and being taught by a teacher they will never meet. Are we destined to become a society of isolated individuals whose lifelong companions are computers? Not necessarily, argues author John Naisbett. In the book *Megatrends,* Naisbett describes a probable future based on his observations of human responses to technology today.

One example that Naisbett discusses is **telecommuting**—a means of working at a computer terminal in your home rather than traveling back and forth to the workplace every day. Telecommuting is sometimes an attractive option for a working parent who wants to be home with young children. Naisbett points out, however, that most workers choose telecommuting as a short-term arrangement. They prefer the personal contact and social interaction that the workplace provides.

Naisbett predicts that people will continue to compensate for technology in the future by being out in nature more often. We will use our hands and bodies more in leisure activities to balance the constant use of mental energy at work.

Once you have identified possible and probable futures, the next step is to decide which kind of future is preferable. We must decide what is most important to us. Do we want a world without pollution, one that would provide a better life for the animals, plants, and people of this planet? Or do we prefer the conveniences and luxuries that pollution-producing industries and transportation provide us? Is there a way we can have the benefits of both?

The rapid rate of change that Toffler call future shock could be a serious threat. If you are not prepared for the future, you might become confused about who you are and where you are going. You might become irritable or nervous. When you have had too much future shock, you become apathetic, or uncaring. You just sit back and let things happen, whether they are good or bad. You become numb to emotions, people, and things around you.

Working to clean up the environment to make our Earth a better place to live is everyone's responsibility.

We have the power to avoid future shock. We must dedicate ourselves to achieving the kind of future we want. We must manage the future, or else the future will manage us.

If we act individually to slow down the pace of our lives, we shall begin to manage our present and our future. If everyone does this, perhaps our society can be brought back under our control and slowed down. That means doing fewer things, but doing them better. It means hanging onto the jacket or car you were going to get rid of, if only for one more year. It also means making efforts to keep your friendships more lasting. Remembering to send cards and letters to friends, especially on birthdays, holidays, and special occasions, will keep your friendships going. These are only a few things that each of us can do.

Personal efforts are necessary to bring future shock under control in our society. But individual efforts are not enough. The most lasting change is that which has the broadest base of support. It is important to get others to commit themselves to the same goals you have for the betterment of our future. What will be your response to the challenge?

READING REVIEW

1. What responsibility do you have for future generations?
2. How does future shock affect human relationships?
3. What are some ways that you can avoid future shock?

Critical Thinking

4. **Checking Consistency** (see page 25) John Naisbett predicts how people will react to future technology by observing how they react to technology today. Give one or more examples (not from this reading) of human responses to technology. Are they consistent with Naisbett's observations? Why or why not?

EXPERIMENT **10-D**

Public Survey on Challenges for Our Future

In the readings so far, you have read about challenges you will face in the future. You have investigated strategies that will help you prepare for these challenges. And you have had opportunities to examine your own ideas and feelings about the future.

Now you will conduct a survey to find out how other people feel about the challenges of the future. Begin by choosing three adults and five people from your peer group to interview. Use the following questions to design a survey sheet for each person in your group:

1. What are the most significant challenges that will be faced in the future by (a) our world, (b) our country, (c) our community, and (d) yourself?
2. What do you think should be done about each?

3. What can you personally do to make a positive difference in the world, however small it might be?

4. What impact might your action have on others? On the challenge itself?

Record each person's answers or ask each person to write his or her answers on the survey sheet. Study the results and draw conclusions. Be prepared to discuss your conclusions with the class.

Challenge for Your Future: Reducing Poverty and Homelessness

What does it mean to be poor? For some people, being poor means not being able to afford the kinds of designer-label clothes their friends wear. For other people, being poor means only one member of the family has shoes. Poverty is a relative term. In other words, the definition of poverty varies according to time and place.

This homeless family once had to use an abandoned school bus for shelter. Fortunately, they now have a real home.

In the United States, the government measures poverty based on yearly income. Families whose incomes fall at or below the **poverty level** are considered poor. The poverty level is based on the amount of income families need in order to eat adequately without spending more than one third of their income on food. In 1990 the poverty level for a household of four was about $13,000 a year. The level is adjusted according to the number of people in a family. Based on these standards, about 14 percent of the American population is poor.

Certain groups have higher poverty rates than others. For example, 44 percent of all black Americans are classified as poor and 20 percent of all children in the United States are poor. The South has a higher rate of poverty than other regions of our country—about 16 percent.

Because the definition of poverty differs from country to country, it is difficult to determine how many people are poor. United States poverty-level incomes would be considered a fortune in developing nations! During the 1980s, an estimated one fifth of the world's people were so poor that their health and lives were endangered. Such severe poverty occurs mostly in developing countries.

Consider the situation in the Philippines, where 70 percent of the families live in poverty. A squatters' colony of 20,000 people exists on a garbage dump in Manila, the nation's capital. People pick through the mountain of garbage to find bits and pieces of materials they can sell for recycling. Their earnings equal about $2 to $5 a day.

In Bombay, India, one half of all housing consists of shanty colonies. More than 500,000 people live in 80,000 huts in the slum of Dharavi. Raw sewage and garbage are strewn where children play.

Many of the world's poor people live in crowded apartment buildings in inner-city neighborhoods. Others live in dwellings made of scraps of metal or wood, without electricity, running water, or sewage disposal. The United Nations estimates that more than 100 million of the world's people are homeless.

Poverty affects all of us, even if we are not poor. Those who live in poverty are part of our society. Poor people lead less productive lives than those who can afford adequate food, medical care, and education. A portion of the taxes paid by everyone goes toward programs to assist the poor.

Government and private agencies try to fight poverty by attacking its causes. One law provides welfare programs for the poor. These programs include money, food, and medical care. A second law provides educational programs designed to give poor people the knowledge and skills they need to support themselves. A third law provides job opportunities.

Can we reduce poverty and homelessness in our country? In the world? That is the challenge for your future.

READING REVIEW

1. Why is *poverty* a relative term?
2. How does the United States government measure poverty?
3. Describe the kind of severe poverty often found in developing nations.

Critical Thinking

4. **Recognizing Cause and Effect** (see page 35) Discuss the causes and effects of poverty in our society. Why does poverty affect all of us, even if we are not poor?

READING 6

Global Interdependence

Believe it or not, what you did today made a difference in many people's lives. Some of those people are familiar to you. Others are people you have never met. Some live close to you. Others live in different places on our planet. All the people who live on our planet are **interdependent.** In other words, all of us are connected with each other in many ways, even if we don't realize it. Your actions make an impact on others, just as their actions make an impact on you.

Some of your actions today made a positive difference in other people's lives. Did you smile at someone today? That person probably felt better and smiled at another person. One smile can make a positive difference in many people's day. Were you rude or thoughtless with someone? That sort of action also has a way of spreading to many others. Sometimes, it is hard to believe that each person can have such a powerful impact on so many others.

The way you spend your money also affects other people. Everything you bought today helped to keep several people employed. If you bought a radio and a headset, you contributed to the paycheck of people who live in the different parts of the world where all the parts are made and assembled. You also helped to make it possible for people to be employed where you shopped. Those people, in turn, are better able to buy things they need and want for themselves and their families.

Likewise, goods made in the United States and sold overseas bring money into our country. When we make products that people around the world want to buy, their purchases help make it possible for us to enjoy our high standard of living. Of

Two symbols remind us that our world is increasingly interdependent—the UN flag (top) and the sculpture "Let Us Beat Swords into Ploughshares," a gift from the Soviet Union to the UN.

course, if our work is careless and our products fall apart, people will not want them. The quality of work we do in this country affects many people here and in other countries.

Have your ever made a contribution to Unicef or another worldwide relief effort? If you did, your thoughtfulness and your money helped people you may never meet. The lives of those people and their families and communities were changed because of your kindness.

Some of the things you did today might have harmed other people, although you did not know it. For example, if you took a 15-minute shower, you probably used about 105 gallons of clean drinking water. That's 105 gallons that other people in dry areas of our country (and our world) will not be able to drink. Cleanliness is important, but a 15-minute shower is excessive! If you washed the family car or watered the lawn, you used even more water!

"So what?" you might say. "Our planet is covered with water. Why do a few gallons matter?" It's true that most of the Earth's surface is covered with water. Yet less than 3 percent of that water is fit to drink. When we waste pure water, we waste a precious resource that is in very limited supply in many parts of the world. Our thoughtless waste of good water robs others of a chance to use it.

When you unwrapped the things you bought today, what did you do with the wrappings and containers? If you threw them onto the ground, you contributed to our country's growing problem of litter. If you threw them in the trash, you may have contributed to our nation's problem of waste disposal.

The last time you bought fast food, did you ask for paper plates and containers, instead of styrofoam and plastic? Paper will eventually decay and become part of the natural composition of our planet. The plastic you throw away today, however, will still be around hundreds of years from now. Your children and grandchildren will probably have to pay taxes to maintain the garbage dumps where all the trash is kept. What you do today affects people who are alive today, as well as entire generations of people who are not born yet.

Do you take care of the environment? Do you help keep our streams and waterways fresh and clean? Do you buy products from companies that take care of our environment? Do you avoid buying things from companies that are careless about polluting our water, air, and soil?

Futurists want people to enjoy the resources of our planet today and for many years into the future. They are also aware that everyone on this planet is interdependent. We are all connected. What each of us does today will have an impact on our world and its people, today and in the years to come.

READING REVIEW

1. What does interdependent mean?
2. Describe something you did today that made a positive impact on other people.
3. Describe one action you took today that might have had a negative effect on someone else.

Critical Thinking

4. **Creating Good Questions** (see page 20) Create three good questions you could ask your family about the impact of their everyday actions on our environment.

Challenge for Your Future: Eliminating Hunger

Imagine that it is the last period before lunch or your last class of the day. You keep glancing at the clock thinking, "I wish this class would end. I'm *starving!*" For most of us, such temporary "starvation" is remedied easily by a trip to the cafeteria, to the corner restaurant, or by opening the refrigerator as soon as we get home. For more than 1 billion of the world's people, however, hunger never goes away.

Famine-relief efforts worldwide have done much to relieve the suffering of the world's starving people. Yet more needs to be done by each of us to end this problem.

The hunger experienced by hundreds of millions of the Earth's people is an all-consuming, constantly weakening, and painful experience. Hunger keeps people from doing productive work and from thinking clearly. It permanently damages the body and mind. Undernourished people are more susceptible to infection and other illnesses. If hunger persists long enough, it kills.

Consider some staggering statistics: Every year between 13 and 20 million people die as a result of starvation, malnutrition, and hunger-related diseases. One in four children in developing countries will die before the age of 5 from diseases related to hunger.

There are basically two kinds of hunger—famine and chronic, persistent hunger. During a famine, there is a widespread lack of access to food as a result of factors such as drought, flood, or war. Many people die from starvation. A famine generally receives a great deal of media attention. In recent years, dramatic film footage of the ordeal of Ethiopians has often been a part of the nightly news. Despite the great amount of attention given to famines, however, only about 10 percent of the world's hungry people are affected by them.

Chronic, persistent hunger affects 90 percent of the world's hungry people. Chronic hunger is a slow killer. Think about the effects of constant hunger on the human body. Over a period of time, a chronically hungry person eats fewer calories and less protein than the body needs. Finally, the person is too weak to resist diseases or infections, to work productively, or to think clearly. Lack of protein shortens life expectancy and stunts physical and mental growth in children.

Despite efforts to end hunger, such as this soup kitchen, many people in the United States still go without proper nutrition. What solutions might you propose to help end hunger?

A widely accepted way of measuring the existence of hunger in the world is by the **infant mortality rate (IMR).** The IMR measures the number of infants per 1,000 live births who die before they are one year old. A high IMR indicates that pregnant women are unhealthy and infants are poorly fed. Hunger is said to exist as a chronic, persistent condition when the IMR of a nation is greater than 50. About 73 nations have IMRs over 50!

Most chronically hungry people live in developing countries. This is true for a number of reasons. First, hungry people are poor people. They cannot afford the seeds, tools, irrigation methods, storage, and transportation necessary to end their own hunger. Second, many hungry people are landless. They have no opportunity to grow their own food or to make enough money in other ways to feed themselves. Third, the population of many developing nations has grown faster than the food supply. There simply isn't enough food. Fourth, many developing nations are deeply in debt to developed nations. To try to reduce this debt, much of the best agricultural land is used to grow cash crops for exports. Fifth, the much overused soil has been robbed of its fertility, and crops will no longer grow on it.

Many of us think of hunger as a problem only in other parts of the world. Today, however, it is estimated that as many as 5 million children in the United States suffer from hunger for some period of time each month. One measure of this problem is the infant mortality rate in our nation. We have only the 29th lowest IMR in the world, behind almost every other developed nation.

In the 1970s hunger in America was nearly eliminated because of huge govern-ment programs, such as food stamps and school breakfasts and lunches. In 1981 the government cut back drastically on these and other nutritional programs. Signs of hunger in America reappeared almost immediately. Soup kitchens and food pantries have done a heroic job trying to feed hungry Americans. But they cannot begin to meet the urgent demand for food.

Hunger is one of the leading problems facing the world today. What can be done about this crisis? The conclusions of numerous experts on world hunger and economic development are far-reaching. Developing countries must have assistance in education, health care, highways, harbors, storage facilities, marketing, and distribution systems. Assistance in agriculture and industry is just not enough. Short-term food aid alone cannot solve the problem.

Hunger is a global problem, and it requires global solutions. Most experts believe that the world has the necessary resources, technology, and know-how to end hunger on our planet in this century. The world's future leaders must learn to apply this knowledge to end hunger.

READING REVIEW

1. Why is hunger a problem?
2. How is a famine different from chronic, persistent hunger?
3. Where do most hungry people live?
4. What can be done to end hunger?

Critical Thinking

5. **Expressing Problems Clearly** (see page 12) Why does the problem of hunger exist in developing nations? In the United States?

Decision Wheel: What To Do About World Hunger

"Reading 7: Challenge for Your Future: Eliminating Hunger" showed us that we must work together to eliminate world hunger. Some people tend to ignore this problem because they do not believe that individuals can help end this enormous, worldwide, problem. In this exercise, you will make use of a decision wheel to see how individual decisions *can* make a difference in the world.

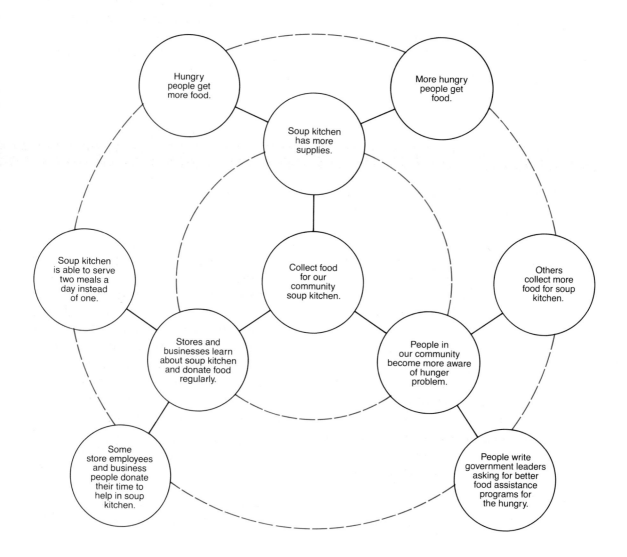

Every decision you make has an impact upon other events or factors. Picture what happens when you drop a rock into a calm pond. As the rock hits the water there is a splash. Then the displaced water flows outward from the point where the rock entered the pond. It spreads in gradually diminishing ripples and reaches across the pond's surface. In a similar way, the effects of your decisions are far-reaching.

Study the decision wheel on this page. The center ring describes a decision a young person made to help eliminate hunger—"collect food for our community's soup kitchen." The first row of rings indicates several possible direct ef-fects of this decision. The second row of rings indicates effects of the central decision based on factors in the first row of rings. In other words, the effects of the decision ripple outward from the center.

Use Handout 10-G to make your own decision wheel. First, make a decision regarding a way in which you could help eliminate hunger. Write your decision in the center ring. In the first row of rings, write several possible direct effects of your decision. In the second row of rings, write the effects of your decision based on factors in the first row of rings. How does the completed wheel help you forecast the possible effects of your decision?

Challenge for Your Future: Making the World More Secure

In the 1950s and 1960s school children practiced air-raid drills and families built bomb shelters or stocked their cellars with food and water. The fear of Word War III threatened personal as well as national security. Fortunately, there was no war between the superpowers—the United States and the former Soviet Union. Air-raid drills are seldom, if ever, practiced today.

Is the world more secure today than it used to be? How can we measure security? First, we must have a working definition of the term. We define **security** as freedom from danger, fear, or anxiety. We can then consider security from personal, social, national, and global points of view.

Studies indicate that individual security has worsened in recent times. Statistics show that between 1989 and 1993 violent crime increased by 17 percent in the United States. In 1993, one violent crime occurred every 16 seconds. One murder occurred every 21 minutes, and one robbery every 48 seconds. About 14 million arrests were made in 1993 alone. Between 1980 and 1992 prison populations nearly tripled. And some experts believe that these trends are likely to continue. Officials believe that much of the increased crime resulted from drug abuse.

Regardless of the cause, many Americans do not feel safe on the streets of their

In recent years crime has become an increasingly serious problem in the United States.

own communities. Many crimes are unsolved. Frustrated citizens have organized many kinds of groups to fight crime. The controversy over handgun control points out that many Americans are arming themselves for protection. Increased sales of home-security systems and attack dogs are other indications that Americans feel unsafe.

On a larger scale, the security of society is sometimes threatened by terrorism.

Bombings, assassinations, and the taking of hostages have occurred in many parts of the world. *Terrorism* is the use of violence to achieve political goals. It instills fear in people because they never know when they might be hurt, captured, or even killed. Terrorism isolates people because they become afraid to travel.

For more than 40 years, the United States considered the Soviet Union the greatest threat to our national security. But the last years of the 1980s saw an end to the cold war, and the arms race between the superpowers was slowed. Relations between the United States and the Soviet Union were better than they had been since the end of World War II.

Other events of the late 1980s further strengthened national security. The Berlin Wall, which stood as a stark reminder of the iron curtain existing between East and West, began to be torn down. Eastern Europeans experienced new freedoms. Dictators tumbled as nations demanded democracy. Communist nations started to experiment with free-market economies.

It seems that some nations have come to the realization that war is a wasteful way of solving problems. The desire for economic cooperation seems to be becoming stronger than the desire for military superiority. A nation that is secure can allow resources to be used for purposes other than weapons.

Still, the possibility of nuclear war continues to threaten our global security. Long-time nuclear powers—the United States, the former Soviet Union, Great Britain, France, and China—have been joined by India, Pakistan, and Israel. Algeria, Iran, Iraq, Libya, North Korea, and Syria may all be working to obtain nuclear weapons. With nuclear weapons in the hands of developing nations, nuclear war between lesser powers may become a new threat. Chemical and biological weapons are also a threat and are the subject of international negotiation.

Let's consider the benefits of security, beginning with the global point of view. When our planet is secure, its nations are free to pursue solutions to critical global problems, such as eliminating world hunger. When our nation is secure, it can devote its strength and finances to exploring outer space and expanding the economy. Likewise, it is free to spend its energies on projects like improving education and saving the environment. When individuals are secure, they can use their talents to find cures for diseases and discover new sources of energy for the future.

The challenge of making the world more secure, like many other issues we have studied, begins with individuals. How can you make the world more secure? There are several ways. You can learn to esteem, or respect, people in other cultures. One way to accomplish this is by gaining a better appreciation of other cultures. Study their histories, religious traditions, arts, literature, and economic systems.

You might also wish to attend or help organize international arts festivals in your community. You can add to the security of society by becoming active in community programs, such as Neighborhood Watch, which is aimed at reporting and preventing crime. Each person can contribute to making individuals, societies, nations, and our entire planet secure.

READING REVIEW

1. How are Americans coping with a lack of security in their own society?
2. How has our national security changed recently?
3. How is planetary security still threatened today?

Critical Thinking

4. **Drawing Conclusions** (see page 42) If the nations of the world no longer need to spend vast amounts of their finances on weapons, how might the global community be able to help all of the Earth's people?

The Delphi Technique: What To Do About Global Security

The **Delphi technique** is an effective method of gathering and analyzing information to make projections about a specific topic by exchanging questions and answers among experts in the field. Here is how it works: Questionnaires are sent to a group of experts. The experts send back their answers, which are then given to another group of experts and also fed into a computer. More questions, based on the analyses of the second group of experts and the computer, are then sent back to the original group of experts.

The experts then comment on the results and new questions. The process continues in this way until there is enough information to make projections.

Now let's use the Delphi technique to study the challenge of global security in the future. You will play the role of experts on international security. Divide your class into groups of four or five students. Each group should use information from "Reading 8: Challenge for Your Future: Making the World More Secure" and its general knowledge about global security to come up with five good, open-ended questions. Open-ended questions cannot be answered with a simple "yes" or "no." They require thought and analysis. Here are some examples:

1. How can the world become free from the threat of international terrorism?
2. How should the United States change the amount of money it spends on defense now that the threat of war between the United States and the Soviet Union seems to be decreasing?

When your group has written its questions, pair up with another group, which has also written a set of five questions. Exchange your questions with the other group. Then meet with your group to discuss possible answers to the questions you've been given. Send your written answers back to the group that wrote the questions. That group will also send back their answers to your questions.

Now each group should generate five more open-ended questions based on the answers to its first questions. Exchange the new questions with the group you were paired with earlier.

Again discuss possible answers with your group and write down the answers you agree upon. Return your group's answers to the group that created the questions. This process should be repeated several times. At the end of the experiment, discuss the following questions:

1. What have you learned from each other about global security?
2. What were the most important questions asked? Why were they important?
3. Why is it important to create as many good questions as possible when you are facing a problem or challenge?
4. What can you and your group do with your findings to make a positive difference in global security?

Challenge for Your Future: Fighting Drug Abuse

What is our nation's number-one problem? More than 70 percent of Americans identify drugs as the nation's toughest challenge for the 1990s.

The following facts support this conclusion: America is the world's largest market for illegal drugs. Millions of Americans are addicted to some form of drugs, on which they spend $100 billion a year. One in three American families is affected by drug abuse. Drug abusers frequently begin to use drugs at 12 years of age.

If you have not already encountered the drug problem, you will. One expert predicts that almost every American between the ages of 12 and 14 will be called upon to make a decision about drugs and alcohol! In a recent poll, more than 4 million students between the ages of 13 and 17 reported that they had been offered illegal drugs in the previous 30 days. In another survey of 200,000 junior and senior high school students, more than 45 percent said that they drank alcohol.

Advertising campaigns such as this one help people become aware of the dangers of using drugs.

We cannot ignore the problem. But drug and alcohol abuse are so prevalent in our society that we sometimes tend to ignore the consequences. Here are the facts about the effects of some common drugs. Smoking marijuana can impair memory and reduce the ability to concentrate. Hallucinogens, such as PCP, produce distorted images that affect perception. Sedatives, such as tranquilizers, can cause unconsciousness and death. Stimulants, such as amphetamines, can cause malnutrition, sleeplessness, depression, and brain damage. Cocaine, the most widely abused stimulant, can kill by causing suffocation, heart attack, or stroke. In addition to the effects of the drugs themselves, addicts also risk contracting AIDS and other diseases from using unsterile needles.

Alcohol and tobacco are not illegal, but they are dangerous drugs. The short-term "high" produced by alcohol causes dizziness, dulling of the senses, and loss of coordination. These conditions cause thousands of automobile accidents each year. Long-term abuse of alcohol damages the liver, heart, and brain. Tobacco is a major cause of respiratory problems, including lung cancer. Alcohol and tobacco can become addictive.

We have seen what drug abuse does to a person's mind and body. But what about the other consequences? How does drug abuse affect a person's life? A drug addict's entire life may center around the need to obtain and take a certain drug. This need overshadows everything else—eating, personal health, family life, friendships,

Many serious automobile accidents result from drunken driving or drug abuse. What might you do to help solve this problem?

school, and career. Young addicts lie to their parents and often steal from them to buy drugs. Drug addicts are irritable and have abrupt changes in mood, so they tend to lose friends. School, social events, and sports activities—the center of life for most teenagers—become unimportant to a drug addict.

Drug abuse is not an individual problem. It takes a toll on our whole society. The United States has spent more than $75 billion fighting drug abuse. Over 1 million people were arrested in 1993 for drug-abuse violations. Drug abuse overburdens our court system and overcrowds our prisons. We cannot even estimate the loss of productivity in the workplace because of drug abuse. Perhaps the greatest tragedy of drug abuse is the waste of talent, brainpower, and leadership in our country.

America is taking a stand against drugs. Our government is working with the leaders of other nations to stop the flow of drugs into our country. Americans are waging war on drugs in their neighborhoods. In New York City, for example, teens have begun a program to "take back the parks." They have planned such activities as concerts and movies to attract crowds of people into the parks at night, thus driving away drug dealers. Drug-prevention programs have been started in our schools as early as the primary grades.

If we are to achieve a drug-free society, however, every individual must make a commitment to fight drug abuse. That means avoiding abuse of all drugs. Become informed about the consequences of drug abuse and share this information. Studies show that people who understand the danger of drugs are less likely to use them. Report illegal drug activities to the proper authorities. You can play a part in beating back drugs. The challenge is great, but ordinary individuals can accomplish extraordinary things.

READING REVIEW

1. Why are drugs America's number-one problem?
2. How does drug addiction affect a person's relationships and values?
3. How does drug abuse affect American society?
4. How can young people help fight drug abuse?

Critical Thinking

5. **Predicting Consequences** (see page 36) What might happen to American society if the rate of drug abuse continues to climb?

EXPERIMENT 10-I

Cross-Impact Matrix: Making Personal Decisions About Drug Abuse

One method of considering the effects of decisions is called the **cross-impact matrix,** or CIM. This method analyzes the impact, or effect, of a certain factor upon a specific area of consequence. The simplest kind of CIM is a table showing horizontal (across) rows and vertical (up and down) columns. At the beginning of each horizontal row, one of a group of related factors is listed. Along the top of each column, the specific areas of consequences are listed. Each factor in a row is matched with each area of consequence listed in a column, one at a time. The matching of factors and areas of consequence raises the question: What impact does one factor have on one area of consequence?

Below you will find an example of a CIM. This CIM is about making personal decisions regarding drug abuse. The rows list several different drugs. The columns list the specific areas of consequence. Let's move from left to right along the row labeled "tobacco." We can now begin to analyze the impact (effect) of tobacco on each area of consequence.

Start with square 1. Here the factor "tobacco" is matched with the area of conse-

	Relations with My Parents		Peer Relationships		My Body		My Mind		Financial Situation		My Education	
Tobacco	Ⓖ 1 S My parents do not approve of using tobacco.		Ⓖ 2 S My peers think using tobacco is obnoxious.		Ⓖ 3 S Cardiovascular and respiratory problems are caused by smoking tobacco.		G 4 Ⓢ Tobacco is not known to be a mind-altering drug.		G 5 S		G 6 S	
Alcohol	G 7 S		G 8 S		G 9 S		G 10 S		G 11 S		G 12 S	
Marijuana	G 13 S		G 14 S		G 15 S		G 16 S		G 17 S		G 18 S	
PCP	G 19 S		G 20 S		G 21 S		G 22 S		G 23 S		G 24 S	
Cocaine	G 25 S		G 26 S		G 27 S		G 28 S		G 29 S		G 30 S	
Heroin	G 31 S		G 32 S		G 33 S		G 34 S		G 35 S		G 36 S	

quence "relations with my parents." What is the consequence of using tobacco on your relations with your parents? We could either answer that the impact on the relationship would be great or small, depending on how your family feels about using tobacco. Therefore, either the "G" or the "S" could be circled. We have circled the "G" in the example. A brief explanation has been written in the block.

Now move to square 2. Here the factor "tobacco" is matched with the area of consequence "peer relationships." What impact does using tobacco have on your peer relationships? Again, you could answer that the consequences of using tobacco would be either great or small, depending on how your peers feel about using tobacco. Therefore, either the "G" or the "S" could be circled. Using tobacco would have either a great or a small impact on peer relationships. The "G" has been circled in the example. A brief explanation has been written in the block.

Now move to square 3. What would the consequence of using tobacco be on your body? Because it is known that the nicotine in tobacco is addictive and that smoking causes many health problems, including lung cancer, the impact of smoking on your body would be great. Therefore, the "G" has been circled and a brief explanation written in the box.

In square 4 you analyze the consequence of smoking tobacco on your mind. Because tobacco is not known to be a mind-altering drug, its effect on the mind is small. In square 4 the "S" has been circled and an explanation given. The entire cross-impact matrix may be completed in this way.

Using Handout 10-I, finish this matrix. Match each factor with each specific area of consequence. Indicate whether the impact of each factor on each area of consequence is great or small by circling the "G" or "S" in the block. Then write a short explanation for each of your answers in the block.

Challenge for Your Future: Esteeming Yourself and Others

Psychologists note that every one of us is unique, each with different traits and characteristics. Unfortunately, as you grow up, especially during your teenage years, you tend to lose sight of your unique self. You often become unsure of yourself and look to other people or things for fulfillment. But in our fast-paced, impersonal, techno-logically advanced world, it is important to hold both yourself and others in high **esteem.**

There are many ways to esteem yourself. One way is by saying "no" to substances that are harmful to your body and your mind. Such substances as tobacco, alcohol, and other drugs are easier to avoid when you esteem yourself. People who have a good self-image have been found to be highly resistant to drug and alcohol abuse. The picture they have of themselves does not include using harmful substances. Self-esteem helps people stick with this positive inner vision of themselves.

Esteeming yourself means avoiding eating too many unhealthy foods. Junk foods may have their place in our society, but "living on them" is certainly not a way to esteem your body. Learn to enjoy healthful food choices.

Saying "yes" to things that make your life more fulfilling and more successful is also part of esteeming yourself. If you want a rewarding future, then value your education, stay in school, and achieve the best grades possible.

What things do you like about yourself? Are you friendly? Smart? Attractive? Athletic? Do you have the ability to empathize with others? Make a list of at least 20 things you like about yourself. This list will help raise your self-esteem by forcing you to think about all the likable things about yourself. If you have trouble thinking of 20 items, ask some of your good friends to give you suggestions. What are some of the things they esteem about you? Remind yourself of the list when you are having bad feelings about yourself or your self-worth.

Do you think that you are too short or that your nose is too big? Learn to accept the aspects of yourself that you are not ideal. Nobody is perfect. Self-acceptance is a key factor in esteeming yourself. Low self-esteem comes from self-criticism and a lack of self-acceptance. This often results from trying to adhere to unrealistic standards of behavior. Don't let pressure from your peers or messages from the media affect your self-esteem. Don't depend on others for acceptance. If someone doesn't seem friendly, don't let that lower your self-esteem. Remember that the unfriendliness is more of a statement about the other person than about you. Acknowledge your

Establishing friendships is a key to having a good self-image.

imperfections; don't ignore them. But focus on your good points!

Esteeming yourself means being comfortable with yourself at this point in your life. Set goals for improving yourself, but be sure the goals are realistic. Set both short-term and long-term goals. Reaching your short-term goals helps you see progress toward your long-term goals. Success in achieving short-term goals can help raise your self-esteem.

Working toward better physical and mental health are also part of esteeming yourself. Engage in a fitness program. Take part in sports activities or in aerobic exercise, such as brisk walking, running, or swimming. Discover what kind of exercise you like and then stick with it. Making fitness a prime focus of your life will reap many benefits. You will have more energy, better circulation, better muscle tone, more strength, and you will have greater relief from stress.

Taking care of your mental well-being includes coping with emotions such as jealousy, hate, fear, and anxiety. Learn to deal with the stressful things in your life. Find a hobby you like and take time out from your schedule to enjoy it. Listen to music or relaxation tapes. Try yoga or other meditation-type activities.

Accepting responsibility is also part of esteeming yourself. Be personally responsible for what you say and do. Admit mistakes but don't dwell on them. Try to do a little better the next time. Esteem yourself by keeping commitments you make. If you say you will do something, do it. If you say you will be somewhere, be there. Honor commitments even when it is inconvenient or when something you would rather do comes along.

Establish good, close friendships with a few special people whom you know you can count on when the going gets tough, and who can likewise count on you. Establish these friendships with people who share or respect your values, ideas, and goals. Esteem yourself and others by being a good listener. Give encouragement to others and help them when they need you. Esteeming others, however, does not mean taking on another person's problems. Nor does it mean covering up or making excuses for friends with problems. Don't ignore or overlook other people's problems. Talk things out and come up with workable solutions.

Esteem others by recognizing and appreciating the beauty in ways of living that are different from your own. Don't judge others or their actions until you know all the facts.

Your commitment to self-esteem and to personal and social responsibility is vital to making a better world for yourself and other people as well. It is also essential to making a better world for all the generations of people who will live on our planet in years to come.

READING REVIEW

1. List three ways to esteem yourself?
2. How can you esteem others?

Critical Thinking

3. **Distinguishing False from Accurate Images** (see page 29) How can a person learn to accept the aspects of himself or herself that are both likable and not so likable? How does this affect a person's self-esteem

Making a Commitment to Personal and Social Responsibility

Commitments are like New Year's resolutions—easy to make, easy to break. But commitments to personal and social responsibility are too important to be taken lightly. Keeping a commitment, such as sticking to a diet, is easier if you have a support system. Join a friend or a group with a similar commitment. That way you can support and encourage one another when the going gets rough. In this experiment you will discover how working in S-Teams (the "S" stands for support) affects your commitment to personal and social responsibility.

First, determine three personal commitments in support of your own self-esteem or the esteem of others. Each commitment must be a specific action or set of actions that you are willing to do.

Here are some examples:

1. I will exercise for at least 30 minutes each day.

2. I will write a letter to my parents telling them how much I admire them and how much they mean to me.
3. I will help a friend who is failing a class study for an important test.

Set deadlines for accomplishing the commitments. Determine a way for deciding whether the goals stated in the commitments have been met.

Next, form an S-Team with one or two other students. Discuss each team member's list of commitments. Decide which of your individual commitments you want to dedicate yourselves to as a team. Set up a time frame in which your team's goals are to be accomplished. Then determine a way of measuring your team's progress.

Your team may wish to concentrate on projects to make your school or community a better place. Ask for your teacher's approval before undertaking this sort of project. Report the progress of your team to the class in one week.

Challenge for Your Future: Protecting Our Planet

Family responsibilities, such as cleaning your room, carrying out the trash, or helping with yard work help make your home a healthy environment. But what about our planet? What are we doing to make the

Earth a decent and beautiful place to live for ourselves and for future generations?

Most people are aware that we are making demands on our planet that may harm it. They are also aware that we must make changes to improve our planet. The air we breathe is becoming more and more impure. Lakes, rivers, and oceans are being polluted. The land is being deforested. These problems are interrelated because they affect the Earth's ecosystem.

The burning of fossil fuels—oil, natural gas, and coal—by homes, businesses, and automobiles releases nearly 5 billion tons of carbon dioxide into the atmosphere each year. In addition to creating unhealthy air to breathe, the carbon dioxide traps heat in the Earth's atmosphere causing the planet to warm.

This global warming is known as the **greenhouse effect.** A number of experts have predicted that by 2050 the average temperature of the Earth could rise between 3 and 8 degrees. This rise in temperature would cause great climatic changes throughout the Earth. It might also cause the level of the oceans to rise because the polar icecaps will begin to melt.

The Earth's ozone layer, which protects us from the Sun's deadly ultraviolet rays, is affected by the release of chlorofluorocarbons (CFCs) into the air. This group of chemicals is used in aerosol sprays, air conditioners, foam plastic products, and in the manufacture of microchips.

More than 3,000 gases, including sulfur dioxide, are released into the atmosphere by factories, power stations, and automobiles. When these chemicals combine with water vapor, they create **acid rain.** What are the results? Acid rain damages buildings, bridges, and statues. It poisons soil, destroys forests and crops, and kills fish and other aquatic life by polluting lakes, rivers, and streams.

The goal of urban planners is to make our cities pleasant and enjoyable places to live and work. Urban planners also try to solve such problems as pollution from auto emissions and factories.

The Earth's waters are also being fouled with chemicals and organic wastes from homes, farms, and industries. Untreated sewage is dumped into rivers and lakes, resulting in a decrease of oxygen in the water. Chemicals, such as nitrites used in artificial fertilizers by farmers, are making their way into water supplies through run-off. In this way, our water is being polluted by the chemicals we put on the land. Another threat to our waters are oil spills from tankers and off-shore wells that foul waters and beaches, killing birds and marine life.

In addition to the air and water in our ecosystem, the Earth's land surface is also being polluted. Landfills and dumps are overflowing with trash, and space for more dumps is running out. Toxic wastes from industry and unsafe dump sites are seeping into the soil. Deforestation is taking place at an alarming rate, particularly in developing nations. This often results in soil erosion. Because trees take carbon dioxide from the air, depletion of forests also adds to the greenhouse effect.

Every inhabitant of the Earth is responsible for the care of our fragile environment. Global warming, destruction of the ozone layer, acid rain, and pollution of the air and the oceans are all problems that ignore national boundaries. Therefore, they need to be addressed by the global community. Representatives of 46 nations, including the United States, have agreed to cut production of CFCs in half by 1999. This is a start, but international cooperation must continue. Developed nations must find ways of encouraging developing nations to preserve their environments without damaging their economies.

Government and industry must also work together to solve environmental problems. Providing money for research to find replacements for CFCs and other dangerous chemicals is one way to help. Tax breaks and other incentives could also be made available to encourage industries to recycle their waste materials.

What can you do to protect our planet? First, take responsibility for simple things like recycling glass and plastic containers, aluminum cans, and newspapers. These actions really make a difference in the amount of garbage a household produces. Imagine the effect if everyone in our nation undertook this easy task!

You might also wish to work with others to convince industry and government to accept their environmental responsibilities. You can write letters to industries that are guilty of environmental pollution and to state and federal legislators. Joining environmental organizations gives individuals a collective voice in dealing with government and industry. Take your personal and social responsibilities seriously. Remember, our planet is the only home we have!

READING REVIEW

1. Why is it important to protect our planet?
2. What environmental problems plague the air and the atmosphere?
3. How are the Earth's waters being polluted?
4. Why is deforestation a problem?
5. Who is responsible for the environment?

Critical Thinking

6. **Recognizing Cause and Effect** (see page 35) How might the environment of the United States be affected if car pooling and four-day work weeks were made mandatory?

Earth S-Teams: What To Do About Cleaning Up Our Environment

In "Experiment 10-J: Making a Commitment to Personal and Social Responsibility," you formed S-Teams to support one another in making and keeping commitments. Now you will form S-Teams for a different purpose. You have probably heard the old adage, "two heads are better than one." In this experiment, you will "put your heads together" to come up with a plan for cleaning up our environment.

Form a new S-Team with one or two other students. Brainstorm the following questions with the members of your team:

1. What can we do, individually and as a team, to make a positive difference in cleaning up the environment?
Example: Write to fast-food companies and ask them to stop using foam plastic products to package their foods.

2. What can we do to enlist the active participation of family, friends, and community in our team's work?
Example: Make copies of the letter asking fast-food chains to stop using foam plastic packaging. Ask friends and family members to sign the letters. Get permission to set up a table in a local shopping center and ask people in your community to sign the letters. Collect the letters and mail them to fast-food companies.

Dedicate your team to doing just one thing, however large or small the action or project may be. Set up a time frame in which your team's work will be accomplished. Determine how you will measure your progress. Report your progress to the class in one week. If possible use some form of visual aid to present information.

Challenge for Your Future: Preparing for the World of Work

What do you want to be when you grow up? You probably have been asked that question many times. You probably have changed your answer many times, too. The world of work is changing rapidly. Some jobs that were important 20 years ago are no longer necessary.

Robots and computers have replaced many factory workers and office workers. In the book *American Renaissance: Our Life at the Turn of the Century,* author Marvin Cetron predicts that one half of the manufacturing jobs in the United States will have disappeared by the year 2000. On

Becoming skilled at using highly technical equipment is one way to prepare for the work challenges of the future.

the other hand, whole new occupations will be created to keep up with our changing technology.

How can you prepare yourself to enter the work force when the job market is so uncertain? What kinds of jobs will be available in the twenty-first century? Futurists have made several predictions. For exam- ple, Cetron believes that by the year 2000, one in four Americans will work in hospi- tality industries. These are such places as restaurants, hotels, resorts, and travel agencies. What does this prediction reveal about the values of our society? Why might hospitality industries become even more important in the future?

Experts predict that many new jobs in the future will be created in personal service industries, such as financial planning.

Other "best bets" for future careers include the following: workers who operate, program, or repair computers; workers who design or repair robots; and workers who deal with hazardous wastes in our environment. Futurists foresee a continuing demand for teachers, accountants, nurses, and paramedics. Our nation's aging population will require social workers and many others trained to care for the needs of the elderly.

Futurists also predict a growing demand for personal services. Today, many businesses perform services such as mowing lawns, shopping, and taking care of household chores for working couples. What kinds of services might these businesses provide in the next century? Entrepreneurs will look for opportunities to expand or create new businesses to meet the changing needs of society in the future.

Think about the careers discussed above. Do they have anything in common? What kind of education or training and skills do they require. Thinking skills, reasoning ability, creativity, and dedication will be important in the work-world of the future. Add to these qualities the flexibility to retrain or change jobs if necessary, and you will have a formula for future success.

READING REVIEW

1. Why are some jobs that were important in the past no longer necessary?
2. What kinds of careers do futurists predict will be commonly available in the twenty-first century?
3. How can you best prepare for a future career?

Critical Thinking

4. **Demonstrating Reasoned Judgment** (see page 40) Imagine that you are an employer in the twenty-first century. What qualities would you look for in the people you hire? Explain.

EXPERIMENT 10-L

Decision Tree: Thinking About Life Choices

The readings in this unit have given you some new ideas about life choices for the future. You have come to realize that you can have power over your own future. You know that you have to plan the future you want. Otherwise, your future will be a complete surprise. Happy surprises are always nice, but who wants the other kind?

No one can control totally the experiences and situations of an entire lifetime. Events, situations, and other people will have a great influence on you, no matter how much you plan for the future. But there are ways you can have a firmer hold on future events. Considering the possible results of your decisions is one way to plan for the future.

In this experiment you will be using the **decision-tree** method to explore your life choices. Think for a minute or two about your future career. What decisions will you need to make in the near future to plan for that career? For example, what kind of education or training will you need? How can you help with expenses?

Now turn to the decision tree printed on Handout 10-L. Think of a question that is related to your life choices for the future. For example, should you attend a college near your home? Do you need to get a part-time job to help with expenses? Write your question on the line that appears on the far left of the decision tree under Question 1.

Answer your question with "yes." What would happen if you followed the "yes" answer? Then answer your question with "no." What would happen if you followed the "no" answer? Continue this process as far in the decision tree as you can.

If you complete the decision tree thoroughly, it should be easy for you to decide the best actions and results. Which answer to the first question do you think is better, "yes" or "no"? Why? Explain how the decision-tree method can help you to plan for your future career.

Creating the Future You Want

What would you like your future to be? Do you ever daydream about what the future might bring?

One thing is certain. The future will come whether you are ready for it or not. You will be living the rest of your life in the future. What can you do today to begin preparing for the best possible future? Every day brings you new possibilities. When you get out of bed in the morning, think to yourself, "I am going to make the most of this day because it will never come again. The opportunities I will have today cannot be repeated."

When you are older and out on your own, do you want other people to respect you for your fine work and creative ideas? Would you like to think of yourself as successful? We know that the greatest success is earned by people who work hard to be the best they are capable of being. These people have high expectations of themselves. They know that it is not enough to do work that is just good enough to barely get by. Successful people set goals for themselves and they dedicate all of their efforts to reaching those goals.

When we think about successful people, we often think of those who win in competitions. But the really successful people in life know the value of cooperating with others. In competitive sports, winning is impossible without teamwork. Even individual athletes, such as golfers, swimmers, and gymnasts, cannot compete successfully without a top-notch supporting team of coaches and trainers. It is important to include people in your plans for success. Choose people who are as committed to your success as they are to their own.

The best time to start creating the future you want is right now. You are capable of

Don't Be Afraid To Fail*

You've failed
many times,
although you may not
remember.
You fell down
the first time
you tried to walk.
You almost drowned
the first time
you tried to
swim, didn't you?
Did you hit the
ball the first time
you swung a bat?
Heavy hitters,
the ones who hit the
most home runs,
also strike
out a lot.
R. H. Macy
failed several
times before his
store in New York
caught on.
English novelist
John Creasey got
753 rejection slips
before he published
564 books.
Babe Ruth struck out
1,330 times,
but he also hit
714 home runs.
Don't worry about
failure.
Worry about the
chances you miss
when you don't
even try.

© United Technologies Corporation, 1981

*From United Technologies Corporation, *Don't Be Afraid to Fail.* (See Acknowledgements, pages 595–596.)

achieving great things in your lifetime. The greatest successes often come to those who begin training early in life. If you begin today to improve your work in school and your awareness of the world around you, it will be much easier for you to achieve success later in life.

Start today to expect the best of yourself. Set solid, realistic goals for your self-improvement. Give yourself definite deadlines for reaching those goals. Give serious consideration to the sacrifices you will need to make to reach those goals. Then think about how good you will feel about yourself when you finally achieve your goals.

Most importantly, never be afraid to take a chance to achieve a worthy goal. Some of the most successful people actually fail many times on their way to the top. Babe Ruth, one of the most outstanding baseball players of all time, struck out twice for every home run he hit. Babe Ruth knew that real success often depends on taking the chance you will not succeed in everything you do. The most important thing is to give it your very best planning and effort.

Are you ready to begin creating the future you really want for yourself? Don't let another day go by. Start now!

READING REVIEW

1. Why is it important to start right now to do the best work you can do?
2. Why is it a good idea to work with others to achieve success?

Critical Thinking

3. **Predicting Consequences** (see page 36) Describe five possible consequences if you were to begin today to do the very best school work you are capable of doing.

Social Scientists Look at Space Exploration

How do the ways futurists think about a subject compare to the ways other social scientists think? Below you will explore these similarities and differences as you examine a selection about life in space. Read the passage from Isaac Asimov's novel *Foundation and Earth* and then answer the questions that follow under "Comparing the Social Sciences."

"Pelorat looked at the thick crescent of light on the viewscreen and said thoughtfully, 'It was called "moon" in at least one of Earth's languages; "Luna" in another language. Probably many other names too. Imagine the confusion, old chap, on a world with numerous languages—the misunderstandings, the complications, the—'

'Moon?' said Trevize. 'well, that's simple enough . . . I'm looking at it now and wondering.'

'Wondering what, Golan (Trevize)?'

'At the size of it. We tend to ignore satellites, Janov. They're such little things, when they exist at all. This one is different, though. It's a *world*. It has a diameter of about thirty-five hundred kilometers.'

'A world? Surely you wouldn't call that a world. It can't be habitable. Even a thirty-five-hundred-kilometer diameter is too small. It has no atmosphere. I can tell that just looking at it. No clouds. The circular curve is sharp, so is the inner curve that binds the light and dark hemisphere.'

Trevize nodded. 'You're getting to be a seasoned space traveler, Janov. You're right. No air. No water. But that only means the moon's not habitable on its unprotected surface. What about underground?'

'Underground?' said Pelorat doubtfully.

'Yes. Underground. Why not? . . . We know that Trantor was underground. Comporellon has much of its capital city underground. . . . It's a very common state of affairs.'

'But, Golan, in every one of these cases, people were living on a habitable planet. The surface was habitable too, with an atmosphere and with an ocean. Is it possible to live underground when the surface is uninhabitable?'

'Come, Janov, think! Where are we living right now? The *Far Star* is a tiny world that has an uninhabitable surface. There's no air or water on the outside. Yet we live inside in perfect comfort. The Galaxy is full of space stations and space settlements of infinite variety, to say nothing of spaceships. . . . '"

Comparing the Social Sciences

Psychologists study human emotions. If you were a psychologist, would this passage lead you to believe that people in the future will feel and react to things much the way we do? Explain your answer. (*Making Comparisons*)

Sociologists study groups in a society. As a sociologist, what questions would you want to ask Golan Trevize and Janov Pelorat about the society of the future? (*Creating Good Questions*)

Anthropologists study cultures. As an anthropologist reading this passage, do you think that the culture of the future world will be very different from today's world? (*Making Comparisons*)

Geographers study the ways people change the environment. What innovative ways of meeting their needs would you as a geographer note about the people of the future? (*Identifying Alternatives*)

Historians study the past. As a historian, what comparisons might you make between these space travelers and previous voyagers to new, unexplored lands? (*Making Comparisons*)

Political scientists study government and power. What can you, as a political scientist, learn about the government of the future from this passage? (*Determining Relevance*)

Economists study the ways goods are made and distributed. As an economist, what new ways do you think the future world will have of producing and distributing goods? (*Predicting Consequences*)

Traveling through space

GLOSSARY OF TERMS

acid rain   precipitation that is mixed with airborne pollutants (such as sulfur dioxide, nitrogenoxide, and other poisonous chemicals from smokestacks and car exhaust) and that ruins the environment (page 573)

cross-impact matrix (CIM)   a method of understanding the future that examines the impact of one thing in relation to other things (page 544)

decision tree   a method of analyzing the future based on the effects of "yes" and "no" answers to questions about decisions to be made in the present and in the future (page 544)

decision wheel   a method of analyzing the future; it examines the direct and indirect effects of a decision (see page 543)

Delphi method   a method of projecting into the future in which questionnaires are sent to experts in a field, asking their opinions; the replies are sent to other experts for their input and are also fed into a computer for analysis. This information is then sent back to the original experts for additional insight. By repeating this process, accurate projections can be made. (page 544)

esteem   respect and appreciation for oneself and others. Self-esteem means appreciating one's own worth and importance; having the character to be accountable for oneself and to act responsibly toward others. Esteeming others means recognizing and appreciating the beauty in ways of living that are different from your own. (page 569)

Future Shock   a book by Alvin Toffler; the term *future shock* refers to the dizzying feeling that changes are occurring faster than you are able to accept those changes. (page 548)

greenhouse effect   the global warming that is caused by the release of carbon dioxide and other chemicals into the air (page 573)

infant mortality rate (IMR)   a measure of the number of infants per 1,000 live births who die before they reach the age of one (page 559)

interdependent   connected; of or referring to the dependency among people or countries (page 555)

poverty level   the amount of income families need in order to eat adequately without spending more than one third of their income on food (page 554)

projection   a method of predicting the future in which information about a topic is gathered and conclusions based on that information are used to predict likely outcomes (page 543)

scenario   a description of life in the future based on current trends (page 543)

security   freedom from danger, fear, or anxiety (page 561)

telecommuting   a means of working at a computer terminal in one's home rather than commuting back and forth to a workplace (page 551)

trend   the way in which something is going or changing (page 541)

trend analysis   another name for *projection;* (see *projection*) (page 543)

Index

Acknowledgements

Photographs

Photo sources that have been abbreviated are as follows:
SB = Stock Boston
PR = Photo Researchers, Inc.
SM = The Stock Market
WC = Woodfin Camp & Associates
PE = PhotoEdit

Photo positions are indicated as follows:
T = Top
TL = Top Left
TM = Top Middle
TR = Top Right
M = Middle
B = Bottom
BL = Bottom Left
BM = Bottom Middle
BR = Bottom Right
L = Left
R = Right

Front Cover
Earth: Tom Van Sant and Van Warren/courtesy of Stardent Computers. **Background:** Chris Alan Wilton/The Image Bank.

Back Cover
Larry Lawfer

Front Matter
i, ii (starry sky) TSW. **i, ii (earth)** Tom Van Sant and Van Warren/courtesy of Stardent Computers. **ii (moon)** Ed Pritchard/TSW. **vi** *Fox Trot* by Bill Amend, 1989. **vii** MMA, Gift of Christian A. Zabriskie, 1950. **viii** Dennis Simon, artist for National Geographic. **ix** C.O. Rentmeester/Life Magazine. **x** Camera Press London/Globe Photos. **xi** UPI/Bettmann Newsphotos.

Unit 1   Critical Thinking Skills
xii–1 Tony Freeman/PE. **3** Susan Lapides. **4** Jackie Curtis/PR. **5** P.W. Grace/PR. **10** United Features Syndicate, Inc. **13** Freeman/Grishaber/PE. **14** David Gamble/Sipa Press. **15** from *Fox Trot* by Bill Amend 1989. **15 T.** Bob Talbot. **16** David Dempster/Offshoot Stock. **20** NASA. **21** Susan Van Etten. **24** Wally McNamee/WC. **26 T** from *Fox Trot* by Bill Amend 1989. **26 B** Library of Congress. **27** Richter, 1971, The New Yorker magazine. **28** E.R. Degginger/Animals Animals. **29** Bill Nation/Sygma Photo News. **30** Robert Frerck/TSW. **33** Roy Morsch/SM. **35** AP/Wide World Photos. **39** Gerhard Gsheidle/The Image Bank. **42** Frank Siteman/Taurus Photos. **45** Mark Antman/The Image Works. **46** Gerhard Gsheidle/The Image Bank. **47** Bill Nation/Sygma Photo News.

Unit 2   Effective Study Skills
48–49 Tony Freeman/PE. **51** Sepp Seitz/WC **53** Kevin Meade. **55** E. Trina Lipton. **57** J.P. Laffont/Sygma Photo News. **59** J. Berndt/The Picture Cube. **63–64** file photos. **66** Owen Franken/SB. **67** Educational Research Council of America. **70** Fredrik D. Bodin. **73** Peter Menzel. **74** Anna Zuckerman/PE. **81** UPI. **82** Wide World Photos. **83** file photo. **85** Owen Franken/SB. **86** reproduced by permission of The British Library. **89** courtesy University of Georgia Libraries. **91** natural history ms., 1297, The Pierpont Morgan Library. **91/109** Richard Howard. **92** Camerique. **93** U.S. Postal Service. **98** Ron Chapple/FPG. **103** MMA, gift of Christian A. Zabriskie 1950.

Unit 3   Psychology
106–107 Tony Freeman/PE. **111** Elizabeth Crews/SB. **112** Bruce Roberts/PR. **113** George Holton. **115** UFS. **117, 118** Susan Lapides. **119** Lou Jones. **121** Ann Hagen Griffiths/Omni-Photo Communications. **123** Marc Bernheim/WC. **124 B.** I. Ullman/Taurus Photos. **127/143** file photos. **128/133** Escher Foundation, Haags Gemeentemuseum—The Hague. **136** Shackman/Monkmeyer Press. **137** Cole Photography. **139** Norris Taylor/PR **140** Eunice Harris/PR. **145** Superstock. **147** Sportschrome.

Unit 4   Sociology
150–151 Rory Lysaght/Gamma-Liaison. **153** Stacy Pick/SB. **154** Alec Duncan/Taurus Photos. **155** Frank Siteman/Taurus Photos. **157 R** J. Barry O'Rourke/SM. **157 TL** Charles West/SM. **157 BL** Nancy Pierce/PR. **158** Larry Lawfer/courtesy The Genji Restaurant. **159** Philip Bailey/Taurus Photos. **162** Joel Gordon. **163** file photo. **164** SB. **165** Museum of Modern Art, New York/A. Conger Goodyear Fund. **167** Paul S. Conklin. **169** Susan Lapides. **171** Paul S. Conklin. **172** Sybil Shelton/Monkmeyer Press. **174** Ira Kirschenbaum. **176** Fujihara/Monkmeyer Press. **177 B** Eric Kroll/Taurus Photos. **177 T** file photo. **179** Institute of Outdoor Advertising. **181** The Granger Collection. **183 TL** Eva Demjen/SB. **183 TR** Owen Franken/SB. **183 BL** Michael Keller/SM. **183 BR** Peter Southwick/SB. **184** Owen Franken/SB. **186** Peter Southwick/SB. **187** Courtesy of Saturn Corp. **189** Cary Wolinsky/SB. **191** Superstock. **192 L** Bill Gillette/SB. **192 R** Owen Franken/SB. **193** Susan Lapides. **195** David Austen/SB. **196** Lenore Weber/Taurus Photos. **197** Stephen Brown/The Picture Group. **199** Matt Herron.

Unit 5   Anthropology
202–203 Tony Freeman/PE. **205** Craig Aurness/WC. **206** Paolo Koch/PR. **209 (1)** Craig Aurness/WC. **209 (2)** Richard Hutchings/PR. **209 (3)** Sepp Seitz/WC. **209 (4)** Seth Goltzer/SM. **209** Ted Horowitz/The Stock Market. **209 (7)** Sepp Seitz/WC. **209 (8)** Carl Purcell. **210** file photos. **211 TL** SB. **211 TR** The Granger. **211 BL** The Granger Collection. **211 BR** file photo. **213** Gountei Teishu/Tsuneo Tamba Collection. **215** Anthony Edgeworth/SM. **216** file photo. **217** Thomas Hopker/The Image Bank. **219** file photo. **221** Reuters/UPI/Bettmann. **223** J. Berndt/SB. **225** Owen Franken/SB. **226** file photo. **228** Arthur Richmond. **230** Ira Kirschenbaum. **231** Gabe Palmer/The Stock Market. **233** courtesy of the Trustees of The British Museum. **234** Eric A. Roth/The Picture Cube. **240** file photo. **242** Mark Antman. **243** Wide World Photos. **245** file photos. **247** Bill Weems/WC. **248** file photos. **250, 251** file photos. **252 TL** MFA Expedition Fund, courtesy Boston Museum of Fine Arts. **252 TR** Robert Azzi/WC. **252 M** courtesy Boston Museum of Fine Arts, Egyptian Collection. **252 B** The Metropolitan Museum of Art, New York. **253 TL** Erich Lessing/Magnum. **253 TR** Dick Durrance/WC. **253 BL** courtesy The Metropolitan Museum of Art, New York. **253 BR** Marc Bernheim/WC. **254** Harriet Gans/The Image Works. **257, 259** Adam Woolfitt/WC. **261** Dennis Simon, artist for National Geographic. **263** Paolo Koch/PR.

Unit 6   Geography
264–265 Stephen McBrady/PE. **267** Anne Zuckermann/PE. **269** John Flannery/Bruce Coleman Inc. **271** Robert Semeniuk/SM. **280** Steve & Mary Skjold/PE. **287** Taurus Photos. **289** Teuters/Bettmann Newsphotos. **290** Bettmann Archive. **292** Rube Goldberg/King Features Syndicate Inc. **293** Carnegie Library of Pittsburgh. **294** Jim Rudnick/SM. **297 LL** T. Rhodes/Taurus Photos. **299** Ted Horowitz/SM. **302** Alan Oddie/PE. **303/308** Superstock. **309** Luis Villota/SM. **311** UPI/Bettmann Newsphotos. **312** Frank Siteman/The Picture Cube. **313** H. Armstrong Roberts. **315** Joel Gordon. **318** Luis Villota/SM. **331** Sam Mikulis/UPI/Bettmann Newsphotos. **335** Richard Hutchings/InfoEdit. **336** H. Armstrong Roberts. **339** Globe Photos.

Unit 7   History
342–343 Tony Freeman/PE. **345** Peter Vandermark/SB. **348** Nelson-Atkins Museum of Art, Kansas City, MO. **349** SB. **354** file photo. **356** National Archives. **357** The Bettmann Archive. **358** Sygma Photo News. **359 T** Yoran/WC. **359 B** BANDPHOTO. **360 A, B, C, D** BANDPHOTO. **354 LR** Library of Congress. **366** file photo. **368** Peter Menzel/SB. **369** file photo. **370** Cary

594   Acknowledgements

Wolinsky/SB. **374 TL** Documentary Photo Aids. **374 TR** The Bettmann Archieve, Inc. **374 BL** Brown Brothers. **374 BR** Historical Pictures Service, Inc. **376** Elizabeth Barry/The Picture Cube. **377** SB. **381, 382** Wide World Photos. **382 inset** UPI/Bettmann Newsphotos. **384** N.Y. Times, August 5, 1964. **385** UPI/Bettmann Newsphotos. **386, 389** UPI/Bettmann Newsphotos. **391** Wide World Photos. **395** Vernon Merritt/Black Star. **396** Nik Wheeler/Black Star. **399** David Worrall/Pennsylvania Gazette. **401** C.O. Rentmeester/Life Magazine. **402 T** file photo. **402 B** Peter Menzel/SB. **403** file photo.

Unit 8   Political Science
404–405 Don Black/Globe Photos. **407** Martucci/McClenagham Collection and The J. Doyle Dewitt Collection. **409 T** Reuters/Bettmann Newsphotos. **409 B** Wide World Photos. **411** file photo. **413** AP/Wide World Photos. **415** painting by B. West, 1772. **417, 418** file photos. **425** Betsy Cole/The Picture Cube. **427** AP/Wide World Photos. **428** AP/Wide World Photos. **432** Bohdan Hrynewych/SB. **434** Courtesy Publishers-Hall Syndicate. **435** Courtesy Western High School, Baltimore, MD. **436, 437** Theodore Roosevelt Room, Mugar Memorial Library, BU/A&B Photo. **439** AP/Wide World Photos. **441** Cole Photography. **442** Nancy Harp/Monkmeyer Press Photo Service. **444** Arnold Jarmak/Chelsea Press Inc. **445** UPI/Bettmann Newsphotos. **446** J. Pat Carter/Gamma-Liason. **448** Joel Gordon. **450** E. Trina Lipton. **451** Charles Gatewood/SB. **453** UPI/Bettmann Newsphotos. **454** Universal Press Syndicate. **455** Camera Press London/Globe Photos.

Unit 9   Economics
458–459 Robert Brenner/PE. **461 T** Frank Siteman/Taurus Photos. **461 BL** Stacy Pick/SB. **461 BR** Owen Franken/SB. **463** Pierce Fund, courtesy of The Boston Museum of Fine Arts. **465 T** Cary Wolinski/SB. **465 B** Ken Karp/Omni-Photo Communications. **468** John Marmaras/WC. **472** The Pierpont Morgan Library, New York. **474** E. Trina Lipton. **475 L** Jim Harrison. **475 R** courtesy The Johnson Family and Stop & Shop Supermarkets. **493** Wide World Photos. **496** Sepp Seitz/WC. **498** Mark Antman. **501** UPI/Bettmann Newsphotos. **503** Simon Nathan/SM. **505** Colonial Williamsburg. **506** Alain Walsh/SM. **507** Lincoln Russell/SB. **511** John Lei/Omni-Photo Communications. **512** John Bryson/PR. **514** The Granger Collection. **515** Eric Poggenpohl/WC. **517** Alain Nogues/Sygma Photo News. **519** Louise E. Jefferson. **520** Peter Menzel. **524 L, 527** Joel Gordon. **529** Patricia Lanza/Folio. **532** Robert McElroy/WC.

Unit 10   The Future
534–535 FPG: **538** Joel Gordon. **540** Bill Gleasner/SM. **542** S.P. Laffont/Sygma Photo News. **543** Mark Antman. **544** Charles F. Borniger. **548** Robert Srenco/Superstock. **551** Superstock. **553** David H. Wells/The Image Works. **555 T, B** courtesy The United Nations. **557** Mariantonietta Peru/UNICEF. **558** Alan Oddie/PE. **562** Rick Mansfield/The Image Works. **565** Tony Freeman/PE. **566** Bar Harbor Police Department. **570** Bill Bachman/PR. **576 T** J.P. Laffont/Sygma Photo News. **576 B** Barbara Alper/SB. **581** Joel Gordon.

Text

Unit 1   Critical Thinking Skills
15 From Amend, Bill. *Fox Trot*, p. 36. Kansas City: Andrews and McMeel, 1989. **21** From The Earthworks Group. *50 Simple Things You Can Do to Save the Earth,* p. 20. Berkeley, California: The Earthworks Group, 1989. **26** From Amend, Bill. *Fox Trot*, p. 72. Kansas City: Andrews and McMeel, 1989.

Unit 2   Effective Study Skills
58 Adapted from Lorayne, Harry. *The Memory Book.* New York: Stein and Day Publishers, 1975. © 1975 by Harry Lorayne. Used by permission. **60** Adapted from Lorayne, Harry. *The Memory Book.* Chelsea, MA, Scarborough House, 1974. © 1974 by Harry Lorayne. Used by permission. **62** Adapted from Lorayne, Harry. *The Memory Book.* New York: Stein and Day Publishers, 1975. © 1975 by Harry Lorayne. Used by permission. **68** Material adapted from "Steps in the SQ3R Method" from *Effective Study,* 4/ed. by Francis P. Robinson. © 1941, 1946 by Harper & Row Publishers, Inc. © 1961, 1970 by Francis P. Robinson. Reprinted by permission of Harper & Row Publishers, Inc. **70** Material adapted from "Steps in the SQ3R Method" from *Effective Study,* 4/ed. by Francis P. Robinson. © 1941, 1946 by Harper & Row Publishers, Inc. © 1961, 1970 by Francis P. Robinson. Reprinted by permission of Harper & Row Publishers, Inc. **71** From Kolevzon, Edward R. and John A. Heine. *Our World and Its Peoples.* Boston: Allyn and Bacon, Inc., 1977. Used by permission. **75** The reading and diagrams are adapted from Carman, Robert A. and W. Royce Adams. *Study Skills: A Guide for Student Survival.* New York: John Wiley & Sons, Inc., 1972. **80** Adapted from Leinwand, Gerald. *The Pageant of American History.* Boston: Allyn and Bacon, Inc., 1975. Used by permission. **81** From Toppin, Edgar A. *The Black American in United States History.* Boston: Allyn and Bacon, Inc., 1973. Used by permission. **83** From *The Challenge of Change.* Learner-Verified Edition II. Prepared by the Social Science Staff of the Educational Research Council of America. © 1975, 1971 by the Educational Research Council of America. Used by permission. **84** From Leinwand, Gerald. *The Pageant of American History.* Boston: Allyn and Bacon, Inc., 1975. Used by permission. **102** From Henson, Kenneth T. *Secondary Teaching Methods.* Lexington: D.C. Heath and Company, 1981. Used by permission of Kenneth T. Henson.

Unit 3   Psychology
131 All three parts of this experiment are adapted from Engle, T. L. and Louis Snellgrove. *Record of Activities and Experiments* for use with *Psychology,* Fifth Edition. © 1969 by Harcourt Brace Jovanovich, Inc. Used by permission of the publishers. **142** The discussion of the eight stages of life is adapted from Erikson, Erik H. *Childhood and Society.* New York: W. W. Norton & Company, Inc., 1950. Used by permission. **144** Adapted from U.S. Department of Labor. Bureau of Labor Statistics. *Occupational Outlook Handbook.* Washington, D.C.: 1989. **146** From Scheiber, Dave. "And She's Only 13!" in *Sports Illustrated.* March 19, 1990. Used by permission of Dave Scheiber.

Unit 4   Sociology
163 Adapted from Quinn, James A. *Living in Social Groups.* Revised edition, pp. T16–T19. Philadelphia: J. B. Lippincott Co., 1976. Used by permission of Harper & Row Publishers, Inc. **194** Adapted from Longfellow, Layne A. "Body Talk." In *Psychology Today.* New York; Ziff-Davis Publishing Co., 1970. Reprinted by permission from *Psychology Today* magazine. © 1970 (PT Partners, L.P.) **197** Adapted from U.S. Department of Labor. Bureau of Labor Statistics. *Occupational Outlook Handbook.* Washington, D.C.: 1989. **198** From Ruskin, Cindy. *The Quilt: Stories from The NAMES Project.* © 1988 by The NAMES Project. Reprinted by permission of Pocket Books, a division of Simon & Schuster, Inc.

Unit 5   Anthropology

208 Adapted from Linton, Ralph. "One Hundred Per Cent American." In *The American Mercury.* April 1937, pp. 427–429. Used by permission. **222** Adapted from Priester, Susan, Gloria Cohen, Charles Bullwinkle, Jim Kilmurray, and George Renwick. "Friendship Module." An unpublished paper: circa 1974. Used by permission. **236** Adapted from Priester, Susan, Gloria Cohen, Charles Bullwinkle, Jim Kilmurray, and George Renwick. "Friendship Module." An unpublished paper: circa 1974. Used by permission. **260** From *The Emergence of Man: The First Americans.* By Robert Claiborne and the Editors of Time-Life Books © 1973 Time-Life Books, Inc. Used by permission.

Unit 6   Geography

268 Adapted from "Five Themes in Geography." In *Guidelines for Geographic Education,* prepared by the National Council for Geographic Education and the American Association of Geographers. Used by permission. **290** The discussion of open and closed systems was adapted with permission from *Teaching About Spaceship Earth, Intercom #71* © The American Forum for Global Education. **292** The reading and diagram are adapted from Commoner, Barry. *The Closing Circle,* pp. 33–46. New York: Alfred A. Knopf, Inc., 1971. Used by permission. **298** From Lehrer, Tom. "Pollution." From the recording *That Was the Year That Was.* © 1965 by Tom Lehrer. Used by permission. **310** Information in this experiment based upon several sources including the two listed here. The first is Heifer Project International, as reported in *USA Today,* August 15, 1989. The second is Heilbroner, Robert L. *The Great Ascent: The Struggle for Economic Development,* pp. 33–37. New York: Harper & Row, Publishers, Inc., 1963. Used by permission. **336** Adapted from U.S. Department of Labor. Bureau of Labor Statistics. *Occupational Outlook Handbook.* Washington, D.C.: 1989. **338** From Ellis, William S. "Rondônia: Brazil's Imperiled Rain Forest." In *National Geographic.* Vol. 17, No. 6. Used by permission.

Unit 7   History

363 From Saxe, John Godfrey. "The Blind Men and the Elephant." In *The Poetical Works of John Godfrey Saxe.* Boston: Houghton Mifflin, 1899. Reprinted by permission of Houghton Mifflin Company. **364** The concept sequence presented here is adapted from Block, Jack. *Understanding Historical Research: A Search for Truth.* Glen Rock, New Jersey: Research Publications, 1971. Used by permission. **365** From Dodge, Professor Robert, trans. *The History of the USSR During the Epoch of Socialism,* 3rd ed. Moscow: USSR Ministry of Education, 1974. (Professor Dodge is affiliated with Washington and Jefferson College, Washington, Pennsylvania.) **365** From Mehlinger, Dr. Howard, trans. *Contemporary History (1939–1984).* Moscow: USSR Ministry of Education, 1985. (Dr. Mehlinger is affiliated with Indiana University, Bloomington, Indiana.) **371** From the *Independent Journal.* Reprinted by permission of the Associated Press, New York, N.Y. **371** From the San Francisco *Chronicle.* © 1966 Chronicle Publishing Co. Reprinted by permission of the Associated Press, New York, N.Y. **372** From the *Sunday Ramparts,* Nov. 6–3, © 1966. Reprinted by permission. **372** The three newspaper articles on pages 371 and 372 were drawn from material from Messner, Nancy Shingler, and Gerald Messner. *Patterns of Thinking.* Belmont, Calif.: Wadsworth Publishing Co., Inc., 1968. **373** From Leinwand, Gerald. *The Pageant of American History.* Boston: Allyn and Bacon, Inc., 1975. Used by permission. **380** From *The New York Times,* August 3, 1964. © 1964 by The New York Times Company. Reprinted by permission. **383** From the *Los Angeles Times,* August 4, 1964. Reprinted by permission. **384** From the *Washington Post,* August 5, 1964. **387** Congressional Resolution, from the Public Paper of the Presidents, United States Government Printing Office, Washington, D.C., 1964. From the *Chicago Tribune,* August 5, 1964. Press Statement, from the Public Paper of the Presidents, United States Government Printing Office, Washington, D.C., 1964. **389** Statement at the LBJ Ranch, from the Public Papers of the President, United States Government Printing Office, Washington, D.C., 1964. From Johnson, Lyndon Baines. *Vantage Point: Perspectives of the Presidency, 1963–1969.* New York: Holt Rinehart Winston, 1971. **392** From the *New Statesman,* August 14, 1964. **393** From the *National Guardian, August 15, 1964.* Reprinted by permission of The Guardian, formerly the National Guardian. **400** Adapted from U.S. Department of Labor. Bureau of Labor Statistics. *Occupational Outlook Handbook.* Washington, D.C.: 1989. **400** O'Brien, Tim. *Going After Cacciato.* © 1975, 1976, 1977, 1978 by Tim O'Brien. Used by permission of Delacorte Press/Seymour Lawrence, a division of Bantam, Doubleday, Dell Pubishing Group, Inc.

Unit 8   Political Science

452 Adapted from U.S. Department of Labor. Bureau of Labor Statistics. *Occupational Outlook Handbook.* Washington, D.C.: 1989.

Unit 9   Economics

494 Game concept adapted with permission from two sources. The first is Joseph, Myron. "Role Playing in Teaching Economics." *The American Economic Review.* May 1965. The second is Schultze, Mindella. *Economics Readings for Students of Twelfth Grade American Democracy.* Prepared by the Developmental Economic Education Program of the Pittsburgh Public Schools: 1968. **526** Adapted from U.S. Department of Labor. Bureau of Labor Statistics. *Occupational Outlook Handbook.* Washington, D.C.: 1989. **528** "We Can Save the World" Reprinted by permission of Bonjour International, Ltd.

Unit 10   The Future

545 This experiment is adapted from Hanvey, Robert G. *Explorations in the Emergent Present, Intercom #77* [circa 1974]. © The American Forum for Global Education. Used by permission. **548** Adapted from Toffler, Alvin. *Future Shock.* New York: Random House, Inc. Alfred A. Knopf, Inc. 1970. Used by permission. **567** The discussion on the cross-impact matrix, together with the CIM diagram, is adapted from LaConte, Ronald T. and Ellen LaConte. *Teaching Tomorrow Today.* © 1975 by Bantam Books, Inc. **577** The discussion on the decision tree is adapted from LaConte, Ronald T. and Ellen LaConte. *Teaching Tomorrow Today.* © 1975 by Bantam Books, Inc., New York, N.Y. **579** A message as published in the *Wall Street Journal* by United Technologies Corporation, Hartford, Connecticut 06101. Reprinted by permission of United Technologies Corporation. **580** Excerpts from *Foundation and Earth* Isaac Asimov. © 1986 Nightfall, Inc. Used by permission of Doubleday, a division of Bantam Doubleday Dell Publishing Group, Inc.